Designing Storage for Exchange 2007 SP1

Designing Storage for Exchange 2007 SP1

Pierre Bijaoui

Juergen Hasslauer

SYNGRESS®

Amsterdam • Boston • Heidelberg • London • New York • Oxford
Paris • San Diego • San Francisco • Singapore • Sydney • Tokyo

Digital Press and Syngress are imprints of Elsevier

Digital
Press

Digital Press and Syngress are imprints of Elsevier
30 Corporate Drive, Suite 400, Burlington, MA 01803, USA
Linacre House, Jordan Hill, Oxford OX2 8DP, UK

⊗ Recognizing the importance of preserving what has been written,
Elsevier prints its books on acid-free paper whenever possible.

Library of Congress Cataloging-in-Publication Data
Bijaoui, Pierre.
  Designing storage for Exchange 2007 SP1 / Pierre Bijaoui, Juergen Hasslauer.
    p. cm.
  Includes index.
  ISBN 978-1-55558-308-8 (pbk : alk. paper) 1. Microsoft Exchange server. 2. Client/server
computing. 3. Electronic mail systems. 4. Computer storage devices. 1. Hasslauer, Juergen. II. Title.
  QA76.9.C55B4757 2008
  00.5.7'1376—dc22

2008023960

British Library Cataloguing-in-Publication Data
A catalogue record for this book is available from the British Library.

ISBN: 978-1-55558-308-8

For information on all Digital Press and Syngress publications
visit our website at www.books.elsevier.com

Typeset by Charon Tec Ltd., A Macmillan Company.
(www.macmillansolutions.com)

Printed in the United States of America

08 09 10 11 12   10 9 8 7 6 5 4 3 2 1

Working together to grow
libraries in developing countries

www.elsevier.com | www.bookaid.org | www.sabre.org

ELSEVIER   BOOK AID International   Sabre Foundation

Pierre Bijaoui's dedication
Pour Paul, Marianne et Nathalie

Juergen Hasslauer's dedication
For my parents

Contents

Foreword

Storage and email systems are usually the domains of different IT experts in large companies. Some folks look after storage design, allocation, tuning, and support, and some serve the same function for the email servers. It is often true that the larger the environment, the bigger the gap that exists between the two teams. When this happens, you may find that mail server performance suffers as the storage fails to cope with I/O demand, you spend too much money on storage, or you have problems achieving the kind of business continuity that you need for mission-critical applications like email.

The gap exists because the storage community usually takes a hardware-centric approach to technology while the email team looks at things from a software perspective. The gap is fine as long as you can isolate technology in such a way that the storage and email teams can work in mutually exclusive vacuums. Unfortunately, as email servers scale up to deal with massive amounts of data, and companies place more importance on business continuity, no such vacuum exists. The storage and email teams have to work together to achieve a common goal: to deliver highly resilient, performing, and cost-effective email services based on the right server and storage platform.

Microsoft has made many changes to Exchange in the 2007 release. They trade memory to reduce disk I/O and take advantage of 64-bit hardware platforms. There are several different ways of shipping transaction logs that can be exploited to replicate store data. There's a new transport engine and a few esoteric components to understand, such as the transport dumpster. Exchange still supports traditional clustering, but the advent of log replication may indicate that its heyday is past. All of these questions are posed by software changes and have implications for storage architecture and design, so it is great to have a comprehensive guide to the technology that puts these questions into a common context for the storage and email teams.

Pierre and Juergen are well known to everyone who has attended conferences such as Microsoft TechEd or Exchange Connections. If you attended their sessions, you know that they have a rare expertise that covers Exchange, storage, systems management, architecture, and planning, and the need to achieve business results. This mixture of skills and expertise comes through in this book, and I believe that it will add value to anyone who is struggling with how best to deploy Exchange 2007 in medium- to large-scale IT infrastructures, especially with regard to all of the storage questions that arise.

Tony Redmond

Acknowledgments

Many people have contributed to this book, sometimes knowingly, and sometimes unconsciously. I would like to thank them for giving me the support, the energy and the inspiration that turned this project into a reality. If I have forgotten people, please be sure that I have not forgotten them in my heart.

The very first people I have in mind are Tony Redmond and Juergen Hasslauer. Juergen because he's my co-author and he proves to be a patient and friendly tandem rider. Tony, because he gave many of us the inspiration to write books and stretch ourselves to progress and bring better contributions to the industry. Many thanks to both of you!

I would also like to thank the other three tutor members of my Academy team: Kieran McCorry, Kevin Laahs, and Donald Livengood. It's always great when you can combine work and fun in such a productive way. Of course, this extends to the other members of the team, including our lab masters and rats!

Ten years ago, I ran my first-ever industry presentation at the Microsoft Exchange Conference in Boston. There, I presented on I/O for Exchange. Over those 10 years, many people have helped me in the realization of my work and provided mentoring. Of all of my mentors, a special mention is due Christophe Dubois of HP StorageWorks, who is a fantastic sparring partner. Hardly anywhere will you get people with opinions that make a difference to you, your work, and your relation with your customers. Christophe is one of them, in addition to being a very knowledgeable person. Exactly the kind of mentorship a professional would dream to have.

Many thanks to the great people at HP who work hard to create value and differentiation of HP in the industry, especially when it comes to Microsoft Exchange storage deployments! A few teams inside HP do significant and innovative work and research on how to best align storage and services with Microsoft's technologies The Customer Focused Testing (CFT) and Solutions Alliance Engineering teams are great examples and I wish to thank in particular Rich Gianattasio and his team, Maria Jordan and Jacky Bouskila, for supporting me for writing this book by generously giving me access to their labs, time and competencies. Steve Tramack for leading a talented team, which includes Evan Morris and Stuart Ladd. Many talented people in HP Services deliver high-quality jobs on a daily basis on Microsoft Exchange deployments in particular and on storage designs. The HP IT organization with Mike Ireland and Kathy Pollert has been a great source of work and research: Thank you for helping us do our work (which was also to help you)!

I would like to thank Microsoft for being so open and collaborative. Perry Clarke, Laurion Burchall, Nicole Allen, and Matt Gossage have always been very helpful and open for discussion and argumentation. The prospects for success are always much better when you know the design rationale and internal operations. As more and more information becomes available from Microsoft and the Exchange team blog ("You had me at EHLO"), the industry benefits and customers have a better experience with their Microsoft Exchange deployment. Juergen and I have often worked on joint customer projects, and dealt with particularly advanced customers. I could quote many customers, and I know they will appreciate the necessary confidentiality of our relationship. My sincere thanks, anyhow, to Mike Rheinsberg for the purposeful collaboration he had with Juergen and I.

Thanks to our publisher, and in particular, Tiffany Gasbarrini, Monica Mendoza, and David George for dealing with us, with the same ongoing goal of getting this book to the market with quality and value.

Finally, I have special thoughts for my family, for the care they gave me, for the time I spent away from them, and for their tolerance while I was working on this book project. I love you for the rest of my life!

Pierre Bijaoui

I'm not a star and I did not win a GRAMMY © award. I'm only a co-author of a book.

However this is the right place to thank my parents for raising me and forming my character. I'm proud to be straightforward and ambitious. Without this education it would have been impossible to finish this sportive challenge that has eaten up all my free time in the last months.

I want to thank Pierre for his trust and providing me with interesting opportunities. It started with his question as to whether I would like to deliver a session at Microsoft Tech Ed South Africa 2004. Initially I considered declining because I was unsure if I was good enough to stand in front of a crowd and talk about Exchange performance tuning. Luckily, I accepted and the week in Sun City was one of the best in my life. There were many other rewarding challenges including this book. The apprentice learned a lot from the MASTER of Exchange and storage performance.

There is one man I cannot thank enough: Tony Redmond. It started with a book he gave me for my first HP Knowledge Briefs. The award was very inspiring and I like his belief in the value of knowledge sharing for a services organization. This provided me opportunities that I had never imagined a few years ago. Discovering an email from Tony in my inbox asking if I would like to provide comments on a chapter of his upcoming book on Exchange Server 2007 was a welcome surprise. However, the main reason for this acknowledgment is the assistance he provided me when I encountered a lot of hassle. It was great to see that a small consultant can get excellent support from a top manager. I will never forget that!

Being selected as a speaker at Microsoft Exchange Connections is an honor. I would like to thank Paul Robichaux, Kieran McCorry, and Kevin Laahs for their help. Connections is always a very nice week in the year.

Gaining practical experience with Windows Server 2008 failover clustering without the help of Dave Lalor and Chanmuny Dy from Microsoft would not have been possible. Matt Gossage was very helpful in finding answers to my countless questions about technical details. For me, lost log resiliency would be like magic without the information provided by Laurion Burchall. Erin Bookey and Jeff Mealiffe provided a lot of insight into the details of LoadGen. Joseph Grisolia of Symantec was a big help in learning Volume Shadow Copy Services–based backup when Exchange Server 2007 was still in early beta.

You cannot write a book without reviewers. Let's start with a very special one: Linda Gallacher. My writing would be worse without the many changes I always found in the documents that she reviewed. This was a perfect training. Many colleagues helped me to learn Windows- and Exchange-related topics and then write articles about them: Aric Bernard, Christophe Dubois, Daragh Morrissey, Donald Livengood, Dung Hoang Khac, Evan Morris, Guido Grillenmeier, Jan De Clercq, Joe Sullivan, Ken Meier, Mike Ireland, Shree Vishwanathan, Tonino Bruno, and many more. Finally, I want to especially thank friends who reviewed chapters of this book in their free time: Blair Parkhill, Bob Snyder, Gary Ketchum, Maarten Piederiet, Maria Jordan, Mike Rheinsberg, Stuart Ladd, and Thomas Strasser. Their review comments helped to significantly enhance the quality of this book.

I would also like to thank Tiffany Gasbarrini, Monica Mendoza, David George, and Matthew Cater from Elsevier for their patience and support for us as we finished this book.

Juergen Hasslauer

Introduction to Exchange 2007 Storage

In this chapter, we review aspects of storage design for Exchange 2007 that you should be aware of. This "launch pad" provides background information on the purpose of this book.

Where to Start?

Deploying Exchange 2007 will require you to make decisions about the type of storage you will need to provide to one of the most critical business application on the market. Microsoft Exchange is a dominant mail and messaging platform, often used also as a corporate address book and time management application.

If you think about it, email is about sending and receiving data; for users, it's having a repository of relatively unstructured data and querying that repository similar to a database. Storage is therefore a critical component in your deployment. In fact, given the tremendous progress made in the world of processors, and the adoption of 64-bit computing by Exchange 2007, storage is the most critical component in your design. This is the thing to get right from the beginning, or you run the risk of continuous problems in your deployment, eventually delivering an email service that does not help your users or customers.

When dealing with Exchange storage, we always find it necessary to first work the requirements for the storage and then figure out the best solution. Those requirements can be quite simple (e.g., I want a 5-GB mailbox) or more complex (e.g., ability to recover all Tier-1 users within 4 hours after a major disaster).

The logical flow of handling your requirements could be similar to Figure 1-1 (nonexhaustive sample).

The flow in Figure 1-1 is based on standard architecture methodology and does not pretend to be the only approach to handling requirements. In fact, many customers of Exchange 2007 already have such methodology. The

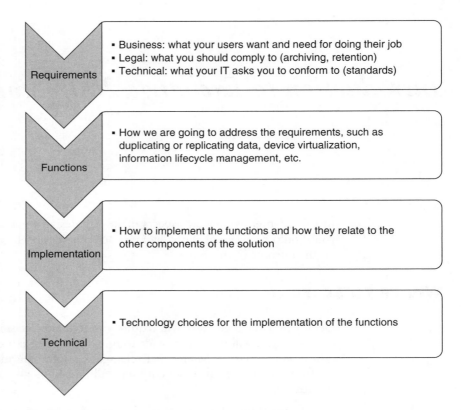

Figure 1-1
*Handling
requirements
for storage in
Exchange 2007*

Requirements
- Business: what your users want and need for doing their job
- Legal: what you should comply to (archiving, retention)
- Technical: what your IT asks you to conform to (standards)

Functions
- How we are going to address the requirements, such as duplicating or replicating data, device virtualization, information lifecycle management, etc.

Implementation
- How to implement the functions and how they relate to the other components of the solution

Technical
- Technology choices for the implementation of the functions

need for such a structured approach is there to ensure that you provide the best solution to your problems, and not attempt to replicate a solution that, after all, does not address your problems, but others' problems. For example, are you certain that you wish to create an ISP-type mail environment with large mailboxes and no service level? Or perhaps you will want a combination of both? Or, you may want to have 1-GB mailboxes with *absolutely* no loss of data and to be able to sustain a natural disaster within a 100-mile/kilometer radius.

What's new with Exchange 2007?

Microsoft with Exchange 2007 has embarked on a journey that started with the 64-bit route. 64-bit computing has been possible since Windows NT4 (with Digital's Alpha processor). However, Microsoft focused their development of subsequent versions of Microsoft Exchange for the i386 instruction set (processors manufactured primarily by Intel and AMD), running on 32-bit address space. It really was not a problem until the data sets (the database hosting the mailboxes) used by Microsoft Exchange grew to a point where it was necessary to break the single private Information Store model to allow for easier manageability.

With Exchange 2000, we saw the adoption of a multiple database model, where mailboxes could be held in several smaller databases, instead of just one big database in a single file. This was further extended with Exchange 2007 (up to 50 databases can be defined for a single server), now that the barriers of the Virtual Address space (3 GB and a few bytes) of the Information Store process are broken, thanks to 64-bit computing. Many more databases can be handled by a single Exchange 2007 server, allowing for a better granularity when dealing with individual databases and transaction log files. The databases can be smaller in size, or even better, you can have the same number of users per server, but with a much larger mailbox size, while keeping a reasonable size for the individual databases (200 GB is considered the practical maximum).

You may wonder why we discuss 64-bit computing in a book about storage. In fact, much of the storage optimization and improvements found with Exchange 2007 are due to the ability to use larger quantities of RAM (up to 10 times more RAM should be used for a high-end server compared to Exchange 2003, allowing for effective database page caching). While we discuss those new functions later in this book, you will have to remember that choosing the right memory sizing for your server is extremely important to relieve the Microsoft Exchange–induced I/O pressure on the storage subsystem components. Reducing that pressure will result in better user experience, better behavior in shared storage environments (by decreasing the burst of I/O requests and making Exchange less dependent on high-performance storage), and the ability to have more choices for your storage components.

Public folders still exist in Exchange 2007, yet Microsoft definitely put the emphasis on Microsoft Office SharePoint Server for collaboration and shared information. It means basically that if you currently run a Microsoft Exchange environment, and you use public folders, you will still have the possibility to continue using them, but you should seriously consider an exit strategy, because public folders are not likely to get any attention from Microsoft in the long run.

Microsoft touched the tip of information life-cycle management with Exchange 2007 with the use of managed folders. These will provide great assistance for environments where you wish to keep email for compliance purposes, yet not clutter users' mailboxes. The data are still preserved in the Microsoft Exchange databases, but a special area is created to host messages and items that are governed by a retention policy (Figure 1-2).

Exchange 2007 administrators can create management policies that define how long content can exist in user folders and whether content within that folder should deleted or journaled. These policies can be established on standard folders or custom (as defined by an administrator) folders. Custom folders are provisioned in the user's mailbox and are useable via Outlook 2003 SP2, Outlook 2007 and Outlook Web Access. They are just like any other folder except they cannot be deleted, unless the administrator decides to no longer manage them.

Figure 1-2
*Managed folders
with Exchange
2007*

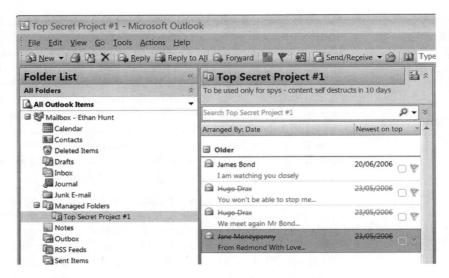

Messaging records management is therefore a way for administrators to comply with corporate policies for message retention and lifecycle. As you deploy this function, you will have to be careful about the overhead, both from a transactional standpoint (incurred by the action of moving messages, scanning mailboxes or deleting messages) and from a capacity standpoint: keeping messages around can bust your users' mailbox quota and lead to further problems in Outlook 2007 cache mode. Because the Outlook 2007 cache is based on PST technology (but called an OST), it suffers from the same "issues" found with large PSTs: an excessive number of I/O requests are required each time you add, delete, or modify items in the OST, every time you browse folders, or perform information scanning and retrieval. The result is a degraded user experience, and until Microsoft improves the local cache technology in Outlook, we suggest keeping the mailbox size to approximately 2 GB.

The real novelty brought by Exchange 2007 is the database replication: the ability to continuously, although with a slight delay, keep a replica of a database up-to-date, and use that replica in case the source database fails. Think of it as a log shipping mechanism, except that it is fully integrated in the product, with proper instrumentation (e.g., using PowerShell), monitoring, and ease of use. It means that if you are ready to double your storage capacity, you can bring your messaging service to new levels of availability and possibly amend backup and recovery policies in a way you never imagined for an Exchange server (e.g., daily differential + weekly full).

The result is that the best practices for storage that we used with previous releases of Microsoft Exchange must now be revisited, because Microsoft changed the product, and also because the industry has made progress in certain compartments of storage technology.

In summary

Thus, we take you on a journey for designing the best storage solution for your environment. Remember that what is best for you today may not be optimal 3 years from now and may not be for a company equivalent to yours. That's a challenge relevant to our industry, that is, the fact that we deal with changing technology, and that storage as we know it today will probably be significantly different 5 years from now from both technology and functionality standpoints.

The important matter is to solve your business requirements with the most appropriate technology and implementation, and to conform to best practices.

Exchange 2007 Server Roles and Usage of Storage

Figure 1-3 describes the server roles for Exchange 2007 at RTM. With Exchange 2007 SP1, you can now run Microsoft Exchange on Windows Server 2008, in addition to Windows Server 2003 SP1 and later.

In this section, we review the storage requirements for each of the roles.

Common requirements

Whatever the role of your server, you will need to provide a boot volume to the Windows operating system. The purpose of the system disk is to host the binaries of the operating system and applications, and to host the page file, which allows for virtual memory management on Windows. Little performance is required from system disks on Windows and Exchange servers. There is no significant paging activity because the Microsoft Exchange database engine will ensure using physical memory as it becomes available. If the server gets low on physical memory, Exchange will proceed to decrease its utilization of physical memory. This is particularly true for the mailbox role. It can apply as well to other roles, such as the Hub Transport Server role that will make full use of RAM for caching messages during transfer, thus preventing slow storage access. Of course, if you use complementary software to your Exchange 2007 server setup, such as a file system antivirus, a backup application, or any kind of monitoring software, you will need to ensure that indeed the system is not paging excessively. This can be monitored quite easily using the Windows performance monitor that we discuss in Chapter 11.

It's generally a good idea to have ample room on your system disk. Given the rather large size of disks, a disk fill-up condition on Windows servers these days is a pretty nasty situation to explain to your manager. You can't get disks smaller than 72 GB? Fine! Make use of them and create partitions

Figure 1-3
*Exchange Server
roles*

Figure 1-3 Exchange Server roles

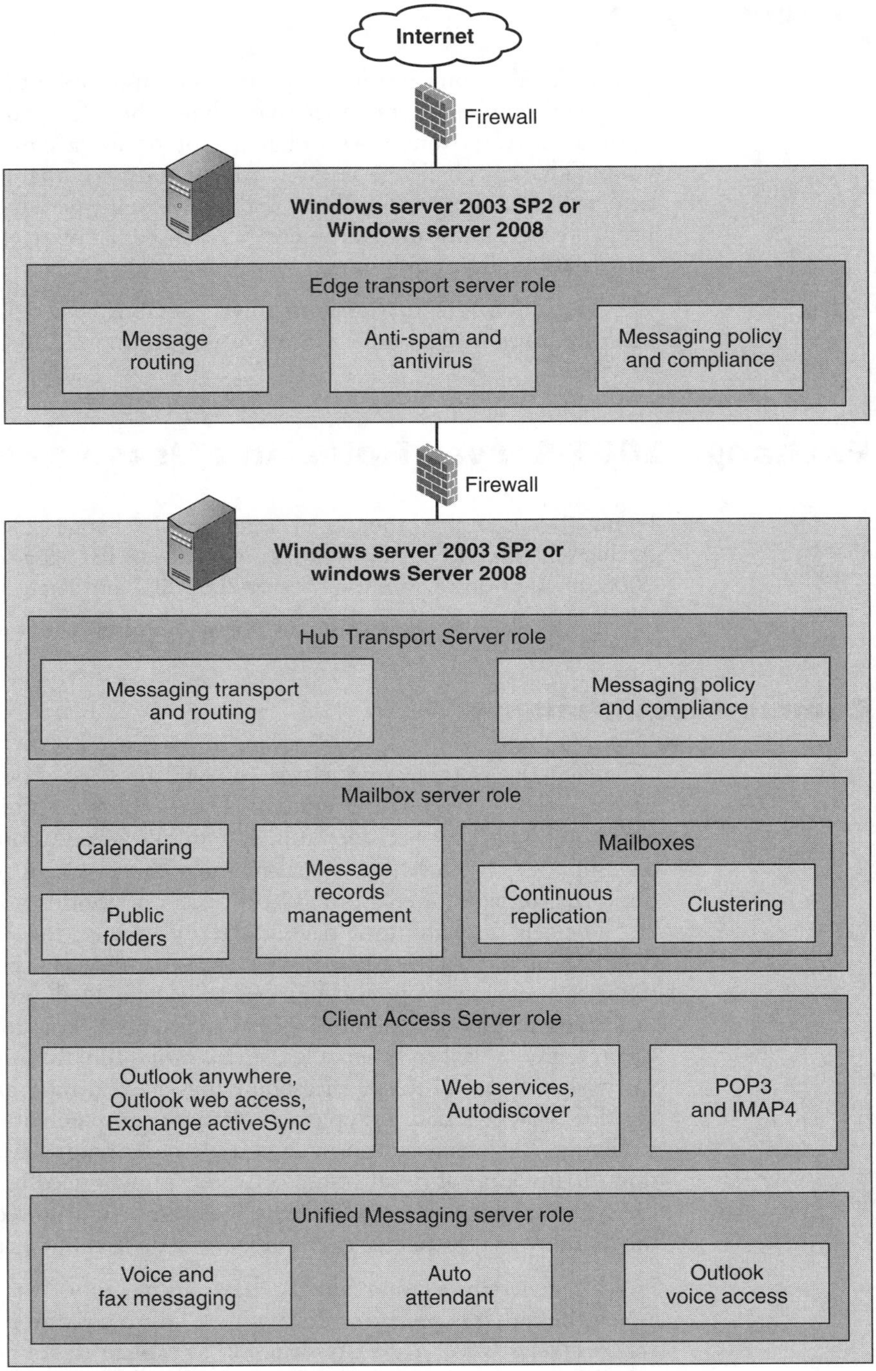

for the operating system that prevent file fragmentation and disk-full events, and comply with your crash dump management and performance monitoring policies. You might also want to break this 72 GB mirror set in two or more partitions in order to create separation between vital system storage and storage that the system needs but will not cause downtime in case it gets full. For example, we frequently recommend to our customers to create a separate partition of the Windows Event and Internet Information Server log files.

Mailbox server storage

Mailbox servers are by far the most important role in an Exchange 2007 deployment when it comes to storage design. The purpose of mailbox servers is to hold a number of databases (50 maximum per server), and each database holds the mail for mailboxes homed to that database. The structure of the database is a series of tables (Figure 1-4) that contain the following:

- The list of the mailboxes

- For each mailbox, the list of folders

- For each folder, the list of messages or items

- For each message or item, a list of body part, attributes, and attachments

There is no hard-coded limit to the number of mailboxes, folders, or items that can be stored in an Exchange database. There are some practical limits, such as the number of items in the critical path folders. The critical

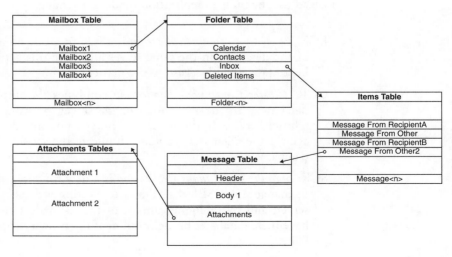

Figure 1-4
*Tables inside the
Exchange 2007
database*

path folders are Inbox, Calendar, Sent Items, and Contacts. These folders are used regardless of the user being connected (Inbox and Calendar) or for sending email. If you have too many items (5000 or more), the server will start getting more load than usual, and the user experience for normal operations will be degraded due to the large number of items in the folder. The size of the items is not important: it is the count that matters. You can have a very large number of items in a folder (e.g., 15,000 emails) as long as you do not use this folder often. If you have so many items in your Inbox, every time a message is delivered to you, it will cause more I/O to the database. Opening your client will also cause a larger than usual count of I/O requests. The net result is a larger footprint of Microsoft Exchange on your storage subsystem, where you will obtain two to three times more I/O per second than if you had proper maintenance.

The databases for Exchange 2007 mailbox servers are important: If the database is not available, and then logging on to Exchange 2007 is not possible. Therefore, users cannot send and receive emails, create calendar appointments or contacts, nor work with any other kind of item. Because databases in Exchange 2007 are so important, they should be allocated to storage that provides availability, performance, and reliability. In Exchange 2007, there is the concept of an active database, that is, the primary database where the user mailbox is located. This is no different than previous versions of Microsoft Exchange. Exchange 2007's new feature is the ability to maintain a separate copy of the database, called the passive database (or replica) that you can use in case the primary database fails.

Storage industry trends have been constant reduction in the cost per gigabyte, as well as constant increase in data density. As a result, it became natural for Microsoft to implement data duplication functions inside their product, so you do not have to create complex storage infrastructures, and instead use the built-in replication mode of Exchange 2007 SP1, namely:

LCR: *Local Continuous Replication* is a way to create an additional copy of the database on the same server and have this copy continuously kept updated with regard to the master copy.

CCR: *Cluster Continuous Replication* combines the duplication of the database with the availability of the server, by using the Microsoft Cluster Service. In this environment, you not only duplicate the storage for the databases, you also duplicate the servers that serve these databases.

SCR: *Standby Continuous Replication* is a new function introduced with Exchange 2007 SP1 that allows replicating a database to a standby server, and by taking advantage of the database transportability, to have these databases brought online if the primary copy of a database fails.

In addition to these built-in data duplication techniques, you can also take advantage of infrastructure-based storage duplication as typically found in Storage Area Networks. The principle is the same—you duplicate a data block on another storage device, possibly located in another physical location. The idea is that if the primary database copy fails for some reason, you can quickly recover from a replica of the database. We discuss these modes of replication in greater detail later in the book.

Besides the user mailbox environment (represented by databases and transaction log files), which is by far the largest storage volume for a mailbox server, you need to pay attention to two additional storage requirements:

Online content conversion: Because mail items are transmitted in SMTP/MIME form but are stored as a series of MAPI properties, a place for temporary storage of content that needs conversion is required. This typically happens in memory; however, if the item is too large to fit in memory, a temporary storage area will be utilized (typically pointed by the TEMP environment variable, that is, C:\Temp for most servers). This conversion may also take place on the Hub Transport Server or the CAS server, depending on the client interface used and path of the message.

Content indexing: The ability to search your mail is critical. Traditional search techniques have been replaced advantageously by indexing techniques in the past 15 years. The principle is to create an index of all the terms used in the content that you wish to index, and point that index to the place in the file, message, or item that contains the indexing term. Present since Exchange 2000, content indexing has been through a major rework for Exchange 2007, and is now built in to the mail (or item) creation process: As items get stored in the database, they are automatically indexed as background activity. Indexes are typically stored in the same volume as the mailbox databases. They are not replicated by Exchange and they can be rebuilt in the background, using an efficient throttling mechanism that prevents server overload by indexing activities when it is actually required by the users during peak hours, or if the index must be rebuilt entirely (such as in the event of a database failover or recovery).

Additional considerations for storage design are typically overruled by the requirements of the databases hosted on a mailbox server. The need for additional space in modern mail environment has caused Microsoft Exchange administrators to create large storage areas to store databases. It is common to build a server with a total capacity of 1 TB of mailbox server storage. As you grow the size of your mailbox databases, you will have to keep in mind that these databases must be manageable. In fact, this is the real challenge for the Microsoft Exchange administrator, and we explain ways to deal with that particular challenge in this book.

Hub Transport Server

The Hub Transport Server role is different from the mailbox server role due to the fact that data are stored temporarily and are never used except in recovery conditions. It is very important, however, because all mail delivery, should it be local to a database or to a remote server, will transverse a Hub Transport role. That role is strategic in an Exchange 2007 environment, as you can guarantee that all mail delivery will go through the same code path. In there, you can implement a more secure and systematic message hygiene process (antivirus, antispam) and compliance (journaling).

When relaying messages, the Hub Transport Server will write messages to disk as well as caching those messages into memory. If the server can relay the message immediately, the data are read from memory instead of being read from disk. Therefore, the majority of the disk accesses is in write mode, and seldom read, except in a recovery condition. A recovery condition can happen, for example, if the server fails, and crashes: The content of the system memory is lost and the data must be retrieved from disk. The Hub Transport Server will proceed to rebuild its in-memory queues based on the Information Stored on disk. The key benefit brought by Exchange 2007 is the ability to use an ESE database engine for storing messages and keeping those messages around for more time than necessary. If you lose the active copy of the database and if the passive copy of that database is not completely updated, the mailbox server can turn around to the Hub Transport Server and ask for resubmission of the mail items. This allows for making the environment resilient by storing very recent information in different places. It diminishes the risk of information loss in case something really bad happens on the mailbox servers. Known as the *transport dumpster*, that feature was not present in Microsoft Exchange 2003 and earlier because the equivalent server role of the Hub Transport, known as the *bridgehead server*, was not used for all mail delivery: Some mail delivery could be local or remote.

Other server roles: Client Access and Unified Messaging

The other Exchange 2007 roles have minimal need for storage. They only keep information in transit (for the case of the Unified Messaging server). You should therefore ensure that there is ample room on the system disk for Windows to run; however, you will not have to deploy special engineering efforts in sizing and designing the storage units for those server roles. Since the introduction of Exchange 2007, we have commonly seen Client Access and Unified Messaging servers deployed with two local disks configured in RAID1 (mirroring technology) to ensure business continuity, but not necessarily to protect data.

Information Store Service

On mailbox servers, there is a single process than controls the database engines (storage groups): the Information Store. It is by far the most critical process for a mailbox server. The Information Store takes advantage of Windows 64-bit computing for caching as much data as possible given the constraints of physical memory on the server. The benefit of caching is clear: Instead of reading data on disk in 10 ms, you can read the data from cache in 50 ns. The difference is immense, and the goal of Information Store is to use as much RAM as possible for caching data. If you have a 32 GB-RAM server, and if you notice that only 50 MB of free physical memory is left, don't panic! You are not dealing with a memory leak of some sort, but rather an extremely efficient use of your server resources.

With Exchange Server 2003, the maximum database cache can be up to 2.1 GB. However, in reality Microsoft has issued a recommendation to tune the database cache to 896 MB (see Microsoft KB Article 266768) on mailbox servers. This limitation is primarily due to the 3 GB, user-mode Virtual Address space, which is also used for other operations other than caching database pages. Exchange 2007 operates in a 64-bit native Windows Server 2003 environment, so the user-mode Virtual Address space can theoretically be as large as 8 TB (1 terabyte = 1000 GB), but in practice, will be limited to the quantity of RAM that can be allocated to the Information Store process, while preventing excessive memory paging from Exchange or any other process running on the Windows server. The current recommendation for large servers is 32 GB of RAM; you may use more, and Exchange will take advantage of it, but it might break the cost-efficient model for your design because high-density RAM tends to be quite expensive.

In Figure 1-5, you can see that the massive benefits brought by 64-bit computing to Exchange 2007: A large address space will allow for better caching and I/O optimization as we will see later. Note that even though you have an 8 TB Virtual Address space, not all servers today can scale to that quantity of RAM. In fact, x64 systems (Intel or AMD processors that extend the x86 instruction set to 64-bit) typically do not accommodate more than 128 GB of RAM. Things will evolve as multicore processors (four or more cores) are delivered by the industry: Indeed, if you have lots of processing power, you will need lots of RAM to keep those processors busy.

Databases and storage groups

Each database must be mounted in a storage group. The storage group is simply an instance of the ESE database engine executing in the Information Store process. This engine, used by Microsoft Exchange and the Windows

Figure 1-5
*Comparing 32-bit
and 64-bit systems*

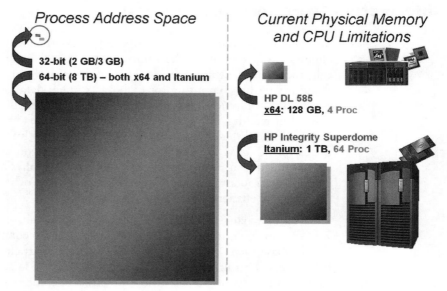

Active Directory services (to name a few), takes it roots from the Joint Engine Technology (JET) efforts made by Microsoft to create two database engines that would be used by their software: JET Red (for Microsoft Access) and JET Blue (for Microsoft Exchange). There is as much difference between those two engines as between red and blue! They are different and do not share the same code base. JET Blue was created with a few considerations specific to the mail database world:

- First, the database engine should be crash-proof. If you have a system crash, abnormal application termination, or power loss on the server, no data should be lost and the database should be left in a recoverable state.

- Second, the database engine was designed based on the fact that disks are slow. Even though that consideration was made more than a decade ago, it still holds true today. Disks and in general any I/O (including to network devices) are considered slow when you compare them to the sheer processing speed of modern processors. Therefore, you should use as much RAM as possible to cache and buffer data before it has to go to disk, or instead of reading it from disk. We will return to the fundamental differences between buffering and caching in Microsoft Exchange later in this book.

- Third, the database should not require any administration tasks, such as tuning the amount of cache to be used. This aspect of ESE has vastly improved since Microsoft Exchange 5.5. In fact, there is no tuning to be done on the database engine before you can take advantage of the full processing and physical memory of a server.

■ Finally, the database should not be taken down for any reason, not even for backups. Initially, a streaming API was created with Microsoft Exchange to back up the database while running. We will see that with Exchange 2007 and Windows 2003, the emphasis is on different technologies, such as volume shadow copy.

Inside, the database engine consists of a balanced tree with backward and forward links, designed to reach any particular data page with a minimal number of disk I/O to meet the high-performance requirements of email (Figure 1-6).

Figure 1-6
Exchange 2007 database page structure

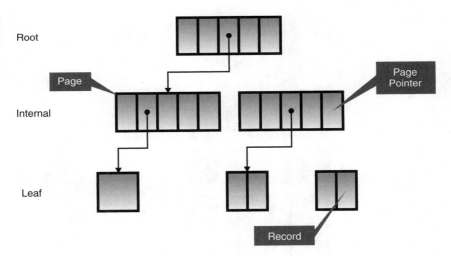

The rather large percentage of write operations compared to read operations is what makes the Exchange database particular in its design. If you wonder why Microsoft is not using its SQL Server database engine, consider the unique nature of the mail environment, and the fact that almost as much information is deleted as is stored during the life cycle of a server. The SQL Server database engine is a more traditional engine in which a large number of items are stored, typically during ETL (Extract, Transform, and Load) operations; during peak activity, you mostly read from the database. With Exchange 2007, the activity is 50% read and 50% write, and as such, you need a database engine that can process semistructured data of extremely variable size (from the 1 KB "Hello" message to the 20 MB PowerPoint presentation). With Microsoft Exchange 5.5, there was a single storage group with two possible databases in this storage group: the private Information Store and the public Information Store. With Exchange 2000, the intended number of storage groups increased to 15; however, due to

Virtual Address space constraints imposed by the 32-bit Windows operating system, Microsoft finally decided to enable only four storage groups for hosting up to five databases per storage group. With Exchange 2007 and the use of a 64-bit Windows operating system, there are no real constraints for the Virtual Address space of the STORE process, and you can have up to 50 storage groups and up to 50 databases in total. This means that you can deploy 10 storage groups with five databases each or 50 storage groups with one database each. As discussed later, using one database with one storage group is actually a best practice from an availability standpoint (Figure 1-7).

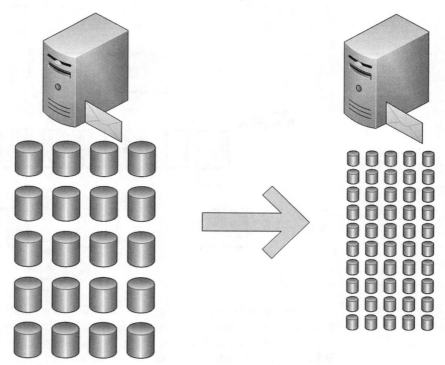

Figure 1-7
*From 20 to 50
databases per server*

Each storage group has a series of transaction log files. They are extremely important to Microsoft Exchange, because they represent the logging of transactions happening in the database as modifications occur. The transaction log files must be stored in a place where you have ample capacity. If you run out of space on a transaction log disk used by a storage group, your database will be dismounted. As a consequence, the entire mail service will be unavailable to the users whose mailboxes are located on a database mounted in that storage group. Transaction logging is a key capability of modern database engines, and they are required for implementing fast transaction processing and ACID properties. ACID properties are common in the database world and they represent the following:

A: Atomicity. The ability to make either a full transaction or no transaction at all. For Exchange 2007, it means that a message cannot be stored partially in the database or that a transaction is not done in halves. There can be a significant delay between the time you write the header of a mail message, and the time you finish writing the last byte of a large attachment to that message. During this time, you must ensure that the message is not partially stored in the database. It's an all-or-nothing transaction processing strategy.

C: Consistency. The ability for a database to be consistent at all times. In addition, while a message is being delivered to a mailbox, the user of that mailbox does not see parts of the message.

I: Isolation. There can be many concurrent access operations to the same parts of the database. For example, during the delivery of a message, the transport component will write a message in the Inbox of the user, while the user browses through that very same folder. The isolation allows the transaction to occur and not interact with other transactions in progress until those are fully committed.

D: Durability. Once a transaction is committed, it must be guaranteed permanent storage in the database (as opposed to being stored in the cache of the server, and possibly being lost if the server is abruptly shut down).

There is nothing specific to Microsoft Exchange regarding ACID properties; they are common for all professional database engines. To implement these properties, the Exchange database engine uses a dual-phase commit. Simply put, this method allows saving transactions to a log file when the transaction starts. The transaction consists of a series of database page modifications (such as insertion, modification, deletion). When the transaction ends successfully, the transaction is considered complete and the database pages are updated first in RAM for speed reasons. Then, a background process (known as the *checkpoint*) proceeds to write the modified pages to the database. If the transaction fails for some reason (e.g., loss of network connection), the in-memory page modifications are discarded as part of the transaction roll-back. Because the vast majority of the transactions succeed, you will rarely see roll-back activities on an Exchange server, and in fact, the use of memory for buffering and caching takes place on the server in an optimal way.

Capacity Considerations

For a start, you need to determine the global amount of data that you will need to deal with. A rough estimate is the number of mailboxes multiplied by the maximum size of those mailboxes, often associated with the mailbox quota. If you plan to deploy Exchange 2007–based database replication (in the form of LCR, CCR, or SCR), you need to factor in additional storage space. A simple approach is to multiply the storage quantity by 2. A more thorough approach will indicate that there is much more than quota and database replica. You also need to account for *growth*: Storage design is not something you will want to redo every 6 months or every year. You need to reach agreement with your business users on the estimated growth of storage, which may result from mergers, acquisitions, or simple organic growth. Because growth patterns are often not predictable, you will have to focus on a scalable design, that is, one that does not need architectural changes as you need to increase capacity or throughput or both! Common practices are to start with annual growth (15% is reasonable), and periodically revisit the topic with users (e.g., every 6 months or so).

Besides the fact that you need to provide storage to host the Microsoft Exchange data, you will also have to *manage* the storage: backup, recovery, expansion, and so on. The latter step is currently one of major turn-offs for modern companies to provide large (2 GB and above) mailboxes for their business users. Although the acquisition cost of storage drops on a regular basis, the cost of management and the need to have data readily available does not help the IT manager to provide large quantities of storage to users.

For Exchange 2007 and its database replication functions, the job of administering the storage is somewhat different, because replica databases are readily available in case the active database fails. It does not mean that the job of recovering a database does not exist anymore; however, this process can be largely simplified and improved when using database replicas.

One particular aspect of the Exchange 2007 database engine is the utilization of single-file databases. In other words, and unlike with Microsoft SQL Server, an Exchange 2007 database is a single file. If you have a database with 200 GB of data, you will have a single file of 200 GB for that database. This means that if a single page in that database gets corrupted, you may have to recover 200 GB of data instead of recovering that single page. This peculiarity of the ESE engine has caused many headaches to storage administrators for the following reasons:

- There is no index area. This is good and bad—typically, indexes are "hot" areas in a database, as they get updated when data are inserted or removed from the database. This represents both a challenge and an opportunity: It's a challenge because there is no possibility of focusing optimization techniques found in traditional high-end storage (e.g., solid-state disks or controller cache optimization).

- I/O is scattered across the entire database seek range. It's an opportunity because the I/O is actually spread across the entire volume, and if you use RAID (redundant array of independent disks) techniques such as those described in Chapter 2, you will benefit from having many small disks to host a database, rather than a few high-bandwidth disks.

- You need to create *big* volumes. How big is big in storage terms these days is quite a subjective consideration, but you will have to create, for high-end servers, volumes of 200 GB, 500 GB, or more for hosting the single-file databases, with no ability to store parts of the database on multiple logical units, channels, controllers, or disks, although it is possible to create volumes that *span* multiple LUN, controllers, and so on.

Regarding storage, these reasons make Exchange 2007 different from other commercial database engines such as the Microsoft SQL Server or Oracle's databases, just to name a few. It also means that the way to manage storage is quite different when you work with Exchange 2007 compared to SAP applications. This has been a big headache for Exchange administrators and Microsoft when dealing with Storage Area Network (SAN) administrators who designed storage for capacity purposes, and forgetting about essential characteristics of the Microsoft Exchange engine. It resulted in many critical situations where we got involved as Hewlett-Packard (HP) professionals, in order to explain the application requirements and demonstrate that high-performance storage had to be provided in terms other than pure MB/s (data rate).

Performance Considerations

The performance of the storage designed for Microsoft Exchange is critical to the overall user experience. Slow storage solutions for Exchange 2007 will lead to message queuing, sluggish response time, and delays in performing certain actions.

Introduced with Outlook 2003, the cache mode creates a local copy of the user mailbox on the client machine running Outlook, and performs background synchronization, in a relatively seamless manner. Initially designed for shielding the user experience from network conditions, the cache mode will also hide storage performance issues to a certain degree. However, this is not the only access mode for Microsoft Exchange, and users of Outlook Web Access will "feel" directly the performance deficiencies of the storage hosting the Microsoft Exchange databases.

The real value brought by Exchange 2007 is the utilization of the 64-bit Virtual Address provided by Windows 2003 x64. Having a large address space means that more data can be loaded in RAM; loading more data in RAM allows getting much better optimization out of the database engine

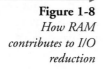

Figure 1-8
How RAM contributes to I/O reduction

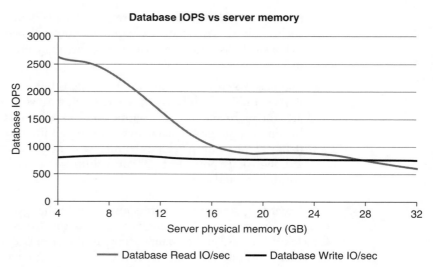

by caching data instead of accessing it to disk. Figure 1-8 shows an example of such reduction for a 2000-user workload with Exchange 2007 RTM.

It also allows delaying any disk access by turning a large number of small I/O operations into a smaller number of larger I/O operations. The best expression of this kind of improvement came with the increase of the database page size from 4 KB to 8 KB. The size of electronic mails is such nowadays that the chances to store a single message inside one database page was slimmer compared to 10 years ago. An 8 KB page size means that twice as much data go to disk in a single I/O compared to 4 KB page size.

Because using more RAM means that more pages are cached, Microsoft could proceed to further optimization by employing I/O coalescing techniques. The idea is to gather dirty pages that are contiguous on disk into a single larger I/O to disk as illustrated in Figure 1-9.

Figure 1-9
Benefits of I/O coalescing

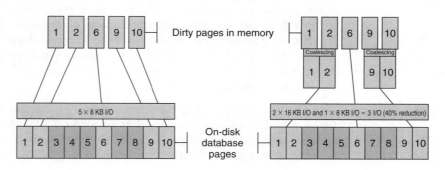

The resulting I/O request size is larger, but the request rate is smaller: instead of issuing five I/O in the above example, there are three I/O requests. While this may not be of importance for small servers (500 mailboxes and less), it contributes to making Exchange 2007 a viable application for low- to medium-performance storage as well as shared storage.

Challenges and Opportunities

By moving to Windows 64-bit computing, Microsoft opened itself to the comfort of a 64-bit Virtual Address space and the ability to use more RAM to cache data and increase the possibility for code optimization that eventually led to a significant decrease of I/O per second per user. By diminishing the I/O requirements, Microsoft made Exchange 2007 a much better citizen for shared storage environments such as Storage Area Network. Reduced requirements also enabled consideration of much less expensive storage technologies, such as serial ATA drives (SATA). The choice is left to the IT administrator and in particular the person in charge of storage management. We would like to emphasize that there is no good or bad choice, only one that is right for a given environment, comprising acquisition and management costs, as well as availability and recovery requirements.

The benefits just described come at a price: Rolling out Exchange 2007 means that you need to replace your servers and that you cannot perform an in-place upgrade, even if your Exchange 2003 already operates on 64-bit–capable processors. From a storage viewpoint, it means that there will be important movements of data, and that during a transition phase, which consists of moving mailboxes from legacy Exchange 2003 to Exchange 2007, you will need to oversize your transaction log files volumes to accommodate the massive addition of data in newly deployed Exchange 2007 databases.

If you must migrate from Exchange 2007 to Exchange 2007 SP1 *on Windows Server 2008*, you will need a similar approach; or even better, take advantage of the database transportability feature of Exchange 2007 and simply point your new servers to the "old" Exchange 2007 RTM databases. This is more or less easy depending on the underlying storage infrastructure. We have a preference for SAN when dealing with database transport because that technology does not require cabling or data transfer between servers. A wealth of information on this topic is available from the excellent Microsoft TechNet article located at http://technet.microsoft.com/en-us/library/cc296562.aspx.

With these requirements and characteristics of the Exchange 2007 in mind, you should now consider your options based on your requirements. This will lead you to challenges ("how can I satisfy both by business and IT requirements?") and opportunities ("which value will I deliver to my businesses?"). In this section, we review the most common challenges and opportunities; you may recognize your deployment scenario in one or several of them.

Large mailboxes: Breaking the 1 GB barrier

Corporate deployments of Microsoft Exchange have typically limited the quantity of mail per user store (i.e., the mailbox). Mailbox quotas are generally set to 20 MB (Exchange 4.0) to 200 MB (Exchange 2003). The reason for implementing a quota lies in the cost of managing and acquiring storage. The reality of modern businesses is that much of a company's business actually depends on email. Until 5 years ago, it was tacitly acknowledged that the business world would use email; however, email was not considered mission critical. Nowadays, email is commonly used in any kind of business. In fact, if you do not use email, you may find it difficult to do your job, even if picking up the phone, printing documents, and faxing them is still an option for communication. The increased use of the email function means that the data and Information Stored in the form of email is growing at a very fast pace. You cannot respond to user needs with 50 MB mailboxes, or you expose yourself to the generalized utilization of Outlook Personal Stores (PST files), which are local archives to the Outlook folder, and quite an inappropriate way to deal with email for several reasons:

- PST files can be quite large (>1 GB) and are implemented as single files. If you have one bad block on that file, you run the risk of losing all PST contents. The original PST file design was a size limit of 2 GB. With the introduction of Unicode-PST with Outlook 2007 you can create much larger PST files (5 GB and above); however, the PST design is rather inefficient for large files (>2 GB) and you will see significant performance problems characterized by frequent and inefficient disk accessing for information retrieval (browsing a folder, opening a message, etc.).

- PST files are opened in write mode. They cannot be stored on DVD if you intend to use them out of the box with Outlook. If you use a WORM (write-once, read-many) device for PST file archiving, you will have to copy the file to disk (read/write device) before you can actually open the file with Outlook 2007.

- Using PST files creates copies of corporate data on local PC disks, or file servers. Instead of bringing data together for better management, using PST disseminates the data, which renders its management and utilization far more difficult. For example, if a user deletes an item from a PST file, there is no dumpster and no way to restore that item, unless the PST files are restored. Another example is a legal search, which is rendered far more difficult if you have to search for email evidences (as part of a court order) across multiple PSTs scattered all over the place in your IT, and especially on desktops.

- Storing PST data outside the boundaries of the Microsoft Exchange server environment moves the data beyond the control of IT and notably of data management policies (e.g., archiving and retention).

You may expose your company to serious trouble if you permit data to be spread across your environment, and you could be held liable for it.

- A local backup of the client computer will back up the complete PST file every day, although only a small fraction of the file was changed.

Thus, PST files are problematic, but they have been useful to the user because they allow keeping data around, just in case. While this is a challenge for the IT administrator, it is also an opportunity to proactively tackle the problem by offering a reliable data management strategy that allows users to do their jobs, while simultaneously archiving email in an extremely efficient manner for users as well as administrators and legal auditors.

This opportunity can be implemented in various ways. With Exchange 2007, you will have two choices:

1. Keep mailbox size relatively small (<100 MB) and implementing a data management solution.

2. Make mailbox size large (2 GB) and implement additional data management solutions.

In both cases, you will want to get rid of the PST—not the data inside the PST, but the way of storing that data. In both cases, you will also want to implement a data management solution if you intend to get value from that data.

Because storage costs less every month, you have a good opportunity to provide the best of both worlds.

The value of archiving and data management

You can implement large mailboxes (500 MB and above) and apply policies on information retention using out-of-the-box solutions, such as Messaging Records Management, or implement relatively small mailboxes (200 MB and less) and still apply policies using Enterprise archiving solutions, such as HP Integrated Archiving Platform (http://h18006.www1.hp.com/products/storageworks/rim/) or Symantec Enterprise Vault (http://edm.symantec.com/enterprisevault/nam/#section=Home). These types of solutions are interesting for two reasons:

- They offload the Microsoft Exchange online storage from items that are seldom accessed. Microsoft Exchange Stores in online databases all the data related to a mailbox, regardless whether it is 1 year old or 1 hour recent. The challenge is that in an email system, the user needs the *most recent* information, not the one that is 1 year old. In other words, you need an environment that has high performance and that quickly recovers the last week or month of data, and it can be slightly slower for the data that is 1 year old, *because it is less frequently accessed.*

With Exchange 2007, there is no difference between frequently and infrequently accessed data in terms of performance. Each item in a database is stored in the same way, and this uniform way of managing data removes the possibilities to use a more optimized data storage mechanism. Getting data out of the way of Exchange 2007 database storage is also a good way to enable *rapid* migration (see later).

■ Data are stored in such a way that they can be categorized, indexed, and easily retrieved. In short, they turn data into information (i.e., data with additional data about the data—metadata). Turning data into information means that you can *leverage* the value of the data to support the business. In short, the email system is not a cost to the business, but can be a power engine to the business, because it has information that the business can exploit. In addition, you can leverage additional tools that help in electronic discovery (aka eDiscovery).

We are currently at the infancy of using email data and information for delivering value to businesses. Most of the business value of the solutions derives from legal search cases, that is, being able to significantly reduce time for information retrieval. They provide cost-cutting benefits for reducing online storage and getting rid of PST (an archiving solution that gives you unlimited mailbox quota, in substance).

In the course of various projects that we have been involved with, the quantity of data to migrate or transition to Exchange 2007 was the basic driving factor for the duration of the project (Figure 1-10). Why is this? The mass migration from one version of Microsoft Exchange to another, as is the case between Exchange 2003 and Exchange 2007, requires transferring the mailboxes from one server to another. While this can be done using a simple PowerShell command, the problem becomes more complex if you have to deal

Figure 1-10
The weight of data in a migration/transition project

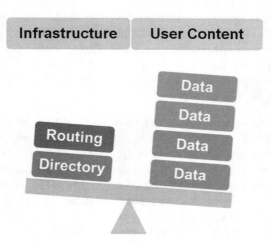

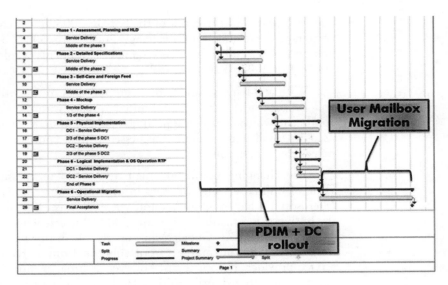

Figure 1-11
Infrastructure migration versus mailbox migration for a 120,000 mailbox project

with tens of thousands of mailboxes as shown in Figure 1-11. This project schedule has been sanitized; however, it was used in a real-life project where we were asked to provide information for migrating and consolidating 120,000 mailboxes into a single (dual-redundant) data center. Focus on comparing the infrastructure migration (PDIM means plan, design, implement, and manage in the HP Services project methodology) with the data migration.

The migration of the infrastructure is relatively simple and straight-forward. The migration of data are comparatively more complex, given the large quantities of mailboxes and associated data to move between servers over local or wide area network links. The problem with migration is that it is directly proportional to the quantity of data to move: If you reduced that quantity of data to, for example, 10 MB per user, you can migrate 4000 to 5000 mailboxes per week in a very safe way (metric used from a real-life Lotus Notes to Microsoft Exchange migration project).

The way to get rid of these data is to put them into an archiving system before the migration, migrate the mailboxes, and leave the data in the archiving system, because it is much better managed than in the online Exchange 2007 storage (single binary block storage across the entire data set, no need for online backups, etc.). In any event, very few of your users will need access to on 1-year-old email. They will need their most recent email online, for sure.

In summary

Unlimited quotas for free is what everybody wants. In reality, there are no free lunches or quotas, so you have to make compromises. Exchange 2007 offers management tools and storage efficiencies that allow you to considerably scale up the mailbox size, out of the box. In 2008, it was common to observe corporate deployments of Exchange 2007 with 500 MB and 1 GB mailbox quotas. In 2003, those very same environments would have considered 100 MB or 250 MB at most.

With archiving solutions that can pull data out of Microsoft Exchange, you can consider *virtually* unlimited quotas without PST. This type of approach, which is quite appealing in the corporate deployment, is often used in small and medium businesses with accompanying archiving/data management solutions.

The changing nature of email, its use in businesses, and the rising value of online services will help in evolving your approach to email. As a Microsoft Exchange administrator, you will have difficulty explaining why the business user mailboxes are only 200 MB in size when anyone can obtain a 5 GB mailbox with Google Mail for free. With this in mind, if your focus is mailbox size, you may get your solution from a free or low-cost email service provider. If your focus, however, is broader more than mailbox size (such as guaranteed availability or additional enterprise-level services), you will probably need to consider running your own deployment, although with reduced or limited mailbox quotas.

Because of the evolving nature of business requirements and market drivers, we recommend that you adapt your approach. This adaptability is based on the innate and unique ability of the human being to throw an object and hit a moving target (Figure 1-12).

Figure 1-12
Using ballistics to evolve your service

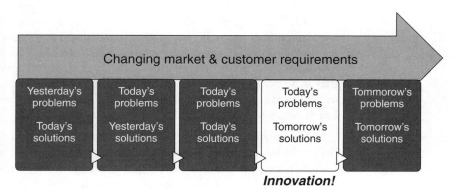

Based on this technique, identify your business users' problems—we assume that your IT problems are the same over many years: cost, cost, and cost. If you have more IT problems (e.g., lack of standards, political struggles), it means that you can have them resolved before you eventually get to how to reduce/optimize your costs. By the time you tackle the cost issues of your service, you can use ballistics techniques and study where your users and your company market are going, and provide a solution for existing problems. Don't try to spend time on trying to identify future problems. Focus on today!

Today, the mailbox size is a concern for many users (go and ask them) and the consumerization of IT as described by the Gartner analysts group during the Gartner Symposium/ITxpo in October 2005 (http://www.gartner.com/press_releases/asset_138285_11.html) in 2006 is real. Why pay in-house for something you can get for free outside? The answer lies in the value that your mail and messaging service can deliver to your business, and before you can determine the value in your environment, you need to go, search, and understand, *in situ*, the problems faced by your customers. So, don't neglect this very simple aspect of email, and make sure that whatever size of mailbox you provide to your users satisfies both the users and your financial controller. Exchange 2007 and its new and flexible storage management methods can be the answer; however, it might provide only 60% of the solution, and you might have to think out of the box.

Consolidation

Much of the value of the data, as mentioned previously, is enabled by gathering the data in a single location. Why? Because in a consolidated environment, you can mine and exploit data, and simplify and deliver standardized and cost-effective solutions. Distributed environments seldom allow this capability, or at least their full potential is not realized when being scattered around.

The globalization of the Internet, the growing speed of network connections (optical fiber at 100 Mbps is available for consumers in most advanced industrialized countries), and the major improvements made in Microsoft Exchange with its interaction with Outlook clients deliver a new way of email management. A worldwide consolidated environment is now feasible by offering a central service to anyone on the globe from a single location.

The Exchange 2007 storage techniques express their benefits in such an approach: They provide scalable and highly reliable storage management functions, with few requirements to the underlying storage technologies. This makes Exchange 2007 suitable for low-end storage as well as a much better citizen for shared storage deployments.

Beyond storage, there are other considerations to bring to the environment, such as the presence of secure network connections, and data center facilities suitable for 24 × 7 operations. These considerations or requirements cannot be neglected in your consolidation project.

Keep in mind that as part of a consolidation exercise, Exchange 2007 storage technologies support a much larger plan comprising network consolidation and rationalization and client desktop migration (not everyone runs Office 2007!).

Automation

Exchange 2007 comes with a new management paradigm, with the support and enhancement of PowerShell scripting. Even if you are not a big fan of scripting or command line interfaces, you will have to get used to PowerShell, because there are many management functions that can only be done from the Exchange Management Shell (EMS). In this section, we are going to study those commands that relate to storage management with Exchange 2007.

PowerShell comes with a verb–noun structure for each command. For each verb, you have an associated noun, and for the nouns, you have the ability to view properties and apply methods to the object or the component in focus pointed to by the noun. You need to know about EMS because it is a superset of the Exchange Management Console (EMC). Therefore, as we discuss Exchange 2007 storage design and cover some management aspects, we use EMS commands as examples that you can possibly transpose into your test, learning, or production environment. Beyond commands, there is the surrounding logic (e.g., conditional statements) to create scripts that can do fairly advanced work. For example, see the commands you should use to seed/re-seed a database in a CCR environment:

1. Open the Exchange Command Shell.

2. Suspend-StorageGroupCopy "<CMS Name>\SG Name>".

3. Clear out the files on the Passive node, and remove all files and directories in the SG directory on the Passive node.

4. Update-StorageGroupCopy "<CMS Name>\SG Name>". (This may take a few minutes depending of the size of the database.)

5. Resume-StorageGroupCopy "<CMS Name>\SG Name>".

You do not really have the option of avoiding EMS. You will quickly become accustomed to using the command line environment and pipelining commands. Then you might try to create scripts that carry several commands with associated logic.

A reminder: EMS enhances the local PowerShell environment with Exchange 2007–related cmdlets. There are system cmdlets that relate to storage manipulation. However, you might check with your storage vendor for cmdlets that go beyond the Windows environment and reach out to storage components. Regardless of the use of DAS or SAN, there are always management actions that need to be done on the storage subsystem, such as creating a new RAID set or migrating a clone volume. These commands can be either implemented via the VDS framework and the use of a VDS provider that talk to your vendor storage, or by using direct scripting/extensions.

Over 300 cmdlets are installed with the Exchange 2007 PowerShell snap-in. This is not the place to explore all of them. In the remaining portion of this section, we provide a task-oriented description of the commands, based on how and why they should be used rather than by their definition.

We mentioned previously that EMS is a superset of EMC. Any command that you activate through the graphical user interface (GUI) provided by EMC is actually implemented and executed as an EMS command. By using EMC, you often get the equivalent EMS command that will be executed—this is a fairly good way to quickly learn EMS, that is, studying EMC's utilization of EMS. You will rapidly get acquainted with executing these commands locally, without going through the user interface.

Some of the management functions in EMS are not implemented in the GUI-oriented EMC. Therefore, avoiding EMS is *not* an option, at least if you intend to do some relatively advanced management or use certain functions of Exchange 2007. For example, you can use PowerShell to monitor continuous replication status, create the remote CCR database, and seed or re-seed the database (Figure 1-13).

Figure 1-13
Export-Mailbox:
Allows exporting
the contents of a
mailbox to a PST
file with Exchange
2007 SP1.

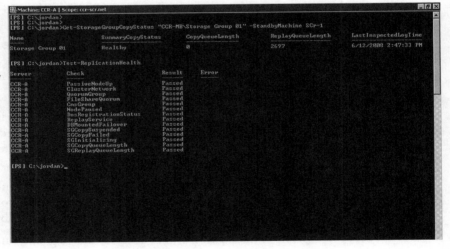

Overview of PowerShell commands

- Use the Get-* command with the appropriate noun, such as a database or a mailbox.

- Use the Set-* command with the appropriate noun for setting properties or status of the component.

Beyond setting and viewing properties, you have additional commands that actually change the object, and possibly its existence in the Exchange organization, such as Move, Rename, Delete, and so on. Each of the commands comes with a confirmation request by default (just to be sure), and some of them allow you to use the *whatif* switch, which is quite handy to determine how far can a command go in its processing.

- New-*
- Disable-*
- Remove-*
- Move-*
- Export-*
- Connect-*: Equivalent to the Mailbox Recovery Center (MRC) in Exchange 2003. It allows you to connect a mailbox to an AD account.

For more information about PowerShell commands for Exchange 2007 SP1, we recommend *Professional Windows PowerShell for Exchange Server 2007 Service Pack 1*, by Joezer Cookey-Gam, Brendan Keane, Jeffrey Rosen, Jonathan Runyon, and Joel Stidley (Wrox, 2007; ISBN: 978-0-470-22644-5).

Back to our focus: Exchange 2007 storage

In EMS, there are a few commands that relate to the management of Exchange 2007 storage. In this section, we list a few of them by the nature of work related to storage.

- Mailboxes can correspond to many things, in fact, including a user, a conference room, some office equipment (video projector), and a car (from a company fleet). They can also be linked to external accounts, particularly important in multi-forest deployments.

- Legacy mailboxes appear when they are still hosted in the Exchange 2003 environment. By the time you move them to an Exchange 2007 server, they become mailboxes (as in native mailboxes).

- Resource mailboxes are to be used for meeting, and can be given custom properties, such as the availability of coffee breaks or seating or other equipment. You must define the property in advance.

Managing quotas and determining mailbox size information are useful in determining the amount of white space in your environment (i.e., the actual size of data vs. the allocation space of the Exchange 2007 databases). The other functions found in PowerShell commands for managing storage components follow:

- Managing storage group properties (logs and databases locations)
- Identifying the database status (e.g., replication status)

- Finding about the database contents
- Creating and managing databases
- Continuous Replication management commands

Implementing policies to defining a common setting to a large set of objects is recommended. With Exchange 2003, you could define policies using ESM, and have them applied to objects, such as databases. Note that the mailbox quota was never one of them, even if it seemed like an obvious pick. One of the reasons is that changing the mailbox quota by mistake could have serious consequences on the follow-on operations of the server, such as getting in a full-volume situation (Figure 1-14).

```
[PS] C:\>get-mailbox | set-mailbox -ProhibitSendQuota 1GB  -ProhibitSendReceiveQ
uota 4GB -verbose
VERBOSE: Set-Mailbox : Beginning processing.
VERBOSE: Set-Mailbox : Administrator Active Directory session settings are:
View Entire Forest: 'False', Default Scope: 'nwtraders.com', Configuration
Domain Controller: 'SMBEX01.nwtraders.com'.
VERBOSE: Set-Mailbox : Searching objects "nwtraders.com/Users/Administrator" of
 type "ADUser" under the root "nwtraders.com/Users".
VERBOSE: Set-Mailbox : Previous operation run on domain controller
'SMBEX01.nwtraders.com'.
VERBOSE: Set-Mailbox : Processing object "nwtraders.com/Users/Administrator".
VERBOSE: Setting mailbox "nwtraders.com/Users/Administrator".
VERBOSE: Set-Mailbox : Applying RUS policy to the given recipient
"nwtraders.com/Users/Administrator" with the home domain controller "$null".
VERBOSE: Set-Mailbox : The RUS server that will apply policies on the specified
 recipient is "SMBEX01.nwtraders.com".
VERBOSE: Set-Mailbox : No properties changed for the object
"nwtraders.com/Users/Administrator".
WARNING: The command completed successfully but no settings of
'nwtraders.com/Users/Administrator' have been modified.
VERBOSE: Set-Mailbox : Saving object "nwtraders.com/Users/Administrator" of
type "ADUser" and state "Unchanged".
VERBOSE: Set-Mailbox : Previous operation run on domain controller
'SMBEX01.nwtraders.com'.
VERBOSE: Set-Mailbox : Administrator Active Directory session settings are:
View Entire Forest: 'False', Default Scope: 'nwtraders.com', Configuration
Domain Controller: 'SMBEX01.nwtraders.com'.
VERBOSE: Set-Mailbox : Searching objects "nwtraders.com/Information
Technology/Spencer Low" of type "ADUser" under the root
"nwtraders.com/Information Technology".
VERBOSE: Set-Mailbox : Previous operation run on domain controller
'SMBEX01.nwtraders.com'.
VERBOSE: Set-Mailbox : Processing object "nwtraders.com/Information
Technology/Spencer Low".
```

Figure 1-14
Managing quotas using PowerShell

This should therefore be a big caveat in the utilization of PowerShell commands against a large set of objects, especially when dealing with storage: You should carefully weigh the consequences of, say, changing the mailbox quota for all users on a server. For instance, you might want to grow the database volume size to meet a "worst-case scenario" and perhaps carry out the operations gradually (e.g., one database at a time) rather than all at once.

How many users per server?

This is a tough question, because the main driving factor is unlikely to be related to technology in general and storage in particular. The maximum number of users per server will depend on soft factors such as the recovery time objective and the recovery point objective, two key metrics in service-level definitions.

In addition, some organizations index the cost of their IT to the sheer number of servers they deploy rather than the complexity of those servers.

From a pure scalability viewpoint, Microsoft Exchange can scale to 10,000 users and above for a standard workload using Outlook 2007 clients. If the client is configured in cache mode, that workload will vary and possibly shield the clients from temporary performance issues.

From a pure manageability standpoint, you should consider how many users should be impacted if a server fails. That consideration derives from the answer to two questions:

- How likely is my server to fail?
- How fast can I recover if my server fails?

Let's discuss the extremes. If your server never fails, never slows down, and if it never crashes, never requires any sort of downtime for maintenance purposes, there is no reason to not load that server to the maximum server capability. If, for some reason, that server fails but it only takes 5 minutes to bring the service back to the users, you have no real reason not to load as many users as possible.

On the other hand, if your servers fail every month for two hours, you might step back and study the maximum impact you will want to have on your user community. There are other examples such as the following:

- If you require 2 hours of downtime per month, you will find it acceptable for 500 users, but not for 5000 users, because of a too large impact to your company.
- If your server only fails once a year, but it requires 3 days to restore all data from the last backup set, then you might be out of business.

What we are trying to explain here is that there is no single answer to the question, and much will depend on the technology and operational processes. (For documentation, see the Information Technology Infrastructure Library, http://en.wikipedia.org/wiki/ITIL for more information.)

Service levels

Before you make a decision on how to size your servers, how many databases you will have per server, and the corresponding technology to employ, you need to determine your service levels. Storage is at the center of the service available for Microsoft Exchange, even if Exchange 2007 comes with a set of key availability functions, such as continuous replicability.

To determine your service levels, ask yourself the following two questions:

- How much downtime is tolerable to my users?
- How much data am I ready to lose in the event of a disaster?

Often the first answer from the business users to the first question will be "zero minutes," and the answer to the second question will be "none." However, building such a solution can be significantly more complex and expensive compared to a solution with "30 minutes" for the first and "1 hour" for the second. The reality is that technology delivery by Exchange 2007, in terms of continuous replication, is very effective when dealing with "reasonable" answers to your service-level question.

In the past, we used to deal with additional figures for service levels related to performance, such as "ability to open a 1 KB email in 3 seconds." This kind of key performance indicator is of less and less importance because of the Outlook cache mode operation, and because performance with Exchange 2007 tends to be less of a concern. Why? The I/O reduction and the increased power of modern CPUs make high-end servers (5000 users and more) relatively safe to deploy from a resource consumption viewpoint.

Later in this book, we review service levels in greater detail, and we will see that they can be implemented in many ways.

SAN or DAS?

With Exchange 2007 and the application-level data management functions (such as Continuous Replication), the need for a strong storage infrastructure that delivers these functions has significantly diminished. In fact, the world of storage and applications has evolved in such a way that the utility model applied to storage becomes less relevant. Let's take an analogy: An infrastructure utility service is like the provisioning of electricity to companies and households. This model regarding storage was valid until we had a situation in which every household item actually needs its own power scheme. Instead of using 220 V/50 Hz AC power, we have one appliance that needs a 12 V DC input, another that requires 380 V in tri-phase mode, and so on. Look at your data center and applications and determine whether all applications require all the storage functions in your SAN infrastructure. Do all the applications share the same procedure for backup and recovery? Do they use the same mechanisms for data replication and recovery from it? Probably not. So, when Microsoft Exchange comes with its own data management functions, you can legitimately ask yourself if you should continue the same storage approach that you adopted in the past.

You first need to determine how storage is typically provisioned to your application servers. There are two different approaches:

- Storage is an infrastructure component, provided as a utility service to servers. These servers consume storage by capacity units (e.g., units of 8, 16, 32, or 64 GB). If your application server needs storage capacity (beyond a local boot/swap disk unit), you need to contract the storage provisioning organization for the required capacity.

■ Storage is a server add-on. When you order your server, you size whatever disks your server requires, and you provision this storage in the best possible way. For example, it can be local disks or a dedicated SAN array for your application.

With Exchange Server 2007, some companies take an application-driven approach, favoring DAS components, while others take an infrastructure-driven approach, favoring a strictly standardized SAN infrastructure.

The two approaches are not mutually exclusive. You may very well decide to implement the Exchange Server 2007 replication functions using SAN back-end storage components. This is the approach taken in many environments that have standardized SAN storage for their applications and prefer to take advantage of the built-in Exchange replication rather than use SAN-based replication. You may also decide to take advantage of some of the key SAN features for Exchange 2007, such as the ability to rapidly transport databases from one server to another. This is something that cannot be achieved when using local disks.

We do not wish to dismiss the value of SAN or DAS right away, and in fact, we will examine later the value points for each technology. Instead, we prefer to give you a heads-up on the kind of change that you can envisage if you have a degree of liberty. Some companies have strict policies that discard the use of local storage, not just for technology reasons, but also for operational and process reasons.

Top 10 Topics for Exchange 2007 Storage

In this section, we would like to provide with the top 10 key topics you will need to address as you design storage solutions for Microsoft Exchange 2007 SP1 by increasing order of importance. They are based on our experience, and you may have additional considerations.

Topic 10: Know your users

Are all your users equal? You may provide different SLA to reduce the total cost of the solution because the concierge does not need the same highly available mailbox that the CEO would like to have. You may also determine that for email to be a power engine to your business, you need to significantly exceed the current mailbox size for certain users.

Topic 9: Who does what?

Who is responsible for which component of the Exchange environment, such as the storage infrastructure for the SAN department or the Exchange team. Will the backup department/team or the Exchange team run backups and restores?

Topic 8: Measure and monitor

You should consider how you monitor the environment from the beginning and not as an afterthought.

Topic 7: Automate

Any setup of storage subsystems and Exchange servers should be done in an automated way (e.g., by using scripted PowerShell commands) instead of manual procedures. Manual procedures are error-prone, and will not allow you to meet your recovery time objective.

Topic 6: Archiving

Will you use archiving? There are two reasons: legal reasons for compliance purposes, and ease of data management. We believe that you should have archiving in the scope of your design, even if you do not implement it immediately with your Exchange 2007 roll-out.

Topic 5: Mailbox size

The size matters when you eventually get to design Exchange 2007 storage. You may overengineer your solution design and calculate the various nitty-gritty details of a storage design, but understanding the sheer storage capacity you have to deal with is very important. A 500 GB system gets implemented with different tools and technologies than a 10 TB system.

Topic 4: Cost

What is driving cost in your storage environment? Is it the size, acquisition, or running operational cost? As technologists, we have a natural tendency to ignore costs, but they have major importance in the way you design your solutions, such that you do not rush for a cheap solution that will only deliver incremental operational costs, or an expensive solution that will deliver little benefit. The right solution is a balance, and technical matters alone are inadequate for mail solutions.

Topic 3: IT standards

Ruthless standardization is a key driving factor for cost reduction and simplification in an IT environment. You must determine the standards in place and determine whether they (1) need to be improved or (2) must be followed. In the world of Exchange 2007 storage, the first standard you will be confronted with is whether you should use SAN or DAS. We return to this aspect later in this book, but you have to make a decision, and we prefer that you make that decision based on your IT standards rather than on fugitive product capabilities.

Topic 2: Service levels

Storage design for Exchange 2007 is not possible unless you know your service levels. They do not need to be expressed in a 50-page document; a simple table, such as in Figure 1-15, will suffice.

Figure 1-15

Sample service levels for Exchange 2007

	Bronze	Bronze	Premium
Mail Quota (MB)	75	300	1,000
Anti-spam	•	•	•
BlackBerry		•	•
ActiveSync	•	•	•
Calendaring	•	•	•
Outlook Anywhere		•	•
OWA		•	•
Single Item/Mailbox Restore		•	•
Deleted Item Ret	7	14	30
Recovery Time Objective	24h	8h	2h
Recovery Point Objective	24h	4h	15mn
Encrypted Email		•	•
Fax		•	•
Disater Tolerance		○	•
One DC	n/a	n/a	n/a
Two DC	RTO = 24h RPO = 24h	RTO = 2h RPO = 24h	RTO = 1h RPO = 24h
Archiving + e-Discovery		•	•
Dedicated Forest	•	•	•
AD Hosting	•	•	•
Legacy Public Folder		•	•
Estimated count	90,000	30,000	4,000

Topic 1: Requirements

Don't start any deployment without understanding the business and user requirements. They represent your problem statement, and if you do not have a good problem statement, you will not have a good solution. If you do not have a *simple* problem statement, you will not be able to develop an optimal solution. Examples of business requirements for your Exchange 2007 storage design appear below. Perform your own analysis and compare it with ours.

Good Sample Requirements	Good or Bad?
Unlimited quota	
No downtime	
No data loss	
99.9% availability	
20% cost reduction per year over next 5 years	
2€ per month per mailbox	
No more than 15 minutes of data loss	
Open 1 KB message in less than 2 seconds	
BlackBerry support for 10% of users	
Maximum length of a single outage is 2 hours	
Maximum length of a single outage is 2 hours	
Each backup set has to be retained for 1 year	
Full VSS backup has to be performed each day and the split-mirror volume has to be available for 7 days for instant recovery	
Each server role must run at least three different virus scanner engines.	

Turn the page for the solutions to the exercise.

Solution to exercise		
Unlimited quota	Bad	It's a good requirement but incomplete—it needs to be complemented with other requirements, such as the user environment (always on, distributed, mode of access, etc.).
No downtime	Bad	Again, a good requirement, but not precise enough—perfection is a fine target, but difficult and expensive to implement. It could be a good requirement if complemented with other requirements.
No data loss	Good	This is a good requirement because it is precise; however if there are *transactions* that should not be lost, you may even reconsider whether a general-purpose email solution is the best approach.
99.9% availability	Good	Simple, standard, and easy to measure. It could be better if accompanied by mutually acceptable measurement techniques.
20% cost reduction per year for next 5 years	Ugly	Why do people have to make things so complex? Who will be around 4 years from now to ensure that metric? What cost are we talking about anyway? Acquisition, operations, or both?
2€ per month per mailbox	Good	Simple figure—not easy to calculate, but that is just a requirement. This is easy to monitor, even if it's hard to actually implement, because there is more to the cost of a mailbox.
No more than 15 minutes data loss	Good	Realistic requirement.
Open KB message in less than 2 seconds	Bad	Very precise but unrealistic to measure. This requirement is a good basis for improvement, however.
BlackBerry support for 10% of users	Good	Simple (again!) with enough details to allow solution designers to implement the function with the right technology.
The maximum length of a single outage is 2 hours	Bad	This is a bad requirement because it does not define whether the RTO starts at the time that a user opens a support ticket or at the time the operational staff have finished troubleshooting and starts with the recovery procedure. This requirement is also bad because it was for an environment with 70,000 mailboxes. Do all 70,000 mailboxes need this high SLA (i.e., not all users are equal)? Are you willing to pay the necessary hardware and operational cost for the necessary leading-edge configuration?

(Continued)

Solution to exercise (Continued)		
Each backup set has to be retained for 1 year	Ugly	Backup is not archiving, and backup is not the method to meet compliance regulations.
A full VSS backup has to be performed each day and the split-mirror volume has to be available for 7 days for instant recovery	Bad	You should rework this kind of requirement. It is unlikely that you are going to spend the money for eight times the storage space that is required for your database and log file disk volumes.
Each server role must run at least three different virus scanner engines	Good	Virus protection is very important. Running multiple and different virus scanner products and putting in place multiple layers of protection comprises common best practice, but security has to be reasonable. A better approach, for example, would be to use product A on the edge, product B on the HT, product C on the mailbox server, and product D on the client—and this procedure is already extreme.

2

Basic Concepts of I/O Systems

This chapter is dedicated to key storage terminology and concepts that are used later in this book.

Start with Basics

Storage is inevitable in any kind of computing environment; the goal is to have a place where you can keep data at rest. This term is often used for making the difference between volatile and temporary data, compared to data that are supposed to be stored for a certain amount of time, sometimes years, depending on the retention requirements of that piece of data.

Storing data can be done in the following ways:

- Randomly—Data are written anywhere on the mass media. This is often the case for disk access and a bit of nuisance when it comes to high performance.

- Sequentially—Data are stored in sequence. The second block is written after the first block, and the third block has to wait for the second block to be written before it can be processed.

The mass media on which you store data varies depending on the density, speed, and frequency of access. Often called the duty cycle, this access frequency is important to best judge the type of device you should use. To keep it simple, let's consider that there are two distinct families of mass media: disks and tapes.

Magnetic and optical disks

This type of media allows random access to data; however, some media, such as magnetic disks, are best performing with both sequential and random access because of their relatively slow, head seek time and rotation speed (Figure 2-1).

Disks are composed of a series of plateaus that rotate around the same axis. They are simultaneously accessed by one or more heads, reading or writing

Figure 2-1
*HP's small form
factor 72 GB disk
drive*

more information, more rapidly, for the same head movement. Disks are mechanical devices and as such are vulnerable to all sorts of physical disturbances, including heat, water/humidity, and shocks. While it's unlikely that your Microsoft Exchange server will be subject to shocks, it is very likely that you will have to deal with power specifications and cooling for your storage environment, as well as making sure that devices do not interfere with each other by their relative vibrations.

You may think that heat is generated by rotation of the disk, but in fact, it is primarily due to the disk accesses made by the head (also known as the *actuator*). The frequency of access to the disks somehow conditions the lifetime of the disks. Some disks are designed to be infrequently accessed, while others are designed to be accessed all the time. This has some importance for when you will need to choose storage disks for your Microsoft Exchange environment, given that not all disks are created equal.

Disks include SMART (self-monitoring, analysis, and reporting technology) functions that allow a disk drive to auto-diagnose its performance. Over time, the disk determines whether error rates or time to spin up the plateau or the data throughput degrade. If they do, it will signal to the host (the unit that the drive is connected to) that disk replacement should be considered. This kind of technology is excellent for catching aging drive conditions. It does not prevent, however, the loss of one or more drives because a fan failed in a disk shelf (quite common, actually), resulting in severe heat across many disks!

Magnetic tapes

Mounted on streaming devices, the magnetic tapes used to be the mass storage media for the computer in the 1970s. At that time, data were stored on tapes, and tapes were sequentially accessed. They still are nowadays, except that their density is much greater, resulting in high capacity for a relatively low volume. The key benefit of tapes is that they can be transported to a fire-proof vault (for example) with minimal effort. If you keep your data only on disk devices, you have to find a way to have the data transmitted over a network link or some removable media for it to be duplicated *and* located on another site. We will return to the concept of offsite storage later.

Offsite storage is mostly relevant if you wish to use or process your data in a different location than the production environment. This is primarily required for disaster recovery, and prevents information loss—one of the worst things that could happen to your company.

Figure 2-2 shows an HP Ultrium tape cartridge for LTO tape drives (linear tape open, a standard developed by HP, IBM, and Seagate). Magnetic tapes typically can stream data in and out *faster* than a single disk. If you need to stream data even faster, backup software solutions can stream data to multiple tape drives at the same time. You can back up your 1 TB of data in less than an hour, but it will be more expensive, because it will require an infrastructure that can transfer 1 TB in 1 hour (approximately 300 MB per second) and enough tape drives to save those 1 TB of data!

Figure 2-2
HP Ultrium tape cartridge

Units of measurement

When dealing with storage, you have to understand key terminology for the measurement of the storage device. In this section, we explain some terms that will be used throughout the book.

Capacity measurement unit: Gigabyte (GB)

One gigabyte (GB) is 1 billion bytes, using the giga prefix from the Système International (in French in the text). There are in fact two ways of expressing a billion bytes:

Decimal: 1 gigabyte = 10^9 (1,000,000,000) bytes

Binary: 1 gigabyte = 1024^3 ($1024 \times 1024 \times 1024$)

In reference to RAM size and file sizes, the GB unit will be in binary form. Regarding network transmission, the giga prefix will be 10^9 instead of 1024^3. The same goes with raw storage. This is one of the reasons why a smaller capacity expressed by Windows is typical compared to the actual capacity of the disk drive. For the rest of the book, we refer to the binary form of the gigabyte, that is, 1024^3.

Data rate measurement unit: Megabyte per second (MB/s)

The data rate is the quantity of data that can be transmitted during a particular time lapse. The second is often used as the referent time period, but you will find in the various Exchange 2007–related literature that people refer to MB per minute or GB per hour. The data rate is often used in activities that involve the transmission of a large quantity of data. For Microsoft Exchange, this is primarily for database copy operations, backup, and recovery (Table 2-1).

Table 2-1   *Transfer rates for different types of storage media and interconnect*

Disk	30 MB/s
LTO-3 tape	80 MB/s
Optical fiber	100 MB/s (FDDI mode)
Optical fiber	1000 MB/s (gigabit Ethernet)
Copper wire	1000 MB/s (gigabit Ethernet for <100 m)
Internet backbone	2048 MB/s and above

Request rate measurement unit: I/O per second (IOPS)

The request rate is a critical measurement in Exchange 2007 deployment. It defines the maximum number of input or output operations that you can issue to a disk drive or a logical unit. Such an operation is often abbreviated as "I/O".

When you make a request to a storage component, you in fact involve protocol commands and mechanical movements of disk heads that cause the particular request to drain resources and be limited in the number of operations that you can do during a defined time lapse.

With Exchange 2007, we often refer to the I/O per second as the request rate or IOPS (the acronym for I/O per second). Modern disks typically have a 160 IOPS request rate capability. Interestingly enough, even though we notice some significant improvement in the capacity and data rate of disks (double at least every 2 or 3 years), the request rate has not progressed as much.

Response time: Seconds

This is a simple time unit that indicates how long it took between the moment the data was requested to the application, and the moment it was made available to that application. The response time is primarily important for the request rate: You may issue a large number of requests to a device; however, these requests might not be returned at the same response time for each of them. This can depend on placement of the disk and heads of the disk drive at the time you requested that information. It can also depend on the quantity of data requested.

We often qualify a logical disk by the number of I/O that it can perform. We should always associate this number of I/O to a given response time. Let's use the analogy of filling a car's gas tank. Assume that you fill your gas tank in, for instance, 5 minutes, but if there are five cars in front of yours, the total time spent at the gas station, to get the gas tank filled, will take approximately 5 minutes per car (if they have a gas tank of a similar size, plus some marginal time for payment). The big question is can you afford to wait? It depends:

- You can wait if you were on your way back from work and aiming to relax on the porch of your house. After all, whether you come home at 5:30 pm or 5:50 pm will not make a big difference.

- There are times where you just can't wait. For instance, if you have to fetch your kids from school, you probably do not want to have them stay on the street for long. The school's staff have many other things to do after class and kids want to go home.

Put this back in perspective with Exchange 2007: When the server reads a database page from disk, what is potentially behind each demand? Users are directly affected by wait times on storage, and this is why it's so important to not only consider how many I/Os you can get out of a logical or physical volume, but also how fast you can get this I/O completed.

Let's consider a disk drive that can perform 400 I/O per second at 35 ms response time, and another disk drive that performs 150 I/O per second at 15 ms response time. Which one is best? For Microsoft Exchange, because the response time is important, the disk drive that responds the fastest will be the best for transactional access, that is, managing the end user workload. However, you will need to ensure that the disk can indeed satisfy the demand;

otherwise, you will have the same problem as you had at the petrol station—queuing! Disk queuing will increase your response time to a point that can render your application virtually unusable for your users.

We often see that storage administrators focus on the request rate and data rate, but forget to associate a response time figure to those rates. Although not so important for the data rate, the response time for the request rate is a very important criterion to use in determining whether the storage device meets the performance requirements of the application, in our case, Exchange 2007.

Relation to each other

If you need to tune a logical or physical disk for request rate, you may adopt a different strategy than if you tune it for data rate. For example, if you try to access a file in a sequential manner, you will have a very high data rate if the data are contiguously located on media, regardless of the actual support. This is a good example of why tape drives continue to have excellent performance over the past few years, despite the growing presence of cheap storage devices.

On the other hand, if you need to access relatively small pieces of information in a random way, that is, at various offsets of a file, you will need to focus on the request rate capability of the logical or physical disk instead of its data rate capability. Considering that you often have intervening disk access protocols, such as SCSI and fiber channel, and controllers, the access data pattern and throughput (IOPS or MB/s) can significantly vary depending on the optimization found in such components.

Let's look at Figure 2-3, which is based on simple mathematics. If you have a large I/O size, you will require far more I/O to achieve a given data rate, and inversely, if you issue a large number of small I/O, you will *not* have a high data rate.

The reason is that the data rate is a function of both the request rate and the size of the request. In other words, the larger the I/O, the more data you will transfer in a single request. Because hard disks tend to be bound by the number of I/O that you can issue, applications that need to transfer large quantities of data use large I/O sizes, ensuring that they do not overwhelm the request rate capability of the device, instead use as much of the bandwidth for transmitting data as possible.

In Figure 2-3, we outline three different I/O sizes:

- **256 KB** is typically the size used by backup applications. Of course, in order to issue a 256 KB I/O size, you must be able to have 256 KB of contiguous data (hence the need for contiguous files in general-purpose Windows environments). Note that you quickly saturate a Fibre Channel connection (4 Gbps) with less than 250 IOPS.

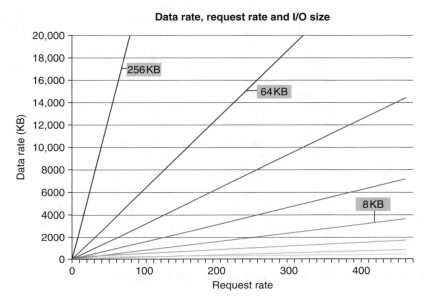

Figure 2-3
Request rate versus data rate

- **64 KB** is sometimes found in Microsoft Exchange environments for log file flushes and certain sequential accesses to the database (such as during an online backup).

- **8 KB** is the page size of the database engine for Exchange 2007, and represents the majority of the I/O size on a Microsoft Exchange server, despite the presence of I/O coalescence introduced (in fact reinforced) with Exchange 2007.

With this in mind, you should now realize that the request rate is a far more important metric for Microsoft Exchange than the data rate.

What is important to Exchange 2007

For Exchange 2007, you will first need to ensure that you can provide online storage that is reliable and fast. The storage speed for Microsoft Exchange depends on the activity you perform on the server. For regular online access to email, you need to have a good I/O throughput (request rate). The size of the I/O is typically that of a database page, set to 8 KB with Exchange 2007 (with previous version of Microsoft Exchange, this was 4 KB). It may be much larger in case you can bring pages together via a single request, or if you run a backup job that does not really care about the page-level structure of the database.

For backup and recovery purposes, you need to have a good throughput (data rate). The disk throughput in 2008 can be in excess of 125 MB per second for a single disk drive (Seagate Cheetah, http://www.seagate.com/www/en-us/products/servers/cheetah/). In fact, if you optimize the disk layout, and use, for example, several disks combined in a single logical volume (RAID), you can exceed that data rate. For sequential access devices, such as tape drives, a single LTO3 tape drive can exceed a throughput of 200 MB per second in native rate. Add to that hardware compression and you can assume that those devices that sustain pretty data transmission rates for backup and recovery. Of course, they are not used on their own, and they often depend on the surrounding infrastructure and server connectivity that can have a bottleneck impact from a performance viewpoint.

Finally, we believe that it is important to make the point that the performance data explained here are based on a single component only: disk or tape drive. In reality, you will need to assemble disks together to create larger and more powerful disk units that can sustain the workload applied by hundreds of users. That is the topic of the next section.

Anatomy of a Storage Controller

Because a CPU accesses data directly from RAM, but certainly not directly to disk, there is a requirement to connect that CPU (or CPUs) to disks by the means of a storage controller, schematized in Figure 2-4.

Figure 2-4
Logical view of a storage controller

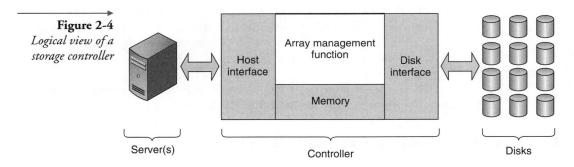

The key components of a storage controller follow:

- On the left, we have a host interface. In the next chapter, we discuss further ways to connect storage to a server. For now, think of it as a power adapter that you have to plug in the wall to power your iPod, unless you wish to fry it.

- On the right, we have a bunch of disks. They are connected using a bus, which has standardized physical and electrical properties. Typically, disks have their own power entry, and source their power from infrastructure components that we will not describe at this point.

- In the middle, we have the array management function (AMF). Implemented as microcode (firmware) for small controllers, the AMF's goal is to manage the server requests and communicate and transform them into commands that can be sent to the disks. For example, "give me logical block #189" will translate into "give physical block #12 on disk #1 and physical block #45 on disk #2". One of the key functions of the AMF is the implementation of RAID (see next section) or other optimization algorithm aimed at improving request speed to storage.

- To assist the controller in certain AMF operations, there is a memory area. The goal of this memory area, called the "cache," is to store data that has been read or written, just in case it is accessed again.

That's it. A controller, regardless of its price, basically consists of those functions. Not all of them are equal in their implementation. For example, the controller may be implemented with a redundant processing mechanism, either by running two AMF on separate chips, or by implemented AMFs that can in fact communicate to each other, and create a redundant solution. Storage is so important to Microsoft Exchange in particular and business applications in general, that redundancy is key, and you have many extreme ways to implement that model, from the one comprising a simple ASIC (application-specific integrated circuit), to the one comprising a large enclosure with dedicated management consoles and redundant cooling and power supply.

In the next section, we discuss two key features of controllers that matter a lot to Microsoft Exchange: RAID systems and the controller cache.

RAID

In the late 1980s, Berkeley University documented a way to assemble many small disks to create larger disks. Known as *redundant array of inexpensive disks* (RAID), this model aimed at using small cheap disks that could be arranged into bigger volumes from the server viewpoint. Even if you were to use four disks of 10 MB to create a 40 MB volume, the resulting solution would be cheaper than buying a single 40 MB disk at the time. In 2008, disks of large capacity are no longer expensive. In fact, the progress made in storage technology is such that large disks will tend to be cheaper by GB than smaller disks.

RAID, later used for *redundant array of independent disks*, is a technique that combines several independent disk drives into a single logical volume. It presents characteristics that are similar to using only a single disk. These characteristics follow:

Availability. By building redundancy in the array, you can sustain the loss of an individual member in a RAID set.

Performance. By combining several disks, you can get increased through-put in terms of both data rate (MB per second) and request rate (I/O per second).

Size. The resulting volume can be made larger than a single disk drive, quite suitable for environments in which the data cannot be broken down, such as with Microsoft Exchange databases.

Cost. For any given US dollar or euro amount, you get a certain quan-tity of usable storage space. Depending on requirements, you can get factors of 10 or 20 between any two configurations. Cheap con-figurations typically have a low level of redundancy and do not per-form very fast. On the other hand, the performance requirements for Microsoft Exchange have vastly changed with Exchange 2007 and the 64-bit computing model. Slow and cheap disks may represent acceptable options again, as long as they are reasonably reliable.

RAID comes in many levels, with the base levels ranging from 0 to 5. Additional levels have been developed, such as 10, 0+1, and 6 or 7. Combining RAID volumes into stripes is common, as is appending the indi-vidual volumes RAID level with a 0 (e.g., RAID50 for a stripe of RAID5 volumes, RAID10 for a stripe of mirrors, etc.).

Some of these levels have value in the Microsoft Exchange environ-ment, whereas the storage manufacturers seldom implement others. For Microsoft Exchange 2007 and other Microsoft server technologies such as SQL Server, RAID5, RAID1, and RAID0+1 (aka RAID10) are the most relevant because they combine data redundancy with increased performance levels, and that's what makes choice relevant. In the following, we examine the most common RAID levels and briefly state their advantages and incon-veniences, and then we compare them.

RAID0

The basis of RAID0 is *disk striping*. The idea is to combine several disks into a logical volume, the resulting size of which is the sum of the size of each disk making up the volume. In RAID0, all disks must have the same capacity and geometry. Depending on the controllers, you can mix drives of varying size (geometry), but the lowest common denominator will always be used.

The advantages of RAID0 are to obtain the maximum quantity of storage (the sum of the capacity of each drive), and the maximum level of performance (the sum of request rate of each individual drives).

For instance, five 72-GB disks combined in a RAID0 array will yield a total raw capacity of

$$5 \times 72 \text{ GB} = 360\text{GB}$$

This combination has the ability to sustain up to 650 random I/O per second (if you consider that each single disk drive can handle 130 I/O per second), no matter whether the I/O request is a read operation or a write operation. (We will see later that a write request is more "costly" than a read request.) Depending on the I/O size and the low-level formatting of the array (mainly the chunk size), you may get a little less throughput, but you get the overall idea. Later in this chapter, we focus on the necessity of properly configuring the chunk size, if that is at all possible (or relevant) on your controller.

The main disadvantage of RAID0 is the lack of data redundancy. If you lose a single member of the RAID0 set, you lose all volume content and get an opportunity to check how good your last backup was.

Figure 2-5 describes the layout of data blocks in a RAID0 disk subsystem. The correspondence between the virtual volume blocks and the actual disk blocks is done by a component of the RAID controller called the array management function. Consider the logical disk obtained from the RAID0 disk array described in Figure 2-5.

Figure 2-5
RAID0 disk
structure

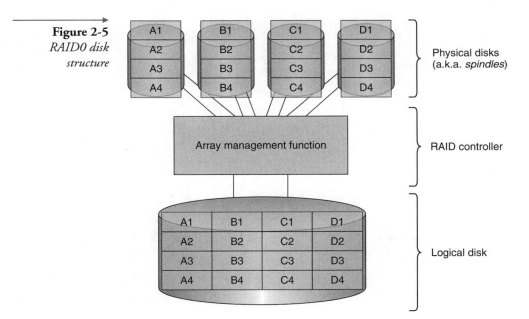

A single "layer" of blocks at the same level (e.g., A1, B1, C1, and D1) is called a *stripe*. The size of each block is called the *stripe depth*, also known as the *chunk size*. Chunk size is important in performance optimization, depending on the I/O size. This subject is covered more fully later in this chapter. The size of a stripe is determined by the number of members multiplied by the size of each chunk or stripe depth.

RAID0 is implemented at times in benchmarking environments to avoid the storage subsystem's presenting itself as a bottleneck. This is an arguable tactic; although it gives the best results, it can indicate great performance in a configuration that wouldn't be suitable for a production environment, given the hassle of having to resort to restore operations and the negative impact it has on service availability. Besides, you may obtain better performance gain by adjusting the disk controller configuration or simply using RAM. (Remember, 64-bit is golden for Microsoft Exchange!)

RAID 1

RAID1 is another fundamental RAID level that keeps and maintains the exact same content of a disk drive on one or more additional disks. RAID1 is often referred to as *disk mirroring*, and carries the great advantage of duplicating the contents of a given disk drive onto another drive. Should the initial drive fail (or any member of the RAID1 set), operations can still continue by getting data on other valid members of the RAID1 set (Figure 2-6).

Figure 2-6
RAID1 disk structure

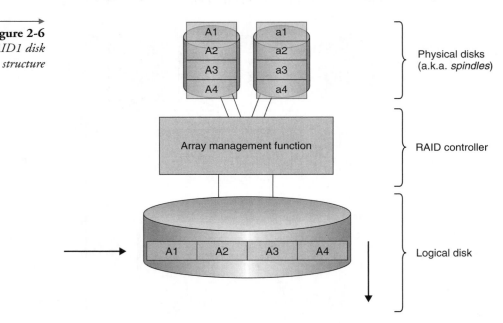

The advantage of RAID1 is the high level of data redundancy and availability. In fact, it carries other advantages, especially in the area of point-in-time backup operations, which is discussed later. The disadvantage of RAID1 is that you lose capacity. If you combine two 72 GB disk drives in a RAID1 array, the resulting raw capacity is 72 GB. You've just lost the capacity of the mirroring drive. The same thing applies if you arrange three drives together: The resulting capacity is still the size of one disk.

From a request rate perspective, the deal is somewhat different depending on whether you mostly read from the volume or write to it. In read operations, the RAID controller can read from either of the two volumes (in a two-volume RAID1 set) and yield a performance level of 200 I/O per second, given that your individual disk drives can sustain 100 I/O per second.

When it comes to write operations, the data have to be written to both volumes at the same time, and in some cases, the resulting response time is dependent on the slowest drive to complete the operation. Therefore, a two-disk RAID1 set has a write performance of 100 I/O per second. This is the first instance in which we see that the read/write ratio gains importance in the actual performance of the volume. When we compare the RAID levels, you will see that the R/W ratio can weigh significantly in choosing the most appropriate level for your environment.

Figure 2-6 describes the block layout of a RAID1 volume. Note that for two disks, the contents are the same. As mentioned earlier, you could combine more than two drives in a RAID1 set. A three-member RAID1 volume can handle the loss of two disk drives (really, the probability of losing two drives in a three-disk RAID1 set is quite small). The other advantage is that you can "break" the mirror (without necessarily affecting the current operation of the drive, although it's best to do this with a "quiesced" volume), and in a matter of seconds you have a duplicate copy of your original volume. This is a fast way to back up data. Given the decreasing price of storage these days (in terms of $/GB), this can be an interesting approach, and we'll see that in high-end environments, this becomes a sound data duplication strategy for backups of the replica database of Exchange 2007 CCR passive nodes.

RAID5

We skip RAID 2, 3, and 4, because not only do they carry little advantage in terms of performance and availability, but they are seldom implemented in modern controllers. RAID5 is by far the most popular RAID level in a production environment, sometimes rightly and sometimes wrongly. You'll see why shortly.

RAID5 builds on the notion of disk striping. But unlike RAID0, where there is no data redundancy, RAID5 introduces the notion of extraneous parity information, which can be used should a member of a RAID set fail. The parity information is *distributed* across all members of the RAID set and is a simple logical XOR of each data block of each volume. This parity information is stored in place of data in a member of a RAID5 set. Whereas RAID3 dedicates a drive for storing parity, RAID5 distributes the parity across all members of a disk. Locating the parity on a single drive can quickly turn that drive into a hot spot where time is spent waiting for the total write operation to complete.

When data must be read from a RAID5 volume, the performance and access pattern of the disk drive is similar to a regular stripe set (RAID0). The big difference comes in when data must be written or updated to the volume, and the parity information must be maintained. An application write to a RAID5 volume consists of updating the parity information from the stripe set and updating the data block supposed to hold the data. First, consider the structure of a RAID5 volume—it is composed of a set of stripes. Within each stripe, for N drives, there are $N - 1$ stripe chunks, and one parity chunk. As the data are written to the stripe chunks, the parity information is computed by an XOR operation between all the $N - 1$ stripe chunks and stored in the parity chunk, as described in Figure 2-7.

Figure 2-7
*RAID5 disk
structure*

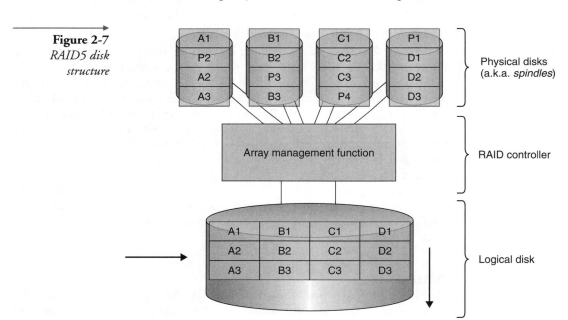

In the example shown in Figure 2-7, P3 is the stripe parity chunk, calculated from A3, B3, and D3. The calculation is done the following way:

$$P3 = A3 \oplus B3 \oplus D3$$

If the disk that holds B3 is lost for some reason, B3 can be computed from

$$B3 = A3 \oplus P3 \oplus D3$$

The XOR calculation is very straightforward. In hardware RAID implementations, it can be as simple as implementing it in a dedicated integrated circuit that calculates the parity data as they are transferred. In software

RAID, this operation is usually left up to the processor, which is not the best way to use your CPU cycles (the disadvantages of software-based implementations of RAID are discussed later), and it carries certain risks because of the write-hole problem (see below).

The value of the parity information is present only if you maintain it as the data are updated. Writing on block A3, in our example, will involve first "subtracting" the knowledge of A3 to the parity block P3, and then proceeding to generate a new parity. For writing to a RAID5 subsystem, you need to read the data block, read the parity block, update the parity block, and write back both the data block and the parity block. This is what we usually call a *compound write operation*, which can seem innocent at first; however, note that to maintain the integrity of the overall stripe, you need to write two blocks of data at once. First, the parity block must be written back, and then the data block. Typically, the controller will return a successful status when both operations are complete.

RAID5 write-hole

What if the controller has a problem right between those two write operations? You get an inconsistent volume: The parity block is out of sync with the corresponding data blocks. This is known as the RAID5 *write-hole*, and is addressed differently depending on the storage vendor and controller model.

This write-hole can be quite dangerous—if you're lucky, you will get a volume corruption straight away. You will need to address it, but it will not go unnoticed. However, if the controller does not flag this error, you will most likely get a volume corruption notice by the time the data are actually needed.

We observed this at a customer site, and the process is quite painful to recover from (basically, you need to restore the entire volume). To prevent this, RAID controllers have implemented various techniques as they evolved. First, were models of controllers that would, after a system crash, regenerate the parity blocks for the entire volume. This can be annoying, since the volume is unavailable, in fact, for the controller that was implementing this feature; the entire system was not available because this operation was happening at boot time.

Other controllers verify parity information every now and then as a non-disruptive background task. Finally, high-end controllers will retain an area of their cache for multidisk I/Os, and even if you operate in write-through mode, it will still keep track of the disk I/Os that must absolutely be done. But since this last feature is using cache memory in the controller, you must make sure that before the volume is online, the cache battery is fully charged. Modern controllers will prevent bringing a unit online before the cache battery is fully charged. So, it is a good idea to power the RAID array in advance of any operation on the RAID volume so that the batteries can go through a full charge cycle. (This is a typical development when you ship a test environ-ment to a production site and the batteries have discharged in the meantime.)

In software-based implementations, you can hardly guarantee that the two write operations will be successful. If you write a parity block, you must write the data block that is "contained" on the parity block; otherwise, you lose consistency. Even if the I/O is effectively reported as not carried out by the operating system, you can have unmatched parity and data blocks for a given stripe, should a system crash occur at a bad time (is there any good time for a system crash anyway?) during the write operation. Some operating systems, such as HP's OpenVMS, go as far as using six-disk I/Os for the par-ity and data block updates, instead of the traditional four-disk I/Os.

Impact of disk number in RAID5 volume

RAID5 comes in a minimum of three disks. Typical large RAID5 volumes can grow up to14 disks and beyond, but there are downsides to building large RAID5 volumes. For instance, if you lose a member in a RAID5 array, you need to replace it. Typically, the controller will do this operation auto-matically (hot swap feature). However, during the rebuild of the volume, every single data block of each member of the RAID5 set has to be read for regeneration of the data and the parity. For large volumes, that can be a lengthy operation (several hours). Furthermore, during this operation you have no more redundancy in the volume. In the unlikely event of disk loss during volume rebuild, you would lose the entire volume and have to use your backups to restore the volume. Because there are a large number of disks, the backup duration may tend to be lengthy, and therefore, the overall downtime of the application and/or its data hosted on the volume is greater than what it should normally be. So, although theory implies that you could have 30 or 40 disks in a RAID5 volume, practical implementation rarely goes beyond 14 or 15 disks, which is an acceptable limit in most cases.

Another approach is to logically group disks in a RAID5 volume by a certain number determined at the initialization time of the array, or simply as part of the array architecture (this is the case for HP's StorageWorks EVA and XP SAN arrays). Using four or five disks, you can make up a RAID5 set, even though the total number of disks can be much larger. The result is an increase in performance (because of a large number of drives) with-out the risk of frequent occurrence of volume repair mode (because of the small number of drives making up the RAID5). The parity arrangement can cycle across disks; it's just that the parity is calculated on a smaller number of blocks than the number of blocks making up a stripe (minus one, of course).

As an example, let's study the grouping on a 4+1 basis (4 data disks and 1 parity disk) without restricting the maximum number of members in a RAID5 volume to 5 (distribution of data may occur on several "groups" of 4+1 disks), as shown in Figure 2-8. Reducing the number of members reduces the stripe length. The smaller the stripe length, the greater the chance of updating an entire RAID5 stripe and avoiding the RAID5 write penalty. The disadvantage of this approach is the fixed loss of capacity (20% when using a 4+1 scheme; 25% in a 3+1 scheme), regardless of the number of disks.

Figure 2-8
Rotating parity scheme in a 4 + 1 RAID5 implementation

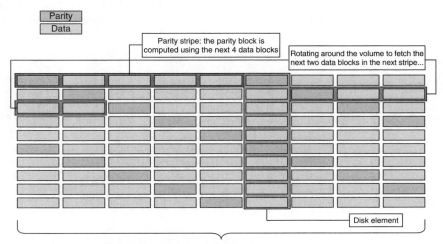

9-disk volume using a 4 + 1 RAID5 parity scheme

The major advantage is decreased dependency on the number of disks used to achieve a full stripe update: Because the data portion of a parity stripe is four chunks, if your chunk size is 8 KB, you only need 32 KB in a write (aggregated or not) operation in order to bypass the parity update, and avoid the write penalty.

For all implementations, the minimum number of drives comprising a RAID5 array is three. This is necessary for generating parity information, which can be used to recover a lost member.

In addition, for all implementations, there is no read penalty. For this reason, and given the vendor-specific optimizations for handling the parity updates and RAID5 write-hole, RAID5 (or RAID-S) volumes are commonly used when the transactional access pattern is read only, even if batch mode operations use write transactions. Data archiving and data mining are common examples of processes that suit RAID5 deployments. User transactions are typically read operations, and write operations are performed in batch mode in a noninteractive manner, and with a flow of data that large controller cache modules (32 GB and above) can deal with efficiently.

RAID6

Another approach is the one used in RAID6, seldom implemented by manufacturers, which provides two levels of parity (instead of one as in RAID5) distributed on two separate member sets, and can sustain the loss of two disk drives at the same time or the loss of a single disk drive during volume reconstruction. This extra security increases the time needed for write operations, since you now need to maintain two parity blocks instead of one.

In the Smart Array controller, HP implements RAID6, called Advanced Data Guarding (ADG). The block parity layout is actually shown in Figure 2-9.

Figure 2-9
RAID6 principle (also called Advanced Data Guarding)

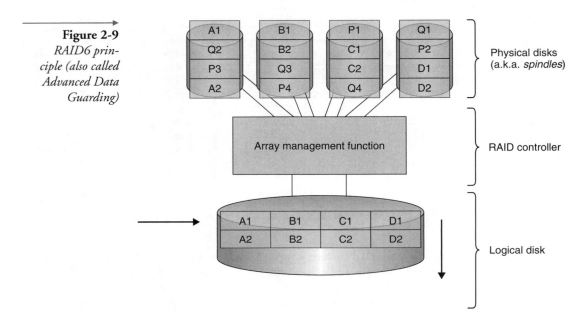

With HP's implementation of the Smart Array 6400 (which is a PCI-based controller), you can use up to 56 disks in a RAID array. By using ADG, you decrease the impact of an unlikely second disk failure during reconstructing time. However, by using lots of disks in the array, the reconstructing time will be quite significant, and although it is running at a lower priority than normal data traffic, it can be inconvenient. The likelihood of a disk failure within a given module will tend to increase as you increase the number of drives in that volume; if you have a 20% chance of losing a disk in a four-disk volume, you have a 40% chance of losing a disk in an eight-disk volume.

Hybrid models: RAID0+1 or RAID10

Because RAID1 provides the most redundancy and RAID0 gives the best performance, combining the two RAID levels into one, RAID0+1, became a reality. RAID0+1 consists of striping (RAID0) mirrors (RAID1) together. The resulting volume has good capacity (half of the overall disk capacity thrown in the volume) and splendid performance (up to N × 100 I/O per second for N drives). RAID0+1 is costly to implement, yet is popular because of the low cost of disk drives these days, the high density of storage, and the ability of modern controllers to handle a large number of disks.

Figure 2-10 shows a RAID0+1 disk structure. Here, we see a four-disk RAID0+1 volume, where two disks are being mirrored and then striped. Note that you could do the reverse—stripe two disks and mirror them. This is also referred to as RAID10. There is little difference between the two approaches from a performance and capacity perspective. Your I/O through-put is theoretically equivalent to:

$$\text{Total I/O} = (\text{read \%}) \times (\text{Total number of disks}) + (\text{write \%}) \times (\textbf{Total number of disks/2})$$

Yet, from a management and operations perspective, there are differences that may force or incline you to choose between one and the other.

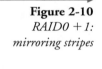

Figure 2-10
RAID0 + 1:
mirroring stripes

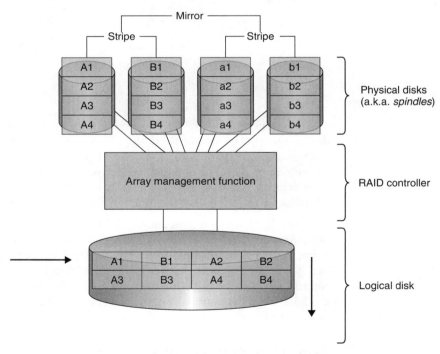

Let's look at a small visual comparison. Figure 2-11 describes the mir-roring of two stripes. From the RAID controller perspective, you have to deal with three units: two stripes and one overall mirror of these two stripes. If we were to arrange the same number of disks in RAID0+1, we would obtain what is described in Figure 2-11.

Figure 2-11
RAID10, striping
RAID1 members

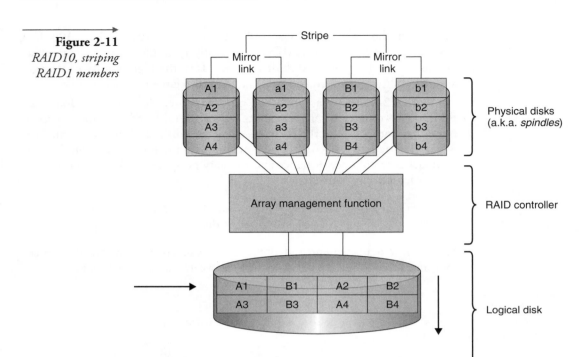

The downside of RAID10 is how gracefully the controller can handle a disk failure. In the case of RAID0+1, if a disk drive fails, the controller will tap into the hot spare pool of disks, and proceed to rebuild a single mirror. In the case of RAID10, if a disk goes wrong, it is the entire stripe that needs to be rebuilt. The consequence, notably the rebuild time, as well as the overall tolerance to disk failure are much different for the two techniques.

Another issue is redundancy. A RAID10 volume can sustain the loss of one drive, perhaps more if the subsequently failing device is part of the same stripe as the original failing drive. A RAID0+1 volume made of N disks can handle the loss of N/2 disks only if these failures are impacting each mirror and never twice the same mirror. Failures can be of several orders, from a regular disk burnout, to an entire back-end bus failure, which has been observed before at several customer sites.

Concatenation is *not* striping

There is a fundamental difference between concatenation of disks (also known as *drive spanning*) of volumes and striping. With concatenation, you collate volumes together. As you traverse the volume through each of the logical block, you hit the first member, then the next member, and so on, until you reach the end of the volume. Concatenation is often proposed in array architecture for expansion of volumes, and is really interesting for capacity purposes, not performance.

When studying Figure 2-12, if you fill up 40% of a concatenated volume, you only access data from two disks. If you fill up 40% of a stripe, you access data from five disks. The difference is important for Microsoft Exchange database workload because of the sensitivity on the response time and throughput of random I/O. Because I/Os to the database are random, you can reasonably plan on the fill space being accessed almost uniformly. But if you leave spare space, the disks hosting that spare space will not be used in a concatenated volume, whereas in a stripe, all disks will participate in the I/O, no matter the fill ratio.

Figure 2-12
Concatenating 5 disks and filling them at 40%

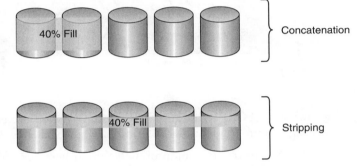

Comparing RAID levels

There are many ways to compare RAID levels depending very much on your prime requirement. First, is availability a priority? If this is the case, RAID0 is no good for you. Do you need capacity? In this case, RAID1 can be seen as a costly implementation, especially compared with RAID0, which yields the most capacity, and RAID5, which grants the most capacity while keeping redundancy. Finally, is performance more important?

For performance, RAID0 is excellent, and so is RAID1 or RAID0+1; RAID5 comes in last, unless you have a majority of read operations. (In Exchange 2007, this can be the case. For example, ISPs want the maximum level of performance for their POP users, which, when they retrieve their mails, only read from the database!) The key thing to remember is that there is no free lunch in the world of storage, and you will always have to make compromises among *availability*, *performance*, and *cost*. Figure 2-13 quickly summarizes the comparison.

JBOD stands for just a bunch of disks. JBOD literally means that you use the disks as individual units and you do not try to arrange them into a RAID level. With the introduction of application-based data duplication

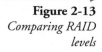

Figure 2-13
Comparing RAID levels

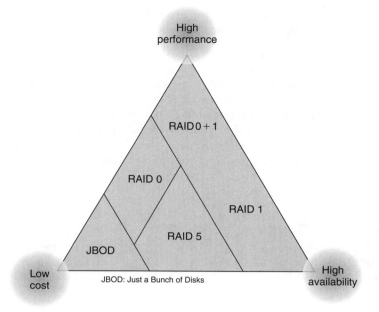

and recovery (LCR, CCR, and SCR), you may want to venture into implementing a nonredundant disk solution for your Exchange 2007 servers.

As you can see, the compromise solution here lies with RAID5, which gives a good cost figure (in terms of capacity), good availability (it can sustain the loss of one member of the volume), and a reasonable performance, provided that you don't spend your time writing to the volume (as with the replica databases or transaction log files in Exchange 2007).

What's more important, because of a potentially significant financial impact on the resulting solution, especially in high-end environments, you need to determine your priorities up front and stick with them. For example, assume that you wish to build a volume that hosts 360 GB. Table 2-2 summarizes how many drives are involved and the resulting cost and performance

Table 2-2   *360 GB Volume Characteristics*

	RAID0	RAID0+1	RAID5	RAID6 (ADG)
# of 72 GB disks	5	10	6	7
Request rate	600	1,200	558	630
Cost	$1,000	$2,000	$1,200	$1,400
Price per GB	$2.77	$5.55	$3.33	$3.88
Price per I/O	$1.66	$1.96	$2.15	$2.22

levels that would be obtained. This table assumes a \$200 cost for a 72 GB disk drive and 100 random I/O per second at 20 ms response time, which a good worst-case scenario.

The RAID0+1 solution is quite appealing from a performance perspective, but not from a cost perspective; it is quite understandably more expensive than RAID0 and significantly more expensive than RAID5. Beyond the pure capacity requirement, you then have to decide whether you wish this volume to be protected, and/or to offer performance, and more important, whether you actually can afford the volume.

Note that to obtain the request rate, we chose a 70% read/30% write ratio. If we were to have a majority of read operations, RAID5 would rapidly become an appealing solution, because the overhead resulting from the write I/O does not get in the way too often, and that makes it acceptable. This is important, and we will take the opportunity, once again, to reinforce the great advantage—if you've been running a Microsoft Exchange environment-of capturing performance counter information and establishing a baseline, a pattern of behavior of Exchange in your particular environment.

As you can see, it's not black or white, red or blue, love or hate. It's all a question of determining, in your own particular environment, what the load looks like, because it may turn out to be a massive cost savings given that the most performance is needed for read accesses. In the majority of the situations that we have had the opportunity to diagnose, the read/write ratio of the Exchange ESE database with Exchange 2003 SP2 is around 70/30 (60% read, 40% write); while the ratio for the transaction log volume is a clear 100% write (during operations). This has evolved most notably since Exchange 2003, and during the follow-on Service Packs (SP1 and SP2) as Microsoft worked hard to reduce the I/O footprint and flow of the database engine, helping notably in storage replicated environments. With Exchange 2007, we're on a 50/50 read/write ratio for the databases, which improves the table above even more.

Based on this preliminary information (preliminary because there is much more to include in the picture such as cache optimization), it is definitely appropriate to separate the transaction log files from the database files, not only from a pure data recovery perspective, but also because the I/O pattern is so radically different that it's easier to tune two separate volumes that are in line with the workload generated by the Microsoft Exchange database engine. Because we can have up to 50 storage groups in Exchange 2007, this means that you will need either many logical units, or "gather" storage areas of Exchange 2007 by function and access pattern. For example, create a single volume that will host four databases from four different storage groups, and another volume for the corresponding four transaction log files set.

There is another way to compare RAID levels, and that is from a pure cost perspective (your financial manager will love this). First, you must determine whether your concern is space or performance. Given the massive processor scalability that the industry in general, and Intel in particular, has given us, it would be a pity to hook a 3800-hp engine on a four-wheel drive vehicle with all the brakes on. In other words, you may bring all the processing power of the world, but it will be relevant only if you can submit the data for processing at a fast enough speed. When we visit a customer site to tune the systems, we approach the situation from a performance perspective. That is what will matter most to your end users, including the CEO and the CIO, who will not find a $100,000 solution acceptable if it fails to respond when *they* decide to use it (this is the objective of tuning a system for transactional access compared to tuning a system for batch execution) (Figure 2-14).

Figure 2-14

Cost comparison for RAID levels

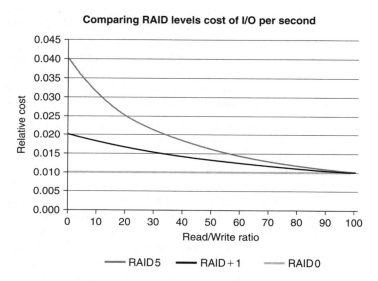

When you study the relative cost per GB for each of the RAID levels of interest, RAID0, RAID0+1, RAID5, and RAID6, you should note that the cost of RAID0+1 does not vary: It's always twice as much as the cost of RAID0, simply because you need twice as many disks than in RAID0 to build up the redundancy. Compared to RAID1, the cost for RAID5 will always closer to the cost of RAID0 because of the smaller number of disks required to achieve target capacity requirements. Then comes RAID6, followed by RAID0+1. Depending on the array technology, the distributed parity of RAID5 and RAID6 may be against a fixed number of disks (between four and five) and result in a net overhead of 25% or 20%, regardless of the number of disks that make up the array.

The other way to compare RAID levels is in terms of request rate or I/O throughput (I'm not referring here to data rates—i.e., MB per second—but to I/O per second). The write performance penalty of RAID5 does not play in its favor, quite clearly (Figure 2-15).

Figure 2-15
*Comparing RAID
depending on read/
write ratio*

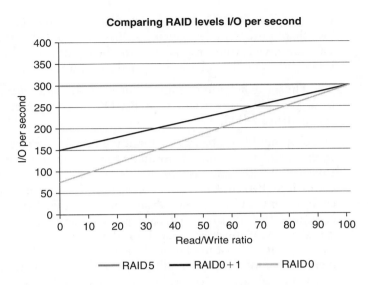

Four-disk I/Os being required for any application write creates a lot of over-head, which will have a direct impact on the response time of the individual I/O and on the overall request rate capacity of the disk subsystem. Now, keep in mind that the parity overhead in RAID5 occurs only for write operations. If you know that the majority of your I/Os are going to be read operations, RAID5 has a lot of value for the redundancy it brings in the subsystem as well as the cost per MB that we have just reviewed. It is even worse with RAID6 (six-disk I/O for each write operation); however, this brings additional redundancy and resiliency, such as the ability to lose two members in a RAID6 volume.

For Exchange 2007, we typically observe a read/write ratio at 50/50 (50% read and 50% write). That might be slightly different during the nec-essary transition phase when migrating from Microsoft Exchange 2003 to Exchange 2007 for example, the PowerShell command (move-mailbox is typically write intensive for the target host).

The read/write ratio can vary if you have agents that performance post-processing of mail information, such as BlackBerry Enterprise Servers that perform device reconciliation or selective archiving that extracts items from users' mailboxes for archiving purposes. We have found differences on pro-duction servers, but not enough to require a design change just for those par-ticular cases; it is better to focus on the production workload (e.g., Outlook clients in cache mode).

In a production environment, you will hardly see RAID0 because of the lack of data protection. The reliability (MTBF = mean time between fail-ures) of a RAID0 volume is proportionally less compared to the reliability of the disk drives that it is made of. Therefore, if you create a three-disk RAID0 volume (great for I/O throughput), you have three times more chances to lose that entire volume than if you have one disk for the overall capacity. Of course, you would not be able to obtain the same throughput from the single disk (spindle) volume compared to a multidisk RAID0 set.

Thus, if your prime requirement is to obtain a satisfactory request rate from your disk subsystem, then RAID0+1 is a better, more economical choice than RAID5.

You should also be careful about the benchmark results that use RAID0 as the main storage for Microsoft Exchange. As you plan your production environment, do not rush to double the storage by transforming RAID0 drives into RAID0+1. This approach works only in a pure 100% write environment, and that is not always the case in Exchange 2007; even if you continuously write to the database, you will never get 100% writes. Because it uses a transaction-based model, for the database engine to update its database pages it will first need to read the page, execute the page modification in memory, record the page modification in the log buffer, flush the log buffer when the transaction (consisting of several page modifications) is committed, and update *asynchronously* the dirty (modified) data page located in the cache memory back to disk.

A 50% read/write ratio should generally used when sizing and choosing RAID levels for Exchange 2007 databases. For transaction logs, the story is different: You have one read for each write; however, the read is shortly after the write, and the likelihood that the read operation will be serviced directly from the NT cache or from the controller cache is quite high. You should still plan for 100% write for performance, considering that it is the write operation that matters in the case of transaction logs. The read operation can be slightly slower, but not too much; indeed, if you get too far behind on your replication, you render it useless.

Software-based implementation versus hardware-based implementation

Windows Server dynamic disks allow the building of software-based stripe sets, which could include distributed parity (RAID5) or mirror sets that protect the volume by duplicating data between any two dynamic disks. Furthermore, you can use this technology across many disks and partitions, thereby creating load balancing at the system level as opposed to the storage subsystem level. This is especially important if you wish to take advantage of multiple independent controllers that would otherwise present independent logical units (and therefore partitions and drives).

By default, any new device discovered by Windows Server is defined as a basic disk. You need to upgrade the basic disk to a "dynamic" disk in order to use the advanced volume management tools available from the Disk Management MMC snap-in. You can access the disk management snap-in by right-clicking on the My Computer desktop item and selecting the Manage option. From there, you can select the Disk Management component under the Storage container. Figure 2-16 shows how to upgrade a basic disk to a dynamic disk.

Figure 2-16
*Converting basic
disk to dynamic
disk*

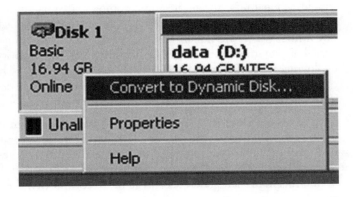

Then you can create your host-based RAID implementation using the Disk Management MMC snap-in from Windows (Figure 2-17). Volume P is a software-based RAID5 volume.

Figure 2-17
*Dynamic disks and
host-based RAID
with Windows*

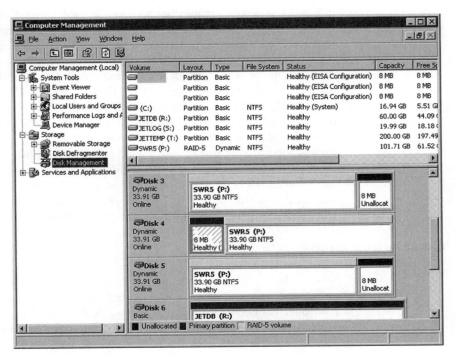

The issue concerning software-based RAID implementations is twofold. First, you are soliciting the CPU of the system to perform tasks around block device management (simple striping of disks can be addressed with low overhead, but striping with distributed parity requires CPU cycles to compute the parity blocks during a write operation). Second, the recovery steps required should a dynamic disk fail are more complex, manual, and typically prone to operation mistakes. This action typically requires unavailability and service downtime, which are not in line with the goal of increasing volume and data availability by the means of RAID. To this effect, the majority, if not all, of the deployments of Microsoft Exchange, use hardware RAID, which can be implemented with added features such as hot-swap and hot-spare device management, independently and transparently from the operation system and the application.

There are situations in which host-based striping provides an effective advantage, such as in the example where the target storage array has limited striping capabilities in favor of high availability and resiliency (e.g., HP StorageWorks XP 12000 array, based on Hitachi Japan Ltd. technology). While this approach generates a little more complexity, the return is the benefit of a super-scaling solution that can deal with the highest workloads, provided that you have effectively at leveled the resource utilization, comprised of the host port interface and cache and back-end disk buses and units.

All in all, you should take advantage of RAID and the volume management functions offered by PCI-based RAID controllers, as well as the external, possibly shared, storage enclosures that will offload the CPU resources from the parity calculation and disk block management and offer advanced features. The declining prices of entry-level PCI-based RAID arrays should definitely decide you to go that way. Note also that this practice is becoming more and more common; some computer vendors (e.g., HP) are embedding on their motherboard design a RAID-on-chip logic (ROC) that provides basic RAID management (mirroring, read cache, no writeback cache), without the need to use a PCI slot for a back-plane RAID controller. This is a common practice in high-density server environments, where 1-U servers, such as the HP ProLiant servers, include this ROC chipset and allow building a RAID1 mirror set for the system disk volumes at no additional hardware cost. Blade servers go a level beyond and propose a special slot for a *mezzanine* card that sits on top of the motherboard (in the same plane), and provides excellent performance for local system disk requirements (Figure 2-18).

Controller cache

Storage disks are seldom attached directly to the I/O bus of the server. They are typically connected by a storage controller, which can be either a local controller connected on a PCI-Express (PCI-X, but PCI also works) of the server, or located as a component of a Storage Area Network. The SAN components are discussed later, but for now, the focus is on the storage controller.

Figure 2-18
*Mezzanine storage
controller boards
on a Blade server*

In the storage controller, there is an area of memory (high-speed RAM) that is used to *cache* I/O requests. When a host queries information from a storage volume, it issues, for example, an 8 KB I/O. The controller will figure out, by virtue of the AMF, which disks host this information, and proceed to read it from the disks and return it to the host. Fetching this information can be at the minimum 4 KB, but in certain product lines (such as EMC DMX, Hitachi TagmaStore, or HP StorageWorks XP series), the controller will actually fetch a fixed quantity of data, regardless of the I/O size (128 KB is common). The net effect is that 128 KB of data are pulled from the disks and stored in the controller's memory, and the queried 8 KB of data are returned. At this point in time, you have 120 KB of data in cache that are there, but not used because they are not expected. If the host queries the next 8 KB of data, and these data happen to be part of the remaining 120 KB, you get a cache hit, and instead of the usual 12 to 15 milliseconds response time, you obtain a submillisecond response, which is of course very good!

A large cache is very important for two reasons:

1. If you have many *sequential* I/O, you will provide a lightning-fast response to each host query, and therefore greatly help the transaction workload.

2. If you have many *random* I/O, you need lots of cache to cater for the 124 KB trashing that occurred when the host queried the small I/O.

Ideally then, you would want your host to make few very-large reads, instead of many small-reads. Most of the time, this is decided at application design time. With Exchange 2007, the optimization made to the database engine to favor I/O coalescence leads to larger and fewer I/Os, reducing the pressure on the disk request rate, to better exercise the data rate.

For write operations, the same principle applies. The controller, by caching the write operation, will decouple the response time to the host from the actual completion time, as shown in Figure 2-19.

Figure 2-19
Improving write response time with controller cache

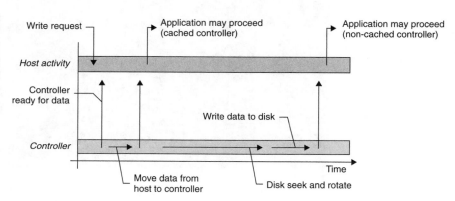

What is the right size?

The questions then are how much cache is needed for a given volume of host I/O, and more importantly (given that cache size is not infinite), how will the cache flush, how will the controller behave during cache flush, and how often does your host really stress the controller (peak duration). For most transactional applications using databases, the write cache has to be enabled, and the read cache does not really matter (except during backups). Consider the case of Exchange 2007 and a 32 GB RAM machine: If a page of data is not found in the database cache, what are the chances that this page is in the controller cache? None. The read cache is actually useful for pre-fetching data (read-ahead), in case the host has a sequential access to data (e.g., block-based backup). Write cache is good for caching I/O and offering a quick response time to the host that makes the write request. It does not have to be big, because once the data page in cache has been written to disk, you can discard these data and free controller cache memory. Thus, depending on how the controller is attached to the computing resources (one server using a PCI-Express interface or hundreds of servers over a Fibre Channel network), the required cache size will vary. Small controllers (local PCI-Express boards) typically have 256 MB or 512 MB of cache. Mid-range Fibre Channel controllers have 4 GB, and high-end multiprotocol controllers can scale up to 512 GB.

As to the right size for that cache, there is no single answer, and worse, there can be many good answers. The controller's abilities to report its workload and response times are very important, and unfortunately, not always well implemented. Often, my team has found no performance problem on a controller, whereas Microsoft Exchange on the server was not getting good response time. Because of this discrepancy, you should use host-based performance information, which, in a platform such as Microsoft Windows Server, can be extremely detailed with enough indicators provided to help you determine how well your volumes and overall storage combination handle the workload proposed by the application(s).

Virtualization

Some storage controllers implement virtualization. You probably know about virtual machines and the concept of running a PC inside another PC. Virtualization with storage is slightly different: Instead of creating hard-defined storage volume by assembling five physical disks together into a single logical volume, you may want to create volumes that do not depend directly on the five physical disk drives, but can be laid out in many possible ways, for example, across 20 disks. The capacity used is still one of five disks, but the throughput used is one of 20 disks. The result is that you can benefit from a large number of disks for throughput, instead of benefiting only from the capacity. That's the basis for virtualization: You dissociate the data from its actual physical placement. It could be on 5, 10, or 100 disks; it does not matter to the application. What does matter is that you have the ability to share and benefit from many components instead of being bound to just a few of them.

Virtualization can be implemented at various levels:

Disk level—Your logical disks can be implemented on a large quantity of *shared* physical disks; therefore, you have the throughput capability of this large quantity of disks at a single point in time, as long as all applications do not demand that throughput all at the same time.

Controller level—Your server does not communicate with one controller, but rather communicates to a series of controllers that can be placed in several locations or enclosures, and that can provide resilient and high-performance functions that would not be otherwise available from a single controller.

Network—Your server connects to a cloud. It gets storage from a cloud of storage in the form of a logical unit that has been uniquely identified. You need not to worry about the cloud implementation, and you are immune from the changes occurring in that cloud. You are also independent of the downtime of any component of the cloud, because it is resilient by design.

Virtualization is therefore appropriate to separate the persistent data storage from its actual implementation. It is a way for the Microsoft Exchange administrator to spend time on managing the application, rather than the specific components used for that application. It is a way for storage administrator to offer storage as a service or a utility and make significant economies of scale in operating that environment, instead of managing different storage solutions from different applications.

Finally, virtualization allows making changes to the application without impacting the hardware implementation. If you wish to extend a volume, you do so without downtime, just by extending or migrating the data volumes to a larger occupation space. On days where availability is really important, the ability to create one or more degrees of liberty between the application and hardware implementation is a winning feature for uptime and flexibility. Storage networks are key enablers for virtualization, and they are covered in the next section.

Storage + Network = Storage Networks

Storage networks are inevitable in large enterprises. The initial idea was to share the benefits of a strong storage environment among different servers (or storage consumers). Storage networks typically come in two modes:

- File-level access: This is the classical file share implementation that we are all familiar with; a standardized protocol runs on top of a networking protocol (TCP/IP) to access files.

- Block-level access: This is the SAN implementation type in which the devices are presented to the application server, but the storage controller has no concept of files or directories.

SANs are typically implemented using a Fibre Channel protocol over a dedicated infrastructure. The use of TCP/IP as a networking protocol is an alternative, known as *iSCSI*. IP SAN (iSCSI protocol) and FC SAN (Fibre Channel protocol) sit on the same level from a *functional* standpoint.

The benefits found in SAN environments follow:

- The ability to virtualize data across many independent physical devices or paths. The benefit is that you can quickly add more storage to a server (e.g., provide more log space during a move mailbox operation) without taking the server down. This virtualization is often accompanied by pooling disk resources, as found in the HP StorageWorks EVA platform.

- Advanced management (copy, clone, mirror, and replication) of volumes in the back-end environment, at the storage array level. This often is done at a much greater efficiency than at the host level. You implement it once, and it's available (in theory) for all applications. In practice, there is a level of integration that is necessary and usually complex, because the SAN vendor is rarely the application vendor. Despite industry efforts to provide "open SAN" specifications, this integration can be problematic.

- The ability to *transport* a particular SAN logical disk unit from one server to another, and share storage components such as network fabrics, controllers, or disk drives. With Exchange 2007, this is particularly interesting during a Windows 2008 server upgrade, as it eliminates the need for using the move-mailbox PowerShell command and instead simply present logical units to an upgraded server.

- Increased availability with redundant paths and components. Each server can access a disk unit through more than one path, including redundant host-bus adapters, network switches, interconnects, and controllers. Because many servers depend on your SAN, it better be available, and resiliency is typically implemented by duplicating components in the infrastructure.

Implementing a SAN and enabling storage management and virtualization functions at the SAN level often mean that *all* applications/servers that use this SAN will benefit from such features. To be able to do this, you first have to consolidate your servers—so if you have a highly distributed environment, you may find the value of SAN significantly diminished (Figure 2-20).

Considerations for Microsoft Exchange Server

Fundamentally, a SAN is all about sharing storage resources. When you construct a SAN, you provide access to a pool of storage resources (disks, tapes) for servers that need this storage capacity. This type of environment needs the right level of management, monitoring, and change control for delivering a satisfactory level of service to the application servers. Tools, professional services, and best practices are available to SAN administrators for prevent a SAN failure that would affect *all* the servers that depend on it.

From a Microsoft Exchange Server administrator standpoint, if you have to deal with a storage administration group, make sure that you treat the group as a service provider: the clearer your requirements, the better will be your service. SAN technology is a great approach if you have the right people, the right processes, the right policies, and the right products. Training and consulting services are available to develop capabilities for your storage team and ensure proper configuration and management of your storage configuration for Microsoft Exchange.

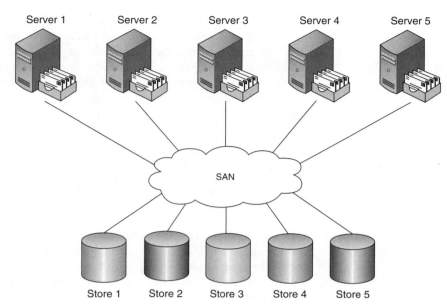

Figure 2-20
*Five servers
accessing storage
across a SAN*

Capacity and performance can change, and result in slower response times for Exchange users over time. This rarely happens at the network fabric level, but is more likely to happen at the disk level and sometimes at the controller level. Microsoft has helped their customers and systems integration/consulting partners with guidelines on how to properly configure and monitor their environments to help avoid performance problems. In addition, storage resource management solutions, such as HP's Storage Essentials, can be helpful in monitoring the configuration to keep performance at expected levels.

In Summary

There are many ways to provide storage to application servers, and the only thing we are sure of is that storage technology will continue to evolve in the directions of lower costs, higher density, and faster access. You can provision 400 GB of storage to a server in many different ways. The server, infrastructure, and cost considerations typically drive the choice for the right solution. With Exchange 2007, Microsoft really worked hard in taking the most advantage of the 64-bit processor architecture, and use more RAM and less disk I/O. This results in a general improvement of the situation in two ways:

■ Microsoft Exchange is a much better SAN citizen than previously. It can coexist with other applications on a SAN without being impacted by those applications (64-bit benefit).

- Microsoft Exchange is more resilient (and this trend will continue with Exchange 14, the next major release of the product), and does not *need* the many functions offered by storage networks and virtualization, such as replication (continuous replication benefit).

The challenge, for the Microsoft Exchange administrator, is to make the right choice. Low cost of purchase and low cost of operations do not necessarily go hand in hand. With the scope of Microsoft Exchange, the use of SAN is arguable in favor of the use of DAS, that is, storage that is directly and exclusively connected to a server. If you extend the scope of your storage design to the data center, the use of SAN delivers far more benefits, because you can leverage functions from your SAN from many servers.

3

Storage Technologies

In this chapter, we are going to review the major storage technologies available in 2008. Of course, this section has a somewhat limited lifetime because of rapid evolution. However, some fundamentals remain the same, and we often use certain principles that were well established 10 years ago. Naturally, technology has improved, and will continue to improve in several dimensions: capacity, performance, and cost. The relatively recent appearance of serialized protocols such as SATA (Serial ATA) and SAS (Serial Attached SCSI) have changed the way storage can be configured. These protocols provided cheaper interconnects and more flexibility at a lower cost per GB.

First, we will review disk technology—the physical components and connectivity options—and how it fits together. As HP employees and shareholders, we have a particular interest in that company's technology; however, very little in this chapter is solely relevant to HP—in fact, it applies to other major storage vendors such as EMC, HDS, and IBM as well.

Leveraging Storage Technologies

The trend for Exchange storage is one of continuous growth, even though many companies attempt to control information size by enforcing quotas and maintaining user mailboxes by removing unwanted messages. As companies strive to reduce their infrastructure and operational costs, they move to server consolidation and centralization, aiming at reducing the number of servers that they have to manage, and taking advantage of global network connectivity.

You may tackle the problem one way or another, but you should always keep in mind that in any consolidation scenario, data remain; typically data quantity does not decrease and will quite probably increase in terms of availability requirements, because of the necessity to manage data *as well as* servers and services. As you were planning to redeploy a computing infrastructure to reduce costs, you have to increase your storage capabilities, which are very important for mission-critical applications such as messaging.

It might not imply increased cost because of the way the price per GB has evolved in the last few years.

As companies evolved into creating large data centers that host massive quantities of computing power and are built around high-speed networking accesses, the concentration of data has to be addressed in three perspectives—cost, performance, and availability. Apart from these three criteria that should shape your final technology solution and strategy, the manageability of this information is increasingly important. Today you can build a server that serves 1 TB or even 1 PB of data, but making these data manageable is another problem. This was first addressed with Microsoft Exchange 2000 by allowing for a single Exchange server to serve more than one mailbox store: Instead of gathering a large quantity of information into a single file database, you can now create more than one of these databases, all managed and processed by a single server. With Exchange 2007, you can now have up to 50 databases per server!

This is a serious scalability advantage of Exchange 2007 and a big improvement compared to any previous generation of Microsoft Exchange. It can lead to more flexible designs that take advantage of new technologies. It also leads to more choices and more decision points.

When building any Exchange 2007 server, you must first determine how much space you should plan for hosting the user mailboxes and optionally, shared information (public folders). In short, you will have to build storage solutions that implement to various degrees the following attributes:

- Capacity
- Availability
- Performance
- Manageability
- Cost (affordability)

Throughout this chapter, we will return to those key aspects because they represent the roots for any storage design decisions you make. As we cover the storage technologies that you can (and you cannot) use with Microsoft Exchange, you will quickly realize that there is an advantage in having a sound storage strategy for your enterprise, both from a management perspective and from a storage platform acquisition standpoint.

It is generally a good idea to appoint a storage administrator as part of your administration staff; this person will be responsible for looking up these issues, not only across your Microsoft Exchange environment but also across your Windows Server environment (including file and print services), and probably beyond the Windows Server platform by including such environments as UNIX or other high-end operating systems (not that Windows Server is not a high-end operating system).

We mentioned in Chapter 2 how storage embraced the networking paradigm: Project yourselves into the past and think about how networking was introduced in IT infrastructures, how it evolved, and how it is run today. With storage, you will find the same pattern of server-specific components, which then get deployed in an interconnected way. Then you need to address the redundancy, performance, and security of the interconnecting components and links. Finally, you will need to address a level of multivendor interoperability, which is best addressed by standards implementation.

For the remainder of this section, we are going to cover three key storage technologies and their relevance to Exchange 2007:

Direct-Attached Storage: This is really about local disks in servers. The networking and high-performance interfaces still do not allow building diskless servers for all solutions. In some cases, this is appropriate and it is covered later in the book. Interestingly enough, when great emphasis was focused on networking functions (see below), direct-attached storage technologies evolved more recently and get a new fame this is correct for Microsoft Exchange deployments today and in the future.

Storage Area Networks: Built using a standardized protocol, Fibre Channel, these networks are designed for high-performance block-mode access to raw devices. SAN-attached devices have no concept of file systems, a notion that remains at the operating system. After being placed in complex and high-end infrastructures, SAN are now making their way into the smaller Small and Medium Business (SMB) market. Much of the upcoming challenge of the storage industry is to propose simple ways of managing relatively complex storage components.

Network Attached Storage: The NAS fundamental is the utilization of a data network protocol, IP (and more precisely, TCP/IP) to a file-share protocol. NAS made its way from file-sharing appliances, which rapidly evolved into mature storage components.

Comparing these technologies and claiming that one is better than the other would be a limiting, counterproductive exercise. In fact, you will find that each of these storage approaches has pros and cons, all of which depend on the objectives you are pursuing, the revision of Microsoft Exchange and Windows Server that you intend to use, and your operating model. So our primary goal is to cover these technologies as they are present in 2008, and indicate areas of improvement, bearing in mind that storage is a moving target which constantly changes—as a customer and implementer of Microsoft Exchange, you will be astonished by the type of problems you encounter when deploying a mission-critical application, which is probably one of the most demanding on the market when it comes to storage.

Our second goal—only second by order of citation—is to educate you in one of the favorite sports in France: getting good wine at a fair price. Instead of buying wine, we will buy and manage storage. It's very easy to get an excellent wine at €1,000 ($1,300) a bottle; it is very difficult to find a pleasant wine that perfectly fits your palate and your meal at a fraction of this price. For storage, the situation is more difficult: Getting the best storage solution for your Microsoft Exchange environment is not obvious if you pay for the most expensive one. In fact, it is rarely the case. The reverse is also true, as the cheapest storage solutions might not deliver to your expectations either!

Disk Technology

Disks come in various size and form factors. Typically, you will deal with 3.5" and 2.5" form factors. The former are found in detached storage arrays, while the latter are now appearing in servers, enabling greater local storage capacity and performance. Only a few companies manufacture disk drives: Seagate, Western Digital, Samsung, IBM, Fujitsu, and Hitachi Global Storage Technologies. The rest? They OEM; in other words, they go to the disk manufacturers and buy disks that meet certain specifications, depending on the targeted use and requested price. Mergers and acquisitions, and spin-offs and consolidation have occurred, too, in the disk drive industry, and it should be no surprise that when you open an HP drive cage, for example, you will see a Seagate drive.

The important thing to consider is that not all disks are born equal, and some can be far more expensive than others. Disks are built to different specifications, and are guaranteed for different MTBFs (mean time between failures) or *duty cycles*.

Connector and bus technology

In this section, we discuss the way that you can connect disks to controllers or servers. This part of the technology has vastly improved over the last decade and in particular since 2005, with the introduction of serialized protocols (the S in SATA or SAS). Serialization enables to deal with smaller connectors, longer distances, and increased performance and reliability. When it comes to Microsoft Exchange, you *do not* want a bit that is set to 0 instead of 1. In fact, when Microsoft first introduced ECC (Error Correcting Checksum) in Exchange 2003, 60% of the causes of database checksum failures were found to be due to a single bit flip—not a page full of rubbish, but just one bit that is set to 0 instead of 1.

Disks communicate using a particular set of commands. There are two big families of commands (and they do share common genes):

- SCSI: small computer system interface
- ATA: AT attachment

Initially, both standards provided physical and protocol specification for connecting disks to servers. SCSI was first introduced for connecting optical disks to workstations (enterprise origins). ATA was first introduced for connecting disks to personal computers equipped with Intel's Advanced Technology processors (80286).

SCSI disk commands

SCSI (pronounce *scuh-zee*) provides both a physical and protocol standard for connecting devices to computers. The SCSI protocol contains the concept of initiator and target. The initiator is typically a host (server), and the target is a logical unit number (LUN).

The relation is similar to a master/slave: The initiator establishes a connection and sends requests. The target responds to the request (e.g., with data or with the status of a write operation).

SCSI commands are sent in a command descriptor block (CDB). The CDB consists of a 1-byte operation code followed by 5 or more bytes containing command-specific parameters. At the end of the command, the target returns a Status Code byte.

ATA disk commands

It is interesting to see how two pieces of technology were born from different sources: one from the high-end computing world (SCSI), and the other from the personal computing world (ATA). These are now blending happily in enterprises data centers, and this is one of the first indicator of what Gartner analysts call the *consumerization* of IT, that is, the use of consumer technology for corporate IT.

First, ATA started to include the SCSI protocols to allow the connection of CD drives to ATA motherboards. CD drives were first introduced with SCSI command set support with SCSI interconnects. As their price diminished, they came to the attention of the consumer market and ATA was *extended* to support a protocol called ATAPI (ATA Packet Interface), which encapsulates SCSI commands into ATA interfaces. ATAPI is part of the Extended IDE standard. Several iterations of ATA came to the industry as disks increased in capacity and bus speed requirements increased.

The big difference between ATA and SCSI is that although SCSI works with commands and packet responses, ATA works with commands written into a command register. In addition to the command register, you also have a status register and an error register. In such mode, you execute each I/O in sequence. One I/O cannot be requested to the disk before the previous one has completed. This is extremely detrimental to the performance of single-threaded sequential write operations (as found in Microsoft Exchange transaction log file access).

SCSI, on the other hand, supports *command queuing*. With this mode, a disk drive can process multiple outstanding commands and complete them in the most time-efficient order. SCSI and SAS disk drives have queuing support. The SATAII standard provides *native command queuing (NCQ)* support.

Physical interconnects

To carry these protocols, there are two families of disk interconnect (the physical interface):

■ Parallel bus interconnects. Implementations are known as IDE, EIDE, ATA, Ultra-ATA, UDMA, and SCSI. The name difference basically comes from the evolution brought to buses (faster, wider, and varying types of peripherals). Note that ATA (and members of the ATA family) is now referred to PATA (parallel ATA) since the introduction of SATA (see next bullet). Parallel buses are easily recognized by their big connectors, thick cables, and relatively short distances.

■ Serial interconnect. Implementations are known as SAS (serial attached SCSI), SATA (serial ATA), FC-SCSI (Fibre Channel SCSI), and FATA (Fibre Channel ATA). Because they are serial, these interconnects only require a handful of copper wires (5 to 10) or a single optical fiber. Their connectors are simple and require little footprint on the motherboard or devices, and they are less prone to bent pins and electrical interference.

Network interconnects

The serial protocols for SCSI or ATA can be transported on other media than serial copper buses. In fact, these protocols are appropriate for use inside networks, such as Fibre Channel–based networks or TCP/IP networks. We describe later in this chapter how Fibre Channel and iSCSI can be used to transport SCSI commands.

What's best? SCSI or ATA? Serial or parallel?

Before 2003, it was almost automatic to associate parallel SCSI (SCSI as in transport) with direct-attached storage, and in fact, it represented the majority of disk interconnects (80%) (Figure 3-1).

By applying serialization of electrical signals to both SCSI and ATA disk access protocols, two disk access specifications emerged:

■ SATA: Serial ATA, positioned for the entry-level servers, and low-cost ($/GB) and high-capacity, low-performance disks

Figure 3-1
"Old" SCSI cables

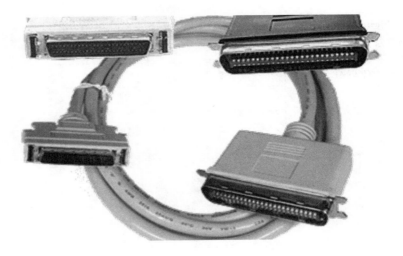

Figure 3-1
"Old" SCSI cables

- SAS: Serial attached SCSI, positioned for high-performance disks, with relatively smaller capacity

Currently, both of these interfaces are predominant in the server market, and address some of the problems initially found with parallel SCSI, such as limitation in the number of devices attached to the bus, arbitration of access to the disks, and cable length restrictions. In SAS disk enclosures, you are now able to plug both SATA and SAS drives. This helps in building storage solutions that have high performance for a part and high-capacity at reduced cost for another part (Figure 3-2).

Figure 3-2
MSA70 with dual SAS and SATA disk hosting capability

When SCSI is often associated with high-end (enterprise-class) disks, ATA is associated with consumer-grade disks. What are the important differences between the two?

SAS is a point-to-point architecture in which all storage devices connect directly to a SAS port. It inherits its command set from parallel SCSI, frame formats from Fibre Channel, and physical characteristics from SATA. SAS and SATA both offer low-voltage differential signaling, 8-bit/10-bit encoding, and full duplex communication. Figure 3-3 shows the differences

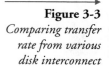

Figure 3-3
*Comparing transfer
rate from various
disk interconnect*

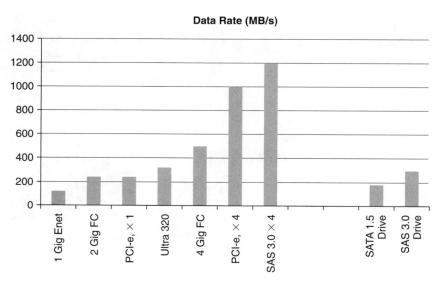

between various bus bandwidth technologies and compares the disk data rates (i.e., MB per second).

As seen here, the parallel SCSI standard, Ultra320, was challenged by PCI-Express (PCI-e) in single width mode, and largely overtaken by PCI-e in quad-speed mode (most motherboards or controllers can now operate in PCI-e x16, i.e., 40 Gb/s) and in serial SCSI (SAS 3.0 $\times$ 4). The serialization of protocols not only led to more reliability but also greater data throughput!

So which to choose? We propose the following breakdown, based on your *requirements*:

- SATA for the best price advantage for entry server and bulk storage deployments with low workloads. For example, a departmental (200 mailboxes) deployment with 2 GB mailboxes and Exchange 2007 with continuous replication falls in this category.

- SAS for the maximum performance, reliability, and heavy workloads for mission-critical applications. This is the sweet spot for Exchange 2007 in continuous replication mode for moderate workloads and very-large-capacity disks.

- Fibre Channel (FC) for the highest-performance, mission-critical availability and largest-scale storage systems for SAN-based storage operations. This is currently the situation for consolidated solutions (from 10,000 mailboxes to hundreds of thousands of mailboxes) that take some (not all) advantage of the continuous replication feature of Exchange 2007, and instead leverage on *infrastructure* services from SAN.

Direct-Attached Storage

The most common way to provide storage to a Windows Server is to use locally attached storage device controllers. In fact, many servers today come with on-board controllers that are directly integrated in the motherboard. You may use backplane controllers (named after their position in the server) and connect using PCI, PCI-X, or PCI-Express. From these controllers, you can connect at least one drive (for the smallest servers, such as "blades"), more often two or four, and sometimes a dozen.

The storage capacity and performance offered by these locally connected devices are limited to the server—you can distribute or share some of this capacity by means of file sharing protocols, but really, the disks are to be used by this server and not another. This storage is directly attached because it has no intermediate networking components other than the RAID controller and the electrical wires that connect to the disk electronics that control the drive rotation and head movements.

Onboard controllers are now predominant because operating systems that run on industry-standard servers typically require a local boot device. Windows Server 2003 makes certain assumptions about this boot device and specifically about the fact that a direct path is always available for memory dump operations after a system crash. Typically, the boot device contains the operating system components and pagefile (swap space for virtual memory management). Further components, such as Microsoft Exchange databases and transaction log files, are assigned to additional disks, for performance, management, and redundancy purposes, but not always.

You can use PCI-Express disk controllers to store the Exchange 2007 databases and logs. This is quite common for small environments: For less than 500 users, direct-attached storage with network backup and recovery is a very appropriate and cost-effective solution. With Exchange 2007 and its continuous replication features, the need for high-speed and resilient storage is somewhat diminished. Considering direct-attached storage for large capacity servers (2,000 users per server and more) is increasingly common. However, you need to weight the implications of such an approach, especially in terms of backup, recovery, and overall availability.

In the same way that information in your Microsoft Exchange infrastructure has varying value, you are able to align this information storage on varying components that best fit the criticality of the information and its access rate (Figure 3-4).

In this example, you have 1.2 TB of raw storage in three drives, compared with 560 GB of raw storage in four drives. Of course, the resulting capacity will depend on the type of RAID level you use for these disks and how you decide to assemble them together. The net result is that at a lower

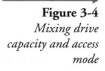

Figure 3-4
*Mixing drive
capacity and access
mode*

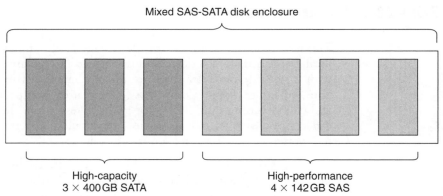

Mixed SAS-SATA disk enclosure

High-capacity
3 × 400 GB SATA

High-performance
4 × 142 GB SAS

cost and space, you can store massive amounts of information, but not at the same throughput (I/O per second).

While there are similarities in terms of electrical signaling between SAS and SATA, the major differences can be summarized as follows:

- SATA drives are less expensive (30 to 40% cheaper for similar capacity).

- SATA drives use the ATA command set.

- SAS drives can be dual-ported, use faster rotation speed, and lower latency, and can be configured using variable sector size.

- The SATA backplane cannot host SAS drives. (But the inverse is true: SAS enclosures can host SATA drives; as in other examples, such as PCI buses, using devices with varying response time may result in degrading overall performance.)

- SAS drives are responding to stricter specifications than SATA drives, resulting in greater MTBF (mean time between failures) and duty cycles: 1,500,000 hours with a duty cycle of 100% for SCSI drives versus 500,000 hours at a duty cycle of 20% for the SATA drives. The duty cycle simply means the percentage of time that the drive is in use.

Which to choose then? You may consider that SATA drives provide greater capacity at lower cost, and aim your choice toward this technology. However, Microsoft Exchange is a demanding application in terms of transaction throughput (I/O per second), and it uses that storage *all* the time. When SATA drives come with a third of the reliability for five times less use than SAS drives, you can ask yourself a quite legitimate question, "What's best for my mailboxes?," given that they will be accessed *all* the time. Second, the data typically found in Microsoft Exchange cannot easily be partitioned between what's really important (3 months worth of mailbox or shared documents) and what's not important (the mails exchanged 2 years ago, but that are kept, just in case).

The net result is that there is a requirement for hosting the Microsoft Exchange databases to fulfill the capacity requirement at the same time as transaction throughput. While the SATA drives appear to be very cost effective for capacity, they do not offer the same level of transfer rate and reliability that is often demanded for Microsoft Exchange, even in the smallest environments (200 users or more).

Therefore, you should investigate the use of SATA drives for hosting backups or shadow copy images of production volumes, which should be hosted on SCSI or SAS drives. This modus operandi enables your company for the greater availability and performance of production volumes (online databases), while the sheer capacity delivered by the SATA drives is used for storing backups, and therefore is less subject to utilization than the SCSI drives. Furthermore, because direct-attached drives are components of more advanced solutions, such as in network storage servers (NAS) or small to medium SAN arrays, you should extend to this recommendation when using these components.

One of the problems with direct-attached storage is the inability to transparently scale up to the demands of both capacity and performance requirements. As your user base grows and demand increases, by taking advantage of Exchange 2007's ability to use multiple databases, you will quickly get into a situation where you may not be able to add units and where the expansion of existing units will require downtime. For example, it is not possible to dynamically expand a volume using direct-attached storage technology without bringing the service down. You may, however, envisage this type of operation during planned downtime of your servers.

For example, suppose that you have a storage group, with a single database and with 200 users, and that you need more space for doubling the quota of those users. You could use the following sequence:

- Add more disks to the controller (possibly an additional shelf of disks). Whether this can be done online or requires downtime depends on the *capabilities* of your SAS/SATA controller.
- Create a new RAID volume.
- Create a new storage group.
- Host the database of the new storage group on this new volume.
- Move users to the new storage group.
- Run offline defrag to reclaim the saved space from the old database (optional step).

While the lack of expandability on a particular bus-attached controller can be noted, you may argue that you can add additional controllers to the PCI bus. This is true, but the current host I/O bus technology and the way Windows Server handles it is such that by adding more controllers, you will introduce more interruptions in the processing of the server and in fact decrease the server's performance—its ability to perform optimally. Furthermore, lower-priority bus addresses and requestors can quickly become starved as higher-priority entities (network cards or others storage controllers) grab the bus bandwidth. Slow response time on certain devices can have an overall negative effect on the computing capability of the server, and worst of all, the response time of user transactions.

Direct-attached storage is an excellent strategy for small- to medium-sized servers that do not require immediate expansion. PCI-based RAID controllers are faster and faster, and although they are often pointed out as a single point of failure, they have proved to be reliable to the point that you can deploy them with confidence, provided that you accompany this type of deployment with advanced data management and fast backup and recovery. With these controllers you can use advanced storage optimization techniques such as RAID5 or RAID0+1, and, most important, write caching, which will boost performance for the response time of your transaction log traffic and your database accesses.

Servers can ship in high-expansion models, by which drive cage and bays are prepared in the server enclosure. This carries great advantages for expandability reasons, but it shouldn't be assumed that new high-capacity drives will be supported in these existing configurations. Some manufacturers, such as HP, have made the effort, however, to build drives around the same form factor and plug characteristics, thereby enabling you to interchangeably use disks between servers of various models, and even external storage shelves.

Given the above, many deployments that we have worked on are targeted to last for a minimum of 2 to 3 years. The cost of the hardware upgrade is certainly considered, but, most important, the cost of downtime and the cost of servicing typically prohibit "touching" to already deployed servers. Thus, new ways of providing storage to clients and servers were developed, almost on demand, and built around architecture that allows easy expansion, management, and monitoring. This leads to SAN implementations that shift from bus-oriented storage to network oriented storage. The network paradigm is applied to storage components, coming with incurred flexibility, yet with more complexity and more choices to choose from. Which choice is the right one becomes then a significant equation to solve, and can only be made if you have clearly identified your requirements.

Controllers and buses

SAS and SATA controllers share a number of parts together. Let's have a look at an HP-branded Smart Array controller for SAS peripherals in Figure 3-5.

First, you have a 2 GB/s PCI-Express (PCI-e) × 8 bus interface. Then there is a RAID on chip that implements hardware-based calculations for RAID5 and RAID6 parity. The board supports up to eight SAS links and has a transportable, battery backed-up write cache. "Transportable" basically means that if the controller burns down for some reason, the contents of the cache can be preserved as you service the controller and replace it with a new one.

Figure 3-5
*Anatomy of an
HP Smart Array
controller*

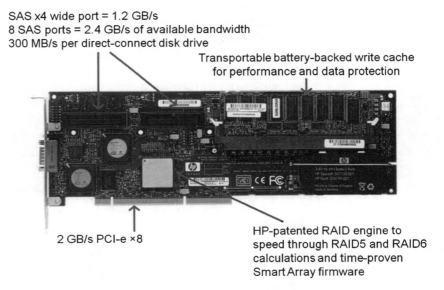

SAS x4 wide port = 1.2 GB/s
8 SAS ports = 2.4 GB/s of available bandwidth
300 MB/s per direct-connect disk drive

Transportable battery-backed write cache
for performance and data protection

2 GB/s PCI-e ×8

HP-patented RAID engine to
speed through RAID5 and RAID6
calculations and time-proven
Smart Array firmware

Shelves and disks

For direct-attached storage, you need to connect your local controller to either internal disks using relatively high-capacity servers, as shown in Figure 3-6, or use external shelves as seen earlier in Figure 3-2.

The best approach depends on your needs. In servers, we see space available because the components inside the server, such as the DIMM slots for

Figure 3-6
*HP ProLiant
DL585 with 16
local SAS disks*

memory or the CPU sockets, require space. However, if you intend to create a 2 TB server with some form of RAID redundancy, you will need a fair quantity of disks, and using an external shelf might be better.

Disks can come in various shapes and footprints. There are two big families: large form factor, that is, 3.5″ disks, or small form factor, that is, 2.5″ disks. The 3.5″ disks (LFF) are typically found in today's data centers. They have a greater power consumption compared to 2.5″ disks (SFF) and a greater capacity per unit (500 GB and above vs. 250 GB and below). However, in terms of providing I/O per second for the GB, the clear winner is the SFF disk family, because these disks provide similar MTBF compared to the LFF (~1.75 million hours at 100% duty cycle for a SAS SFF), as well as similar throughput. Table 3-1 provides a summary when comparing disk technologies for direct-attached storage.

Table 3-1   *Comparing disk technologies*

	PATA	SATA	SCSI
Built for:	Price	Price	Reliability
Price/MB	1/3 Fibre Channel	1/3 Fibre Channel	A bit less than Fibre Channel
Performance			
RPM	5400	7200	10000/15000
Average seek time	9.5 ms	8.5 ms	4–5 ms
Reliability			
MTBF	1M + hr	1M + hr	1M + hr
Duty cycle	20–30%	20–30%	80–100%
Start/stop cycles	>50,000	>50,000	Never stops
Ports	Single port	Single port	Single port
SMART	Available	Available	Yes
Limited warranty	1–3 years	1–3 years	3–5 years
External shock	Limited protection	Limited protection	Greater protection
Acoustics	Average	Average	Minimized
Internal components— actuators, magnets	Low cost	Low cost	Higher quality

Of course, because of changes in technology between the time we wrote this book and the time you read it, you should check with your storage (server?) vendor for specifications of the disk drives you plan to use for your direct-attached storage solution.

In summary

Design specifications and the different *requirements* for SATA and SAS disk deserve careful consideration before you move to SATA-based storage. Indeed, SATA disks are built for the best capacity for the price, while SAS disks are built for the best *performance* for the price. Therefore, you should use SATA drives for non–mission critical applications and reference information storage, and SAS for mission-critical applications and transactional data.

The local server attachment specific to DAS makes the combination of scaling disks and performance deployed across single point of failures (a disk controller does not have any form of redundancy). For this reason, you should exclusively use direct-attached storage on the following conditions:

- Your Microsoft Exchange service does not require high availability (99.7% and above) and can sustain the loss of service of several hours.

- You deploy continuous replication, preferably at the Microsoft Exchange level, or at the operating system level.

Storage Area Networks

Storage Area Networks basically represent a paradigm shift in the storage world by applying the best concepts of networking to storage. Note that this is also true for NAS, but NAS has a separate and not competitive place in Exchange 2000 data centers. In fact, despite an attempt by Microsoft to support file-based protocol shares with Exchange 2003 (Thunderclap feature pack for Windows-based storage servers), this never really took off, and instead, the standardization and generalization of iSCSI made Microsoft Exchange capable of using IP-based storage, albeit not file shares. SAN became popular because of the following virtues:

- Scalability
- Flexibility (especially with virtualization)
- Performance
- Consolidation
- Manageability
- Availability

You have certainly heard about SANs if you have to manage a large-scale environment and if you've been attentive to developments within the storage industry. Given that storage represents approximately 60% of IT spending, administrators certainly have had to care about it. For IT directors, data storage should have a strategic orientation, and CIOs just want it to work while the company carries on its business without worrying about details and shortcomings of one implementation or another.

The important thing, really, is that when we build large Microsoft Exchange infrastructures for hosting massive quantities of data, the servers are of much less concern to us than the storage.

With Microsoft Exchange 2000 and 2003, we moved from a host-centric approach to a storage-centric approach: Evaluating the storage capacity as well as its performance became the key decision criteria for the architectures. When using SAN technology, we have to focus on considerations beyond the disk and RAID systems by including the networking components, typically Fibre Channel switches and hubs and host-bus adapters (HBAs), which are special controllers that enable the server to enumerate and access the logical units defined on the back-end SAN controllers, as shown in Figure 3-7.

Figure 3-7
SAN in a Microsoft Exchange network

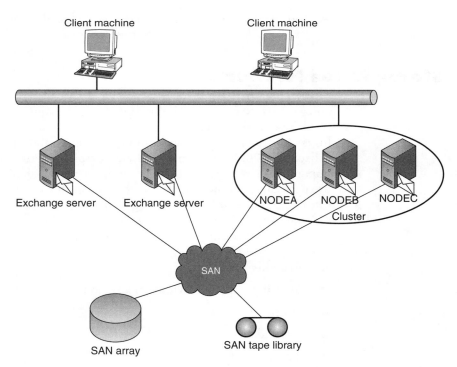

The exercise must consist of establishing solid and reliable connectivity between the servers and the SAN array controllers, building controllers that can support the peak and aggregated workloads anticipated, and then issuing servers that will run the Microsoft Exchange services and access the units over the SAN. These units are accessed independently between servers, and cooperatively between servers that are part of a Microsoft cluster.

Figure 3-8 illustrates the approach to a server-centric design, where client computers connect to servers by means of a network infrastructure (typically LAN, but can be expanded to a WAN in highly centralized environments) and application servers are provided by servers, each of which has its own server-tethered storage. With Exchange 5.5, this type of deployment was extremely common because SAN was not yet mature. The application itself is confined to the realm of resources, processor, and memory, and, most important, storage, all of which are available on the server.

Figure 3-8
Server-centric approach

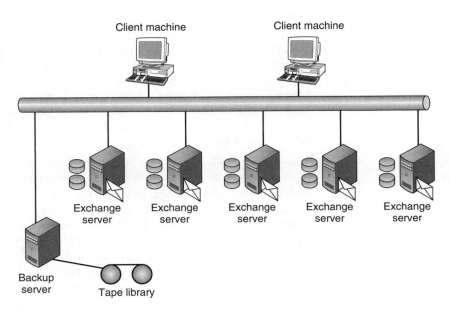

By contrast, Figure 3-7 exhibits a storage-centric approach, where servers have minimal local storage resources and share one or more common storage cabinet to access mainstream data required by the application. Some deployments can even go as far as using diskless servers that can boot directly from the SAN infrastructure. We are in this case building a redundant array of independent servers (RAIS), a proposal that is quite attractive when clustering Exchange 2007 for mailbox servers does not comply with the customer's requirements. Servers are becoming almost "throwaway" items; if one breaks down, replacing it is relatively simple. In what are sometimes called "N + 1" configurations, N servers are active and one server is kept as a cold-standby server; the latter is not online, although you may want to have it powered up to keep it updated with BIOS and firmware. This configuration may be implemented in many ways. Clearly, the ability for a SAN adapter to boot into a SAN greatly simplifies the process of replacing the existing failed server with a new one. All that is needed is granting access to the boot and data volumes to the new server (this can usually be done at the storage cabinet level by enabling access to the volumes for the host-bus adapter of the recovery server).

SANs enable you to do the same things that you did before, only differently and with greater flexibility. It would be a mistake to buy a SAN solution for its performance, unless you need the performance of high-end storage cabinets. In that case, you will concentrate on deploying an *island* of SAN, which is, admittedly, a common practice at the moment. SAN is an enabling technology that improves on certain aspects of data storage operations, such as the following:

Backup and restore—The ability to localize the bulk of the backup and restore data transfer to the SAN, without the need to build a separate high-speed LAN or use-dedicated, locally attached tape drives, while keeping the same levels of performance. Remember that SANs are typically gigabit networks (400 MB/s, i.e., 4 Gbps, and more in the future) that are perfect for backup applications that can take advantage of such a large bandwidth.

Advanced disaster tolerance—The ability to implement distant mirrors, clones, or snapshots of individual volumes much more easily than with direct-attached storage. In fact, with DAS, it's almost impossible to build such solutions, unless aiming for a software-based solution, which does not always address the strict requirements of data consistency and performance required by an application such as Exchange 2007. Disaster tolerance, or what we could simply reduce to availability is important, and if you ask anybody, the basic requirement will fall to $7 \times 24 \times$ forever, no matter what.

Easy growth—SAN storage cabinets can usually grow beyond several terabytes, not that it would be a wise thing to build 1 TB logical units or volumes; this can have a major impact on the manageability of the volume (see subsequent discussion of RAID volumes and how large they should or can be). Local storage capacity to servers typically is limited by physical space, and sometimes connectivity. The important concern in storage growth is not always capacity; often it's the requirement to maintain the same levels of performance and availability, especially when adding third-party applications such as antivirus or other mobility-enabling solutions such as RIM's BlackBerry Enterprise Server.

Cost recovery—The ability to serve storage to many servers helps to reduce the somewhat incremental cost of a SAN-based solution. You can realize economies of scale by sharing advanced features of the SAN, such as data replication for disaster tolerance and recovery purposes.

Ability to deploy disk-less server farms—Also known as *redundant array of independent servers* (RAIS). This is accomplished by enabling a boot device to be located in the shared SAN.

Cost recovery is a key factor for most IT directors, given that established shared-storage vendors will attempt to offer their storage services to the Exchange 2007 servers for use in many environments, thereby reducing the overall cost of the storage solution. This aspeFct of sharing is quite important. As you invest tens of thousands of dollars in a storage solution, it will provide certain availability features that you will not find on PCI-based RAID controllers, such as cache mirroring, bus redundancy, or controller redundancy. The benefits of tape automation, disk hot spares, and emergency access to temporary storage (e.g., making a 100 GB volume available to several servers for database offline defragmentation or maintenance operation or debugging) also come into play.

Finally, the notion of online growth and expansion without taking down the service is particularly important when building Microsoft Exchange networks. For any storage design for Microsoft Exchange, you will want to build in your design adequate capacity for growth: estimated at between 20 and 50% per annum, the growth rate depends on your business. Your company can (will) grow, either organically or by acquisition. The quantity of data also grows, both in terms of quantity of messages processed per day and per employee and in terms of individual size, by using rich documents, media, digitized information, and so on. Figure 3-9 shows the expansion of

Figure 3-9
IDC disk storage system forecast

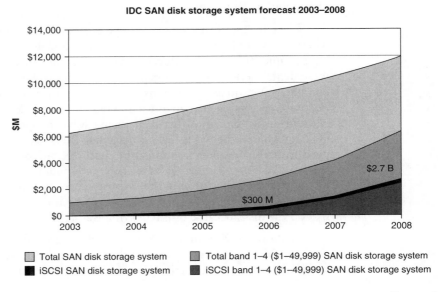

IDC SAN disk storage system forecast 2003–2008

$2.7 B

$300 M

Total SAN disk storage system   Total band 1–4 ($1–49,999) SAN disk storage system
iSCSI SAN disk storage system   iSCSI band 1–4 ($1–49,999) SAN disk storage system

SAN storage and the relative growth of iSCSI with respect to the total SAN solution delivered.

Just like any consumer, ask yourself the three following questions:

- How much was a GB last year?
- How much is it today?
- How much will it be in 1 year down the road?

We think you will find that the trend of ever decreasing storage costs, combined with improved footprint (and therefore required infrastructure) and somewhat improved performance, implies that the storage infrastructures of today will be different 3 years from now. The modern IT infrastructures are therefore designed to adapt, and use only what they need: This is the concept of "on demand" that can be applied to storage components or even application services. You pay for what you use, period.

Note that this model does not apply to all companies, either because of technology (lack of) readiness, culture, or other parameters. However, you should keep this model in mind, and understand that SANs are key enablers for building such flexible infrastructures: adding a server on a SAN is far less costly than building a server with its own server-tethered storage, simply because you can build on existing practices (processes) and staff and technologies, instead of adding additional units.

Again, we wish to stress that SAN is not a unique solution for all environments, but it is beneficial in most environments with a somewhat increased acquisition cost. This cost increment is basically the value you obtain with such technologies.

The concept of sharing can also be extended to an entire RAID volume, where you would define a 10-disk array, partitioned into several independent logical units (LUNs) of reduced capacity. The advantage is that you get an incremental performance boost by using a volume with many disks that can handle a large quantity of transactions. The disadvantage, and you should be aware of this, is that in most implementations, the LUNs are accessed without any cooperation between them. What happens if you share a single large volume between several Exchange 2007 servers, and suddenly you need to perform a database integrity check on one of the databases on one server? The other servers will suddenly get "polluted" by the sheer request rate of the server performing the integrity check and their performance may be seriously affected. Sequential I/O from one host might turn into random I/O on the disks because of interleaving traffic.

In short, sharing in a SAN is a good concept and can be extended to volumes, but you must make sure that you have sufficient capacity so that individual servers can effectively maintain their respective workloads.

SAN protocols: Fibre Channel and iSCSI

Fibre Channel (as a protocol) provides high levels of bandwidth, connectivity, and flexibility. Today's SANs are deployed using multiport switches that can provide nonblocking 400 MB/s (megabyte, not megabit) per port with any-to-any connectivity. Although early implementations were seen on copper (serial cable type interface), Fibre Channel moved very quickly to optical fiber, which provides a flexible approach to connectivity, including long-range connectivity (up to 100 km and above) that is appropriate when building secondary disaster recovery sites. But this is not all; the Fibre Channel runs at 4 GB/s in 2008 and is projected to grow to 10 GB/s very soon. Most implementations are based on switch deployments and sometimes combine switches in rings or cascades. Be warned, however, that although switches from different vendors can have the same origin (e.g., Brocade switches are distributed by many vendors), differences in the firmware may appear and cause incompatibility.

iSCSI is basically the transport of SCSI commands over a TCP/IP connection. So instead of using the Fibre Channel protocol, which requires a specific infrastructure, you can provide *block-mode* storage to servers over Ethernet, IP, and TCP. From a capability viewpoint, iSCSI is almost on par compared to Fibre Channel. The difference is found in cost of components and performance. iSCSI is relatively new compared to Fibre Channel, so you should not be surprised that some components, such as high-end tape controllers, do not natively support the iSCSI protocol. More importantly, TCP and IP were created for unreliable and slow networks—the Fibre Channel protocol, on the other hand, has been designed for high-speed and high-quality networks. The two networking protocols are a world apart. FibreChannel quickly became dominant in the Enterprise Data Center market, while iSCSI grew from the increasing reliability of commodity networks. It grew on the opportunity to use these reliable and high-speed data networks for something other than client–server applications or web browsing, and benefit from networked storage.

Figure 3-10 shows how you can define the iSCSI attributes of a virtual disk in an HP StorageWorks EVA array. While this LUN can be exposed on a Fibre Channel network, it can also be presented on a LAN, and reachable over TCP/IP.

Figure 3-10
Choosing iSCSI parameters on a multiprotocol SAN controller

You can also use *host-based* iSCSI solutions to present disk containers on your network. All you need is the target "side" of the iSCSI protocol to be implemented on your server.

At this juncture, you may wonder when to use iSCSI. Table 3-2 shows a simple summary with key points to remember. Do not forget, however, that the relevance of these criteria depends on your environment. If you do not have a Fibre Channel infrastructure at present, yet wish to exploit the benefits of consolidated and shared storage infrastructure, you should seriously consider iSCSI. If on the other hand, you have a strong Fibre Channel infrastructure, you should enhance your benefits from it, rather than building a separate iSCSI environment that delivers little relative benefit.

Today, simple SANs are built on low-cost switches (with small number of ports, 8 or 16) with a single array, designed to serve a handful of servers (Figure 3-11). The switches are connected by means of an inter-switch link

Table 3-2   *Comparison of Fibre Channel and IP storage networks*

FC SAN	IP SAN
Consolidated storage: ease of installation, configuration management	
Dedicated network for storage	Recommend dedicated network for storage
Uses Fibre Channel	Uses Ethernet
FC HBA, FC Switch, Transceiver required	Ethernet NIC (Network Interface Card), Ethernet switch
For Performance needs	For Lower cost of ownership and lower infrastructure cost needs

Figure 3-11
Simple SAN with two redundant switches

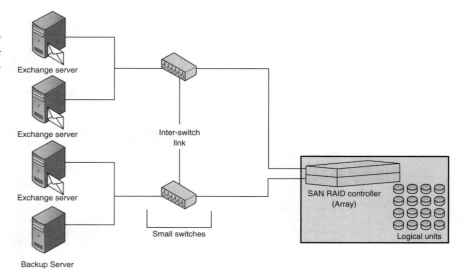

(ISL). If a switch breaks, the path to the storage array is still available to the other switch. The problem with this approach is that the more switches you add, the more ISLs you need to bring to guarantee path availability and performance. Adding an ISL to a switch is basically wasting two ports, one for each switch.

Ports are a scarce resource in SAN environment because switches are relatively expensive. A new approach that has been considered in recent years is using a series of switches at the center (core) of the Fibre Channel fabric, and another series of switches for connecting to this core at the edge of the fabric. Core switches can scale up in ports and performance and run multiple protocols (particularly interesting for consolidation of networking infrastructures for mixed iSCSI and SAN deployments). Known as a *core-edge SAN infrastructure*, this type of approach is schematized in Figure 3-12.

Figure 3-12   *Simple core-edge SAN design*

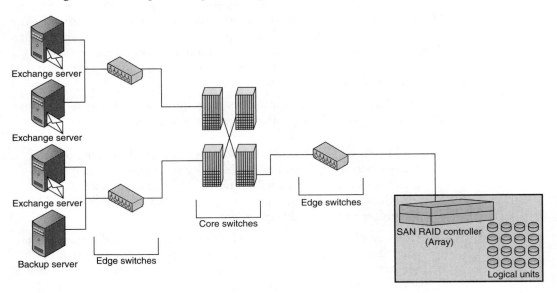

Core-edge SAN designs are now well established in high-end SAN environments because they enable some level of separation between servers (particularly useful in mixed-vendor server environments) and also between back-end storage components. In addition, the mesh at the core can connect to remote switches, that is, switches connected over long distance by the means of multimode and single-mode optical fibers and possibly Fibre Channel extenders. Deciding when to move to a core-edge infrastructure really depends on the number of ports available on your switches. In the past, switches would not scale in footprint and performance beyond 32 or 64 ports. Therefore, in order to accommodate 500 or 600 port access, you had to multiply these switches, multiply the ISL, have many ports wasted and finally, many resources wasted. Cascading the switches is a possibility, but only if you can keep the number of hops minimal (three hops is considered a maximum within a data center—one edge, one core, one edge).

In SANs, it is common to create a logical separation with the implementation of zones. Known as *zoning*, this method allows resource partitioning for management and access control purposes. A common configuration is to create two zones per Exchange server. Zone A contains the servers' HBAs and the backend storage array. Zone B contains the servers' HBAs, the tape library, and Fibre Channel-to-SCSI bridges.

With such an approach and the combined usage of zoning, you also have the possibility of creating a protocol-level isolation, which carries the advantage of avoiding servers impacting each other (Microsoft clusters, for instance, use SCSI commands with the SCSI miniport driver, which can be disruptive to other servers, even if they are not running Windows Server). Although fabrics are migrated with the goal of merging SAN islands, the core-edge approach enables bridging islands, and sometimes continents (because they are so large), and has a common physical infrastructure for manageability and cost recovery perspectives. The variations become too numerous to describe in this book.

We've seen two basic approaches, but then, as a Microsoft Exchange administrator, you will be confronted with two approaches:

- Build your own SAN and control it. In this case, depending on your budget, you might consider core-edge scenarios, but generally, a simple dual-switch approach will work well for a small number of servers (less than a dozen). Make sure that proper knowledge is developed by the people managing this environment.

- Use (reuse?) the corporate SAN infrastructure, typically built in a core-edge approach. In this case, you become a subscriber to a storage network service, and you will need to face the same advantages and problems as a customer: ensuring that you have full and reliable access, dealing with congestion, and so on. In such an approach, defining clear and measurable service levels is essential to determine whether the SAN delivers the throughput required at an acceptable latency. Without SLA (service level agreements), an Exchange administrator is vulnerable to SAN service quality fluctuation, with few possibilities of making changes.

This is a just a quick summary, but as you can see, the network paradigm applied to storage, as mentioned earlier, comes with its own set of problems. They are not unsolvable—it's just that in Microsoft Exchange environments, we have not always been accustomed to these notions, especially when we grew out of server-tethered storage. With Exchange 2007 and the much improved usage of storage, shared and virtualized infrastructures represent an opportunity; your role as a designer or artist will consist of getting the right quantities of resources for dealing with the majority of your workload, and ensuring that you have some head room for peak periods (high traffic due to business or external reasons) without overengineering the solution.

On the other hand, do not be surprised if Microsoft pushes for direct-attached storage solutions, because that is one of the design centers for Exchange 2007 and for the next generation of Microsoft Exchange (code named Exchange 14).

SAN controllers

Storage area network controllers typically range from small units that can handle a limited number of disks (200 or so), to larger units that can handle 1000 and more disks. This is not the only comparative piece of information between the low and high ends of the spectrum.

At HP, we have defined this spectrum in the following four parts. Other companies may use different categories.

Workgroup: A small storage appliance that can be used by several servers in a department, store, or office. This type of storage typically provides high-performance internal/external storage with PCI-class storage controller technologies.

Branch office: For the branch office, you will look for shared storage that requires a minimal infrastructure, allows for simple migration from server-based storage to SAN-based storage, and provides relatively good availability (e.g., by using redundant controllers in active/passive mode) for a low price.

Departmental: This type of storage, used with a maximum of 20 to 30 servers, is flexible and scalable. Positioned as entry-level or medium-range Fibre Channel storage, departmental SAN controllers can be scalable and deal with multiple host operating systems. They boast a relatively good price for high scalability. HP StorageWorks EVA and EMC Clarion storage lines are good examples of such storage controllers. They provide data replication functions and can typically handle up to 120 TB of raw storage.

Enterprise: This type of storage plugs into the data center network fabric to maximize scalability and availability for hundreds of connected servers and controlling 1000-plus drives. You typically have the highest level of availability and connectivity (multiple protocols and attachments), and provide extremely high availability (99.999% or <5 mn of downtime per year) and disaster-tolerant functions, such as instant (minutes) site failover with no data loss. With this type of high-end solution, you aim at multi-PB (petabyte = 1000 TB) solutions for many hosts.

In each category of storage arrays, you will encounter a varying number of features. In the enterprise class, hot-swaps of each and every component are common, as well as online upgrade of firmware, such that there is virtually *no* downtime required once you have powered up the array. In Figure 3-13, we provide an overall view of such large array. In Figure 3-14, we have a closer view of the connectivity inside such an array.

The disk cabinet access (DCA) is the heart of the system and contains up to eight back-end buses for connecting to dual-ported Fibre Channel disks. The DCA is comprised of the disk cabinet controller (DCC) unit, which has also a small disk cabinet unit (DCU) for hosting a few disks. Then the array can expand on "both sides" with DCUs (DCU-Lx for left side, DCU-Rx for right side) that contain disk units. The first DCA set supports up to 384 disk drives. The other DCA sets support 256 disk drives.

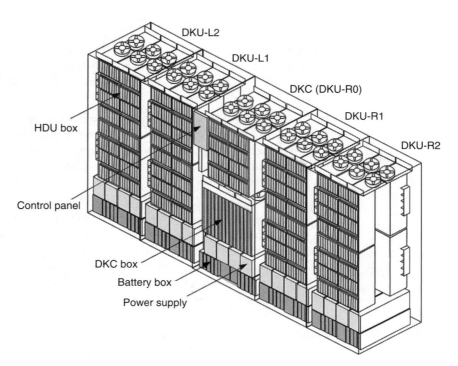

Figure 3-13
Enterprise storage block diagram (XP12000 by HP StorageWorks)

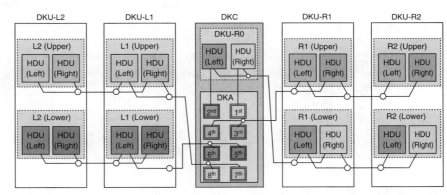

Figure 3-14
*Redundant connec-
tivity paths for the
HP StorageWorks
XP24000*

The dual-ported disk drives are active on both ports. Each disk unit (DCU) consists of four HDU boxes where disk drives are installed. Each HDU box supports 64 disk drives for a total of 256 disk drives per DCU.

In a midrange array, you will have similar features but fewer connectivity options (e.g., support for Fibre Channel and iSCSI, no support for mainframe connectivity), and you might require a controller reboot for firmware upgrade.

Figure 3-15 shows the logic diagram of the EMC DMX series. The interesting part of this high-end array is the central place given to the controller cache. The cache is quite large (up to 512 GB in size) and is central for any operation. With Exchange 2007, large caches lend little value because the servers already hold a lot of data that are accessed randomly. However, a large cache presence helps for sequential operations and isolates (with more or less effectiveness) busy disk conditions from the hosts.

This cache-centric design is in fact a key characteristic of high-end arrays that were initially designed for mainframe environments. When many designs are made on the basis that the contention points are the host connection and the cache size, we see trouble in addressing Microsoft Exchange workloads. Why? Because Microsoft Exchange has a database workload pattern (random across a large seek range) that does not lend itself well to cache operations; when the database engine calls for a disk-read operation, it means that the data are not in the cache of the system (in RAM, 32 GB per server connecting into the SAN environment). So the chance that the controller cache has the data is quite minimal. For this reason, you should never design a storage system based on the assumption that the cache will solve disk access. Instead, design on the basis that a cache miss will be the norm.

Midrange solutions, which include the HP StorageWorks EVA line of products (shown in Figure 3-16) differ according to the number of host connections and number of ports. In the illustration, you can see that there is no central place for the cache. The cache is an integral part of each controller, and the controllers are interconnected by means of internal ports

Figure 3-15   *EMC DMX logic diagram (Source: EMC documentation)*

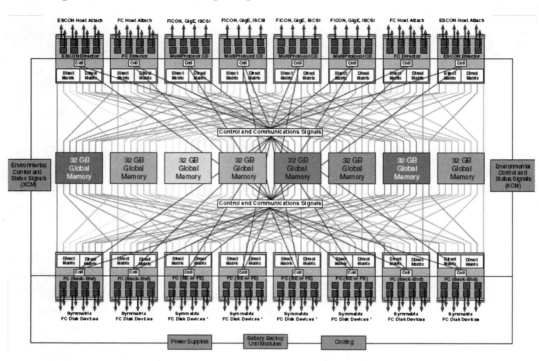

Figure 3-16
*HP StorageWorks
EVA architecture*

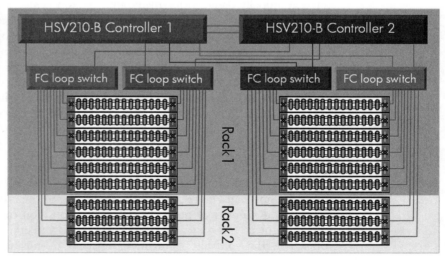

(known as *mirror ports*). Each access to the disks is fully redundant, and in fact, each disk has two paths: one to each controller. Each host has also two paths (or more) to each controller. This shows that although the SAN array can be seen as a single basket where you put all your eggs, it also has many redundancy features that help in protecting data (RAID or virtualized RAID across many disks) and the path to the data (redundant ports, controllers, buses, and disk ports).

In branch office and workgroup solutions, you are basically dealing with a network extension of the back-end controller class. These solutions are characterized by a small quantity of disks attached to the shelf, as well as entry-level redundancy features, such as the active/passive controller model, or no ability to hot-swap a controller component from the SAN solution. This is due to the design objectives of this type of controller.

Virtualization

As discussed previously, virtualization is the ability to dissociate data placement from physical elements. In modern storage technologies, this virtualization happens in several ways.

Virtualization occurs at the disk level by using techniques such as those found in the HP StorageWorks EVA platform, where data are spread across as many disks as possible. If you need more IOPS, you just need to add disks. If you need more capacity, you add more disks as well. This type of disk-level virtualization is ideal for *thin-provisioning*. The principle is to provide as much storage as necessary and as little as possible, and grow accordingly. With the storage management benefits of Windows Server 2008, such as LUN shrink and expand, this approach can make excellent use of your assets and prevent overengineering your solution. For an example using the HP StorageWorks EVA, see Figure 3-17.

At the controller level, by abstracting the implementation of disk storage, you can use either local disks or externally attached storage systems, or both. The pooling of heterogeneous volumes into a single reservoir results in increased capacity utilization, by dynamically reallocating capacity. On high-end storage arrays (HP StorageWorks XP platform, based on Hitachi hardware), you can go as far as placing data on heterogeneous back-end storage systems, as shown in Figure 3-18.

The benefit of such an approach is that the storage volumes are presented in the exact same way and managed using the same tools, from the client operating system viewpoint. On the back-end viewpoint, you have a variety of options, including leveraging existing assets and recycling them in profit of more cost-effective and performing solutions. This dissociation of the data life cycle from the hardware life cycle is indeed quite important, because you know you will have data storage requirements for quite some time, and you know that your hardware will evolve over time. They should

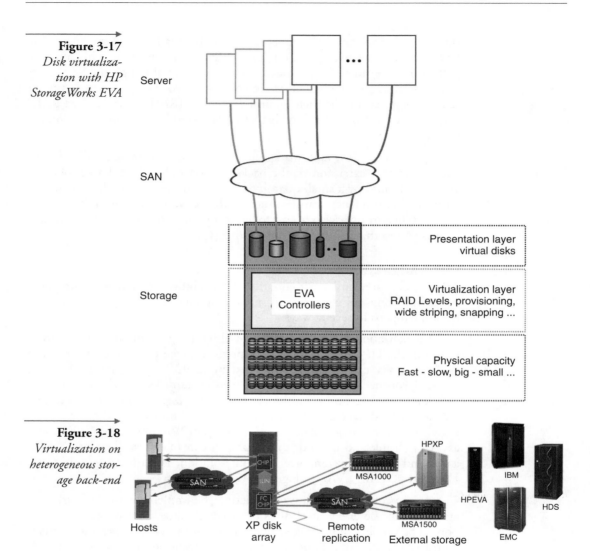

Figure 3-17
Disk virtualization with HP StorageWorks EVA

Figure 3-18
Virtualization on heterogeneous storage back-end

not be tied together, but if they are, the migration should be made transparent to the users and the business application.

Virtualization, which is just another word for abstraction, masks the particulars of the physical resources behind logical objects. It also allows the organization to dynamically change the composition of the logical objects—in effect mixing and matching different physical resources and their attributes—while remaining transparent to the application. In short, virtualization enables the organization to achieve what the application ideally has wanted all along, which is transparent access to the most appropriate resources when and how it needs them.

You may wonder if virtualization has any disadvantages. One of its downsides is that because you cannot relate application requests to physical components, troubleshooting issues may take longer than in a direct-attached storage environment, for example. There you need to spend enough time in properly engineering your solution so that the *sharing* nature of SAN does not counter its benefits.

For this reason, virtualization must not be limited to the physical storage, fabric, and server resources. All the management capabilities that present infrastructure components (in fact, the entire management path from the application to the physical device) must provide functions that enable proper management of the solution life cycle. To the application, everything—physical devices, operating systems, software, management services, and components of all sorts—is a transparent resource that exists to serve its needs. To the IT administrator, it means extra effort to manage a somewhat more complex environment than a direct-attached solution; however, this effort is beneficial to many applications, not just Microsoft Exchange.

Replication

In a SAN, replication is quite easy to implement because it does not require much involvement from the application or the server. To express this, let's consider Figure 3-19. This somewhat complex diagram shows how the continuous access solution for the XP array links two XP arrays that could be miles apart, and establishes a link between primary volumes (P-VOL) and secondary volumes (S-VOL). This link allows storage of a replica of the data in a

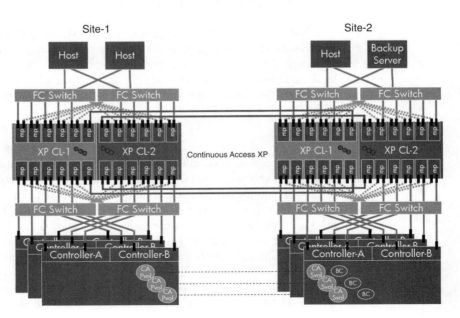

Figure 3-19
HP SAN Replication with XP array (source: HP)

separate site. However, it does not require any specific implementation from the host (upper part of Figure 3-19), and the data "created" on the second site (Site-2) can then be accessed for backup purposes. The abstraction made possible by the SAN topology makes implementation of site-level replication similar for all hosts and all applications. This is a key benefit of SAN approaches. Sharing infrastructure and functions among many hosts leads to standardized storage management practices. It does require some level of adaptation or integration with the application, and this is where the Windows storage management components such as VDS and VSS (discussed in Chapter 4) are very useful.

In Summary

Storage Area Networks are versatile enterprise resources whose value depends on how much is shared. In other words, sharing is profoundly the nature of SANs, and if you intend to dedicate a SAN to a server or a group of servers, you basically defeat the purpose of the SAN.

SANs are designed to bring benefits to many servers at once. These benefits can be summarized as follows:

- Improve efficiency of storage utilization
- Reduce time and cost of server management
- Simplify storage management
- Enhance data protection and availability
- Enable virtualized server infrastructures

For example, the use of SAN, combined with database transportability delivers significant value if you do not wish to use move mailboxes with Exchange 2007. Instead, you point a database volume to a *different* server, regardless of the database size, and refer the mailbox attributes to this new server (using the PowerShell command move-mailbox in configuration change only).

Tape Systems

Since the beginning of modern computing (1951), tapes have been in use, from small cartridges to large reels operating under vacuum. The objective of tape technology is to store large quantities of data in a sequential access pattern. This is in contrast to disk drives that store data and access them in a random way. Tapes are often used for putting data on a medium that can be transported *away* from the production site, and to later be used for recovery purposes. The industry has evolved in the following aspects:

1. In response to exponential data growth, companies such as HP try to help by bringing some context to these data (relative

importance, frequency of change), moving into the information management arena and content addressable storage (CAS), but the reality is that there is a growing quantity of information to protect and recover from, with defined retention policies.

2. Tape technology has evolved but has some shortcomings: access is sequential and random access to a single piece of information (such as a file) can be too slow. As an analogy, just remember how easy it is to change tracks on a CD compared to a conventional magnetic tape when you listen to music.

3. Disk technology is getting faster (especially for sequential access) and the cost per GB has dramatically decreased.

4. Information is important for enterprise survival. It is often classified—along with the application that uses it—as mission critical. If data are lost, the business closes; if a piece of data is lost, it must be recovered quickly, for operational or legal purposes. Not only does data need to be rapidly recovered (known as recovery time objective [RTO]), the most recent data possible must be recovered (known as recovery point objective [RPO]).

5. Backup windows (time-wise) are shrinking. The 8am–6pm workday might not map to the production workload of your environment, not to mention other projects such as a data center consolidation exercise that may host applications and users in multiple time zones. With mobility and global access to data networks, the 24 × 7 production hour requirement is justified.

In summary, you have to deal with constant data growth, be able to classify the data, and most importantly, protect the data (with shrinking backup window) and retrieve the data (as fast as possible). To address these needs, the storage industry has a number of solutions that can be grouped into six families:

- Low-cost disk arrays: A good example is the HP MSA family of arrays that can use relatively low-cost SATA or SAS disk drives of large capacity (250 GB and above per disk unit). The industry is indeed moving into an era where the disk capacity per spindle (unit) continues to increase. For example, Hitachi recently announced a 1 TB disk drive.

- Virtual library system: The VLS is easily integrated into an existing backup and recovery framework (implemented using industry standard solutions, such as HP Data Protector, VERITAS NetBackup or BackupExec, EMC Legato Networker or IBM's TSM). The objective of the VLS is to combine ease of use and rapid random access of disk technology with the emulation of a commonly used tape library, in such a way that you can rapidly integrate disk-based technology in conventional tape-based backup environments.

- Array business copy: The ability of a storage array to create two or more copies of a logical volume is combined with the capability of recovering from a failed unit by using a mirror copy. There are many ways to implement such a feature, such as in the HP StorageWorks XP or EVA lines of products.

- Host-based volume management: Application and drivers can be installed on a given operating system. This service combines logical units from various arrays to create mirrors, for instance, for duplicating data, independently of application *capability*. HP OpenView Storage Mirroring is a good example of such an application.

- Application-based replication: This is the ability of an application to manage its own data duplication and recovery in a more or less automated way. Such ability has existed for quite some time in the database world (Oracle ASM), and it is now appearing in Microsoft Exchange 2007.

- Continuous data protection: The CDP objective is to save changes as they occur. The particularity of a CDP solution, compared to application-based replication, is its ability to be implemented at a relatively low level (by the means of a filter driver) and to walk backward in time to the desired point of recovery (e.g., Mendocino RecoveryONE technology).

You may wonder whether tape is going to disappear as it did in the music industry. In the long run, probably—but for now, tape libraries and media have a useful place in modern data centers, even if many tasks that used to be given to tape devices can now be accomplished by disk drive technologies.

Myth Debunking and other considerations

In this section, we would like to eradicate a few myths associated with tape technology.

Myth #1: Disk is faster than tape

This is not correct; In fact, let's consider a common scenario illustrated in Figure 3-20. In this scenario, the application server runs a backup of its databases to an intermediate backup unit and the backup software will then back up that unit to media. This type of approach is valuable if your disk capacity

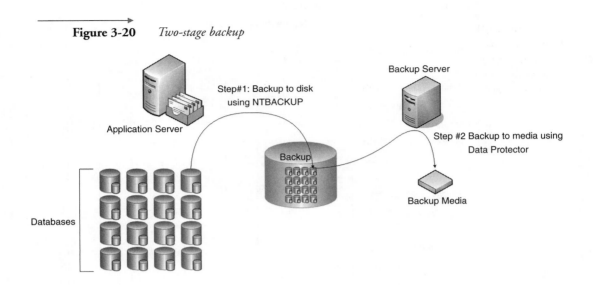

Figure 3-20   *Two-stage backup*

and throughput largely exceeds the backup media capability. However, be aware that most mainstream operating systems (such as Windows Server) are not precisely optimized for such data transfer. It could be far better to back up directly to the media, be it a tape drive or a virtual tape library. We have seen customer environments where-disk based backups used file servers (using CIFS over Ethernet), and performance was terrible.

Currently LTO-3 tape technology can stream data in excess of 200 MB/s. If you cluster these tape drives together (typically, it's a function of the backup media solution), you can achieve a much higher throughput (Figure 3-21).

If you use multiple tape drives, you can generally aggregate those rates, if your storage infrastructure allows it! Note that these are native rates: If the data allows, compression can be twice as much on the tape media, resulting in doubling the data rate (close to 1 TB/hr for an LTO-4 tape drive). See Table 3-3 about the HP product set using LTO-3 and LTO-3. Similar solutions are available from other vendors.

Thus, tape libraries can be really fast with appropriate infrastructure support, and the capacity of tapes exceeds that of disks.

Myth #2: Restore is longer than backup

There is technology inside tape drives, called buffering, that enables writing faster than reading, but generally speaking, the backup and restore speed are also driven by the type of application data. In other words, a RAID5 volume that hosts a database may be slower to write to than to read, and this has nothing to do with the backup media, be it tape or disk. So, if you think

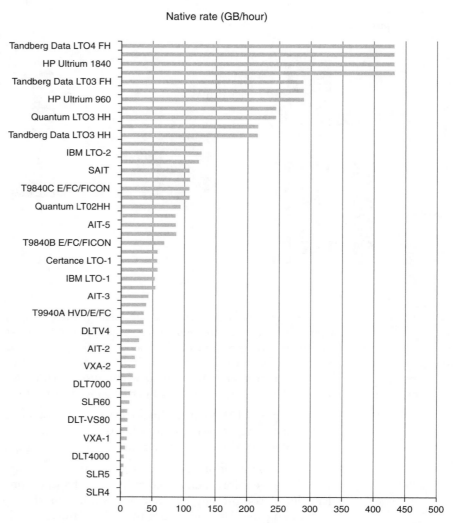

Figure 3-21
*Comparative data
rates for tape
technology from
various vendors*

your tape backup is slow, think twice before assuming that moving to disk-based backup and recovery technology will be beneficial.

Myth #3: Tape lasts

Whether you are working in computers or in music studios, if you have ever shot some videos, you will realize that tape media fades with time. It's not as obvious as in the introduction of the famous "Mission: Impossible" TV series; however, it is expected that tapes should/must be re-created in newer media every 3 years. With the data retention policies in certain industries, tape technology alone can be a burden to the administrator. Disk drives typically have a longer lifetime, in the range of 5 to 10 years.

Table 3-3 *Comparing tape library technologies*

	EML 103e Base	EML 442e High Performance	EML 505e High Capacity
Maximum capacity[a]	41.2TB (LTO 3) 20.6TB (LTO 2)	176.8TB (LTO 3) 88.4TB (LTO 2)	202TB (LTO 3) 101TB (LTO 2)
# slots	103 98 data, 5 load port	442 407 data, 35 load port	505 470 data, 35 load port
Maximum throughput[a]	1.15TB/hr (LTO 3) 0.43TB/hr (LTO2)	4.6TB/hr (LTO3) 1.7TB/hr (LTO 2)	2.3TB/hr (LTO3) .85TB/hr (LTO 2)
# drives	4	1–16	1–8

[a] uncompressed mode

Moving away from tapes: The simple approach

The simplest approach is to mount a physical disk or logical unit (LUN) as a local disk to the operating system, and run your backup on the local disk. Production data are read from the system and written to the local disk. The benefit from such an approach is that it is extremely simple to implement.

Benefits

- Data does not traverse the network.
- It's a local operation. There is no need to involve a storage administrator for performing backup or recovery, which can be easily handled by the application management team.

Problems

- It's a deviated use of your application server. Beyond running the application, the server has also got to be running backups and it may not necessarily be tuned for optimal performance. In certain environments, such as Windows, the operating system, the I/O stack, and the backup application might not be making the most of the resources to deliver the best throughput. You have not eliminated your backup window problem, but only displaced it until the volume of data gets too large.
- Running backup is not only about reading and writing data; there can be a significant CPU consumption. Again, this means that the

impact to the application server is quite important, because of both incurred I/O and CPU consumption.

- Consider that backing up to a local disk is only an intermediate operation. Most storage management policies will mandate that data are transported to an alternate physical site for disaster recovery purposes or otherwise written to some media that can be used for archiving and recovery.

All in all, backup to a local disk is a simple way to do disk-based backup, but by far is the least efficient and beneficial way of using disk technology in backup and recovery environments. It is relatively storage agnostic, and can reveal as a great band-aid solution in case you deploy a recent application that does not integrate with your backup and recovery framework.

Library emulators

Virtual library systems (VLSs) are a good example of adopting disk-based technology as seamlessly as possible in a production environment. They emulate most industry-standard tape drives and robotics, and are implemented using a dedicated operating system and server components (such as host-bus adapters), specifically tuned to run backups.

Benefits

- You have a seamless integration of random access disk technology into a backup environment. If you want to retrieve a 10 KB file from a 200 GB backup save set, you do not have to sequentially traverse the backup save set media, unlike with tape devices, which are sequential devices by design.

- Therefore, you remove *latencies* due to tape search operations.

- You suppress the effect of shoe-shining found in tape drives that operate at a data rate that is not in sync with the source/target volume data rates.

Problems

- Using a VLS will not necessarily provide a greater throughput compared to a tape-based solution, especially if your tape libraries are based on relatively recent technology, such as LTO-3.

- You still stream data in and out of the VLS; data access is sequential from the application viewpoint (when performing backup or recovery). If you have a very large database, using a VLS might not deliver better performance compared to traditional tape-based backups. If you have a large file system (such as a volume with *millions* of files), you will not suppress the problems of backing up a lot of small files.

■ You do not suppress the requirements for a backup window. Because the application or the volumes where the data reside are backed up using traditional backup tools, you have not really eliminated the backup window (Figure 3-22).

Figure 3-22
Managing a VLS

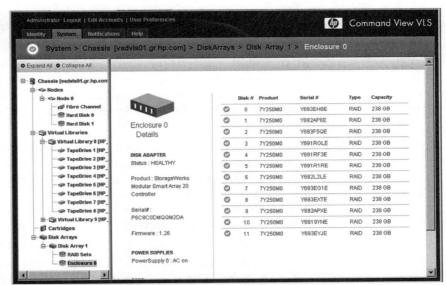

We have found that VLSs are probably the best choice for disk-based intermediate backup solutions. They are much better than tape devices if you have to retrieve relatively small quantities of data, because the transfer time is much smaller compared to the tape search and head position operations. If, on the other hand, you have a large database to back up, going with a VLS might not deliver a significant performance increase, if any at all, for either or both backup and recovery. A VLS will seamlessly integrate into current data protection paradigms. It will optimize the bandwidth utilization of the backup environment by allowing for high write and read data rates. Because the data are written to relatively reliable media (disks), you suppress media errors from the most time-critical operations (backup and recovery of recent data). Finally, the cost per GB is far less than for SAN storage, so you have a cost-effective solution.

Continuous data protection

Continuous data protection (CDP) is an emerging approach that is based on the principles that data are backed up as they are created/changed. In such an approach, you have a system that tracks all changes made to volume, and cares about backing up those changes. In addition, CDP solutions will allow you to traverse back in time and present a volume in the state it was at a particular point in time. This technology is relatively emergent and not always applicable in all environments, and certainly not exclusive to "traditional" backup and recovery infrastructures.

Benefits

- Each change is incrementally logged and archived/saved; there is no more backup window per se.

- Most implementation will be independent from the application and the operating system. You do not need to have application-specific code or procedures to place applications into a continuous data protection scheme. This is particularly true of the CDP solution is implemented at the filter driver level.

- It's the best way to deal with legacy applications, or when the application is complex, business critical, and has no backup integration. Typically, these applications will require no downtime and have a reduced or no backup window, and they have no extension that enables them to fit in a backup and recovery framework (i.e., an API that allows capturing the application data in a consistent way).

- Metadata stored along with the data changes enable the association of a time index with the backup of information, and most of the time, point-in-time recovery at any time in a defined recovery windows (typically between 24 hours and a few days). The use of application-specific event markers allows capture of a consistent data set even if the data to back up are spread across multiple volumes.

Problems

- The technology is emergent and needs maturing. It might be ready for *any* kind of environment, and you must first understand the sweet spots of such an approach before rushing into it.

- The CDT might not be implemented at the application level (such as with log shipping), but instead in a more generic way at the operating system level, using a filter driver. Like it or not, if the filter driver sits on the critical path of an I/O write operation, it will be the first suspect in cases of bad write performance, and its presence might delay case resolution.

- You might need to have a special way of marking events in your CDP solution, such that you can record a consistent data set.

- There is a general lack of experience, integration, and characterization information available to solutions architects. It is not uncommon to see these solutions fall apart if you run them in an environment that deviates significantly from those in research and development labs.

This is by far the most promising approach for removing backup windows and having flexibility in data recovery. In addition, this type of solution can be implemented on a variety of storage components, and is relatively agnostic from the application and operating system viewpoints. CDP does not suppress the need for traditional backups, offsite storage, or disaster recovery.

Beyond the media technology, do pay attention to the management and integration software. It can serve as a constraint (e.g., you *must* use a backup tool of certain brand), or as a key enabler (e.g., you can manage the entire media life cycle at the click of a button) or as a difficulty area (e.g., you need to assemble a series of complex components).

After defining your data plans and methods, make sure that you train people. If this is something that you do not wish to burden your IT with, start investigating outsourcing rather than sourcing it yourself.

In Summary

Storage Area Networks are standardized and have reached a plateau of functionality in terms of virtualization and storage management. The introduction of iSCSI for SAN made them far easier to deploy than for Fibre Channel SAN, because of the strong presence of TCP/IP in data centers. That said, the introduction of better and scalable (from capacity and performance viewpoints) direct-attached storage, combined with the storage management functions of Microsoft Exchange 2007 make the decision somewhat more difficult for IT administrators. The basic question is how much do you need to place between the host SCSI initiator (the driver, driven by the application) and the disk array (Figure 3-23)?

For Microsoft, the issue is simple: either operate over complex and hard-to-troubleshoot SAN environments, or take radical steps and operate on simple storage and provide the functionality required out of the box. This is what happened with Exchange 2007, and the vision encapsulated therein will continue.

To storage vendors, it's more difficult. There is a lot of research, development, and intellectual property in high-end storage networks. They come at an acquisition cost per GB that is substantially higher compared to DAS. The value of SAN is less obvious with Exchange 2007 compared to Exchange 2003, for example. The differences in disk technology found in DAS and SAN dwindle.

Figure 3-23
*Positioning from
application to
storage device*

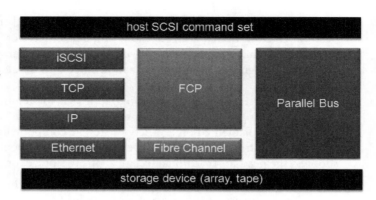

To the Exchange administrator and customer, it's even more difficult. SAN vendors worship their technology, Microsoft recommends DAS because it helps lower their support costs and improves the value of their product, and the CIO wants a cheap solution that works, given that the equivalent is often found for free on the Internet (e.g., Google email). The most important matter is to determine the scope of your storage strategy. If you have a data center–wide strategy based on *ruthless standardization,* then you should go for SAN. If you have flexibility in storage provisioning and not-so-strict SLA, then DAS is appealing. Just make sure that your cost focus is not on acquisition alone, but includes the cost of *running* the environment.

From a backup media perspective, it is not a one-size-fits-all proposition—it's a mixture of problem analysis, education, and know-how that helps to implement disk-based solutions for protecting your most critical data. There are strong precedents in the industry that suggest the elimination of tape media, such as in the music or video industries (how about creating optical storage in crystal stones?). However, with existing record retention policies and increased data usage, the exclusive use of backup-oriented disk technology is not effective just yet. You may end up using a mix of tape *and* disk technologies to create the best solution for your backup environment.

4

Windows Storage

You have learned the basic concept of I/O systems and we have discussed the different storage technologies you can use with Exchange servers. Regardless of whether you go with a Fibre Channel attached storage array or with Direct Attached Storage (DAS) you have to make the disks available to the Windows operating system. In this chapter, we describe technologies to manage disk storage using Windows management applications. We describe the things you have to consider when you create a file system on top of the raw disks presented to your server.

Figure 4-1 shows the Windows Storage Stack and whether the components we will discuss in the following sections are implemented in user mode or in the

Figure 4-1
Windows Storage
Stack (Source:
Microsoft)

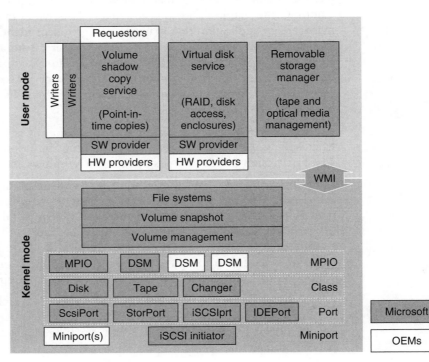

kernel of the operating system. We do not touch on all components shown in the picture, for example, we don't explain the Removable Storage Manager. The Volume Shadow Copy Services (VSS) facility is described in Chapter 8.

If you are interested in the changes that Windows Server 2008 introduced to the Windows Storage Stack, then we encourage you to download the presentations available on the Microsoft WinHEC website. For example, "Enterprise Storage Advances in Windows," from the Windows Hardware Engineering Conference 2007 provides many details about the topics discussed in this chapter.

Virtual Disk Service and Volume Shadow Copy Services

Two key components of the storage stack are the Virtual Disk Service (VDS) and VSS. VDS and VSS provide an abstraction layer that hides the hardware specifics of the underlying storage subsystems from storage management applications and applications like Exchange that want to take advantage of VSS (Figure 4-2).

VDS provides a single interface to manage multivendor storage environments. It eliminates the necessity that a Windows administrator understands several different vendor-specific storage application interfaces, for example, HP StorageWorks Command View EVA or an application of the EMC ControlCenter family. With this abstraction layer, you can envision a storage management application that manages storage independently of the hardware implementation. The management is transparent if the storage is connected to a backplane RAID controller, Fibre Channel or an iSCSI network. You could use the same management application and the same procedures for management tasks independently of whether the storage subsystem was manufactured by vendor A or vendor B.

Figure 4-3 provides an example of this vision; it is a screenshot of the Microsoft Storage Manager for SANs running on Windows Server 2008. The first version of this tool was included in Windows Server 2003 R2.

This vision of a hardware vendor independent storage management is achievable in a "Microsoft-only" environment. In large environments other operating systems are present, and therefore storage administrators have to understand additional storage management interfaces. Additionally, not all features of high-end storage subsystems are utilizable using the VDS interface. Some vendors try to differentiate them from their competition by providing special features that often do not have a corresponding VDS interface.

You can find a detailed description of the VDS architecture, including the picture in Figure 4-2 on Microsoft TechNet. Other good sources for details about VDS and VSS are Jose Barreto's Blog and the Microsoft whitepaper, "Storage Management Using VDS and VSS."

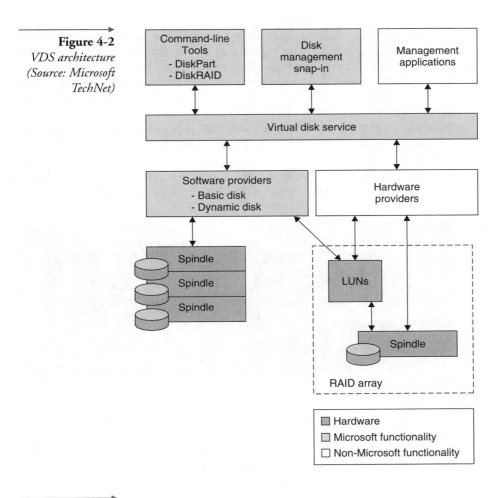

Figure 4-2
*VDS architecture
(Source: Microsoft
TechNet)*

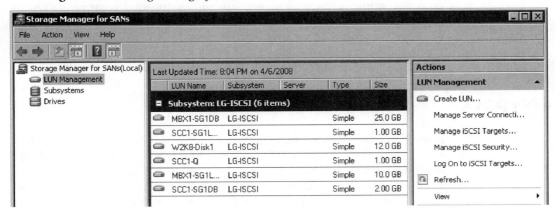

Figure 4-3   *Storage manager for SAN*

Microsoft changed the way how newly discovered disks are managed by the operating system. The behavior how new disks are presented to the operating system can be configured with the VDS SAN Policy. In Windows Server 2008 versions that support failover clustering, Windows Server 2008 Enterprise and Windows Server 2008 Datacenter, disks on a shared bus are now by default kept offline and not brought online in read/write mode. This is an important change that allows installation of Windows Failover Clustering without the need to bring down all cluster nodes but one for the initial setup. Windows Server 2003 tries to grab all disks that are visible to the operating system. Therefore, it was necessary to manually control that only one cluster node was online before the cluster service was installed and configured.

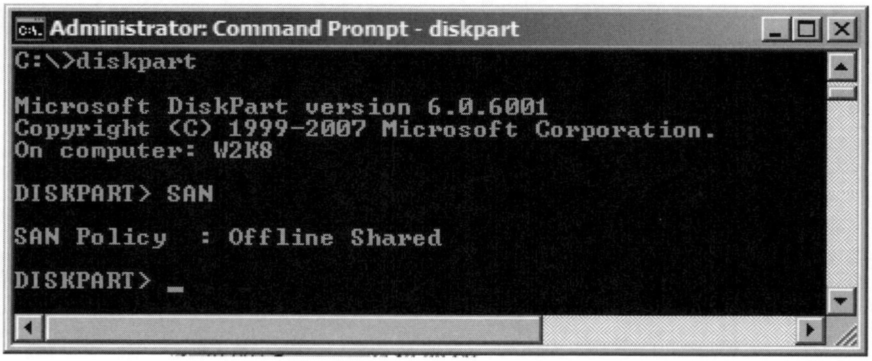

Figure 4-4
SAN Policy

```
C:\>diskpart

Microsoft DiskPart version 6.0.6001
Copyright (C) 1999-2007 Microsoft Corporation.
On computer: W2K8

DISKPART> SAN

SAN Policy  : Offline Shared

DISKPART> _
```

Figure 4-4 shows how you can use DISKPART to display the current policy. You can change the policy with DISKPART as well. Windows PE allows you to configure the SAN Policy during an unattended setup. You can use the Windows PE tool SETSANPOLICY.CMD to make any necessary changes during the installation.

See Chapter 8, "Backup" for an introduction to VSS. This chapter describes using VSS for backing up and restoring Exchange databases. For readers interested in software development and the internals of VSS, we highly recommend visiting Adi Oltean's ANTIMAIL Weblog, and the article, "Diskshadow, the New In-Box VSS Requester in Windows Server 2008," on Jose Barreto's Blog.

Storport

Before Windows Server 2003 was released, the SCSIport driver was used as a device driver for storage devices. The SCSIport architecture was developed at a time when it was common to only have a few disk drives connected to a server. Direct-attached storage (DAS) arrays were mainly used, and only up to 15 devices were attached to a parallel bus. Nowadays it is common to use Fibre Channel networks and to have a much higher number of devices connected to servers. In a large enterprise you will find hundreds of devices connected to a Fibre Channel network. The SCISIport driver model was not designed for this kind of complex environment and had several limitations; for example, it issues a complete bus reset instead of using a hierarchical reset method by first resetting the faulty logical unit. According to the Microsoft Knowledge Base Article 887017, attaching disk volumes and tape devices to the same SCSI bus using the SCSIport driver is not recommended. Doing so on a Microsoft failover cluster with shared storage can cause problems.

With Windows Server 2003, Microsoft released a new driver architecture called Storport. The related Microsoft whitepaper describes the manageability and performance improvements of Storport for Fibre Channel networks and hardware RAID configurations. A brief overview of Storport and a comparison with the SCSIport driver model is available on the Emulex website. Table 4-1 summarizes the key points.

Table 4-1   *Comparison of Storport and SCSIport*

	SCSIport	Storport
Error handling	Reset of complete bus	Hierarchical reset (LUN, target, complete bus)
I/O processing	Half duplex	Support for full duplex
I/O queue	254 outstanding I/O requests regardless of number of attached devices	254 outstanding I/O per attached LUN. Total outstanding requests = 254 × number of attached LUN
Queue management	None	Miniport driver can prevent a device with I/O backlog from stopping other attached devices receiving I/O

Storport allows you to have different configuration parameters per Host Bus Adapter (HBA). For example, it is not required to use the same queue depth for all HBAs of a server. You can use a different figure for the HBA connected to a tape device and the HBA connected to disk storage. This is an additional advantage over the SCSIport model. Even if it is supported with Storport to connect tape devices and disk storage to the same port of the HBA it is still a best practice to use dedicated ports for backup devices. Configurations with separate ports for backup and disk storage are more reliable and provide better performance. Chapter 8 provides details about this topic.

New server deployments use the Storport driver model. You should check the website of the storage vendor to verify which Storport driver version and firmware revision must be used. For example, EMC publishes support matrixes on their EMC E-Lab website, and HP provides the Enterprise Backup Solutions (EBS) compatibility matrix. The storage vendor is your main contact person if you want to know whether specific configuration parameters must be set. Usually the installation routine of the device drivers automatically sets the required parameters in the registry and there is no need for tuning. Don't make modifications without consulting the hardware vendor. These kinds of tuning tweaks have the disadvantage that you cannot know if they will still be valid with the next service pack. Every configuration tweak that you have to configure in addition to the default installation is additional work for the change management process, additional time for the staff that installs the server, increases solution complexity, and thereby makes troubleshooting more difficult.

Multi Path I/O

If a server has only a single path to the storage device, as seen in Figure 4-5, then this path is a single point of failure. Additionally, the operating system cannot distribute the I/O load over multiple paths and thereby increase performance.

Figure 4-5
Single path configuration

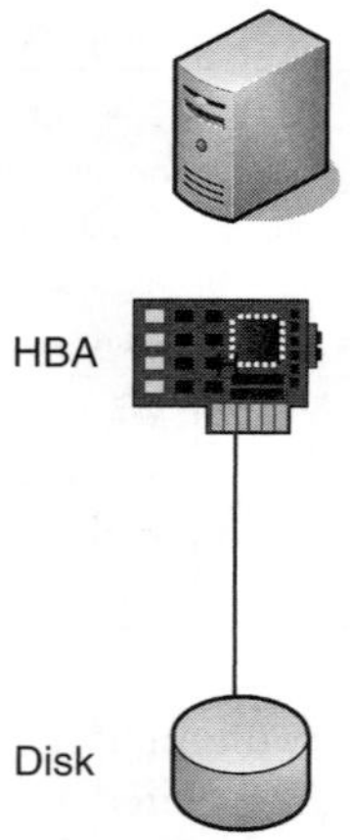

HBA

Disk

In Figure 4-6, the operating system has two paths to access the disk; the single point of failure no longer exists. But the operating system now has to prevent that this single disk appears as two separate disks to the upper layers of the operating system. Solving this issue is the responsibility of a Multi Path I/O (MPIO) solution. In the past, MPIO solutions were provided by storage vendors. In Windows Server 2003, Microsoft provided a MPIO framework that allows vendors to develop a solution that enables the server to access mass storage in a highly available manner. The framework in Windows Server 2003 provides the device-independent functions of the solution, and vendors could use a common set of functions to build their application. The storage vendor develops a device-specific module (DSM). The DSM uses the functions provided by the MPIO framework and implements the storage-specific functions. A major benefit of the MPIO framework is the possibility of connecting storage arrays of different vendors to the same server while being able to take advantage of MPIO for all arrays. Before the advent of the Microsoft MPIO framework, you had to use a vendor-specific solution, such as HP SecurePath, and often it was not supported to install MPIO software solutions from different vendors on the same server. This was especially an issue when you wanted to change the storage array vendor and had to migrate data from array A to array B.

Figure 4-6
Multipath configuration

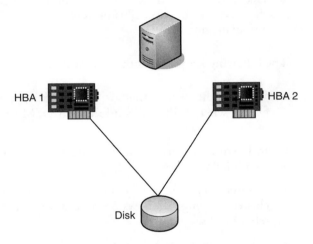

The MPIO framework is implemented as kernel mode drivers and consists of the following three major components:

1.   Port filter driver MPSPFLTR.SYS

     ■ Informs MPIO about arrival and removal of new disks on a HBA.

     ■ Changes the hardware ID of a new disk from a generic disk to an MPIO disk.

2.   Bus driver MPIO.SYS

     ■ Creates a pseudo LUN for the new disk devices. The pseudo LUN is a representation of the individual path seen by the HBAs in the server to a single disk. MPIO.SYS exposes this pseudo LUN to upper layers in the operating system and ensures that a physical disk is only seen once by the upper layers.

- Implements the API that is used by the DSM, and it implements a Windows Management Instrumentation (WMI) interface that can be used to manage the pseudo LUNs.

- Sends I/O requests for a disk to the DSM.

3.   Replacement class driver MPDEV.SYS

- Informs MPIO.SYS about changes in the paths from the server to the disk. It recognizes whether a path failed or discovers new paths to a disk.

- Helps to prevent direct I/O by claiming all seen paths from the server to the disk. This prevents DISK.SYS from claiming and managing a disk.

The following list provides the responsibility of a DSM:

- It claims the devices that are hosted on its storage array. This occurs when MPIO.SYS informs all DSMs about the arrival of a new device.

- It determines whether an I/O request needs to be retried or if a path failover should occur.

- It interprets the SCSI command that a Windows failover cluster running Windows Server 2003 is using to reserve and release disks.

- It implements a WMI interface to allow applications to manage the devices.

- It provides routing information from the server to the device.

In Windows Server 2003, there are two kinds of DSM available: the basic DSM and the Full-Featured DSM. The basic DSM has no user interface; it only supports path failover and provides no support for load balancing. The Full-Featured DSM includes a Microsoft Management Console (MMC) snap-in that allows you to manage the paths to a device or you can use a command-line utility for path management. The MPIO DSM Manager MMC enables you to easily see which storage device is hosted on which storage subsystem. This is especially important in a large Storage Area Network with various storage arrays connected to the same network. The Full-Featured DSM is able to send notification about critical events via email and it provides performance information via WMI.

You can configure different load-balancing policies for MPIO. This allows you to optimize disk I/O performance. The following settings are available in Windows Server 2003:

- Preferred Path: The I/O is sent over the user-selected preferred path.
- Round Robin: All active paths from the server to the device are used in a round-robin mode.
- Shortest Queue Bytes: The active path with the least number of outstanding bytes is used for this I/O request.
- Shortest Queue Requests: The active path with the least number of outstanding I/O requests is used for this I/O request.
- Shortest Queue Service Time: The active path that is considered as the fasted path is used for this I/O request.

Shortest Queue Service Time (SQST) is the default policy, and usually there is no need to select a different load balancing policy (Figure 4-7).

Figure 4-7   *MPIO DSM Manager in Windows Server 2003*

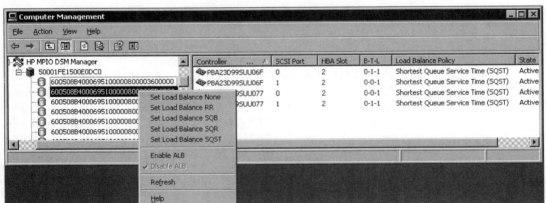

Microsoft changed the architecture of MPIO in Windows Server 2008. The functionality of MPDEV.SYS and MPSPFLTR.SYS has been integrated into the core operating system. The two separate drivers have been eliminated. Microsoft ships a DSM with Windows Server 2008 that you can use with Fiber Channel and iSCSI storage arrays. MPIO is now an installable feature through Server Manager. If you want to learn MPIO and do not have access to a Fiber Channel attached storage array, then you can use MPIO in combination with an iSCSI target.

Note that Microsoft changed the names for the load-balancing policies in Windows Server 2008. Figure 4-8 shows an MPIO-enabled iSCSI disk on a server running Windows Server 2008.

Figure 4-8
*MPIO-enabled
iSCSI disk in
Windows Server
2008*

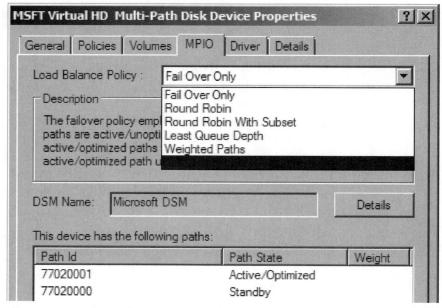

You still can use a vendor-specific DSM such as the one from HP for the EVA. A vendor-specific DSM provides benefits if you use additional vendor-specific features of the storage array, such as Continuous Access or Business Copy in the case of HP. Additionally, the current DSM shipped by Microsoft does not provide a MMC to manage the configuration of all disks in one place. You have to use the MPIO tab of each individual disk for management purposes.

Windows Server 2008 Storage Explorer

With Windows Server 2008, you can use Storage Explorer to gain an overview of your storage infrastructure. Storage Explorer is an MMC snap-in that uses WMI to gather information about all components in the storage infrastructure (Figure 4-9).

The data are displayed in a tree structure similar to the way that Windows Explorer shows information about the file system. You can use the tool to detect resources that have been added to your storage infrastructure, and it shows you configuration information such as the Word Wide Name (WWN) of a Fibre Channel HBA. Storage Explorer works very well with iSCSI networks and provides an overview of your iSCSI fabric.

Figure 4-9   *Storage Explorer*

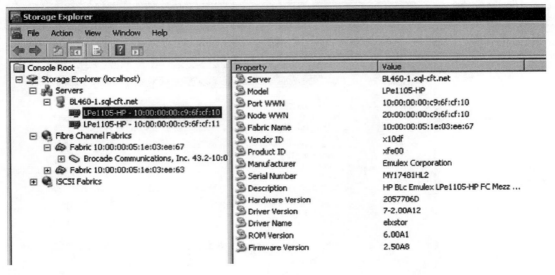

Basic versus Dynamic Disks

The Windows operating system offers two types of disks: basic and dynamic disks. Basic disks are the default type and this type has been available with all previous operating system versions. Dynamic disks were introduced with Windows Server 2000. Dynamic disks are required if you want to span a volume over multiple disks or if you want to use the operating system to create fault-tolerant volumes. Microsoft TechNet provides a very helpful description about this topic in the section "Disks and Volumes".

Microsoft TechNet clearly states that using basic disks for all Exchange server roles is a best practice. Therefore, there is usually no need for endless discussion. If you think it is a good choice to regularly extend the disk volumes that host your Exchange data, then we (a) do not agree, and (b) you can do this with DISKPART for basic disks. The second point is that dynamic disks are not supported by default as shared disks in a Windows failover cluster. You need, for example, VERITAS Storage Foundation for Windows if you want to use dynamic disks as shared disks in a cluster. If you install this third-party tool, then Symantec is your contact for issues related to these disks. This is documented in Microsoft Knowledge Base Article 237853. If you still want to use dynamic disks, then you should at least read Knowledge Base Article 816307, which describes best practices related to dynamic disks.

There is one situation where you might want to consider using dynamic disks. Let's assume that you have to create a large disk volume, and the storage

Figure 4-10
Dynamic disk

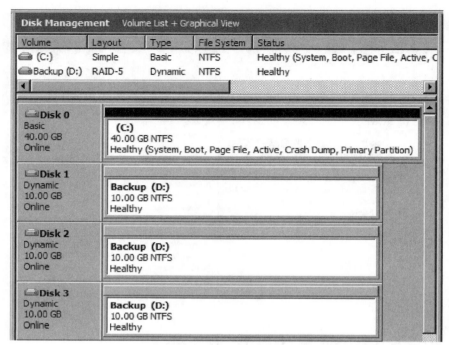

space is provided by a storage subsystem that provides higher performance if you present multiple smaller disk volumes to the Windows server via separate connections to the Fibre Channel network. Some storage arrays have multiple so-called front ports that are used to connect the array to the Fibre Channel network on one side and the internal array logic on the other. In this case, you get higher performance if you combine smaller disks using a dynamic disk in the Windows operating system compared with a large disk presented via a single front port. However, please note that you gained performance but increased the complexity of the solution. Do you really need large disk volumes? In Exchange Server 2003, you only can create up to 20 databases, but with Exchange Server 2007 you now can have up to 50 databases. Therefore, it might not be necessary to have a disk volume with a giant capacity for Exchange databases. The TechNet section, "Mailbox Server Storage Design," describes two alternatives how you can layout the disks: (1) two disks per Exchange storage group, and (2) two disks per backup set.

We recommend using two disks per Exchange storage group because this eases the usage of hardware-based VSS providers. For hardware-based VSS solutions, hosting only the files of a single storage group on the two disks is preferred; otherwise, a recovery would affect files from multiple storage groups. A hardware VSS provider will likely swap or re-sync the disks with the one created by the last backup. This recovery would then also change the disk that is used by storage groups that are healthy. Consequently, dismounting databases of multiple storage groups would be required, although only a single database is corrupt. One possible way of mitigating this disadvantage is to present the shadow copy volume to an alternative path on the server. In this case, you can use a manual file copy to recover a single database instead of replacing everything in one step.

If you host the databases of multiple storage groups on a single disk, then you need a disk with a large capacity. This approach leads to fewer disks per Exchange server, but there are issues related to recovery and file system corruption.

Another reason for large disk volumes is if you run disk-to-disk backups. Figure 4-10 shows such a configuration; we combined three small dynamic disks in a larger RAID 5 volume. Please ignore the actual disk size; this is an example from a small virtual machine based lab.

In summary, we recommend using basic disks and we do not advise creating disks with multi-TB capacity. In our view it is better to manage multiple smaller disks and be prepared to take advantage of hardware based VSS solutions. However, it is up to you to make the final decision. For example, you can decide that fewer disks to manage are more important to you, and that you do not plan to use a hardware-based VSS solution in any case. Therefore, you combine the files of four storage groups on two disks.

Partition Style: MBR versus GPT

By default, the Windows operating system uses the master boot record (MBR) partition style to organize partitions on a disk. Initially, only the 64-bit version of Windows was able to use the new globally unique identifier (GUID) partition table (GPT) partition style. Starting with Windows Server 2003 hot fix 919117 or Service Pack 1, you can use GPT disks with the x86 version of the operating system.

GPT disks enable you to use disks and partitions with more than 2TB of capacity. This might sound like a good idea, but consider the following points before you venture into the creation of multi-TB partitions:

- Understand how long CHKDSK will run on such a disk. Large numbers of files will cause CHKDSK to take longer than you want, especially if the volume was found dirty at boot time.

- Determine proper management tactics for such large volumes, and validate with tools like JetStress if the performance does not decline with larger volumes.

GPT disks support up to 128 primary partitions per disk. We assume that you will not take advantage of this because a single partition per disk is recommended for simplicity. GPT disks store multiple copies of the partition table and use cyclical redundancy check (CRC) to protect the partition table. This increases the reliability of GPT disks compared with the MBR partition style.

The decision between MBR and GPT disk might lead to a religious dispute. In the past, MBR was the commonly used partition style. If you follow our advice and create small disks instead of multi-TB disks, then MBR-style disks are still a good decision. In this case, the only downside is that you would not be able to take advantage of the greater reliability of the partition table on GPT disks.

Disk Alignment

In Windows Server 2003, you should align partitions on a sector boundary. Misaligned partitions can have as much as a 20% reduced performance. Details of this issue are described in the Microsoft Knowledge Base Article 929491. Aligning the partition provides no performance benefit in some storage arrays because the storage array controller handles this transparently. However, there is also no disadvantage to aligning the partition. Therefore, you should always align partitions. This saves you needless discussion with support staff if the misalignment is the reason for performance issues. You probably don't have time for this.

The easiest way to read the current alignment of a partition is to use the old DISKPAR command of the Windows Server 2000 Resource kit. DISKPAR requires that you specify the *DriveNumber* as a parameter on the command line. You can see the DriveNumber of a disk in the Disk Management MMC snap-in, for example, 9 in Figure 4-11.

Figure 4-11   *DiskNumber*

If you divide the StartingOffset by the allocation unit size of the NTFS file system, which is 4096 bytes in the example shown in Figure 4-12, then the result is 7.875. This is not an even number, so the partition is not aligned. The article titled, "How to Align Exchange I/O with Storage Track Boundaries" on TechNet, or the Exchange Team Blog article, "Why Should You Use Diskpar (Diskpart in W2003 SP1)?" describes the procedure to align the partition using DISKPART:

```
Select Disk <DiskNumber>
Create Partition Primary Align = X
Assign letter = <DriveLetter>
```

Figure 4-12 *DISKPAR*

Command Prompt
D:\Software\MS-Tools>diskpar -i 9
---- Drive 9 Geometry Infomation ----
Cylinders = 7296
TracksPerCylinder = 255
SectorsPerTrack = 63
BytesPerSector = 512
DiskSize = 60011642880 (Bytes) = 57231 (MB)
---- Drive Partition 0 Infomation ----
StatringOffset = 32256
PartitionLength = 60003385344
HiddenSectors = 63
PartitionNumber = 1
PartitionType = 6
End of partition information. Total existing partitions: 1
D:\Software\MS-Tools>

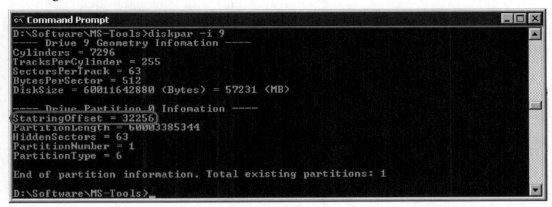

You should always ask the storage vendor about the correct partition offset for their storage array. If you don't have this information, then use X = 64 in the previous command. A good source for the correct offset value for your storage array is consulting the Exchange Solution Reviewed Program (ESRP). You should use a storage subsystem that was tested with the ESRP and refer to the solution documentation for this kind of configuration setting.

Figure 4-13 *Alignment in Windows Server 2008*

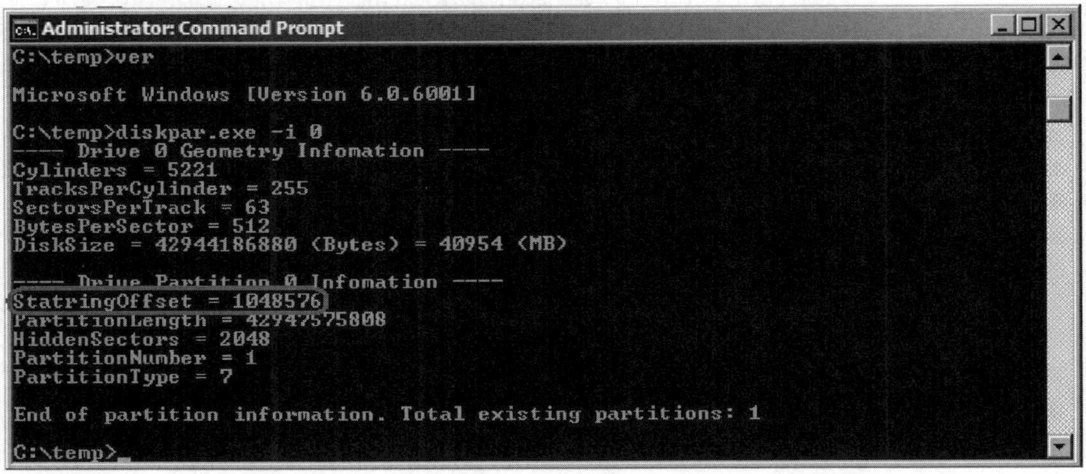

Administrator: Command Prompt
C:\temp>ver
Microsoft Windows [Version 6.0.6001]
C:\temp>diskpar.exe -i 0
---- Drive 0 Geometry Infomation ----
Cylinders = 5221
TracksPerCylinder = 255
SectorsPerTrack = 63
BytesPerSector = 512
DiskSize = 42944186880 (Bytes) = 40954 (MB)
---- Drive Partition 0 Infomation ----
StatringOffset = 1048576
PartitionLength = 42947575808
HiddenSectors = 2048
PartitionNumber = 1
PartitionType = 7
End of partition information. Total existing partitions: 1
C:\temp>

Starting with Windows Server 2008, you don't need to manually align partitions. Windows Server 2008 does it for you automatically. This is a good improvement (Figure 4-13).

New Technology File System

The New Technology File System (NTFS) was introduced by Microsoft with the Windows NT operating system. Microsoft Knowledge Base Article 100108 provides an overview of NTFS and the file systems that Windows previously used. NTFS is the file system that you now mainly use on all client and server versions of the Windows operating system. You can find the NTFS technical reference for Windows Server 2003 on TechNet. Windows Server 2008 provides enhancements related to transactional file operations on the NTFS file system. Details about this topic are available on Microsoft TechNet and Microsoft Developer Network. A good collection of information about NTFS is available on the website www.ntfs.com.

Partition allocation size

Using the correct NTFS allocation unit size is a method to optimize the performance of the NTFS file system. If you store a new file on the file system, then a so-called cluster is allocated to store this file. If the file is large, then multiple clusters are allocated, and if the file is very small, NTFS has another option that does not require allocating a new cluster. We can ignore the details of how tiny files are stored for now. It is only important to remember that usually at least one cluster has to be allocated if you want to store a new file.

The cluster size influences the performance of the NTFS file system. Bigger clusters often have better performance but they waste disk space. A cluster is not shared by multiple files. If the cluster size is 4 KB and your file is only 1 KB, then you waste 3 KB of disk capacity—to use a very simplified example.

If you format a new NFTS file system, then the size of the partition determines the default cluster size. The default cluster size is documented in Microsoft Knowledge Base Article 140365. All disk partitions larger than 2 GB have a default cluster size of 4KB. You can overwrite this setting and use one of the large cluster sizes—8 KB, 16 KB, 32 KB, and 64 KB.

In the "Partition Design" section on TechNet, Microsoft recommends using an NTFS allocation size unit of 64 KB for the file system with the Exchange databases. This provides performance benefits for the large sequential read operations of Exchange backups. The streaming online backup and the checksum verification of the database after a VSS backup tries to read the database file with an I/O size larger than the default 4 KB.

You do not have to change the default NTFS allocation unit size for the file system with the transaction log files. Performance tests have not indicated that using a larger allocation unit size for the log file volume provides benefits.

NTFS CHKDSK and self-healing

Windows Server 2008 also made enhancements to how corruptions of the file system are repaired. This feature, called self-healing NTFS, is explained on TechNet. Starting with Windows Server 2008, you might be lucky and not have to take a server offline to run CHKDSK to fix an NTFS corruption. Enhancements in the NTFS kernel code might be able to resolve this issue while the file system is online and accessed by applications.

The time required to fix file system corruption with CHKDSK depends on the size of the volume and the number of file stored on it. This is one reason why it is not reasonable to create volumes with terabyte capacity. The article, "Microsoft Storage: Fact and Fiction," states that the performance of CHKDSK has been significantly increased since Windows NT: "To check 17 million non-fragmented files, for example, the NT4 test was cut short at 2880 minutes; Windows Server 2003 (beta version), by contrast, was complete in 210 minutes."

You might encounter a situation in which the file system was shut down dirty. Windows will automatically run CHKDSK/F the next time you boot the server. This can be very time consuming and may be inconvenient; for example, you may prefer to have the Exchange server up and running, and just let the storage group with the affected disk volume be offline. Microsoft Knowledge Base Article 160963 describes how you can use the tool CHKNTFS to postpone this check.

File system defragmentation

File system fragmentation occurs when Windows is not able to store data of a file in contiguous disk blocks. This reduces the throughput because the write–read head of the disk has to seek for the next data block and move the head to this location before it can continue to read the file. You can find a good description of file system fragmentation on Wikipedia and in the Windows Sysinternals article, "Inside Windows NT Disk Defragmenting."

Regularly checking the fragmentation of file systems used by a file server is a best practice. On a file server, running defragmentation is a common operational procedure; otherwise, performance suffers, especially during backups. You will find related recommendations in the manuals of your backup software, such as "HP Data Protector 6.0 software Advanced Backup to Disk Performance Whitepaper." The Windows operating system includes a tool to defragment the file system, which is based on the well-known product from Diskeeper.

However, Exchange is not a file server and you should *not* run a file system defragmentation of the disk volumes used to store Exchange database or log files. This is clearly stated in the article, "Do we need to file-level defragment Exchange database drives?" on the Exchange Team Blog. Usually the online database defragmentation of the databases is sufficient. There are very rare occasions when you have to run an offline database defragmentation. Microsoft Knowledge Base Article 328804 explains how to defragment Exchange databases.

Mount points

It is a best practice to use separate disk volumes to store the database and log files of a storage group. This enables you to separate sequential write I/O to the disk volume with the log files from random read–write access to the Exchange database. Another even more important reason for this best practice is the possibility of using the last backup set and the transaction log files on a separate disk volume to perform a roll-forward restore if you lost the database volume. If you host the database and the log files on the same disk volume, then you only can perform a point-in-time restore. All new transactions since the last backup would be lost if you lost this disk volume due to hardware failure or file system corruption!

Exchange Server 2007 supports up to 50 storage groups, which results in at least 100 disk volumes. It is a best practice from a recovery point of view to use a separate disk for the operating system files and the Exchange program directory. The 26 characters of the alphabet do not provide enough letters to assign a drive letter to each disk volume.

Volume mount points are the solution for this problem. They were introduced by Microsoft with Windows Server 2000. You can mount an additional disk volume to an empty NTFS directory. An application accesses data stored on this disk volume transparently; the application is not aware that the data are actually stored on a different disk volume. A user can see the difference in Windows Explorer; the mounted disk volume appears as a drive icon in the path in which it is mounted.

Microsoft Knowledge Base Article 280297 describes how to configure mount points on a failover cluster and provides best practices related to mount points. You should use a dedicated root volume that hosts only the mount points but does not store any additional data. This simplifies the recovery procedure if you have to restore this volume, and minimizes the time required for running CHKDSK.

It is not necessary to create a root volume with gigabytes of capacity when a few megabytes would be sufficient. However, do not be stingy. A colleague wasted a lot of time troubleshooting a strange error of the search indexer that turned out to be the consequence of insufficient free space on the root volume. This issue is described in the Microsoft Knowledge Base Article 944554. We do not create volumes that are smaller than 1 GB in size.

Do not use a single root volume to host all your mount points. In Exchange Server 2007, you can have up to 50 storage groups; if all storage groups use the same shared root volume, then all mailboxes of the Exchange server depend on the health of this single volume! This is especially ridiculous if you do this on a cluster. The most important principle of a cluster is "no single point of failure", so use multiple root volumes to reduce the sharing ratio and minimize the impact if a root volume is unavailable. Figure 4-14 provides two examples of how you can group your mount points.

Please be aware that if you use Volume Shadow Copy Services to back up data stored on a disk volume and this disk volume contains mounted drives, then the mounted drives are not automatically included in the created shadow copy set. This is described in Microsoft Knowledge Base Article 812547.

Figure 4-14   *Mount points*

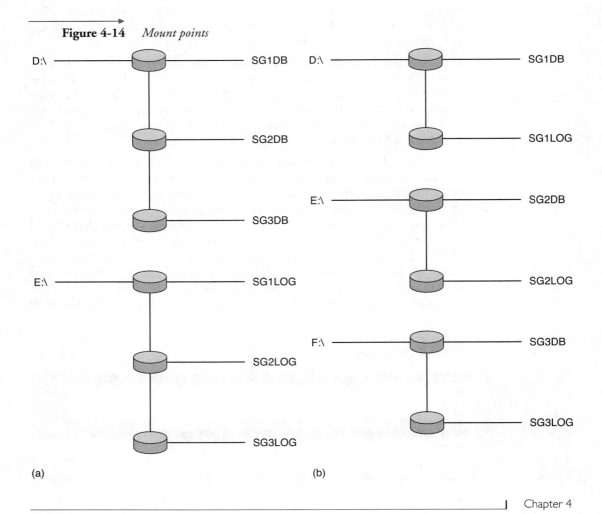

(a)   (b)

Microsoft Developer Network and Knowledge Base Article 205524 explain how to use the MOUNTVOL command to manage mount points from the command line. Another option is to use the *assign* command in DISKPART, which is explained in Knowledge Base Article 300415.

Online Volume Expansion and Shrinking

The section about basic versus dynamic disks stated that it is not a best practice to regularly expand disk volumes. Extending a disk volume is easy, especially in a SAN environment. However, there is the risk that you as an administrator may make a mistake and affect the health of the production data stored on this volume. You have to make the decision about whether you wish to run this risk, or if you prefer to create a new larger volume. You then can either move your database from the small disk to the larger disk, which requires downtime, or you can create a new database on the larger disk volume and perform a move mailbox operation.

Microsoft IT published the IT showcase document "Volume Expansion Using Diskpart.exe." This document describes how Microsoft IT uses DISKPART to extend a disk volume as part of their "just-in-time" storage model. With DISKPART, you can increase the storage capacity of a disk volume that an application is accessing in online mode; bringing the application down is not necessary.

Figure 4-15 shows the two disks used by a storage group. Assume that you increased the mailbox quota of your users from 200MB to 1GB, and then ran out of disk space on the database volume. You decided to give the "just-in-time" storage model a go, and want to increase the disk volume hosting the database. How you extend a disk seen by the Windows operating system depends on your storage subsystem. It is recommended to restripe the existing data over the additional storage space assigned to the Windows disk. If your storage subsystem only concatenates additional disk space at the end of the existing disk seen by Windows, then your performance will be impacted. The procedure shown in this section was performed in a virtual machine based–lab using the Microsoft

Figure 4-15   *Original disk configuration*

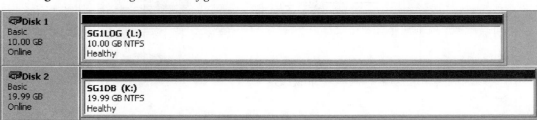

iSCSI target software. Extending a virtual disk is straightforward: right-click the disk in the Microsoft iSCSI target MMC, select Extend Virtual Disk, and use the wizard to specify the additional storage space, which is 5GB in our example.

Figure 4-16 shows the free space at the end of disk 2 after Rescan Disks in Disk Management MMC.

Figure 4-16   *Free space*

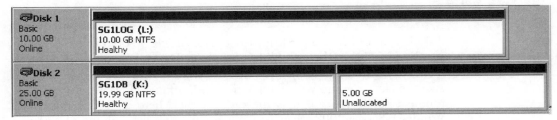

Figure 4-17 shows the necessary commands in DISKPART. You can see the 5GB of free space in the output of the List Disk command.

Figure 4-17   *DISKPART Extend*

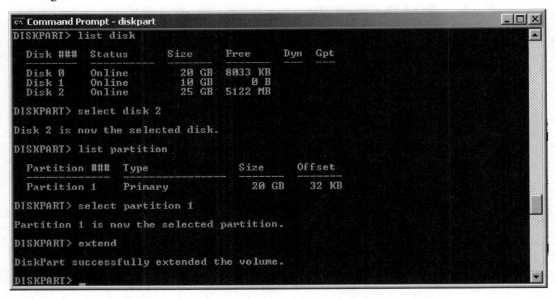

Figure 4-18 shows the database disk volume with its size increased from 20 to 25GB. It is possible to extend the disk volume of a clustered shared

Figure 4-18   *Increased capacity*

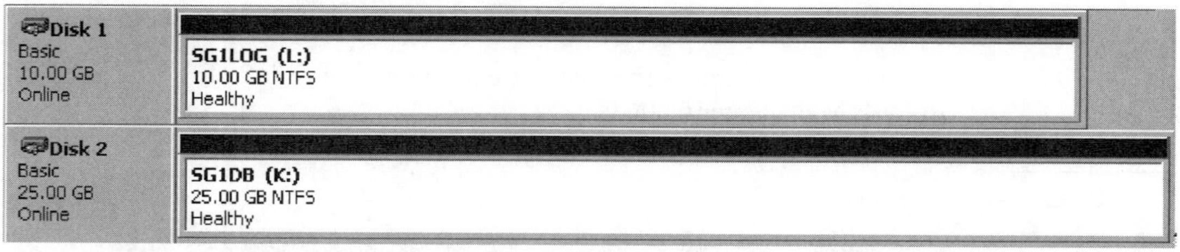

disk. If you read Microsoft Knowledge Base Article 304736 you will understand why this can be an offline procedure. Depending on your environment, it might be necessary to shut down all cluster nodes but one, and
take the cluster group with the physical disk offline. However, if your environment supports it, as it is the case for the Microsoft iSCSI target and
Windows Server 2008, then you can extend the disk volume of a shared
physical disk while Exchange is online and uses this disk volume. Obviously,
you should create a backup before you perform maintenance tasks like this.
Windows Server 2008 has extended your options related to storage management. Now you can shrink a volume and make free space available at the
end of a volume.

Figure 4-19
Shrink

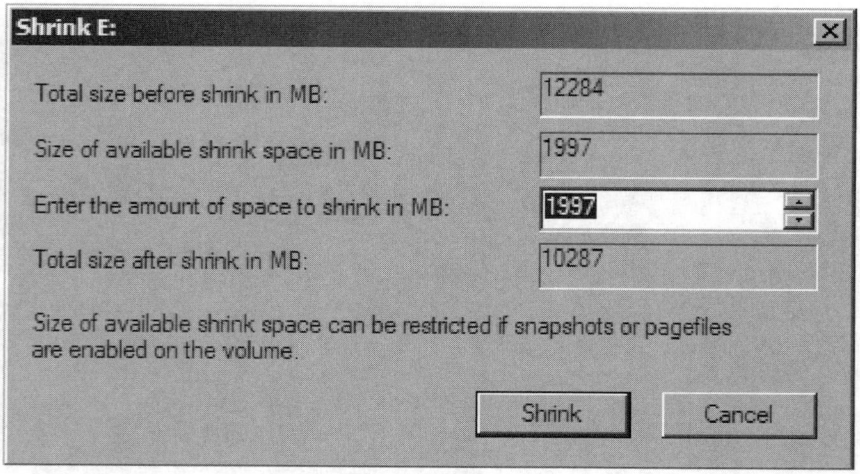

You can either reduce the size of the volume using the Shrink command in DISKPART, or as Figure 4-19 shows, within the Disk Management
MMC. However, you cannot shrink a volume by more than 50% of the original volume size. The reason for this limitation is that a copy of the Master
file table (MFT) is located in the middle of the disk. In brief, you cannot
shrink a volume that was previously extended behind the last extended area.

5

Designing Your Exchange 2007 Server

Your server design will be based on the Exchange server role and expected server workload. For example, a mailbox server will largely depend on the number of mailboxes it should support. A server with the Hub Transport (HT) role will be defined based on the number of mails sent and received in the environment, and possibly on journaling and content-scanning policies. The design for a server with the Client Access Server (CAS) role will depend on the protocols used by the clients and the access mode.

Microsoft created the MAPI Messaging Benchmark (MMB) program to provide administrators with useful indicators. The goal was to measure the performance and scalability of computers running Microsoft Exchange Server. While MMB has served its purpose, it also had limitations in helping customers compare solutions. One of the most significant limitations was that MMB did not take into account variation in end-user usage profiles, modification and updates to storage solutions, differences in customer topologies, and impacts of other features or applications on performance. MMB compares single servers, but does not compare solutions. As a result, Microsoft discontinued the program for Microsoft Exchange Server 2007 in fall 2007.

Microsoft continues to provide the tools necessary to allow partners to perform their own performance and scalability benchmark analysis for Exchange Server. These tools include Exchange Server JetStress, Exchange Load Generator, and Exchange Server Stress and Performance (which is being merged into LoadGen).

What are we left with? We have some estimates for processor and memory sizing, based on testing done by Microsoft and partners. Microsoft's data can be found in the Exchange product group blog, "You Had Me at EHLO" (http://blogs.technet.com/exchange/). In this chapter, we review these estimates. Note that they do not replace in-house testing or solution-based testing. Additionally, we describe the choices you have to make for designing your Exchange servers. Do you want to use conventional rack mount servers, or do you prefer to take advantage of blades? Do you fear Windows Failover

Clustering and prefer booting from SAN? And what about virtualization—should you deploy your Exchange servers as guests of a hardware virtualization product? At the end of this chapter, we also introduce you to high-availability options for the mailbox server role.

Service Level Agreements/Service Level Objectives

Service level agreements (SLAs), which are commitments made to customers by companies, or service level objectives (SLOs), which are agreed upon by departments of a company, have been the starting point for Exchange designs in the past. This did not change with Exchange Server 2007, and will not change with upcoming versions. The business needs of the company and its users dictate the requirements that your Exchange messaging solution must fulfill.

You have to define recovery time objectives (RTOs) and recovery point objectives (RPOs) based on business needs. Figure 5-1 shows a graphical representation of the two terms and the method you can use to meet the SLA, such as a traditional restore from tape or a high-tech solution based on data replication and clustering. The SLA will determine how many users with a certain mailbox size you can deploy on a single mailbox server. Additionally, you have to be able to regularly back up the Exchange databases in a reasonable timeframe. A reasonable backup window is approximately 4 to 5 hours. Avoid the temptation of hosting 10,000 users with multigigabyte mailboxes on a single server, and thinking that Exchange Server 2007 continuous replication precludes the need for running daily backups. You might decide to switch from daily full backups to full weekly and daily differential backups, but you still have to run backups with continuous replication. Backups via the public local area network (LAN) are also not an appropriate solution for a business-critical Exchange Server 2007 deployment. The throughput would be so slow that you would never meet your SLA.

Figure 5-1
Recovery point versus recovery time

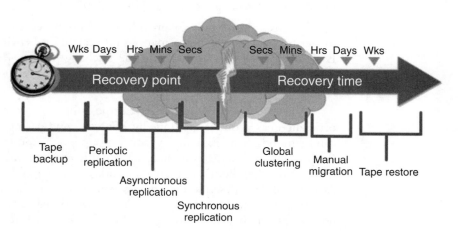

You should define various RTOs. For instance, if you specify only that "the messaging environment has to be available within X hours after a failure", then you will end up with an extremely expensive solution. Defining an RTO for the following recovery scenarios is recommended:

- Single email
- Single database/storage group
- All storage groups of a server
- The complete server including operating system, applications, and Exchange databases
- The storage array used by your Exchange servers
- All servers within your data center

It is also likely that not all users are equal. You can provide different SLAs for different user groups, such as hosting VIPs or mailboxes used by business critical applications in smaller databases that can be recovered faster. You have to define the priority in which the applications used by your business will be recovered after a disaster. Although Exchange may have high priority, there are likely other more business-critical applications for your company. SAP or a Oracle databases used by a business critical applications are two examples. If you are not prepared and have to start this discussion after a disaster hits your data center, then you will not be able to meet the SLA. The risk is high that you will lose business afterwards because you were not able to provide services to users within the expected timeframe.

Microsoft Exchange Solution Reviewed Program

Prior to beginning the design process for Exchange servers, Microsoft's excellent Exchange Solution Reviewed Program (ESRP) must be mentioned. This program aims at listing the characteristics of fully tested storage configuration from vendors. Microsoft jointly validates, with the partner, a whitepaper that describes the methodology and performance results of full-blown storage solutions for Exchange Servers. The solutions include small configurations with only 1 to 1000 mailboxes, but goes up to complex configurations with 5000 and more mailboxes. The whitepaper typically contains a full outline of the environment, bill of material, and performance characterization for the storage configuration. ESRP is an invaluable source for Exchange storage–related information. It is *by far* the most reliable (because fully tested) source of information for complete storage solutions for Exchange 2007 RTM and SP1.

Please be aware ESRP is not a Microsoft certification, qualification, or logo program for storage. You can use the configurations published on the ESRP site as starting points for sizing your servers. Another option is to manually design your servers based on the information described in the following sections, and then afterward compare your result with the configurations published on the ESRP website.

User Profiles

For sizing the hardware of your Exchange servers, knowing the messaging behavior of your users is very important. Do they only send five emails a day, or are they subscribed to newsletters, and synchronize their inbox with Outlook running on their desktop, while at the same time ActiveSync notifies their Smartphones about the arrival of new email? Do your users use ActiveSync or do they use BlackBerry devices? You will find the following in the TechNet section titled, "What Causes Exchange Disk I/O?"

> With previous versions of Exchange, users accessing their mailbox with BlackBerry devices placed additional demands on the server. In the field, many customers saw an increase in database disk I/O of two to four times.

Do your users know that they can use SharePoint to collaborate? Do they know the difference between SMTP and FTP, or do they send their 30 MB marketing slides each day to an Exchange distribution list? Have you told them that they should structure their mailbox and stay below 3500 to 5000 items per folder as described in Microsoft Knowledge Base Article 905803?

For sizing your Exchange environment, we recommend to take advantage of the knowledge worker profiles that Microsoft has published on TechNet and is referring to in their literature (Table 5-1).

Table 5-1   *Knowledge worker profiles for Outlook users*

User profile	Sent and received messages (~50 KB) per day
Light	5 sent/20 received
Average	10 sent/40 received
Heavy	20 sent/80 received
Very Heavy	30 sent/120 received

We are sure you will ask how I can assess the messaging behavior of my users. If you already have an Exchange deployment then you should take advantage of your existing environment. We recommend using the Exchange Server Profile Analyzer (EPA) to obtain these valuable data. We recommend the corresponding Exchange Team blog article or the description of the EPA tool on MSExchange.org.

Figure 5-2 shows the overall statistics of an analyzed Exchange Server 2003 environment that we had to migrate to Exchange Server 2007. EPA provided important information about the existing environment. Details about the message size shown in Figure 5-3 and message frequency are very helpful for sizing the new environment.

If you have to design a new Exchange Server 2007 environment for a migration from another email system such as UNIX *sendmail* or Lotus Notes, then you can consider using a commercial tool for reporting and

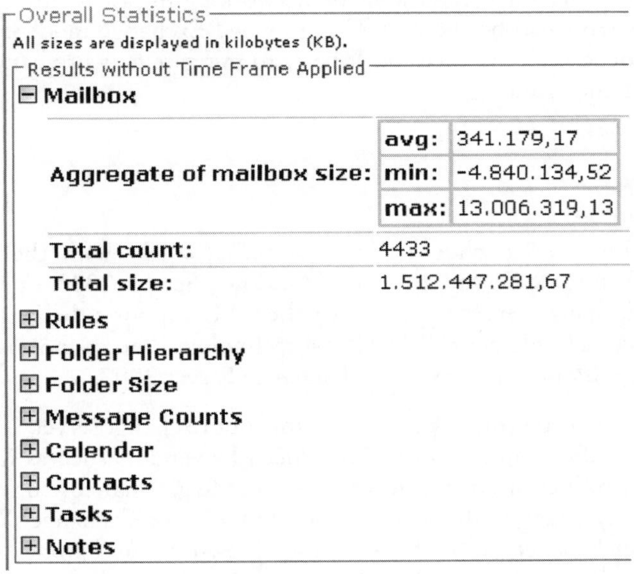

Figure 5-2
EPA overall statistics

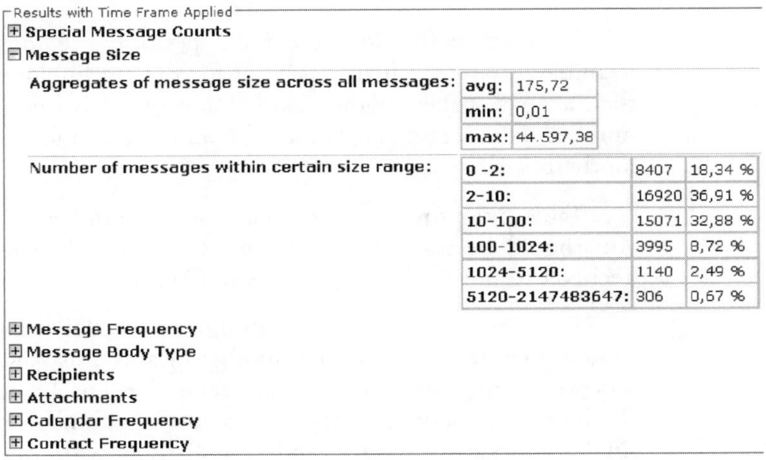

┌─ Overall Statistics ─────────────────────────────
All sizes are displayed in kilobytes (KB).
┌─ Results without Time Frame Applied ──────────────
⊟ **Mailbox**

Aggregate of mailbox size:	**avg:**	341.179,17
	min:	-4.840.134,52
	max:	13.006.319,13
Total count:	4433	
Total size:	1.512.447.281,67	

⊞ **Rules**
⊞ **Folder Hierarchy**
⊞ **Folder Size**
⊞ **Message Counts**
⊞ **Calendar**
⊞ **Contacts**
⊞ **Tasks**
⊞ **Notes**

Figure 5-3
EPA message size

┌─ Results with Time Frame Applied ─────────────────────────
⊞ Special Message Counts
⊟ Message Size

Aggregates of message size across all messages:	avg:	175,72		
	min:	0,01		
	max:	44.597,38		
Number of messages within certain size range:	0 -2:		8407	18,34 %
	2-10:		16920	36,91 %
	10-100:		15071	32,88 %
	100-1024:		3995	8,72 %
	1024-5120:		1140	2,49 %
	5120-2147483647:		306	0,67 %

⊞ Message Frequency
⊞ Message Body Type
⊞ Recipients
⊞ Attachments
⊞ Calendar Frequency
⊞ Contact Frequency

analysis. Quest Software MessageStats, for instance, is a helpful tool that you can leverage for the assessment of an existing messaging environment. You can continue to use MessageStats after the migration for reporting and analysis within your new Exchange Server 2007 environment.

Another important topic is whether your users use Outlook in cached Exchange mode or continue to work in online mode. Using cached Exchange mode helps to reduce the I/O read request rate on the backend mailbox server. A client can reopen a message stored on its local disk that was downloaded to the local offline store file (OST). The client does not have to bother the Exchange server and the networking infrastructure every time this email is reopened by the user. Using cached Exchange mode is often a prerequisite for server consolidation. It helps to mitigate network bandwidth and network latency issues.

CPU Sizing

You have to choose a processor that works with the x64 version of the Windows Server 2003 or Windows Server 2008 operating system. The Exchange server requires that the CPU supports the Intel extended memory 64 technology or the AMD64 technology. You cannot use a system based on the Itanium processor for Exchange Server 2007.

Sizing your CPU resource for your Exchange server will vary as time passes, based on rapid changes introduced by vendors such as Intel and AMD. The introduction of multicore processors (e.g., dual-core or quad-core) has radically changed the way we size the CPU for Exchange. We typically can use dual-socket motherboards (also known as *dual processors*) instead of using multisocket motherboards (quad processors and above) that are significantly more complex and expensive for the value they deliver.

In other words, for pure CPU performance for the Exchange 2007 technology, using dual-socket quad-core technology is more effective than a quad-socket motherboard. However, it is important to balance the number of processor cores and the amount of memory installable on the motherboard.

Table 5-2 provides an estimate of the number of processor cores that you should be using for Exchange 2007 SP1. The table is based on the TechNet section, "Planning Processor Configurations."

There are several factors that influence the CPU configuration that you should pick, for example, the number of antivirus scanner engines that the server runs, or whether the mailbox server has Local Continuous Replication (LCR) enabled storage groups. As a rule of thumb, you can assume that a single processor core can handle 1000 users with an average user profile.

Table 5-2 *Processor Configuration*

Role	Minimum	Recommended	Maximum Recommended
Edge transport	1 × processor core	2 × processor cores	4 × processor cores
Hub Transport	1 × processor core	4 × processor cores	8 × processor cores
Client Access Server (CAS)	1 × processor core	4 × processor cores	4 × processor cores
Unified Messaging server (UM)	1 × processor core	4 × processor cores	4 × processor cores
Mailbox server	1 × processor core	4 × processor cores	8 × processor cores
Multirole (hub, CAS, UM, mailbox)	1 × processor core	4 × processor cores	4 × processor cores

Users with a heavy user profile reduce the number by 50%. LCR requires about 20% more CPU performance because the mailbox server has to manage the active database and the passive database at the same time.

You not only have to define the number of processor cores for the individual Exchange server roles, you also have to balance the ratio of processor cores among the Exchange server roles. The starting point for your calculation is the number of processor cores in the mailbox server.

The rule-of-thumb figures in Table 5-3 are based on the information in the TechNet section titled, "Planning Server Role Ratios." Using 64-bit domain controllers (DCs) allows you to consolidate your DC/global catalog (GC) servers. It is important to remember that the 1:8 ratio is only achievable if you are able to load the complete AD database in RAM. You can examine the size of the NTDS.DIT file on a GC to estimate the required amount of RAM. Please refer to the Exchange Team blog article, "Guidance on Active Directory Design for Exchange Server 2007," for additional details.

The information in this section is only a starting point. As motherboard and symmetric multiprocessing (SMP) technology implementations evolve,

Table 5-3 *Server role ratios*

Server role ratio	Processor core ratio
Mailbox : HT	7 : 1 without antivirus scanning on HT
	5 : 1 with antivirus scanning on HT
Mailbox : CAS	4 : 1
Domain controller : Mailbox	1 : 4 (32-bit)
	1 : 8 (64-bit)

the recommended quantity of processor cores and their implementation will vary. The discussion about an intelligent design of the interprocessor communication paths, and whether the memory controller should be integrated into the processor or be a separate chips is a hot topic. If you are interested in the technical details of the enhancements in upcoming Intel and ADM CPUs, you can read the reports published at www.realworldtech.com or www.anandtech.com. We recommend that you seek advice and request Exchange 2007–specific collateral from your server vendor. There is one additional option: Running CPU performance–related tests yourself. This option can be time and resource consuming, so make sure that your results bring a business advantage to your implementation.

Memory Sizing

In Exchange Server 2007, memory sizing is somewhat simpler than CPU sizing. With the 32-bit version of Exchange Server, you had to spend a lot of time on troubleshooting memory issues and tuning the memory management of your servers. Luckily the issues described in Microsoft Knowledge Base Article 912376 and 815372, and the Exchange Team blog article, "Microsoft Windows Kernel Memory Management and Microsoft Exchange Server," are problems of the past. As a consultant, you can use them to encourage your customers to start the migration to the 64-bit world of Exchange Server 2007.

Exchange 2007 must have adequate memory in order to use it. With 64-bit computing, you can use 8 GB and more RAM and reap major benefits from it, such as an increase of kernel resources or a reduction of IO per second (IOPS) due to improved caching. Table 5-4 is based on the TechNet article, "Planning Memory Configurations." Please be aware that Microsoft significantly changed the recommendation from Exchange Server 2007 RTM to SP1.

In Table 5-4, we quote the quantity of RAM based on two factors:

- *The number of cores*. The more processor cores, the more memory should be used. This is first due to the computing power available. A core with too little RAM will be idle, and too much RAM for a single core will cause data loaded in RAM to be left unused or unprocessed.

- *The number of users*. This is for the mailbox role. The more users (logged-on mailboxes), the more RAM will be required to cache database transactions, reduce the read I/O request rate sent to disks, and increase RPC operations throughput. The user profile of the mailboxes hosted on the server determines if you have to calculate 2 MB (light), 3.5 MB (average), or 5 MB (heavy) per mailbox. This is a significant

Table 5-4 *Memory configuration*

Role	Min	Recommended	Maximum
Edge ransport	2 GB	1 GB/core	16 GB
		(2 GB minimum)	
Hub Transport	2 GB	1 GB/core	16 GB
		(2 GB minimum)	
Client Access	2 GB	2 GB/core	16 GB
		(2 GB minimum)	
Unified Messaging	2 GB	1 GB/core	4 GB
		(2 GB minimum)	
Mailbox	2 GB	2 GB	32 GB
	Also depends on number of storage groups	+2–5 MB/mailbox	
Multiple roles	4 GB	2 GB	32 GB
	Also depends on number of storage groups	+2–5 MB/mailbox	

change from the previous 32-bit version of Exchange. As described in Microsoft Knowledge Base Article 815372, you could have a maximum of 1200 MB allocated to the database cache in Exchange Server 2003. Assuming that 5000 mailboxes are hosted on the server, there was a cache size of about 245 KB per user. This is far less than the amount of memory a server running Exchange Server 2007 will use to cache database pages accessed by active users. Such quantity of memory helps to significantly reduce the number of read I/O requests, and thereby enable the reduction of the I/O footprint of Exchange.

■ The number of storage groups configured on a mailbox server is an additional parameter that you have to consider to determine the minimum amount of RAM. Table 5-5 lists the minimum amount of RAM that you need to receive support from Microsoft. The figures are provided on Microsoft TechNet. The requirements have changed from RTM to SP1 because of the changes made to the Extensible Storage Engine (ESE). Details about the changes in SP1 related to ESE are available in the blog article, "Exchange Server 2007 SP1 ESE Changes—Part 1 and Part 2."

The move to 64-bits has vastly changed the way that memory for servers is sized. With Exchange 2003, 4 GB was the maximum usable by the

Table 5-5   *Minimum memory based on number of storage groups*

Number of storage groups	Minimum physical memory required with Exchange Server 2007 SP1
1–4	2 GB
5–8	4 GB
9–12	5 GB
13–16	6 GB
17–20	7 GB
21–24	8 GB
25–28	9 GB
29–32	10 GB
33–36	11 GB
37–40	12 GB
41–44	13 GB
45–48	14 GB
49–50	15 GB

product; therefore, there was little decision making necessary. In the case of Exchange 2007, the challenge is that you can put 64 GB or 128 GB of RAM in a server, but its cost ($/GB) differs significantly, depending on whether you use high-density RAM (4 GB or more per DIMM). The previously mentioned 32 GB RAM maximum is therefore not an architectural limit for Exchange Server 2007. There is no source code in Exchange Server 2007 that says ignore all RAM above 32 GB RAM. This is a recommendation based on comparing the cost of additional RAM versus the benefit that you get from a performance point of view. After a certain amount of physical memory is installed in the server, you will see less benefit if you add more RAM. In addition, the larger amount of memory mainly reduces the read I/O request rate; there is a much smaller reduction in write I/O. New email messages have to be written to disk regardless of whether you have 4 GB RAM or 32 GB RAM, and the frequency of new emails arriving on a mailbox server does not depend on the amount of physical memory installed.

We presented the following chart in Figure 5-4 at an Exchange Connections event in 2007. Although the chart may be outdated by the time you read this book, the important element here are the differences among the various RAM form factors.

The price per gigabyte is more than doubled if you use high-density DIMM. Furthermore, the number of memory slots, which determines the required RAM density, varies based on the motherboard design. Dual-socket motherboards will typically have less DIMM slots than quad-socket

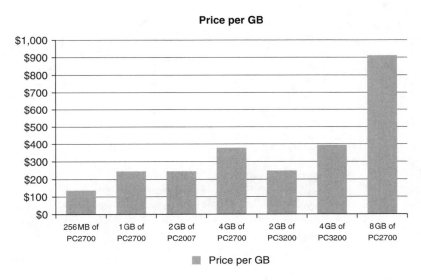

Figure 5-4
Price per gigabyte

motherboards. The number of slots will also vary from one vendor (HP) to another (IBM), and from one model (rack-mounted) to another (blade-mounted) for a given vendor. Therefore, it is important to pick a mother-board that provides a good balance between the number of processor sockets and memory DIMM slots.

Before moving on to the next topic, we would like to make you aware of the following two issues. First, assume that you opted for a large amount of physical RAM to reduce the I/O footprint of your mailbox server. Figure 5-5 highlights that it will take some time until you can harvest the benefits of the large database cache. The left vertical axis is the database read IOPS and the right vertical axis is the database cache size. Initially, the cache is cold and the store process has to read several database pages from disk until you actually see a reduction in disk transfers per second. Therefore, a higher read request rate is seen in the beginning after a server booted. The data in Figure 5-5 are from a LoadGen test. The server was rebooted just before the test started. The same effect would occur in a production environment, for example, after a failover of a clustered mailbox server.

Second, there are nontransactional workloads that you have to consider during the sizing of the mailbox servers. Two well-known examples are backups and online maintenance. These nontransactional workloads require disk perfor-mance. Adding more than 32 GB of RAM might not significantly reduce the necessary storage performance for these nontransactional workloads.

In summary, we believe that you should never compromise on the min-imum quantity of recommended RAM, and that you carefully select your server form factor and model based on other aspects, such as standardiza-tion, power and cooling, blade format, and so on. The right choice for your environment will combine those factors to meet your requirements.

Figure 5-5
Cache warming

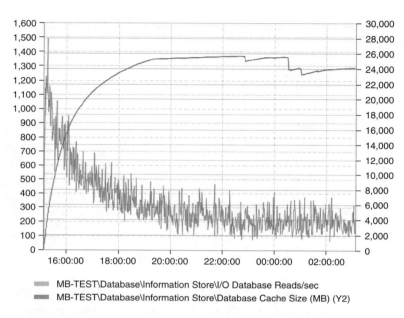

MB-TEST\Database\Information Store\I/O Database Reads/sec
MB-TEST\Database\Information Store\Database Cache Size (MB) (Y2)

Storage Considerations for Server Roles

In this section, we describe a few considerations that are specific to each server role when designing server storage. So far, we have seen the recommendations for the CPU and memory sizing. For storage, which is the main topic of interest to us, we need to consider the following facts:

- Mailbox server storage is the most critical point of design, and the one that can cause the most arguments between you and your storage administrators. We will review the proper tactics to employ.

- HT and Edge Servers require local storage for keeping track of messages in transit. The faster the storage, the better the performance. However, this storage location does not need to be very large because it is only used for temporary data. You may even discard the backup of such a storage location, and focus on the full server backup for recovery purposes, even though an HT server or an Edge Server can be rebuilt from scratch in case something goes bad. However, you would lose the information stored in the transport dumpster of the server with the HT role.

- Servers with the CAS role require no specific storage other than the boot volumes. There are some general considerations to bring to the topic regarding proper layout of Windows operating system partitions.

Mailbox Server

Storage sizing of mailbox servers will first depend on one basic parameter: the size of the mailbox and the number of mailboxes that you wish to host on your server. This should give you a rough idea of the kind of volume size you have to deal with. Beyond that, there are other areas of Exchange that require storage, along with the typical overhead (aka the "fluff factor") of the Exchange database engine, such as:

- Whitespace
- Disk fill-up policy
- Deleted item and deleted mailbox retention
- Content indexing
- Frequency of backup (specific to the transaction log space requirements)
- Database replication (local)
- Special operations: mailbox move and database maintenance

However, *never* forget to consider performance requirements. This was especially important with 32-bit versions of Exchange. The increased database cache size reduced the I/O footprint of Exchange Server 2007, but it is still important to stay within the physical disk latency boundaries. Therefore, we put them at the top of our list.

I/O per second requirements

We have been working on this topic for the last 10 years with Microsoft Exchange technologies. Every release from Exchange 4.0 to Exchange 2007 SP1 brought improvements in this area. The IOPS requirements for storage groups, transaction log files, and databases are therefore significantly different from one version of Microsoft Exchange to another. They also depend on the type of client used (e.g., Outlook 2003 in online mode vs. Outlook 2007 in cache mode). For example, Microsoft estimates that a user with a 250 MB mailbox and Outlook in online mode causes about 1.5 times more read I/O than a user with Outlook in cached Exchange mode. Internet clients and Outlook Web access are less storage friendly than Outlook in cached Exchange mode. You might see twice the number of IOPS.

Table 5-6 presents rule-of-thumb figures from Microsoft TechNet for a mailbox server. This information is based on the assumption that users run Outlook 2007 in cached Exchange mode. If you use Outlook in online mode, then you will have a higher number of read requests. The read/write ratio in Exchange Server 2003 was about 2:1 or 66% reads. The larger database cache in Exchange Server 2007 reduced the read percentage significantly. With Outlook

Table 5-6   *IOPS per user depending on user profile*

User profile	Messages (~50 KB) sent/received per day	Database cache per user in MB	Estimated IOPS per user
Light	5 sent/20 received	2	0.11
Average	10 sent/40 received	3.5	0.18
Heavy	20 sent/80 received	5	0.32
Very heavy	30 sent/120 received	5	0.48

2007 clients in cached Exchange mode, the ratio is about 50% read and 50% write requests. If you had 100 I/O requests to the database volume in Exchange Server 2003, then you could measure approximately only 10 I/O requests at the same time going to the log file volume. In Exchange Server 2007, we have less read I/O on the database volume; therefore, the ratio between I/O to the log file volume and I/O to the database volume is now about 3:4 or 3:5. Please be aware that if you enable a storage group for continuous replication, there will be read I/O to the disk volume hosting the log files. The exchange replication service has to pull closed transaction log files from the log file directory of the active storage group to the inspector directory of the passive storage group. Therefore, it is not a mistake to see read I/O requests if you analyze the physical disk performance counters of the log file disk.

Microsoft documentation about IOPS/mailbox figures, such as "Optimizing Storage for Exchange Server 2003," refers only to the read-and-write I/O on the database volume. These numbers do not consider I/O going to the log file volume.

Besides, direct multiplication between the number of spindles that constitute a volume for an Exchange 2007 database, and the IOPS capability of each spindle is not correct. We understand that you might be disappointed by this kind of statement and not have a formula that you can directly use for sizing your environment. In the following, we provide a method for the correct IOPS requirements and provisioning:

Step 1. Know yourself. As Steve Tramack of HP often quotes in his famous TechEd sessions, you have a lot of information readily available in your environment. A simple monitoring of your database and transaction log disk/Logical Unit Number (LUN) will be greatly superior to *any* of the simplified IOPS calculations you can get on the market. Consequently, our advice is to spend a bit of time monitoring the environment, preferably during peak hours, and determine the kind of I/O demand you have from your environment.

Step 2. Believe what you see. Do not assume that if you have 10 spindles (disks) for a volume, you will get 10 times the throughput of each disk. RAID levels and array optimization come in place, and in fact can deliver much better or lower performance, depending on how optimistic the storage vendor was with the IOPS/disk information and the access pattern. To see the performance of a volume, use Jetstress. If Jetstress does not work, go no further. Make it work. Jetstress is ultra-simple, and it delivers excellent information for the implementation and viability of your server solution.

Step 3. Ask for help. There are many resources available on the Internet (e.g., Microsoft Exchange Team blog, a form of refined marketing and information sharing, or HP's Active Answers). Use them, read them, and if needed, call in for a consult. The reason we mention this is that we have been in situations where the storage does not perform adequately, and the solution is already in production. The impact on the user is negative, and fast action is required. To use an analogy, consider changing engines on an aircraft at 30,000 ft. It's better to get ready before deployment, run a simple validation, and burn in the additional three to four days that will make a difference to your deployment.

Simply put, in Step 1, you have determined your storage performance requirements; in Step 2, you determine the storage capabilities; and in Step 3, you use readily available collective or individual intelligence (this book is a good example).

One important topic to remember is that storage models (DAS or SAN, high-end or mid-range) will make a different translation between the number of IOPS available from a single disk and the number of IOPS available eventually to a LUN used by Microsoft Exchange. Let's take an example:

- Assume that a single disk does 160 IOPS (50% read, random).

- Next, you create an LUN from 10 of those disks.

- Using RAID0, the estimated throughput would be $10 \times 160 = 1600$ IOPS.

- Using RAID1, you would have to take into account the write penalty, that is, each LUN write operation actually translates in two disk write operations.

- Using RAID5, you would have to consider that each LUN write requires four disk operations (two disk reads and two disk writes for data block and parity block updates).

- Using a high-end storage array, the IOPS to disk are (positively) affected by cache policies (write-back cache, aggregation, etc.). Therefore, writing to RAID0 in our above example might actually achieve *much* higher transactions than 1600 IOPS!

- If you use a high-end storage array with a virtualization layer between the physical disks in the array and the LUNs presented to the

Windows hosts, then you have to consider another topic. The virtualization layer might group a set of physical disk spindles together and then carve individual LUNs out of the spindle set. With this approach, you gain performance by spreading I/O requests to a LUN over the complete set of physical disk spindles. However, sequential write I/O issued by the Windows host will be random write I/O on the array back-end. You have to consider that the achievable IOPS figure for random writes is lower compared to sequential write I/O.

- Using a low-end storage array, you might get into contention issues at the back-end disk bus, array memory throughput, or host port connectivity.

In summary, there are so many factors that contribute to the IOPS requirements and capabilities of storage devices that it's nearly impossible to make a precise calculation. Instead, we recommend that you make a simple conservative first estimate and later verify that information with tools such as Jetstress. Making that conservative estimate requires a couple of assumptions:

- You do not use cache optimization. In other words, you consider that any cache benefit should not be in your calculations. If you are told that storage array A will solve all your disk latency issues because of its larger cache size, then you already know that this person works in the sales department. Most of the time the cache in the storage controller is shared among all connected hosts, and therefore is significantly smaller than the database cache size of your 64-bit Exchange Server 2007 with 32 GB or more RAM. Additionally, the controller cache is not Exchange aware—it has to work with all applications running on the different hosts connected to the array. Therefore, 1 GB RAM used by the database cache on the Exchange server is much more valuable compared to 1 GB of RAM in the array controller.

- You do not use RAID0. RAID0 is not applicable to Exchange 2007 technology. While it delivers great performance, it opens great risk of losing data, even though you can implement Exchange-based replication (SCR, LCR, or CCR).

As a result, we suggest that you start with the following formula (courtesy of our colleague Christophe Dubois):

$$\text{Total IOPS} = 1 / [1 - (\text{RAID Penalty} - 1 / \text{RAID Penalty}) \times \text{Percent Read}] \times (\text{Number of disks/RAID Penalty}) \times \text{Drive Max IOPS}$$

The RAID penalty parameter is the number of additional disk accesses for each LUN write operation. The percent read is the percentage of read access (a high read access percentage diminishes the impact of the RAID penalty). The drive max IOPS is obtained from the vendor's disk characteristics. Assume that a 15,000-rpm disk will typically deliver 170 IOPS, while a 10,000-rpm disk delivers 125 IOPS.

This formula is a typical example of arithmetic used in a conservative way. It compensates for the relative imprecision of calculating the I/O requirements per active user, server, or mailbox. It also compensates for the fact that life is not a quiet river, and sometimes problems occur that stress production (e.g., recovery of a database on a Monday morning). This oversimplification does not take into account the access pattern (sequential vs. random), drive density, or cache benefits. If you want to take these into account, you should consult with your storage vendor and obtain full volume characterization or use vendor tools (such as HP's Storage Calculator for Microsoft Exchange) that integrate characterization testing. Trying to devise an all-purpose formula has led to many situations where storage was inadequately tested and sized and production was impacted. Mail is vital for most businesses. It is the only application that impacts all users, immediately and constantly.

In Chapter 11, "Performance Monitoring and Analysis," we describe in detail how you can verify the health of your disk subsystem. Here we provide just three very simple rules. The subsystem does not meet the expectations of Exchange if:

- The average read-and-write latency is greater than 20 milliseconds for the database volume.

- The average write latency is greater than 10 milliseconds for the disk volume hosting your log files.

- You see spikes greater than 50 milliseconds that last for more than a few seconds. Yes, it is acceptable to see spikes, but not peaks that last for multiple seconds. This is why we will teach you the usage of the percentile function in the upcoming performance and analysis chapter of this book.

Whitespace

Whitespace is the space left unused inside the databases. For example, if you have an 8 KB page with 1 KB of data, the 7 KB remainder is called whitespace. Whitespace with Exchange 2007 will increase if you do not have enough time to get online database defragmentation to take place. That operation is designed to rearrange data such that access and data placement are optimized inside the page structure of the database. To start with, you can estimate the whitespace to no more than 5% of the database size. If you have little movement inside a database, that percentage will be smaller. For example, if you deploy 50 GB databases with 50 users per database, the databases will contain much more data at rest than if you were deploying 500 users per database.

Disk fill-up policy

This policy consists of determining the level of occupancy of your storage volumes. A common policy is no more than 80%. In other words, 20% of the space on a disk (or partition) should be available at all times. In fact, some companies prefer to set this at 50%, and others overlook this aspect and get downtime simply because the transaction log disk volume fills up. (The transaction log files area tends to grow much faster than the database or content indexing ones.) We recommend that you set this policy to a value that you can monitor, and then be able to react fast enough (e.g., by adding more disks and extending the LUN) before the service goes down. We also learned another very good trick from a customer. A few large files are created on the disk volumes used to store Exchange databases and log files. This is done during the installation phase of the Exchange server. If issues with file system free space occur later, the files are deleted and you very quickly gain new free space.

The drive fill-up policy also depends on your recovery strategy. If you have to restore a database from your last backup, then you should not be forced to overwrite the assumed damaged database. You might need it as a last resort or for troubleshooting purposes. If you have to copy the database first to another disk volume, then you lose valuable time for the file copy, especially if you consider that the database size might be in the range of 100 to 200 GB. One approach to solve this issue is to always have free space on the disk volume for an additional database, or you can assign a new disk volume to the server before you start the database recovery. This is one instance in which you reap great benefits by deploying Exchange using SAN instead of DAS.

Deleted item and mailbox retention

We have found that if you deal with small mailboxes (100 MB or less), the overhead for the deleted items will vary according to the figures in Table 5-7. Note that these are ballpark figures; every environment is different, so don't be surprised if yours looks different. Because the retention is expressed in time units and the overhead in the actual percentage of mailbox size, if you vary the mailbox size (e.g., to 1 GB), the overhead will in fact correspond, roughly, to the quantity of mail that a user gets during the retention period. One hundred percent of a 100 MB mailbox is just 10% of a 1 GB mailbox.

Table 5-7   *Deleted item and mailbox retention overhead*

Retention period	Overhead
7 days	15%
14 days	50%
30 days	100%

Make sure that as you use these guidelines for your storage requirements, and you take into account this aspect of the sizing.

Content indexing

Content indexing basically consists of scanning the Exchange databases and creating an index. That index is roughly 10 to 15% of the database size. This may vary, however; you can easily monitor it in your existing Exchange 2007 environment by looking up the size of the folder.

You may decide to disable content indexing. For example, in an Exchange 2007 deployment where most/all of your clients operates in cache mode, the index is little used. Instead, the client-side indexing takes over the bulk of the search requests for the users. There are, however, more and more frequent situations where the server-side index will be of benefit, such as in the case of ActiveSync mobile devices. A little-known feature of those devices (from Windows Mobile 6.1 onward) is the ability to search the server by sending a simplified search query. The server will return the resulting hits and the mobile device can be used to download items of your choice. This is an example in which getting content indexing to operate, even if you are in cache mode, will be largely beneficial for your users.

On the other hand, turning off content indexing brings benefits other than saving space, such as saving CPU cycles. We have found that disabling content indexing during scale-up testing and database item creation was necessary to keep up with workload demand. Normally, and outside a special benchmark or database creation condition, you should let content indexing run. Therefore, our recommendation is to size your server appropriately and keep the default configuration that is content indexing enabled.

Backup frequency

The space requirements for your Exchange 2007 server need to take into account your backup policy. This is especially important for the transaction log volume size. That volume size needs to be calculated based on two key factors:

- How many log files do you generate per day?
- How many days do you accept on your log files without running a backup?

Traditionally, with Exchange 2003, we recommended running full backups on a daily basis. With the increase in mailbox size in Exchange 2007, the daily full backup may not be achievable anymore. In fact, you might think that backups are no longer required, given the use of built-in or storage-based database replication. A weekly full backup might be sufficient, with intermediate daily incremental or differential backups. Keep in mind that you need to have enough free space to restore all log files that have been created since your last full backup. For example, if you run your last full backup on Sunday and have to perform a restore on Friday, then you need space for all log files generated since Sunday!

The number of log files generated per user (on a daily or weekly basis) largely depends on the user activity on the server, and in particular the number of emails received by the user. The best way to determine this information is from empirical data, that is, from your existing Exchange environment, try to figure out how much log files are generated per storage group on a daily basis and divide by the number of users on that storage group (provided that you have a relatively uniform user population). You will have a figure that you can then reuse for your sizing calculation. Bear in mind that previous Exchange versions had 5 MB log files, and in Exchange 2007 log files are only 1 MB in size.

If you have to migrate mailboxes from a non-Exchange environment, then you can take advantage of Table 5-8. It shows the estimated number of log files per user based on their messaging behavior. It assumes an average message size of 50 KB. The table is also valuable if you have to migrate mailboxes from a previous Exchange version to Exchange Server 2007 SP1 because the number of log files generated in SP1 is different from previous Exchange versions. This is due to the changes in the ESE.

Table 5-8   *Transaction logs per mailbox*

User profile	Sent/received messages (~50 KB) per day	Logs generated/mailbox/per day
Light	5 sent/20 received	6
Average	10 sent/40 received	12
Heavy	20 sent/80 received	24
Very heavy	30 sent/120 received	36

Microsoft estimates that an average message size of 100 KB instead of 50 KB will generate 1.9 times more log files. This information is published in the "Mailbox Server Storage Design" section on TechNet.

Special operation: Database maintenance

On top of the estimated mailbox database size (number of mailboxes × quota + fluff factor), you will need to size the storage units such that you can perform database maintenance activities according to your policies, and such that you can prevent a disk fill-up condition at any time. Database maintenance typically requires as much space as the original database plus 10%. So if you have a 50 GB database, running an operation such as offline defragmentation (e.g., as requested by Microsoft Support Services), you will need 55 GB of free space for storing the target repaired database. Sourcing these additional 55 GB can be done in two different ways:

- Using a spare LUN as a temporary workspace for database maintenance. This has the advantage of offloading the source database LUN from the workload of the target database. The benefit is that this "temporary" LUN can be used for other purposes. The downside is that once the database has been repaired, it must be copied back to the original source database location (after verification of the maintenance results).

- Doubling the allocation space for your volumes and using that additional space for database maintenance. This radical approach simply consists of setting a disk-fill ratio policy of no more than 50%. With the low cost of storage space ($/GB), this option does not have a large impact, except if you multiply the overhead by many databases.

The right approach will depend on your deployment characteristics and the way you source storage. We typically prefer to have temporary LUNs allocated to the servers instead of doubling the storage requirements for the database. We also recommend a disk fill-up ratio of about 75% maximum.

Special operation: Mailbox move

In-place upgrades are not always possible, especially when transitioning from Exchange 2003 to Exchange 2007. Move mailbox migrations lead to a cleaner environment. Typically you will not want all the legacy entries in the registry and all the unused files in the file system. We recommend using the move mailbox procedure and to stay away from in-place upgrades.

The database target area may be sized correctly; however, during the move operation, *all* the data transferred will also be stored in the transaction log files area. Therefore, you should plan for sufficient space, for the transaction log volumes, and for both normal operations and mailbox move operations. For this, you may need additional space temporarily or permanently.

Special operation: Recovery Storage Group

Do not forget to reserve additional space for the Recovery Storage Group (RSG). You need at least the capacity to restore one database and all transaction log files of a production storage group. We have frequently reviewed designs where the RSG was praised during the presales phase and then the storage requirements of the RSG were forgotten during the design phase.

In summary

If you were to code a formula for storage space calculations, the following could be used as an example:

Database LUN size = (# of mailboxes × quota) + (% content indexing) + (% disk fill-up) + (% deleted items retention) − (% of single instance store)

There are lots of pluses and little minuses, but considering the increased density of storage and lower prices, this formula is quite acceptable to prevent disk fill-up conditions that would render the service unavailable!

For the transaction log files volume, the formula is different:

Transaction log LUN size = (# of logs per day) + (number of days between full backup) + (% disk fill-up) + (estimated quantity of move data between backups)

The transaction log files volume should *never* be sized as a percentage of the database volume—this is absolute nonsense, because databases represent data at rest, while the transaction log represents data getting into the database (from a size perspective).

Warning

These kinds of arithmetic calculations can be difficult (i.e., garbage in, garbage out [GIGO]), especially if you deal with a medium or large (>2000 users) environment. Therefore, you should be extra cautious with your calculations and have them verified by your storage supplier/administrator.

If you source your storage from DAS (local devices on the server), be aware that any change to the storage setup will require some form of downtime or service degradation. Therefore, plan your storage size generously; however, keep in mind that many fluffs can lead to suboptimal deployments from space, power, cooling, and cost perspectives.

Disk volume design

Exchange databases and the transaction log files must be stored on separate disk volumes. This is required from a recovery point of view and it provides performance benefits as well. During normal operations, there is random read and random write access to the database and sequential write access to the log file volume. Separating these I/O patterns can increase the performance of your solution. However, the main reason is to be able to take advantage of the transaction log files stored on another disk if you are unlucky and lose the database volume. If you host the database and the log files on the same disk volume, then you can only perform a point-in-time restore. You will not be able to roll the log files forward that have been created since your last backup. This would mean you lost all data created since the backup!

You have mainly two options in how you design the layout:

- Two disk volumes per storage group
- Two disk volumes shared by multiple storage groups

If you use separate disks for each storage group, then you have the benefit that you increased the reliability of your configuration. Only one storage group is affected if you lose a disk volume. Another advantage is that it eases the usage of a backup product that takes advantage of a hardware-based Volume Shadow Copy Services (VSS) implementation. A VSS solution might rip and replace a disk volume during the recovery. Often a hardware-based VSS provider will swap disk volumes or perform a block-by-block re-sync from the created shadow copy volume to the production disk volume. If you share one disk volume between multiple storage groups, then a corruption of a single database affects multiple storage groups during the recovery. You can mitigate this issue by performing a restore to an alternative file system location and manually copy the database file to the production directory. However, with this approach, you lose the "instant recovery" feature that likely caught your eye in the marketing brochure of the VSS solution vendor. If you do not intend to use a hardware-based VSS solution, then you can consider hosting the files of multiple storage groups on a shared disk volume. This has the benefit that you reduce the number of disk volumes you have to manage. See Chapter 4, Windows Storage, for a description of how you can take advantage of mount points to overcome the insufficient number of characters in the alphabet to assign a drive letter to each disk volume.

Hub Transport Server and Edge Server

Microsoft TechNet provides a separate section titled, "Transport Server Storage Design." Both roles use an ESE database, mail.que, to store all the mails they process. The database uses an 8 KB page size and is randomly accessed. The log files of the mail queue could remain on the system disk, which is hardly used after boot time. Log files are sequentially written with an I/O size of 512 bytes up to the log buffer size.

If you wish to leverage from the transport dumpster feature of the HT role in continuous replication scenarios, then you should build resiliency into the storage components. One approach is to use a local disk controller with a battery-backed-up cache, tune the cache to 100% write (to ensure that you do not get hit by write performance), and choose RAID5 or RAID1 (preferred) for the disk unit that will host the mail queue database. Another approach is to use SAN attached disk volumes to store the mail queue. This allows you to replay the mail queue of a failed HT on another server.

Using different disks to store the ESE database and the log files of the mail queue database is recommended to increase reliability and the performance. By default, Exchange Server 2007 uses the same directory in the Exchange

Figure 5-6
*Mail queue data-
base and log file
path*

```
add
    key     QueueDatabasePath
    value   C:\Program Files\Microsoft\Exchange Server\TransportRoles\data\Queue
add
    key     QueueDatabaseLoggingPath
    value   C:\Program Files\Microsoft\Exchange Server\TransportRoles\data\Queue
```

program folder to store the database and log files of the mail queue (Figure 5-6). See the Microsoft TechNet section, "How to Change the Location of the Queue Database," for the relocation procedure, and pay attention to the file system permission that you have to apply to the new mail queue directory.

In addition, you can improve performance by moving the TMP folder from the drive with the operating system to the disk volume hosting the mail queue database. Transport servers use the TMP folder during content conversion. Messages received in an Internet format are converted to the MAPI format before they are delivered.

From a capacity viewpoint, having at least 500 MB of free space on the disk volume with the database is important; otherwise, you will see back pressure warnings in the event viewer. Exchange servers with the transport engine monitor system their resource utilization, and if resource usage is above the limits configured in the EdgeTransport.exe.config file, then they stop accepting new connections. This helps to complete the delivery of existing messages in the queue. New connection requests will only be accepted after resource utilization falls below the configured limits.

Table 5-9 provides rule-of-thumb figures for I/O requests per message. The data are published on Microsoft TechNet. You have to adjust the values if you use features like journaling or transport rules. However, they are helpful for giving you a rough idea of I/O requirements.

Table 5-9   *Hub Transport role I/O requirements*

I/O per message (~40 KB)	Transport dumpster enabled	Transport dumpster disabled
Total IOPS	17	4
Sequential log write	7	2
Random database write	7	2
Random database read	3	0

For calculating the required disk capacity hosting the mail queue database, you can use the following rule of thumb formula:

- Maximum number of items in the mail queue multiplied by the average message size
- +Transport dumpster size = MaxDumpsterSizePerStorageGroup multiplied by the number of Exchange storage groups in the local AD site with Local or Cluster Continuous Replication enabled

- +Space reserved for Message tracking logs
- +Space for SMTP send and receive protocol logs, connectivity logs, and agent log files.
- +at least 20% free space

For the maximum number of items in the mail queue, you can use the worst-case scenario figure 500,000, or a value that you have measured in your existing Exchange deployment. See Chapter 7 for a description of the Transport dumpster and the MaxDumpsterPerStorage Group variable.

Please refer to the previously mentioned TechNet section or other blog articles available on the Internet for additional details.

Client Access Server

Client Access Servers (CASs) usually do not require storage other than local boot devices. However, we emphasize that event logs and Internet Information Services (IIS) logs are particularly important for the CAS role. As the CAS acts as a broker between Web services and back-end servers, such as Active Directory domain controllers or mailbox servers, the role of IIS is central. Any connection issue or service interruption from IIS will get logged in both the IIS HTTP error logs and the application event log. In high-end environments, you must prevent disk fill-ups due to log files.

Therefore, we recommend using a dedicated disk partition to store the IIS logs and event viewer logs. You should reserve ample space—for example, 20 GB—for these logs in an enterprise deployment. You will then need to modify your Windows server installation to ensure that the IIS logs and event logs store their information in that secondary partition. You do not need to worry about performance. Local disk access with enterprise-class disks (10,000 or 15,000 rpm) will be just fine.

If you have a large number of clients who connect to mailboxes using POP3 or IMAP4, then you should move the TMP folder to a faster disk and not use the default configuration where TMP is located on the system disk. The transport engine converts all incoming emails to the MAPI format before the message is forwarded and stored in the Exchange database. If a POP3 or IMAP4 client then wants to read the email, the CAS is is responsible for converting it back into the Multipurpose Internet Mail Extensions (MIME) format.

Unified Messaging Servers

Unified Messaging (UM) servers do not require storage outside of local boot devices. Please refer to the TechNet section, "Planning for Unified Messaging Servers," for information about the Unified Messaging server role.

Exchange Server Sizing Tools

In the previous section, we discussed details about designing Exchange servers. We are sure you will ask: Do I have to do the sizing manually? Isn't this very time consuming?

Luckily, Microsoft provides a tool for this purpose, the Exchange 2007 Mailbox Server Role Storage Requirements Calculator. The tool allows you to perform the previously described calculations for a mailbox server using an Excel sheet. You have to provide your requirements such as number of mailboxes, mailbox quotas, and server type (CCR or SCR) in the input tab.

Figure 5-7 shows the entry fields for the server configuration and Figure 5-8 shows the mailbox and client configuration steps of the requirements gathering phase.

Figure 5-7   *Server configuration*

Storage Requirements Input Factors - Server Configuration				
Step 1 - Please enter in the appropriate information for cells that are blue and choose the appropriate drop-downs for cells that are red concerning your server configuration.				

Exchange Server Configuration		Standby Continuous Replication Configuration	
Exchange Server 2007 Version	SP1+	Number of SCR Targets	0
Number of Exchange Mailbox Servers	1	SCR Log Replay Delay (Seconds)	86400
Continuous Replication (CR) Model	CCR	SCR Log Truncation Delay (Seconds)	0
Content Indexing?	Enabled		
Dedicated Maintenance / Restore LUN?	Yes		
LUN Free Space Percentage	20%		

Exchange Data Configuration		Database Configuration	
Deleted Item Retention Window (Days)	14	Use Recommended Maximum Database Sizes?	Yes
Data Overhead Factor	20%	Maximum Database Size (GB)	0
Mailbox Moves / Week Percentage	0%		

IOPS Configuration	
I/O Overhead Factor	20%
Additional I/O Requirement	0.00

Figure 5-8   *Mailbox and client configuration*

Storage Requirements Input Factors - Mailbox & Client Configuration	
Step 2 - Please enter in the appropriate information for cells that are blue and choose the appropriate drop-downs for cells that are red concerning your mailbox population. If the server(s) will house multiple mailbox types, then please enter that information in the Tier-2 and Tier-3 User Mailbox tables. Otherwise, only use the Tier-1 User Mailbox table.	

Tier-1 User Mailbox Configuration		Client Configuration	
Total Number of Tier-1 User Mailboxes	5000	User Concurrency	100%
Projected Mailbox Number Growth	0%		
Send/Receive Capability / Mailbox / Day	10 sent/40 received		
Average Message Size (KB)	50		
Tier-1 User Mailbox Size Limit (MB)	500		
Predict IOPS Value?	Yes		
Tier-1 User IOPS / mailbox	0.00		
Tier-1 Database Read:Write Ratio	0%		
Outlook Mode (Majority of Clients)	Cached Mode		

Tier-2 User Mailbox Configuration		Tier-3 User Mailbox Configuration	
Total Number of Tier-2 User Mailboxes	2000	Total Number of Tier-3 Mailboxes	100
Projected Mailbox Number Growth	0%	Projected Mailbox Number Growth	0%
Send/Receive Capability / Mailbox / Day	20 sent/80 received	Send/Receive Capability / Mailbox / Day	30 sent/120 received
Average Message Size (KB)	50	Average Message Size (KB)	50
Tier-2 User Mailbox Size Limit (MB)	1024	Tier-3 User Mailbox Size Limit (MB)	2048
Predict IOPS Value?	Yes	Predict IOPS Value?	Yes
Tier-2 User IOPS / mailbox	0.00	Tier-3 User IOPS / mailbox	0.00
Tier-2 Database Read:Write Ratio	0%	Tier-3 Database Read:Write Ratio	0%
Outlook Mode (Majority of Clients)	Cached Mode	Outlook Mode (Majority of Clients)	Cached Mode

The result that the Excel sheet provides is vendor neutral. The sheet does not provide vendor-specific information; for example, the calculator does not differentiate among storage subsystems from NetApp, EMC, or HP. The storage requirements results pane shown in Figure 5-9 provides an overview of the necessary disk capacity and the required IOPS.

Some vendors have created Exchange sizing tools that consider the specifics of their own hardware. We would like to mention two examples: Dell provides the "Dell Exchange Advisor Tool," and HP provides the "HP Sizing and Configuration Tool for Microsoft Exchange Server 2007" and the "HP Storage Planning Calculator for Microsoft Exchange Server 2007." Using these vendor specific tools has the benefit that they have know how about hardware internals that a vendor neutral tool has to neglect to be applicable for storage subsystems from all vendors. Because we work for HP, we would like to take the opportunity to share our enthusiasm about the HP sizing tools.

Figure 5-9
*Storage require-
ments results*

Storage Requirements Results Pane

User Mailbox Configuration	Tier-1	Tier-2	Tier-3
Total Number of User Mailboxes	5000	2000	100
User Mailbox Size (within Database)	537 MB	1097 MB	2158 MB
Database Cache / Mailbox	5 MB	5 MB	5 MB
Transaction Logs Generated / Mailbox / Day	12	24	36
IOPS Profile / Mailbox	0.17	0.34	0.51

Solution Configuration	Single Server	Total for all Servers
Recommended RAM Configuration (GB)	31 GB	--
Recommended Number of Storage Groups (Databases)	25	25
Recommended Number of Mailboxes / Database	284	--
Number of Tier-1 Mailboxes / Database	200	--
Number of Tier-2 Mailboxes / Database	80	--
Number of Tier-3 Mailboxes / Database	4	--
Total Number of Mailboxes	7100	7100

Transaction Log Requirements	Single Server	Total for all Servers
User Transaction Logs Generated / Day	133920	133920
Average Move Mailbox Transaction Logs Generated / Day	0	0
Average Transaction Logs Generated / Server / Day	133920	133920
User Transaction Logs Generated / SG / Day	5357	--
Average Move Mailbox Transaction Logs Generated / SG / Day	0	--
Average Transaction Logs Generated / SG / Day	5357	--

Disk Space & Performance Requirements	Single Server	Total for all Servers
Number of Data Copies	2	
Database Disk Space Required / Replica	5969 GB	5969 GB
Log Disk Space Required / Replica	262 GB	262 GB
Database LUN Disk Space Required / Replica	7834 GB	7834 GB
Log LUN Disk Space Required / Replica	327 GB	327 GB
Restore LUN Size / Node (and / SCR Targets)	1558 GB	1558 GB
Required Database IOPS / Replica	1905	1905
Required Log IOPS / Replica	700	700

The results of the HP Sizer include an order list and catalog price of the solution. Figure 5-10 shows that this tool allows you to compare the total hardware cost of a configuration using RAID 1+0 and one using RAID 5. The calculation considers the capacity and performance needs of the storage subsystem. The tool shows you whether capacity or performance requirements lead to the proposed number of disk spindles. You can easily change the disk drive model (146 GB to 300 GB, or 10,000 rpm to 15,000 rpm) or switch between the available storage subsystems to investigate the impact on hardware cost. As seen in Figure 5-11, the calculator provides hardware-specific details such as the HP StorageWorks EVA disk group configuration.

The screenshots in Figures 5-10 and 5-11 are from the HP Storage Planning Calculator, which you can use for sizing the storage of mailbox

Figure 5-10   *HP Storage Planning Calculator for Exchange Server 2007*

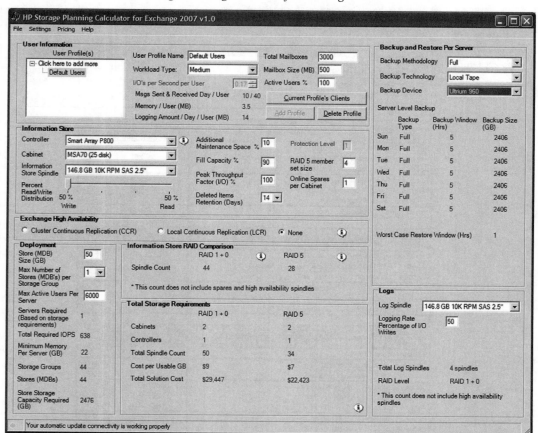

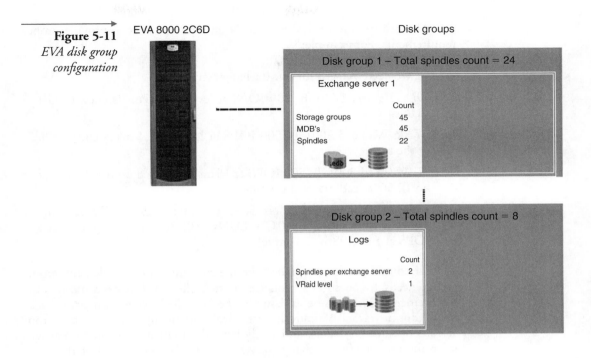

Figure 5-11
EVA disk group configuration

servers. The HP Sizing and Configuration Tool for Microsoft Exchange Server 2007 supports sizing the complete environment, not only mailbox servers. It provides you with a complete solution, including servers holding the HT and CAS role and the backup infrastructure. You can download a guide describing how to use the HP Sizing and Configuration Tool from the HP Active Answers website.

Dealing with SAN Administrators

The process of designing your storage solution started with your Service-Level Objectives or Agreements (SLOs or SLAs). Then you need to bring in considerations for capacity and throughput, and then you can choose the right technology for implementation of the storage solution. However, there are situations where that last step (technology and implementation) is outside of your control as a Microsoft Exchange administrator, as it is controlled by the storage management team or the entity in your company that manages storage resources. If that is the case, you must properly outline your requirements in order for them to be properly addressed. Failure to do so will result in an impact to your application service level and general user dissatisfaction because Exchange does not work.

The proper way to deal with SAN administrators is to provide proper requirements. For example:

BAD: We need 300 GB for our Exchange server.

GOOD: We need 300 GB, 500 IOPS at less than 15 ms latency, 60 GB LUNs.

BETTER: We need 300 GB, 500 IOPS at less than 15 ms latency, 95% of the time.

BEST: We need 300 GB, 500 IOPS at 15 ms (measured on the Windows host), 50% read, 95% of the time.

ULTIMATE: 2 × 100 GB LUNs, 50% read, 200 random IOPS at 15 ms (95th percentile), 2 × 50 GB LUNs, 100% write, 80 sequential IOPS at 5 ms (98th percentile).

Of course, the more detailed the metrics, the more detailed the monitoring needs to be so that you can ensure the SAN storage meets your requirements. This can be an issue in the large SAN environment, because SAN administrators typically have to deal with many hosts (servers) from various operating systems, and rarely have the right tools to micromanage/micromonitor the few Exchange servers from their management platforms.

This is the point where you need to make friends with your SAN administrators, take them to lunch, and discuss how they can meet your requirements. The difficult part of monitoring the performance of Exchange is that if you have a failure, everybody will notice it *immediately*, and your operations staff may actually be the last to know. Therefore, you have to closely monitor the servers if you are beginning the roll-out of an environment. You have to catch resource contention and remediate it as soon as possible. In Chapter 11, we discuss in greater detail the performance-monitoring strategies you can employ.

SAN Boot Versus Local Boot

In Windows server environments, a SAN Boot is a convenient way to create a redundant server infrastructure without having to implement Microsoft failover clusters. The idea is to build on the notion of Redundant Array of Independent Servers (RAIS, see later), and to place the boot volume of one or more servers in a SAN environment in order to enable error-free and semiautomated server failover.

SAN boot can be used without standby servers, such as in a disaster-tolerant environment where the boot volumes are replicated in real time to a remote site hosting a mirrored hardware configuration. In the case of a site failover, you only need to break the replication link, and then present the LUNs to the remote servers and start them.

Standby servers are useful when recovering from a server hardware error; however, if you have a software problem (at the application, operating system, or file system levels), using a standby machine will probably not solve your problem. When you design such an environment, you should always plan on using advanced server monitoring tools that can report and diagnose problems on the physical server. Note that this is the principal weakness of such an approach. Microsoft Failover Clustering, for example, provides a Cluster Resource Manager that can monitor and move resources between nodes in a cluster.

Figure 5-12 shows the principles of RAIS and SAN boot. Servers are configured with no local disk, and use their Host Bus Adapters (HBAs) to communicate with a storage array on a SAN, using SAN-based LUNs as boot volumes. In this example, we have four production servers (A, B, C, and D) and one standby server (Z); each has boot volumes hosted in a SAN array (Boot A, B, C, D, and Z).

Figure 5-12
SAN boot
schematics

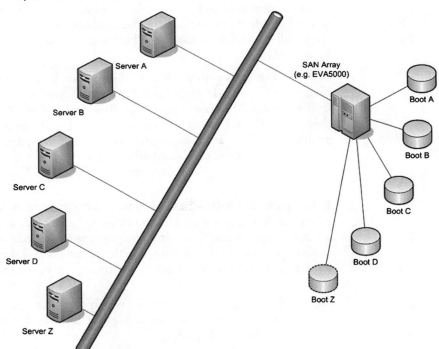

How does it work?

SAN booting is typically enabled on servers by programming the HBA BIOS to look up a logical unit on a SAN as a boot device. This procedure is based on the following assumptions:

- You have programmed the server's own BIOS to enable HBA boots.

- You have selected the correct LUN in the HBA BIOS configuration.

HP StorageWorks has published a very comprehensive whitepaper describing how to enable a SAN boot in HP storage environments, available from http://h18006.www1.hp.com/storage/networking/bootsan.html. If you use HP servers, you should read and understand this particular article "HP StorageWorks Booting Windows Server 2003 and Windows Server x64 Edition Systems from a Storage Area Network Application Notes (AA-RS2US-TE, February 2007)". See also the Microsoft article, "Boot from SAN in Windows Server 2003 and Windows 2000 Server." This article provides a good overview of the pros and cons for SAN boot for a Windows server, as well as some generic server and HBA configuration guidelines.

The downside of boot volumes located on a SAN is the crash dump analysis. When executing a STOP instruction, Windows Server expects to generate a memory dump on the system partition volume. When booting from a SAN volume, a crash dump stack is created based on the Fibre Channel path used to locate the boot volume on the SAN. If, for some reason, this path is not available at the time of a STOP error, the crash dump stack will be unable to locate the boot device and a memory dump will not be created.

You can ensure that memory dumps can be created in your environment using the Ctrl-Scroll Lock-Scroll Lock key sequence. The procedure is described in Microsoft Knowledge Base Article 244139. One might argue that you will rarely want to perform server debugging using a crash dump analysis, but there are cases where this has been requested by Microsoft support during complex troubleshooting.

Best practice 0: Master your environment

From the field experience viewpoint, completely mastering the entire environment is paramount, as many components are interdependent. In particular, any operations staff who work with the servers and the hardware and key operating system features should have knowledge of the following:

- SAN Management Appliance, which provides a user interface and automation facility for managing the SAN back-end array (in our case study, an HP EVA)

- SAN back-end array and the fabric topology (including zoning information, which is typically defined at the Fibre Channel switch level)

- HP host-bus adapters, server boot BIOS, SAN fabric and path definition, and SAN boot in general

- Host operating system (in our case, Windows 200x Server) and any critical applications

Last, but not least, all these management interfaces are generally deployed with their own security identification mechanism. A Remote Integrate Lights-Out Interface (RILO/iLO) board requires a user name and password, as does the SAN Management appliance and the Fibre Channel switches. This is required in addition to operating system–level credentials. Make sure that you have all of this information at hand before you start implementing/troubleshooting your solution.

Best practice 1: Create a boot volume for standby server

It is usually a good idea to create a small (8 GB) LUN for the standby server, ensuring that the machine is present on the network and can be managed. That way, you can monitor the standby server's hardware components, flash BIOS, and ROMs, and possibly use the machine for testing purposes. Of course, you need to give priority to the production server's work, but it is always good to be sure that the standby server, seldom used in failover scenarios, can indeed be failed over.

Given that the standby server will be used in the network for monitoring purposes, remember to include it in your software and hardware maintenance processes, such as Service Pack upgrades, hot fixes, and security conformance.

Best practice #2: Preconfigure HBAs of standby server

A standby server is designed to impersonate a production server that fails to operate properly. For this "impersonation" to occur, you need to boot the standby machine on the boot LUN used by the now-defunct server. This means that standby server Z must be capable of booting off the boot volume of server A, B, C, or D.

For each of the A, B, C, and D servers, you will typically point the HBA BIOS to boot from one LUN (referenced by the controller's worldwide port name and LUN). In Figure 5-13, we select LUN 01 on the controller port

Figure 5-13
Selecting boot LUN in HBA BIOS

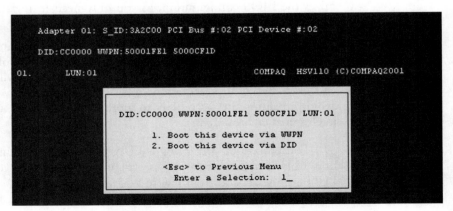

"50001FE1 5000CF1D". This port is defined at the controller level, similar to a NIC MAC address. In the case of an HP EVA storage array, the controller's host port can be viewed from the Command View utility, as shown in Figure 5-14.

Figure 5-14   *Locating the controller's WWPN*

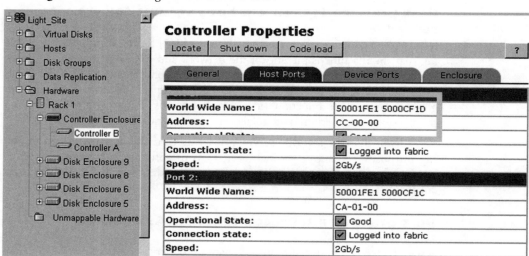

Alternatively, given that the HBA BIOS needs the WWPN of the host controller interface as well as the boot LUN, you can simplify this definition process by always using the same LUN (e.g., 1; don't use 0, which is reserved for controller commands) for each boot volume. This minimizes the BIOS configuration, as you only need to register the SAN array WWPN.

Figure 5-15 shows how various servers can use a volume presented with the same LUN (1 in this case). This is achieved by virtue of the presentation (masking) of the LUN from the SAN array. No conflict will occur as long as you keep the LUN presentation consistent across the servers (and therefore avoid presenting the same LUN to more than one server, unless you operate in clustered environments).

The process of presenting a LUN consists of selecting a preregistered host from a hierarchical view (see Figure 5-16) and optionally selecting a LUN number, as shown in Figure 5-17.

Figure 5-15   *LUNs as "seen" by the servers*

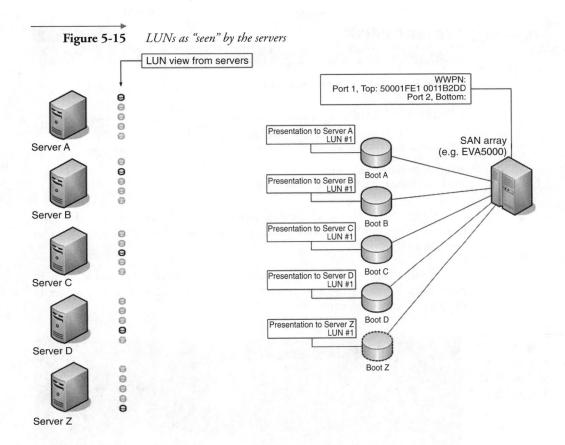

Figure 5-16

Selecting a host from a predefined list

Present Vdisk

Present Vdisk	Select None	Select All	Assign LUN	?
Cancel				

Select one or more hosts to which your Vdisk will be presented. Only those hosts without existing presentations to your Vdisk are shown.
Click the **Present Vdisk** button after you have made your selections.

HSV Storage Network
└ Hosts
  ├ Amethyste
  ├ Diamond
  ├ Emerald
  ├ Ora01
  └ Saphire

Figure 5-17
Choosing an LUN during presentation

Present Vdisk

| Previous step | Finish | Cancel | | ? |

Complete the steps below to present your Vdisk.

STEP 2: Select a LUN:

Available LUNs for this host: 6 ?

STEP 3: Present your Vdisk
Click the **Finish** button to present your Vdisk.

Figure 5-18 shows an extract from an HP document that describes how to select the SAN LUN (located using the WWPN of the controller and the LUN).

Finally, you should make sure that the fabric zoning (partitioning used for a Fibre Channel infrastructure to create virtual islands) does not get in the way of the failover process.

Figure 5-18
Selecting SAN boot LUN in BIOS settings of HBA

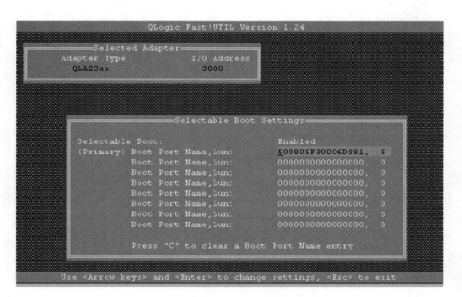

Best practice 3: Use RILO (iLO) and Insight Manager for operations

When using SAN boot, and unlike with a Windows Failover Clustering environment, there is no process or technology provided with Windows Server that enables you to monitor your server and its applications and make *educated* decisions for the failover process. Depending on your server vendor, you should take advantage of server management tools (e.g., Insight Manager from HP) when performing hardware monitoring to ensure that you can predict or be sure that a server failover will indeed solve your problem.

Best practice #4: Use snapclones for boot volumes

The Business Continuance Volumes (BCV) or clones represent a physical duplicate of a volume. They are typically used for hosting business-critical data that must be rapidly recovered, such as databases. If you decide to host your boot volumes on a SAN, it is appropriate to create a block-by-block copy (do *not* use snapshots) of a boot volume to allow for fast recovery in case the boot volume becomes physically or logically corrupted. This has happened previously in a customer environment, where the only option was to perform a baremetal recovery of the operating system. Of course, depending on the backup and recovery product you use, this operation can be more, or less, complex. However, it is not as simple as presenting a LUN to the server.

Another use of SAN array capabilities is to create a snapshot copy (read-only) that is used to generate an RDP image that can be flashed later on.

Protection, yes, but rollback too! By booting a standby server from a cloned volume, you keep the production system disk intact. If, in the process of recovery, you need to install critical operating system or application updates, you have a "safety net" that allows you to roll back to the original boot volume if things turn sour. This is an example of how you can take advantage of SAN abilities in your server farm environment.

Best practice 5: Use a local pagefile volume in replicated environments

A pagefile usually contains transient information that is not required after a reboot. If you operate in a replicated environment where each volume is replicated by means of a disaster recovery group (EVA terminology), carrying paging operations across to the remote site is not necessary. If there is a site failover, the information will be of no value. While you can still host your pagefile volume on the boot volume or another volume on the SAN, make sure that you do not pollute the intersite link with paging operations.

Paging over the SAN is not necessarily a good thing. For a server that pages excessively, you should use a local volume. Microsoft documents how to track possible problems when using SAN-hosted pagefile volumes in Microsoft Knowledge Base Article 305547.

Note the significantly increased capacity requirement for the pagefile. In Exchange Server 2007, you are not limited to 4 GB RAM! The size of the pagefile should be 10 MB larger than the amount of physical RAM in the server. This is documented in the "Exchange 2007 System Requirements" section on Microsoft TechNet. Microsoft Knowledge Base Article 889654 provides additional details about this topic.

Summary

SAN boot is a very effective approach for ensuring business continuity with reduced complexity. You should take advantage of the technology, but always remember what your goals are. Using RAIS with SAN boot is not a one-to-one replacement of Failover Clustering. In fact, esome of the operations listed here can be quite complex, and even more so than clusters.

You should keep in mind that this type of approach is not a replacement for any slack in operations and administration. While it can deliver value in well-maintained environments, this approach is completely counterproductive if you do not have best-in-class operation processes (such as backup and recovery) and if you have not thoroughly reviewed the architecture and failover processes.

Remember that technology alone does not solve all the problems and that your processes and operations staff are the key success factors for such an implementation. Do not neglect process and training!

Blades Versus Conventional Rack Mount Servers

Conventional rack-mount servers typically come with the ability to host many more internal components than blade servers. On the other hand, blade servers are optimized for sharing as many components as possible between other blade servers that are part of the same "blade system" (Figure 5-19). This results in a change of the server computing landscape that only really started in 2006.

Where rack-mount servers are used, you should ask yourself whether using blade servers would provide an advantage. The following criteria will help you get to the right answer:

1.   Are you operating a consolidated environment? If that is the case, you have multiple servers (a farm) that could possibly be hosted in a reduced number of blade systems, reducing your power, cooling, and footprint requirements. The weight per square meter or square foot might be increased, so you need to consider some key environmental conditions first.

2.   Do you have power, cooling, cabling, and space concerns? These are the sweet spots for blade server computing. Power and cooling are typically addressed by using a shared power unit that can *vary*

Figure 5-19
*Rear and front
views of an HP
blade system*

(a)

(b)

its consumption based on the CPU utilization of the individual blades. This approach is similar to the conventional laptop computer that varies the processor speed depending on whether it is busy. The net result and benefit are immediate: Less power means less heat dissipation, which in turn means less cooling requirements! Cabling and space requirements are addressed by sharing connectivity components via integrated hub technology for (data and storage) networking inside the blade system, thereby using fewer cables. The savings are not in the cables, by the way. They are in the required core infrastructure needed to support the servers.

3.   Get quicker return on investment from consolidation and virtualization: By consolidating your servers and virtualizing your infrastructure, you get quicker benefits for your investments. You can reduce your operational costs by simplifying a server replacement (2 mn rack-and-replace operation for a blade vs. 2 hr for a conventionally cabled rack mount server). You may think that we exaggerate the figures here, and that's probably true, but if you have ever replaced a server in a rack, you will know exactly what we mean.

With Exchange 2007, the choice of blade versus rack-mount is a worthwhile consideration. Because the deployment model for Exchange 2007 is based on roles, and because it is *simpler* to have single-role servers, you will require several servers for your deployment. Depending on the nature of your deployment, you will have to consider blades or rack-mount servers according to the following criteria:

For blade servers:

Scalable infrastructure.

Simplify provisioning and maintenance.

Deploy/reprovisioning resources often.

Have a distributed infrastructure.

See Total Cost of Ownership (TCO) associated with modular, integrated computing environment.

Application requires many servers/processors.

Building service-oriented architectures/clusters/grids.

For traditional rack-mount servers:

Not a data center deployment.

Fewer than five servers.

Special PCI slot requirements.

Require local storage and tape streaming.

Require highest reliability/scale up (beyond eight processing cores).

Cable and space consolidation are not concerns.

Use of blade servers has consistently increased in recent years due to several factors: the consolidation of computing resources, the need for more computing resources, and finally, the necessity of reducing power consumption and cooling requirements. Blade systems have vastly improved, and some of the smaller models (e.g., HP's BladeSystem c3000) can now be used in office environments, as long as you keep the environmental temperature to less than 36°C.

In summary

Major growth in blade server computing has occurred in recent years and this trend will continue. However, be aware of the storage requirements of your servers, and especially if you decide to adopt DAS technology. The latter may not be suitable for blade server deployment if you would need to scale too many disk units for each server.

Virtualization

Server virtualization has been in use for quite some time, and we just can't write a book about Exchange 2007 storage without touching on virtualized environments for two reasons:

■ Some customers already use fully virtualized Exchange 2007 deployments in production. They leverage some of the motion capability of the virtual machines for their disaster recovery scenario, and they deal with a relatively modest concurrent workload.

■ Microsoft has fully embarked on the virtualization model, and in particular, for Windows Server 2008. Therefore, sooner or later you will have to explain why you need to deploy your Microsoft Exchange environment on physical servers, whereas the underlying virtualization and hardware technologies allow you to virtualize the environment. In addition, you may generate benefits that you had not previously considered, such as the ability to failover an execution environment from one location to another or to drive further server consolidation for small deployments while keeping server roles apart on individual servers.

In the long term, the technology evolution and the value brought by those innovations will drive the choice of deployment. It is not realistic to embark on all Microsoft Exchange deployments in virtualized environments. However, you should be aware of what is coming your way.

Virtualization products

Describing the architecture of virtualization products is beyond the scope of this book. We recommend Massimo Re Ferre's blog article, "A Brief Architecture Overview of VMware ESX, XEN and MS Viridian." Another interesting article that would familiarize you with this topic is *AnandTech*'s "Hardware Virtualization: The Nuts and Bolts" (http://www.anandtech.com/).

It is obvious that VMware Infrastructure is the clear leader related to market share and functionality as of summer 2008. VMware released its first hypervisor product, VMware ESX, in 2001. The role of Citrix XenServer and Microsoft Hyper-V, the successor to Microsoft Virtual Server, will definitely increase in the upcoming months. Customers will benefit from this completion, as it will increase available functionality and reduce the price of the products.

VMware has a website dedicated to Exchange—"Virtualize Your Exchange Server 2007." This website provides links to storage vendor–specific whitepapers and case studies.

Microsoft support statement

Exchange Server 2003 was supported in a virtual machine running on Microsoft Virtual Server 2005 R2 if several requirements were fulfilled. The details are described in Microsoft Knowledge Base Article 320220. If you want to run Active Directory (AD) domain controllers in a virtual environment, then you must adhere to the requirements documented in the whitepaper "Running Domain Controllers in Virtual Server 2005," and you should read Knowledge Base Article 888794. AD is not happy if you suspend a domain controller for several days or start a domain controller from a previously created snapshot. This problem is more likely to occur in a virtual environment compared to a physical deployment.

Microsoft does not support running Exchange Server 2007 and Exchange Server 2007 SP1 in a virtual environment. This is explicitly stated in the TechNet article, "Exchange Server 2007: Platforms, Editions, and Versions." At the time of this writing, spring 2008, Microsoft had no virtualization product that supported running 64-bit guests. This support statement very likely will change after Microsoft releases Hyper-V. Hyper-V is capable of running 64-bit guests.

What other options do you have? Does Microsoft support running Exchange Server 2007 in a VMware Infrastructure environment? The answer is no.

Microsoft does not test and does not support Microsoft software running in a non-Microsoft hardware virtualization product. This is described in

Microsoft Knowledge Base Article 897615. If you do not have a Premier support contract with Microsoft, then you first have to reproduce the issue in a physical environment. If you have a Premier support contract, then Microsoft will use "commercially reasonable efforts to investigate potential issues."

Virtualization certainly provides benefits, but do they outweigh the increased risk? You might be the first to encounter a situation that has not yet occurred in a physical environment. Do you accept longer downtimes because you first have to reproduce the issue in a physical environment? Is "commercially reasonable efforts" the level of support you desire for your business-critical Exchange environment?

If you purchased VMware software through a server OEM, such as HP, DELL, or Unisys, then the support issue is mitigated because these vendors provide end-to-end support for Microsoft products running on VMware virtual machines. You will have to decide on your own if this completely solves the supportability issue for you.

Backup and restore

A major issue related to virtualizing Exchange mailbox servers is the backup and recovery of Exchange databases. Sadly, this is not highlighted on the websites of solution vendors. Available whitepapers as of spring 2008 only described how Exchange running in a virtual machine can handle the load generated by Microsoft LoadGen. There is no available whitepaper that describe how to back up and restore Exchange databases within a virtual machine. It is not sufficient that a virtual machine can handle the user load; the virtual machine must also be capable of providing a solution that fulfills RTO and RPO.

VMware Consolidated Backup (VCB) is not integrated with Exchange Server 2007. VCB does not dismount the Exchange database to ensure that the backup data are consistent. VCB does not interact with Volume Shadow Copy Services (VSS). There is one product available that claims support for VSS and has a VCB integration module – Vizioncore vRanger Pro.

Using VCB to back up Exchange is comparable to a hot-split snapshot backup. According to the Microsoft Knowledge Base Article 311898, the vendor of the hot-split backup solution is your primary support contact in the event of problems with hot-split backups. It is likely that you even get less support from Microsoft if you have issues with restoring an Exchange database from a VCB-created backup set.

What other options do you have? You can use the streaming API and back up the Exchange Information Store via a LAN connection to a backup server. The backup server then sends the data to a tape device. The throughput that you can achieve with a LAN backup is by far less compared to a backup via a Fibre Channel connection. Using LAN backups heavily reduces the amount of data that can be backed up within a reasonable backup window and restored within your RTO. You should not be surprised if you can only achieve about 50 GB/hour throughput. This is ridiculous compared with the more than 200 GB/hour that you can achieve with a Fibre Channel attached LTO3 tape device on a physical mailbox server. The upcoming support of 10 Gbps network infrastructures might solve this issue.

Another option is to use the streaming backup API to back up the Information Store to disk, and then use VCB afterward to back up the guest including the disk volume storing the backup set. However, this approach has a significant disadvantage. If you have to run a recovery, and the data that you need to restore is not available anymore on the disk volume attached to the guest because it has already been overwritten by subsequent backup jobs, then you have to perform a lengthy recovery procedure. You first have to recover the file that contains the Exchange database backup set.

This should not be the first time that you recognize that the term "back up" is part of VCB but not restore. VCB helps you with running backups; it does not help with restore. The aim of VCB is to offload resource demands during the backup job from the ESX server to a backup proxy server.

For the restore of the backup file, you can use a backup agent running in the virtual machine. The backup data are sent via a LAN to the virtual machine. The throughput will again be slow. Finally, you restore the backup set using the Exchange streaming API. Clearly, this lengthy process is not appropriate for enterprise deployment with a short RTO defined in the SLA.

You might argue that there is a third option. You could use the VMware tools script started by VCB backup to quiescence the Exchange database. VMware Knowledge Base Article 5962168 provides such an example. This is a handcrafted solution for a lab environment (in our point of view). If you use this for a business-critical Exchange deployment, then you should not be surprised if you have to update your resume.

Appropriate use cases

What are appropriate use cases for running Exchange in a virtual environment? If in the future Microsoft changes the support policy, then you can run Exchange as a guest in hardware virtualization solutions without worries about support issues. Until such time, we recommend using virtualization for lab environments. This is what we do on a daily basis—it's a perfect test environment. There are only a few things that you cannot test in a virtual environment, such as VSS-based backups using VSS hardware providers.

Let's assume that you accept the reduced support or that Microsoft has already changed its support statement. What are the most appropriate

Exchange server roles to be deployed in a virtual environment? You have already learned that there are issues with backup and restore of large mailbox servers. If you have strict mailbox quotas and the database size is manageable for LAN backups, then you can consider the mailbox server role. Other interesting options are using Standby Continuous Replication (SCR) to create database copies on a mailbox server running in a remote virtual environment. Once again, this is interesting for smaller deployments; if you have to activate the SCR target, then the virtual machine has to handle the resource requirements of an active mailbox server accessed by clients. For small environments you can create a cost-efficient recovery data center using virtualization.

CAS or HT servers are a better fit compared to mailbox servers. These roles do not hold large amount of data that you have to back up on a daily basis. You might only back up servers with the CAS and HT role after a configuration change. The I/O demands of these roles are rather low compared to a mailbox server. So you can consider the CAS and HT roles.

If your RTO allows it, then you can think about running a small mailbox server in a virtual environment. We do not doubt that a VMware ESX server can provide adequate performance for a mailbox server during a regular user workload. It is the lack of appropriate backup and recovery methods that are the reason why you should think twice about whether it is a good idea to run a large mailbox server in a virtual machine.

Configuration options

Starting with ESX 3.5, you can assign up to 64GB RAM to a single virtual machine and take advantage of up to four-way virtual Symmetric MultiProcessing (SMP). We recommend the documentation about resource management on the VMware website before you rush to use these extreme configurations. Less memory and a single virtual CPU often provide adequate performance for the virtual machine.

VMware has published a whitepaper that documents it is a myth that using Raw Device Mapping (RDM) provides significant benefits from an I/O performance point of view.

High Availability Options for Exchange 2007 Mailbox Server

There have been many changes in the implementation of high-availability functions since Exchange 2007 was introduced. Primarily due to the new software functions of Microsoft Exchange, such as the continuous replication, the typology of a typical high-available Exchange server deployment has changed a lot, because there are now many more options. In this section, we review these options and provide background information to assist you in making the right choice (Table 5-10). This section provides an overview before we dive into the details of Windows Failover Clustering and data replication solutions for Exchange in Chapters 6 and 7.

Table 5-10   *High availability options for server roles*

Server role	Redundant array of independent server	DNS round robin	Network load balancing	Continuous replication
Edge	X	X		
Hub Transport	X	X	X (requires SP1)	
Client Access	X	X	X	
Unified Messaging	X	X		
Mailbox				X

Exchange Server 2003 supports using a single clustered server to host multiple services in addition to the private and public Information Store databases. For example, it was possible to provide mail transport services or Outlook Web Access (OWA) services from a clustered mailbox server. In Exchange Server 2007, only the mailbox server role can be installed on a cluster. If an Exchange Server 2003 deployment, consisting of only one system, the clustered mailbox server, has to be migrated to Exchange Server 2007, then additional machines have to be purchased. In addition to the mailbox cluster, at least one, or for high-availability purposes two, additional servers are required. These servers host the HT and CAS roles.

The following section provides a brief overview of the possible mailbox server architectures that you can use with Exchange Server 2007. The focus is on the question of how you can protect the data stored in a mailbox database. Starting with Exchange Server 2007, Microsoft provides a kind of log file shipping solution to create an additional copy of the database. This log file shipping solution, called continuous replication, is an application built-in solution for data replication. Details about data replication solutions are provided in Chapter 7 and details about failover clustering are explained in Chapter 6.

Single Copy Cluster

High-availability mailbox servers in Exchange Server 2003 deployments are based on clusters. These clusters store Exchange data on a disk volume that is shared between the nodes in the cluster. All nodes of the cluster have potential access to the shared disk volumes. The cluster service governs access to the disks and prevents corruption due to simultaneous access. Microsoft changed the terminology: the Exchange *Virtual Server* in Exchange Server 2003 is now called the *Clustered Mailbox Server* (CMS) in Exchange Server 2007. The cluster architecture using continuous replication is called *Cluster Continuous Replication* (CCR), and the solution using shared disks is called *Single Copy Cluster* (SCC). This highlights the fact that in SCC (Figure 5-20) there is only a single copy of the Exchange database. By default, SCC is a single data center solution. You can combine SCC with a third-party data replication solution, and deploy it as a geographically dispersed configuration across multiple data centers.

Figure 5-20
Single copy cluster

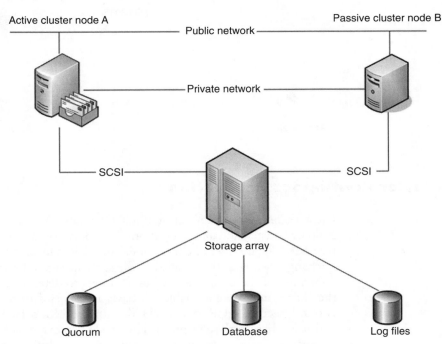

Local Continuous Replication

Local Continuous Replication (LCR) creates a replica of the database on a disk volume visible to the server as a local disk. This replica can be used as a first line of defense if database corruption has been detected. Usually a time-consuming restore from backup media would be necessary. With LCR you can use the replica database for recovery purposes. LCR is a single-server solution aimed at small- to medium-sized deployments within a single data center. Currently there are no architectural limits known so theoretically you could host several thousand mailboxes on a single server with LCR-enabled storage groups, but this was not the design goal of LCR (Figure 5-21).

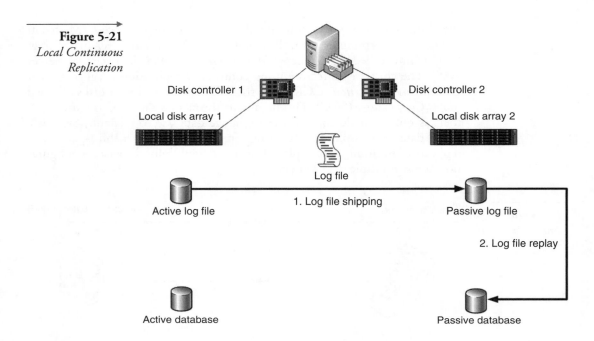

Figure 5-21
Local Continuous Replication

Cluster Continuous Replication

Cluster Continuous Replication (CCR) requires a Majority Node Set (MNS) Failover Cluster, and allows creation of a replica database on the passive cluster node. The number of cluster nodes in CCR is limited to two servers with Exchanger Server 2007 installed. A file share located on a separate server, not a member of the cluster, is used as a witness to determine if the majority of the cluster nodes are available, and as a note board to track which node is currently active. CCR extends LCR with protection from a server failure, and it is Microsoft's solution for large-scale deployments for Enterprise customers. We recommend it as a highly available solution within a single data center (Figure 5-22).

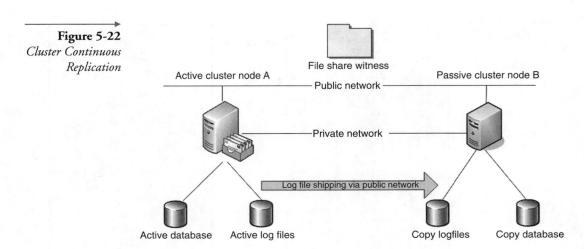

Figure 5-22
Cluster Continuous Replication

Standby Continuous Replication

Initially, Microsoft marketed CCR as the final solution for geographically dispersed deployments. Because of limitations within Windows Server 2003 clustering, and requirements of Exchange Server 2007, Microsoft now recommends Standby Continuous Replication (SCR) for stretched deployments (Figure 5-23).

If you enable a storage group for SCR, Exchange creates a replica of the database on a second server. You can use SCR with single servers and with clustered mailbox servers. You do not have to enable all storage groups of the server for SCR, and you can replicate storage groups of multiple source servers to a single target server. For example, you can use a single mailbox server at a remote data center as a target for the most important storage groups of all production servers in your main data center.

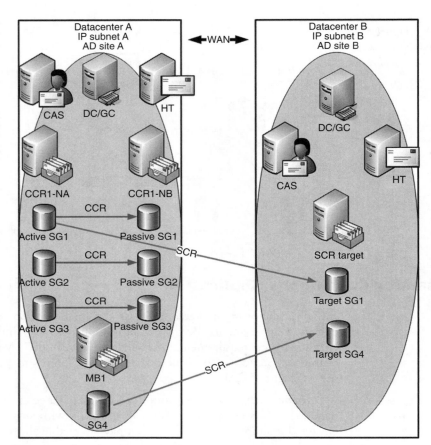

Figure 5-23
*Standby
Continuous
Replication*

6

Exchange Server 2007 Failover Clustering

This chapter provides an introduction to Windows Failover Clustering (WFC) in Windows Server 2003 and Windows Server 2008, followed by a discussion of Exchange Server 2007 Clustered Mailbox Servers. In the past clustering was called Microsoft *Cluster Service* or Windows *Server Clustering*. Starting with Exchange Server 2007 and Windows Server 2008, Microsoft renamed it WFC. The creation, usage, and management of clusters in Windows Server 2008 have been made easier.

Introduction to Windows Failover Clustering

The majority of Exchange Server 2003 deployments are using standard servers; consequently, many Exchange administrators have limited exposure to clustering technologies. There were many valid reasons why running Exchange on a single server was the preferred solution. With the introduction of Cluster Continuous Replication (CCR) in Exchange Server 2007, the pros and cons for clustering Exchange may have to be reevaluated. Therefore, Exchange administrators should have at least a basic knowledge of the WFC concept to understand the various cluster architectures used by the two implementation alternatives for a Clustered Mailbox Server (CMS) in Exchange Server 2007, CCR, and Single Copy Cluster (SCC).

Typically, a clustered deployment is considered if you want to increase the availability of your messaging service, or if your business continuity requirements demand a geographically dispersed deployment with relatively short recovery time objectives. The following sections provide an introduction to the WFC architecture, including the hardware and software requirements for building a CMS.

The mailbox server role is the only role in Exchange Server 2007 that can be deployed on a cluster. In Exchange Server 2003, a cluster could provide additional Exchange services such as Outlook Web Access or transport services. In Exchange Server 2007, these services are provided by the Client Access Server (CAS) and Hub Transport (HT) server role. Both roles cannot be installed on a WFC. A server with the HT and another with the CAS role must be online in the same AD site; otherwise, users cannot send and receive emails or connect to their mailbox using Internet protocols. *It does not make sense to deploy the mailbox server role on a cluster using leading edge technology, and at the same time have a single server holding the HT and CAS roles.* The minimal configuration is four Exchange servers: two clustered nodes for the mailbox server and two multirole servers with both the HT and CAS role installed. Additionally, you need two Active Directory (AD) global catalog servers.

Windows Clustering Solutions

Clusters are multiple computers that appear to users as a single highly available system. The concept was introduced by Digital Equipment Corporation (DEC) in the 1980s with the VAXCluster. The objective was a "no single point of failure" configuration. If one component fails, another component takes over the responsibility, and the service offered by the cluster should not be affected from an end-user point of view. This principle is very important if you design a WFC.

Microsoft provides three clustering solutions. The first, referred to as WFC, supports the failover of a service or application to another node in the cluster if the node currently hosting the application fails. WFC can be used to provide highly available mailbox servers.

Another form of clustering in Windows is called Network Load Balancing (NLB). The service provided by a NLB cluster is accessed using the Internet protocol (IP). You can use NLB to combine multiple web servers to a web farm. End users cannot differentiate which server of the web farm is processing their request. NLB increases the scalability of a service. If the user load increases, you can scale the NLB solution by adding more servers to the NLB cluster. In Windows Server 2003, NLB is horizontally scalable up to 32 nodes. NLB is suitable for services that are state-less. Alternative solutions are DNS round robin or hardware-based load balancers such as the BIG-IP series from F5 Networks. An issue with NLB is that traditionally it has not been aware of session state, which made it a very poor candidate for front-end servers in Exchange Server 2003. Only the CAS role of an Exchange Server 2007 Release to Manufacture (RTM) deployment could take advantage of NLB. Starting with Exchange Server 2007 SP1, you can use NLB for the HT role. Now you can provide highly available inbound SMTP connections for line-of-business applications that submit mails to Exchange.

Microsoft introduced the Windows Compute Cluster Server (CCS) with Windows Server 2003. A CCS combines multiple-commodity x64 computers to provide a High-Performance Computing (HPC) solution. The aim of CCS is to provide supercomputing power to the workgroup level in a familiar Windows-based environment. The target market for CCS is, for example, computer-aided engineering or geoscience used in performing simulation and modeling tasks. The successor to CCS is called Windows HPC Server 2008. Exchange does not require this kind of number-crunching performance and has more IO-related demands. CCS cannot be used for Exchange deployments.

Availability Goals

The main reason for deploying WFC is to minimize application downtime. The following events can cause application/service unavailability:

- Planned downtime for installing software patches, upgrading application versions, or performing hardware maintenance.

- Unplanned downtime because of server hardware failures, infrastructure failures such as power outages, or natural disasters including floods or earthquakes.

WFC can provide reduced application downtime for maintenance tasks compared to standard server deployments. Maintenance tasks including installation of patches can be performed on the passive cluster node without affecting end users connected to the application running on the active node. It has to be noted that some service packs require taking the clustered application offline for specific upgrades. For example, upgrading Exchange Server 2003 SP1 to SP2 requires that Exchange is taken offline for a few minutes. This timeframe is far shorter compared to the outage on a single server, but the upgrade is not fully transparent to end users. See Microsoft Knowledge Base Article 328839 for information about applying Exchange Server 2003 hot fixes.

The same is true for Exchange Server 2007. You upgrade the Exchange binaries on the passive node, and then the CMS on the active node is stopped. Starting from this point, Exchange clients cannot connect to their mailboxes on the Exchange server. The CMS is then moved to the passive node and then the CMS is upgraded by running *Setup /upgradecms*. After this step, the CMS comes online again and users can connect to their mailbox. The CMS is only offline during failover and until *Setup /upgradecms* finishes, but there *is* a minimal time that the CMS is actually unavailable.

To give you an idea of the duration, for a CCR server with about 8000 mailboxes in a customer environment, it was 15 minutes. An assumption of no downtime for the cluster would be incorrect.

Clustering protects against unplanned downtime caused by hardware failures and certain application errors. If the motherboard of a cluster node fails, then WFC will automatically (after fail over to another node in the cluster) attempt to restart applications on one of the remaining cluster nodes.

You have to realize that clustering is not an insurance against all kinds of errors. It is important to be aware of cluster limitations and requirements. Clustering increases solution complexity, and therefore requires additional skills for designing, deploying, operating, and maintaining the solution. This is especially true for clusters a using shared storage architecture, because disk volumes must be made available to all cluster nodes, and WFC will control the ownership of the disk volumes. For these kinds of clusters, you must have at least basic Fibre Channel or iSCSI knowledge. If a new hot fix introduces a bug in a database application, then this software bug will affect database health, independent of whether the application is running on a single server or a cluster. Initiating a failover to another cluster node will likely not help because the database may still be corrupt; the other cluster nodes are running the same application and even possibly access the same database file. Clustering does not remove the necessity to be prepared for a recovery. You still have to run regular backups. In fact, you need different recovery procedures for Exchange installed on single servers and clustered Exchange servers. Do not forget the dependencies of the applications that you have deployed on the cluster. Exchange depends on infrastructure services like Domain Name System (DNS), AD, or network routers. Even if you have a highly available Exchange mailbox server running on a cluster, unplanned downtime of these infrastructure services can prevent your end users from accessing their mailboxes. You have to keep the complete picture in mind if you want to provide a highly available messaging service. Figure 6-1 highlights that WFC can only be used in a very small area of your Exchange Server 2007 deployment. Can you spot the small circle?

To summarize and realistically set your expectations: The main benefit of WFC is that it can help to reduce planned downtime. It may prevent unplanned downtime caused by a server failure. You should not expect reduced downtime caused by bugs in application software, and you should not forget the infrastructure services that Exchange depends on. Be prepared to acquire additional skill sets if you want to use clustering. Finally, you should consider that you will now have to maintain additional hosts. For a two-node active/passive cluster, you double the host count. This is something you should think about when you estimate the associated labor time.

Figure 6-1
WFC and server roles

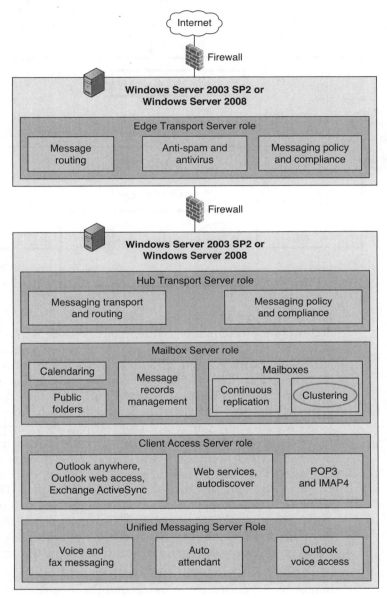

Introduction to the Failover Clustering Architecture

Figure 6-2 shows an example of a WFC. The following sections explain the components displayed in the picture. The description is mainly based on Windows Server 2003. Later sections in this chapter highlight the changes introduced with Windows Server 2008.

Figure 6-2   *Failover clustering architecture*

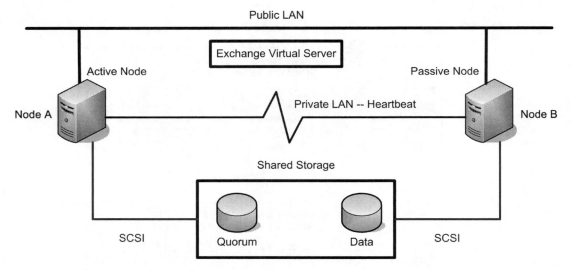

Cluster Nodes

A cluster consists of multiple cluster nodes. A node is usually a physical computer system, although you can use virtualization solutions like Microsoft Virtual Server or VMware ESX to create nodes to form a Windows cluster. Some virtualization solutions allow you to combine virtual and physical nodes to form a cluster. For production deployments, physical nodes are definitely preferred and virtual nodes should only be considered as an alternative for self-study purposes. In an active/passive cluster model, only the active servers provide services that are accessed by end users. For example, in a two-node active/passive cluster, only one server provides a service to end users. The other node is in a "standby" mode, and waits until it has to take over the responsibility of the currently active node. The cluster resource manager constantly monitors the active server; when it recognizes that the active server fails, WFC brings the resources/application online on the passive node and starts to serve user requests from this node. Up to that point the server is passive and does not provide any services to end users.

Microsoft Knowledge Base Article 288778 summarizes the maximum number of supported cluster nodes and the required shared disk configuration. With Windows Server 2003, up to 8 nodes can be part of a cluster. In Windows Serer 2008, the maximum number of cluster nodes was increased to 16, but you can only use up to 8 nodes in an Exchange Server 2007 SCC. CCR is limited to a two-node active/passive cluster. Various combinations of active nodes and passive nodes can be used—for example, one active and one passive in a two-node cluster, or two active nodes and one passive node in a three-node cluster. The ratio of active to passive nodes depends on the number of passive nodes you can afford, and the number of failed nodes you want to be prepared for. You can use a feature called cluster group affinity to control the failover behavior in a cluster with more than two nodes. This allows you to prevent a cluster group/application to fail over to a node that is already running an instance of the same application.

In a two-node active/active configuration, all cluster nodes are active and provide services to end users. For an Exchange cluster, this would mean that the Exchange services would be running on node A and node B. There would be two Exchange servers from an end-user point of view, hosting various mailboxes at the same time. This model was initially supported with Exchange Server 2000. Because of memory fragmentation issues, this model was not recommended by Microsoft with Exchange Server 2003. With Exchange Server 2007 it is no longer supported, although there should be no memory fragmentation issues with the 64-bit version of Windows Server 2003/Exchange Server 2007.

In Exchange Server 2007, the number of CMS instances is always less than the number of physical nodes in a cluster. There must be at least one passive cluster node that can take over a CMS instance from a failed cluster node. This is referred to as an "N + m" configuration. "N" is the number of cluster nodes with Exchange running, and "m" is the number of cluster nodes that can be used for Exchange, but do not run its services. The maximum number of active cluster nodes/CMS is seven with Exchange Server 2007.

It is a best practice to use an Exchange cluster only for Exchange and to not provide any additional services from the same cluster. If you spend a significant amount of money on having a highly available Exchange server, then it is a bad idea to increase the solution complexity and the likelihood of a failure by hosting additional services on the Exchange cluster. This is still true even for simple services like print or file services. An Exchange cluster should be an Exchange cluster and nothing else. If you cannot afford a passive node, then you should not deploy a cluster!

For SCC on Windows Server 2003, all cluster nodes must be listed in the cluster solution category of the Microsoft Windows Server Catalog. If the SCC is geographically dispersed, then the nodes must be listed on the geographically dispersed cluster solution category. For CCR, the nodes are not mandatorily listed in the cluster or geographically dispersed cluster solution category; being part of the server catalog is sufficient. This significantly reduces the hardware costs for CCR compared to SCC.

Microsoft Knowledge Base Article 309395 describes this support policy and contains hyperlinks to the hardware compatibility list and Windows server catalog. The support policy for third-party components used by the cluster is described in Microsoft Knowledge Base Article 814607. A subsequent section in this chapter explains that the support policy for WFC with Windows Server 2008 has been significantly simplified.

You must use the Enterprise edition of the Windows operating system on all nodes of the cluster. All nodes of the cluster must run either the 32-bit or the 64-bit version of the Windows operating system. All cluster nodes must use the same drive letter and file system path configuration for the Windows boot and system files, and for the Exchange binaries. Only the Enterprise edition of Exchange Server 2007 supports SCC and CCR.

Virtual Server

End users access the service provided by the cluster using a virtual server identity. The virtual server identity has a unique IP address and a network name that is different from the IP address and network name of the individual cluster nodes. The IP address and network name is registered in DNS. From an end-user point of view, whether the service is provided by a single computer or a cluster is transparent, and which cluster node is currently providing the service does not matter. If the node that is currently providing a service fails, then the cluster initiates a failover of the service to a remaining node. How long a failover takes depends on several factors like the application or user workload. Usually a failover does not require more than a few minutes. During the failover, the services provided by the clusters may appear to be offline to end users. In the case of Exchange, to minimize the impact of these short outage periods, end users can use Outlook in cached mode. In the past it was necessary to create the Exchange virtual server manually within *cluadmin.exe*. With Exchange Server 2007, you use the setup program to create the virtual server, which is now called CMS. The fact that you now can automate the setup of the Exchange cluster is a major step forward.

Cluster Resources and Cluster Group

A cluster manages the resources that an application requires, and the resources managed by a cluster are called cluster resources. There are several resource types available by default, and cluster-aware applications like Exchange provide their own resource types. Examples of these cluster resources are a physical disk resource, an IP address resource, or the Exchange-System Attendant resource. A cluster can provide multiple services at the same time to end users. Usually the services provided by one application are combined in a so-called cluster group. This group combines all resources that are required by the application. During a failover, the cluster group is moved as a whole from one cluster node to the other.

It is possible from a technical point of view to host different applications on a single cluster. For example, one cluster can provide file services and Web services at the same time. In Exchange deployments, dedicated Exchange clusters that do not host any other applications at the same time are common. With Exchange Server 2007, Microsoft does not support hosting other applications such as Active Directory (AD) domain services on the same cluster.

Each cluster has a default group known as the *cluster group* (Figure 6-3). This group is created during the cluster setup, and it hosts the cluster resources necessary to form the cluster.

Figure 6-3   *Default cluster group*

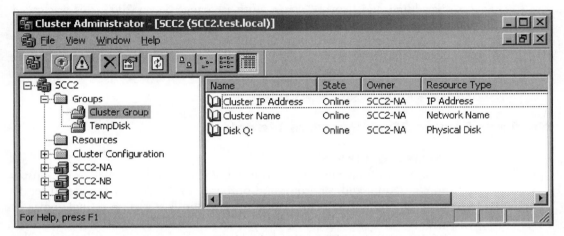

A standard cluster installation creates a cluster group with the following resources:

- Cluster IP address
- Cluster name
- Quorum disk Q:

The cluster IP address and network name comprise the identity of the cluster virtual server. This virtual server is not accessed by end users; it is only used by administrators for management purposes. Disk Q is a physical disk resource that stores configuration information about the cluster. This disk is called the *quorum disk*. The quorum is also used to track the cluster node that currently owns a clustered application.

What is a quorum? Wikipedia defines the quorum as the minimum number of members of a deliberative body necessary to conduct the business of that group. If fewer members are present, the group is unable to vote.

WFC implements a share-nothing model, and only one cluster node can own and access a resource at a time. In a so-called "shared quorum" deployment, all cluster nodes can potentially access these shared disks, but the WFC enforces that at a given point in time only one node has access to a disk.

This model makes ensuring the integrity of a clustered resource like a database easier. The share-nothing model is also the reason why WFC cannot provide load-balanced access to a clustered resource. Cluster solutions that implement a shared resource model require a distributed lock manager that coordinates parallel access to a shared resource. This is more difficult to implement, but allows load-balanced access to a clustered resource.

An Exchange cluster has a separate cluster group with the cluster resources that are required by Exchange. This cluster group has its own identity with an IP address and network name. With Exchange Server 2003, this was called the Exchange Virtual Server (EVS). In Exchange Server 2007, this is called the CMS. The network name of the CMS cannot be longer than 15 characters. Exchange Server 2007 installs the following three application-specific cluster resources: Exchange System Attendant, Exchange Information Store, and Storage Group/Database.

Windows Server 2003 Quorum Models

Shared Quorum

As explained previously, the quorum disk is used to keep track of the cluster configuration, and for arbitration purposes, to decide which node currently owns an application. This critical information is stored on a single physical disk resource, the quorum disk in Figure 6-4. Although the physical disk resource can be implemented by a hardware RAID set, it is still the Achilles heel of the cluster. If the Storage Area Network (SAN) that provides the quorum disk fails, then the complete cluster solution is unavailable. You can design a redundant SAN to minimize the likelihood of this failure, but if you lose the data center with the storage array, the cluster fails.

A cluster using a single shared physical disk as a quorum resource is not an adequate solution if you want to be protected against a fire, flood, or earthquake that can destroy your data center. For this kind of requirement, it is better to have an additional copy of the quorum disk. This can be achieved using third-party storage replication solutions. An example of such a solution is HP's StorageWorks Cluster Extension software, or EMC SRDF Cluster Enabler, previously called GeoSpan.

Majority Node Set

Microsoft implemented the Majority Node Set (MNS) quorum model (Figure 6-5) to overcome the limitation of a "single quorum instance." Each node in a MNS cluster stores the cluster configuration on a local disk instead of a shared cluster disk. The data that describe the cluster configuration are synchronized between the cluster nodes using the Server Message Block (SMB) file share protocol. Therefore, an MNS cluster does not require access to a shared disk array connected to a storage network using the Fibre

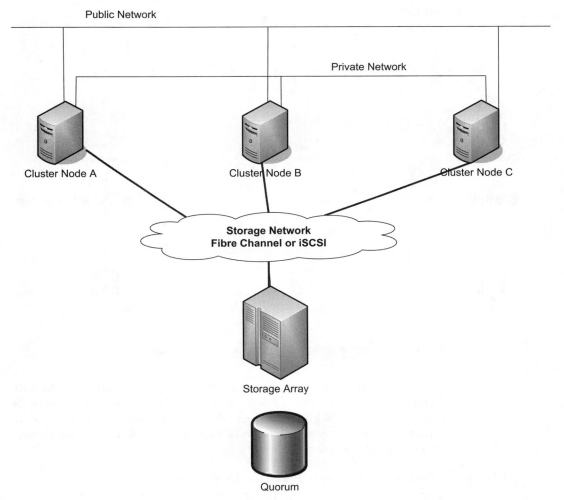

Figure 6-4 *Shared quorum cluster*

Channel or iSCSI protocol. Only TCP/IP network communication is required between the cluster nodes. MNS clusters are better suited for geographically dispersed deployments.

An important characteristic of MNS is that the majority of nodes must be running and be able to communicate with each other; otherwise, WFC will shut down the cluster service. In a shared quorum model, one node of a two-node cluster can be switched off and the remaining node will continue to provide services to end users. In a two-node MNS configuration, WFC will shut down the cluster service as soon as one node is switched off, although the other node is still running. In the MNS configuration, forming a cluster

Figure 6-5   *Majority Node Set*

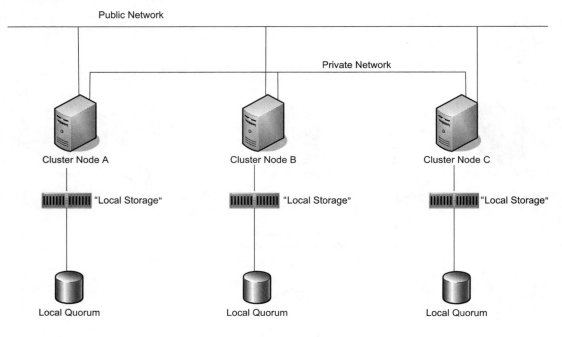

with at least three nodes is recommended, and the total number of nodes should be an odd number. Each node in the MNS configuration counts as a single vote when WFC determines whether the majority of the nodes are available. Table 6-1 shows the allowed number of node failures for clusters with up to eight nodes.

Table 6-1   *Number of cluster nodes by allowed number of node failures*

Number of cluster nodes	Allowed number of node failures
2	0 (1 with FSW)
3	1
4	1
5	2
6	2
7	3
8	3

Microsoft introduced the possibility of using a file share as an alternative vote. The File Share Witness (FSW) is described in Microsoft Knowledge Base Article 921181 and on Microsoft TechNet in the section on CCR. The FSW is a file share that is used instead of the third node to determine whether the majority of cluster nodes are up and running. The file share has to be located on a server that is not a member of the cluster. Microsoft recommends hosting the file share on a server holding the Hub Transport (HT) role for a clustered Exchange deployment. The reason for this recommendation is that it should be a server where the Exchange staff has administrative control.

The file server is not part of the cluster and does not communicate with the cluster nodes. The FSW is not used to store the complete cluster configuration; it is used only as a note board to track the cluster node currently controlling the cluster. If the MNS cluster has more than two nodes, then the FSW is ignored in Windows Server 2003. The active cluster node takes control of the note board. If the cluster nodes cannot communicate with each other because all networks enabled for cluster communication are unavailable, then each node will try to get control over the note board.

If Node A was active before the heartbeat network failed, then Node B tries to take control of the note board. But this attempt will fail because Node A still locks the note board. This prevents Node B from starting its cluster resources and reduces the likelihood of the so-called split brain syndrome. A split brain syndrome occurs if both cluster nodes think that the other node is dead and each independently starts the application. In this case, two instances of the application are running and both applications can access the same data, which may lead to data corruption.

The FSW also helps to reduce the likelihood of the so-called partition-in-time problem. Let's assume that the cluster is online on Node A and Node B is switched off. During this time, it is possible that the cluster state information is changed or the configuration of a cluster resource is modified. Node A stops running and Node B comes back online. Node B tries to start the cluster but this will be unsuccessful. The cluster service on Node B recognizes that the note board states Node A was the last active cluster node. The cluster service on Node B decides to stop and wait until Node A comes back online. If Node B would be able to start the cluster, then Node B would run the cluster with outdated state information. Node B is not aware of the changes made to the cluster while it was offline. The operating system of Node B will automatically restart the cluster service after 1 minute, by default. The cluster service will then perform the check again. You will find a similar message in the event viewer system log (Figure 6-6).

A single server can host multiple file shares that are used as witnesses for separate MNS clusters. You can use a clustered file server to host the shares on a highly available server. To reemphasize: The shares are used by separate Exchange clusters.

Figure 6-6

Partition in time

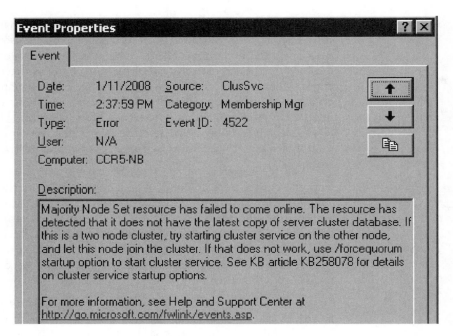

The file share cannot be a DFS share because the share is used for arbitration purposes, and DFS would make the share available through multiple servers. If multiple cluster nodes would think that they acquired the FSW, this would lead to a split brain syndrome.

The location of the server hosting the FSW is an important topic in a geographically dispersed configuration. Hosting the FSW in a third data center has the advantage that an outage of a data center cannot affect the active cluster node and the FSW at the same time. This topic is further described in the article "Placement of the File Share Witness (FSW) on a Geographically Dispersed CCR Cluster" on the Exchange team blog. If you only have two data centers then we recommend hosting the FSW within the data center where the CMS will be online most of the time. This reduces the risk that an outage of the network link between the two data centers will bring the CMS down.

Initially, Microsoft recommended using a Canonical Name (CNAME) instead of the Fully Qualified Domain Name (FQDN) of the file server to access the share. The idea was to update the alias in DNS if the original server hosting the FSW was unavailable. It turned out that in large and complex DNS topologies, this procedure is prone to unpredictable behavior such as replication latencies. Reconfiguring the cluster quorum to use a different Uniform Resource Locator (URL) pointing to another file share is recommended. For a detailed description of this topic, see the Microsoft

Exchange Team Blog article, "New File Share Witness and Force Quorum Guidance for Stretched Exchange 2007 Clusters."

Another issue emerges when using a CNAME for the file server. If the file server is running Windows Server 2003, then you have to disable strict name checking on the server providing the share.

```
REG_DWORD
HKEY_LOCAL_MACHINE\System\CurrentControlSet\Services\
LanmanServer\Parameters\DisableStrictNameChecking = 1
```

Otherwise, you will see the error message "System error 52 has occurred. A duplicate name exists on the network." This problem is described in Microsoft Knowledge Base Article 281308. If the FSW is hosted on a server running Windows Server 2008, this registry modification is not necessary.

If fewer than the majority of nodes are available after a disaster, you can start the cluster service on a remaining node with the parameter */forcequorum:<ListOfRemainingNodes>*. This is explained in the Microsoft Knowledge Base Article 258078.

By default, the cluster service verifies the health of the file share every 4 minutes. This interval can be configured with the MNSFileShareCheckInterval property. If a cluster node loses communication with the other cluster node, the node will try to obtain the "vote" of the FSW. The cluster service, by default, waits 4 seconds before it tries to obtain the FSW. This delay can be configured with the property *MNSFileShareDelay*.

You can use the script shown in Figure 6-7 to create the share on the HT. You should verify that the file share is accessible from both cluster nodes using the cluster service account.

Figure 6-7
Creating file share witness for Windows Server 2003

```
REM This script creates the file share that is used by the MNS cluster
as file share witness
Echo On
REM The recommended name is MNS_FSW_<ClusterNetworkName>
set FileSharePath=C:\MNS_FSW_CCR1
set ShareName=MNS_FSW_CCR1
set ClusterServiceAccount=e12.local\cl-svc
mkdir %FileSharePath%
REM no space between ',' and FULL!
net share %ShareName%=%FileSharePath%
/GRANT:%ClusterServiceAccount%,FULL
cacls %FileSharePath% /G BUILTIN\Administrators:F
%ClusterServiceAccount%:F
```

New Quorum Models in Windows Server 2008

In Windows Server 2008, Microsoft provided a new quorum model that is a combination of the shared quorum architecture and MNS. The disk volume hosting the quorum resource is no longer a single point of failure. The new architecture is very similar to an MNS configuration that takes advantage of an FSW.

Figure 6-8 shows a screenshot of the quorum configuration wizard that allows you to configure the components that will receive a vote. The votes will be counted when determining whether the majority of votes are available.

Figure 6-8   *Select Quorum Configuration on Windows Server 2008*

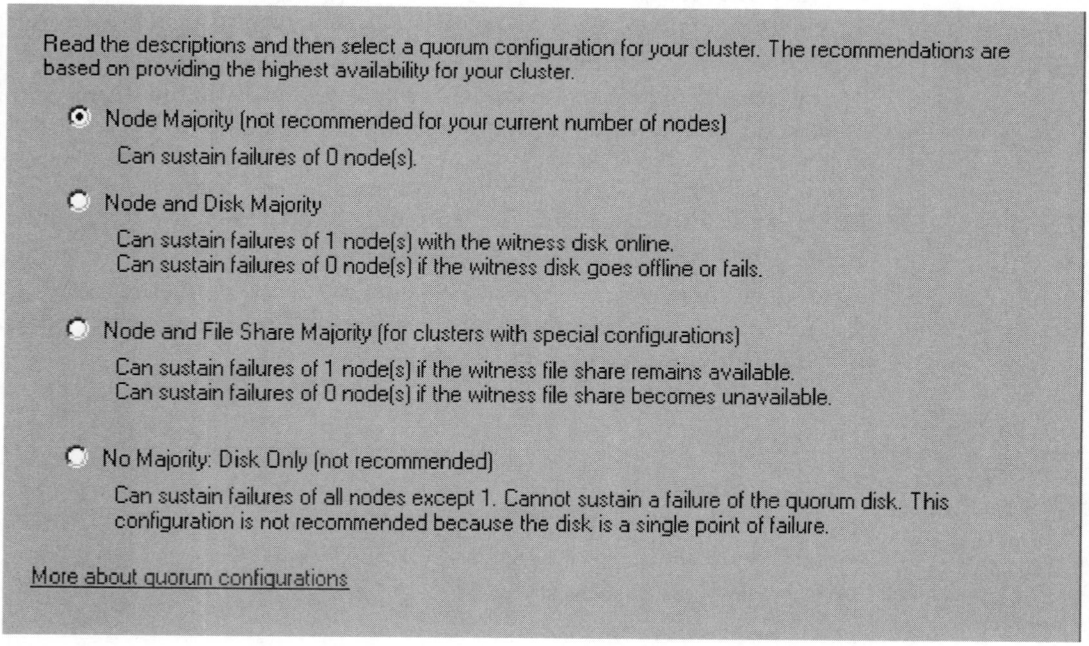

Read the descriptions and then select a quorum configuration for your cluster. The recommendations are based on providing the highest availability for your cluster.

○ Node Majority (not recommended for your current number of nodes)
   Can sustain failures of 0 node(s).

○ Node and Disk Majority
   Can sustain failures of 1 node(s) with the witness disk online.
   Can sustain failures of 0 node(s) if the witness disk goes offline or fails.

○ Node and File Share Majority (for clusters with special configurations)
   Can sustain failures of 1 node(s) if the witness file share remains available.
   Can sustain failures of 0 node(s) if the witness file share becomes unavailable.

○ No Majority: Disk Only (not recommended)
   Can sustain failures of all nodes except 1. Cannot sustain a failure of the quorum disk. This configuration is not recommended because the disk is a single point of failure.

More about quorum configurations

You can assign a vote to the following components:

- Cluster node
- Shared disk
- File share

No Majority Disk Only (not recommended)

Figure 6-9 shows a configuration that is identical to the legacy quorum architecture. Only the quorum disk gets a vote. The cluster stays up even if one node is down and only one node has access to the disk. The new terminology for the shared disk volume hosting the quorum is "Witness Disk."

Figure 6-9
Witness disk

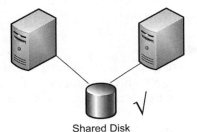

Shared Disk

By default, no drive letter is assigned to the witness disk, that is, no $Q:\backslash$. It is possible to map the volume, for example, to drive $Q:\backslash$ if you prefer the old configuration. You can change the drive letter assignment within the Failover Cluster Management user interface. Not assigning a drive letter to the witness disk reduces the likelihood that it is accidentally modified because it shows up in the Explorer. The disk must have at least 512MB capacity, and it have to be formatted with NTFS. Windows Server 2008 automatically selects the smallest disk that fulfills these requirements as the witness disk.

The "No Majority Disk Only" configuration is not recommended. You should use one of the following configurations instead.

Node Majority

Figure 6-10 is directly comparable to the MNS configuration in Windows Server 2003. Only the cluster nodes get a vote. You need a solution that enables the cluster nodes to have access to the "same data." This can be a third-party data replication solution like EMC SRDF, or an application integrated solution like Exchange Server 2007 CCR.

Figure 6-10
Node majority

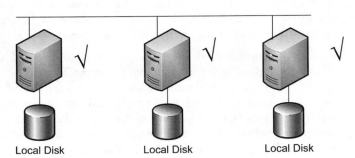

Local Disk   Local Disk   Local Disk

The allowed number of failed nodes provided in Table 6-1 is enforced for this quorum model as well. It is important to keep Table 6-1 in mind when performing maintenance tasks on a cluster. You should not be surprised when the cluster goes down automatically because you switched off too many cluster nodes.

Windows Server 2008 automatically selects this configuration if the number of nodes in the cluster is odd.

Nodes and Disk Majority

Figure 6-11 is the new enhanced shared quorum configuration. Windows Server 2008 automatically selects this configuration if the number of nodes in the cluster is even and you have a shared storage device.

Figure 6-11
Node and disk majority

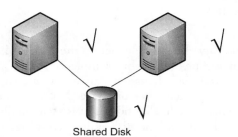

Shared Disk

Both cluster nodes and the disk witness get a vote. The cluster service stays up even if the disk witness is not accessible from both nodes because the majority of votes are still available. You need to consider whether the application that is hosted on this configuration can really take advantage of this.

Let's assume this is your Exchange mailbox server, and the Exchange databases and log files are stored on a physical disk in the same storage array that hosts the quorum disk. If you lost access to the storage array, the cluster service is still up and running in Windows Server 2008, but do your users have any benefit from it? They cannot access their mailboxes because there is only a single instance of the Exchange database available, which is stored on the lost storage array. The single instance of the Exchange database and log files is still a disadvantage of the SCC configuration.

The recommended quorum model is nodes and disk majority on Windows Server 2008 for an Exchange Server 2007 SCC. The disk majority quorum configuration should be used with a local shared storage configuration; it should not be used with a replicated storage configuration. If you use a third-party storage replication solution, you should ask the storage replication vendor about the recommended configuration. It is very likely that the vendor will suggest the node and file share majority configuration.

Node and File Share Majority

Figure 6-12 is directly comparable to the configuration of Exchange Server 2007 CCR on a Windows Server 2003 MNS cluster. This configuration is the recommended configuration for a CCR deployment on Windows Server 2008. The node and file share majority configuration is also recommended for geographically dispersed deployments with a storage replication solution.

Figure 6-12
Node and file share majority

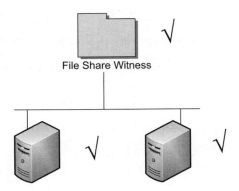

File Share Witness

An FSW is used to determine whether the majority of nodes are up and running. The FSW allows surviving the loss of a single node in a two-node cluster setup. This enables you to perform maintenance tasks on one node while the CMS on the other node is still online.

The information provided in the Windows Server 2003 section about the FSW is also applicable to Windows Server 2008. The only major difference is that Windows Server 2008 does not use an AD user account as the cluster service account. The cluster service, which is using the *LocalSystem* account, impersonates as the cluster computer account when it tries to access the FSW. Therefore, you have to provide the cluster computer account access permission to the share. This complicates the cluster setup procedure. You cannot set up the FSW before you have created the cluster. The cluster computer account is created in AD during the cluster setup and does not exist previously.

For a related description of this procedure, see the TechNet section, "How to Configure the Node and File Share Majority Quorum." In Windows Server 2003, the FSW can only be used with up to two nodes. In Windows Server 2008, this limitation does not exist, and you can use the FSW with more than two nodes. Exchange Server 2007 does not take advantage of this, and it is still not possible to have more than a single CMS instance in CCR, but you can use an FSW in a multinode SCC deployment.

In the Windows Server 2003 section about the FSW, we explained how to start the cluster service using the *option /forcequorum*. For example,

```
REM This script creates the file share that is used by the MNS cluster
as file share witness

REM This script is for a cluster running Windows Server 2008

Echo On

REM The recommended name is FSW_<ClusterNetworkName>

set FileSharePath=C:\MNS_FSW_CCR4

set ShareName=MNS_FSW_CCR4

REM In Windows Server 2008 the cluster runs under the Local System
account

REM The cluster service impersonates as the cluster computer account
when it accesses the FSW

REM You have to add "$" at the end of the computer account

set ClusterComputerAccount=test.local\CCR4$

REM ClusterAdmins is a group / user that has permission to change the
cluster configuration

set ClusterAdmins=test.local\Administrator

mkdir %FileSharePath%

REM no space between ',' and FULL!

net share %ShareName%=%FileSharePath%
/GRANT:%ClusterComputerAccount%,FULL /GRANT:%ClusterAdmins%,FULL

cacls %FileSharePath% /G BUILTIN\Administrators:F
%ClusterComputerAccount%:F
```

this is necessary in a geographically dispersed deployment if you lost the site with the majority of the cluster nodes. You can use the same procedure with Windows Server 2008. The Microsoft Knowledge Base Article 947713 describes the implications of this option in Windows Server 2008.

Network Configuration

Best practices for configuring cluster networks are documented on Windows Server TechCenter and Microsoft Knowledge Base Article 258750. Figure 6-14 shows that each cluster node must have at least two network cards. One card is used for public network access. This is the connection that the clients use to access the CMS, and the CMS uses this network to access other Exchange servers, DNS servers, and DC/GCs. One network card is dedicated to cluster internal communication. This is often referred to as a private LAN or cluster heartbeat. The private and public network must not have a component in common that can cause both networks to fail simultaneously. Therefore, using a single network interface card (NIC) with two ports to connect to both the public and private network is not supported, nor is using a single network switch for both the public and the private network. In a geographically dispersed deployment, setting up only a single

Figure 6-14 *Network configuration*

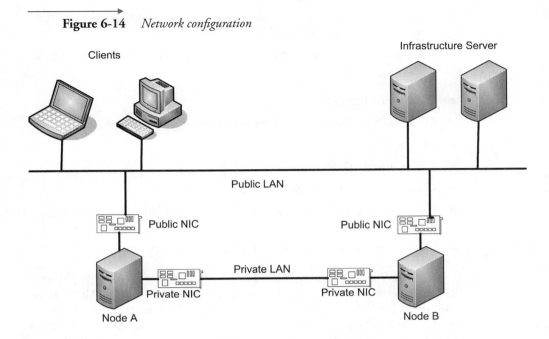

VLAN is therefore not supported. In this instance, both cluster networks, the public and private network, share a single component that would be a single point of failure.

For a two-node active/passive cluster, you need the following IP addresses:

- Node A public IP
- Node A private IP
- Node B public IP
- Node B private IP
- Windows Cluster IP—This IP address/network name is used for administrative purposes only.
- Exchange CMS IP—This is the IP address/network name used for the Outlook MAPI profile and for the Exchange server-to-server communication

Using static IP addresses for the public and private network is recommended. In Windows Server 2008, using DHCP-assigned IP addresses is supported, but the documentation provided by Microsoft states that using static addresses or unlimited lease durations for Exchange Server 2007 deployments is still recommended.

The public network requires the following components to be enabled/configured:

- Client for Microsoft Networks
- File and Print Sharing for Microsoft Networks
- Internet Protocol (TCP/IP)
- Assign a static IP address.
- Configure a default gateway for this network.
- Configure a DNS server and specify that the IP address is registered in DNS.
- Do *not* disable NetBIOS over TCP/IP on the WINS tab.

Microsoft clearly documented in Knowledge Base article 837391 that Exchange Server 2000 and Exchange Server 2003 require NetBIOS name resolution. NetBIOS name resolution is equivalent to using a Windows Internet Name Service (WINS) server or broadcasting name resolution requests. Many administrators hoped that they would not need WINS servers, and thus could completely disable support for NetBIOS with Exchange Server 2007. This is not the case. Microsoft TechNet states in the section, "How to Configure Network Connections for a Single Copy Cluster," that you have to enable NetBIOS on the public network of an Exchange cluster. For CCR, enabling NetBIOS on the public network and on all redundant networks used for log file shipping is also required.

The private network has the following requirements:

- Internet Protocol (TCP/IP)
- Assign a static IP address
- Leave the DNS server address blank and specify that the IP address is not registered in DNS.
- Do not configure a default gateway. The private network is a non-routed subnet.
- Disable NetBIOS over TCP/IP on the WINS tab.

It is explicitly noted in the above-referenced Microsoft website that the private and public networks must use distinct subnets. The private network must be a nonrouted subnet from the Windows operating system point of view on Windows Server 2003. For example, if the private IP address of Node A is 192.168.1.1 with a subnet mask of 255.255.255.0, then the private IP address of Node B must use an IP address of the same Class C subnet, such as 192.168.1.2. It is not possible to use, for example, 172.16.1.1 as a private IP for Node B in this instance. This would require that the operating system must forward heartbeat packets to a router that connects the 192.168.1.0/24 network with the 172.16.0.0/16 network.

But you can set up a VLAN for the private network. A VLAN hides the fact that the IP frames actually travel over a routed network such as a WLAN intersite link. The Windows Server 2003 requirement of a nonrouted subnet for the cluster internal communication is a significant obstacle that may prevent the deployment of geographically dispersed clusters with this operating system release. Network administrators may be reluctant to configure a VLAN over a WAN intersite link that connects two data centers. The VLAN would enable broadcast traffic to consume expensive WAN bandwidth.

Windows Server 2008 removes this limitation and supports routed subnets between cluster nodes. The point-to-point round trip latency must be less than 500 milliseconds. Microsoft Knowledge Base Article 921181 describes a fix that enables you to configure WFC on Windows Server 2003 to be more tolerant of missed heartbeats, which may be required in geographically dispersed deployments. By default, a heartbeat packet is sent every 1.2 seconds.

If you configure a cluster with a shared quorum model, a file-sharing protocol should not be selected in the private network. For a Windows Server 2003 MNS cluster, you should enable the file sharing protocol on the private network. Windows Server 2003 MNS clusters use a file-sharing protocol to replicate the cluster configuration between the cluster nodes. If only the public network has the file sharing protocol enabled, the public network would become a single point of failure.

The passive node in a CCR deployment is pulling transaction log files from the active node via the TCP/IP network. The active node exposes the transaction log files of each storage group via a file share *activenode*\ *StorageGroupGUID$*. The Exchange Server 2007 RTM build is not capable of using the private network for log file shipping. Starting with Exchange Server 2007 SP1, you can configure the network to be used for log file shipping. It is likely that there will be deployments that use three network connections for CCR: the public network for client and infrastructure server access, an additional log file shipping network, and a dedicated network for cluster internal communications. Additional details about this topic are provided in Chapter 7.

Network card priority has been defined within the Windows operating system as follows:

- Public network
- Private network
- Remote access connections

Otherwise the operating system will first try to reach a client or an infrastructure server via the private network. In Windows Server 2003 deployments, we have seen many instances of an incorrect binding order as the root cause of cluster related problems.

You can use network adapter teaming for the public interface, but be aware that the hardware vendor is responsible for supporting this configuration. Teaming is not supported for the private network. You can configure multiple independent network ports for cluster internal communication, but it is not supported to team private network ports. You should not team together two ports that are provided by the same network card. This network card would become a single point of failure.

You should regularly verify whether Microsoft has changed the recommended network configuration settings by checking the TechNet section, "How to Configure Network Connections for Cluster Continuous Replication" for updates.

Active Directory and DNS Requirements

Windows Server 2003 uses an AD user account as a service account to run the cluster service. All cluster nodes must use the same service account, and all cluster nodes must be members of the same AD domain. In Windows Server 2003, the public IP addresses of the cluster nodes must be within a nonrouted IP subnet. In this way, the cluster nodes will belong to the same AD site. Using separate service accounts for each cluster is considered a best practice; otherwise, a disabled user account would affect all clusters at once.

The cluster service account must be a domain user account that is a member of the local Administrators group on all cluster nodes. The user should not be a member of the Domain Admins group for security reasons. The cluster service account does not need any Exchange organization permission. See the Exchange Server 2007 section titled, "Permission Frequently Asked Question," on Microsoft TechNet for additional details.

In Windows Server 2008, the cluster does not use an AD user account as a service account; the cluster service runs under the Local System account of the cluster nodes. Another change is that clusters running Windows Server 2008, by default, use Kerberos authentication and not NT LAN manager (NTLM) authentication, which was the case in Windows Server 2003. These are two examples of the increased security in Windows Server 2008. The security model used by Windows Server 2008 clusters is described in Microsoft Knowledge Base Article 947049.

All nodes of an Exchange Server 2007 cluster must be members of the same AD domain, and the same AD site. This is the case, regardless of whether Exchange is installed on Windows Server 2003 or Windows Server 2008. Exchange Server 2007 requires that all cluster nodes are members of the same AD site. CCR only talks to servers holding the HT role if they are located in the same AD site. After a lossy failover, CCR would not be able to take advantage of messages stored in the transport dumpster of HT servers in AD site A if the cluster Node B would be a member of AD site B. This is the reason why Exchange requires that all nodes of the cluster are within the same AD site, although Windows Server 2008 would support nodes of a cluster that are assigned to different AD sites.

The ideal configuration is an AD integrated DNS zone, allowing secure dynamic updates for DNS records. Otherwise you have to create a DNS A record for each cluster node and the CMS.

Storage Configuration

The SCC stores the Exchange database and log files on shared physical disks. With CCR you can host the database and log file on disk volumes that appear as local disks to the computer. It is not required that the disk volumes are provided by a Fibre Channel or iSCSI attached storage array. CCR does not store Exchange data on shared physical disks; each cluster node has its own local copy of the Exchange database and log file. This is a huge advantage of CCR that enables reduction of the hardware cost of a clustered Exchange server. This will increase the number of Exchange clusters deployed in Small and Medium Businesses.

The rest of this section describes topics related to physical disk resources in a SCC; they are not relevant for a CCR deployment.

With Windows Server 2008, you can only use disk storage accessed via Serial Attached SCSI (SAS), iSCSI, or Fibre Channel. Support for parallel SCSI, which was used in legacy cluster-in-a-box solutions, has been removed. SAS provides better performance and especially scalability compared to parallel SCSI.

In the past, Windows Server 2003 only supported a disk that uses the Master Boot Record (MBR) format. Support for the GUID Partition Table (GPT) disk partitioning scheme was added to Windows Server 2003 clusters via hot fix 919117. Windows Server 2008 provides support for GPT disks out of the box. This allows you to use disks and partitions with multiple terabyte capacity, but do not forget how long CHKDSK.EXE will run on such a disk. Another benefit of GPT disks is the built-in redundancy on how information about the partition table is stored. GPT stores multiple copies of the partition table and uses Cyclical Redundancy Check (CRC) to protect the partition table. The increased reliability of GPT disks is the reason why you should consider to use GPT disks instead of disks with the MBR format on Windows Server 2008. Chapter 4 provides additional details about this topic.

Windows Server 2008 changed the way that shared disk volumes are reserved. It now uses SCSI-3 Persistent Reservation. You have to verify whether the storage device drivers are compatible with this new mechanism. The cluster validation wizard explained in the next section is able to perform this check. The advantage of SCSI-3 Persistent Reservation is that Windows Server 2008 does not use SCSI bus resets to break reservations. Windows Server 2003 is using SCSI bus resets, which has the disadvantage that it impacts all disks connected to this bus. Only with Storport drivers was it possible to initiate a target reset instead of a bus reset.

WFC is using disk signatures to identify each physical disk resource. Microsoft Knowledge Base Article 309186 explains how a disk is reserved and how WFC in Windows Server 2003 brings a disk online. It was important to back up the signatures of clustered disks because you need this information during recovery of a failed disk volume. You can run an automated system recovery (ASR) backup to save this information, or use the command CONFDISK.EXE from the Windows Server 2003 resource kit. In Windows Server 2003, the tool CLUSTERRECOVERY.EXE is used to replace a failed physical disk. Knowledge Base Articles 305793 and 280425 provide information related to replacing failed disk volumes in Windows Server 2003. The procedure was rather complicated. Luckily, this is simplified in Windows Server 2008. Windows Server 2008 additionally uses SCSI inquiry data to identify a disk volume. Now WFC can "self-heal" certain disk-related issues if one of the attributes that identifies a disk is unavailable. Additionally, the Failover Cluster Management GUI provides a Repair button on the properties tab of a disk volume that lets you replace a failed disk volume with a new volume exposed to all cluster nodes. Reading and modifying the signature of a disk has been integrated into DISKPART.EXE in Windows Server 2008. The command *uniqueid disk* enables you to read and write the signature. It is also possible to use the disk signature as an identifier when you create a new clustered disk resource.

```
CLUSTER . resource "DISK X:" /priv DiskSignature=
<disk_signature>
```

Microsoft improved the maintenance mode of shared clustered disks to provide better support for hardware-based creation of Volume Shadow Copy snapshots. During maintenance mode, the cluster service provides another application with temporary exclusive access to a shared disk. For example, this is used by a Volume Shadow Copy Services (VSS)—based backup product that swaps the disk volumes assigned to a mount point or driver letter during a recovery.

In Windows Server 2003, you had to power down all nodes of the cluster but one before you could install the cluster service. This was necessary to prevent multiple cluster nodes from accessing the shared physical disk at the same time, which could cause file system corruptions. Windows Server 2008 made enhancements to the partition manager, and the Virtual Disk

Service (VDS) includes a SAN policy that allows keeping all disks offline on the SCSI bus, which is different from the one the operating system disk is connected to. This new feature allows having all nodes up and running while you install WFC—another example of how Windows Server 2008 has simplified clustering.

Several Microsoft webcasts are available on WFC in Windows Server 2008, and in particular, storage-related changes. After reading this section, you should be aware that the shared disks used by an SCC are the reason for the additional complexity of a CMS using a shared storage architecture.

Cluster Validation

Microsoft recognized that several support calls were related to configuration mistakes. Therefore, Microsoft introduced the Cluster Configuration Validation Wizard (*ClusPrep*). You can use this tool to validate the configuration of Windows Server 2003 clusters. *Clusprep* is available as a download from Microsoft. *Clusprep* and another tool called ClusDiag are explained in an article on MSExchange.org.

Starting with Windows Server 2008, the installation and configuration of a WFC are greatly simplified. One reason for this enhanced user experience is the integration of an updated version of the cluster validation wizard (Figure 6-15) in the Failover Cluster Management GUI. This wizard is run before you create the cluster to perform an inventory on all cluster nodes and to validate the cluster nodes configuration. This allows you to identify

Figure 6-15   *Validate a Configuration Wizard*

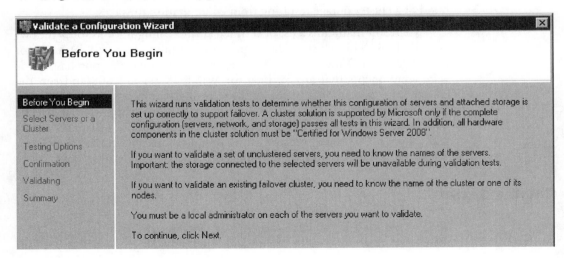

configuration errors before you run into issues during the cluster setup. Figure 6-16 shows that the validation compromises several storage-related tests including verification of whether the attached storage array supports SCSI-3 Persistent Reservation.

Figure 6-16
Storage validation

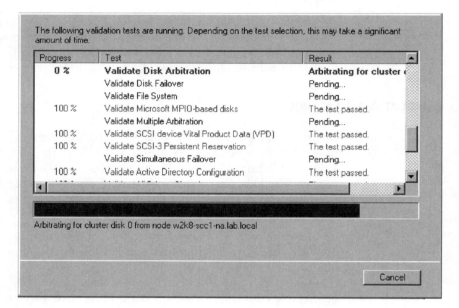

You can also run the validation wizard after you deploy the cluster in production. Including the cluster validation in your proactive maintenance schedule will allow you to determine, for example, that a hot fix was installed on Node A but not on Node B. This tool will significantly reduce the likelihood of a cluster outage resulting from configuration mistakes.

Microsoft maintains a list of certified cluster configurations for Windows Server 2003. This cluster Hardware Compatibility List (HCL) will not be provided for Windows Server 2008; instead, you have to purchase hardware components that are certified for Windows Server 2008 and run the cluster validate tool on your own. If the configuration passes the validation test, the configuration is supported by Microsoft. See Microsoft Knowledge Base Article 943984 for more details. Hardware vendors will likely maintain a list on their own websites with configurations that passed the cluster validation test to promote their products.

Cluster Setup

You can set up a WFC with the GUI or perform the setup from the command line. A setup from the command line is advantageous in that you can script the process. An automated installation procedure is a requirement for an agile infrastructure.

Figure 6-17 creates a two-node Windows Server 2008 cluster. Initially, the cluster is configured in the same way as the node majority quorum mode. This configuration is not recommended with two nodes (Figure 6-18).

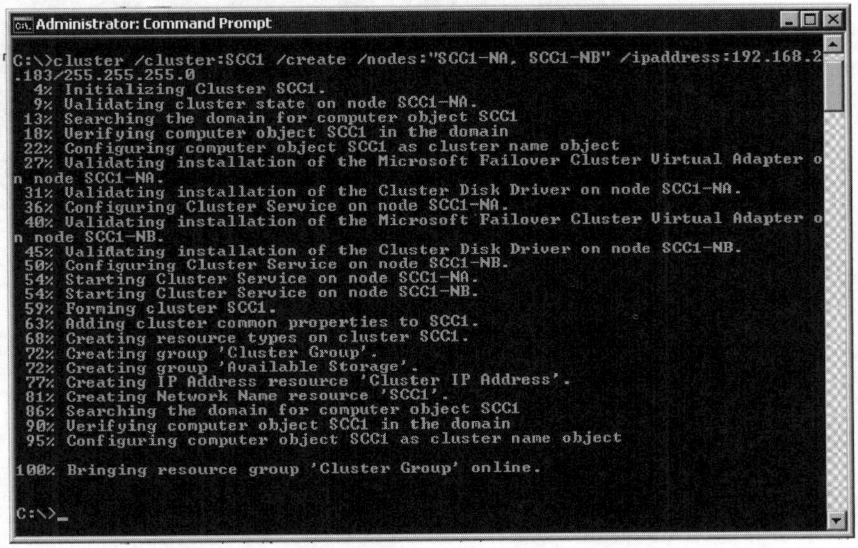

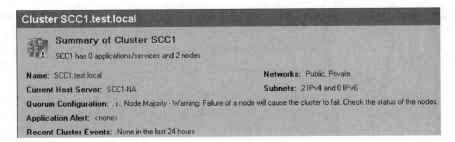

Figure 6-17
Create cluster command line

Figure 6-18
Node majority warning

In CCR, you configure an FSW, and for SCC, you change the configuration to a node and disk majority. This configuration change can be done from within the GUI with the wizard shown in Figure 6-8, or via the command line (Figure 6-19).

In Windows Server 2003, you have to configure the type of traffic the cluster sends over available network connections. Table 6-2 describes the available options.

In an SCC configuration, you usually configure one network as a cluster internal network and the other network as mixed. If you configure one network

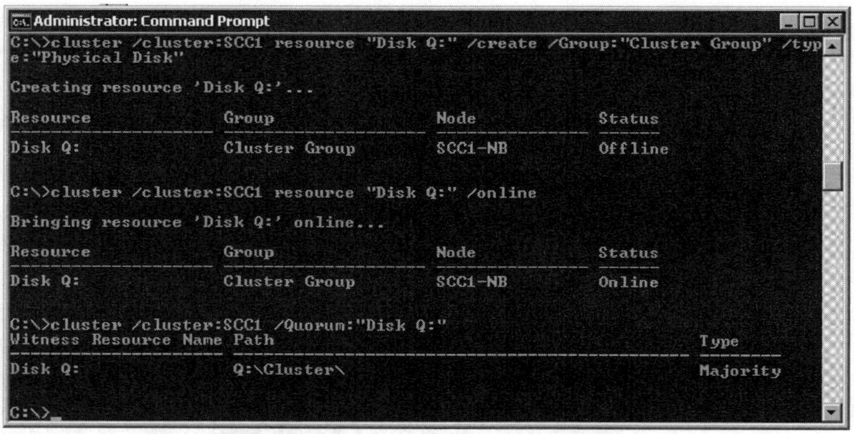

Figure 6-19
Configure disk majority

Table 6-2 *Cluster network options in Windows Server 2003*

Option	Description
Client Access only/public network	The network is only used for external communication and not for cluster internal communication.
Internal cluster communication only/ private network	The network is only used for cluster internal communication but not for communication with clients or other infrastructure servers. Cluster internal communication is often referred to as *heartbeat.*
All communications/mixed	The network is used for communication with clients and for heartbeat traffic.

as Client Access only and the other network as internal communication only, then the private network would be a single point of failure. Therefore, you should allow the cluster to use the "public" network for heartbeat traffic when the private network fails. Figure 6-20 shows the related section of a script.

Figure 6-20
Cluster network configuration

```
REM Role=1 --> private communication; Role=2 --> public communication
Role=3 --> mixed

C:\WINDOWS\system32\cluster /cluster:%ClusterName% net "Private" /prop
role=1

C:\WINDOWS\system32\cluster /cluster:%ClusterName% net "Public" /prop
role=3

REM Network priority for Cluster internal communication

C:\WINDOWS\system32\cluster /cluster:%ClusterName%
/setnetpri:"Private","Public"
```

For CCR, the setup is more complicated. In Exchange Server 2007 RTM, only the network that is used for client communication can be used for log file shipping; log file shipping does not occur over the private network. In Exchange Server 2007 SP1, you can use multiple networks for log file shipping. If you want to enable a network for log file shipping, you have to configure the network as mixed in Windows Server 2003.

In Windows Server 2008, the network configuration has been simplified. A cluster in Windows Server 2008 creates a virtual adapter on each cluster node called "Microsoft Failover Cluster Virtual Adapter." To see this adapter, execute *IPCONFIG.EXE /all*. The adapter is used by the fault-tolerant network driver NETFT.SYS, which replaces CLUSNET.SYS of Windows Server 2003. NETFT.SYS has its own internal routing table and ensures connectivity between cluster nodes (Table 6-3).

Table 6-3   *Cluster network options in Windows Server 2008*

Option	Description
Allow the cluster to use this network	The network is only used for cluster internal communication, but not for communication with clients.
Allow the cluster to use this network and allow clients to connect through this network	The network is used for communication with clients and for heartbeat traffic. This was referred to as a mixed network in Windows Server 2003.
Do not allow the cluster to use this network	If you select this option, then the cluster will not use the network for internal communication, and clients will not connect to the network. You can use this option for management networks.

Windows Server 2008 by default enables all networks for cluster use. When a network has a default gateway configured, Windows Server 2008 automatically enables this network for Client Access. This is comparable to a mixed network in Windows Server 2003. The cluster sends heartbeat packets across all cluster-enabled networks, and you cannot define a priority of the networks. In Windows Server 2008, execute the commands shown in Figure 6-20 is not necessary.

The cluster setup of Windows Server 2008 labels the networks *Cluster Network <n>*. You can use the commands in Figure 6-21 to rename the networks with more meaningful labels.

Figure 6-21
Renaming cluster network

```
C:\WINDOWS\system32\cluster network "Cluster Network 1" /rename:Public
C:\WINDOWS\system32\cluster network "Cluster Network 2" /rename:Private
```

Cluster Maintenance

If the cluster setup fails or if you have to troubleshoot the cluster at a later stage, you can take advantage of the information stored in the cluster hive of the registry. The cluster has a so-called cluster database, which is a set of keys stored at *HKLM\Cluster* on each cluster node. The cluster service synchronizes the information among the nodes and stores an additional copy of the database on the quorum resource. See the Microsoft Developer Network for additional information about the cluster API and the cluster database.

You have to consider WFC in your backup and recovery procedures. A detailed description of this topic is beyond the scope of this book; we will provide two helpful pointers only. For WFC running Windows Server 2003, see the article, "Server Clusters: Backup and Recovery Best Practices for Windows Server 2003". Windows Server 2008 simplified backup and recovery of clusters by integrating it into the VSS framework. This is described in the blog post, "Backing up and Recovering the Failover Cluster Configuration Database," on the Microsoft Clustering team blog.

Exchange Server 2007 Clustered Mailbox Servers

Single Copy Cluster

In previous Exchange Server releases, most CMSs used the shared storage architecture, and had only a single copy of the Exchange mailbox and public folder databases. This architecture is known as SCC in Exchange Server 2007. Figure 6-22 provides a visual representation of a SCC.

You can start with your SCC self-study in a small virtual machine—based lab using an iSCSI target software as the storage solution. If you want to use Windows Server 2008 as the operating system, the iSCSI target software has to support SCSI-3 Persistent Reservations. RocketDivision's StartWind and the Microsoft iSCSI Target are one of the available options. The open source iSCSI Enterprise Target currently does not support SCSI-3 Persistent Reservations, so you cannot use it for a WFC running Windows Server 2008, but it works fine with Windows Server 2003.

In Exchange Server 2003, you had to use a third-party solution for a geographically dispersed deployment. The third-party solution was responsible for storage replication, and a synchronous replication solution was highly recommended for supportability reasons. See Microsoft Knowledge Base Article 895847 for additional details about the support boundaries of multisite deployments.

Data replication was usually implemented using the functions of a high-end storage array in a SAN. You can, for example, use the EMC Symmetrix

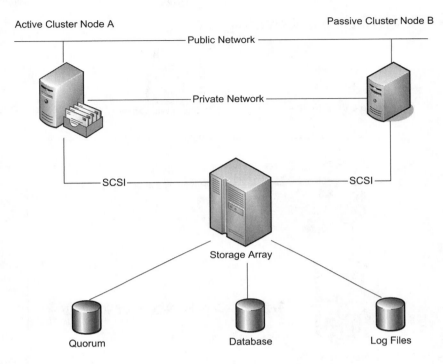

Figure 6-22
Single copy cluster

Remote Data Facility (SRDF) or Veritas Storage Foundation for Windows for this kind of deployment. Note that data replication uses the SAN environment to send data from Array A to Array B. Data do not travel over the Ethernet network connecting the cluster nodes. The replication uses a dedicated storage connection between the data centers via a "Dark Fibre" connection. These stretched deployments are often based on the Majority Node Set (MNS) cluster architecture.

It is very important to highlight that the design shown in Figure 6-23 is still an SCC. Exchange data on storage Array A and Array B are synchronously mirrored. The databases always have identical content, and the log file volume always stores identical log files on storage Array A and array B. This is true as well when problems occur! If a database has a logical corruption, then the databases on storage Array A and Array B are damaged. If you have a physical failure of the RAID set used to store the database on Array A, then you might be lucky and the database file hosted on Array B may be unaffected and still healthy, but there is no guarantee despite what the sales rep may tell you. Chapter 7 provides additional details about data replication solutions.

The OEM clustering solution determines how the disk volumes hosted on storage Arrays A and B are presented to the cluster nodes. Some solutions present the disk volumes on Array A to the active and passive cluster nodes. There are other stretched cluster solutions available that present the disk

Figure 6-23   *Stretched SCC using MNS*

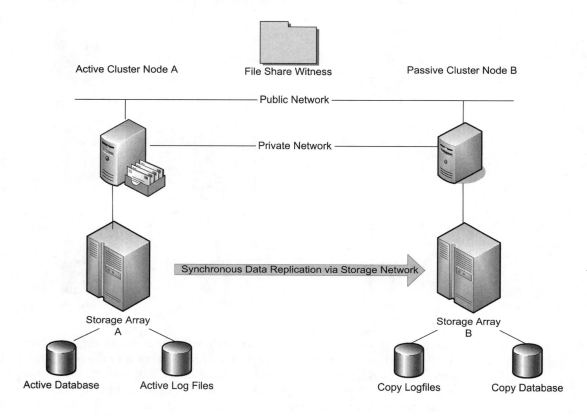

volumes of Array A only to the local cluster node, and the volumes of Array B only to the cluster node in the remote data center. The solution vendor's implementation affects the cluster failover procedure. The failover procedure in a stretched deployment is far more complex than a configuration within a local data center.

WFC is only able to failover the cluster server nodes. By default, WFC is not able to perform a storage array failover including reversing the direction of the data replication. Initially, this was always a manual procedure where the Exchange staff had to collaborate and rely on colleagues working in the storage department. This is not an optimal condition for a fast failover in a disaster situation. It is not the best solution if you first have to set up a meeting or telephone conference with another team, especially if you are trying to fulfill service-level agreements related to a site failover. Therefore, some vendors enhanced the WFC solution and integrated their own logic into the clustering service to automate the storage failover procedure. For example, HP provides the HP StorageWorks Cluster Extension

(CLX) software for the EVA and XP arrays. CLX enables a transparent storage array failover, which is seamlessly integrated into the Microsoft cluster management tools. Figure 6-24 shows the CLX resource within the cluster administrator. A similar WFC solution, SRDF Cluster Enabler, is available from EMC.

Figure 6-24
CLX cluster resource

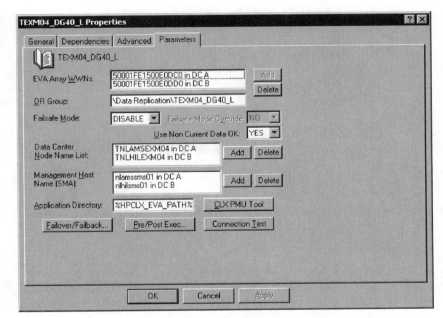

Cluster Continuous Replication

With the release of Exchange Server 2007, Microsoft now provides an application built-in data replication solution that can be used for a stretched deployment. The main benefit of CCR is that it is an application-aware replication, and the solution is provided by the application vendor. No third-party solution is required for the data replication. The data replication implemented by Exchange Server 2007 is based on a log file shipping mechanism, which has been used in database applications for years.

Figure 6-25 shows an illustration of a CCR deployment. The CCR uses the MNS architecture; you can create only a single CMS instance per cluster. It is possible to use three cluster nodes to set up a CCR, but typically two nodes are used and a FSW hosted on the server holding the HT role.

Continuous replication ships the closed log files via the TCP/IP network. Data replication in Exchange Server 2007 continuous replication does not occur via a storage network. This has the disadvantage that the Ethernet

Figure 6-25   *Cluster continuous replication*

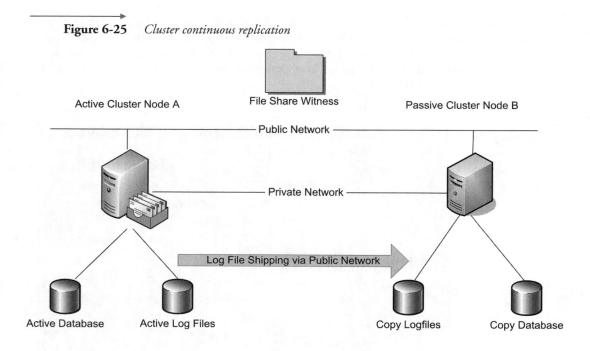

infrastructure must be capable of handling the additional load; otherwise, log file shipping will affect client traffic. Continuous replication puts additional load on the Exchange servers because the server is responsible for data replication. Data replication is not performed by the storage array controller.

One significant advantage of CCR over a SCC implementation is that when a database is logically corrupted, then the database on storage Array A is damaged, but because of the log file checking and verification built into CCR (during log shipping), the probability of a corruption on Array B is slim to none. In the event of a physical failure of the RAID set that is used to store the database on Array A, you will be able to fail over to the database file hosted on storage Array B, which would most likely be unaffected.

Chapter 7 describes Exchange Server 2007 continuous replication in detail.

For Microsoft's point of view about CCR and SCC, see the TechNet section titled, "Advantages of CCR over SCC."

Installing Exchange on Clusters

In the following sections, we assume that your AD is already prepared for Exchange Server 2007 and you previously installed other Exchange 2007 servers.

In Exchange Server 2003, a clustered Microsoft Distributed Transaction Coordinator (MSDTC) had to be configured before you could set up Exchange on a cluster. MSDTC was also required for workflow applications and during the installation of service packs. This is described in the article, "The Story of the MSDTC Resource and Exchange 200x Cluster Servers" on the Exchange Team Blog. In Exchange Server 2007, this requirement has been removed. Do not configure this resource for Exchange Server 2007.

In Windows Server 2003, the MSDTC resource requires a clustered disk resource and this would complicate the CCR configuration. CCR uses local disks and not shared physical disks. Adding a clustered disk resource to a CCR configuration would greatly complicate the deployment, management, and failover of the cluster. In SCC you have shared disk resources, but as Exchange Server 2007 does not need the MSDTC, creating an MSDTC resource in the cluster is *not* recommended. Adding an MSDTC resource to an SCC would increase complexity and the likelihood of failures. You should change the startup type of the MSDTC service from automatic to manual in the SERVICES.MSC.

You can perform the installation of the Exchange binaries and create the CMS using the command line or the GUI. The setup wizard is appropriate for your first Exchange cluster deployment in a lab, but for a production deployment, using a scripted setup is recommended. The following scripts can be used for installing Exchange on Windows Server 2003 and Windows Server 2008.

```
Setup /mode:install /roles:mailbox
```

The previous command installs the Exchange binaries on the hard disk. The next step is to create a new CMS. If you create the CMS on the first node before you have installed the Exchange binaries on the second node, you will encounter the following error messages in the event viewer from the second node: "The Cluster Resource Monitor could not load the DLL exres. dll for resource type Microsoft Exchange Database Instance."

```
Setup /newcms /cmsname:<CMSnetworkName>
/cmsipaddress:<IPaddress>
```

This step is comparable to creating the Exchange System Attendant resource of an Exchange Server 2003 cluster using the CLUADMIN.EXE GUI. With Exchange 2007 this can be done from the command line, and thus implemented from a script. In the past, it was not possible to automate this step, as it was always a manual procedure. The *CMSnetworkName* can contain up to 15 characters only.

Figure 6-26 shows the Exchange configuration in the cluster administration tool.

Figure 6-26   *Exchange Cluster Group*

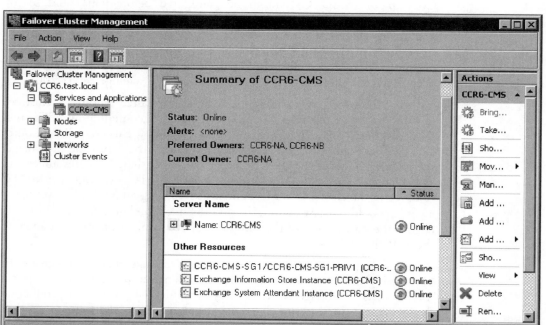

SETUP.EXE /newcms created a new cluster group with the name that you specified for the CMS network name. It is important to note that you cannot create a cluster group with this name in advanced. Setup will fail if a group with the same name already exists. This is especially important if you set up a SCC.

SCC stores the Exchange database and log files on shared physical disks. You have to create a temporary cluster group with the physical disk resources that Exchange will use before you run *SETUP.EXE /newcms*. This temporary cluster group cannot have the same name that you are going to specify as the CMS network name. As a second step, you will move the physical disk resources from the temporary cluster group to the group created by the Exchange setup program.

Installation of the Exchange binaries for the mailbox server role adds the computer account of both cluster nodes to the following security groups:

```
CN=Exchange Servers, OU=Microsoft Exchange Security
Groups, DC=<Domain>, DC=<Domain>
```

```
CN=Exchange Install Domain Servers, CN=Microsoft
Exchange System Objects, DC=<Domain>,
DC=<Domain>
```

The Exchange CMS configuration is stored in AD in the following hierarchy:

```
CN=<CMSnetworkName>, CN=Servers, CN=Exchange
Administrative Group (FYDIBOHF23SPDLT),
CN=Administrative Groups, CN=<ExchangeOrganization>,
CN=Microsoft Exchange, CN=Services, CN=Configuration,
DC=<Domain>, DC=<Domain>
```

The entries in the AD configuration container are created during *Setup /newcms*.

Log files of the installation procedure are automatically created in the directory *C:\ExchangeSetupLogs*. You can use the log files for troubleshooting purposes.

You now have an Exchange cluster with the default configuration and without any custom optimizations. PowerShell cmdlets are your best friend to adjust the storage group/database configuration of the cluster and perform additional optimizations.

Uninstall

During your self-study, you might encounter issues with the configuration and want to start again from scratch. If so, you can use the following steps to uninstall the Exchange cluster. Although this section provides scripts, it is likely that you will have to execute the commands manually. It is unlikely that *uninstall* will run smoothly if your configuration is corrupt. Therefore, consider the scripts as a reference of the necessary steps.

You have to move all mailboxes from the CMS before you can remove the CMS.

```
Setup /removeCMS /CMSName:<CMSnetworkName>
```

You can uninstall the Exchange binaries from both nodes after you have removed the CMS. It is also possible to remove just one node from the CMS by uninstalling the binaries from this node.

```
Setup /mode:uninstall
```

Uninstalling the binaries does not delete the old database and log files. You should remove these files, including the Exchange program directory, before you perform a new Exchange installation. For a production deployment, reinstalling Exchange is *not* recommended. Formatting the hard disk, reinstalling Windows, and reinstalling Exchange will create a more predictable configuration.

You can use the script in Figure 6-27 to remove the passive node from the cluster and finally uninstall the cluster by evicting the last node.

Figure 6-27
Cluster uninstall

```
REM Uninstall the cluster
Echo On
set ClusterName=CCR1
set DefaultClusterGroup="Cluster Group"
set ClusterNodeA=CCR1-NODEA
set ClusterNodeB=CCR1-NODEB
C:\WINDOWS\system32\cluster GROUP %DefaultClusterGroup%
/MOVETO:%ClusterNodeA%
C:\WINDOWS\system32\cluster /cluster:%ClusterName% node %ClusterNodeB%
/STOP
C:\WINDOWS\system32\cluster /cluster:%ClusterName% node %ClusterNodeB%
/EVICT
PAUSE
C:\WINDOWS\system32\cluster /cluster:%ClusterName% node %ClusterNodeA%
/EVICT
REM C:\WINDOWS\system32\cluster /cluster:%ClusterName% node
%ClusterNodeA% /FORCECLEANUP
```

If the uninstall procedure fails, you have to perform a manual cleanup. For example, deregistering the Exchange cluster resources may be necessary (Figure 6-28).

Figure 6-28
Delete Exchange resources

```
cluster CCR1 resourcetype "Microsoft Exchange DAV Server Instance"
/delete /type
cluster CCR1 resourcetype "Microsoft Exchange Database Instance"
/delete /type
cluster CCR1 resourcetype "Microsoft Exchange Information Store"
/delete /type
cluster CCR1 resourcetype "Microsoft Exchange System Attendant" /delete
/type
```

You might have to delete Exchange-related registry entries, which are located in *HKLM\Software\Microsoft\Exchange*. You have to check if the cleanup of the objects in the AD was successful. Verify whether the computer account objects were removed from the Exchange security groups, and whether the CMS objects were removed from the AD configuration container. It is obvious that deleting registry keys or using ADSIEDIT to remove entries in AD is something you should avoid in a production environment. Deleting registry keys can have an adverse affect on the operation of the Windows environment and thereby should only be conducted by an expert.

Management of Exchange Clusters

You can manage the Exchange cluster using various tools. The WFC can be managed from the command line using CLUSTER.EXE or the Failover Cluster Management GUI. The Exchange Management Shell (EMS) or the Exchange Management Console (EMC) also provide cluster-specific management functions. Which tool should you use to manage an Exchange cluster? This issue is discussed in the article, "Exchange Tools vs. Cluster Tools: What's the Deal?" on the Exchange Team Blog.

It is possible to initiate a failover from Node A to Node B with the Windows cluster management tools, but Microsoft prefers that you use the Exchange-specific tools for most tasks. The EMS and EMC verify the health of data replication to the passive cluster node before it initiates the failover in a CCR deployment. The WFC tools do not perform these safety checks. Additionally, the Exchange tools allow you to specify a reason for the failover to the passive node. The requirement to use the PowerShell commands and not integrate these health checks into the standard WFC tools has disadvantages. Application-specific skills are necessary to manage the Exchange cluster. It is very likely that only a few staff members will be available after a disaster renders one data center unavailable, and all applications used by the company have to be brought online in the second data center. If the administrators could use the same commands for all applications running on WFC, the business continuity procedure would be simplified and the likelihood of a successful and timely failover would be much higher.

A manual move of the CMS from the active node to another node is called *handoff* in Exchange Server 2007 terminology.

```
Move-ClusteredMailboxServer -Identity:<CMSName>
-targetmachine:<NodeName>-movecomment:<Reason>
```

You should move the CMS to another cluster node if you want to shut down the active cluster node because the Windows shutdown function is not Exchange-aware. If all other nodes in the cluster are already down, you should stop the CMS using the *Stop-ClusteredMailboxServer* PowerShell cmdlet before you shut down the active cluster node.

```
Stop-ClusteredMailboxServer -Identity
<MailboxServerIdParameter> -StopReason <String>
[-DomainController <Fqdn>] [<CommonParameters>]
```

The reason for stopping or moving the CMS is written to the Application Event Viewer log. The Source of the Event Viewer entry is *MSExchangeRepl* and the description field contains the specified reason. Stopping the CMS before a shutdown is especially important in a CCR deployment. You should try to bring the CMS online on the same node where it was online before you shut down the cluster nodes. If not, the former passive node might not have all the latest log files and would have to pull them from the previously active node. If you reboot or start both nodes at the same time, then you cannot be sure which node will be first up and will then try to bring the CMS online.

You can check the status of the CMS using the command shown in Figure 6-29.

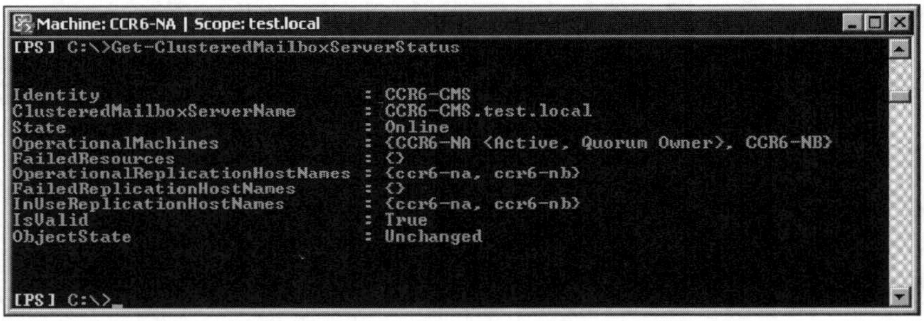

Figure 6-29
*Get-ClusteredMail
boxServerStatus*

Exchange Server 2007 Cluster Resource Behavior

Microsoft changed the default configuration of the Exchange cluster resources in Exchange Server 2003 with the release of Exchange Server 2007. Previously a failed resource always initiated a failover of the complete cluster group. In Exchange Server 2007, only the IP and network name resource initiates a cluster group failover. This is the case for SCC and CCR deployments; both cluster architectures have the same behavior. For the CCR, this is automatically configured during the CMS installation. For the SCC, it is only partially accomplished during CMS setup. It is your responsibility to make the necessary adjustments. This section describes the necessary steps.

The new default configuration makes much more sense. Why should a failover be initiated if a single database failed and the other databases are healthy? Are the mailboxes in this database more important than the mailboxes in the other databases? The monitoring and alerting procedure should be capable of alerting operational staff, allowing them to make an informed decision on whether a failover should be initiated.

The failover can afterward be initiated using a script. You should use an automated but not an automatic failover. This is a small but significant difference, especially in a geographically dispersed deployment. Some customers might prefer an automatic failover because it is easier to blame Microsoft for an unnecessary or failed failover than deciding who is responsible for determining if a failover should occur. You probably want to decide for yourself if a disaster renders your data center unavailable, rather than delegating this far-reaching decision to a few lines of code.

This failover behavior is controlled by the so-called "Affect the group" property of a cluster resource. Figure 6-30 shows that in Exchange Server 2003 this box was checked for all resources in the Exchange cluster group. Figure 6-31 shows that "Affect the group" is not checked for the Information Store resource in Exchange Server 2007. Another very important difference is that in Exchange Server 2003, the Information Store resource managed all storage groups and databases on the cluster. In Exchange Server 2007, there is still only one Information Store resource, but now there is a separate cluster resource—the Exchange Database Instance resource--for each database in the Exchange cluster.

Figure 6-30
"Affect the group"
in Exchange Server
2003

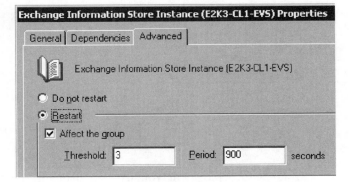

Figure 6-31
"Affect the group"
in Exchange Server
2007

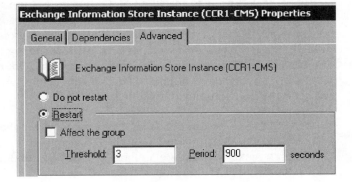

Figure 6-32 depicts the cluster resource dependency in Exchange Server 2007, and shows whether a resource has the "Affect the group" property set.

Figure 6-32   *Cluster resource dependency*

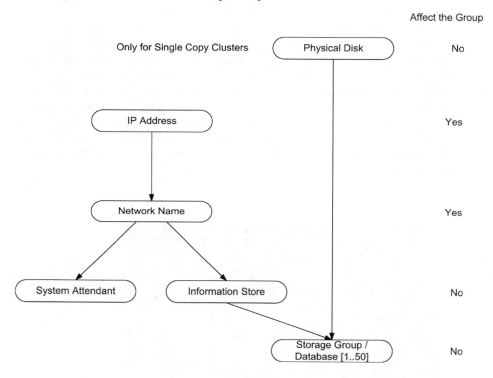

In an SCC deployment you have to manually configure the dependency of the database resource on the physical disk resource. The Exchange setup program requires that the physical disk resource is already online in the cluster if you want to install an SCC, but it does not automatically create the corresponding dependency. If you forgot this manual step, you will have problems if you perform a failover. The database resource will not come online because the two disk volumes used to store the log files and the database file will still be online on the previous node and your new active node has no access to the disk volumes. The Exchange Store cannot access the files stored on the disk volumes and will fail.

```
CLUSTER.EXE <ClusterName> resource <DatabaseResource>
/AddDependency:<DiskResource>
CLUSTER.EXE <ClusterName> resource <DiskResource>
/properties RestartAction=1
```

The previous two commands add the dependency and disable the "Affect the group" property. RestartAction=0 disables restarting a failed resource, RestartAction=1 enables restarting a failed resource, but deselects the "Affect the group" property, and RestartAction=2 selects the "Affect the group" property. The "Affect the group" topic is described in the TechNet section, "Single Copy Cluster Resource Model."

Table 6-4 provides examples of possible failures and specifies whether the cluster service will automatically initiate a failover of the CMS. The TechNet section titled, "Cluster Continuous Replication Recovery Behavior," describes expected recovery actions for additional failure scenarios, and the section, "Scheduled and Unscheduled Outages," provides additional background information about the behavior of CCR. Microsoft Knowledge Base Article 947712 provides Windows Server 2008—specific information about the behavior of clustered resources.

Table 6-4   *CMS behavior*

Failure	Automatic failover
Motherboard of active cluster node fails	Yes
Network name or IP address resource of CMS fails	Yes
Exchange System Attendant resource fails	No
Exchange Information Store resource fails	No
Exchange database gets dismounted because of database corruption	No
Physical disk hosting Exchange databases is lost	No

Geographically Dispersed Clusters

Windows Server 2003 did not support using a routed subnet between cluster nodes. You had to use a nonrouted subnet for the public network and you had to use a separate nonrouted subnet for the cluster internal network. For a geographically dispersed deployment, it was necessary to stretch a VLAN across the WAN.

The round-trip latency still must be below 500 ms if the heartbeat timeout has not been adjusted. Microsoft Knowledge Base Article 921181 describes how you should adjust heartbeat parameters to prevent an unnecessary cluster failover because of dropped or delayed heartbeat packets.

Network administrators do not like this configuration because this allows broadcast traffic to be sent over the expensive WAN connection. Additionally, the routers and switches have to be compliant to the 802.1Q standard. This was one reason why several large enterprises decided to wait until Windows Server 2008 is available with their stretched cluster deployment.

In Windows Server 2008 you can set up a WFC using a routed network for the public and private network (Figure 6-33). You can assign the cluster an IP address from Subnet A and an IP address from Subnet B. During the CMS setup, the same method is used—you assign an IP address from Subnet A and an IP address from Subnet B to the CMS (Figure 6-34).

Figure 6-33   *Create geographically dispersed cluster*

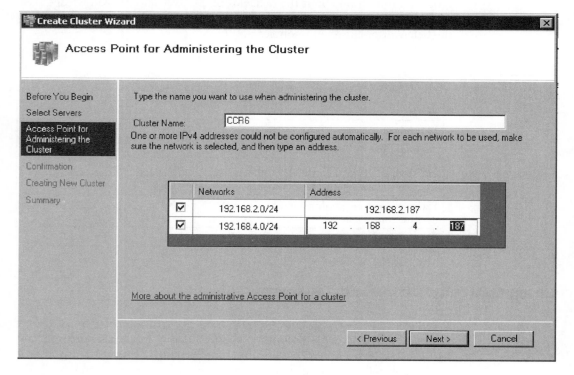

Figure 6-35 shows the two IP addresses in the Failover Cluster Management GUI.

Figure 6-36 illustrates that the network name of the CMS is online if either the IP address 192.168.4.188 or the IP address 192.168.2.188 is online. The Failover Cluster Management GUI allows you to create such a dependency report of the cluster configuration. This is very helpful for troubleshooting purposes if you had not set up the cluster.

Figure 6-34 *Create geographically dispersed CMS*

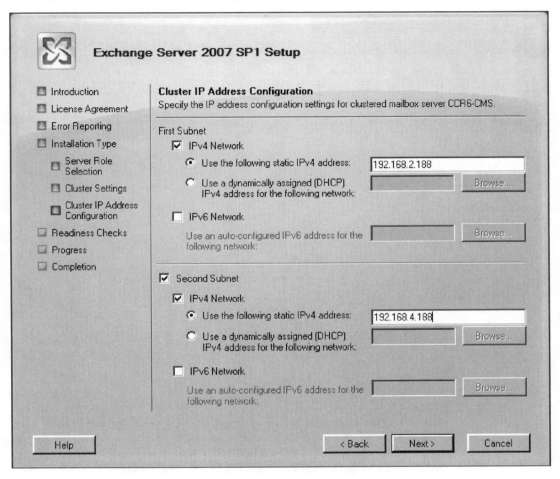

Figure 6-35
*CMS with two IP
addresses*

Name	Status
Server Name	
⊟ Name: CCR6-CMS	⊙ Online
IP Address: 192.168.2.188	⊙ Offline
IP Address: 192.168.4.188	⊙ Online

If you deploy an Exchange server on a WFC configuration that is using various IP subnets for the cluster nodes, the CMS has a different IP address after the failover. You cannot bring an IP address of Subnet A online in Subnet B. This affects your users; they access their mailbox via the Fully Qualified

Figure 6-36   *Dependency report*

represents 'AND' relationship: all child resources must be on-line

represents 'OR' relationship: at least one child resource must be on-line

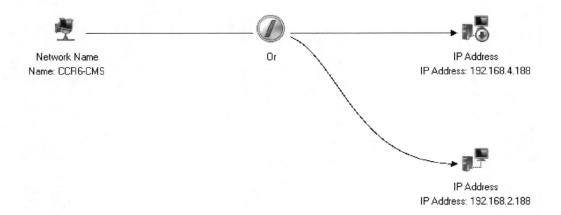

Domain Name (FQDN). The Outlook client will continue to access the mailbox server via the cached IP address that corresponds to this FQDN. The cluster will update the DNS A record after the failover, but clients will not be aware of the change until the cached DNS record expires. The default time-to-live (TTL) figure is 20 minutes. Therefore, you should define a low value for the TTL property of the A record, such as 5 or 10 minutes (Figure 6-37).

Another option is to instruct users to execute *IPCONFIG /flushdns* to manually flush the cached DNS records and fetch the updated IP address of the CMS, but this is not practical in an enterprise environment. You should also select the property "Update associated pointer (PTR) record" if you want to keep the reverse lookup information current. Microsoft Knowledge Base Article 947048 provides additional information about deploying WFC on routed subnets and 318803 describes client-side caching of DNS records.

From a Windows Server 2008 operating system point of view, it is possible to assign cluster Node A to AD Site A and cluster Node B to AD Site B. However, Exchange Server 2007 does *not* support this! This is because of the transport dumpster functionality. Exchange will contact the HT servers

Figure 6-37

Time to live (TTL)

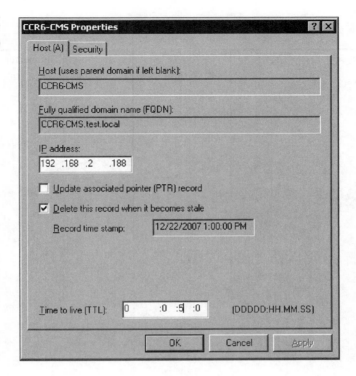

in its own AD site and not in other AD sites after a lossy failover of the CMS in a CCR deployment. See Chapter 7 for additional details about lossy failovers and the role of the transport dumpster. Exchange Server 2007 requires that the cluster nodes are located in a single AD site (Figure 6-38).

The Exchange server roles select their communication partners based on the AD site membership. A mailbox server role will select a server with the HT role in the same AD site, and a server with the CAS role will select a mailbox server role in the same AD site. This can lead to a situation where a mailbox server in data center A is selecting a HT/CAS in data center B. In this case, the IP packets are sent via the expensive and slow WAN link. This can affect end-user experience because the Exchange server roles expect LAN-quality connections for server MAPI/RPC—based communication.

Figure 6-39 shows an AD site configuration that restricts the CMS to use servers with in data center A. AD Site 2 will not be used during normal production; these servers are reserved for site resiliency purposes.

If you lost Data center A because of a disaster, you must modify the configuration to obtain an AD site with all required Exchange roles and AD domain controllers. In the TechNet article, "Site Resilience Configurations," Microsoft recommends moving the other Exchange roles to the AD site of

Figure 6-38   *Single AD site*

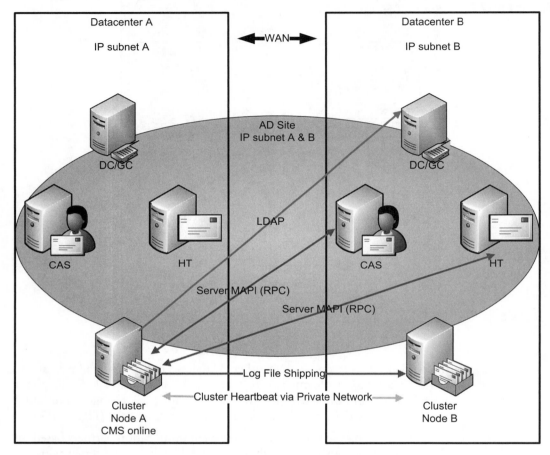

the CMS (Figure 6-40). This can be achieved by changing the AD site definition or changing the IP address of these servers.

Microsoft does not recommend moving the CMS to another AD site. If you select the recovery approach shown in Figure 6-41, Exchange servers located in other AD sites--branch offices, for example—have to adjust their planned mails routes for messages sent to recipients hosted on the CMS. Another disadvantage is that the CMS would not ask the HT servers in the old AD site/Data center A to resend mails that are available in their transport dumpster if you manage to recover Data center A. Additional

Figure 6-39 *Two AD sites*

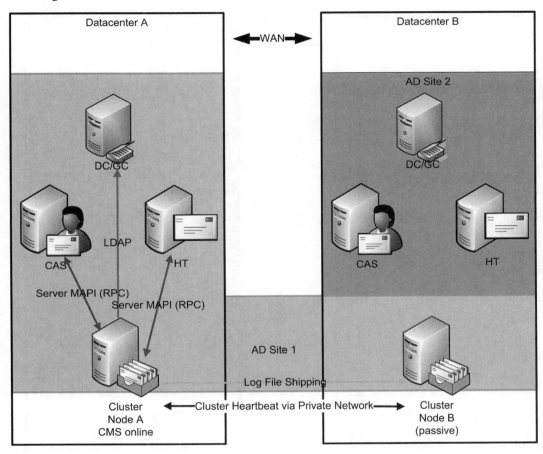

information about this topic is available in the IT Forum 2006 presentation, "Exchange Server 2007 Availability Strategies."

The described site resiliency solution for a geographically dispersed cluster is not perfect. If you run into problems with the bandwidth or latency of the WAN link and have to use the previously described tweaks, you should consider using Standby Continuous Replication (SCR). After Exchange Server 2007 Service Pack 1 was released, Microsoft tried to reposition CCR as the high-availability solution within a data center and SCR as the preferred site-resilient configuration.

Figure 6-40   *Move other Exchange roles*

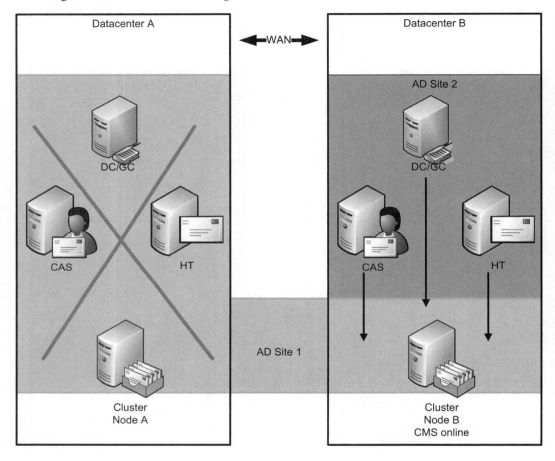

Figure 6-41 *Move CMS*

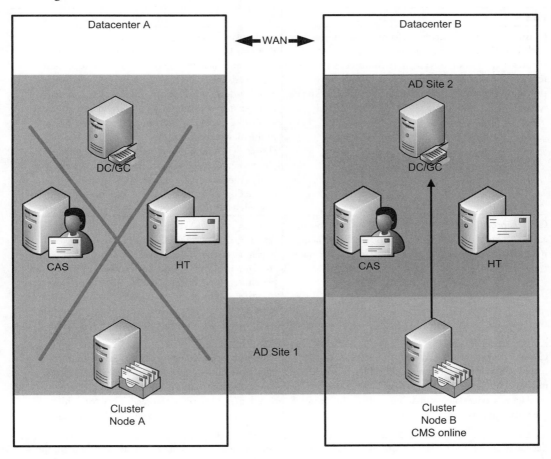

Pros and Cons for Exchange Clusters

The advantages and disadvantages of an Exchange Server 2007 deployment using WFC are summarized in Table 6-5.

Table 6-5   *Pros and cons of Exchange Server 2007 clusters*

Pros	Cons
Clusters allow you to update software (including service packs) on a rolling basis, one node at a time. This ensures that you can provide more continuous service to clients because you do not have to take the server providing the messaging service totally offline to update software.	If you plan software upgrades properly, schedule them for low-demand times (like Sunday morning), and communicate the necessary downtime to users well in advance, you can take a server down to apply an upgrade without greatly affecting users. Routine maintenance is necessary for all systems, so planning a software upgrade at the same time is not a major problem. Microsoft hot fixes may be untested on clusters when they are first released to customers. Therefore, it is a mistake to assume that you can apply every patch to a cluster. Also, third-party product upgrades do not always support rolling upgrades and can be applied only to the active node.
Clusters provide greater system uptime by allowing an administrator to transition work to other cluster nodes if a problem occurs on the currently active cluster node.	Clusters are more expensive compared to single servers from a hardware acquisition point of view. Exchange Server 2007 does not support an active/active configuration, and at least one passive server is required per cluster. It is not supported to use this passive server for other application services such as an SQL server or an Active Directory domain controller. More servers mean higher operational costs because you have to manage more systems.
Clusters provide protection against failures in components such as motherboards, CPUs, and memory. WFC automatically tries to restart the messaging services on a remaining node in the cluster if the active node is lost.	Clusters provide no protection against shared storage failures, so clusters have an Achilles heel. Exchange Server 2007 introduced a new clustering model that does not use shared storage. Therefore, this disadvantage only applies to clusters with a shared storage configuration.
Exchange Server 2007 Cluster Continuous Replication allows a faster and simplified failover procedure compared with Local Continuous Replication or single servers that are configured as Standby Continuous Replication targets. There are far fewer commands to execute if you want to take advantage of the database replicas hosted on the passive cluster node.	Due to the fact that clusters are not widely used, the number of add-on software products is smaller for both Windows and Exchange.
	Clusters require greater experience, knowledge, and attention to details from administrators than standard servers.
	Only the mailbox server role of Exchange Server 2007 can be installed on a Windows Failover cluster. A highly available messaging solution from an end-user point of view requires that the components the mailbox server depends on are highly available as well.

7

Data Replication Solutions for Exchange

From users' point of view, the most important piece of an Exchange environment is their mailbox or the data stored in their mailbox. Information Stored in mailboxes is often business critical. Mailboxes contain an enormous amount of a company's intellectual property. We assume that you agree that this information has to be especially protected. However, before the advent of Exchange Server 2007 Continuous Replication (CR), mailbox data were the only data that could only be stored once using built-in features. For several years, it has been possible to replicate data stored in public folders. Multiple Exchange servers can synchronize public folders using public folder replication. Public folder data are then stored in multiple public folder databases. Information about mailbox users, distribution lists, and contacts are stored in the Active Directory (AD). AD replication is utilized to increase the availability of this information.

Customers demanded a solution to better protect mailbox databases. Exchange administrators requested a solution to make a second copy of the information available for business continuity purposes.

With Exchange Server 2003 you had to use an application-aware backup program to make a copy of the mailbox data available on a second medium. For a geographically dispersed deployment, you had to use a host- or storage array–based replication solution from a third-party vendor. Additionally, there are products available that extract contents of the Exchange database and use these data for business continuity purposes. You should be aware of Microsoft's support policy described in Knowledge Base Article 904845 before you make the decision to use such a product. You should always clarify the supportability boundary and make the decision if your business critical application should rely on a product provided by a small company.

Availability and business continuity solutions for Microsoft Exchange are an interesting market segment. Several vendors provide appealing solutions in this area. We recommend spending the time to read the brochures of Quest Software Availability Manager for Exchange or Mimosa Systems NearPoint for Microsoft Exchange Server.

With Exchange Server 2007, Microsoft now provides a built-in mechanism to duplicate your mailbox databases and keep them constantly in loose synchronization. This data replication solution is based on a type of log file shipping called CR. As of this writing in spring 2008, Exchange Server 2007 was released more than a year ago. Looking back, it is obvious that CR, along with the move to 64-bit, two of the main reasons why Exchange Server 2007 is so successful.

In this chapter, we discuss the methods you could use in previous Exchange versions to replicate Exchange databases and we describe the details of CR. This will enable you to make an informed decision whether you utilize a traditional data replication solution with Exchange Server 2007 or jump on the CR bandwagon.

Host- and Storage-Based Data Replication Solutions

Figure 7-1 shows the main components of a data replication solution for a geographically dispersed Exchange deployment. At the left is the production site with the server accessed by your users. This server stores its data on a local storage subsystem. This local storage array is often called the *source*.

Figure 7-1
Data replication terminology

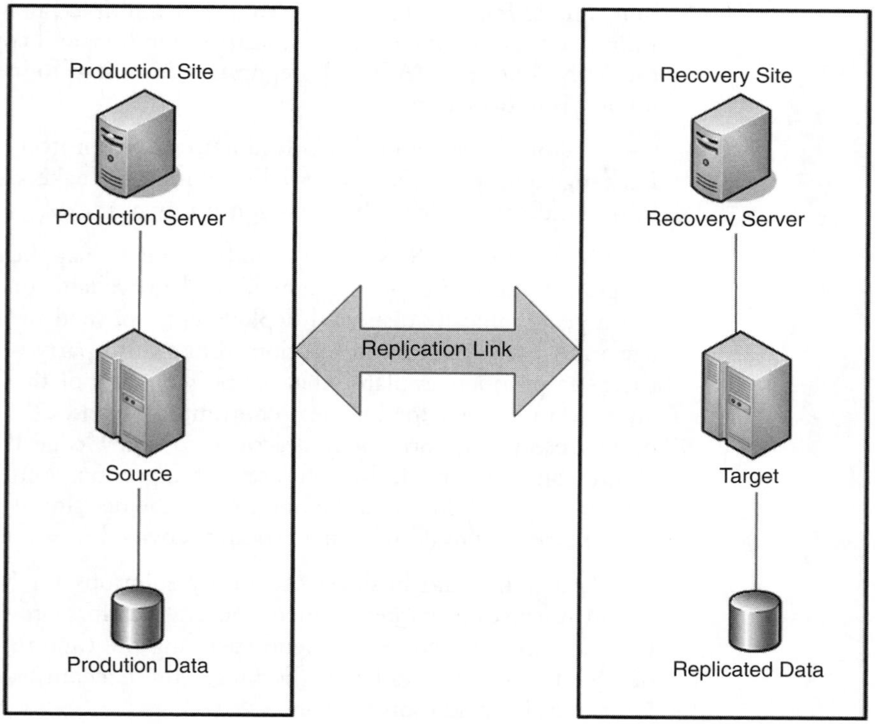

Production Site

Production Server

Source

Production Data

Replication Link

Recovery Site

Recovery Server

Target

Replicated Data

On the right is the recovery site, which is used for business continuity purposes. If the production site fails, the servers available in the recovery site have to take over the tasks of the lost servers. The recovery server uses the data stored on the storage array at the recovery site. This storage array hosts a replica of the data at the production site.

Data are replicated from the production site to the recovery site over a replication link. The storage array in the recovery site is called the target because it receives the replicated data. The replication link can be implemented using different methods. It can be a Fibre Channel connection, often called Dark Fibre, but there are many alternatives, such as an IP network. You can use an IP connection to tunnel storage traffic. This is called Fibre Channel over IP. For example, the Cisco Systems whitepaper, "Data Center: SAN Extensions for Business Continuance," provides a lot of details about such a configuration. In a Fibre Channel network, the link is called an *intersite link*, or if it is a direct link between two Fibre Channel switches, an Inter Switch Link (ISL). It is obvious that the characteristic of the replication link is an important topic for a data replication solution. The link has to have a short round-trip latency; otherwise, it is not possible to meet the disk write I/O latency requirements—20 milliseconds for database I/O and 10 milliseconds for log file I/O. It is important to know that only write I/O is sent over the replication link from the source to the target array. In most solutions, read I/O is only fetching data from the local array.

The link must have a high bandwidth; otherwise, it is impossible to replicate large databases from the source to the target. It is important to consider bandwidth requirements not only during normal operations, but also the bandwidth required to update the target after you have performed a database restore on the source. The link must be resilient; it should not go down if a single component fails. Usually, you have multiple ISLs. How should the storage array behave if the replication link is unavailable? Should the write I/O fail or should the I/O be buffered in a write history log on the source and be sent to the target array after the link comes up again? For the HP storage arrays, these two modes are called FAILSAVE mode and NORMAL mode. In FAILSAVE mode, the local storage controller will signal to the host that the write I/O command failed as soon as it recognizes that the target cannot be reached. In NORMAL mode, the write I/O is cached in a buffer on the local array and can be sent to the target after the link is available again. Most of the time, Exchange environments are configured in NORMAL mode because it is a catastrophic event for the Exchange Store process if a write I/O failed.

A crucial topic for a replication solution is the integrity of the data at the remote site. Microsoft defined strict supportability boundaries for data replication solutions in Microsoft Knowledge Base Article 895847. For a database application, it is very important that the write I/O order is preserved. All write I/O of the Exchange Information Store to the volume hosting the log files, and also all write I/Os of the Information Store to the volume hosting the database must arrive at the remote array in the same sequence that the Exchange Store process performed them. It is very important to realize that the order must be preserved, not only for the I/O targeted to a specific volume, like the log file volume. The order has to be preserved for the alternating I/O issued by the store process to the log file volume and the database volume of a single storage group.

In an asynchronous replication solution (Figure 7-2), the Exchange developers cannot enforce write ordering. The operating system already receives an I/O acknowledgment as soon as the write I/O arrives in the cache of the local storage controller. It is the responsibility of the replication solution to update the data stored on the remote disk volume and ensure that write ordering between the disk volume hosting the database and the disk volume hosting the log files is preserved. There are third-party vendor asynchronous replication solutions available that preserve write ordering by utilizing so-called consistency groups.

Figure 7-2
Asynchronous data replication

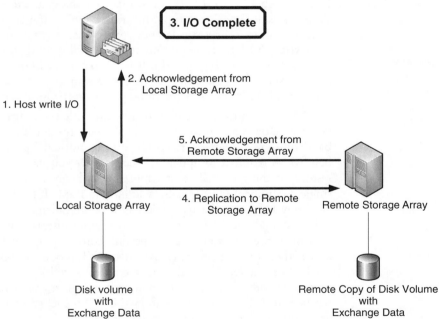

Microsoft only supports replicating online Exchange data in a synchronous mode (Figure 7-3). With a synchronous data replication solution, the Exchange developers can be sure that a write I/O is completed when the operating system receives an acknowledgment from the local storage array.

If you deploy an asynchronous replication solution, the vendor of the replication solution is your main support contact and is responsible for the

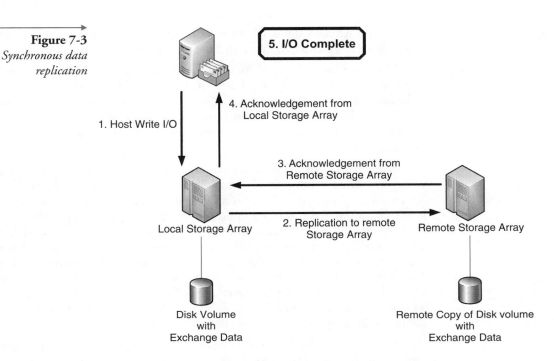

Figure 7-3
Synchronous data replication

5. I/O Complete

1. Host Write I/O

4. Acknowledgement from
Local Storage Array

3. Acknowledgement from
Remote Storage Array

Local Storage Array

2. Replication to remote
Storage Array

Remote Storage Array

Disk Volume
with
Exchange Data

Remote Copy of Disk volume
with
Exchange Data

solution. However, you can still call Microsoft Product Support Services (PSS), and they will help to a certain extent. See the supportability statements in Microsoft Knowledge Base Article 895847, and the description available in the whitepaper, "Deployment Guidelines for Exchange Server Multi-Site Data Replication." The Knowledge Base Article contains, for example, this statement: "Any data that has been replicated asynchronously is supported only by the storage vendor."

The advantage of asynchronous replication is that it enables data replication over longer distances with a reduced risk of breaking the write I/O latency boundaries defined by Microsoft. An asynchronous storage replication solution acknowledges the I/O request as soon as the data arrive on the source array and does not wait until the data are replicated to the remote array as a synchronous replication solution would. Additionally, under asynchronous replication, a temporarily unavailable replication link to a remote storage array that undergoes maintenance tasks does not stop your Exchange server from accessing the source storage array.

Most storage replication solutions provide a method called write history logging. If the link to the remote array is unavailable, write I/O is logged in a buffer area on the local array and the write commands are automatically forwarded to the remote array as soon as the link comes up again. Therefore, you cannot be 100% sure that with a synchronous data replication solution, the write I/O has really already arrived on the target array when Exchange received the acknowledgment for the I/O request. It is possible that the array is operating in NORMAL mode and the replication link is currently down.

Microsoft provides the following estimates in the abovementioned whitepaper: "Synchronous replication can cause as much as a 75 percent reduction in mailboxes/server scalability.... Generally, 100 KM is considered to be the threshold for synchronous storage replication of Exchange Server data. This threshold value can vary depending on the solution implementation."

We consider the 75% reduction of mailboxes per server as a kind of worst-case scenario. For example, according to the previously mentioned Cisco Systems whitepaper, you will see an additional latency of about 5 microseconds/km if data must travel over an optical network (the speed of light through a fiber). If we now assume that each write I/O requires two round trips, we have a latency of 20 microseconds per kilometer. If our two data centers are 50 km apart, then we will have an additional latency of about 1000 microseconds or 1 millisecond. With a decent storage array configuration, you should not have any problem meeting 10-millisecond latency for writing to the log file volumes. This is still true even when we consider the additional latency introduced by the networking equipment used to connect both data centers.

Spreading the Exchange data over multiple storage groups and using multiple replication links among the storage arrays is recommended. For the storage controller of the storage array, managing multiple smaller disk volumes compared to only a few large disks is usually easier. For example, the HP StorageWorks Enterprise Virtual Array (EVA) uses the concept of Data Replication Groups (DR Groups). You have to combine the database and log file disk volumes of a storage group within a single DR Group to ensure write ordering. Creating a separate DR Group for each Exchange storage group is better than using a single DR Group for all Exchange storage groups of the server. You should also take advantage of the possibility of creating more than four storage groups in Exchange Server 2007. Multiple storage groups spread over multiple DR Groups is the recommended configuration.

Another option you should consider in a Greenfield deployment is using multiple medium-sized storage arrays per site instead of one large storage array per data center. The storage controller often has a limited number of resources available for data replication. If you increase the number of storage arrays, you also increase the number of storage controllers and thereby the amount of resources available for data replication. Another benefit of this approach is that the impact of a storage array outage is reduced. This is something you should keep in mind, although failure of a complete storage array is very unlikely.

Replicating the storage group files (*.edb, *.chk, *.log) of an Exchange Server 2003 and Exchange Server 2007 mailbox cluster is mandatory. Replicating the disk volume hosting the SMTP queue of an Exchange Server 2003 cluster is recommended. Replicating the tracking log files is considered optional. You have to verify whether the solution is able to provide latency figures for RPC operations and disk access within the supported thresholds. See Chapter 11 for specific figures. Chapter 10 explains how to verify the solution before you migrate production mailboxes to the new environment.

Storage vendors provide storage array–based data replication solutions that can be configured synchronously or asynchronously. HP offers, for example, Continuous Access for EVA and XP arrays. The EMC Symmetrix Remote Data Facility (SRDF) can also be set up in synchronous and asynchronous mode. DoubleTake Software provides host-based data replication solutions working only in an asynchronous mode.

A major disadvantage of host- and storage array–based replication solutions is that they are not application aware. The replication solution has no notion of the database structure and contents explained in the TechNet article, "Extensible Storage Engine Architecture." Therefore, the solution cannot utilize information like page-level checksums available within the Exchange database and log files. The solution only sees bytes or disk blocks. This is the reason why a solution that replicates online disk blocks will replicate logically corrupt data to the remote site as well.

You can mitigate this issue only by switching to an offline replication architecture where you replicate, for example, the volume hosting a shadow copy created by a Volume Shadow Copy Services (VSS) backup. This architecture is shown in Figure 7-4. With this architecture, you can run an offline consistency

Figure 7-4
Offline data replication

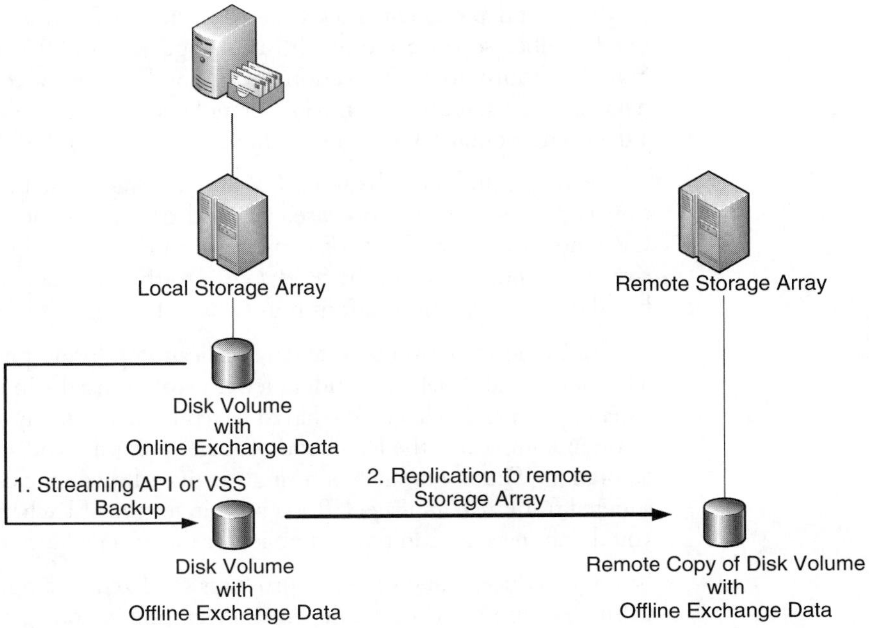

Local Storage Array

Remote Storage Array

Disk Volume
with
Online Exchange Data

1. Streaming API or VSS
Backup

2. Replication to remote
Storage Array

Disk Volume
with
Offline Exchange Data

Remote Copy of Disk Volume
with
Offline Exchange Data

check before you replicate the data to the remote site. Offline data replication solutions raise the question of how many times a day you should perform a replication to the remote site. The answer really depends on how many transactions you are willing to lose after a site disaster. Everybody will be reluctant to provide a figure of acceptable data loss or the acceptable number of minutes or hours to go back from a recovery point of view.

Exchange Server 2007 Continuous Replication

With Exchange Server 2007, you can deploy a data replication solution without the need for a third-party solution. Microsoft implemented a feature that had been available in other database applications for many years: log file shipping.

CR is a built-in Exchange function that asynchronously copies closed transaction log files to another file system path on the same server, or over a TCP/IP network to another server. Exchange uses these log files to automatically create a replica of the database in the background. This database copy is your first line of defense if your active database is damaged, and you previously had to perform a time consuming restore of your last backup set. With Exchange Server 2007, you can use the replica database for the recovery, which is much faster compared to, for example, streaming data back from tape media.

With the Release to Manufacture (RTM) version of Exchange Server 2007, you could choose between Local Continuous Replication (LCR) for a single server deployment and Cluster Continuous Replication (CCR) for a clustered mailbox server. Starting with Exchange Server 2007 SP1, you also can use Standby Continuous Replication (SCR). SCR creates a copy of the Exchange database on a standby system. This standby system can be used to recover from a data center outage. CCR aims at high availability, and SCR at site resiliency.

A major difference between CR and a storage-based data replication solution is the kind of network used to send data from the source to the target. CR sends data over a TCP/IP network from the active cluster node to the passive cluster node or from the SCR source to the SCR target computer. Storage-based data replication solutions mostly use a Fibre Channel network.

CR is an application-aware data replication solution provided by Microsoft. This has several benefits, including fewer involved parties in the event that a consistency or a performance issue has to be resolved. Too many suppliers increase the solution complexity, the likelihood of finger pointing, and required time for collaboration. The importance of a single contact heavily increases if you ever have suffered from such an issue. CR is a built-in feature of Exchange Server 2007, and you do not need an additional supplier for the data replication solution.

CR reduces the number of products the Exchange operational staff has to learn, and also removes the dependency among various products and the team responsible to operate them. With Exchange Server 2003, you had to investigate whether the latest Exchange Service Pack is already supported by the vendor of your third-party data replication solution. Now Microsoft is responsible for verifying the compatibility of Exchange Service Packs with the built-in data replication function. In large enterprises, you often find that Team A operates the storage environment, Team B operates the Windows operating system, including failover clustering, and Team C is responsible for Exchange. This separation of responsibility does not make troubleshooting and disaster recovery easier. If you use storage-based data replication, Team A is responsible for it, and the Exchange team often fights with Team A to get a configuration that is suitable for Exchange. With CR, the Exchange team has data replication back under control.

However, there may be a company-wide strategy to use a storage-based data replication for disaster recovery purposes with an application-independent solution enabling a common recovery procedure. This is a very important topic if you consider how many applications a company typically uses. Following a disaster, if the remaining operational staff has to be able to successfully fail over, for example, 50 applications from Data center A to Data center B, and all 50 applications use different methods for business continuity, you can imagine how challenging this job will be. It will also reduce the likelihood of a successful failover, and increase the time required to fail over all applications. Therefore, the company-wide strategy may prevent you from taking advantage of CR.

In the event that yours is a Microsoft-only company, you may argue that this problem does not exist. Unfortunately, the problem exists in this scenario as well. Just consider the four main Microsoft applications you will likely use: AD, Exchange, SQL, and file servers. You use AD replication, CR for Exchange, database mirroring with SQL, and distributed file system replication for file servers. For these four applications, you have to understand four replication solutions.

A benefit of CR is you can use built-in tools to manage the replication. For example, you can write a PowerShell script to create a new database replica, suspend or resume the replication, and perform a recovery using the replica database. It is not necessary to learn an additional vendor-specific scripting language or an additional Graphical User Interface (GUI) to manage the data replication solution. This lowers the costs of operating the solution.

The *most* important benefit is that the replication mechanism is *Exchange aware*. Exchange can utilize its knowledge about the database and log file structure. It is now possible to check data consistency before data are applied to the replica of the database by utilizing existing information such as page-level checksums. This eliminates the previous issue of replicating corrupt data to the remote site by host- or storage-array data replication solutions. In CCR you have two copies of your databases and not just one, as is the case with a Single Copy Cluster (SCC). If the disk volume hosting your active database is damaged, you still have the chance that your copy database is healthy and not affected by the failure. This is a big advantage. With SCR you can even create multiple replica instances of a database located on different standby servers.

But you have to be aware that any data replication solution does not protect you from human error, such as the CEO accidentally deleting a very important email in his inbox. Log file shipping and a traditional storage-based data replication solution will delete the email in the active database and the copy database. Therefore, you have to keep in mind that CR is *not* a replacement for backups!

CR architecture is explained in Microsoft TechNet, various blogs of members of the Microsoft Exchange Team, and presentations delivered at industry conferences, including Microsoft Exchange Connections. The remaining sections are based on these sources, information available on the Internet, and experience gained during our customer projects.

Log File Shipping

Figure 7-5 shows the steps of how transaction log files of the active database are used to create a passive copy of the database. The Information Store service creates log files to write the database transactions to disk. The log files have a fixed size of 1 MB. The size was reduced in Exchange Server 2007 from 5 MB to 1 MB to ease replication over a Wide Area Network (WAN) link, and a smaller file reduces the amount of data loss if the last log file has not yet been shipped. The Information Store closes the current log file and creates a new log file when the file is full.

The Exchange Replication service copies closed transaction log files of the active storage group to the inspector directory on the passive storage group. In a CCR deployment, the active log files and the inspector directory of the passive storage group are located on two different cluster nodes. The active log files are on the active cluster node, and the inspector directory is on the passive cluster node.

The active cluster node exposes the log files via a file share to enable the Replication service to pull them to the passive cluster node (Figure 7-6). The log files are copied by the passive cluster node over the TCP/IP network.

Figure 7-7 shows that only the Exchange Servers security group has permission to access the share. The Exchange Servers security group contains the computer accounts of all systems with the Exchange Mailbox, Hub Transport, or Client Access Server role installed. The access permissions are very restrictive, and it is not an error if you do not see Full Control, Change, or Read ticked. You have to use the commands in Figure 7-8 to view the actual share permissions.

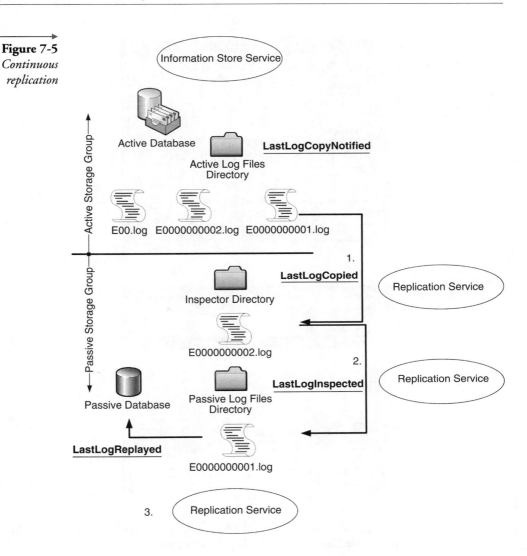

Figure 7-5
Continuous replication

In SCR the method used for log file shipping is comparable to the one used by CCR. The major difference is that the database replica is created on a server that is not a member of the cluster where your active database is hosted. In LCR there is no share for the log files because the Exchange Replication services can directly access the files. LCR creates the second instance of the database on the same server.

Copying closed log files from the active storage group directory to the inspector directory is an asynchronous process, and it is referred to as log file shipping. The checksum of the copied log files is verified by the Replication service. This is equivalent to using the command line utility *ESEUTIL.EXE /K*

Figure 7-6
Log file share

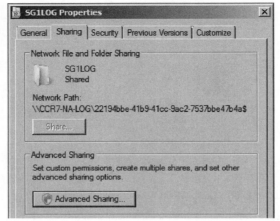

Figure 7-7
*Log file share
permissions*

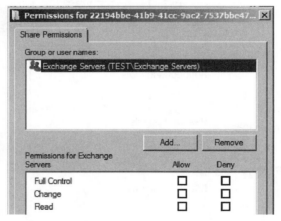

to verify the checksum of the log files. If the checksum is invalid, this log file is recopied from the active log file directory.

Healthy log files are moved to the target directory—the passive log file directory in step 2 of Figure 7-5. The Replication service afterward replays the log files to the passive database—step 3. This last step creates the copy database. The active database and the copy database are loosely coupled; the copy database is a few transactions behind.

In the RTM version of Exchange Server 2007, the log files are replayed in batches of at least 10 files or if the last replay occurred more than 60 seconds ago. The replay Extensible Storage Engine (ESE) instance was destroyed after each batch. The database cache that was built during the log file replay was also destroyed. This was a very inefficient method that did not take advantage of caching database pages. Therefore, the I/O rate on the disk

Figure 7-8
*Share permission
command line*

```
Administrator: Command Prompt                                              _ □ ×
C:\Program Files (x86)\Windows Resource Kits\Tools>net share 22194bbe-41b9-41cc-
9ac2-7537bbe47b4a$
Share name      22194bbe-41b9-41cc-9ac2-7537bbe47b4a$
Path            C:\MSXDATA\SG1LOG
Remark          CCR7-CMS\CCR7-CMS-SG1
Maximum users   No limit
Users
Caching         Manual caching of documents
Permission      TEST\Exchange Servers, UNKNOWN (0x120089)

The command completed successfully.

C:\Program Files (x86)\Windows Resource Kits\Tools>subinacl /share 22194bbe-41b9
-41cc-9ac2-7537bbe47b4a$

================================================
+Share 22194bbe-41b9-41cc-9ac2-7537bbe47b4a$
================================================
/control=0x0
/audit ace count  =0
/perm. ace count  =1
/pace =test\exchange servers     ACCESS_ALLOWED_ACE_TYPE-0x0
      ACCESS_READ -0x1            ACCESS_EXEC-0x8              ACCESS_FINDFIRST
-0x80
      READ_CONTROL-0x20000       SYNCHRONIZE-0x100000

Elapsed Time: 00 00:00:00
Done:       1, Modified        0, Failed        0, Syntax errors        0
Last Done : 22194bbe-41b9-41cc-9ac2-7537bbe47b4a$

C:\Program Files (x86)\Windows Resource Kits\Tools>
```

volume hosting the passive database was several times higher than the Disk Transfers/sec on the disk volume hosting the active database.

Figure 7-9 shows a chart that a colleague from the HP Customer Focused Testing (CFT) team provided to me. The storage back-end array exposes the performance counter, "Total Host Req/s," to the Windows operating system. This counter corresponds to the physical disk, Disk Transfers/sec. The chart verifies that the active cluster node performed less read-and-write I/O compared to the I/O done by the passive node.

Figure 7-9
*CCR RTM Total
Host Req/s*

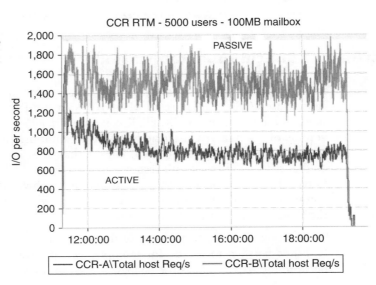

In SP1, the replay is not performed in a batched manner, and the replay ESE instance is not destroyed. The replay instance now can take advantage of the RAM installed on the passive server and build a "warm" database cache. This enables a reduction of the I/O demand compared to the RTM version. Figure 7-10 shows that in SP1, the number of I/O requests of the passive cluster node is lower than the I/O requests of the active cluster node. According to the article, "Exchange 2007 SP1 ESE Changes—Part 2," on the Microsoft Exchange Team Blog, with SP1 the I/O on the passive node is estimated to be 50 to 100% the I/O of the active node.

Figure 7-10
CCR SP1 Total
Host Req/s

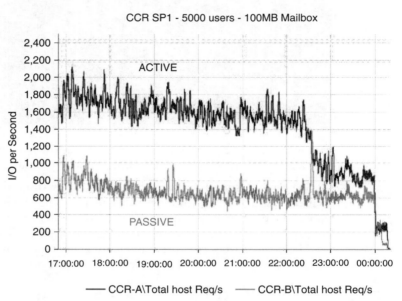

Restrictions of Continuous Replication

LCR creates a copy database on a local disk volume of a single server. You cannot use LCR on a Clustered Mailbox Server (CMS). Therefore, you cannot combine SCC and LCR. CCR creates the database copy on a local disk volume of the passive cluster node. CCR does not use shared physical disks. It is a Majority Node Set (MNS) cluster that does not use a disk volume configured as a physical disk resource in the cluster. LCR and CCR can use Direct-Attached Storage (DAS) or disk volumes provided by a storage array connected to the server via a storage network. The storage network can use the Fibre Channel or iSCSI protocol.

You can create only one copy of the active database with LCR and CCR. It is not possible to create, for example, two passive copies. The time lag between the active and passive database is fixed for LCR and CCR. You cannot tune the log shipping behavior in LCR and CCR. Therefore, you cannot specify that the passive database is always 1 hour or 100 log files behind.

You have to use SCR if you want to create multiple copies of the active database or configure how far the database replica is behind the active database. SCR can be combined with LCR, CCR, and SCC. The SCR source server can use LCR, SCC, or CCR, but the target server cannot use LCR or be a fully configured CCR or SCC system with a CMS instance. The target SCR server must be a single server without a storage group enabled for LCR or a failover cluster with the Exchange binaries installed but without a CMS configured.

CR requires that the storage group enabled for replication has only a single database. It is possible to have storage groups with LCR enabled and storage groups without LCR enabled on the same mailbox server. With CCR all storage groups of the cluster have a copy database. It is not possible with CCR to have storage groups without data replication. This is important in a small environment when only a very limited number of mailboxes have business needs for data resilience.

CR requires that the database be a mailbox store; it cannot be a public folder database if your Exchange organization has multiple public folder stores. Public folder replication always occurs if you have two or more public folder databases. You cannot combine public folder replication and CR. CR is available for mailbox data, and public folder replication is available to duplicate public folder data. This is important to keep in mind when you design your Exchange Server 2007 mailbox servers. You might be tempted to deploy only CCR mailbox servers, but this is not a good idea. If you still rely on public folders, and have not migrated all public folder data to SharePoint and migrated all legacy Outlook clients to Outlook 2007, then you should deploy a few single servers. These servers host your public folder databases, and use public folder replication to create a database instance at a remote location and provide a redundant copy of the data. Initially, you might consider this as a big disadvantage. However, this is not the case. In a geographically dispersed deployment, we recommend a single server per data center to take advantage of the Recover Storage Group (RSG) for single mailbox recovery. We do not recommend using your highly available mailbox clusters for this purpose. You can host your public folder replicas on this single server, and on demand create an RSG.

How to Enable Continuous Replication

CR is automatically enabled if you create a new storage group in CCR. You can use the commands in Figure 7-11 to enable a storage group for LCR on a single server.

For an existing storage group/database, you have to use the PowerShell commands *Enable-StorageGroupCopy* and *Enable-DatabaseCopy*. The commands

Figure 7-11
Create LCR-
enabled database

```
New-StorageGroup -Name LCR1-SG1 -Server LCR1.e12.local -
CopyLogFolderPath C:\MSXDATA\LCR-SG1LOG -CopySystemFolderPath
C:\MSXDATA\LCR-SG1LOG -HasLocalCopy $true -LogFolderPath
C:\MSXDATA\SG1LOG -SystemFolderPath C:\MSXDATA\SG1LOG

New-MailboxDatabase -Name LCR1-SG1-PRIV1 -StorageGroup LCR1\LCR1-SG1 -
CopyEdbFilePath C:\MSXDATA\LCR-SG1DB\LCR1-SG1-PRIV1.edb -EdbFilePath
C:\MSXDATA\SG1DB\LCR1-SG1-PRIV1.edb -HasLocalCopy $true
```

to enable a storage group for SCR are explained in a later section of this chapter.

Seeding Process

The next step after enabling a storage group for CR is seeding. This is an important term for CR. It is the process of creating the initial copy of the replica database. It is automatically performed when you create a new CR-enabled database and the first log file (Exx00000001.log) is available.

You have to manually seed a database after you have recognized database or log file corruption. Manual seeding can be performed using the *Update-StorageGroupCopy* command or by using an offline copy of the active database. You have to suspend replication and delete existing files in the directories used by the copy database and log files. CR is in a healthy state after seeding is complete.

You can run multiple reseed jobs in parallel. You can achieve a total reseed throughput of about 300 GB/hour over a Gigabit Ethernet network with multiple parallel jobs. You have to open multiple Powershell command windows and run *Update-StorageGroupCopy* in each window for a different storage group.

Monitoring of Continuous Replication

The Exchange Management Console (EMC) shows the summary status of the replication (Figure 7-12), and you can see additional details by selecting the property tab of the storage group in EMC.

Figure 7-12
Copy status in
EMC

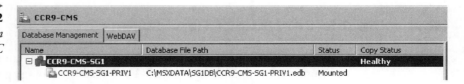

A full list of the attributes that describe the replication status is provided with the command shown in Figure 7-13.

Figure 7-13
Get-Storage
Copy Status

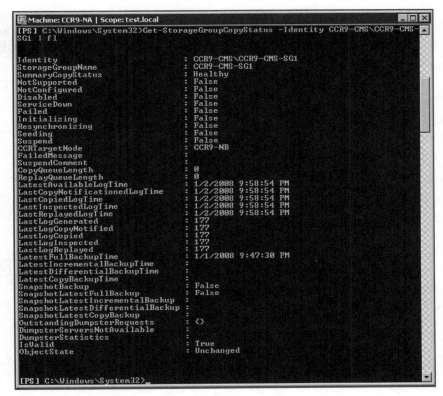

In the RTM version, the status of the replication was fetched from the registry (LCR) or from the Windows Failover Cluster database (CCR). SP1 improved the capabilities for monitoring CR. Now the information is directly retrieved from the Exchange Replication service. Additionally, a new PowerShell command was introduced. Figure 7-14 shows the new command, *Test-ReplicationHealth*, which is very handy for checking the health of CR.

Figure 7-14
Test-Replication
Health

```
Machine: CCR9-NA | Scope: test.local
[PS] C:\>Test-ReplicationHealth

Server          Check                   Result      Error
------          -----                   ------      -----
CCR9-NA         PassiveNodeUp           Passed
CCR9-NA         ClusterNetwork          Passed
CCR9-NA         QuorumGroup             Passed
CCR9-NA         FileShareQuorum         Passed
CCR9-NA         CmsGroup                Passed
CCR9-NA         NodePaused              Passed
CCR9-NA         DnsRegistrationStatus   Passed
CCR9-NA         ReplayService           *FAILED*    The Microsoft Exchange Re
                                                    plication Service is not
                                                    running on computer 'CCR9
                                                    -NB'.

CCR9-NA         DBMountedFailover       Passed

[PS] C:\>
```

The Replication service provides performance counters within the object MSExchange Replication that you can use to monitor CR. The counters correspond to the information that you can manually fetch using the PowerShell command *Get-StorageGroupCopyStatus*.

Figure 7-15 shows at what step in the log file shipping process the related counters are updated.

Figure 7-15
Continuous replication counters

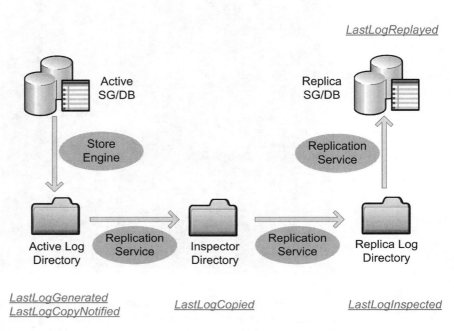

LastLogGenerated: Last log generation seen in the source directory.

LastLogCopyNotified: Last log generation seen in the source directory that the copy is aware of.

LastLogCopied: Last log generation copied by the Replication service to the inspector directory.

LastLogInspected: Last log generation inspected and moved to the target log file directory.

LastLogReplayed: Last log generation replayed into the database replica.

It is highly recommended to use a framework like Microsoft System Center Operations Manager 2007 and the Exchange Server 2007 Management Pack to proactively monitor your Exchange environment. Assuming that you can monitor a large Exchange Server 2007 deployment by manually browsing

Figure 7-16   *Replication in Operations Manager*

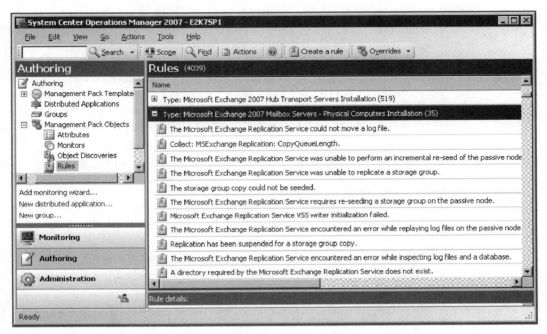

through the event viewer of all your servers and once a week opening *PERFMON.MSC* is unrealistic. The Operations Manager provides specific rules to monitor CR (Figure 7-16). This allows you to trigger actions when a counter value passes a threshold, such as the length of the copy queue or the replay queue. The Management Pack uses the thresholds shown in Table 7-1 These thresholds are from the Management Pack that was released before Exchange Server 2007 SP1 was available. The thresholds do not consider SCR. For example, SCR has a hardcoded minimal replay lag time of 50 log files. This means the SCR target would always have a critical error related to the replay queue length. A useful article titled, "Monitoring Exchange Server 2007 Using MOM 2005," is available on MSExchange.org.

Table 7-1   *Continuous replication thresholds*

	Warning	Critical error
Storage group copy queue length	>7	>15
Storage group replay queue length	>7	>15

Management of Continuous Replication

Understanding that CR verifies only the checksum of the shipped log files is critical. The Exchange Replication service does not verify the health of the passive database. It is recommended to regularly suspend replication using the Suspend-StorageGroupCopy command and manually verify the health of the database copy using ESEUTIL.EXE /K <database>.edb. During tests performed by the HP CFT team, ESEUTIL.EXE /K on a 188 GB database took about 10 Minutes. You can resume replication after the checksum verification is complete with the *Resume-Storage GroupCopy* command.

You can minimize the duration with CR suspended if you use VSS to create a shadow copy of the volume with the database. In this case, you can resume replication after the shadow copy has been created, and you don't have to wait until the database verification is finished. The following screenshot is from a small test lab: please pay attention only to the logic and not to the database size and required time for checking the health of the small database.

Please be aware that the *VSSADMIN.EXE* command in Figure 7-17 creates a copy-on-write shadow copy that uses disk blocks from the same volume hosting your production database. Every time *ESEUTIL.EXE* fetches a database page, it is actually accessing disk blocks used by your production database as long as this page has not been modified in the meantime. You can throttle the I/O request of *ESEUTIL.EXE /K* by introducing an artificial pause after the number of I/O requests specified with the option */p*.

Regularly checking the health of CR created databases is especially important if you only run streaming online backups. With streaming backups, you can only back up only the active database. This procedure does not verify the health of the passive database. In this case, a damaged passive database would be identified only if the Exchange Replication service accesses a damaged database page during the log file replay.

If you use VSS to back up the passive database, the likelihood of an unidentified corruption of the passive database is reduced because the VSS backup process performs checksum verification at the end of the backup process. But what about checksum verification of the active database when you run VSS backups from the passive database? Theoretically, you could regularly perform a controlled failover/handoff to the passive cluster node and thereby alternate the database that is backed up. This is impractical and would also not be a solution for an LCR-enabled storage group. The "failover process" to the passive database is more complicated in LCR, and this is not a reasonable solution to the problem.

Microsoft introduced a solution to this problem in SP1. A new task was added to the online maintenance process—database check summing. This task is disabled by default but you should consider switching it on if you run

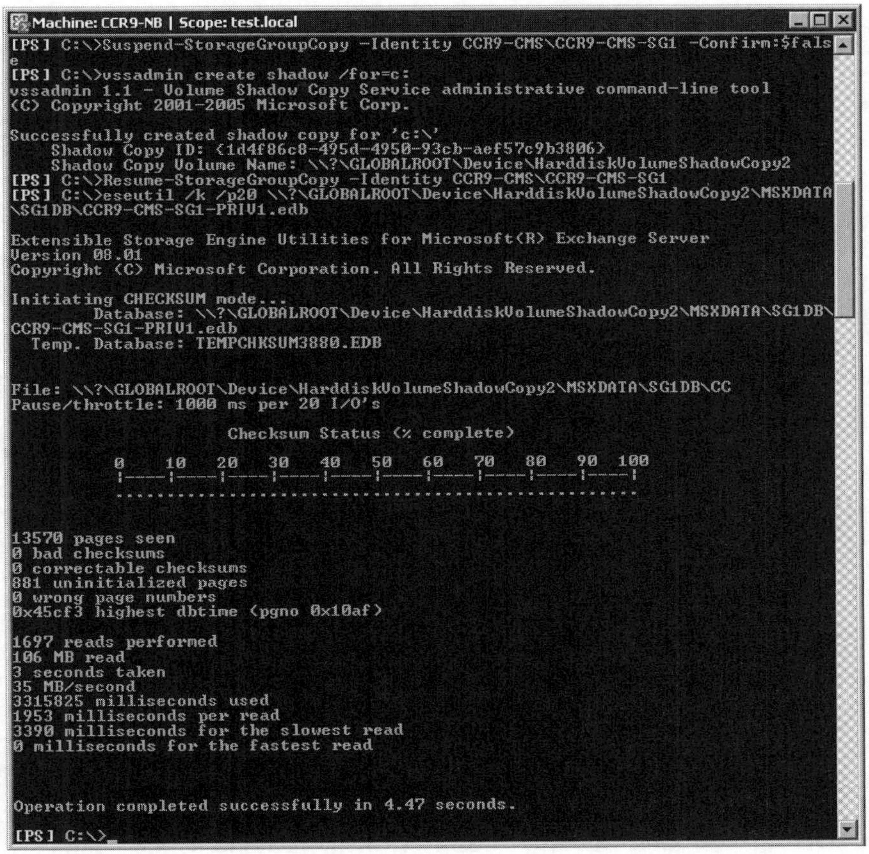

Figure 7-17
*Using ESEUTIL
on a shadow copy
volume*

Figure 7-17
*Using ESEUTIL
on a shadow copy
volume*

VSS backups of the LCR or CCR created copy database. The method that *ESEUTIL.EXE* uses and the method used in online maintenance to verify the checksum of the database pages are similar. The main difference is that *ESEUTIL.EXE* reads larger chunks of the database in a single step, and is therefore less friendly to the storage array.

The article, "Online Maintenance Database Scanning in Exchange 2007 SP1," on Microsoft TechNet describes the necessary registry key changes to switch on checksum verification during online maintenance. SP1 introduced additional performance counter objects and event viewer entries to monitor the checksum process.

Lost Log Resiliency and *AutoDatabaseMountDial*

In LCR, the Exchange Replication service is running on the local server and copies transaction log files from the directory where the Exchange Server generates them to another file system directory on the local server. In CCR and SCR, the Exchange Replication service running on the passive cluster node or on the SCR target pulls closed log files to its local file system. This process is asynchronous. Therefore, you cannot expect that all log files already arrived at the copy location when you have to immediately activate the copy for recovery purposes.

In previous Exchange versions, the Information Store did not mount a database if one or more recently generated transaction log files are missing. After a server crash, the ESE goes through a soft recovery process and verifies whether the database has been cleanly shut down, which is very unlikely, or if the contiguous log file sequence specified in the database header field "Log Required" is available. If this is not the case, then Exchange Server 2003 did not mount the database.

If log files are missing, you could restore your last backup and recover to the point in time you created the backup set. All data created since that time would be lost. Additional options are to run a hard repair using *ESEUTIL/P*, or try to recover up to the point of the last contiguous log file using the process described in Microsoft Knowledge Base Article 296843.

The Lost Log Resiliency (LLR) feature introduced with Exchange Server 2007 enables you to recover a database even if the most recently generated log files are damaged or lost. LLR delays writes to the database until a certain number of log file have been created. The number of log files is referred to as LLR depth.

Having a basic grasp of how the ESE works is helpful for understanding the following description of LLR. An introduction to the ESE is available on Microsoft TechNet in the section, "Understanding the Exchange 2007 Store." This section contains information about ESE architecture and transaction logging. Additionally, we will refer to information that you can get using the *ESEUTIL.EXE* file dump mode. Another source for information about ESE is Wikipedia.

ESE uses a dual-phase commit for transactions, and the transactions meet the ACID (Atomicity, Consistency, Isolation, and Durability) test. A transaction is not a single operation, but rather a series of database page modifications that is treated as a single logical unit. All page modifications are completed and permanently saved, or none of the modifications are saved. For example, when you receive a new email, both the email and all attachments are saved and the properties of the inbox folder such as the number of items in the inbox are updated, *or* none of these changes occur. You would not be happy if Outlook tells you that a new email has arrived in your inbox and the number of items in the inbox folder was increased, but the email is not visible in your inbox because it could not be saved by Exchange. Thus, either all operations are successful and the transaction is visible to you, or the operations are undone and no change is visible to you.

Operations are modifications of database pages. The following steps occur when ESE modifies a database page:

1. The database page is fetched from disk if it is not already stored in the database cache.

2. A log record is added that describes the operation to the in-memory log buffer.

3. The database page is modified and the page is marked as "dirty."

4. The database page is linked to the record in the in-memory log buffer. This prevents the database page from being flushed to disk before the log record is written.

Log records represent individual page modifications. Transactions are implemented as follows: When a thread starts a transaction, a "begin transaction" log record is added to the log buffer; when the transaction commits, a "commit transaction" log record is added to the log buffer and the log buffer is written to disk.

After a system crash, ESE performs a recovery. During recovery, the ESE always reruns operations found in the transaction log files and if no "commit" record is found for a transaction, all the operations performed by the transaction are undone. This ensures that no partial transaction occurs.

An important note is that dirty pages are not really written to disk in the same order they are modified in RAM. Several other factors affect the flush order, such as database page number, location in RAM, and so on. This means that a log file is not necessarily "committed." Instead, ESE flushes dirty database pages and calculates the current recovery point—the checkpoint—every 30 seconds. In addition, ESE aggressively flushes pages that are impeding checkpoint advancement. ESE is using continuous "fuzzy check pointing" as opposed to the CHECKPOINT system of the SQL server, which is a discrete action.

What does this mean for LLR? Write ahead logging already requires that a log record is flushed to disk before the modified database page is written to disk. LLR just changes the page update sequence:

1. The database page is fetched from disk if it is not already stored in the database cache.

2. A log record is added that describes the operation to the in-memory log buffer.

3. The database page is modified and the page is marked as "dirty."

4. The database page is linked to the record in the in memory log buffer. This prevents the database page from being flushed to disk before the log record is written *and* N more transaction log files are written.

LLR enforces that in step 4 ESE has to wait until N more transaction log files are written before the dirty database page can be written to disk.

As already discussed in the previous section, the ESE uses a sophisticated process for its database transactions. Changes are first made in memory, and then written to log files and finally to the database file. Figure 7-18 shows a greatly simplified version of this process. The main purpose of the illustration is to visualize the terms *checkpoint*, *waypoint*, and *current log file* that we use in following sections when we describe the difference between a planned outage and a lossy failover.

Figure 7-18
LLR depth

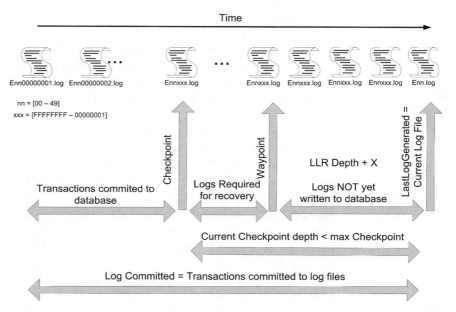

Each transaction log file has an internal log file generation number. The ESE uses this number to identify the sequence of the log files. If the current log file is closed and a new log file is created, the new log file has a generation number that is 1 greater than the generation number of the previous log file. A log file can be in one of the following three ranges:

- Log File Generation < Checkpoint: All transactions with a begin transaction log record and a commit log record have been applied to the database file on disk. Transactions existing in the log file without a commit log record have not been applied to the database file on disk.

- Checkpoint ≤ Log File Generation ≤ Waypoint: Some changes described in the log file have been written to the database file on disk and some have not. Which database pages have been written is essentially random.

- Waypoint < Log File Generation: No changes described in the transaction log file have been written to the database file on disk.

All transaction log files between the checkpoint and the waypoint are required for a recovery. The waypoint marks the last log file that is required. Log files between the waypoint and the current log file are not required to be able to mount the database. If you lost these log files, you are still able to bring the database online, but you have lost the transactions in these log files. Recall the ACID test mentioned earlier in this section. LLR weakens the durable part of ACID. Although transactions are atomic, it is possible to lose committed transactions if they are in a lost log file. However, you may have not completely lost them because of the transport dumpster. The transport dumpster is explained in a following section of this chapter.

The checkpoint depth references the amount of database pages that have been updated in RAM, but the changes have not been completely written to the database file on disk. Increasing the checkpoint depth enables to store of more updated database pages in RAM before they have to be written to the database file. This reduces the frequency of data being written to disk. A large checkpoint depth can increase performance, but it also increases the time necessary to flush the database cache to disk during a database dismount. The checkpoint depth also determines how long recovery will take. A bigger checkpoint means that there will be more log files that have to be processed during the recovery.

To further reduce the likelihood of data loss, Exchange Server 2007 automatically creates new transaction log files, although there is no user activity. This process is called Transaction Log Roll. The problem the ESE faces is that with LLR a page is pinned in memory until a certain number of log files are generated. If there is no activity on the database to generate log files, the pages can be pinned in memory indefinitely. Rolling over the log files prevents this. The current log file, *Enn.log*, is closed even it is not full. Transaction Log Roll takes only place if there is no user activity. If the server is busy because of user requests, Transaction Log Roll is not necessary.

In the RTM version, you could influence the value of LLR depth on CCR using the *AutoDatabaseMountDial* parameter of the *Set-MailboxServer* command. LLR depth was the numeric value of *AutoDatabaseMountDial* + 1. SP1 allows you to configure the *AutoDatabaseMountDial* parameter in the EMC, but starting with SP1, LLR depth is fixed at 10 on CCR, regardless of the *AutoDatabaseMountDial* setting. For all other mailbox servers, it is still 1. It is important to note that the passive node of a CCR system does not use LLR. The passive cluster node tries to pull closed log files from the active node as soon as possible. There is no lag time between when the log files have arrived on the passive node and the time the Exchange Replication service tries to replay the logs into the copy database. The passive node tries to update its database as soon as possible.

The current value of LLR depth is exposed as the performance counter MSExchange Database → *Instances\ Log Generation Loss Resiliency Depth*. You can use this counter to check the current value and verify if patches or service packs after SP1 modified the LLR depth configuration.

In CCR, you can either manually start a failover of the CMS from Node A to Node B, or the cluster service automatically tries to start the CMS on Node B if it recognizes that Node A is lost. In this case, Exchange has to determine if it can automatically mount the database on Node B. Node B might have not copied all transaction log files from Node A. In this case, the AutoDatabaseMountDial setting comes into play. The value that you have configured for AutoDatabaseMountDial determines whether Exchange can automatically mount a database.

The default value is *BestAvailability*, but you can also set this to *GoodAvailability* or *Lossless*. Availability refers to the ability of the CMS to be able to send and receive new emails; it does not directly refer to the amount of data loss. With *BestAvailability* and *GoodAvailability*, it is more likely that the database can be mounted, but it is accepted that more log files are missing. *Lossless* refers to a configuration that only allows mounting the database automatically if no log file is lost.

The quantity of lost log files is determined based on the copy queue length. Exchange compares the value of the last log file generated on the former active node with the generation number of the last log file inspected by the passive node. The Replication service keeps track of these counters, and this information is also written to the registry in LCR and SCR, or written to the cluster database in CCR. This allows the passive node to know this information even if the former active node is unavailable.

Table 7-2   *AutoDatabaseMountDial*

AutoDatabaseMountDial	Acceptable copy queue length
Loss-less	0
Good availability	3
Best availability	6

If the copy queue is longer than the value provided in Table 7-2, Exchange does not automatically mount the database. Exchange will wait and continue to try to access the log file share on the former active node to copy additional log files.

LLR also affects the *ESEUTIL.EXE* recovery mode. A new switch, */A*, was added to enable recovering a database with missing log files.

Transport Dumpster

In Exchange Server 2007, every email sent has to traverse a server holding the Hub Transport (HT) role. This is the case even if User A sends an email to User B hosted in the same database. This constraint enables the usage of transport rules for compliance purposes. Exchange also takes advantage of this requirement for recovery purposes.

In the past, bridgehead servers used plain files to store emails waiting in a queue for delivery. Exchange Server 2007 uses an ESE database, *mail.que*, for this purpose. The database has a retention area that is used to store emails that have already been delivered to recipients. Mailbox servers can request HT servers in their AD site to resubmit emails stored in this retention area. This is similar to the deleted items cache of the mailbox database that users can take advantage of to recover deleted items. This retention area of the HT database is called the *transport dumpster*.

It is important to emphasize that the transport dumpster only contains emails that have already been delivered and not emails that are pending delivery. It is also important to highlight that certain objects are not protected by the transport dumpster because these objects do not traverse the HT role, such as:

- Appointments
- Updates to the contact folder
- Updates to the task folder
- Property updates to emails like the status update that an email in the inbox has been opened
- Items stored in the drafts folder

In the RTM version, only CCR could take advantage of the transport dumpster. The HT servers were asked to resubmit messages after a failover if log files were missing. Since SP1, LCR is using the transport dumpster to minimize data loss as well. If you execute *Restore-StorageGroupCopy* for an LCR-enabled storage group, the Replication service will request all HT servers in its AD site to resubmit messages. Single servers without LCR or SCC do not use the transport dumpster. SCR does also not use the transport dumpster.

Recall that if you lose an entire data center in a disaster, you lose the mailbox server and the HT servers. In this case, you cannot take advantage of the transport dumpster. This is also true in a geographically dispersed deployment: The passive cluster nodes in Data center B cannot take advantage of the HT servers in Data center A if a disaster completely destroys Data center A.

The Exchange Team blog article titled, "How the Transport Dumpster Works with a CCR Cluster," specifies that at least one recipient must reside on a CCR server for an email to be retained in the transport dumpster. It is likely that this rule was extended in SP1: At least one recipient must reside on CCR or an LCR-enabled storage group.

You can configure the size of the transport dumpster and the maximum time a message stays in the dumpster per storage group. The settings are Exchange organization wide: All storage groups have the same values, and all HT servers have an identical configuration. The configuration can be defined using *Set-TransportConfig* or starting with SP1 set within the EMC.

The parameter *MaxDumpsterSizePerStorageGroup* defines the size of the dumpster per storage group. The default value is 18 MB. Microsoft TechNet recommends setting this value to 1.5 times the size of the maximum message size, or if you have not configured message size limits, to 1.5 times the size of an average message. There are other rules of thumb: The transport dumpster should provide enough space to enable mailbox servers to reclaim all emails that are lost because the corresponding log files have not arrived on the passive CCR node. Accordingly, the dumpster size depends on the expected number of missing log files after a lossy failover.

The necessary space, *MaxDumpsterSizePerStorageGroup*, is allocated per storage group on each server with the HT role in the same AD site as the mailbox server. If you have multiple servers with the HT role in an AD site, then the total amount of space reserved for one storage group is *MaxDumpsterSizePerStorageGroup* × servers with the HT role.

The parameter *MaxDumpsterTime* specifies how long an email can stay in the transport dumpster. The default value is 7 days. The dumpster uses a first in–first out method and *MaxDumpsterSizePerStorageGroup* takes priority over *MaxDumpsterTime*. If a new email has to be stored in the transport dumpster and the dumpster is full, an old message gets removed even if it has not yet been in the transport dumpster for the maximum specified time.

The transport dumpster must be considered during the transport server storage design, and adequate disk capacity for the dumpster on the disk volume hosting the mail queue database must be reserved. The estimated size of the dumpster follows:

MaxDumpsterSizePerStorageGroup × (storage groups on CCR
+ LCR-enabled storage groups in this AD site).

If you use disk volumes provided by a SAN for the mail queues, you can easily increase performance by adding more disk spindles to the disk group if you identify a performance bottleneck. Please keep in mind that in Exchange Server 2007, every email sent will go to a server with the HT role. Do not underestimate the I/O requirements of the HT.

Since SP1, you can use the EMC to configure the transport dumpster; the PowerShell command *Get-StorageGroupCopyStatus* was enhanced and

Figure 7-19

Transport dumpster statistics

```
Machine: CCR9-NB | Scope: test.local                                    _ □ X
[PS] C:\>Get-StorageGroupCopyStatus -DumpsterStatistics | fl name, OutstandingDu
mpsterRequests, DumpsterServersNotAvailable, DumpsterStatistics

OutstandingDumpsterRequests : {HTCAS3(12/29/2007 8:35:13 AM;12/30/2007 12:50:58
                              AM)}
DumpsterServersNotAvailable : {HTCAS3}
DumpsterStatistics          : {HTCAS1(12/29/2007 8:02:52 PM;1078;18427KB)}


[PS] C:\>_
```

now provides transport dumpster statistics. Figure 7-19 shows the statistics that are now viewable:

- *OutStandingDumpsterRequests* lists the HT servers that have not answered a resubmit request and specifies the start and end time-frame of the emails that should be resubmitted.

- *DumpsterServersNotAvailable* lists the HT servers that are currently not reachable.

- *DumpsterStatistics* provides the following information per HT server: time stamp of the oldest email, number of items in the dumpster for this storage group, and currently used size of the dumpster for this storage group.

Failover

In CCR, you can manually start a failover from the active cluster node to the passive cluster node. This is called handoff in Exchange terminology. The Exchange team recommends using the *Move-ClusteredMailboxServer* command for CMS failover. You should not use the command line tool *CLUSTER.EXE* or the cluster GUI to initiate a failover. The PowerShell command *Move-ClusteredMailboxServer* performs continuous replication-specific health checks that the cluster tools do not perform.

You would, for example, start a handoff to perform maintenance tasks on the hardware of the active cluster node. In addition to these scheduled outages, there are unplanned failovers that occur because of a hardware failure. In this case, the cluster service initiates the failover, and the abovementioned health checks are not performed prior to the failover.

It should be possible to move a CMS from the active node to the passive node in less than 2 minutes. One performance improvement for CCR in SP1 is that databases are taken offline without flushing the database cache. This reduces the necessary time for a manual handoff and an automatic failover in case the active cluster node failed. Note that in SCC, the database cache is still flashed before the CMS is move to the other node.

Testing by the HP CFT team has shown that initiating a failover by executing *Move-ClusteredMailboxServer* from the passive node is faster compared with executing the command from the active cluster node. The handoff started from the passive node took less than 2 minutes, but the command required more than 8 minutes when started from the active node.

Note that the 2 minutes comprise the time necessary for the technical move of the CMS from Node A to Node B. A failover resulting from a hardware failure is often more complex, and a failover from Data center A to Data center B because of a site-level disaster requires up-front planning. The Exchange Team Blog article, "CCR, Site Resilience and Sample Decision Making Processes," provides a good description of what has to be considered regarding a failover in a production CCR deployment.

The following section describes the steps that occur in the background during scheduled and unscheduled outages. You can use Process Monitor from Windows *Sysinternals* to monitor the activity of the Exchange services during the failover. Process Monitor allows you to see how the Information Store and the Replication service are working with the transaction log files.

Let's start with describing a manually initiated handoff:

1.   In Figure 7-20, you see that the passive cluster node copies closed log files from the active cluster node.

2.   You request a handoff using *Move-ClusteredMailboxServer*, and specify a comment on why the failover was initiated using the

Figure 7-20
Failover Process
Start

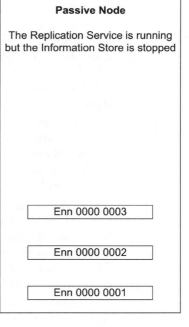

Active Node	Passive Node
Information Store and Replication Service are running	The Replication Service is running but the Information Store is stopped

Enn (Generation 4)

Enn 0000 0003	Enn 0000 0003
Enn 0000 0002	Enn 0000 0002
Enn 0000 0001	Enn 0000 0001

Node A   **Node B**

parameter *MoveComment*. This comment is visible afterward in the event viewer application log.

3. The PowerShell command verifies the health of the CR process and the cluster status. This is comparable to manually executing *Get-StorageGroupCopyStatus*, *Get-ClusteredMailboxServerStatus*, and *Test-ReplicationHealth* to verify whether the current status allows a successful failover to the passive cluster node without the likelihood of data loss or a dismounted database. This health check identifies issues that already occurred in the past.

4. The clustered Exchange resources such as the System Attendant are stopped on the active cluster node. If the services are not reacting in a timely manner, they are forcibly terminated. During this step, the current log file, *Enn.log*, is closed and the passive node is able to pull this log file over.

5. The clustered Exchange resources are moved to the former passive node and then they are brought online on the new active node. First, the IP address and the network name are started. The Exchange specific resources are started afterward because they depend on the network name resource (Figure 7-21).

Figure 7-21
Exchange start on former passive node

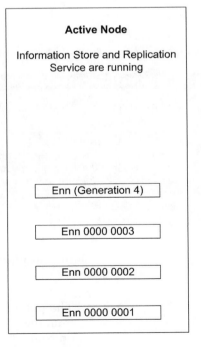

Passive Node	Active Node
The Replication Service is running but the Information Store is stopped	Information Store and Replication Service are running
Enn (Generation 4)	Enn (Generation 4)
Enn 0000 0003	Enn 0000 0003
Enn 0000 0002	Enn 0000 0002
Enn 0000 0001	Enn 0000 0001
Node A	**Node B**

6.   The Exchange Replication service on Node B tries to pull any missing log files from the former active node. If it has not copied *Enn.log* in Step 4, it will copy the file now.

7.   The Exchange Information Store service on Node B starts a soft recovery process and tries to mount the databases. The CMS is now available online to end users and new transaction log files are generated.

8.   The Exchange Replication service on Node A compares the log files with generation number 4 and recognizes that the log file on the active node, Node B, is newer. Therefore, it moves its outdated copy of the log file to the directory *<LogFileDirectory> IgnoredLogs\EnnOutofDate*.

9.   CR continues as normal and the passive node pulls closed log files from the active node.

10. You perform maintenance tasks on Node A, such as shutting it down to replace a failed case fan.

You can use the event viewer to check the successful move in the application log of the former active node (Figure 7-22).

Figure 7-22   *Successful* Move-ClusteredMailboxServer

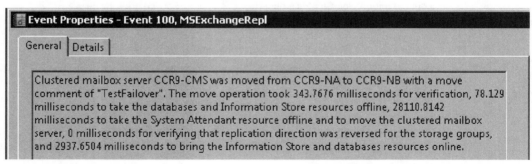

During an unscheduled outage (Figure 7-23), the following steps take place.

1.   The passive node has not copied all closed transaction log files from the active node. Log file generation 3 and 4 are not available on Node B.

Figure 7-23
Start lossy failover

Active Node	Passive Node
Information Store and Replication Service are running	The Replication Service is running but the Information Store is stopped

Enn (Generation 5)

Enn 0000 0004

Enn 0000 0003

Enn 0000 0002   Enn 0000 0002

Enn 0000 0001   Enn 0000 0001

Node A   **Node B**

2. Node A goes down because of a failure.

3. The cluster service on Node B recognizes that Node A is unavailable and tries to start the CMS on Node B.

4. The Replication service on Node B is not able to copy any missing log files from the log file share on Node A because Node A is down.

5. The number of lost log files is calculated. This is the difference between the last log generated on the former active node, Node A, and the last log inspected on the former passive/now-active node, Node B. The Replication service keeps track of the generation numbers, and this information is also written to the Windows failover cluster database. The cluster database is synchronized between the cluster nodes. This allows the remaining node to know the generation number that the active node created before it failed. In our

case, the last log generated on Node A was 5, and the last log file copied and inspected on Node B has generation number 2. Three log files are missing on Node B.

6.   The number of lost log files is compared with the configured *AutoDatabaseMountDial* setting. You lose fewer log files, and this is used as a signal that Exchange can try to automatically mount the database. Figure 7-24 shows a screenshot from a test environment—log generation 1406 and 1407 are missing on Node B.

Figure 7-24
Loss calculation and Automount

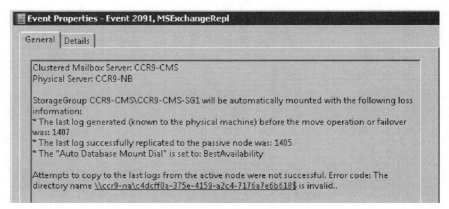

7.   To mitigate the data loss, the HT servers in the local AD site are asked to redeliver emails (Figure 7-25). The lists of unavailable HT servers and outstanding requests are written to the cluster database. You can read these lists in the cluster hive of the registry, or use the command in Figure 7-19 to get the transport dumpster statistics.

Figure 7-25
Transport dumpster redelivery request

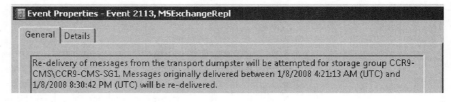

8.   The Information Store starts a soft recovery using all locally available transaction log files. If the recovery is successful, the database will be mounted. The attempts of the Replication service to pull missing log files from the failed cluster node are stopped. As soon

as the database is mounted, it cannot roll forward additional log files that were previously missing.

9. The lossy failover is finished and the now active cluster node creates new transaction log files (Figure 7-26).

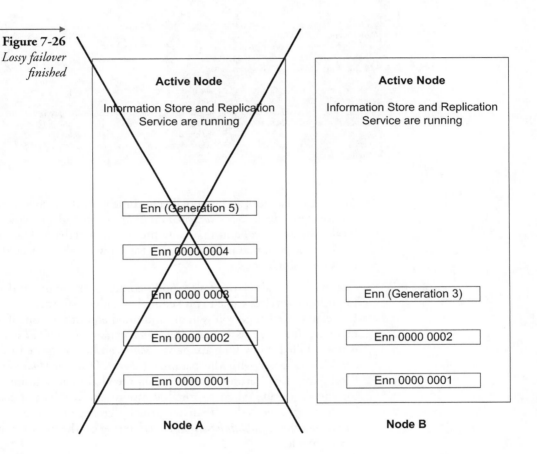

Figure 7-26
*Lossy failover
finished*

Active Node

Information Store and Replication
Service are running

Enn (Generation 5)

Enn 0000 0004

Enn 0000 0003

Enn 0000 0002

Enn 0000 0001

Node A

Active Node

Information Store and Replication
Service are running

Enn (Generation 3)

Enn 0000 0002

Enn 0000 0001

Node B

10. HT servers resubmit messages from the transport dumpster. The Exchange Store is intelligent enough to avoid creating duplicate messages. This minimizes the actual data loss of the lossy failover. The mailbox server will continue for *MaxDumpsterTime* to contact any outstanding HT servers and request a redelivery of messages.

You might be unlucky: The database does not mount automatically because you lost more log files than what is accepted based on the *AutoDatabaseMountDial* setting. In this case, you have the options shown in Figure 7-27.

Figure 7-27
No Automount

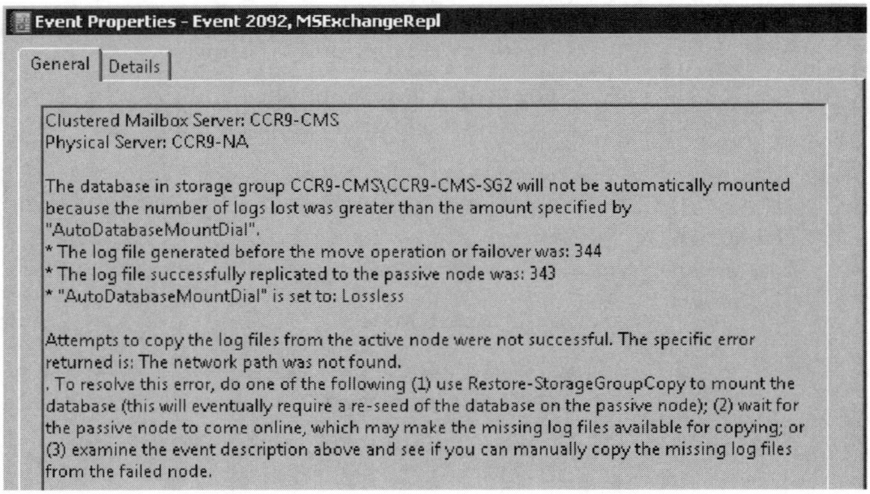

1.   Accept the data loss and manually continue with the recovery pro-
      cedure. Use the *Restore-StorageGroupCopy* command to mark the
      local copy as active, and manually mount the database. This step
      is comparable to manually activating the copy database created by
      LCR on a single server.

2.   Continue to wait if the failed node comes back online and the
      Replication service is able to pull enough log files to the active node.
      By default, Exchange will wait an unlimited amount of time if too
      many log files are missing and the *AutoDatabaseMountDial* setting
      is not fulfilled. How long Exchange waits can be configured using
      Set-MailboxServer with the parameter *ForcedDatabaseMountAfter*.
      Modifying this setting is not recommended. An administra-
      tor should decide when to forcibly mount the database if more
      log files have been lost than are usually considered acceptable.
      Increasing the *AutoDatabaseMountDial* setting on the fly is also not
      recommended.

3.   Try to manually copy log files from the failed node to the remain-
      ing cluster node.

Divergence

Let's assume that you recovered the failed Node A and the node comes back
online. The cluster node recognizes that Node B is now the active node. The
passive node now has to determine the divergence between its local data and
the data available on the active cluster node—Node B. Comparing the database file on Node A and Node B is impractical because the file is usually

several gigabytes in size. The passive node just compares the local transaction log files with the transaction log files on the active node. The comparison process does not perform a byte-by-byte comparison of file contents. The process uses the information in the log file header for the comparison. The Replication service starts the comparison with the latest log file. This is file "Enn (Generation 5)" in Figure 7-28. The Replication service will continue to compare the log files until it finds the first log files that are identical on the local system and on the active cluster node. The previously compared log file is the first divergent log file.

Figure 7-28
Divergence detection

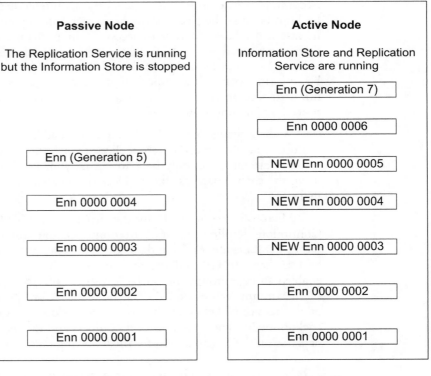

If this first divergent log file is above the waypoint (Figure 7-18), LLR helped to prevent database divergence. In this case, the Replication service can move the divergent log files to the *IgnoredLogs* directory on the passive node (Figure 7-29). The Replication service recopies the necessary log files from the active node.

If the first divergent log file is older than the waypoint, both databases have different content and reseeding the database is necessary.

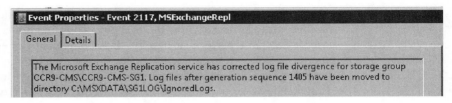

Figure 7-29
*Divergence
corrected*

Maximum Database Size

According to Microsoft, CR removes the requirement to perform daily full backups because the passive copy of the database is your first line of defense in case a database recovery is necessary. In Exchange Server 2003, it was necessary to restore a previously created backup of the Exchange database after data corruption or loss of the volume hosting the database. This could be very time consuming, especially if the database size is large, the backup infrastructure provides only low throughput, or disaster recovery operational procedures are not up-to-date.

With Exchange Server 2007, you have an additional line of defense. You can utilize an almost up-to-date replica of your production database for your recovery attempt. You only have to restore your last backup if the recovery using the passive database failed. Does this enable large databases of unlimited size?

Microsoft recommends in the articles titled, "Planning for Cluster Continuous Replication" and "Recommendations for Configuring Storage Groups and Databases," that databases which are not enabled for CR should be less than 100 GB and the maximum database size for LCR- or CCR-enabled storage groups should be less than 200 GB. The main reason why the maximum recommended database for LCR or CCR is larger is because of the reduced likelihood that you have to do a traditional restore from backup media. These are not fixed numbers and the maximum database size depends on the time required for the following tasks:

Online maintenance. You should ensure that online maintenance is finished for each database at least once every 2 weeks. It is even better if online defragmentation and other tasks performed by online maintenance completes a full pass every week.

Offline maintenance. It may be necessary to run a offline defragmentation or database repair. The larger the database, the longer the task will take, and users cannot access their mailbox in online mode.

Database seeding. If you activate the copy database during a recovery process, then it is necessary to manually reseed a new replica database. Until the seeding process is finished, you do not have your new first line of defense—the database copy. If you are very unlucky and a second failure occurs during this time, you must perform a traditional restore of your last good backup set. To give you an idea how long reseeding can take, we share the results of a test that a colleague performed. The Exchange server hosted 5000 1 GB mailboxes, and reseeding all databases over a 155-Mbps link took 3.5 days!

Traditional restore from backup. In the end, you have to be capable of restoring your mailbox databases using traditional restores from tape devices if your new advanced technology feature has failed! Examples include (1) making a mistake during the recovery procedure and accidentally deleting your healthy copy database instead of the corrupt "active" database, and (2) failure by your virus scanner to recognize a virus outbreak, and the modifications made by the virus were already replayed to the replica database. You should keep such failures in mind when you negotiate recovery service levels. Luckily, starting with Exchange Server 2007 SP1, you can create additional replicas using SCR.

At this juncture, you should be aware that imposing database size restrictions is recommended, and that the advent of CR has not eliminated the best practice of running daily backups.

Backup Integration

Chapter 8 describes Exchange backups in general. This section explains the integration of the backup process with LCR and CCR. Information on how SCR affects the backup process is provided mainly in a later section in this chapter about SCR.

It is important to highlight that LCR, CCR, and SCR do not automatically delete log files after they have been replayed to the passive database. The log files of the passive database are truncated only after a successful backup. This is one reason why you still have to run backups with CR. If you fail to do so, then Exchange will automatically dismount your database because there is no free capacity on the volume hosting your transaction log files.

There is one exception to the above statement. If you enable circular logging, log files are deleted independent of running backups. You should not use circular logging for storage groups hosting production mailboxes. Circular logging makes sense only during *LoadGen* performance testing in the database initialization phase. Circular logging prevents a restore to the point of failure; you can recover only to the point in time you created the backup set because there is no contiguous transaction log file sequence available that you can roll forward.

In CR, log file truncation has to be coordinated with log file shipping. After a successful backup, the database header gets updated by the database engine. The update of the active database header is written to a transaction log file, and this log file is shipped and replayed into the copy database. Therefore, the active and passive database header shows the time of the last successful backup.

With the streaming backup application programming interface (API), you only can back up the active database. You have to use Volume Shadow Copy Services (VSS) to back up the passive storage group/copy database. If you use VSS to back up the copy database, then the backup process does not directly update the header of the copy database. The Replication service coordinates with the Information Store, and the Store updates the active database header first. Log file shipping will replicate the change to the passive side, and the passive database is updated in a second step.

A successful full and a successful incremental backup truncates the transaction log files. Log file truncation has to be coordinated between the active and passive database. On the active storage group only log files that (1) are not needed for recovery, (2) have been replayed to the copy database, and (3) have been backed up can be truncated. Log file truncation has to be deferred if the active database has been backed up while the passive CCR node is unavailable. In an SCR configuration, log files can only be deleted if they have been shipped to ALL SCR targets. The Information Store deletes log files of the active storage group and the Exchange Replication service deletes the replayed log files of the passive storage group.

CR enables you to offload the backup process from the production storage group to the passive CCR node or LCR copy storage group. You can back up the replica database and log files. This enables you to remove the I/O load from the disk spindles hosting the production storage group. With LCR, this only offloads the disk I/O. With CCR, the backup process of the copy database runs on the passive cluster node. This enables you to offload the CPU and memory demand of the backup process to a server not directly accessed by online users.

Additional information about backing up mailbox servers using CR is available in Chapter 8. This chapter also describes the use of VSS to back up the passive database of a CCR deployment.

Microsoft states that CR does not remove the necessity of performing backups, but it reduces the need to perform regular full online backups. The replica database is now your first line of defense, and you only need to restore your last backup if activating the database copy failed. For previous Exchange versions or with Exchange Server 2007 without LCR or CCR, running daily full backups is best practice. As more mailbox servers using Exchange Server 2007 with LCR or CCR are put in production, this best practice might evolve and running full weekly and differential daily online backups for LCR/CCR deployments may be recommended. Be aware that this will complicate the recovery procedure, because you would have to restore your latest differential backup in addition to your last full backup.

You also have to remember that you cannot vault your copy database in a safe. For some environments, creating a copy of the backup data in a remote site—for example, on a virtual tape library—is not sufficient. For your last line of defense, it is still a best practice to implement something like a grandfather-father-son (GFS) backup strategy and store one backup data set offline in a safe for disaster recovery purposes.

Local Continuous Replication

Local Continuous Replication is the implementation of log file shipping on a single server (Figure 7-30). This feature is available with the Standard Edition of Exchange Server 2007. In contrast, CCR requires the more expensive Enterprise Edition of Exchange Server 2007, and the Enterprise Edition of the Windows Server operating system, because it is based on Windows Failover Clustering.

Figure 7-30
Local Continuous Replication

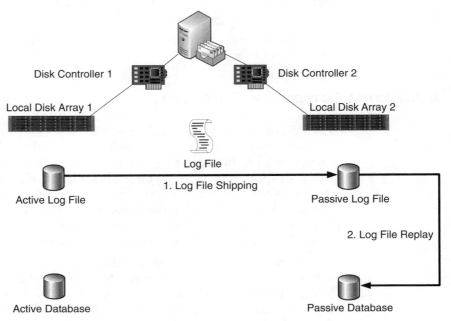

LCR allows you to granularly configure which storage group should take advantage of log file shipping. It is not necessary to enable all storage groups hosted on the server for LCR. LCR allows a granular database recovery. With LCR, you can recover a single database using the database replica without affecting the other databases hosted on the server. With CCR, you have to perform a failover of the complete CMS from the active node to the passive node. A failover affects all storage groups hosted on the cluster.

No automatic activation of the replica database is provided by LCR. A manual/scripted activation is required in the event of a database failure. It is important to note that the copy database location does not contain database search index files. If you activate the copy database with *Restore-StorageGroupCopy*, a re-index of the database will be triggered. Additional information about the behavior of Exchange Search after recovery scenarios is available in the Exchange Search FAQs on the Exchange Ninjas website.

LCR is less complex to operate when compared to CCR. Your operational staff might prefer LCR over CCR. Operating LCR is similar in nature to operating a single/standalone Exchange mailbox server. Managing Exchange Server 2007 LCR requires less training for your staff compared to CCR because Windows clustering is not involved. It is similar to what you already know from managing an Exchange Server 2003 mailbox server.

In the Exchange Server 2007 RTM version, LCR cannot take advantage of the transport dumpster provided by the HT role. Starting with SP1, LCR will request HT servers in its AD site to redeliver emails during the execution of *Restore-StorageGroupCopy*.

The following sections describe topics that you must consider while planning for LCR.

Additional Computing Resources

The mailbox server that is primarily servicing online users must have supplementary computing resources to be able to handle the additional LCR tasks in the background. Log file replication, verification, and replaying the log files to the replica database are handled by the Exchange Replication service running on the same server. You should provide approximately 20% of additional CPU and at least 1 GB of additional memory resources to a mailbox server using LCR. These figures are based on the recommendations provided by Microsoft TechNet in the "Planning Processor and Memory Configurations" section.

Obviously, LCR needs additional storage capacity and especially I/O performance. With Exchange Server 2003, a rule of thumb was that the I/O load on the log file volume is approximately 10% of the I/O load on the database volume. With Exchange Server 2007, this has increased because of the smaller log file size, more storage groups, and the reduction of database reads in Exchange Server 2007. You can assume that there are three write I/Os to the log file volume for every four write I/Os to the database volume. This rule of thumb is independent of LCR.

With LCR, the access pattern on the log file volume will not be only sequential writes. There will be read I/O to this volume because the Exchange Replication service has to read the closed log files stored on this disk volume to copy them to the replica log file volume. Figure 7-31 shows

Figure 7-31   *Read access to log file volume*

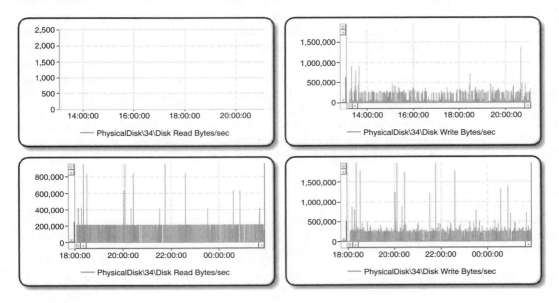

the I/O before the storage group was LCR enabled in the first row, and the I/O after LCR was activated in the second row. The charts were provided by a colleague working for the HP CFT team.

Storage Configuration

Considering the replication process during the storage design is important. The volume used to store the passive database must be a local disk from the disk management perspective, but can be located on a central storage array utilizing iSCSI or Fibre Channel connectivity. It is not possible to host the passive database and log files on a network share.

You can use the same disk volume that is used by the production database and log files for the passive database and log files. However, this a disadvantage: If you lose this volume, you lose the production and the replica database at the same time. For recovery purposes, you should use separate disk volumes for your databases and log files. Otherwise, a failed disk volume means data loss, because you cannot use your last backup and the new transaction logs to recover your Exchange database to the point of failure. Based on these best practices, you need at least five disk volumes for a LCR deployment with a single database! Use of separate disk volumes for the operating system and the Exchange binaries are even recommended. This has advantages for certain disaster recovery scenarios.

With Exchange Server 2007, it is possible to create 50 storage groups. Based on the previously provided recommendation, 202 disk volumes would be required! Is this a manageable configuration? Is the maximum storage group configuration exploited frequently? With the increased maximum value of storage groups, it is easy to surpass the drive letter limitation. You can solve this problem by using mount points. Figure 7-32 shows an example configuration. Mount points provide another very important advantage. You can easily swap the disk mounted at a mount point, which makes the recovery process easier when you want to swap the production and replica database. Note, however, that your operations staff needs time to become accustomed to the mount point concept. Additional information about mount points is available in Chapter 4.

Figure 7-32
LCR disk volumes and mount points

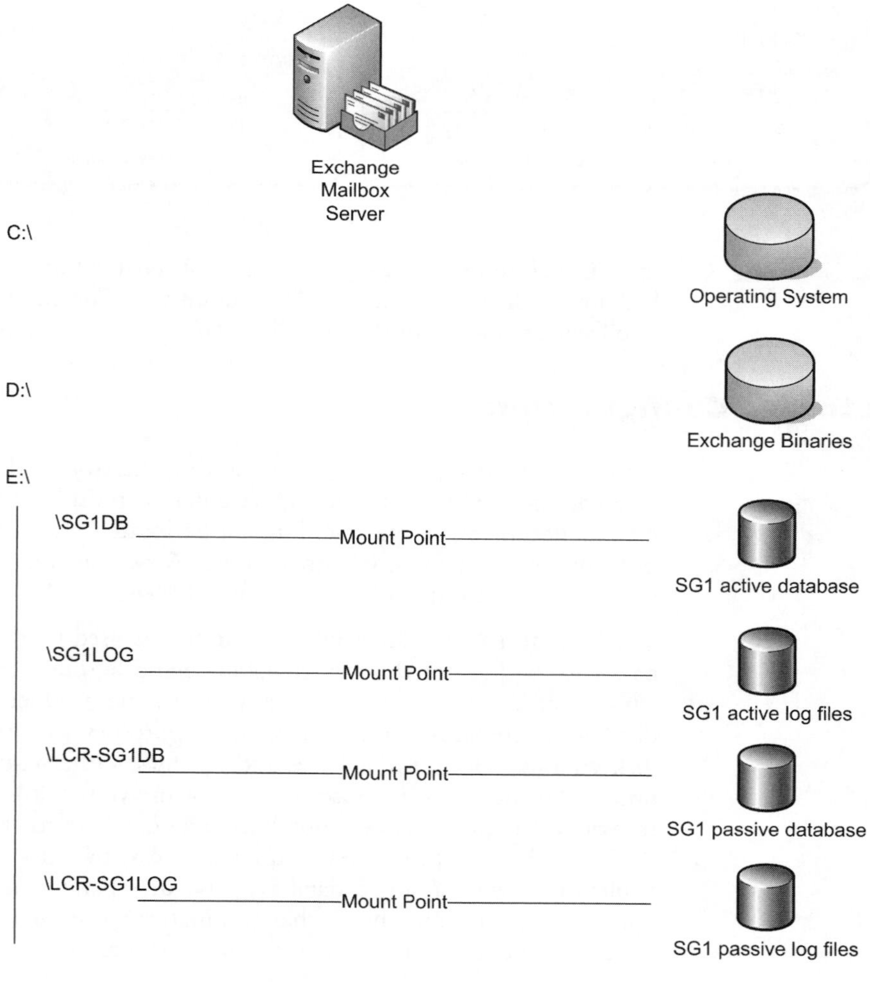

Exchange
Mailbox
Server

C:\ .... Operating System

D:\ .... Exchange Binaries

E:\

\SG1DB ————————Mount Point———————— SG1 active database

\SG1LOG ————————Mount Point———————— SG1 active log files

\LCR-SG1DB ————————Mount Point———————— SG1 passive database

\LCR-SG1LOG ————————Mount Point———————— SG1 passive log files

If you prefer a recovery procedure that modifies the path of the active database to point to the former replica database, you should use a good naming convention for the file system directories and database files. Otherwise, it can be difficult to determine which database is active and which database file is the passive one.

The performance requirements for LCR have to be considered if you are using a modern storage array that lets you carve out individual disk volumes from a fixed set of physical disk spindles. This shared set of spindles has to provide enough performance for the active database and the passive database if you carve out both volumes from the same set of disk spindles. This approach has a disadvantage: If you lose this set of physical disks, you have lost your production data and your first line of defense, the CR-created passive database, at the same time. Another option is to use separate sets of physical disk spindles for the active and passive database volumes.

The next consideration is, "What happens after a recovery?" After a production database failure, you must manually activate the replica database. You have to ensure that the volume hosting the replica database is capable of handling the production load from a performance point of view.

Additionally, if you host your second copy on disks with lower Mean Time Between Failure (MTBF) characteristics, then there is a higher likelihood of a disk failure on the volume now hosting the production data! Therefore, you have to carefully consider the consequences of using low-cost disks for your LCR deployment because of performance and reliability reasons.

If you are using Direct Attached Storage (DAS), then you should think about using separate storage controllers to access the disk volumes hosting your active database and your replica database. You should even consider using separate storage cabinets. Otherwise, if you lose your single storage controller, you lose access to both databases at the same time. Using separate controllers isolates one database from being affected by a controller failure. The configuration comprising two storage controllers is comparable to a no single point of failure configuration using two Fibre Channel host bus adapters in a SAN environment.

Cluster Continuous Replication

Local Continuous Replication does not provide a solution for the failure of your single server hardware. This is the domain of CCR and SCC. CCR is the combination of log file shipping with Windows failover clustering. With CCR, the passive database is created by a second server on its local disks. CCR can be deployed on DAS. A SAN is not required, whether Fibre Channel or iSCSI. This reduced infrastructure requirement lowers the hardware costs. All servers used as cluster nodes must be listed in the Windows Server Catalog, but it is not required that they are listed in the cluster category. This enables a wider variety of supported configurations, which also reduces the hardware costs, because often systems certified in the cluster category are more expensive. With CCR, Microsoft enables small and medium businesses to deploy a highly available Exchange back-end without the need for an expensive and complex SAN infrastructure. Figure 7-33 exemplifies a CCR deployment.

Figure 7-33   *Cluster continuous replication*

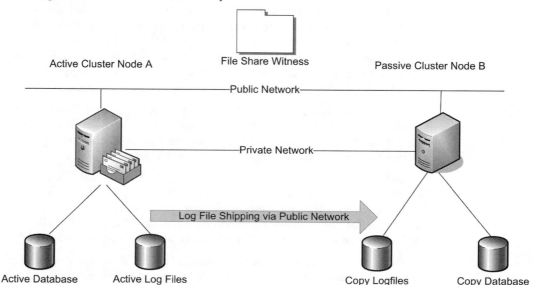

CCR is based on a Majority Node Set (MNS) cluster configuration. You can use a configuration with three nodes, but usually a two-node configuration with a File Share Witness (FSW) is deployed. The FSW uses a file share provided by a separate server that is not part of the cluster as a voter. A single server can provide multiple shares for separate clusters, which reduces the required number of systems, and thus lowering the hardware costs. See Chapter 6 for additional information about Windows failover clustering.

A major difference between LCR and CCR is that Windows clustering automatically performs a failover in case the server hardware of the active node fails. The CMS will *not* automatically fail over if a database is corrupt and cannot be mounted. An administrator has to decide whether the mailboxes hosted in a database are important enough to try a recovery by initiating a failover of the CMS. This failover affects all databases hosted on CCR.

When Microsoft shipped the Exchange Server 2007 RTM version, CCR was proposed as a solution that can be deployed for site resilience purposes. Microsoft advertised CCR as a solution capable of deploying one cluster node in Data center A and the other cluster node in Data center B. Geographically dispersed Exchange clusters have requirements that make this configuration difficult:

- Two nonrouted subnets have to be used for the private and public network with Windows Server 2003. Windows Server 2008 removed this limitation.

- All cluster nodes must be a member of the same AD site. This is a requirement of Exchange Server 2007. Windows Server 2008 failover clustering only requires that the nodes are members of the same AD domain; Windows Server 2008 does not require that the nodes are members of the same AD site.

Starting with SP1, you have another option for a site resilient solution— SCR. You should read the following section titled, "Standby Continuous Replication," and then make your decision about which architecture best fits your business needs.

Log File Shipping Network

Exchange Server 2007 SP1 introduced the possibility of using multiple networks for log file shipping from the active to the passive cluster node. In the RTM version, log file shipping and database seeding only used the public network. In particular, seeding a large database could affect client traffic because the network is congested. The TechNet section, "Continuous Replication over Redundant Cluster Networks," describes additional benefits of using multiple log file shipping networks. Note that continuous replication over redundant networks is only available with CCR and not with SCR.

The network that you going to use for log file shipping has to be configured as a mixed network in Windows Server 2003, or enabled for Client Access in Windows Server 2008. The PowerShell command *Enable-Contin uousReplicationHostName* creates a new network name resource and an IP address in the cluster. Windows clustering does not allow you to create these resources using an IP address on a private/internal use–only network. The cluster assumes that the resource has to be accessed by clients and this would be impossible using this type of network.

The cluster service creates a computer account in AD for this network name, and Exchange uses this account to access the share with the log files of the storage group. The cluster nodes have to be able to resolve this network name to the corresponding IP address of the log file shipping network. Microsoft recommends for Windows Server 2008 that NetBIOS be enabled on the network adapter used for log shipping. In this case, the short name will be resolved by NetBIOS name resolution broadcasts or by queries sent to a configured

Windows Internet name service (WINS) server. If you select "Register this connection's addresses in DNS" for the log file shipping network adapter, you run into the problem that the cluster node tries to register its public IP address and the IP address of the log shipping network adapter in DNS. Clients should access the public network and not the network that is reserved for log file shipping. See Microsoft Knowledge Base Article 302389 for additional information about the cluster network name resource. Microsoft TechNet notes that on Windows Server 2003 you have to disable strict name checking, because Windows Server 2003 does not listen to requests using an alias name. This problem is described in Microsoft Knowledge Base Article 281308.

```
REG_DWORD
HKEY_LOCAL_MACHINE\System\CurrentControl Set\ Services\
LanmanServer\Parameters\DisableStrictNameChecking = 1
```

The first command in Figure 7-34 creates the replication hostname on Node A and the second command on Node B. The two commands create two additional cluster groups. Each group can be online only on the cluster node specified with the parameter—*TargetMachine*.

Figure 7-34
Enable-
Continuous
ReplicationHost
Name

```
Machine: CCR9-NA | Scope: test.local                                    _ □ ×
[PS] C:\>Enable-ContinuousReplicationHostName -Identity CCR9-CMS -TargetMachine
CCR9-NA -HostName CCR9-NA-Log -IPV4Address 192.168.5.3 -confirm:$false
[PS] C:\>Enable-ContinuousReplicationHostName -Identity CCR9-CMS -TargetMachine
CCR9-NB -HostName CCR9-NB-Log -IPV4Address 192.168.5.4 -confirm:$false
[PS] C:\>_
```

Figure 7-35 shows that this group has no Preferred Owners configured. If you omit the TargetMachine parameter, the command assumes that the group should be online on the local cluster node. In this case, you have to execute one command on Node A and the other command on Node B. Otherwise, both replication hostnames would be online on the same cluster node and log file shipping would not use this network interface because of your configuration error.

Figure 7-35
*Log shipping
cluster group*

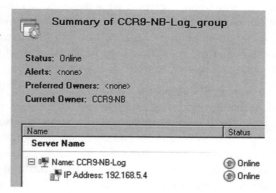

Summary of CCR9-NB-Log_group

Status: Online
Alerts: <none>
Preferred Owners: <none>
Current Owner: CCR9-NB

Name	Status
Server Name	
⊟ Name: CCR9-NB-Log	● Online
IP Address: 192.168.5.4	● Online

Figure 7-36 shows the two new cluster groups and the log file shipping network in the Failover Cluster Management GUI.

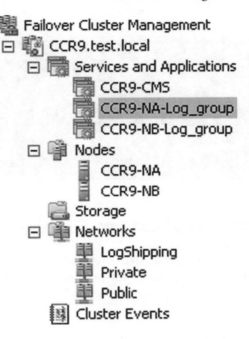

Figure 7-36
Log file shipping host names and redundant networks

The command *Update-StorageGroupCopy* was extended in SP1 and now provides the parameter *-DataHostnames* (Figure 7-37). If you don't use this parameter, the public network is used for seeding. This new parameter enables you to specify that only the log file shipping network and not the public network should be used to seed the database.

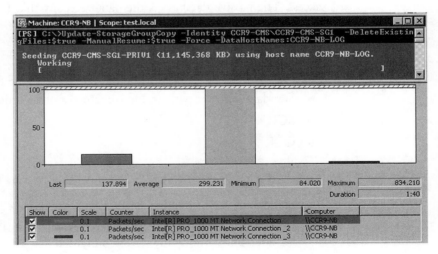

Figure 7-37
Update-Storage GroupCopy *with* DataHostName

The *Get-ClusteredMailboxServerStatus* command in Figure 7-38 shows status information about the configured replication hostnames.

```
Machine: CCR9-NA | Scope: test.local                                          _ □ ×
[PS] C:\Windows\System32>Get-ClusteredMailboxServerStatus


Identity                        : CCR9-CMS
ClusteredMailboxServerName       : CCR9-CMS.test.local
State                           : Online
OperationalMachines              : {CCR9-NA {Active}, CCR9-NB {Quorum Owner}}
FailedResources                 : {}
OperationalReplicationHostNames  : {ccr9-na-log, ccr9-na, ccr9-nb-log, ccr9-nb}
FailedReplicationHostNames       : {}
InUseReplicationHostNames        : {ccr9-na-log, ccr9-nb-log}
IsValid                         : True
ObjectState                     : Unchanged


[PS] C:\Windows\System32>
```

Standby Continuous Replication

With Exchange Server 2007 SP1, Microsoft introduced SCR. The aim of SCR is to provide site resiliency for mailbox databases. SCR uses the same log file shipping technology as LCR and CCR.

SCR Architecture

First, we define terms used in this section to describe SCR. SCR ships log files from a source server to a target server. The SCR source is a mailbox server with the active database, and the SCR target is a mailbox server that hosts the target database. The active database is the database that users access. The passive database is the database copy that LCR or CCR creates, and the target database is the database that SCR creates.

An SCR source server can be a:

■ Standalone server without an LCR-enabled storage group

■ Standalone server with an LCR-enabled storage group

■ SCC

■ CCR

An SCR target server can be a:

■ Standalone server that has no LCR-enabled storage group

■ Failover cluster node with the Exchange binaries of the mailbox role installed but without any CMS configured

If the SCR source and the SCR target is a cluster, then the clusters are two separate Windows Failover Clusters. The SCR source and the SCR target computers are not members of the same cluster!

An SCR source can have multiple SCR targets, but more than four targets per SCR source are not recommended. Log files on the SCR source can only be truncated if they have been inspected on all SCR targets. Increasing the SCR target count increases the dependency and likelihood that a single unavailable SCR target impacts the source.

One mailbox server can be an SCR target of multiple SCR source mailbox servers. Figure 7-39 shows that you can have one SCR target and replicate the most critical mailbox databases from multiple mailbox servers in your production data center to a single SCR target in a remote data center.

Figure 7-39
SCR architecture

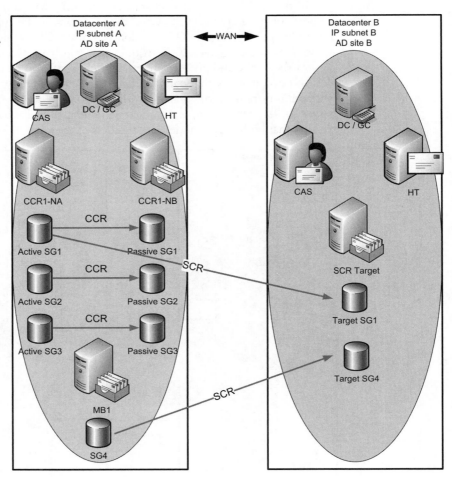

Advantages of SCR

In LCR and CCR, closed log files are immediately shipped to the passive storage group and replayed into the copy database. The SCR target also tries to immediately copy closed transaction log files from the SCR source, but you can configure a time delay before a shipped log file gets replayed into the copy database. This increases the likelihood that a logical corruption is detected before this error also damages the copy database. Let's assume that a new email virus affected all your active databases because your virus scanner does not have a corresponding pattern yet. Your LCR- and CCR-created copy databases will also be affected because the log files are already shipped and replayed. With SCR, you might be able to use the SCR-created database for the recovery, because typically there is a time delay of several hours or a few days until shipped log files are replayed into the SCR database.

In the RTM version of Exchange Server 2007, Microsoft provides limited support for geographically dispersed deployments of the mailbox server role. The only option with the RTM version is to use CCR. Windows failover clustering in Windows Server 2003 requires that you have two nonrouted IP subnets for the public and private subnets. Stretching a Virtual Local Area Network (VLAN) over a WAN that connects two data centers is not a solution that network administrators favor. Starting with SP1 you can deploy CCR on Windows Server 2008, which supports routed networks, but Exchange Server 2007 requires that both cluster nodes are members of the same AD site (Figure 7-40).

Figure 7-40
*Single
AD site*

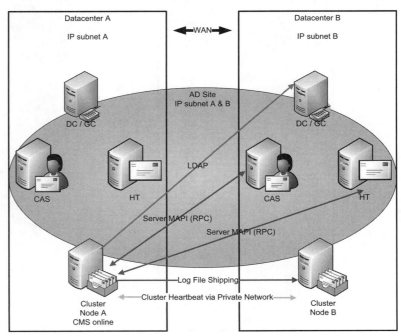

If the servers in Data center A and Data center B are in the same AD site, you cannot prevent a mailbox server in Data center A from picking a server with the HT or CAS role in Data center B as its communication partner. The same is true for AD domain controllers. If a user on a mailbox server in Data center A sends an email to another user on the same server, this mail might travel over the WAN link to an HT server in Data center B and back. Does your WAN link provide enough bandwidth for this communication?

For a site resiliency solution, it is good to have at least several kilometers between both data centers; otherwise, the likelihood is high that a disaster will affect both data centers at the same time. Does your long distance WAN link provide the required low latency? If the latency is too high, you will have a high copy queue length and the passive cluster node might not be able to mount databases after a failover because too many log files are missing. Exchange server-to-server communication uses Remote Procedure Calls (RPC) and assumes a connection with LAN quality.

SCR does not require the usage of Windows failover clustering. This lowers the complexity of the solution, and you can stretch data replication over multiple AD sites (Figure 7-41). With SCR, only continuous replication is using the WAN link between both data centers and the other Exchange server-to-server communication stays within the boundary of the local data center because it is not required to stretch the AD site between the data centers. This reduces the

Figure 7-41
Separate AD sites

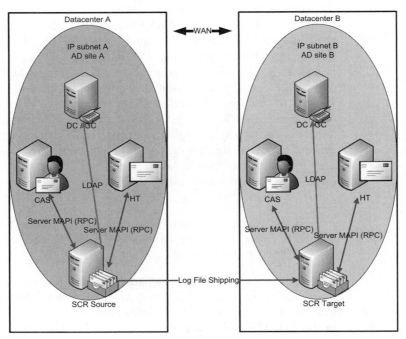

latency requirement on the WAN link and saves WAN bandwidth. The SCR source and the SCR target are members of the same AD domain. Therefore, AD domain controllers will still replicate updates to the AD domain context over the WAN link.

There is one disadvantage that you should be aware of: SCR does not take advantage of the transport dumpster. CCR and LCR can ask all servers in its AD site with the HT role to resubmit missing emails. SCR does not interact with HT servers during the recovery procedure.

SCR requirements

SCR has the same requirements that you are already familiar with from LCR or CCR. For example, a storage group that is enabled for SCR can only have one database, and you cannot combine public folder replication and continuous replication. There are a few additional SCR-specific requirements described in the following.

The SCR source and SCR target can be in different AD sites, but the servers must be members of the same AD domain. Next, SCR is not available with the RTM version of Exchange Server 2007; you need at least SP1. SCR is available with the Standard Edition of Exchange Server 2007. If you use a single server as an SCR target, purchasing the Enterprise Edition of Exchange Server 2007 is not necessary, but if you want to take advantage of the faster recovery procedure for a clustered SCR target then you need the Enterprise Edition of Exchange Server 2007. As discussed in a later section of this chapter, activating a clustered SCR target is pretty simple and fast compared to the steps required for a nonclustered SCR target. With the Standard Edition, you are limited to five storage groups; only the Enterprise Edition of Exchange Server 2007 supports up to 50 storage groups. The SCR source and SCR target can use different Exchange Server Editions. You can, for example, deploy multiple CCR systems with the Enterprise Edition in your main data center, and replicate the five most important storage groups of these clusters to a remote data center, while hosting the SCR target on a single server using the Standard Edition of Exchange Server 2007.

You have to use the same operating system version for the SCR source and SCR target. Using a mixture of Windows Server 2003 and Windows Server 2008 is not supported.

The Exchange installation paths on the SCR source and SCR target must match if you use SCR on a failover cluster. The installation path is written to the AD attribute *msExchInstallPath* of the mailbox server object in the AD. The path must be identical on the clustered SCR source and the

SCR target; otherwise, *setup /RecoverCMS* will fail when you try to activate the SCR target.

The file system path to the database file and storage group transaction log file directory must be identical on the SCR source and SCR target. This can be a problem if you want to use one server as a SCR target for multiple SCR source mailbox servers. Often all servers use the same file system directories to host specific storage groups; for example, storage group 1 is using *C:\ MSXDATA\SG1DB* and *C:\MSXDATA\SG1LOG* on all servers. In an SCR environment, you should consider including the *hostname* in the directory path; for example, you can store the database of storage group 1 in the directory *C:\MSXDATA\<hostname>-SG1DB*. This configuration makes it easier to use one server as the SCR target for multiple SCR source mailbox servers.

Setup and configuration

You can set up and manage SCR only by using the Exchange Management Shell (EMS). The following PowerShell *cmdlets* have been extended in SP1 with SCR-specific parameters:

- *New-StorageGroup*
- *Enable-StorageGroupCopy*
- *Suspend-StorageGroupCopy*
- *Resume-StorageGroupCopy*
- *Update-StorageGroupCopy*
- *Restore-StorageGroupCopy*
- *Disable-StorageGroupCopy*
- *Get-StorageGroupCopyStatus*

The most important new parameter is *-StandbyMachine*. This parameter specifies the SCR target computer. If you use a cluster as an SCR target, which you want to configure as a CCR cluster in case you have to activate the SCR target, then you specify the network name of one physical cluster node as *StandbyMachine*. Do not specify the network name of the Windows failover cluster as *StandbyMachine*. The SCR only ships log files to a single cluster node. The shipped log files and target database are stored on the local storage of this node.

Figure 7-42 shows how to enable SCR on a storage group. The name of the SCR target computer is written to the AD attribute, *msExchStandbyCopy Machines*, of the storage group. One storage group can be replicated to

Figure 7-42
Enable SCR

multiple SCR targets; this attribute is therefore a multivalue one that stores the list of configured SCR targets.

The Exchange Replication service on the SCR target pulls the log files from the SCR source. The log file directory of the SCR-enabled storage group is shared with the globally unique identifier (GUID) of the storage group as the share name. The *<AD domain>\Exchange Servers* security group has access permission to this network share.

This is the same method used by CCR. The passive cluster node pulls the log files via the network from the share on the active cluster node. The Exchange Replication service on the SCR target pulls the log files from the same share on the active CCR cluster node. On a single server, the log file directory is not shared by default. The log file directory will not be shared even if you LCR enable the storage group because the passive database of an LCR-enabled storage group is created on the same server and the Exchange Replication service does not need to access the log files via a network connection. If you SCR enable a storage group on a single server, a share like the one in Figure 7-43 is created.

Figure 7-43
Shared log file directory

How does this work if the SCR source is a cluster? We use Sysinternals Process Monitor running on the SCR target to answer the question. The SCR source is a CCR system with the nodes CCR5-NA and CCR5-NB. The SCR target is the single server SCR-T4. The CMS is currently running on CCR5-NA. As seen in Figure 7-44, the SCR target tries to access a log file on the share *\\CCR5-NA\<StorageGroupGUID>$*. We simulate a failure of the cluster node CCR5-NA and Windows failover clustering will automatically try to bring the CMS online on CCR5-NB.

Figure 7-45 shows the SCR target pulling log files from the cluster node CCR5-NB. You do not have to reconfigure SCR; it automatically recognizes that the CMS is now online on the former passive node.

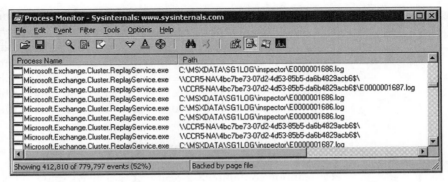

Figure 7-44
CCR CMS online on CCR5-NA

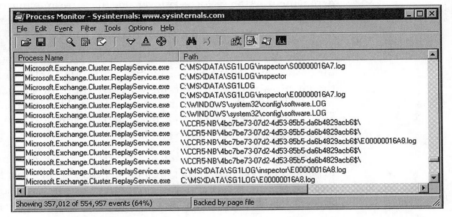

Figure 7-45
SCR Target Pulls Log Files from CCR5-NB

Note that the Exchange Replication service on the SCR target constantly pulls closed log files from the SCR source. You cannot configure a time delay between when a log file is closed on the SCR source and when it gets shipped/pulled by the SCR target. There is no reason that you would want to delay log file shipping.

You can use the following parameters to fine-tune SCR:

- *ReplayLagTime*
- *TruncationLagTime*
- *SeedingPostpost*

ReplayLagTime specifies the time the Replication service has to wait until a copied log file is replayed into the SCR target database. The default value is 24 hours and the maximum delay is 7 days. The format of the value is *Days.Hours:Minutes:Seconds*.

In addition to this lag time, Exchange verifies that a minimum of 50 log files have been shipped to the SCR target before it replays a log file to the target database. This is also the case when you SCR enable a storage group; Exchange does not create the initial SCR target database until at least 50 log files have been shipped. Users with mailboxes in the SCR-enabled storage group must send and receive new emails so that new log files are created on the SCR source and shipped to the SCR target before the database will be created on the SCR target.

Therefore, the actual replay lag time is the maximum of *ReplayLagTime* or "X log files," where X is 50 in the current Exchange Server 2007 build. You cannot configure X because it is a fixed value. This delay minimizes the likelihood that a reseed is necessary after a lossy failover in a LCR/CCR deployment. After a lossy failover, log files are missing on the new active storage group. The SCR source and SCR target are closer together in time because of the missing log files on the SCR source.

The *ReplayLagTime* reduces the likelihood that the active database and the SCR target database have a logical corruption at the same time. You have the chance to recognize the logical corruption on the active database and stop replication before the replay occurs. In LCR and CCR on Exchange Server 2007, there is no such delay and an administrator cannot influence when shipped log files will be replayed.

The parameter *TruncationLagTime* specifies the amount of time that the Replication service has to wait until it can delete log files that have been replayed into the SCR target database. It is important to note that the time period starts after the log file has been replayed into the copy database; the time does not start when the log file has been shipped from the SCR source to the SCR target. This parameter only affects deletion of log files on the SCR target. Log file deletion on the SCR source is not affected by this parameter. The SCR source only has to wait until log files have been inspected on the SCR target. Log file deletion on the SCR source does not require that a log file has already been replayed into the SCR target database. The maximum value for *TruncationLagTime* is 7 days, and the minimum value is 0 seconds. The default value of *TruncationLagTime* is 0. It is important to highlight that *no* log file gets deleted on the SCR target until the log file with the same log file generation number has been successfully backed up on the SCR source.

If you enable an existing storage group for SCR, you can use the parameter -*SeedingPostponed* to specify that you do not want to start seeding automatically and prefer to use the command Update-*StorageGroupCopy* to manually start the seeding process. You have to execute the *Update-StorageGroupCopy* command on the SCR target and not on the SCR source. This enables you to set up and configure SCR during working hours, but postpone seeding to a time with low user activity and utilization of the network. If you do not specify the parameter *SeedingPostponed*, the

SummaryCopyStatus automatically switches from initially disabled to suspended and finally to health.

You have to disable and redo the SCR setup if you want to change the replay or truncation delay settings of an SCR-enabled storage group.

The fully qualified domain name (FQDN) of the SCR target machines are written to the attribute *msExchStandbyCopyMachines* of the storage group object in AD. This attribute stores multivalue strings in the format:

```
SCR-Target; Version; ReplayLagTime; TruncationLagTime.
```

Figure 7-46 shows an example. The version number is currently fixed at 1. Only the SCR source server has an AD object for the storage group in the AD configuration container. The SCR target server has no AD object for the SCR-enabled storage group. If the SCR source and SCR target are members of different AD sites, then you have to keep the replication interval of the AD intrasite link in mind.

Figure 7-46
msExchStandby-
CopyMachines

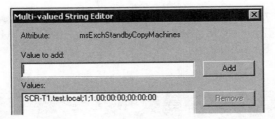

SCR Management

In the current Exchange Server 2007 build, SCR is not visible in the EMC.

Figure 7-47 shows the mailbox server SCR-T1 in the EMC. It is not visible that SCR-T1 is the SCR target of a storage group. Microsoft may add support for SCR management tasks to the EMC in future service packs. In the RTM version, CCR failover management was also only possible using the EMS, and you had to wait for SP1 to be able to manage CCR using the EMC.

Figure 7-47
SCR in Exchange
Management
Console

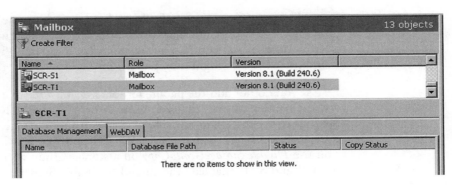

You can use the command in Figure 7-48 to list all the servers in your Exchange organization with an SCR-enabled storage group and display the SCR targets for these storage groups. Note that you have to execute this command on a system with SP1 installed; if you execute the command on a system running the RTM binaries, the command does not display any storage group because the attribute *StandbyMachines* is unknown to the RTM binaries.

Figure 7-48
*SCR-enabled
storage groups*

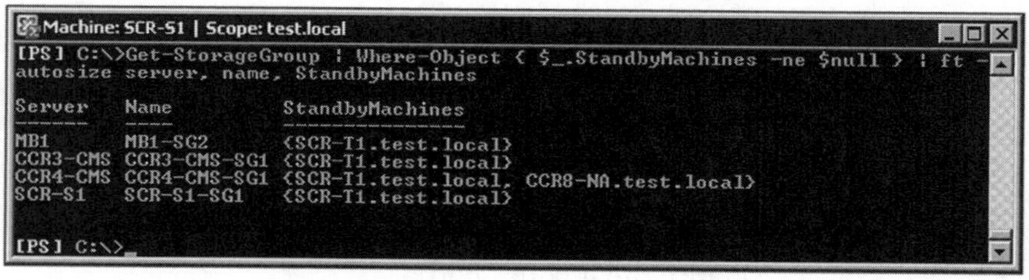

Figure 7-49 shows that the replicated attribute displays only if the storage group is LCR or CCR enabled, but it does not indicate whether the storage group is SCR enabled!

Figure 7-49
Get-StorageGroup

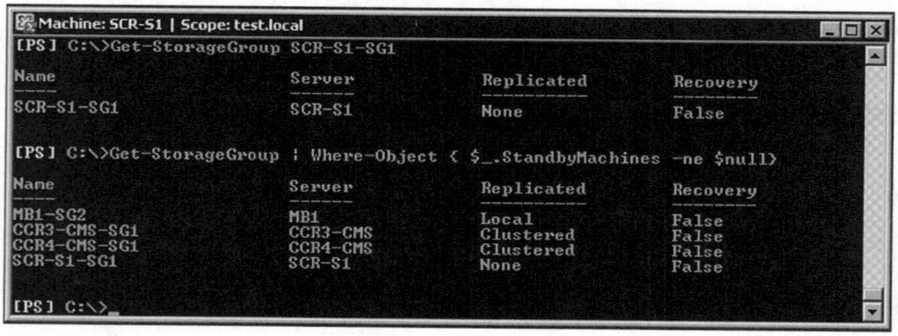

Get-StorageGroup only displays the network name of the standby machines, but it does not display the SCR-specific configuration parameters such as *ReplayLagTime* and *TruncationLagTime*. Figure 7-50 shows how you can display these configuration parameters.

If you do not add the parameter *-StandbyMachine* to a PowerShell cmdlet, the cmdlet assumes that you want to manage the LCR- or CCR-related settings of the storage group. There is no warning message, such as "Are you sure that you want to manage LCR/CCR and not SCR?" For example, if you use *Disable-StorageGroupCopy* on a storage group of a single server that is LCR and SCR enabled, and intend to disable SCR but forget to add the

Figure 7-50
SCR configuration parameters

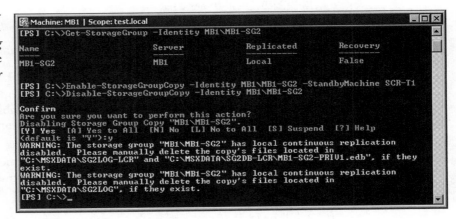

option *-StandbyMachine*, this command will disable LCR for the storage group and not SCR (Figure 7-51).

You should regularly verify the checksum of the SCR copy database using *ESEUTIL.EXE /k<databasefile>.edb*. This is the same as with LCR and CCR: Continuous replication only checks the checksum of the shipped log files, and thus does not verify the health of the LCR/CCR passive database or SCR target database. You have to suspend replication before you start this command and resume replication afterward.

You use the same methods to monitor the log file shipping process for LCR, CCR, and SCR. The PowerShell cmdlets *Test-ReplicationHealth*, *Get-StorageGroupCopyStatus*, and the corresponding performance counter objects let you verify the health of the continuous replication between the SCR source and SCR target. Continuous replication status information is also available under the registry key *HKLM\SOFTWARE\Microsoft\Exchange\Replay\State\<StorageGroupGUID>* on the SCR target.

Backups and Log File Truncation in SCR

You cannot back up the SCR target database using an Exchange-aware API. You can only run backups of the Exchange storage groups on the SCR source. The SCR target database is not being backed up. There is no Exchange-aware backup API available for the SCR target.

A background thread on the SCR target verifies periodically (in SP1 every 3 minutes) whether log files exist on the SCR target that can be truncated. On the SCR target, the following requirements have to be fulfilled for log file truncation:

- The log file generation is below the log file checkpoint of the storage group on the SCR target.
- The log file is older than *ReplayLagTime* + *TruncationLagTime*.
- The log file with the same log file generation number has been backed up on the SCR source.

The only way you can enforce log file truncation on the SCR target without a previous backup on the SCR source is by enabling circular logging. However, circular logging should not be used for storage groups hosting production data.

SCR increases the complexity of log file management on the SCR source. It is important to be aware of all the criteria that must be met before a log file can be truncated on the SCR source.

- A full or incremental backup has been successfully performed. Both backup types copy the log files to the backup media.
- The log file generation sequence is below the log file checkpoint of the storage group on the SCR source.
- The log file has already been replayed to the passive database in an LCR/CCR-enabled storage group, and the passive storage group is online.
- *All* SCR targets have inspected the log file.

The last criterion in particular can cause log files to accumulate if one SCR target is offline or cannot be reached for a long time. You have to consider the changed log file truncation behavior when you calculate the disk volume hosting the transaction log files. Otherwise, you will face the problem that the database of your SCR-enabled storage group gets automatically dismounted because there is no space left on the file system.

Log file truncation on the SCR source does not require that a log file has been replayed into all SCR target databases. The *ReplayLagTime* can be up to 7 days, and this large delay would lead to a huge amount of log files accumulating on the SCR source. Therefore, it is sufficient that this log file has been shipped and inspected on all SCR targets.

Enabling a storage group for SCR does not affect the possibility of making a VSS backup of the passive CCR node or the passive LCR storage group.

Activating a SCR Target

The following section explains the necessary steps to activate an Exchange Server 2007 SCR target. The procedure is based on the Microsoft TechNet article, "Activating Standby Continuous Replication Targets." A small test environment is used to describe the up-front planning and the commands that have to be executed during the recovery.

SCR is used to provide a site-resilient configuration for the Exchange mailbox server role. A mailbox server depends on services provided by other infrastructure servers, such as AD domain controllers. Your business continuity plan has to consider all the components that are necessary to provide a messaging and collaboration service to your users. Creating a business continuity plan is a broad and complex topic. The following sections only consider the Exchange mailbox server role. All other Exchange roles and services like AD or the network infrastructure are beyond the scope of this book.

Assume that your remote data center provides a full infrastructure with AD domain controllers, along with servers hosting the HT and CAS roles. You have configured two separate AD sites. AD site A is in your production data center and AD site B is in your remote data center.

Your primary data center hosts your production Exchange infrastructure. Your mailbox server is a Windows Server 2008 Failover Cluster configured for CCR. For disaster recovery purposes, you use SCR to replicate all storage groups of your CMS to a remote data center. The SCR target is another Windows Server 2008 failover cluster located in the remote data center.

Figure 7-52 shows the topology of the environment. If you use nonclustered mailbox servers, then your recovery strategy is based on database portability. See the Microsoft TechNet article, "Standby Continuous Replication: Database Portability," and Chapter 9 for the corresponding procedure.

The configuration of the CMS is shown in Figure 7-53. This is your SCR source cluster.

The SCR target is located in the remote data center. You have installed the binaries of the mailbox role, but you have not configured a CMS on this cluster. Figure 7-54 shows the cluster configuration of the SCR target.

In Figure 7-55, you can see that one node of the cluster in the remote data center is the SCR target. The cluster in the remote data center is a two-node cluster, but you did not specify the network name of the Windows failover cluster as the SCR target. You decided to use two nodes because this allows you to set up a standard CCR system with two nodes. It is possible to use a cluster with only a single node as a SCR target. A single node cluster would reduce the hardware cost of your site resiliency solution, but has the disadvantage that the cluster in the remote data center would not initially

Figure 7-52
Example environment

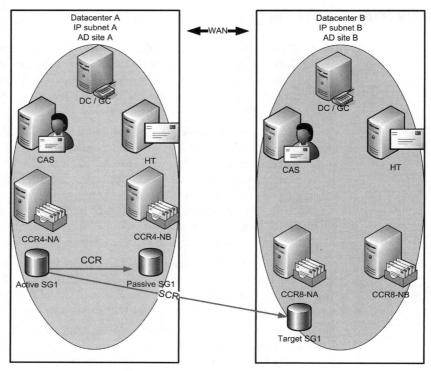

Figure 7-53
SCR source cluster

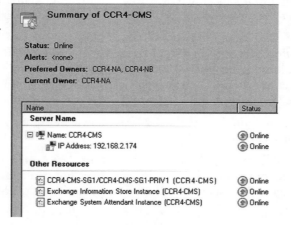

Figure 7-54
SCR target cluster

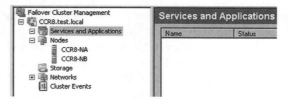

Figure 7-55
Storage group standby machines

provide the same high availability as the cluster in the primary data center. It is possible to install another server in the remote data center and join the new computer to the cluster in a later step.

Initial Preparation

If your production data center and your remote data center use separate IP subnets, the network name of your mailbox server will have a different IP address after you activate the SCR target. Let's assume that your datacenter A uses the IP subnet 192.168.2.0/24, the CMS of the SCR source in datacenter A has the IP address 192.168.2.174, and your datacenter B uses the IP subnet 192.168.4.0/24. You must change the IP address of the CMS if you activate the SCR target. You cannot use the IP address 192.168.2.174 in datacenter B. The IP address of the CMS has to be an address in the IP subnet of datacenter B, such as 192.168.4.8.

You could inform all users to flush the Domain Name System (DNS) cache on their clients using *IPCONFIG.EXE /flushdns* to reduce the time until the clients pick up the new IP address, but this is not a practical solution for a large deployment. A better approach is to reduce the time to live (TTL) value for the DNS A record.

The default value is 20 minutes (Figure 7-56). Windows Server 2008 allows you to configure this property from the command line, for example, to 5 minutes:

```
CLUSTER.EXE resource "Network Name (CCR4-CMS)" /priv
Host RecordTTL = 300
```

In addition to the DNS TTL, you have to consider AD replication latency of the AD-integrated DNS. The default replication interval of an AD site link is 180 minutes, but you can specify a shorter replication interval.

In a Windows Server 2003 cluster, the cluster service account has permission to reset the computer account of the cluster in the AD. If the SCR source and SCR target use the same cluster service account, the SCR target cluster will have no problems in resetting the account during the SCR target-activation process. Microsoft increased the security of failover clustering in Windows Server 2008. The cluster now runs in the security context of the Local System account. This complicates the recovery procedure.

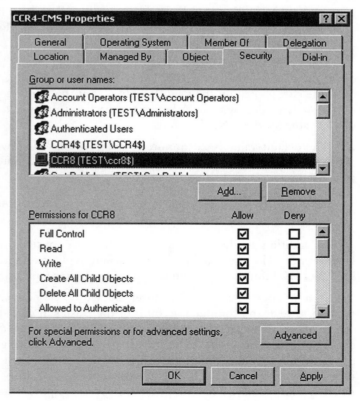

Figure 7-57 shows that you have to assign full control for the SCR target cluster computer account on the computer account of the CMS in the AD.

To reemphasize:

- The permissions are assigned on the CMS computer account and not on the computer account of the cluster that is your SCR source.

- You assign permissions to the computer account of the SCR target cluster and not to the cluster node that you configured as your standby machine. The cluster node will impersonate the cluster computer account when it tries to reset this object in AD during *SETUP. EXE /RecoverCMS*.

- Do *not* delete the computer account in AD; otherwise, the recovery procedure will fail!

Activation

The following section is based on a fictitious scenario. Assume that a backhoe operator damaged the network cable that connects your primary data center to the outside world. You have to continue to provide communication and collaboration services to your users from the remote data center. You do not have any network connectivity between both datacenters.

First, you run recovery steps on your SCR target computer in the remote datacenter as shown in Figure 7-58. The first step is to use the PowerShell command *Restore-StorageGroupCopy*. This informs the storage group on the SCR target that you want to activate the storage group. This storage group then becomes the active storage group and users access this database. *Restore-StorageGroupCopy* terminates SCR from the former SCR source to the SCR target. It marks the database of the SCR target storage group as mountable.

Figure 7-58
Restore-
StorageGroup
Copy

```
Machine: CCR8-NA | Scope: test.local                                    _ □ ×
[PS] C:\>Restore-StorageGroupCopy -Identity CCR4-CMS\CCR4-CMS-SG1 -StandbyMachin
e CCR8-NA -Force
WARNING: Performing a Restore-StorageGroupCopy operation on storage group
'CCR4-CMS-SG1' with the Force option. Data loss is expected for this storage
group.
[PS] C:\>_
```

Restore-StorageGroupCopy does not automatically reconfigure SCR in the opposite direction or shut down the SCR source computer. It only disables SCR for this storage group, and enables you to mount the target database. *Restore-StorageGroupCopy* has to be executed on the SCR target and not on the SCR source. This is especially important to remember if you verify your recovery procedure in a lab and your SCR source is still up and running.

If the CMS has multiple storage groups then you have to execute this command for each storage group, or run the following one-liner on the SCR target:

```
GetSCRSources | Restore-StorageGroupCopy -Standby
Machine $env:ComputerName -Force
```

Restore-StorageGroupCopy is the same command that you use in an LCR configuration to activate the LCR-created copy database for recovery purposes. The main difference is that with SCR you have to specify *-StandbyMachine <SCR-target>*.

The Exchange Replication service attempts to copy missing log files from the SCR source by accessing the shared log file directory on the SCR source. Figure 7-59 shows the corresponding event viewer entry. This attempt fails because the SCR source is unavailable. The SCR target computer cannot connect to the SCR source because the network connection to the other data center is lost. You have to use the *-Force* parameter with the *Restore-StorageGroupCopy* command if you want to activate a SCR target while the SCR source is not available.

Figure 7-59
Attempt to copy log files

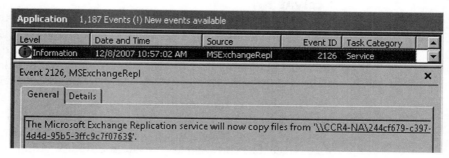

The next step is to delete the DNS A record of the CMS. This step is necessary because in Windows Server 2008 only the computer account of the SCR source cluster has permissions to modify the DNS record.

Figure 7-60 derives from another CMS running on Windows Server 2003. You can see that in Windows Server 2003, the cluster service account has full control on the DNS record. Deleting the DNS record is not necessary in Windows Server 2003 as long as you use the same service account for the SCR source and SCR target cluster.

Deleting the DNS A record of the CMS on Windows Server 2008 cluster is the method described on Microsoft TechNet. We used a different approach in our test. We assigned the computer account of the SCR target cluster full control on the DNS A record created by the SCR source cluster. This enables the SCR target cluster to modify the A record during the recovery procedure. This configuration is comparable to the permission setup in Windows Server 2003. It has the advantage that you can perform the necessary steps during the up-front preparation and you have to remember fewer steps during the disaster recovery. However, verifying whether the modified permissions are still there and have not been changed in the meantime is still recommended.

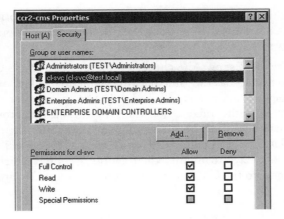

Figure 7-60
*Per missions on
DNS record in
Windows Server
2003*

The next step is the most interesting part of the recovery procedure. The command *SETUP.EXE /RecoverCMS* shown in Figure 7-61 allows you to re-create the same CMS configuration on your SCR target. This command uses the information in the AD configuration container to re-create the CMS. It is important that you specify the same network name for the CMS that was used on the SCR source.

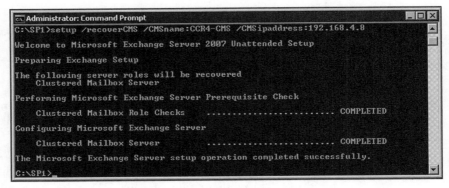

Figure 7-61
Setup/
RecoverCMS

The IP address that you specify can be different. In a two–data-center configuration, it is very likely that the IP address on the SCR source and SCR target are from different IP subnets. In our example, the CMS on the SCR source used 192.168.2.174 and the CMS on the SCR target is using 192.168.4.8. The computer names and the IP addresses of the SCR target cluster nodes do not matter.

However, it is important that the same database and storage group log file directories are available on the SCR source and on the SCR target cluster. This is something you already had to do during the initial SCR configuration because this is a prerequisite for configuring SCR. In brief, it is a requirement for continuous replication, regardless of whether you use a cluster or a single server for SCR.

Figure 7-62 shows the cluster group created for the CMS on the SCR target. The CMS has the same network name that it had on the SCR source, but the new IP address is 192.168.4.8. The two cluster nodes of the SCR target are now the preferred owners of the cluster group. The database resource will be offline. You have to manually mount the database using the *Mount-Database* command. After that users can connect to their mailbox. Users do not have to modify their Outlook profile. Clients will automatically connect to the CMS currently hosted on the SCR target.

Figure 7-62
CMS online on
SCR target

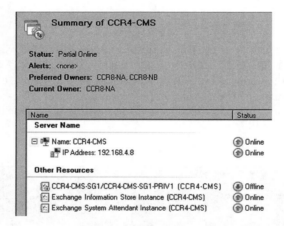

If your SCR target cluster has two nodes and you want to configure the cluster as a CCR system, you have to manually seed the database to the passive cluster node.

Depending on the configuration of your Exchange infrastructures, additional steps may be necessary, such as adjusting the external uniform resource locator (URL) configuration of your CAS roles, or manually retrying the SMTP queues if you do not want to wait until the next automatic retry. If you are never able to bring your primary data center online, you may have to adjust the Flexible Single Master Operations (FSMO) role configuration of your AD because you lost an important domain controller.

Preparation for fallback

If you have repaired your primary data center and started your SCR source cluster nodes, you will recognize that the cluster group of the CMS will fail and the resources do not come online. Exchange recognizes that another computer is already running with the same network name. Therefore, the network name cluster resource of the CMS fails. All cluster resources that depend on the network name, such as the Exchange Information Store Instance or the database resource, will be offline.

To be able to use your old SCR source cluster as new SCR target you have to delete the CMS configuration on the local cluster nodes. The following command removes the configuration from both cluster nodes, but does not touch the configuration stored in the AD. All cluster nodes should be running when you execute this command.

```
SETUP.EXE /ClearLocalCMS /CMSname: <CMS-NetworkName>
```

Figure 7-63 shows a screenshot of Failover Cluster Management after *SETUP.EXE /ClearLocalCMS*.

Figure 7-63
SCR source cluster after/
ClearLocalCMS

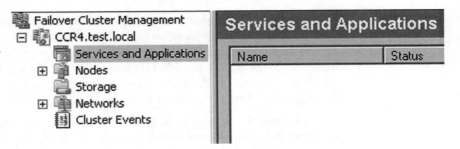

Do not use *SETUP.EXE /RemoveCMS* because this command is intended for uninstalling the CMS from the active cluster node and to remove the CMS from the AD at the same time. This would affect the CMS now running in the remote data center. Luckily, *SETUP.EXE* checks if the CMS hosts mailboxes when you execute */RemoveCMS*.

Now you can begin to reconfigure SCR, but this time the replication will go in the other direction. You should specify one cluster node of your former SCR source cluster as *StandByMachine* with the PowerShell command *Enable-StorageGroupCopy*.

Network Bandwidth and Latency Requirements for CCR and SCR

In CCR and SCR, closed-transaction log files are sent from Computer A to Computer B. The log files are copied via a TCP/IP network connection. What characteristics must the network connection have to be suitable for log file shipping? Network bandwidth and latency are the two main characteristics that have to be considered. *Bandwidth* is the theoretical maximum capacity of data that can be sent in a certain amount of time from Computer A to Computer B. *Throughput* is a related term and often refers to the measured amount of data sent from Computer A to Computer B in a given amount of time, such as megabytes per second. The main difference is that bandwidth refers to the theoretical maximum and throughput refers to the actually measured figure.

Latency is the amount of time is takes to send a single IP packet from Computer A to Computer B. It is measured as round-trip latency—the time Computer A has to wait until it receives the acknowledgment for the IP packet from Computer B. The latency of a network connection depends on the wire distance from Computer A to Computer B and the inherent latency of the network components the IP packet has to pass through. As a rough estimate, you can assume that the IP packet travels at 60% the speed of light over most network connections. The inherent latency of the network devices such as switches and routers contributes a significant percentage to the total latency of the network connection.

If you have a higher bandwidth, you can send more data simultaneously, but the speed of transmission is not faster. A colleague used the following analogy in his whitepaper, "High availability for Microsoft Exchange Server 2007 using CCR with HP StorageWorks EVA8000", about CCR, which is available on the HP Customer Focused Testing (CFT) website: A Boeing 747 is three times bigger than a Boeing 737, but it is not faster.

It is likely that latency is the limiting factor and not available bandwidth. If the network latency is above 50 milliseconds, the log file shipping process can get out of control. In this case, the active node creates new log files faster than the passive node is able to pull closed log files from the active node. This leads to a high copy queue length, and your passive node is many transactions behind the active node. The risk exists that you cannot meet the Recovery Point Objective (RPO) and the Recovery Time Objectives (RTO) of your Service Level Agreement (SLA) if the network latency is too high. After a failover, you may face the situation of your databases not being automatically mounted because the number of missing log files is larger than the *AutoDatabaseMountDial* setting. This was one of the key findings in a test performed by the HP CFT team with 5000 heavy users on CCR over an Optical Carrier 3 (OC-3) link with 30-millisecond latency—some databases had to be mounted manually after a failover to the passive node.

You can tune the TCP/IP stack to increase performance. The most important parameter is the TCP window size, which specifies the amount of data Computer A can send to Computer B without waiting for an acknowledgment for the delivered data from Computer B. The previously mentioned whitepaper provides a description of how to determine an optimal window size and describes the necessary registry changes. For example, reseeding an 11 GB database could be completed in 14 minutes using a tuned TCP stack versus 60 minutes using the default settings in Windows Server 2003. The test used an OC-3 link with 20-millisecond latency. Another very impressive test result is that reseeding all databases of a 5000 × 1 GB CCR configuration over the OC-3 link with 0-millisecond latency required 3.5 days, although the Windows Server 2003 TCP stack was optimized. It is interesting to verify how significant the new Server Message Block version 2 protocol and the Receive Windows auto tuning in Windows Server 2008 will reduce this time frame. At the time this book is released, the result is likely already published on www.hp.com/go/hpcft. This website contains several informative reports written by our colleagues that we recommend.

The section "Optimizing Windows 2003 Networking for SCR" and the corresponding section for CCR on Microsoft TechNet describes network tuning for CR as well. You can use the Exchange Server 2007 Mailbox Server Role Requirements Calculator to estimate the required network link and the registry settings to tune the Windows Server 2003 TCP stack. The calculator provides recommendations based on the number of log files that likely will be generated based on your input figures. In the Input tab of the calculator, you define the Exchange server configuration—for example, number of users and how many emails they send and receive per day. Based on the provided data, the calculator estimates the requirements for log file replication. Figure 7-64 shows an example output of the calculator.

Figure 7-64
Log replication requirements

Log Replication Throughput Requirements	
Transaction Log Data Generated/Day	70 GB
Geographically Dispersed CCR Log Throughput Require	6.67 Mbps
Recovery Point Objective	1 Hours
SCR Log Throughput Required/SCR Target	6.67 Mbps
Total SCR Log Throughput Required	6.67 Mbps

Chosen Network Link Suitability	
Network Link	OC-3 (155 Mbps)
Network Link Latency	30 ms
Is Network Link Acceptable for Geographically Dispersed CCR?	Yes
Is Network Link Acceptable for SCR?	Yes

Comparison of SCC/LCR/CCR/SCR

The information in this closing section of the chapter is intended to help you decide which solution best fits your business needs. Table 7-3 provides a comparison of SCC and the three CR solutions provided by Exchange Server 2007. The SCC configuration considered in this table is based on the Exchange built-in version without the addition of a third-party storage replication solution. SCR requires Exchange Server 2007 SP1.

The Cisco Systems whitepaper titled, "Integrating Microsoft Exchange 2007 in a Cisco Multisite Data Center Design," provides a good description of how you can use Exchange Server 2007 CR for a geographically

Table 7-3   *LCR, CCR, and SCR comparison*

	SCC	LCR	CCR	SCR
Can be combined with other Exchange server roles	No	Yes	No	Yes
More than one server required	Yes	No	Yes	Yes
Hardware from the Cluster category of the Microsoft Windows Server Catalog required	Yes	No	No	No
Requires an iSCSI or Fibre Channel infrastructure enabling shared storage	Yes	No	No	No
Can be deployed in a geographically dispersed configuration	No Requires a third-party storage replication solution	No	Yes	Yes
Mainly intended for site resiliency	No	No	No	Yes
Usable for public folder databases (if more than one database exists)	Yes	No	No	No
Maximum one database per storage group	No	Yes	Yes	Yes
Provides additional copies of the database and log files for recovery purposes	No	Yes	Yes	Yes
Supports more than two copies of the database and log files	No	No	No	Yes
All storage groups hosted on the server have to use this function	No/A	No	Yes	No
Protection for logical database corruption	No	Yes	Yes	Yes But this is not the main purpose of the solution!
A single database can be easily recovered using the copy database without affecting the other databases on the server	No/A	Yes	No	Yes But this is not the main purpose of the solution!

Table 7-3   (*continued*)

	SCC	LCR	CCR	SCR
Protection for server hardware failure	Yes	No	Yes	Yes
Provides the possibility of offloading backups and other maintenance tasks to a "passive" server currently not accessed by clients	No	No	Yes	No
Possibility to verify database consistency without impacting online access to production database	No	Yes	Yes	Yes
Possibility of installing hot fixes/service packs for the operating system and Exchange without impacting online access by clients	Yes	No	Yes	No
Transport dumpster of the hub server can be utilized to recover mails that have been recently sent to the mailbox server, but have not been replicated or backed up yet.	No	Yes Requires SP1	Yes	No

dispersed deployment and integrate Exchange into a highly available network infrastructure.

Now you should be prepared to make an informed decision on which CR solution will fit your business needs. For a highly available and disaster-tolerant solution, you could use a clustered mailbox server, CCR or SCC, inside the data center, and then use SCR to create an additional replica of the Exchange databases in a remote data center. There is no single true answer on whether you should use a storage based data replication solution or depend on Exchange Server 2007 CR. Either of these solutions may be the best answer for a specific requirement.

8

Backup

Planning the Exchange backup strategy and designing the backup infrastructure is a very important task in an Exchange deployment. You need to keep your recovery-related Service Level Agreements (SLAs) in mind when you make your decisions about the number of mailboxes hosted on a single server, or the maximum mailbox size. You may be tempted to host 5000 mailboxes with a 2 GB mailbox quota on a single server. Are you sure that you can back up the server within the backup window and recover your databases according to the SLAs?

Important Terms

Let's start with the definition of two important terms shown in Figure 8-1.

Figure 8-1
RPO/RTO

The Recovery Time Objective (RTO) is the maximum time that your users accept being without the Exchange messaging service. This is the maximum timeframe that you have to analyze an incident and recover the messaging service.

The Recovery Point Objective (RPO) is the allowable data loss that your users accept. For example, if you perform a full online backup of the Exchange storage groups every night, and you lose the disk volume with the database file and the disk volume with the transaction logs, then you lost all data since last night. Do your users accept this? If they don't, are they willing to pay for an advanced solution that, for example, takes advantage of data replication?

319

Why Do You Run Backups?

You run backups because the backed-up data enable you to restore previous existing information in case you have to restore individual data objects or recover your messaging service after a disaster. This could be necessary because of:

- Accidental deletion of data
- A virus outbreak infected or deleted data
- Security intrusion exposed data to modification
- Hardware failure affected a disk volume
- Disaster destroyed your data center

It is important to realize that you perform backups because you want to be able to recover data. End users do not care about your backup strategy; they want their old emails and calendar entries restored in a short timeframe. Backup is a prerequisite to fulfill this expectation.

You should be suspicious if somebody tells you he is working for the "backup department". Ask him, "Who is responsible for recovery?" I once came across a customer who had a "backup team" that provided backup services, but the team did not feel responsible for data recovery and so did not fully consider the restoration of data and recovery of the messaging service. For the backup team, it was convenient to run weekly full and daily differential backups. They only had to back up a small amount of data every weekday. After the customer had to restore an Exchange storage group, they realized the importance of recovery. Transaction log file replay took longer than their RTO. After this outage, they switched to daily full backups. Now they have to back up more data every day, but a restore is much faster and simpler. Only one backup set has to be restored, and only the log files generated since the last night have to be replayed.

You always have to ask the question: What data can be recovered and what is the achievable RTO from an end user point of view? You need to be aware that this includes transaction log file replay. An Exchange database is not online until log files have been replayed. The RTO is more important than the time required to back up data.

Although the streaming backup Application Programming Interface (API) automatically performs a health check of your Exchange database and log files, it is still the main purpose of a backup to be armed for a recovery. The consistency check is not the most important reason for running backups. Another widespread misunderstanding is that backups are run for archiving purposes. There are other dedicated solutions available for records management and compliance regulations, such as Sarbanes Oxley.

What Data Do You Have to Back Up?

The answer to this question is "all data that you have to restore from your backup media to recover the messaging service." During your recovery attempt, you have to decide if it is possible, and maybe faster or easier, to re-create data by other means. One example is an option to re-create the Active Directory (AD) database on a repaired domain controller using AD replication.

You should regularly back up Exchange databases and log files, the system state of your Exchange servers, and AD. Exchange Stores its configuration in AD, and disaster recovery procedures for Exchange servers depend on the information in AD. You should collaborate with your AD team about AD backup and recovery.

The Internet Information Services (IIS) metabase contains Exchange configuration settings. If you back up the server system state, then the metabase is included in the backup, but backing up the metabase separately enables the restore of the IIS metabase as a single component. You can use the VB script *cscript%systemroot%\system32\iisback.vbs\backup* to back up the metabase to the *%systemroot%\inetserv\MetaBack* directory.

It is obvious that you must back up all Exchange storage groups on your server to have a copy of the data stored in the Information Store. It is a best practice to back up a complete storage group and not individual databases of the storage group. With the streaming backup API, you can back up individual databases, but backing up storage groups simplifies the handling of the log file truncation and the recovery process. With the Volume Shadow Copy Services (VSS) API you can only back up a complete storage group. Additionally, a single database per storage group is recommended. If you perform a backup of the Exchange Server 2007 Information Store, then the database index files are automatically included in the backup set. See the Microsoft TechNet section, "Database Backup and Restore," for additional information.

For the Exchange Server 2007 Client Access Server (CAS), backing up configuration settings with a file-level backup is recommended. The Exchange help file provides a detailed list of data that need to be backed up for each Exchange Server role.

Data stored in the offline store (OST) files on the client computers are synchronized copies from the server. If you lose an OST file, you only lose data that have not yet been sent from the client to the server. Data stored in PST files are not synchronized with the Exchange server. If users lose their PST files, they lose the mail data stored in the PST. Therefore, you should forbid using PSTs; otherwise, you might be forced to implement a file system backup of the PSTs on the client computer. This can be painful because your file system backup stores the complete PST files every day to the tape media because the files are very likely modified on a daily basis. PSTs are often several hundred megabytes or even gigabytes in size and this will waste network bandwidth and tape media.

Backing up only data stored on servers is insufficient! You have to capture the configuration of the infrastructure devices such as network routers, SAN switches, tape libraries, and your storage array. You will not be able to restore your last Exchange database backup if you don't know how to re-create the configuration of your storage array after a disaster. For example, you can use the HP Storage System Scripting Utility (SSSU) to capture the configuration of an HP EVA and re-created this configuration if you have to replace the array after a disaster.

Tape Rotation and Offsite Vaulting

An often neglected topic is the question "How many generations of backup data do I need and where do I have to locate the backup media?" If you only use one backup tape and you overwrite your last backup set as soon as you start a new backup job, then you have nothing to restore from when your current backup job recognizes data corruption. You should not store all backup generations on a single tape. If this tape media is damaged, you lose all backup generations stored on this tape.

This rule is still valid with new backup technologies like VSS backups. You should at least have disk space for the following volumes:

- Production data
- Last known good backup
- Volumes for your current backup job

You cannot take advantage of the instant recovery feature of a VSS solution without spending significantly more money for additional disk spindles to host your shadow copies. This is something you have to consider during the planning stage. Several times customers initially requested a large number of shadow copy volume generations during the pre-sales phase, and finally did not use VSS at all because they were not willing to pay for the additional storage capacity.

Keeping generations of your backup data for a very long time—for example, 1 year—is uncommon. A compliance solution is more appropriate for proving what emails your board members exchanged last year. It is unlikely that you are going to restore a 1-year-old database after a server failure. Recalling the purpose of backups is useful when you decide which backup generations you are going to keep. What is the value of a mailbox to a user if it only contains the mail from 6 months ago?

A well-known tape rotation schedule is the grandfather-father-son (GFS) method. GFS is a hierarchical rotation scheme that is likely the most commonly used rotation scheme. Table 8-1 provides an example of a GFS implementation.

Table 8-1   *GFS tape rotation*

	Backup	Write protection
Grandfather	Last Sunday of month	3 months
Father	Sunday	1 month
Son	Monday–Saturday	1 week

The term *backup retention* refers to the time that the backup application should consider a given backup media write protected (i.e., do not overwrite the data with data from new backups). After the retention period has expired, the backup media can be reused and overwritten.

Recently, disk-to-disk backups and VSS backups have become more popular. It is important to realize that these backup methods do not provide the possibility of storing your backup data offsite. You cannot take several disks out of your storage array and put them in a bank safe! You have to complement these methods with a data replication method to protect your backup data from a site disaster. Storing your backup data close to your production data or even on the same storage array would be careless. If a site disaster affects your production and backup data at the same time, you have nothing to restore. You would be forced to re-create your Exchange environment from scratch without any previously existing mails.

Therefore, vaulting backup media offsite or using advanced functions of backup products to duplicate complete tapes or individual backup objects on a remote tape library is considered best practice. If you use the backup to disk step only as a staging area for the following data migration to tape, then it is okay to host the production data and the staging area on the same storage array.

Regular Verification of Backup Data

You should regularly verify your backup data. Backups of Exchange storage groups can be verified by restoring them to the Recovery Storage Group (RSG). Without regular verification, you might recognize after an actual disaster that your backups cannot be restored. It will be difficult to explain to your manager that you had run backups for months, but the backup media cannot be used for recovery.

Backup Types and Schedule

Four backup types are available: full, copy, incremental, and differential. *Full backups* create a complete copy of your database on the backup media. Upon successful completion of the backup, the transaction log files are purged. *Copy* backups also create a complete copy of the data, but a copy backup does not purge the log files or stamp the database header with the date and time of the backup. Copy backups are used to duplicate a database for testing purposes. They are not used within a regular backup strategy.

Incremental and *differential* backups always reference the last full backup. Both backup types only copy the existing transaction log files to the backup media; they do not copy the Exchange database to the backup media. These backup types enable a shorter backup window because less data are written to the backup media. Incremental backups purge existing log files at the end of a backup. You have to remember that in case of a restore, you need enough disk space on your log file disk volume for all transaction log files generated since your last full backup. Differential backups do not delete transaction log files. With differential backups, log files accumulate until you run the next full backup.

You should select a backup type and schedule according to your service level requirements (Table 8-2) and the RPO and RTO.

Table 8-2   *Full/differential/incremental backups*

	Daily full	Weekly full and daily differential	Weekly full and daily incremental
Recovery steps	Last backup set	Last full and last differential backup set.	Last full and all incremental backup sets since the full backup.
Recovery issues	None	Many log files have to be replayed.	Many individual backup sets have to be restored, and many log files have to be replayed. If one incremental backup set is damaged, you can only restore to the last contiguous log file/backup set.
Recovery time	Low	Medium to high	High
Backup time	High	Medium	Low
Media costs	High	Medium	Low

Using daily full backups is a best practice. Even if you have a shorter backup window with the other backup types in Table 8-2, the recovery procedure is more complex and time consuming. Remember that you do not back up for the sake of backups. You only perform backups to be prepared for a fast recovery.

If you made the decision to have large databases because business needs justified the support for mailboxes with gigabyte quotas, you will face the issue that you cannot back up all databases using a daily full backup. Very likely your backup infrastructure is not capable of transferring terabytes of data from the mailbox server to a backup media within the backup window. In this case, you can consider using weekly full and daily differential backups. Table 8-3 shows the corresponding backup schedule.

Table 8-3   *Weekly full and daily differential*

Storage group	Mon	Tue	Wed	Thu	Fri	Sat	Sun
1	**Full**	Dif	Dif	Dif	Dif	Dif	Dif
2	Dif	**Full**	Dif	Dif	Dif	Dif	Dif
3	Dif	Dif	**Full**	Dif	Dif	Dif	Dif
4	Dif	Dif	Dif	**Full**	Dif	Dif	Dif
5	Dif	Dif	Dif	Dif	**Full**	Dif	Dif
6	Dif	Dif	Dif	Dif	Dif	**Full**	Dif
7	Dif	Dif	Dif	Dif	Dif	Dif	**Full**
…	…	…	…	…	…	…	…

Backup Topologies

Local Backup

This decentralized backup topology (Figure 8-2) is typically used in small environments. Local server backups have the advantage that no bandwidth of the public LAN is consumed. Another benefit is that each server has a dedicated tape device and the server does not have to compete with other servers for this resource. This is especially important if several servers have to be restored at the same time.

Local backups are not used in large environments because it does not provide centralized management capabilities, and it is costly since it requires individual hardware and software licenses for each server.

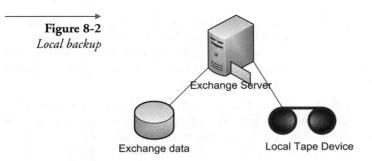

Figure 8-2
Local backup

LAN Backup

A LAN-based backup infrastructure (Figure 8-3) has been widely used in corporate scenarios in the past. It has the advantage of centralized management and the shared usage of tape devices, which enables a higher level of scalability compared to the local server backup.

Figure 8-3   *LAN backup*

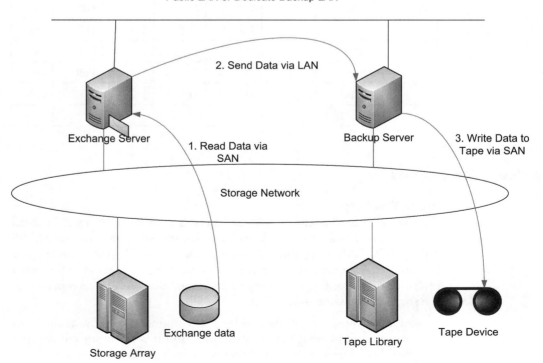

This kind of topology typically uses a multitier architecture with a central backup server handling the backup jobs and control data. Media agents or a media server handle(s) the data movement from/to the tape devices and manage(s) the media resources. Client agents, sometimes called disk agents, are application-specific agents that read from disk/write data to disk. The backup software vendors often use different terms for their solution components but the concepts are identical.

The main drawback of a LAN backup infrastructure is the consumption of network bandwidth by the backup data and the slow throughput. Large environments often have a dedicated backup LAN. A dedicated backup LAN requires a multiport network interface card (NIC) or an additional NIC per Exchange server. This enables the separation of backup data from the general-purpose network traffic. The backup server has a limited number of NICs and the backup server also has limited bandwidth for passing data from the NICs to the tape devices.

In a test environment, it was possible to achieve a backup throughput of approximately 100 GB/hour to a backup target attached via a 1 Gbps dedicated backup network. The CPU utilization was found to be higher in comparison to back ups over Fibre Channel. It is important to state that this is a result from a lab environment, and in production deployments the throughput of LAN backups is often in the range of only 40 GB/hour.

SAN Backup

A Storage Area Network (SAN) using a switched fabric and the Fibre Channel protocol provides higher throughput compared with LAN backup. This is the reason why almost all new infrastructures use the storage network to send data from the Exchange server to the backup library.

SAN-based backups (Figure 8-4) are similar to LAN-based backups; the main difference is that backup data are not sent over the LAN. The LAN is only used to exchange control information between the Exchange server and the backup server. A backup agent runs on the Exchange server and uses the Exchange backup API to access the data stored on disk storage provided by the storage array. Afterward the data are sent by the agent to the SAN attached backup device. Both data transfers (from the disk storage to the Exchange server and from the Exchange server to the backup device) use the SAN and not the LAN. SAN backups do not waste the limited bandwidth of the public LAN, and provide a significantly higher throughput compared to LAN backups.

In large environments, Exchange data are usually stored on disk space provided by a back-end storage array connected to the SAN. Therefore, the disadvantage of the implementation cost of a SAN can be neglected because a SAN is already available. The SAN infrastructure has to be carefully

Figure 8-4   *SAN backup*

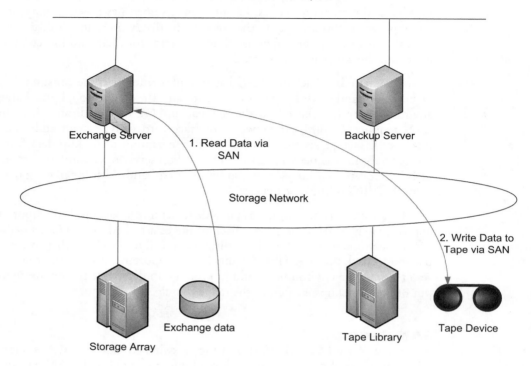

designed and configured to protect the connected devices from being affected by a failed tape device.

Backup to disk/disk to disk backup

With a disk-to-disk (D2D) backup solution (Figure 8-5), the backup data are (initially) stored on a disk volume and not directly streamed to tape. This

Figure 8-5
Backup to disk

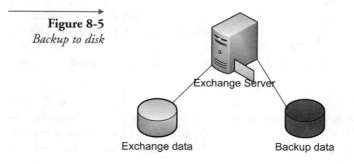

might provide higher throughput compared to a backup using a single standard tape device (DLT or SDLT) as the backup target. New tape devices like LTO3 or LTO4 should be as fast as or faster than a disk target. LTO3 provides a native throughput of 80MB/second, and LTO4 and a StorageTek T10000 tape drive up to 120MB/second.

Another benefit is that D2D does not require transporting tape media from the library magazine to the tape device. This removed step is an advantage for recovery.

The storage location can be provided by cheaper storage building blocks, such as RAID 5 volumes instead of RAID 1 used by the databases, and low-cost disk technologies like SATA or FATA drives.

Backup to disk has the following disadvantages:

- No virus protection compared to tape backup. A virus can access the backup data stored on the file system. This is not the case if the data are located on tape media.

- No hardware compression is available.

- When backup files, such as NTBackup's *.bkf* file, grow to a very large size (>10GB), the server may work too hard, and therefore cause performance degradation for both Exchange and backups.

- No direct offsite vaulting of backup data/media.

- Disks are more difficult to move to a bank safe.

It is important to realize that a staging process is necessary to transfer the backup data stored on the disk volumes to tape media in a second step. A big advantage of this approach is that the migration of the backup data to tape can be offloaded to a separate server, and therefore reduces the load on the Exchange server.

Backup to Virtual Tape Libraries

The cost per gigabyte has dramatically decreased for disks, but tape media prices have not declined as fast. Therefore, enterprises try to move away from tape storage and prefer backups to disk storage systems. Initially, these enterprises performed D2D backups and stored the backup set as a regular file within the file system hosted on a storage array. The disadvantage of this approach is that the storage array is not performance optimized for the access pattern of a backup, and disk drives do not provide support for data compression like tape devices do.

At present, these D2D backup solutions are often replaced by a Virtual Tape Library (VTL). A VTL is a disk storage system with special software that presents the disk storage as tape devices with a tape media pool to the backup server. This virtualization technology has the benefit that the integration of a VTL in an existing environment is simplified. The backup server sees this disk storage as a conventional tape library with well-known tape devices and tape media.

Another advantage is that the VTL is optimized for the access pattern of a backup-and-restore data stream. A conventional storage array has to handle different types of data streams (file server data or database access) at the same time, and therefore cannot be optimized for backup. It is likely that a VTL is faster compared to a disk storage array using the same quality of disks, but you should not expect a VTL to be faster than recent tape devices like LTO4.

You can enable data compression on the VTL; this increases the amount of data that you can store on the library, but it has an impact on the backup and restore performance. A VTL usually has an embedded server that is tasked with emulating the tape devices. If this server also has to handle data compression, the CPU load of the VTL server is increased and reduces the achievable backup performance.

However, a VTL eliminates the problem with tape devices that occurs when you cannot provide a sustained data stream to keep the tape device streaming. This leads to a shoe-shine effect—the tape has to rewind because the backup server did not send enough data to the tape device. This problem mainly exists for the backup of a file server with thousands of small files.

VTLs often use low-cost disks, such as SATA disks. These disks are combined with hardware RAID sets to mitigate the shorter Mean Time Between Failure (MTBF) cycle compared to enterprise-class SCSI or SAS disks. This enables a VTL to provide higher reliability compared to regular tape media.

Both purchase price and operational costs of backup infrastructure are important considerations. You need far less electricity for tape media in a tape library compared to data stored on permanently rotating disks. This includes the power for keeping the disks online and for cooling the data center hosting the storage equipment.

Figure 8-6 shows an environment that integrated a VTL and a conventional tape library. Backup data are first sent to the VTL. Data that have not been accessed for a long time are automatically migrated to a conventional tape library to free up space in the VTL for new backup data. The backup software tracks the location of the tape media and automatically performs a restore from the VTL or from the conventional tape library.

A recent market trend is to include single-instance storage functions in a VTL, referred to as *data de-duplication*. Data de-duplication identifies duplicate data within backup sets stored in the VTL and removes duplicate disk blocks. This significantly increases the storage capacity of the VTL. Some

Figure 8-6   *Backup and restore to a VTL*

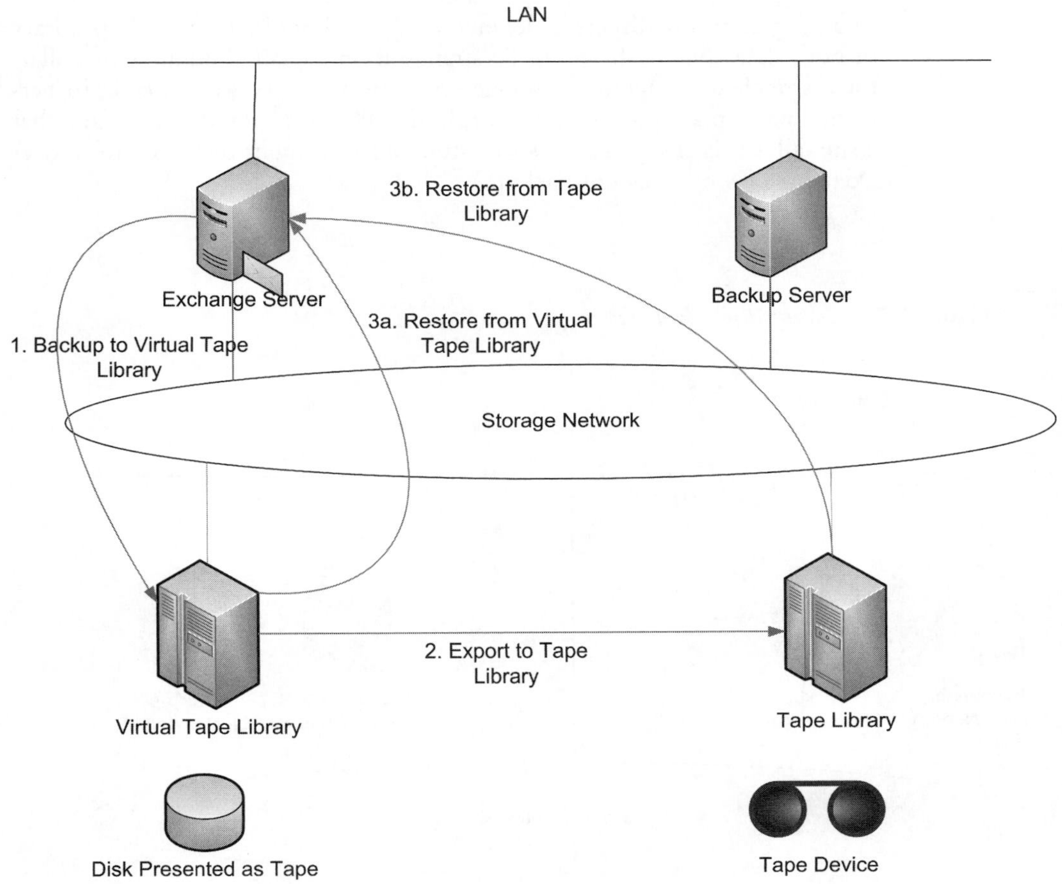

vendors claim that their VTL can store up to 50 times more data because of data de-duplication. This is a significant advantage compared to the 2:1 compression ratio usually provided by a conventional tape library. The compression rate that you can achieve with Exchange depends on the type of attachments that your users send. The more compressible the attachments, the more compressible the data on backup will be.

Meanwhile, however, do not forget the impact of losing a disk block that is referenced by multiple backup sets compared to the effect of losing a single tape media.

Backup for Geographically Dispersed Deployments

In a geographically dispersed deployment, you should have a backup library in both data centers. It would be strange if you spent thousands of dollars for a stretched cluster with storage replication, but you are unable to perform a backup after a site failover. Additionally, you should not assume that a site failover is always 100% successful, and you might be forced to recover a database from a previous backup.

Figure 8-7   *Backup across data centers*

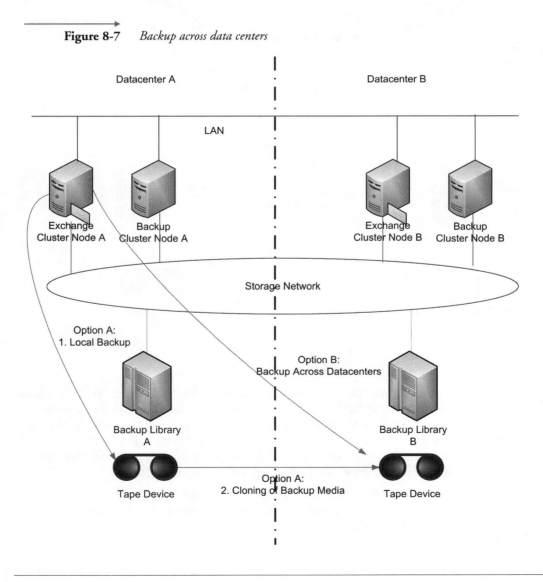

Figure 8-7 shows the two options that you have:

- Back up to a local library and clone the backup media to the library in the remote data center.
- Back up servers located in data center A to the backup library in data center B and vice versa.

Using a clustered backup server in this architecture is advantageous. The backup cluster will have access to all backup media independent of whether the media are located in library A or library B.

An alternative architecture is to host the backup library in a third data center (Figure 8-8). The advantage of this architecture is reduced hardware cost because you only need one backup library.

Figure 8-8   *Backup to third data center*

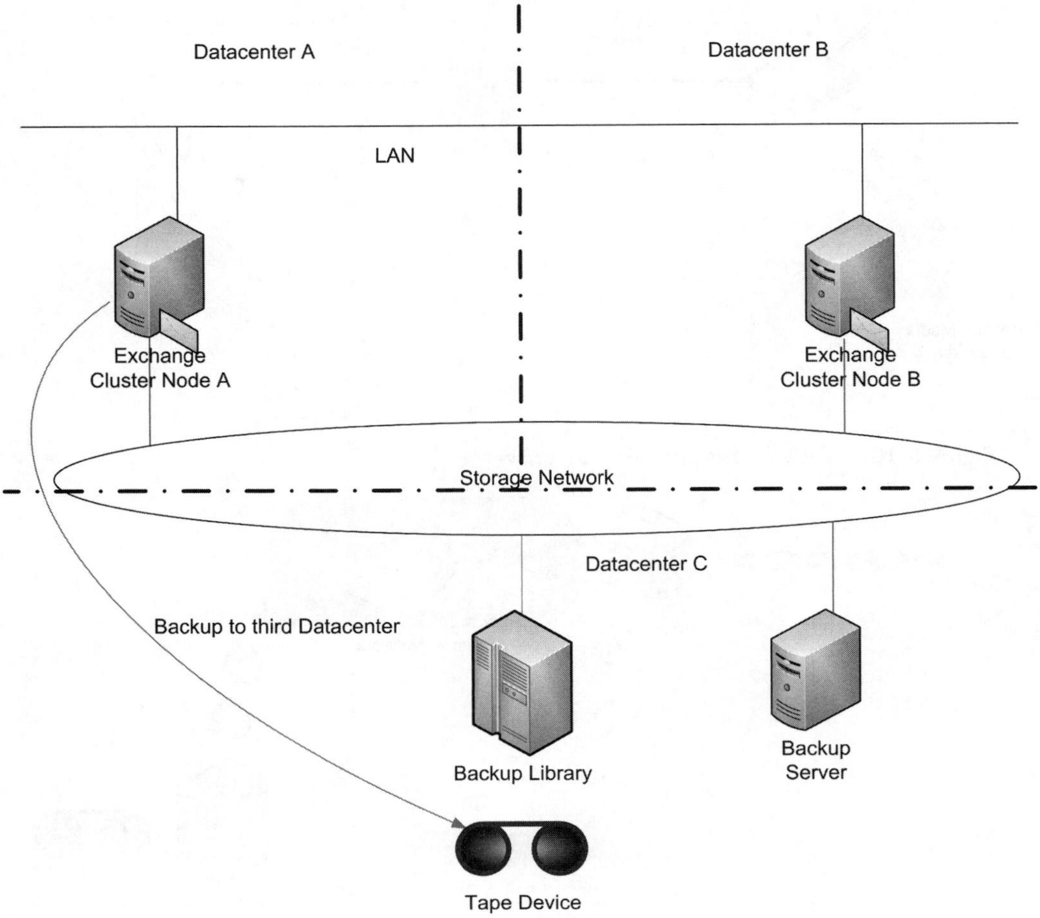

Backup Performance

If you want to estimate the throughput of your backup infrastructure, you have to consider all components from the disk volume storing the Exchange database to the backup target. All components shown in Figure 8-9 can be a bottleneck and the limiting factor for achievable performance. As Figures 8-10 and 8-11 illustrate, you can expect a much higher throughput with a SAN backup infrastructure compared to a LAN backup.

Figure 8-9   *Backup performance*

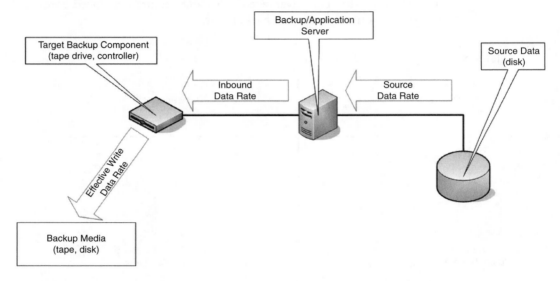

Figure 8-10   *LAN backup performance analogy*

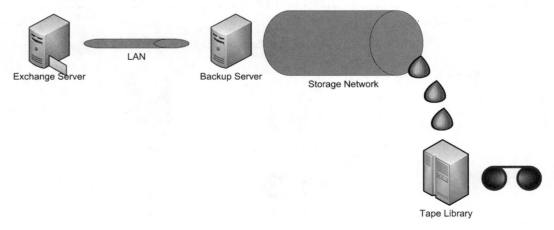

Figure 8-11   *SAN backup performance analogy*

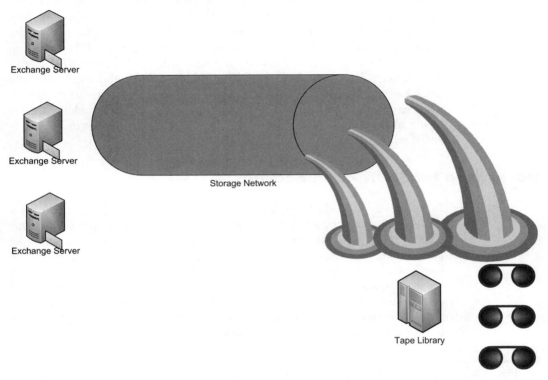

Based on experience from customer projects, LAN backup throughput is often in the range of only 40 GB/hour. With SAN backup, achieving about 100 GB/hour to a LTO2 tape device and above 200 GB/hour to a LTO3 tape device is not uncommon.

Mailbox servers have multiple storage groups and you can back up multiple storage groups in parallel. This allows you to have multiple backup data streams sent to multiple backup targets. You can shrink the required backup window by backing up multiple storage groups in parallel. It is possible to send the backup data of multiple storage groups to a single backup target, but this multiplexing has disadvantages during a restore. For example, assume that you multiplexed four storage groups to tape during the backup, and now want to restore only a single storage group. You have to read back all four storage groups worth of data to get the one you are after. The speed of the restore data stream is again fast, but the time required to restore the single database is longer because you have to read the data of three additional storage groups that you don't want to recover.

Exchange Server 2003 supports four storage groups and Exchange Server 2007 supports up to 50 storage groups. How many storage groups should you back up in parallel? What is the optimal number of storage groups from a backup performance point of view? The answer depends on several factors, including the storage configuration of the Exchange server and the backup software product. In a test performed by the HP Customer Focused Testing team, the fastest backup was achieved with 16 storage groups. It is very likely that the following finding made during tests with SQL Server 2005 is also applicable to Exchange: You should use multiple disk volumes to store the databases and log files. If each backup stream reads data from separate source volumes, then performance is higher compared to multiple backup streams trying to back up storage groups located on a single disk volume. The referenced whitepapers can be found on www.hp.com/go/hpcft.

Information for SAN-based Backups

In a highly available SAN deployment, each server has two Host Bus Adapters (HBAs) to connect to the back-end storage array via multiple paths. This enables multiple paths from the server to the primary storage. The multiple paths protect the Exchange server from losing access to the databases and log files hosted on the storage array if a single component between the server and the storage array fails. Taking advantage of the multiple paths by using load distribution or load balancing between the paths is also possible. The connection to the tape library will only use a single path because multiple path access to tape devices is not supported by most backup products (Figure 8-12).

Figure 8-12
Two HBAs and shared fabric

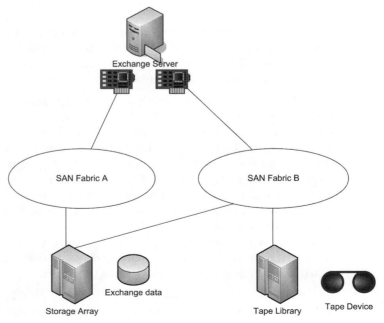

SAN Zoning is a licensed management service of a SAN switch used to create logical device subsets within a SAN. Zoning enables resource partitioning for management and access control purposes. A common configuration is to create two zones per Exchange server. Zone A contains the HBAs and the storage array. Zone B contains the HBAs and the tape library. Another option is to configure a separate zone per HBA port.

Even if the tape library and the storage array are not in the same zone, failure of a tape device may affect access to disk storage. This is possible because the HBAs are in both SAN zones, and the disk array and the tape library use a shared SAN switch infrastructure. See Microsoft Knowledge Base Article 887017 for details.

You can reduce the likelihood of this issue by installing a third HBA per Exchange server or by using one port of a dual-port HBA. This HBA is only used to access the tape library. This setup has three zones, with one zone per HBA. Zone A contains the HBA 1 and the storage array, Zone B contains HBA 2 and the storage array, and Zone C contains the HBA 3 and the tape library. This configuration enables a better separation of disk storage and tape devices (Figure 8-13).

Figure 8-13
Dedicated backup HBA

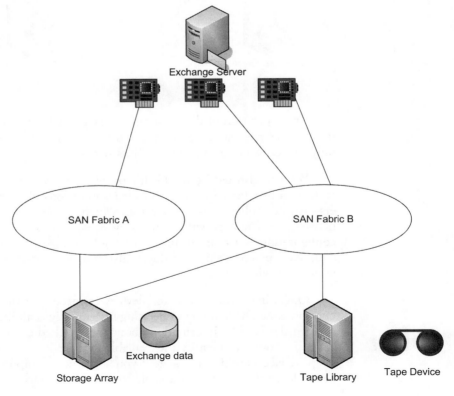

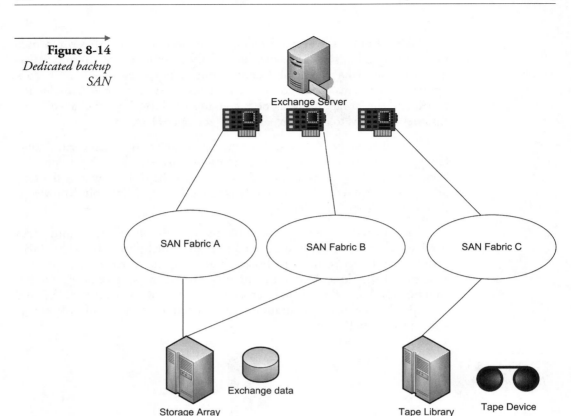

Figure 8-14
*Dedicated backup
SAN*

The separation of disk and tape storage can be further increased if you deploy a completely separate SAN infrastructure with SAN switches used only for accessing the tape library (Figure 8-14).

You can also reduce the likelihood of tape device failures affecting disk storage access by deploying so-called multiprotocol routers. These routers provide multiple routing services, which enable interconnecting devices between SAN fabrics without merging those fabrics. The advantage of this configuration is a more secure and flexible storage networking foundation. This level of connectivity reduces disruptions associated with operational events or device failures.

Operating systems scan for devices connected to the SAN during the boot process. The Windows operating system assigns an identity to each recognized device. The information about the attached devices is used by your backup software to identify the available tape devices. Ideally the identity of a tape device should not change if you add a new component to the storage network, or if you plug in a cable to a different port on the SAN switch.

Maintaining the identity of a device despite configuration changes to the SAN is called *device persistency*.

In UNIX operating systems, device persistency can be achieved for tape drives in the SAN. Several UNIX versions use the world wide name (WWN) of the tape controller to identify the attached tape device. Because the WWN does not change, target identification will not change, despite modifications to the SAN. Microsoft Windows does not offer support for device persistency by default. The device driver of the HBA assigns targets to WWNs in the order of discovery. If a target goes offline or if a target is added, the remaining targets get a different target ID during the next server reboot. If the identity of a tape drive is modified, the likelihood exists that the backup software no longer can access the tape drive and you have to reconfigure existing backup jobs. Some backup applications maintain device persistency in Windows by tracking the serial number of the tape drive. Another option is to use utilities of the HBA manufacturer to configure device persistency, such as *LPUTILNT.EXE* from Emulex.

Introduction to Volume Shadow Copy Services

Since the release of Windows Server 2003 and Exchange Server 2003, it has been possible to back up the public and private Information Store databases of an Exchange server using Volume Shadow Copy Services (VSS). Despite the availability of VSS, most customers decided to stick with a traditional streaming backup solution. Streaming backups have been available since the first Exchange Server versions and represent a very mature data protection solution. VSS is new and has not been widely used in production environments. With the release of Exchange Server 2007, Microsoft declared the streaming backup API "deemphasized."

With Windows Server 2008, Microsoft will further urge customers to switch to VSS. In Windows Server 2008, NTbackup has been replaced with Windows Server Backup. Windows Server Backup uses VSS to back up data. System Center Data Protection Manager 2007 (DPM), Microsoft's enterprise backup product, also uses VSS and not the streaming API.

Exchange administrators and independent solution vendors (ISV) are expected to prioritize their VSS-related activities. Even if you do not intend to switch to VSS right now, you should consider requirements related to VSS during the design of a new Exchange Server 2007 environment. It is difficult to introduce a VSS backup solution later if a few guidelines have not been followed. ISVs that do not have an Exchange Server 2007 VSS solution in their portfolio will definitely lose market share. For ISVs, it is especially challenging because Microsoft will give customers with DPM the chance to drop all components provided by a third party for their backup solution, and buy a complete VSS solution from the application vendor. This is very attractive to customers who used home-grown hot-split solutions from third-party vendors. Hot-split solutions are not fully supported by Microsoft. The term *hot-split* is explained in a following section. In the past, some components of a VSS solution were available only from a third-party vendor and not from Microsoft. The VSS solution vendor is your main support contract for storage-related questions. An Exchange VSS solution from Microsoft reduces the likelihood of finger pointing during troubleshooting issues.

Advantages

Before we cover the technical details, here is a summary of the main benefits of the VSS solution:

- VSS enables faster recovery when compared to fetching data using the traditional restore from tape or a flat backup file stored on a disk. This is called *instant recovery* in marketing brochures.

- VSS allows you to offload resource demands of the backup process to a separate disk volume, or even completely move the CPU and memory load to a separate server.

- VSS might be the only backup API supported in the future. You are investing in a non de-emphasized solution.

The big picture

Figure 8-15 shows the major components that interact with each other during a VSS backup. In the middle of the illustration is the Windows service, Volume Shadow Copy. This service can be compared with an air control system. It is responsible for coordinating the interaction of the other solution components. The requestor is usually integrated in a backup product, and is responsible for initiating the backup or the restore job. The VSS writer is usually integrated into an application, such as Exchange Server or SQL Server. The function of the VSS writer is to ensure that the data stored on the disk volumes are usable for recovery. Before Microsoft made the VSS API available, the backup application developer was responsible for ensuring that the application data were usable for recovery. A backup application developer often does not have access to the necessary information about application

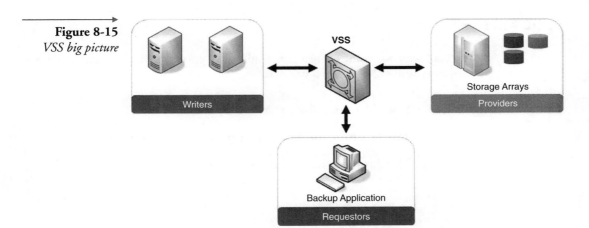

Figure 8-15
VSS big picture

details. The application developer is better aware of what steps are necessary to ensure that the data on the disk volumes created by the VSS backup are usable for recovery. For performance reasons, database applications often implement a "lazy writer" algorithm that defers write I/O to disks until a large number of I/O requests are gathered. The data held in memory have to be considered by the backup and recovery solution. Prior to the advent of VSS, shutting down the application or dismounting the databases was required. This is not an optimal solution for a 24×7 application.

The provider is a disk storage–related software component that abstracts the functions of the underlying storage controller to create a point-in-time copy of disk volumes. Solutions that create a point-in-time copy of the disk volumes without the help of the Exchange writer are called hot-split backup solutions. This type of solution is not recommended; Microsoft's support statement is available in Microsoft Knowledge Base Article 311898. The point-in-time copies of the disk volumes are called *shadow copy volumes* in Microsoft's terminology. This is Microsoft's term for what storage vendors mean when they talk about Business Continuance Columes (BCVs), flash copy, snapshot, clone, and others. In principle, they are all nearly identical. There are only two implementation alternatives of a shadow copy volume.

Shadow Copy Volume Implementation Alternatives

You either get a fully independent copy of the production disk volume, or you get a disk volume that depends on your production disk volume and physically contains only the changes that have been made since the point-in-time copy was created.

Split Mirror

A split-mirror solution usually requires a high-end storage array. An implementation is shown in Figure 8-16.

1.   You add a third disk to a two-disk mirror.

2.   The data from the two-disk mirror are copied to the new disk.

3.   The third disk is split from the mirror.

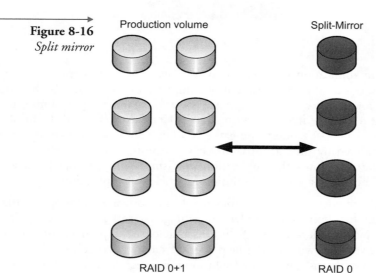

Figure 8-16
Split mirror

The main advantage of this solution is that the shadow copy is fully independent of the production volume. You can use the shadow copy for a restore even if your production disk volume is physically lost. Another benefit is performance related. If you access this disk volume, you do not impact performance of the disk volume still being used by your production Exchange database. This advantage is not cost-free. You need a significant amount of additional disk spindles, or roughly the same amount of disk space for the shadow copy. Some high-end storage arrays allow you to use different RAID levels for the original and shadow copy volume, but you have to be aware of the consequences of this cost reduction. If you decide to use RAID1 for your production data, and switch to RAID5 for your shadow copy, you have to consider this when you define your recovery strategy. You do not want lower performance after a restore.

Copy-on-write

Copy-on-write is shown in Figure 8-17. Initially, the shadow copy volume contains only pointers to your original volume. Every time you access the point-in-time copy you actually fetch disk blocks used by the production disk volume. Only if changes are written to the original volume or to your shadow copy is a copy process started to preserve the data that exist on the disk block at the time the shadow copy was created. Accessing the production disk blocks for every read to an unmodified disk block impacts performance of the disk volume used by your production Exchange data. This is, for example, the case when you verify the checksum of the backed-up database. This is something you should never forget! This copy-on-write implementation is space efficient and requires less additional disk space. How many gigabytes you save depends on the change rate and lifetime of the shadow copy volume.

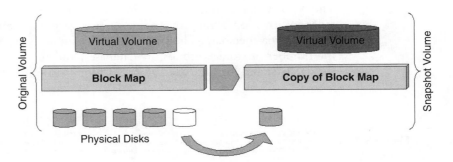

Figure 8-17
Copy-on-write

Bear in mind that the online maintenance process, in particular, tends to modify many disk blocks to optimize the white space within the database file. Copy-on-write volumes are often only used for temporary purposes. For example, you create a copy of the Exchange database and log files on a separate disk volume, map the disk volume to a backup server, and stream the data to a tape library. This offloads the CPU and memory resource demands of the tape backup to a server not accessed by end users. Microsoft calls the feature to transport the shadow copy created on server A to server B *shadow copy transport*. Shadow copy transport is available with split-mirror and copy-on-write shadow copy volumes, but most of the time it is only available with a VSS hardware provider.

Note that a copy-on-write volume is not capable of being used as a production quality disk volume. This has to be considered in your recovery strategy. If you deleted the copy-on-write volume after you send the data on the shadow copy volume to a tape device, you have to use a traditional flat file restore for your recovery procedure. Some solution vendors have implemented a "snap back" function that copies the changed disk blocks from the shadow copy volume back to the original production volume during the restore. This recovery procedure uses the VSS framework for the recovery; the VSS provider is responsible for performing the "snap-back" function.

Components

Requestor

The requestor is responsible for initiating the backup or restore job. Usually the requestor is implemented in a backup product. These products offer a nice GUI that depicts the Exchange storage group configuration, and allows the administrator to select which storage groups/databases have to be backed up or restored. The requestor is also responsible for checking the health of the databases and log files on the shadow copy volumes.

Writer

The VSS writer is implemented in Exchange. The Exchange writer provides information about the Exchange storage group configuration to the requestor via metadata. The metadata comprise an XML file that describes the number of storage groups, its databases, and the file system paths with the database and log files. See Figure 8-18 for an example XML file.

Figure 8-18
Metadata

```
– <WRITER_METADATA xmlns="x-schema:#VssWriterMetadataInfo" version="1.1" backupSchema="791">
    <IDENTIFICATION writerId="76fe1ac4-15f7-4bcd-987e-8e1acb462fb7" instanceId="b481a441-9040-458c-9f12-
      6ff1acdc6f38" instanceName="Exchange Replication Service" friendlyName="Microsoft Exchange Writer"
      usage="USER_DATA" dataSource="TRANSACTION_DB"/>
  – <BACKUP_LOCATIONS>
      <FILE_GROUP logicalPath="Microsoft Exchange Server\Microsoft Information Store\Replica\CCR1-CMS"
        componentName="94abf718-423b-406e-94e6-07d9eadd65a9" caption="First Storage Group"
        icon="KAEAACgAAAAQAAAAIAAAAAEABAAAAAAwAAAAAAAAAAAAAAAEAAAAAAAAAAAAAAAAACAAACAA"
        restoreMetadata="yes" notifyOnBackupComplete="yes" selectable="yes" selectableForRestore="yes"
        componentFlags="0"/>
    – <FILE_GROUP logicalPath="Microsoft Exchange Server\Microsoft Information Store\Replica\CCR1-
        CMS\94abf718-423b-406e-94e6-07d9eadd65a9" componentName="Logs" caption="Logs"
        icon="KAEAACgAAAAQAAAAIAAAAAEABAAAAAAwAAAAAAAAAAAAAAAEAAAAAAAAAAAAAAAAACAAACAA"
        restoreMetadata="yes" notifyOnBackupComplete="yes" selectable="no" selectableForRestore="yes"
        componentFlags="0">
        <FILE_LIST path="C:\Program Files\Microsoft\Exchange Server\Mailbox\First Storage Group"
          filespec="E00*.log" filespecBackupType="3855" />
        <FILE_LIST path="C:\Program Files\Microsoft\Exchange Server\Mailbox\First Storage Group"
          filespec="E00.chk" filespecBackupType="3841" />
      </FILE_GROUP>
    – <FILE_GROUP logicalPath="Microsoft Exchange Server\Microsoft Information Store\Replica\CCR1-
        CMS\94abf718-423b-406e-94e6-07d9eadd65a9" componentName="1bb5d553-e86f-4286-8538-
        704d7d9086a2" caption="Mailbox Database"
        icon="KAEAACgAAAAQAAAAIAAAAAEABAAAAAAwAAAAAAAAAAAAAAAEAAAAAAAAAAAAAAAAACAAACAA"
        restoreMetadata="yes" notifyOnBackupComplete="yes" selectable="no" selectableForRestore="yes"
        componentFlags="0">
        <FILE_LIST path="C:\Program Files\Microsoft\Exchange Server\Mailbox\First Storage Group"
          filespec="Mailbox Database.edb" filespecBackupType="3841" />
      </FILE_GROUP>
    </BACKUP_LOCATIONS>
    <RESTORE_METHOD method="RESTORE_IF_CAN_BE_REPLACED" writerRestore="always" rebootRequired="no" />
  </WRITER_METADATA>
```

A major responsibility of the writer is to ensure that the Exchange data stored on the disk volume is usable for recovery purposes. The writer closes the currently open transaction log file and halts I/O for a few seconds until the VSS provider has created the shadow copy disk volume. Afterward the writer thaws write I/O requests and creates a new transaction log file. After the requestor has successfully verified that the database and log files on the shadow copy disk volume are crash consistent, the writer truncates the log files if this was a full or incremental backup. It was a very good decision on Microsoft's part to assign the responsibility to delete the transaction log files to a core component of the Exchange application. Delegating this critical task to a third-party component—for example, the VSS requestor—would be more error prone.

Exchange Server 2003 has only one VSS writer. Exchange Server 2007 introduced a second writer, the Exchange replication writer. This VSS writer is only used by an LCR and CCR configuration.

Provider

The provider is a software component that abstracts the functions of the storage environment to create and manage point-in-time disk volumes. This abstraction layer allows ISVs to create solutions that can interact with disk arrays from different storage vendors. Three available provider implementations are described in the following.

- System Provider. The system provider is a standard component of the operating system (OS). It creates shadow copies of disk volumes without the need for any third-party component, and it does not need any special disk storage—any hard disk will work. The system provider is, for example, used by the shadow copy of shared folders function on file servers.

- Software Provider. Software providers are installed separately—for example, as part of a third-party volume management solution like VERITAS Storage Foundation for Windows. These providers are often implemented as filter drivers. The Microsoft system provider is also a kind of software provider, but it is referred to as a system provider because it is part of the OS. Software providers are often used in an environment that does not have a high-end Fibre Channel attached-storage array. This is because software providers can be used with Direct-Attached Storage (DAS).

- Hardware Provider. A hardware provider is a software component that abstracts the vendor-specific functions for creating and managing point-in-time copies of disk volumes implemented by a storage array, such as an HP StorageWorks EVA. Hardware provider solutions are very interesting because they can leverage the advanced features of high-end storage arrays. Be aware that it is often the case that the current VSS provider may not take advantage of the newest storage array firmware. A new firmware might have implemented new point-in-time copy features, but you have to wait for the next VSS provider software release until your VSS solution can take advantage of these interesting features.

You always have the system provider installed on your server. The other providers are optional products that you install on an as-needed basis. These additional providers do not replace the system provider; instead, the VSS requestor lets you decide during the backup job creation which VSS provider should be used. If you do not specify the VSS provider in the backup job, then the VSS framework will use the following sequence to determine the VSS provider it will use:

1.   Hardware provider
2.   Software provider
3.   System provider

Backup

According to the official Microsoft VSS documentation, it is possible to back up an Exchange storage group, but you cannot back up an individual database of a storage group. It is likely that some ISV will extend the functions of the "native VSS framework" and provide additional capabilities to differentiate their solution from other offerings. Exchange Server 2007 VSS supports all common backup types: full, copy, incremental, and differential. The Exchange Server 2003 RTM initially only supported full and copy backups; Exchange Server 2003 SP1 added support for incremental and differential backups. The backup program uses configuration information provided by the VSS writer to visualize the Exchange storage group configuration, such as the number of storage groups and number of databases per storage group on the Exchange server that you want to back up. As a prerequisite, you have to ensure that all databases of the storage group you want to back up are mounted.

The first step in the backup process is that the VSS requestor starts a backup job. The second step is that the Exchange writer freezes the I/O for this storage group, and closes the currently open transaction log file. In the next step, the provider creates shadow copy volumes of the disk volumes that are used by the Exchange storage group. This step only takes a few seconds (~10 seconds). Next, the Exchange writer thaws the I/O for this storage group and creates a new transaction log file. At this point, the requestor checks the health of the databases and transaction log files on the shadow copy volumes.

In the past, a VSS requestor used *ESEUTIL.EXE /K* to check the files created by Exchange Server 2003; now the VSS requestor uses *CHKSGFILES.DLL* to verify the Exchange Server 2007 database and log files. This check is very CPU and I/O intensive, and executing it on a separate server is preferable. This can be done using the shadow copy transport

Figure 8-19   *VSS backup sequence*

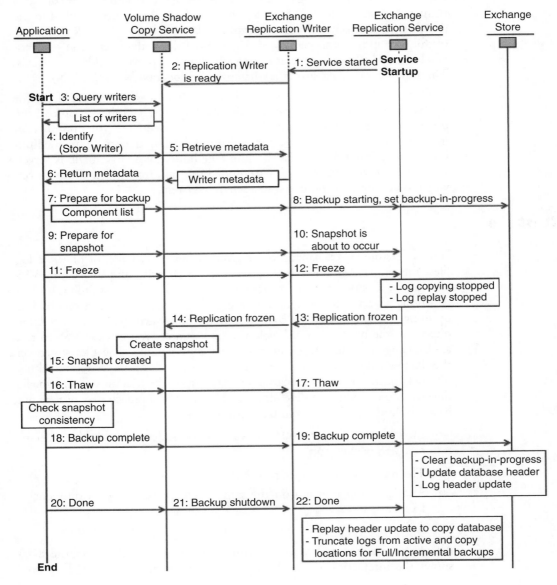

function described above. The shadow copy volume can be mounted to a separate server and this server performs the checksum verification. The database will be in a crash-consistent state. This is different from the clean shutdown state that you achieve by dismounting the database; therefore, some transaction log files are still required to be able to bring the database to a state comparable to a clean shutdown.

If the database and log files are okay, then the requestor informs the Exchange writer that the log files can be truncated if the backup were full or incremental. Exchange will only delete log files that have already been applied to the database. Additionally, the writer stamps the database header to mark that a successful backup has been performed. Figure 8-19 shows the interaction sequence of all involved VSS components during a backup and provides additional details. This flow chart is available on the Microsoft Developer Network (MSDN).

The backup process creates shadow copy volumes that you can use for an instant recovery, or you can use the shadow copy volumes to offload the process that sends the backup data to a tape device from your production mailbox server to a separate server. Streaming backup data to a tape medium is a resource-intensive process that can take hours for a large mailbox server. It is a great advantage to be able to offload this task from the mailbox server, which is accessed by end users, to a separate system.

Restore

You can restore an Exchange storage group, a single database, or only the log files. You can restore only a backup set that was created using VSS with a VSS restore job. It is not possible to restore data created with the steaming backup API using a VSS restore function. However, it is possible to restore files backed up using a traditional flat file backup from a VSS-created shadow copy volume directly to the production disk volume. For example, you can use VSS to run an Exchange backup and create a shadow copy volume. The files stored on the shadow copy volume are then sent to a tape device using a traditional flat file backup. In a recovery scenario, you can restore the files on the tape media directly to the production disk volume. This recovery approach may or may not be available, depending on your backup application.

In Exchange Server 2003, it was not possible with the VSS API to restore a VSS backup to:

- The recovery storage group (RSG)
- Another storage group on the same Exchange server, or a different Exchange server
- A file system path that is not used by an Exchange storage group

All of the above is now possible with Exchange Server 2007. Figure 8-20 shows the interaction of the VSS components during a restore. This flow

chart is also available on MSDN. The administrator is responsible for manually dismounting all databases of the storage group before the restore is
started. For convenience, some VSS solutions have integrated the *dismount*
command with their restore procedure. The VSS requestor, your backup

Figure 8-20 *VSS restore sequence*

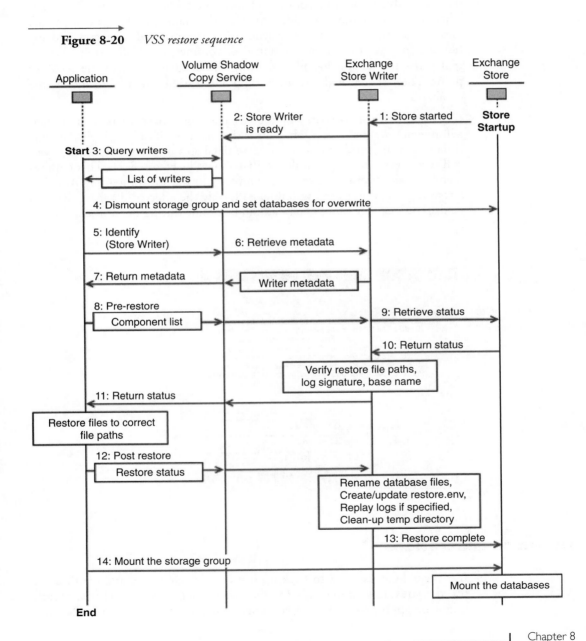

program, initiates a new restore job as a first step. Next, the VSS provider performs the restore of the point-in-time shadow copy volume to the production disk volume. This can be implemented as a disk volume swap or as a block-level re-sync of the disk contents. Be aware of the following disadvantage of a re-sync: If the restore fails you have lost the "damaged" database, which might be your last chance to recover at least a few messages. Therefore, you should consider copying the damaged database to a safe location before you start the re-sync. After the restored databases and log files are in place on the production disk volumes, the VSS writer starts to replay the transaction log files to bring the database back to the recovery point. The last step is that your backup application attempts to mount the databases.

Note that *all* databases of the storage group have to be dismounted before you start the restore job. This is the case even if only a single database is damaged. If you do not dismount *all* databases in the storage group, you will see an error message similar to that shown in Figure 8-21. This require-ment is a significant disadvantage compared to the streaming-only API. For a restore using the streaming online API, only the affected databases have to be dismounted; the other databases can be online during the restore.

Figure 8-21
VSS requires dismount of all databases

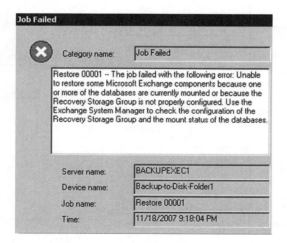

Design considerations

It is possible to use VSS to back up just one storage group and continue to use the streaming online API for the other storage groups. This approach might be appropriate for a server when you want to start to use VSS in a production environment, or if you only have one storage group that needs the instant recovery capability provided by VSS.

Read the VSS solution manual or ask your solution vendor about the VSS solution requirements and what constraints you have to follow. For example, the VSS framework is agnostic to the number of disk volumes you use per Exchange storage group, but your VSS solution might require that all databases of a storage group are stored on a single disk volume. This is important in a recovery scenario. If only a single database of a five-database storage group is damaged, then swapping the disk volume with all the databases back to a previous point-in-time version changes all five databases back to the old version, even though only one of the five is damaged. A similar situation could occur if you use one disk volume to store the databases or the log files of multiple storage groups. These topics heavily depend on the kind of VSS provider you use and how it is implemented by the VSS solution vendor. You can find additional information about this topic in the Microsoft TechNet section, "Mailbox Server Storage Design." This article also mentions the issues you will face with hardware-based VSS solutions when files of multiple storage groups are stored on a single disk.

Is it a clever design practice to only run a VSS backup and keep your backup data on the shadow copy volume? No, it is careless! You should migrate the data on the shadow copy volume to tape media and store at least some generations off-site. This was a best practice with the streaming online API, and there is no reason why you should drop this best practice. If you do not want to use traditional tape devices, you should at least copy the data to a remote site; otherwise, a disaster can easily destroy your production data and backup data at the same time. Realizing that the production data and the backup set are now located on the same storage array is important! You should consult your VSS solution vendor and ask whether having a shadow copy volume as the source for remote data replication is supported.

With the streaming API, it is possible to send the backup data directly to a tape device. With VSS, there is always an intermediate step required before you can send your backup data to a tape media. The first step is always to create a backup on a disk volume that you stream in a second step to tape media. You cannot use VSS to send your backup data directly to a tape device.

These are just a few important constraints that a VSS solution might impose. Read the fine print of the manual and start to gain experience with VSS in a test lab.

VSS and Continuous Replication

Exchange Server 2007 introduced the capability to offload Exchange database backups to the passive node of a mailbox server that uses Cluster Continuous

Replication (CCR). This allows you to move storage I/O, CPU, and memory load from the active cluster node, where the clustered mailbox server (CMS) is online, to the passive cluster node. Note that this is only available with CCR and not with Single Copy Clusters (SCCs).

A backup process is resource intensive and end users appreciate it if their response time is not affected by backups. You may argue that backups occur during the night when no users are online, but this is too optimistic in heavily consolidated data centers. Currently, users in various time zones connect to the same server deployed in a central data center. Additionally, in the near future Continuous Data Protection (CDP) solutions will become popular. CDP solutions run backups very frequently; for example, DPM can run backups of an Exchange mailbox server up to every 15 minutes.

Test environment

Figure 8-22 shows a simplified picture of the test systems used to evaluate VSS on a CCR mailbox server.

Figure 8-22   *CCR test environment*

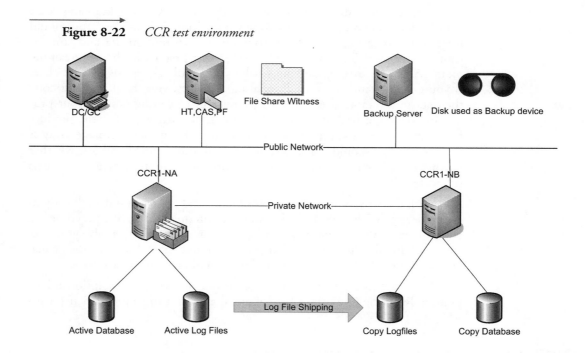

You can set up the environment with virtual machines—for example, the above environment was built with VMware ESX 3.0. The backup server runs Symantec Backup Exec 11d for Windows Servers. In the product manual,

Symantec refers to the backup server as "Backup Exec media server." This server requires a connection to disk and/or tape storage devices. It is possible to co-locate the Backup Exec media server with another application on one system, but in an enterprise environment, using a dedicated system as backup server is recommended. Backup Exec implements a VSS requestor that supports Exchange Server 2007 and is able to back up the copy database created by Local Continuous Replication (LCR) or CCR. The copy database is the replica that the continuous replication function of Exchange Server 2007 creates. This replica should not be mixed up with the database that is stored on the shadow copy volume created by a VSS backup. The shadow copy volumes are created with the Microsoft system provider, or another VSS provider installed on your Exchange mailbox server.

The backup server uses a file system directory as a backup target because the test environment does not have a tape device. In a real enterprise environment you, would use a tape library and the backup data would be sent via the storage area network to the tape library. The public LAN should not be used to transport backup data from the Exchange server to the backup media. You can achieve higher throughput if you send backup data over the switched fabric of the storage area network.

In Figure 8-23, you can see that the CMS is currently online on the cluster node CCR1-NA.

Figure 8-23
CCR1-CMS
cluster group

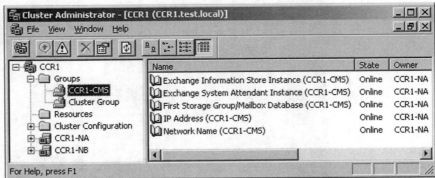

VSS Writers

Exchange Server 2003 has only one VSS writer, the store writer. Deployments of Exchange Server 2007 can have two VSS writers—the store writer and the replication writer. The Exchange Information Store service implements the store writer. The store writer is available on a single server, on the active cluster node of an SCC, and on the active node of a mailbox server using CCR. The Exchange Replication service implements the replication writer. The

VSS replication writer is available on the passive node of a mailbox server that uses CCR, and on a single server with an LCR-enabled storage group. On a server with LCR enabled, you have two Exchange VSS writers—the store writer and the replication writer. There is no VSS writer running on the passive node of an SCC.

Figure 8-24 shows a screenshot of the two VSS writers on a single server with an LCR-enabled storage group.

Figure 8-24
Two VSS writers on LCR

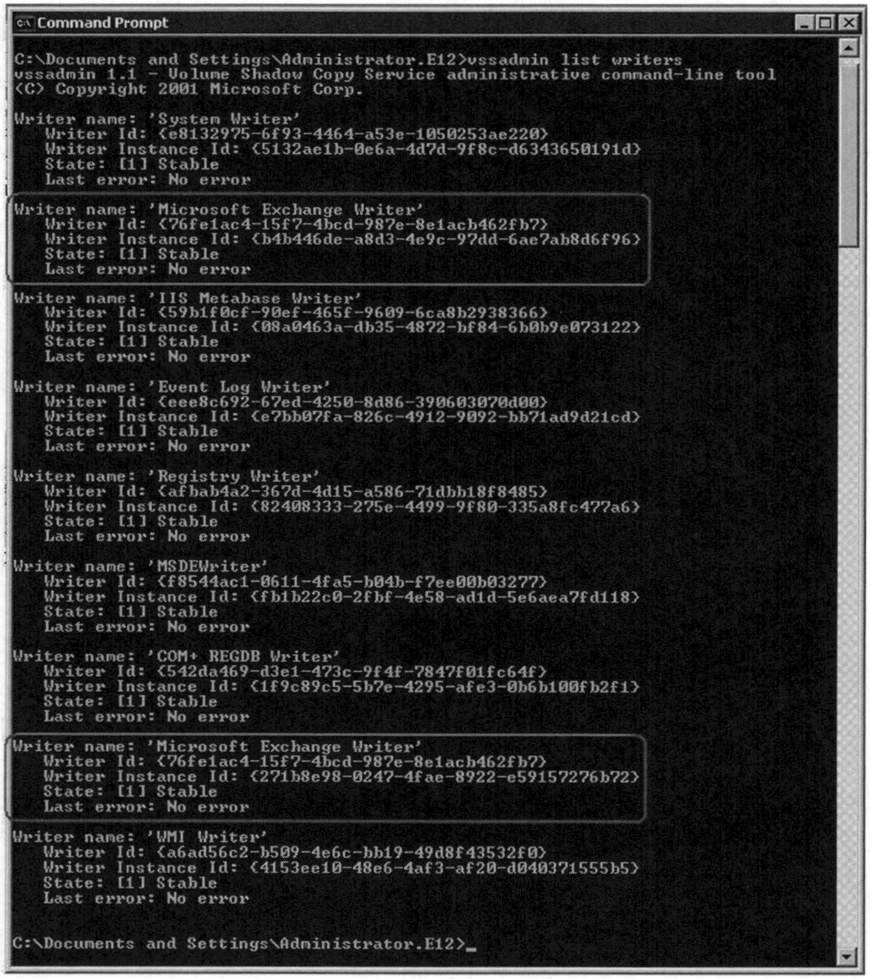

```
Command Prompt                                                          _ □ ×

C:\Documents and Settings\Administrator.E12>vssadmin list writers
vssadmin 1.1 - Volume Shadow Copy Service administrative command-line tool
(C) Copyright 2001 Microsoft Corp.
Writer name: 'System Writer'
   Writer Id: {e8132975-6f93-4464-a53e-1050253ae220}
   Writer Instance Id: {5132ae1b-0e6a-4d7d-9f8c-d6343650191d}
   State: [1] Stable
   Last error: No error

Writer name: 'Microsoft Exchange Writer'
   Writer Id: {76fe1ac4-15f7-4bcd-987e-8e1acb462fb7}
   Writer Instance Id: {b4b446de-a8d3-4e9c-97dd-6ae7ab8d6f96}
   State: [1] Stable
   Last error: No error

Writer name: 'IIS Metabase Writer'
   Writer Id: {59b1f0cf-90ef-465f-9609-6ca8b2938366}
   Writer Instance Id: {08a0463a-db35-4872-bf84-6b0b9e073122}
   State: [1] Stable
   Last error: No error

Writer name: 'Event Log Writer'
   Writer Id: {eee8c692-67ed-4250-8d86-390603070d00}
   Writer Instance Id: {e7bb07fa-826c-4912-9092-bb71ad9d21cd}
   State: [1] Stable
   Last error: No error

Writer name: 'Registry Writer'
   Writer Id: {afbab4a2-367d-4d15-a586-71dbb18f8485}
   Writer Instance Id: {82408333-275e-4499-9f80-335a8fc477a6}
   State: [1] Stable
   Last error: No error

Writer name: 'MSDEWriter'
   Writer Id: {f8544ac1-0611-4fa5-b04b-f7ee00b03277}
   Writer Instance Id: {fb1b22c0-2fbf-4e58-ad1d-5e6aea7fd118}
   State: [1] Stable
   Last error: No error

Writer name: 'COM+ REGDB Writer'
   Writer Id: {542da469-d3e1-473c-9f4f-7847f01fc64f}
   Writer Instance Id: {1f9c89c5-5b7e-4295-afe3-0b6b100fb2f1}
   State: [1] Stable
   Last error: No error

Writer name: 'Microsoft Exchange Writer'
   Writer Id: {76fe1ac4-15f7-4bcd-987e-8e1acb462fb7}
   Writer Instance Id: {271b8e98-0247-4fae-8922-e59157276b72}
   State: [1] Stable
   Last error: No error

Writer name: 'WMI Writer'
   Writer Id: {a6ad56c2-b509-4e6c-bb19-49d8f43532f0}
   Writer Instance Id: {4153ee10-48e6-4af3-af20-d040371555b5}
   State: [1] Stable
   Last error: No error

C:\Documents and Settings\Administrator.E12>_
```

You only can differentiate between the two writers by reading the "Writer Instance Id"; the "Writer name" and "Writer Id" are identical. On the active node of a CCR mailbox server, the Exchange Information Store service and the Exchange Replication Service are running, but only the store writer is active. On the passive CCR node, the Exchange Information Store service has the manual startup type and the service is not running. The VSS store writer is not active on the passive cluster node. The Exchange Replication service is started on the passive node, and the VSS replication writer is active. After a cluster failover, the configuration is automatically changed and the related VSS writer instances are started/stopped.

If you want to back up the Exchange database on the passive cluster node, the store writer on the active cluster node and the replication writer on the passive cluster node must be available. The VSS framework interacts with the store writer on the active cluster node and with the replication writer on the passive cluster node during the backup.

Backup Job

The backup program checks whether the storage group that you want to back up is either LCR enabled, or hosted on a mailbox server using CCR. Symantec Backup Exec enables you to specify that you want to back up the copy database in this scenario (Figure 8-25). Backup Exec verifies the configuration every time you start this backup job. This is quite advantageous because you do not have to modify the backup job after a failover of the CMS to another node in the cluster.

Figure 8-25
Backup source

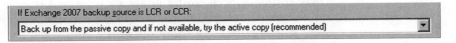

The backup application verifies at the beginning of the backup job that log file replication from the active cluster node to the passive cluster node is healthy. This is similar to manually executing the PowerShell cmdlet *Get-StorageGroupCopyStatus*. The replication is, for example, not healthy if the log file sequence has a gap on the passive cluster node. In this case, the database on the active cluster node will be backed up. You cannot back up the database on the passive cluster node while the database is dismounted on the active cluster node.

It is possible to specify which VSS provider the backup job should use (Figure 8-26). The tests described in this chapter used the Microsoft system provider. No additional VSS provider was installed on the cluster node. The test lab does not have a high-end storage array with a VSS hardware provider such as a HP StorageWorks EVA or XP. The setup for this test does not use a VSS provider from a third-party product like Symantec Storage Foundation

Figure 8-26
VSS provider selection

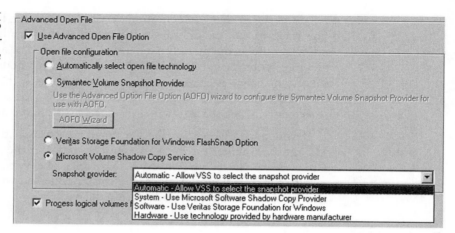

for Windows, or a VSS provider of an iSCSI solution. The lab environment is comparable to a CCR deployment on DAS.

Backup Sequence

You can use the event viewer entries generated during the VSS backup to follow the individual steps of the backup procedure. The entries are very helpful if you have to troubleshoot a failed backup job. By default, the event viewer entries of both cluster nodes are replicated to each other. Therefore, you will find entries from all cluster nodes in the event viewer of a cluster node. It is important to verify the time stamp when the event was created because events replicated from the other cluster node may not appear in the right sequence in the GUI.

In Figure 8-27, you can see that the backup took place on the passive node, CCR1-NB, although the CMS was active on CCR1-NA (Figure 8-23).

Figure 8-27
Backup start on passive node

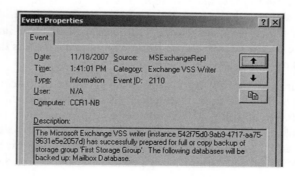

The replication writer freezes the I/O before the VSS provider creates the snapshot (Figure 8-28). Note that read-only access is still possible when the VSS writer freezes a storage group. Exchange can read data from the disk volumes, but it cannot write to the disk volume while the storage group is "frozen."

Figure 8-28
Storage group frozen

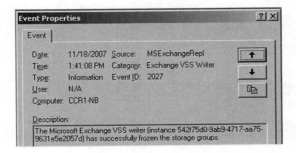

After the shadow copy volume has been created, the writer thaws the I/O again (Figure 8-29). After the Exchange Store thaws the storage group, a new transaction log file is created and the store process continues to write to the production disk volumes.

Figure 8-29
Storage group thawed

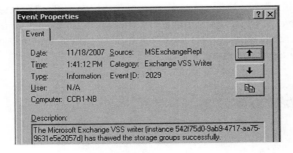

The next step is to verify the health of the transaction log files (Figure 8-30) and the health of the database (Figure 8-31) stored on the shadow copy volumes. This check is very resource intensive, and being able to offload this task to the passive cluster node, which is not accessed by end users, is a significant advantage.

It is very important to realize that the database on the shadow copy is crash consistent and not in a clean shutdown state! The database is only in a clean shutdown state after you dismount the database. VSS performs the backup while the database is online and end users can still send and receive new emails. Therefore, you will need a certain number of transaction log files to

Figure 8-30
Log file verification

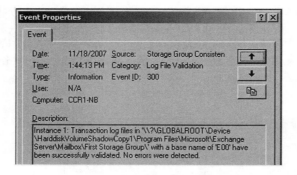

Figure 8-31
Database verification

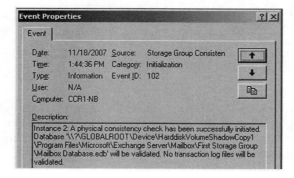

bring the database to a consistent state (Figure 8-32). These are the log files that have not been committed to the database at the time the shadow copy was created. The number of log files requires depends on the server load while the backup runs.

Figure 8-32
Crash consistent

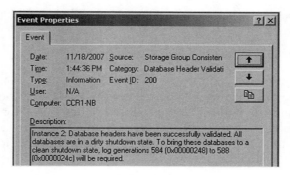

The database header must be updated with the information that a backup has been performed. You can check this information using the *ESEUTIL.EXE /MH <database file>.edb* command, or the property page of the database in the Exchange Management Console (EMC). The update of the database header occurs on the active cluster node. This update modifies the database and creates a new transaction log file. The new log file must be replicated to the passive cluster node before log files can be purged. This information is shown in Figure 8-33.

Figure 8-33
Deferred log file truncation

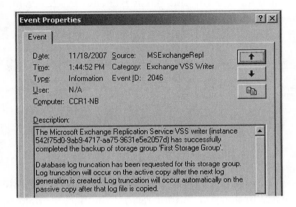

In Figure 8-34 you can verify that the log file deletion on the active cluster node is done by the Exchange Information Store, and on the passive node the log files are truncated by the Exchange Replication service (Figure 8-35).

Figure 8-34
Log file truncation active node

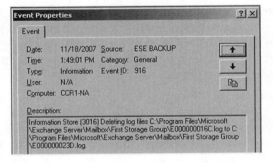

Figure 8-35
Log file truncation passive node

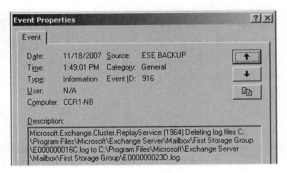

The backup job history in the Symantec Backup Exec GUI (Figure 8-36) documents the successful backup as well. The log file of the backup job specifies that VSS used the default Microsoft Software Shadow Copy provider, referred to as *system provider*, and that the backup was made from the replica database on the passive cluster node. Symantec Backup Exec refers to this database as a "passive copy of the database."

Figure 8-36
Backup job history

```
Backup Set Detail Information

Note: The Microsoft Exchange backup was made from the passive copy of the database.
The consistency check of the snapshot for the Microsoft Exchange transaction log Logs was successful.
The consistency check of the snapshot for the Microsoft Exchange database Mailbox Database was successful.
```

Restore

A VSS backup created on the passive cluster node can only be restored to the active cluster node. You cannot restore the backup data to the passive node. This is a very important point to keep in mind when you plan the recovery strategy of a geographically dispersed deployment of CCR. If we assume that the active cluster node is located in Miami and the passive cluster node is located in Orlando, how can you provide the backup data created on the storage array in Orlando to the active cluster node in Miami that is using a local storage array in Miami? One solution is to perform a CMS failover from Miami to Orlando before you start the recovery. Another possibility is to make the shadow copy volume hosted on the storage array in Orlando available to the server in Miami. However, it is very likely that the read-and-write latency over the long-distance storage network connection will prevent you from using this approach.

All databases of the storage group must be dismounted before you can start a VSS restore. In a CCR and LCR configuration, only one database exists per storage group, but for other configurations this is a significant disadvantage of the VSS API compared to the streaming backup API. With the streaming API, it is necessary to dismount only the damaged database; the other databases of the storage group can remain online during the restore. End users do not appreciate having their mailbox unavailable because a different database in the same storage group is currently being restored.

You have to suspend continuous replication for the storage group before you start the restore job. This can be done with the *Suspend-StorageGroupCopy* PowerShell cmdlet.

You must delete the database, the checkpoint file, and all log files on the passive cluster node after you restore the database to the active cluster node. The next step is to seed the database from the active cluster node to the passive cluster node. Seeding is done with the PowerShell cmdlet *Update-StorageGroupCopy*.

Next, you have to start the continuous log file replication from the active to the passive cluster node with the *Resume-StorageGroupCopy* command. The last step in the recovery process is to verify the health of the storage group replication with the command, *Get-StorageGroupCopyStatus.*

Data Protection Manager

Microsoft's DPM 2007 is a very interesting product for Exchange administrators. The article, "Better Backups with Data Protection Manager 2007," on Microsoft TechNet, and "Protecting Exchange data with DPM" on the Exchange Team Blog provide a good overview of DPM.

DPM provides a CDP solution for Microsoft file servers and Microsoft applications. The first version, DPM 2006, only supported file server backups. Using an application-aware backup program like NTBackup as a first step was necessary. DPM 2006 could only be used to back up the flat file created by NTBackup.

DPM 2007 adds support for Exchange, SQL, SharePoint, Virtual Server, and its virtual machines. Additionally, it extends the depth of backup support by including advanced system recovery tools and bare-metal recovery.

DPM is not an enterprise backup solution for a heterogeneous operating system environment. You cannot back up UNIX servers or non-Microsoft applications like Oracle with DPM. Symantec NetBackup, IBM Tivoli Storage Manager, EMC NetWorker, or HP OpenView Storage Data Protector is a more suitable product for a multivendor environment. However, an enterprise backup solution usually does not provide the same level of seamless integration that DPM offers for Microsoft applications.

Continuous Data Protection

With traditional backups, an administrator has to manually start a backup job or schedule a backup with a task scheduler. CDP does not require that you define the point in time when a backup will take place. Backups are performed continuously. A CDP solution automatically copies every byte written to a protected data object to a second location. A CDP solution for Exchange captures every byte written to transaction log files or an Exchange database. This is usually implemented with a kernel filter driver that intercepts every write I/O to a specific disk volume.

Some CDP products do not implement the duplication of every write I/O, they only mirror protected data objects based on a fixed schedule, such as every hour. The CDP definition by the Storage Networking Industry Association (SNIA) requires that the solution captures every write I/O.

DPM uses a hybrid approach that combines tracking block-level changes to the volumes hosting application data with application-integrated VSS snapshots. Additional information about CDP is available on Wikipedia (en.wikipedia.org/wiki/Continuous_data_protection).

DPM architecture

Figure 8-37 shows the components of a DPM infrastructure. On the left side of the picture you see the Exchange mailbox servers that are protected by DPM. The DPM server in the middle manages the backup and recovery of protected data sources. Protected data sources can be, for example, files on a file server, an SQL database, or Exchange databases. You can use a single DPM server to protect various types of data.

Figure 8-37   *DPM infrastructure*

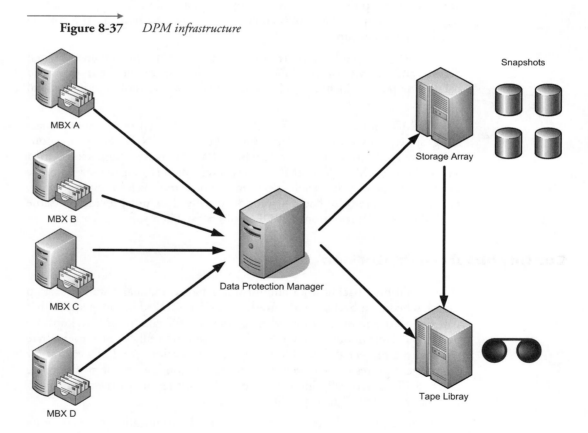

DPM uses disk storage to save a replica of the protected Exchange data. This disk storage can be any local disk from the disk management point of view: DAS, disk volumes hosted in a storage arrays connected via Fibre Channel or iSCSI. It is not possible to use a network share or a USB disk as a data store. The disk volume that you add to a DPM storage pool has to be an unformatted disk. Initially, DPM will not use the full size of the disk. You might be tempted to manually create a partition and file system on the unused disk space, but this is not recommended.

It is possible to migrate the backup data to tape media for long-term storage managed by DPM, but this is optional and not a requirement for DPM deployment. However, it is still a best practice to have a second copy of your backup data at a remote location to be protected for a site-level disaster. Vaulting tape media off-site is a well-established solution for this kind of safeguard.

You can install DPM on Windows Server 2003 SP2 x86 or x64. DPM depends on .NET Framework 2.0, Internet Information Server, Windows PowerShell, Single Instance Storage (SIS), SQL Server 2005, and SQL Reporting Services. DPM 2007 contains the evaluation edition of SQL Server 2005, but it is possible that you use an existing SQL instance on a remote server. Using the evaluation edition is not required, nor is locating the SQL server and DPM server on one machine. SIS is available with Windows Storage Server 2003 R2, or with Windows Deployment Services in Windows Server 2003 SP2.

You have to deploy an agent on each server that you want to protect. This agent consists of a kernel filter driver that intercepts the disk I/O and a service that interacts with the DPM server (Figure 8-38). In DPM 2006, the average performance overhead caused by the filter driver was about 7%.

Figure 8-38
DPM agent components

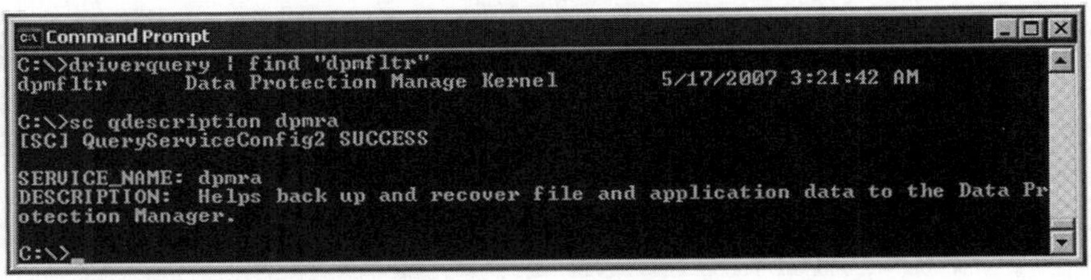

```
Command Prompt                                                          _ □ ✕
C:\>driverquery | find "dpmfltr"
dpmfltr      Data Protection Manage Kernel      5/17/2007 3:21:42 AM

C:\>sc qdescription dpmra
[SC] QueryServiceConfig2 SUCCESS

SERVICE_NAME: dpmra
DESCRIPTION:  Helps back up and recover file and application data to the Data Pr
otection Manager.

C:\>_
```

DPM uses VSS to interact with the Exchange Information Store to ensure consistent data. DPM uses VSS metadata to identify the files that have to be protected—the database file, log files, and the checkpoint file. The kernel filter driver is responsible for creating a map with the changed disk blocks. The driver updates the map whenever a write I/O occurs to these files.

DPM performs a VSS incremental backup to ensure that the current log file is closed and the files stored on disk can be used for recovery. This is a significant advantage compared to a traditional CDP solution because a general CDP solution lacks application consistency. The VSS incremental backups ensure that the backup set is created in an Exchange aware manner.

It is the responsibility of the DPM remote agent service to transfer the modified disk blocks to the DPM server. The DPM server can use these transferred bytes to update its replica of the protected data. The replica is stored in a partition on a local disk of the DPM server.

Figure 8-39 shows that DPM creates two partitions for each protected Exchange storage group. The partitions are located on a disk volume that was assigned to DPM as the storage pool. One partition is used for the replica and contains a full copy of the Exchange storage group. The other partition stores the recovery points created during the VSS incremental backups of the Exchange storage group.

Figure 8-39
DPM storage pool

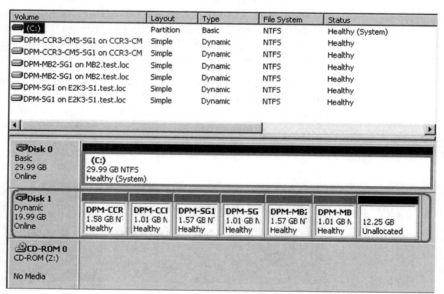

Do *not* manually create a partition on the unallocated space of a disk assigned to DPM. This space is reserved for DPM! You should not change the disk or partition configuration. Do not convert the dynamic disk to a basic disk or modify the mount points of the partitions created by DPM.

These partitions are presented as mount points within the DPM installation directory (Figure 8-40). The *DiffArea* is where DPM stores changed disk blocks. This area is not "human readable," and is used by VSS internally. Beneath the *Replica* directory are mount points to the replicas of the protected data objects, such as the replica of an Exchange storage group. DPM uses the *ShadowCopy* directory to enable a backup of DPM's own database and for the integration of DPM in a third-party backup program.

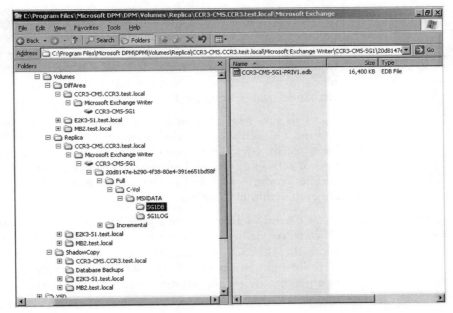

Figure 8-40
Mount points to protected data

In a heterogeneous environment, an administrator of the Exchange team can use DPM to back up Exchange storage groups to disk. In a second step, an administrator of the backup team uses the enterprise backup program to migrate data on the DPM server to a tape library. In a large-scale deployment, different teams being responsible for Exchange and backups to a tape library are common. DPM enables the Exchange team to start backup jobs and restore jobs on their own. The backup team would be responsible for the migration of backup data on the DPM server to tape media. In an environment with only Microsoft operating systems and applications you would directly connect the tape library to DPM, and you do not have to use an additional backup product to stream backup data to tape media.

The initial version of the replica is created when you configure the protection of an Exchange storage group. DPM allows you to create the initial version of the replica by sending all bytes over a TCP/IP network, or copy them to a removable media and import the backup data manually on the DPM server. This is interesting for backups of branch offices when it is impossible to transfer a large amount of data over a WAN link.

In a traditional backup solution, a full backup copies every byte of the source Exchange database to a backup media. DPM allows you to create an express full backup, but the remote agent will only transfer the changed disk blocks since the initial replica creation or the last express full backup from the Exchange server to the DPM server.

A superb feature of DPM is that it can use the Microsoft System VSS provider to create snapshots that are "transportable." In the solutions of their competitors, this is currently only available with a hardware VSS provider, which is much more expensive. The remote agent sends the modified disk blocks to the DPM server and the DPM server builds a full replica of the Exchange databases and log files.

This allows DPM to run the checksum verification on the DPM server and not on the Exchange mailbox server that is accessed by users. This is a huge benefit, especially if you consider that it allows you to utilize the advantage of offloading the backup resource demands from the Exchange server without requiring high-end storage array features. Now you can get this benefit even within DAS or low-end storage arrays.

Currently, all data are sent from the protected Exchange server to the DPM server via the TCP/IP network. DPM allows you to throttle the bandwidth that the agent uses for this data transfer. The usage of the public network for transferring backup data are a big disadvantage of DPM compared to an enterprise backup solution that uses the switched fabric of a SAN to transport backup data.

It is much faster if multiple Exchange servers can directly send their backup data via the SAN to tape devices in a tape library. The network interfaces of the DPM server might be a bottleneck in a large-scale deployment.

Microsoft is collaborating with storage vendors to enhance DPM and add support for transporting backup data via a storage network instead of the public LAN. One possibility is the usage of BCVs. A BCV created on the Exchange server can be mounted on the DPM server or vice versa. This requires that both systems have a storage network connection to the same storage array. The storage array can be accessed using the fibre channel or iSCSI protocol. The BCV can be used for the initial replica creation on the DPM server. Instead of sending all data over the TCP/IP network, DPM is using this custom volume to create the initial replica. You can also take advantage of a BCV for Exchange storage group recovery. Instead of sending the data stored on the DPM replica via the TCP/IP network to the Exchange server, you first create a BCV of the replica. This BCV is afterward mapped to the Exchange server. Mapping a SAN volume can be achieved in a few minutes, independent of the Exchange database size. The data stored on the mapped BCV are used for the storage group recovery. Note that these advanced functions are not seamlessly integrated in DPM, they require additional scripted or manual steps. See the HP whitepaper, "Microsoft Data Protection Manager with HP ProLiant Servers and HP StorageWorks Storage," for additional details on these advanced recovery functions using HP products.

Protection Groups

The Data Protection Manager uses protection groups to logically combine data sources that need to be backed up with an identical configuration. You have to install the DPM agent on the Exchange server before you can add an Exchange storage group to a protection group (Figure 8-41).

Figure 8-41
Protection group members

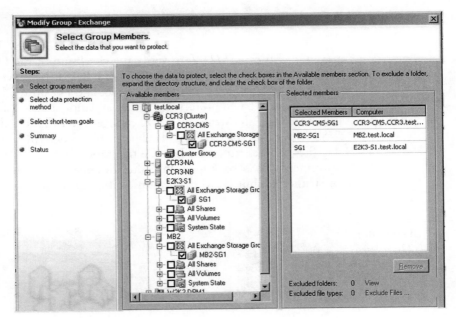

You cannot add a single database or mailbox to a protection group. The protection group granularity for Exchange is the storage group. This is a requirement of VSS; you always have to back up a complete storage group; however, you can restore a single database.

The protection method is defined for every protection group (Figure 8-42). You can configure short-term protection using backup to disk and a long-term protection using tape media. The retention period is set for the backup data of the backup to disk and the backup to tape. You can select between a backup to disk and a backup to tape; using both methods is not required.

Figure 8-42
Data protection method

DPM uses *ESEUTIL* to verify the checksum of the Exchange database and log files of the recovery point (Figure 8-43). As previously mentioned, *ESEUTIL* is executed on the DPM server and not on the Exchange server if you use a disk-based protection. If the validation is successful, DPM informs the Exchange VSS writer on the Exchange server that the data are okay. The VSS writer uses the database checkpoint file to determine which transaction log files can be truncated. Log file truncation is performed after full and/or incremental VSS backups. Only after differential VSS backups no log files are truncated, but DPM does not use differential backups.

Figure 8-43
ESEUTIL integrity check

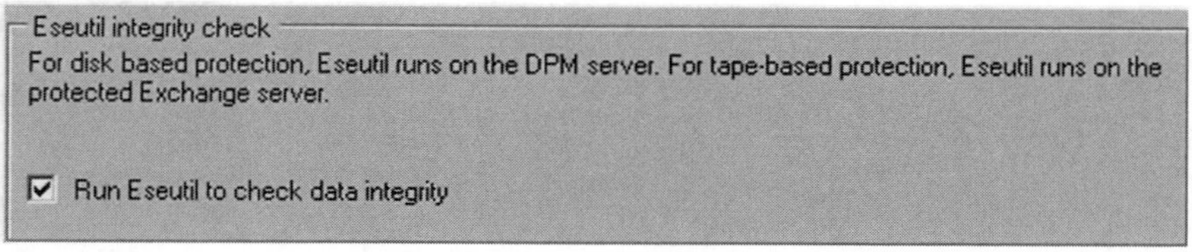

Like most enterprise backup products, DPM recognizes if the Exchange storage group is hosted on a CMS. You have to install the DPM agent on all nodes of the cluster. DPM will afterward show the Exchange storage group beneath the cluster virtual server and not beneath the cluster nodes. This can be seen in Figure 8-41.

DPM automatically connects to the active cluster node in an SCC configuration, and in a CCR configuration provides you with the choice to back up the database on the passive cluster node (Figure 8-44). You do not have to update the backup configuration after a cluster group failover.

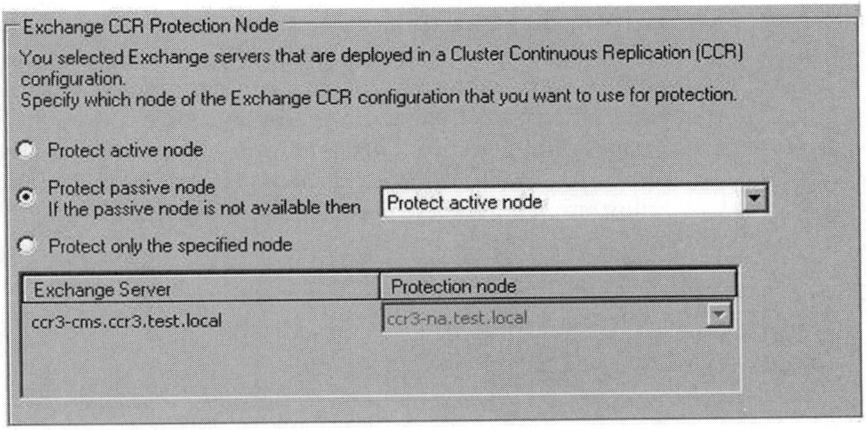

Figure 8-44
CCR protection node

Depending on your recovery objective, you determine how frequently you want to synchronize the changes on the data source to the DPM server. Figure 8-45 illustrates how you can synchronize data between the Exchange server and the DPM server as frequently as every 15 minutes. DPM runs a VSS incremental backup on the Exchange server at the specified synchronization interval and creates a recovery point on the DPM server.

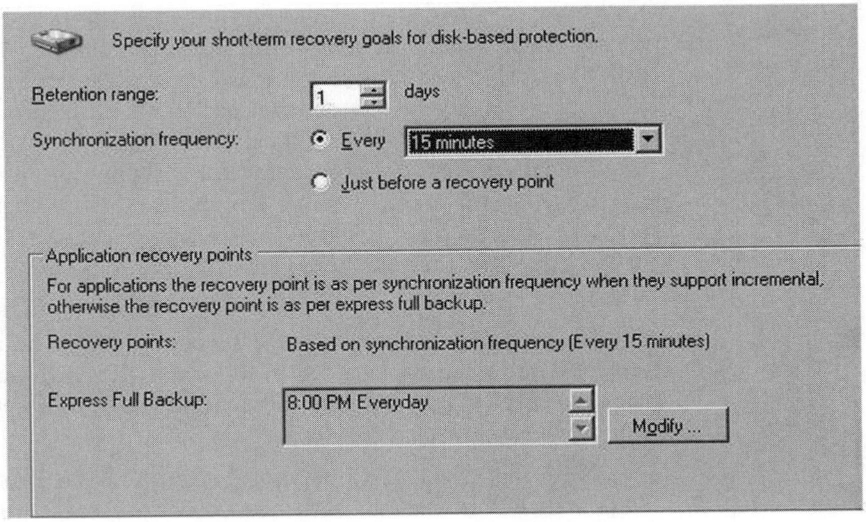

Figure 8-45
Short-term recovery goals

Additionally, you configure the express full backup schedule. An express full backup of an Exchange storage group starts a full VSS backup on the Exchange server and creates a recovery point on the DPM server.

DPM creates a recovery point on the DPM server during the incremental VSS backup and the express full backup. Figure 8-46 shows that DPM only updates the replica of the Exchange storage group during the express full backup. Restoring a replica is faster compared with restoring a replica and all recovery points created by incremental VSS backups since the last express full backup. Therefore, you should regularly run an express full backup. Detailed information about the replica update process and the above illustration is available in the *DPM Planning Guide*.

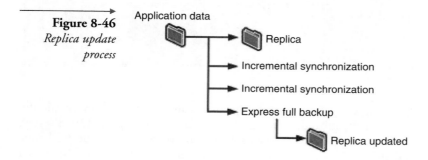

Figure 8-46
Replica update
process

Recovery

DPM has a wizard that guides you through the recovery steps. First, you specify if you want to recover to the point of failure or to a specific point in time. You will try to recover to the latest possible point in time if you recognized that your database was damaged but all your transaction log files were still healthy and available on the Exchange server. In this case, DPM will use the data on its local replica and the existing transaction log files on the Exchanger server for the restore. For this kind of recovery, DPM only supports a restore to the original Exchange Server location. DPM does not copy newly generated transaction log files of the production storage group to an alternative location.

If you perform a restore of a specific recovery point, you are able to restore data to the Recovery Storage Group (RSG), to another database on the same Exchange server or a different server, or to a network share. Figure 8-47 shows this step in the Recovery Wizard.

Note that the DPM does not create the RSG. You have to create the RSG manually before you start the recovery process.

Figure 8-47
Recovery type

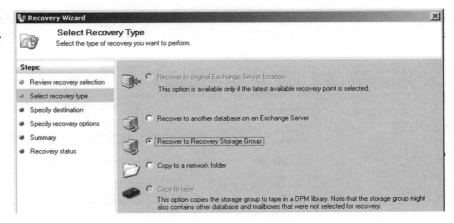

For file server data, the DPM can be configured to allow end-user self-restore. This kind of restore is not available for Exchange. End users cannot use DPM to recover any data that they accidentally deleted and the deleted items retention period has passed. They still need support from an Exchange administrator.

Management

You can choose between a Microsoft Management Console (MMC) snap-in and a PowerShell command line interface (Figure 8-48) to perform DPM management tasks.

Figure 8-48
DPM PowerShell

DPM uses SQL reporting services to create reports about its activities and the status of the protected systems. Figure 8-49 shows the disk utilization report. You should use this report to verify if you sized the DPM storage pool large enough and whether it has sufficient free space. The *DPM Planning Guide* provides formulas to predict the required disk space for the various types of data DPM can back up. The required space depends on the defined retention period of the backup data and the change rate on the Exchange database and log file volume.

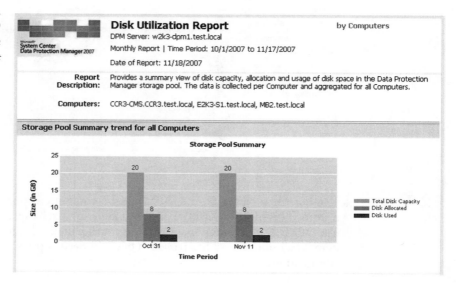

Figure 8-49
Disk utilization report

To assist you in planning the required storage capacity for a DPM deployment, Microsoft has released the Storage Requirements Calculator. This calculator leverages the Exchange Mailbox Storage Requirements Calculator. See the DPM Planning Guide for detailed information about sizing a DPM server.

A good overview of using DPM to back up Exchange is available in the Microsoft whitepaper, "Protecting Exchange Server with System Center Data Protection Manager 2007."

Windows Server Backup in Windows Server 2008

NTBackup is not a component of Windows Server 2008; it has been replaced by Windows Server Backup (WSB). NTBackup used the streaming API to back up Exchange databases. Windows Server 2008 does not include a backup program that supports the streaming API. Microsoft declared the streaming backup API as deprecated with Exchange Server 2007. Additionally, the remote streaming API is by default blocked in Exchange Server 2007 SP1. You have to enable it in the registry if you need it.

```
HKLM\System\CurrentControlSet\Services\MSExchangeIS\
ParametersSystem
```

```
DWORD "Enable Remote Streaming Backup" 0 = disabled
(default); 1 = enabled
```

The streaming API is only supported with Exchange Server 2007 SP1 on Windows Server 2008 if it is used by a third-party backup product with a local agent on the Exchange server. Microsoft does not support using NTBackup on a system running Windows Server 2003 and remote backups of Exchange running on Windows Server 2008. One reason for this is the Secure by Default initiative. Backup data travel unencrypted over the wire if you use the streaming API. Third-party backup applications have to use a local agent installed on the Exchange server to perform a local streaming backup. The third-party backup agent uses its own protocol to send backup data to the backup device. It is the responsibility of the third party backup product to secure the data stream. See the Microsoft TechNet article, "Using Backup to Back Up and Restore Exchange Data," for additional details.

WSB is based on VSS and not on the streaming API. WSB targets customers in the small- and medium-business market segment. WSB is not an enterprise-class backup product.

With WSB, you can back up disk volumes of your Windows Server 2008 system. You can back up complete disk volumes only; it is not possible to specify that you only want to back up a specific file or a specific file system folder. Figure 8-50 shows that you cannot select Exchange-specific components like a storage group or database.

Figure 8-50
Backup items

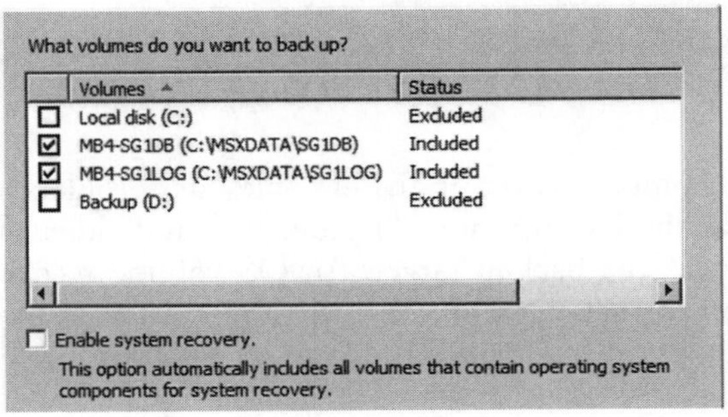

The version of WSB shipped with Windows Server 2008 RTM is not able to perform an Exchange-aware backup. Microsoft would prefer that you buy DPM to back up Exchange data. You can use WSB to protect the OS of the server that runs Exchange, but currently you cannot backup Exchange databases with WSB. Microsoft highlighted this issue related to backing up Exchange Server running on Windows Server 2008 in the Exchange Team blog article, "Exchange Server and Windows Server 2008, Part II." The following paragraphs provide an overview of WSB.

WSB can create full and incremental backup. Differential backups are not possible with WSB. WSB creates VHD files as backup sets-the same file type that is used by the Windows Virtual Server. You can use hard disks or a DVD as backup media. The hard disk must be formatted as the basic disk. Dynamic disks are not supported by WSB. If you want to back up to an USB disk, the disk must be recognized by the operating system as a nonremovable disk. USB flash storage is not supported.

A scheduled backup cannot use a DVD as the backup target; only hard disks are supported for scheduled backups. Backups to DVD media are mainly aimed at creating backup sets for server disaster recovery. WSB does not support backing up and restoring from tape devices. You have to use a third-party backup product if you want to use tape devices with Windows Server 2008.

WSB is capable of interacting with the VSS writer of an application that stores its data on the disk volume. Figure 8-51 shows that you have to specify that you want to perform a VSS full backup to include log file truncation. This is likely the way that future versions of WSB are going to interact with the Exchange VSS writer.

Figure 8-51
VSS backup type

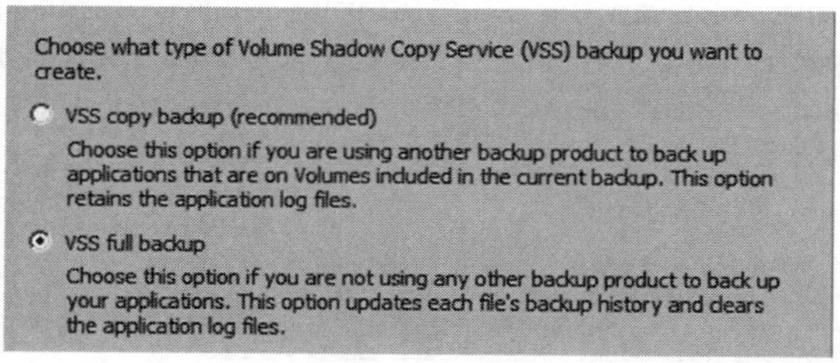

Choose what type of Volume Shadow Copy Service (VSS) backup you want to create.

○ VSS copy backup (recommended)
  Choose this option if you are using another backup product to back up applications that are on Volumes included in the current backup. This option retains the application log files.

● VSS full backup
  Choose this option if you are not using any other backup product to back up your applications. This option updates each file's backup history and clears the application log files.

You cannot recover individual files and folders directly if you use a DVD as the backup target. Recovery of individual files is possible only with disks as the backup target. An OS volume recovery will only restore disk volumes that contain OS files. You start this recovery process from the Windows Server 2008 setup disk by selecting "Repair your computer" instead of performing a system installation.

Integration of Exchange Backups into Heterogeneous Enterprise Backup Solutions

In a large enterprise, the Exchange team is likely using the backup services provided by the backup team. The backup team is responsible for managing a large enterprise tape library and to provide support for heterogeneous operating systems and applications. Backup and recovery are often a complicated task in such an environment.

Backup products often do not have a granular administration model, and you cannot assign permission only to create and run jobs for Exchange servers to a user. If a user has the permission to create new backup jobs or to run existing jobs, it is often impossible to restrict the user's permission to jobs related to Exchange and prevent him from accidentally restoring to an Oracle database.

The Exchange team in such an environment is often using NTBackup to perform a disk-to-disk backup, and afterward the backup team is using the enterprise backup product to back up the flat file created by NTBackup. This allows the Exchange team to run backups and restores independently from the backup team. If the Exchange team has to fulfill a short RTO, this can be a good solution to remove the time necessary to collaborate with the backup team to inform them that they have to start an urgent recovery job.

This two-step backup process was easy to achieve with Windows Server 2003 and NTBackup. Microsoft removed NTBackup with Windows Server 2008, and the future will tell how easily such a procedure can be implemented in Windows Server 2008. If you switch from NTBackup to DPM, you need an enterprise backup product that can integrate with DPM. DPM can either export its backup data to a file system directory using a custom script, or the enterprise backup product must support the DPM VSS writer that enables you to back up the data stored in DPM.

The easiest solution is to use a backup product that seamlessly integrates with Exchange and provides a comprehensive administrative model. But the reality often looks different.

9

Recovery

In this chapter we describe how you can utilize your backup data for recovery purposes. Exchange Server 2007's Continuous Replication provides you the possibility of creating a second copy of your Exchange databases. This replica is your first line of defense. However, don't assume that activating the passive database created by Exchange Server 2007 Continuous Replication is always successful. Sometimes a failover to the passive node of your Cluster Continuous Replication (CCR) deployment does not solve the problem.

You must be prepared for a traditional restore of your last backup set! Additionally, it is good to know the advanced recovery procedures like database portability or how to recover a failed Exchange server.

Basic Recovery Rules

We recommend analyzing previous downtimes of your current Exchange infrastructure to understand potential failures and the weak points in your current environment. This is a prerequisite for designing your new infrastructure and defining the recovery strategy of your new solution.

You should document the configuration of your environment and create a change log to be able to verify why certain settings have been modified. An up-to-date documentation of the setup is very critical for recovery. It is not possible to back up everything and re-create everything by restoring all backup sets. For example, you might not have the same server hardware to recover an Exchange server. In this case, it is nearly impossible to successfully perform a system state restore of the Windows operating system. Documentation of the configuration is also required for other components like the backup library or the setup of the storage network switches.

Frequent verification of your recovery procedure to identify whether a configuration change affected your ability to recover your systems and data is critical. Do not spend thousands of dollars for a leading-edge geographically dispersed Exchange cluster deployment including data replication, but forget to document the necessary steps to perform a site failover in case a data center outage occurs. Finally, do not forget the infrastructure services that Exchange is relaying on. Verifying the failover of your Exchange mailbox cluster by unplugging the power cord from the active cluster node is not sufficient. You have to unplug the power cord of your Active Directory (AD) servers, Hub Transport (HT) server, Client Access Servers (CAS), storage array, network switches, and so on.

Running recovery fire drills is difficult in a production environment. Therefore, you should have a test environment that you also use for validation of service packs before you install them on your live systems.

Disaster Recovery Tools

With Exchange Server 2003, the Exchange Troubleshooting Assistant (ExTRA) bundles the former standalone tools: Exchange Server Mail Flow Analyzer (ExMFA), Exchange Server Performance Troubleshooting Analyzer (ExPTA), and the Exchange Server Disaster Recovery Analyzer (ExDRA). These tools are derived from the ExBPA architecture.

With Exchange Server 2007, these tools are available in the Exchange Management Console (EMC) toolbox. You can start the following two disaster recover tools from the EMC:

- Database Recovery Manager
- Database Troubleshooter

Use the Database Troubleshooter to verify why a database cannot be mounted by the Information Store. The tool reads the database-related entries in the event log, and based on the events, provides you with resources and possible solutions such as tasks within the Database Recovery Manager or links to Microsoft Knowledge Base Articles related to the problem.

Using the Database Recovery Manager you can:

- Analyze log drive space
- Repair a database
- Show database-related event logs
- Verify database and transaction log files
- Create and manage a Recovery Storage Group (RSG)

Brick Level Restore

Single item or single mailbox recovery is a requirement that customers often list in a Request For Proposal (RFP). They want an easy solution to recover items that end users cannot recover using the Recover Deleted Items tool in Outlook. There are many reasons why an item cannot be recovered using this method. For example, the retention period has passed, or the user has performed a "hard delete." See Microsoft Knowledge Base Article 178630 for additional details about hard deletes.

Microsoft's solution for this issue with Exchange Server 2003 is to restore a backup to the RSG and use ExMerge or the Recover Mailbox Data wizard introduced with Exchange Server 2003 SP1 to recover the data. With Exchange Server 2007, the management of the RSG is removed from the EMC and administrators have to use the ExTRA or the Exchange Management Shell (EMS). Additionally, Microsoft removed support for ExMerge in Exchange Server 2007.

Administrators who do not frequently use the RSG often have problems managing the RSG. Third-party tools are available to ease the recovery of single items.

Some backup vendors have integrated a single mailbox backup function in their product. During a single mailbox backup, each mailbox is accessed individually using the Messaging Application Programming Interface (MAPI). A single mailbox backup does not use the streaming backup API or the Volume Shadow Copy Services (VSS) API.

This single mailbox backup requires a user account that has permission to access all mailboxes and read all mailbox contents. This is a contradiction to the enhanced security configuration that is now the default configuration of Exchange Server. A configuration that provides the possibility that one user account can be used to read all mails, including the mails of the board members, is usually not acceptable.

Another disadvantage is that the individual backup of each mailbox does not preserve single-instance storage. A MAPI-based backup creates a much larger backup data set. Single mailbox backups take much longer compared to a conventional backup using the official backup API.

Additionally, a single mailbox backup does not purge the transaction log files. Therefore, you still have to run a conventional backup to purge log files with a supported method. If you do not purge log files regularly, the volume hosting the transaction log files would be filled up and the corresponding databases of the storage group would be automatically dismounted. Using a single mailbox backup is therefore incompatible with the always shrinking backup window in today's business environments.

You can find additional information about MAPI-based backups on www.petri.co.il. This website contains very good documentation about brick-level backups using *EXMERGE* and configuring the necessary access permission for MAPI-based backups.

Some vendors provide products that do not require a MAPI-based backup to be able to restore individual items. These products are able to take advantage of a regular backup set. This is a great advantage because this removes the need for running two backups—the single mailbox backup and the regular backup. For example, Symantec Backup Exec includes the so-called Granular Recovery Technology (GRT) that allows you to restore individual items from a regular backup set (Figure 9-1).

Figure 9-1
Single item recovery with Symantec Backup Exec GRT

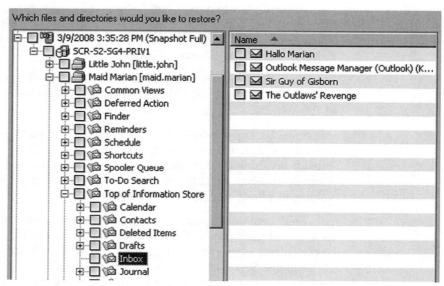

NetApp has a solution for single mailbox recovery that is integrated with their storage array—SnapManager for Microsoft Exchange, which is based on Knoll Ontrack PowerControls. Quest's Recovery Manager for Exchange is another product that enables single item recovery without the need for a MAPI-based backup.

A big advantage of these tools is their nice GUIs that simplify the single item restore process for operational staff who rarely have to do this. Additionally, these tools are capable of working with a public folder database. The RSG cannot be used with public folder databases. Another benefit of these tools is that they have advanced search capabilities, including searching in attachments. This can be very helpful if you are forced to provide electronic evidence because of email compliance laws.

From a storage perspective, it is important to remember that you have to reserve enough disk space to be able to use these products. You either have to restore a previous backup from tape to an alternative location (file system directory), or provide access to an offline database file. Some vendors even provide the possibility of using a VSS-created backup as the source for single item recovery. The database on the shadow copy volume will be in a dirty shutdown state and the recovery tool is using the transaction log files on the corresponding shadow copy volume to bring the database to a clean state.

Recovery Storage Group

In this section, we describe the Exchange Server 2007 RSG in detail, and highlight differences compared to the RSG in Exchange Server 2003.

The Past—RSG in Exchange Server 2003

In Exchange Server 2000, if users accidentally deleted an email that they could not recover from the deleted items folder in Outlook, or using the Recover Deleted Items wizard, setting up a dedicated recovery server in a separate AD forest was necessary. You then had to restore your last backup to this recovery server and use *EXMERGE* to extract the required data from the database.

Introducing the RSG in Exchange Server 2003 made it possible to mount a second copy of the database to the same server, or another server in the same Exchange Server 2003 Administrative Group. This eliminated the requirement of setting up a separate AD forest and an additional Exchange Server within this forest for recovery purposes.

You can extract data from the database in the RSG and make it available to users while the original database is online and accessible by users. Exchange Server 2003 SP1 introduced the Recover Mailbox Data wizard within the Exchange System Manager, allowing you to merge the contents of a mailbox in the RSG with a mailbox in the production database. Another option is to create a new folder in the user's inbox with the name *Recovered Data <date and time>* and copy the entire mailbox contents from the database in the RSG to the mailbox in the production database.

See the Microsoft Knowledge Base Article 824126 for additional information about using the RSG in Exchange Server 2003.

Visible Changes in Exchange Server 2007

With Exchange Server 2007, an RSG cannot be directly created in the EMC and an existing RSG is not visible within the EMC. You have to create and manage the RSG using the EMS, or if you prefer a GUI, with the ExTRA. The Database Recovery Management of ExTRA is started from the Toolbox pane of the EMC. This tool is especially useful for administrators who rarely use the RSG.

Exchange Server 2007 introduced Local Continuous Replication (LCR) and CCR. You do not need to use different commands to create and manage an RSG on a mailbox server using these technologies. The command for managing an RSG is identical on single servers and clustered mailbox servers.

Differences Between the RSG and a Normal Storage Group

The RSG is only used for recovery purposes; therefore, Microsoft imposed the following restrictions on the RSG:

- You only can create one RSG on an Exchange server, and you can only mount databases of a single SG at the same time to the RSG.

- As seen in Figure 9-2, there is no end-user access to the RSG and the databases/mailboxes mounted in the RSG. Only administrators can access the RSG using specific PowerShell cmdlets and recovery tools. All access protocols except MAPI are disabled for the RSG. Although MAPI is enabled, an administrator cannot use Outlook to connect to a mailbox in the RSG.

Figure 9-2
Storage group and
RSG access

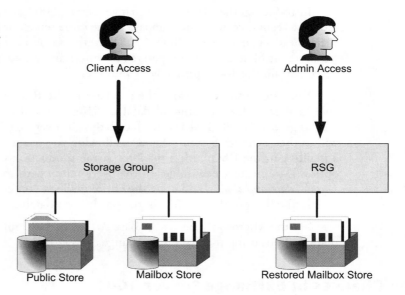

- You cannot use the RSG to recover public folder data, because you cannot mount a public folder store in the RSG. As public folders have been depreciated in Exchange Server 2007, you should not expect enhancements related to public folder recovery to be made available from Microsoft. Therefore, you still need a separate AD forest and Exchange organization to recover items from a public folder.

Permissions

To create an RSG, you need Exchange server administrator permission and you have to be a member of the local administrators group on the Exchange server. You need at least the Exchange recipient administrators permission on the Exchange server where the target mailbox is located and where you want to export data.

Creating an RSG

While sizing the storage array, consider the disk space requirements of the RSG. You need enough free space to restore the database and log files. Additionally, the storage performance needs enough headroom to be able to perform the restore to the RSG during business hours without affecting the experience of users online on the Exchange server. Storage capacity and performance requirements for the RSG are often neglected.

The same cmdlets are used to manage an RSG and a normal storage group. The only difference is that you must set RSG-specific parameters, such as *-Recovery* when you create the RSG, and *-MailboxDatabaseToRecover* to link a production database to a new database in the RSG. The example in Figure 9-3 first shows the existing storage groups and databases on the server CCR1-CMS; an RSG called CCR1-CMS-RSG and a new database in the RSG are then created. The database in the RSG is mapped to the production database CCR1-CMS-SG1-PRIV1. The column *Recovery* indicates whether a storage group or database is used for recovery or production purposes. If you create a new database in the RSG, the AllowFileRestore flag is automatically set to true.

In a following step of the recovery procedure, you use the *Restore-Mailbox* cmdlet to copy or merge data from the database in the RSG to the production database. The database in the RSG is referred to as the *source database* and the production database is called the *target database*. The source and target database for the *Restore-Mailbox* cmdlet have to be from a server running Exchange Server 2007. With Exchange Server 2007 you cannot mount a database from a previous Exchange version to the RSG. In Exchange Server 2003, you can mount the database of a server from the same Exchange organization and within the same administrative group to the RSG. The source and target databases have to be hosted on servers that are members of the same administrative group. Exchange Server 2007 does not use administrative groups as a logical management unit, and in an environment with servers running Exchange Server 2003 and Exchanger Server 2007, all servers running Exchange Server 2007 are shown as members of a single administrative group in the Exchange System Manager.

Figure 9-3
Create RSG

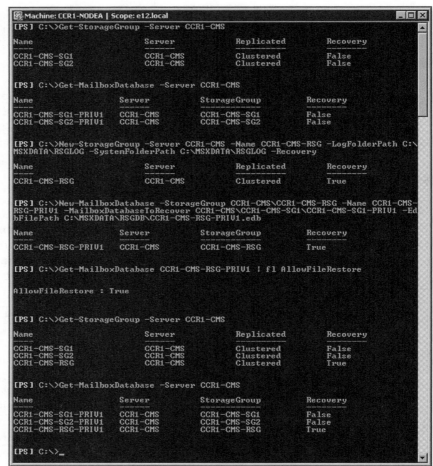

When you add a new database to the RSG on a clustered mailbox server (CMS), this automatically creates the related cluster resource (Figure 9-4). In CCR configuration, the RSG is not replicated from the active cluster node to the passive node (Figure 9-5).

Figure 9-4
RSG on a CMS

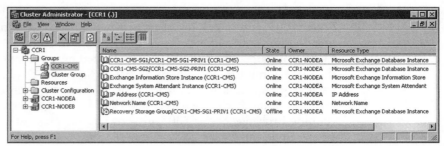

Figure 9-5
Storage group copy
status

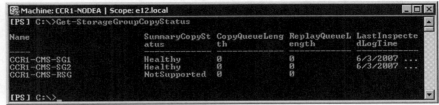

Backup and restore

When an RSG exists on a server, you can continue to back up your production database as before, and NTBackup shows the RSG as an additional storage group that you can back up. The restore behavior is changed from a standard restore if a server has an RSG. If an RSG exists and the database that you want to restore is not in the RSG, the restore job fails. If the database you want to restore exists in the RSG, the restore goes automatically to the database in the RSG and not to the production database. There is no option to explicitly select the database in the RSG as a restore target. This behavior is shown in Figures 9-6, 9-7, and 9-8.

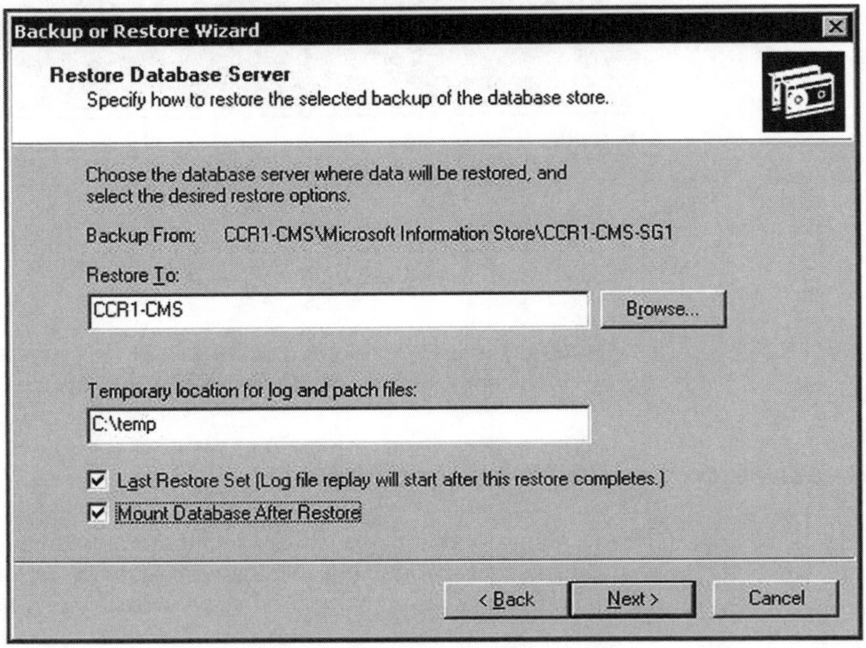

Figure 9-6
NTBackup

Backup or Restore Wizard

Restore Database Server
Specify how to restore the selected backup of the database store.

Choose the database server where data will be restored, and select the desired restore options.

Backup From: CCR1-CMS\Microsoft Information Store\CCR1-CMS-SG1

Restore To:

CCR1-CMS   Browse...

Temporary location for log and patch files:

C:\temp

☑ Last Restore Set (Log file replay will start after this restore completes.)
☑ Mount Database After Restore

< Back   Next >   Cancel

Figure 9-7
Automatic database location change

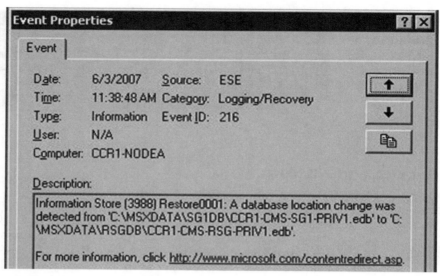

You can override this behavior and continue to restore to the original database location with the following registry key:

```
HKLM\System\CurrentControlSet\Services\MSExchangeIS\
ParametersSystem DWORD Recovery SG Override = 1
```

Restore to an alternate location

If you want to create the RSG on another server and not on the one that hosts your production database, you have to obey the following rules. The storage group names and the database names have to be identical.

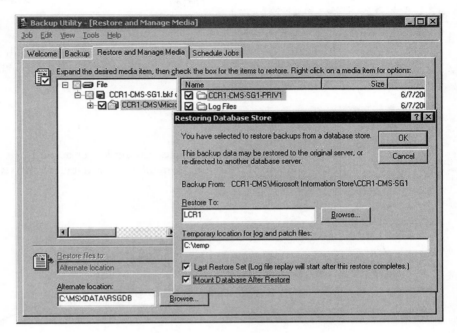

Figure 9-9
*Restore to an alter-
nate location*

The database filename does not matter. For example, assume that you want to recover a mailbox in the database *CCR1-CMS-SG1-PRIV1*, which is a database in the storage group *CCR1-CMS-SG1* on the server *CCR1-CMS*. You want to use the server LCR1 for the recovery. In this case, the name of the storage group on LCR1 has to be *CCR1-CMS-SG1* and the name of the database *CCR1-CMS-SG1-PRIV1*. In NTBackup, you have to specify that you want to restore to an alternate location as depicted in Figure 9-9.

Log File Replay

Let's assume that your last backup job finished this morning at 4:00 AM and your production database fails at 11:00 AM. If you restore only the last backup to the RSG, you would lose the changes made between 4:00 and 11:00. You can copy the log files from the production storage group to the log file folder of the RSG and replay them in addition to the log files from your last backup. Details about this advanced recovery procedure are available in the section, "Transaction Log File Replay: Soft Recovery and Hard Recovery in Exchange Server 2003," of the RSG whitepaper for Exchange Server 2003.

Volume Shadow Copy Support

In Exchange Server 2003, it was not possible by default to restore a VSS backup directly to the RSG. With Exchange Server 2007, this is now supported.

Linkage

Figure 9-10 shows the linkages among a user account, its production mailbox, and the corresponding mailbox in a database that is mounted in the RSG.

Figure 9-10
Linkage

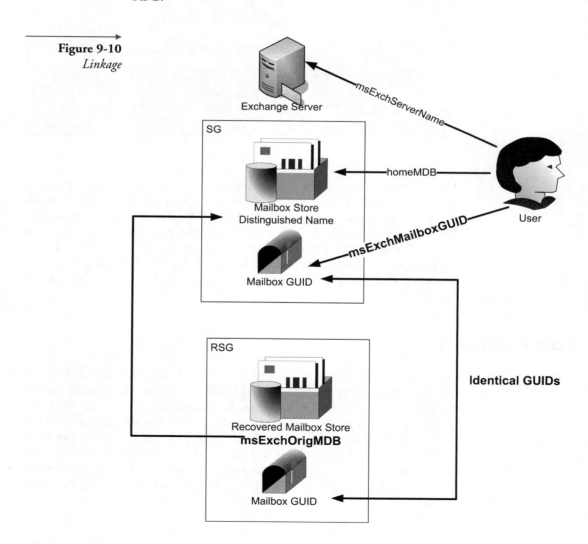

Data recovery

You can use the *Restore-Mailbox* cmdlet to merge the contents of a mailbox in the RSG with the current contents of the corresponding mailbox in a production database (Figure 9-11). The previous section (Figure 9-10) depicts how Exchange determines which mailbox in the production database links to the mailbox in the RSG. You have to be aware that rules and search folders are ignored if you merge data from the RSG to the production mailbox. Access control lists defined on folders are not merged or copied back from the mailbox in the RSG to the target mailbox. If you want to recover this metadata, it is necessary to perform a "database swap" as is often done with the dial tone recovery strategy.

Figure 9-11
Merge

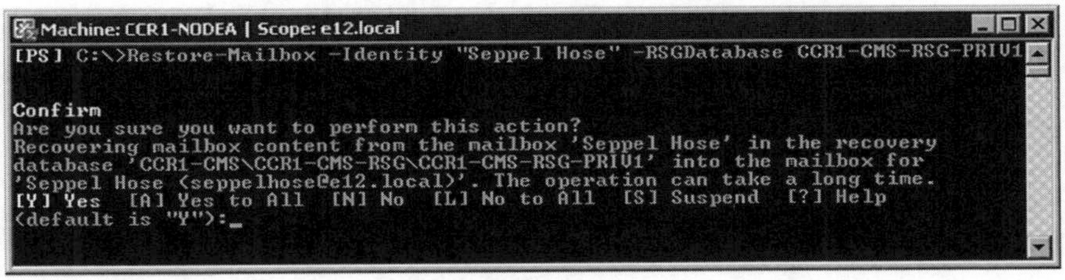

In Exchange Server 2003, you could only copy the contents of the mailbox in the RSG to a subfolder in the same mailbox in the production database. In Exchange Server 2007, you can copy the contents of a mailbox A in the RSG to a subfolder in mailbox B in a production database. It is also possible to specify a start and an end date, filter the messages copied using keywords, or use a wildcard to limit the attachment files that are copied. Figure 9-12 shows a copy example with a filter using a time range.

Figure 9-12
Copy

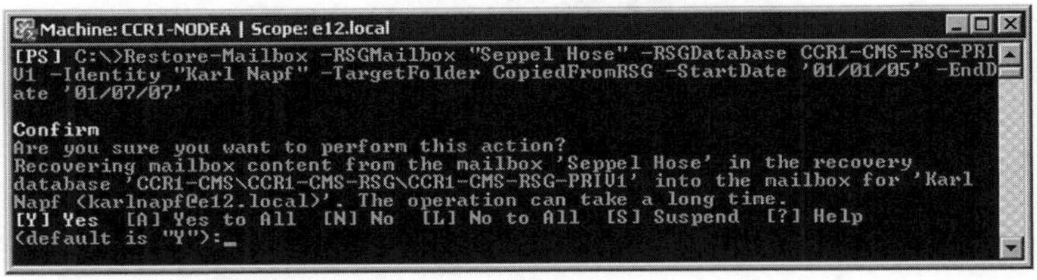

In Exchange Server 2007, the subfolder name where the contents are copied is expanded to contain the name of the source mailbox *Recovered Data—<source mailbox>-<date and time>* (Figure 9-13). If you copy mails from the source mailbox to the target mailbox, data will always be copied to a new subfolder in the inbox of the target mailbox. If you merge the source and target mailbox, no subfolder is created in the target mailbox.

Figure 9-13
Recovered data in
Outlook

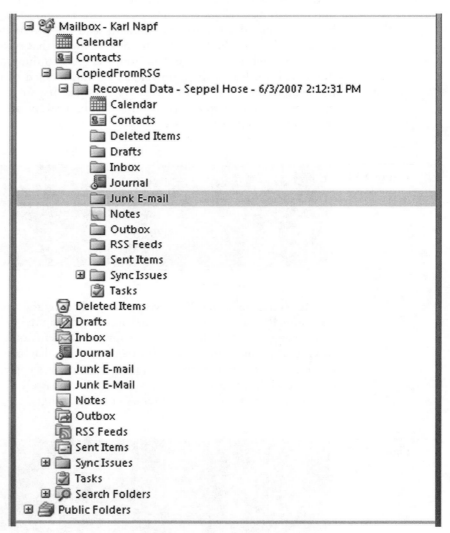

You cannot use the RSG to migrate mailboxes from an Exchange organization in AD forest A to another Exchange organization in AD forest B. The *Restore-Mailbox* cmdlet requires that the source and target mailbox belong to the same Exchange organization. You have to use the *Move-Mailbox* cmdlet for a mailbox migration.

In Exchange Server 2007 SP1 the *Export-Mailbox* command was enhanced. Now it allows you to export data to a PST file. But be aware that you cannot do this for a mailbox that is hosted in the RSG. If you use this command to export only emails containing certain keywords, the command will first export *all* emails to the target mailbox, and afterward it deletes the emails in the target mailbox that do not match the search criteria. You have to consider this when you estimate the required storage space for the target mailbox and required time to finish this task. Using *Export-Mailbox* to export an item from a Mailbox A on Server A to a Mailbox B on Server B is comparable to *Move-Mailbox* of the complete mailbox, not only the single item. This is especially troublesome if you have to do this for thousands of mailboxes.

Cleanup

You should delete the database in the RSG after you have completed the data recovery. This prevents you from troubleshooting strange restore behaviors, such as when you try to restore a backup to the production location while this database is currently mapped to a database in the RSG. Figure 9-14 shows the necessary commands.

Figure 9-14
Cleanup

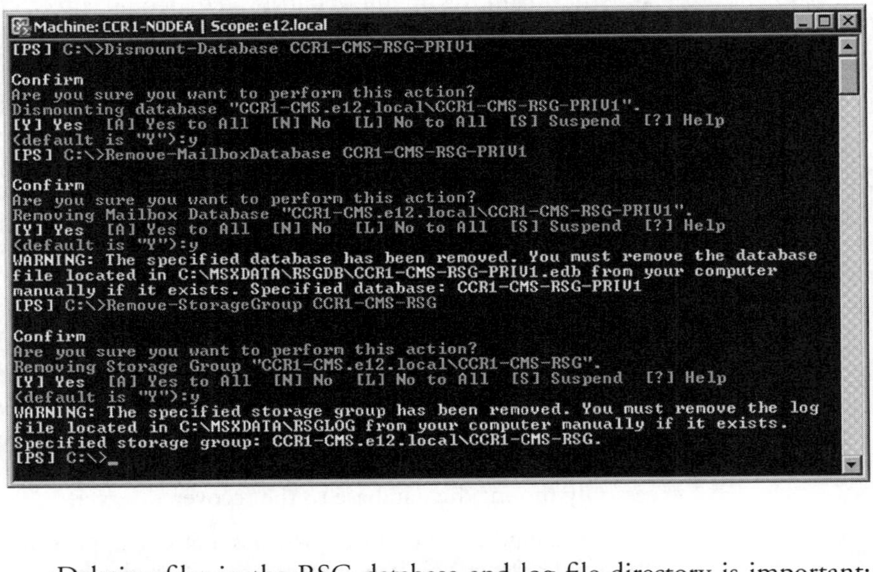

```
Machine: CCR1-NODEA | Scope: e12.local
[PS] C:\>Dismount-Database CCR1-CMS-RSG-PRIV1

Confirm
Are you sure you want to perform this action?
Dismounting database "CCR1-CMS.e12.local\CCR1-CMS-RSG-PRIV1".
[Y] Yes  [A] Yes to All  [N] No  [L] No to All  [S] Suspend  [?] Help
(default is "Y"):y
[PS] C:\>Remove-MailboxDatabase CCR1-CMS-RSG-PRIV1

Confirm
Are you sure you want to perform this action?
Removing Mailbox Database "CCR1-CMS.e12.local\CCR1-CMS-RSG-PRIV1".
[Y] Yes  [A] Yes to All  [N] No  [L] No to All  [S] Suspend  [?] Help
(default is "Y"):y
WARNING: The specified database has been removed. You must remove the database
file located in C:\MSXDATA\RSGDB\CCR1-CMS-RSG-PRIV1.edb from your computer
manually if it exists. Specified database: CCR1-CMS-RSG-PRIV1
[PS] C:\>Remove-StorageGroup CCR1-CMS-RSG

Confirm
Are you sure you want to perform this action?
Removing Storage Group "CCR1-CMS.e12.local\CCR1-CMS-RSG".
[Y] Yes  [A] Yes to All  [N] No  [L] No to All  [S] Suspend  [?] Help
(default is "Y"):y
WARNING: The specified storage group has been removed. You must remove the log
file located in C:\MSXDATA\RSGLOG from your computer manually if it exists.
Specified storage group: CCR1-CMS.e12.local\CCR1-CMS-RSG.
[PS] C:\>_
```

Deleting files in the RSG database and log file directory is important; otherwise, a subsequent creation of a new RSG using the same directory fails. The PowerShell cmdlets do not delete the files; you have to do this manually.

Database Portability

This section explains database portability in Exchange Server 2007. Customers have been waiting for this feature since Exchange Server 4.0—over 10 years! The feature was first introduced with the Release to Manufacture (RTM) version of Exchange Server 2007.

Introduction to Database Portability

In Exchange Server 2003 databases are not really transportable. Information about the Exchange organization and the administrative group is written to the database when it is created. You could move the database to another storage group or to another server in the same administrative group. This requires that the target server runs an Exchange version that is compatible with the source server. The target server has to be the same or a newer version. If the version is newer, Exchange automatically tries to update the database. If the target version is older, portability will likely fail because the target server might not understand the new database structure. For example, Exchange Server 2003 SP1 databases are not backward-compatible because of the error correction code checksum introduced with SP1.

However, the database move breaks the link between the user accounts and the mailboxes in the database. This could affect emails in transition. Fixing the link between the user accounts and the database was a hassle. It was a complex and error-prone manual task. Moving databases was therefore rarely done in previous Exchange versions. The necessary process is described on Microsoft TechNet in the section "Advanced Recovery Strategies" and in Microsoft Knowledge Base Article 555603. Manipulating raw AD attributes is supported by Microsoft according to the above Microsoft TechNet article, but it is not a recommended recovery strategy with Exchange Server 2003.

This issue does not exist if you mount the database to an RSG on a server in the same administrative group.

Another possibility was to restore the mailbox database at the end of a disaster recovery procedure by using the *SETUP /DISASTERRECOVERY* switch. You could either restore a database backup or reuse the old database file (if the database was not affected by the disaster). With this recovery procedure, the name of the Exchange server remains the same and you can successfully mount the database to the recovered server.

Exchange Server 2007 provides better support for mailbox database portability. Now you can mount a mailbox database to another Exchange mailbox server with a different computer name in the same Exchange organization. The portability feature is no longer limited to usage in the RSG. You can mount the database to a production storage group of another Exchange server. You even can use database portability to migrate from Exchange Server 2007 on Windows Server 2003 to Exchange Server 2007 SP1 on Windows Server 2008. Colleagues in the HP Customer Focused Testing team conducted the following study. They had an Exchange Server running on Windows Server 2003 that stored its databases on a Fibre Channel attached disk array. They remapped the disk volumes to an Exchange Server running on Windows Server 2008 and afterward used database portability to re-home the mailboxes. This was much faster compared to a traditional *Move-Mailbox* migration.

A remaining limitation is that the database can only be mounted on Exchange Server 2007 mailbox servers in the same Exchange organization. Therefore, you cannot use database portability for interorganization Exchange migrations.

Exchange Server 2007 does not use the administrative group concept that was used by Exchange Server 2000 and Exchange Server 2003. From the point of view of these legacy Exchange versions, all Exchange Server 2007 systems reside in their own administrative group. You can use database portability between all the Exchange Server 2007 systems in an Exchange organization that still has Exchange Server 2000 or Exchange Server 2003 systems.

This new flexibility enables you to use database portability for additional recovery strategies that are not limited to the RSG or re-setup of an Exchange server. The first possibility is to mount the Exchange servers' mailbox databases in data center A to the Exchange servers in data center B. This is a reasonable disaster recovery strategy if an outage of data center A occurs, especially if you have a storage-based data replication solution in place.

The second possibility is to combine database portability with the dial tone recovery strategy. In Exchange Server 2003, you had to create the dial tone database on an Exchange server with the same computer name. Exchange Server 2007 supports the creation of the dial tone database on another server. You can create empty databases on Exchange servers in Site B and utilize the database files (or previous backups of the databases) from Exchange servers in Site A for the recovery. This recovery strategy is called *dial tone portability* in Exchange Server 2007.

If you relocate the mailbox database to another server, you must update the Exchange-related attributes in the AD of users with mailboxes hosted in this database. This can be done with the PowerShell cmdlet *Move-Mailbox* and the parameter *-ConfigurationOnly:$true*. With Exchange Server 2007, manually manipulating the raw AD attributes is not necessary; the PowerShell cmdlet does this for you.

Public folder databases are not portable. You have to use public folder replication if you want to relocate public folder data to another Exchange server.

Considering the necessary storage capacity and performance for the transported database on the recovery server during the planning phase of your Exchange infrastructure is important. If you do not reassign the disk volumes of Exchange server A to server B, you need additional disks! The possibility of remapping disk volumes is an advantage of a storage network compared to an infrastructure using direct-attached disks. See the user guide for your storage array for the discrete steps to remap disk volumes.

Don't make the mistake of basing your recovery strategy on database portability or the RSG and forget to purchase the required disk spindles to host the data. If you need fast recovery, you should have recovery servers/ standby servers already up and running as Exchange mailbox servers with spare capacity.

The remainder provides a detailed description of the steps you have to perform for database portability.

Database Portability Using an Offline Database

The database should be in a clean shutdown state before you transport it to a new Exchange server; otherwise, you need the corresponding transaction log files at the new Exchange server, and to run a soft recovery on this server. In a disaster recovery scenario, it is likely that you will have to run a soft recovery on the new server because you lost the source Exchange server.

The easiest method for achieving a clean shutdown state is to dismount the databases. In a disaster recovery scenario, it is likely that the Exchange services are no longer running and you have to use what you already have or what remained from the server. Do you have a current backup of the Exchange databases, or did you configure a storage-based replication of the disk volumes hosting your Exchange databases and log files to a remote site?

Figure 9-15 shows how you can verify the state of the database by dumping the database header using *ESEUTIL /MH*. The state is "clean shutdown" or "dirty shutdown."

If the database is in a dirty shutdown state (Figure 9-16), you have to run a soft recovery using the command *ESEUTIL /R*. A detailed description of this command is available on Microsoft TechNet. *ESEUTIL* can determine the location of the corresponding database file from the information available in the log file (Figure 9-17).

By default, *ESEUTIL* will look for log files and the checkpoint file in the local directory. You can specify the directory with the log file, the directory with the checkpoint file, and the database file as an option to *ESEUTIL*.

Figure 9-15
Database state

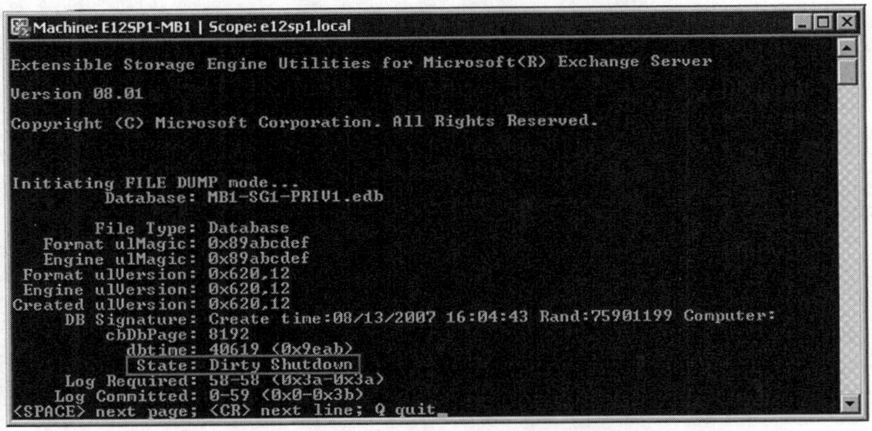

Figure 9-16
Dirty shutdown

In Figure 9-18, the database file is located in the local directory, but the log files and the checkpoint files are in a different directory.

If you don't want to add the database to an existing storage group, you have to create a new storage group on the target Exchange server. Mounting the database using a different database directory name and file name is possible. The directory name is the logical name of the database that you see in the EMC. The database file name is the name of the physical file in the file system, such as *C:\MSXDATA\SG3DB\MB2-SG3-PRIV1.edb*. Figure 9-19 demonstrates the steps to create the storage group and database on the target server.

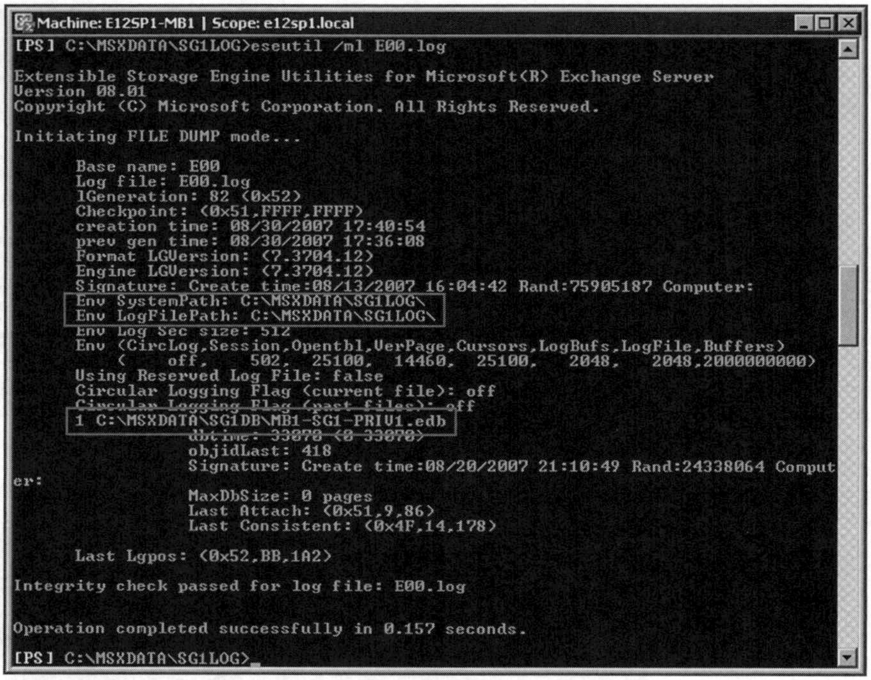

Figure 9-17
Log file dump

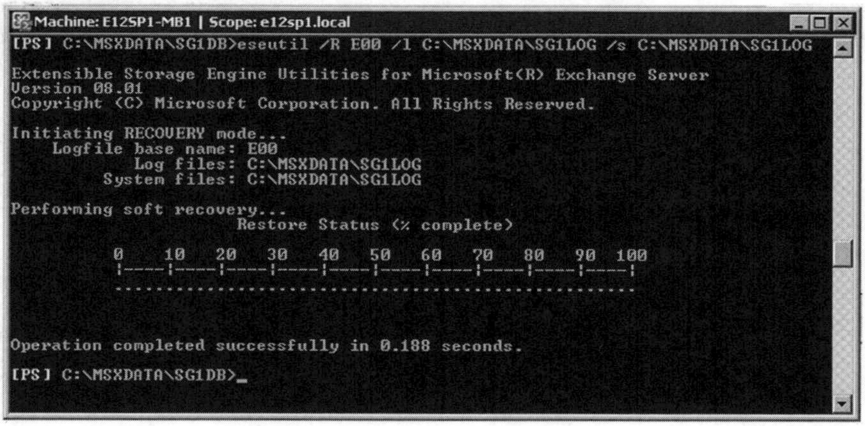

Figure 9-18
Soft recovery

You can use *ESEUTIL /Y* to copy the large database file from the source Exchange server to the target server. The next step is to mount the database (Figure 9-20).

Now is a good time to run a backup of your new configuration. You should back up the Exchange storage group and the system state of the Exchange server.

Figure 9-19
Storage group and database creation

Figure 9-20
Database copy and mount

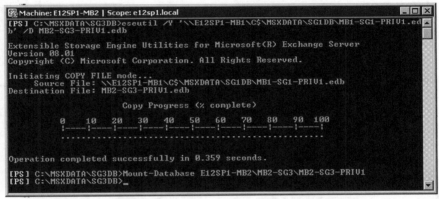

Database Portability Using a Database Backup

Another option for transporting the database to the target server is to restore a streaming API backup set to the target Exchange server. When was the last time you ran a backup and verified that you can restore the database? It is difficult to explain to management that you forgot to take backups or never verified that you can restore data from your backup media. You have to be prepared for a disaster.

The streaming API has several restrictions related to restoring a backup set to an alternate location. Figure 9-21 shows that you have to specify the same directory name for the storage group and the same directory name for the database.

VSS do not enforce the restrictions described for the streaming API. There are no limitations for the storage group and the database name with a VSS restore.

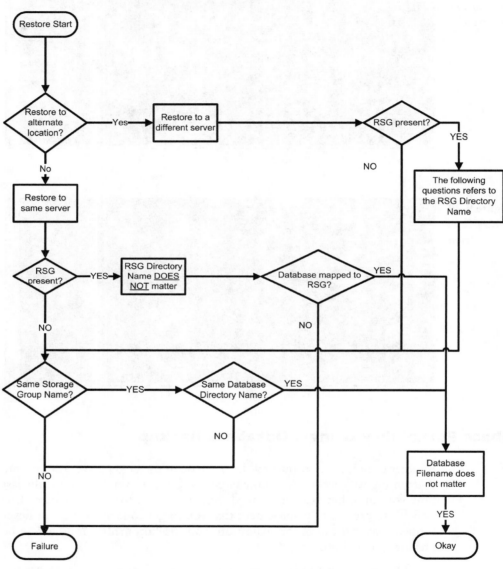

Figure 9-21   *Streaming API restore restrictions*

Updating Exchange-related Attributes in the Active Directory

The last step is to update the Exchange-related user attributes in the AD. The attributes have to point to the database on the new Exchange server.

Updating these attributes in Exchange Server 2003 was a real hassle, and database portability was not recommended. In Exchange Server 2007 this is a simple task using the PowerShell cmdlet *Move-Mailbox -ConfigurationOnly:$true*. You have to provide the mailboxes that you want to move as an input parameter to this command.

What command do you have to use to generate the list of mailboxes? Figure 9-22 shows that *Get-MailboxStatistics* returns the list of mailboxes in the database. This includes mailboxes that are used internally by Exchange Server 2007, including the mailbox of the System Attendant or *SystemMailbox{GUID}*. You should *not* move system mailboxes. An error will occur if you try to move a system mailbox.

Figure 9-22
Get-Mailbox

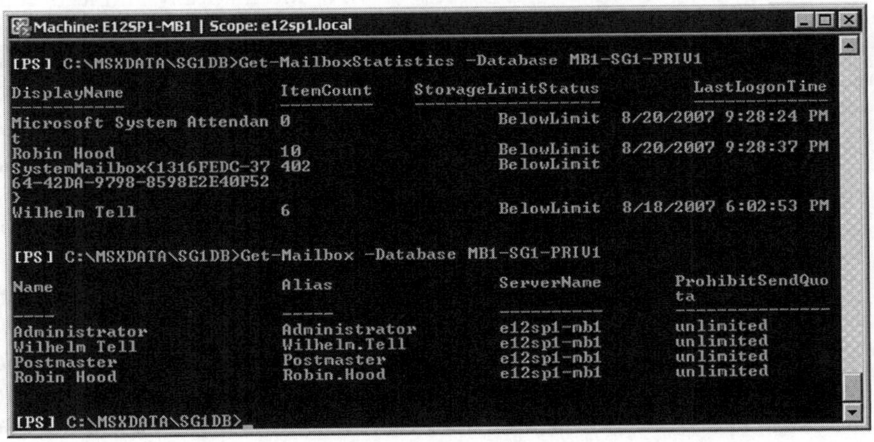

```
Machine: E12SP1-MB1 | Scope: e12sp1.local

[PS] C:\MSXDATA\SG1DB>Get-MailboxStatistics -Database MB1-SG1-PRIV1

DisplayName                ItemCount    StorageLimitStatus         LastLogonTime

Microsoft System Attendan  0                          BelowLimit   8/20/2007 9:28:24 PM
t
Robin Hood                 10                         BelowLimit   8/20/2007 9:28:37 PM
SystemMailbox{1316FEDC-37  402                        BelowLimit
64-42DA-9798-8598E2E40F52
}
Wilhelm Tell               6                          BelowLimit   8/18/2007 6:02:53 PM


[PS] C:\MSXDATA\SG1DB>Get-Mailbox -Database MB1-SG1-PRIV1

Name                       Alias         ServerName    ProhibitSendQuo
                                                       ta

Administrator              Administrator e12sp1-mb1    unlimited
Wilhelm Tell               Wilhelm.Tell  e12sp1-mb1    unlimited
Postmaster                 Postmaster    e12sp1-mb1    unlimited
Robin Hood                 Robin.Hood    e12sp1-mb1    unlimited


[PS] C:\MSXDATA\SG1DB>
```

Only *one* system attendant mailbox should exist on each Exchange mailbox server. This mailbox is automatically created in the default mailbox store—the first mailbox store on the Exchange server. Note that the mailbox store hosting the System Attendant mailbox has to be mounted if you want to move mailboxes in Exchange Server 2003. This is described in Microsoft Knowledge Base Article 264413. Additional information about system mailboxes is available on Evan Dodd's Blog.

You should use *Get-Mailbox* to generate the list of mailboxes that you want to move. System mailboxes are not returned by this command. The list created by *Get-Mailbox* includes mailboxes of users that have not yet logged on to their mailbox or haven't received any emails. Mailboxes for these users have not been created in the database yet, and therefore are not returned by *Get-MailboxStatistics*.

Figure 9-23 shows the command to generate the list of mailboxes and update their AD configuration. If you add the parameter *-Confirm:$false*, you are not prompted to confirm each mailbox move.

Figure 9-23
Move-Mailbox

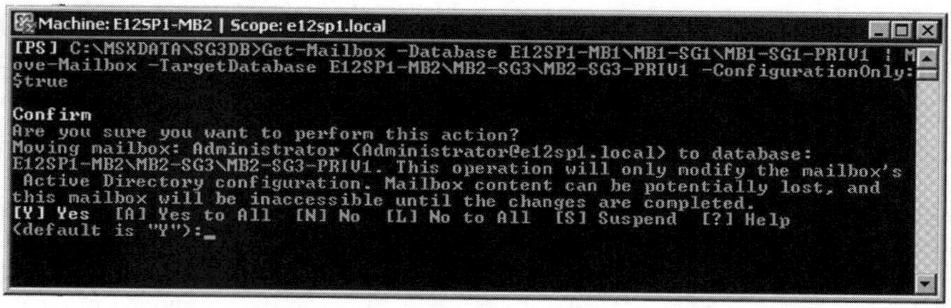

Database Portability and Clients

Outlook Web Access (OWA) automatically connects to the new Exchange mailbox server via the Client Access Server (CAS). Outlook 2007 is redirected to the new server via Autodiscover. Autodiscover and Exchange 2007 are described on Microsoft TechNet and an Autodiscover reference is available on Microsoft Developer Network.

Legacy Outlook clients might require a manual update of the MAPI profile. Tests verified that if the old Exchange server is still running and had at least one database mounted, Outlook 2003 automatically updated the profile. The mounted database was not the one transported to the new Exchange server.

If the old server was running, but had no database mounted, a manual update of the profile was required. A manual profile update was also necessary if the old server was switched off. You can update the MAPI profile using the Exchange Profile Update tool (ExProfRe)—see Microsoft Knowledge Base Article 873214.

Users with legacy clients will appreciate it if you retain the old best practice of keeping the previous Exchange server up and running for several weeks after you move the mailboxes to a new server.

Mail Flow

Will a user lose emails sent during the time when the old database is offline and you run *Move-Mailbox -ConfigurationOnly:$true*? Figure 9-24 shows

Figure 9-24
Mail queue

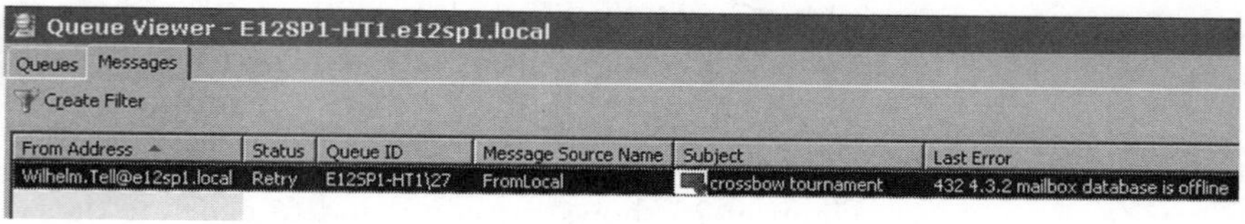

that these emails will remain in the message queue on the Hub Transport Server. The message gets rerouted after the AD attributes of the user have been updated. You can speed up the process by forcing a resubmit of messages in the queue.

Dial Tone Portability

Previously we explained how to use the new database portability function in Exchange Server 2007. This section describes how you can combine mailbox database portability with the Exchange Server 2003 dial tone recovery strategy. Microsoft refers to this recovery strategy in Exchange Server 2007 as dial tone portability. We explain the steps that you have to perform for dial tone portability based on a small test environment.

The key benefit for users is that the dial tone recovery strategy enables them to rapidly send and receive new messages. They do not have to wait several hours until an administrator has completed a restore from the last good backup. While the mailboxes in the dial tone database are empty, administrators can recover data from mailboxes in the failed database in a second step.

We emphasize the impact that this recovery strategy has on the end-user experience. This is a very critical topic and you should be fully aware of the side effects of this recovery strategy before you propose the use of dial tone recovery in a production environment.

The recovery procedure is very complex. Therefore, it is highly recommended that you test and document the recovery steps in your emergency procedures manual before you use it in production. This will minimize downtime and reduce the likelihood of failures.

Test Environment

Figure 9-25 shows the setup of the test environment. The mailbox server *E12SP1-MB4* is used by our test users. *E12SP1-MB5* is a standby server, or it could be a production server hosting additional users.

You can use dial tone portability starting with Exchange Server 2007 RTM. The recovery strategy does not require the use of a specific Client Access protocol or email client version, but the side effects are different.

If you have an Exchange organization with Exchange versions prior to Exchange Server 2007, or if you are running Outlook 2003 or earlier, the

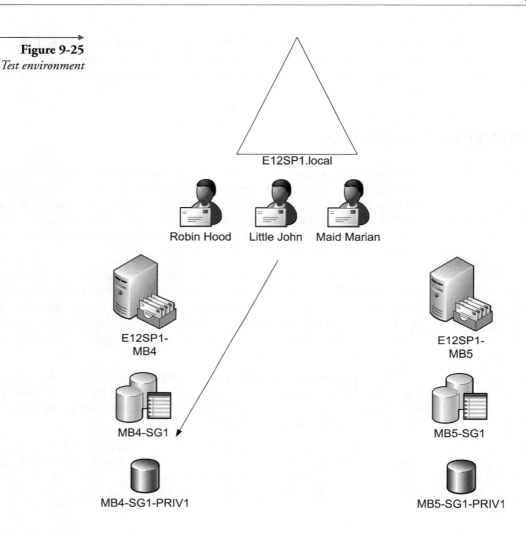

Figure 9-25
Test environment

organization depends on a public folder database to host free/busy information and the offline address book. You cannot recover a public folder database using database portability or the dial tone recovery strategy. It is assumed that the public folder database is hosted on another server that is not affected by the disaster described in the next section.

Figure 9-26 is a screenshot of Robin Hood's inbox and Figure 9-27 shows that he has provided Maid Marian with access to his calendar and has configured a rule in Outlook so that emails from Little John are automatically moved to a subfolder in his inbox.

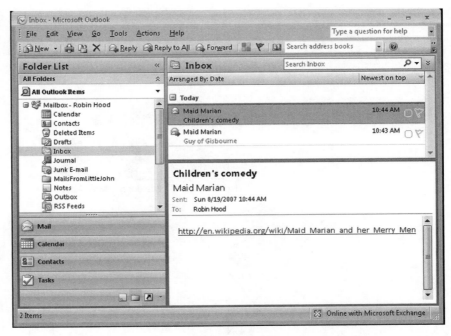

Figure 9-26
Initial inbox contents

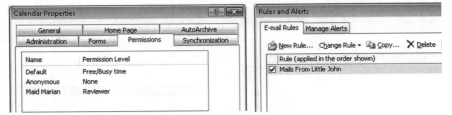

Figure 9-27
Robin Hood's Outlook configuration

The Disaster

Let's assume that the data center hosting the server *E12SP1-MB4* is lost because of a disaster. The business needs of your users require that they need to be able to send and receive email as soon as possible. Recovering mailbox content in a later step is acceptable.

To achieve this goal, you create a new database on one of your remaining Exchange mailbox servers in the same Exchange organization, such as in a recovery data center (Figure 9-28). Additionally, you have to update the Exchange-related attributes of the users in the AD. For example, the attributes *homeMDB*, *homeMTA*, and *msExchHomeServer* have to be updated if the mailbox for these users was re-homed to the database *MB5-SG1-PRIV1*.

The commands to create the storage group and database are provided in Figure 9-29.

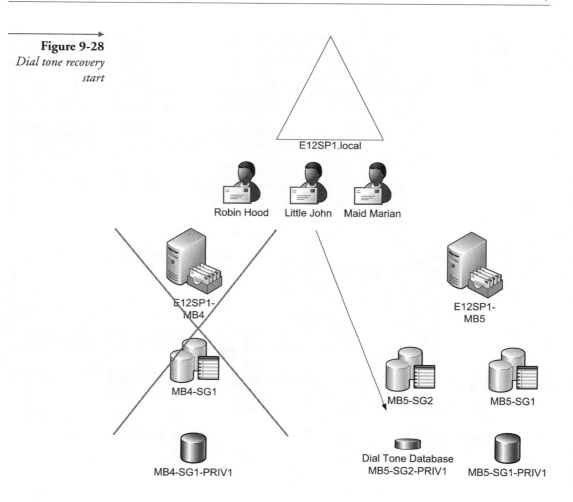

Figure 9-28
Dial tone recovery start

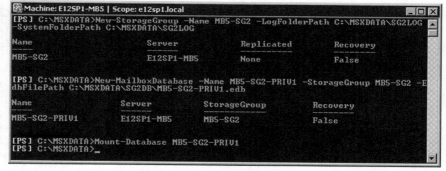

Figure 9-29
Create and mount database

Figure 9-30 shows the command to move the users' mailbox configuration to the new database.

Figure 9-30
Move-Mailbox

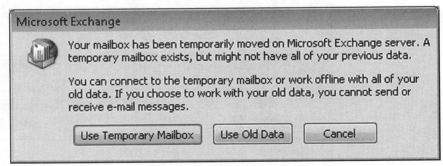

The Shock for Your Users

If a user had the Outlook client open during the recovery procedure, Outlook will display an error message if the user tries to synchronize the offline store file with the inbox on the Exchange server, or there might be a popup window stating that an administrator made a change that requires restarting Outlook.

In the "Database Portability" section, we explained that Outlook 2007 users are automatically redirected to the new Exchange server, and legacy Outlook clients might require a manual update of their profile. OWA users have the most transparent experience; they only have to close their browser and the CAS automatically connects them to the new mailbox server when they log on the next time using OWA.

Outlook 2003 or Outlook 2007 clients who use the cached Exchange mode or users running in online mode using an offline store file will receive a popup and have to choose among the options shown in Figure 9-31.

Figure 9-31
Temporary mailbox

Users are unlikely to understand this message and will flood the help desk with calls. Let's assume that Robin Hood is clever and selects Use Temporary Mailbox because he wants to send an important mail to Little John. It's likely that he may be a little worried if he recognizes that all his emails, folder permissions, and rules are lost (Figure 9-32).

Figure 9-32
Everything is lost

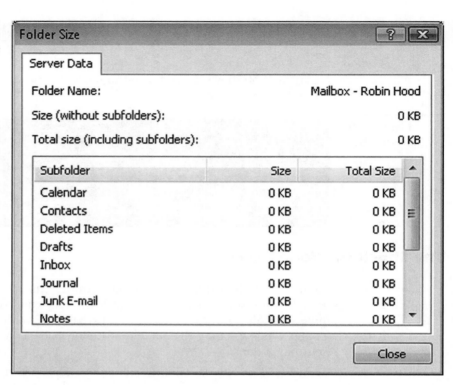

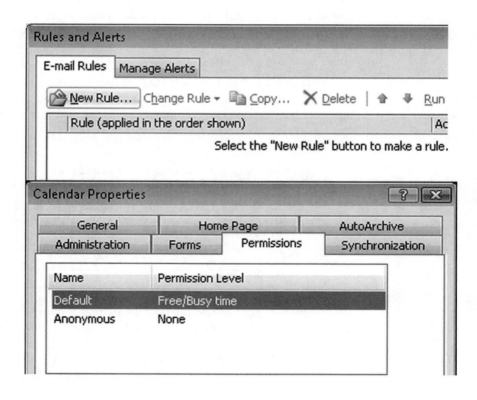

Maid Marian won't be able to access Robin Hood's calendar and won't be able to manage his time. The folder permissions disappear regardless of whether Robin Hood had defined the permission using Tools/Options/Delegates in Outlook or explicitly provided access by selecting Properties/Permissions on one of his mailbox folders.

You have to decide if your users can handle this outcome. Are you willing to provide enough upfront training for them to be prepared for this recovery strategy?

It is very important that you carefully read Microsoft Knowledge Base Article 282496 to understand the effects of resetting a mailbox database! If you create a new database, you lose the metadata stored in the mailbox. These hidden data include offline folder store encryption keys, rules, folder and delegate permissions, personal forms, and custom folder views. If a mailbox is unified messaging enabled, the user also needs a new PIN and must record a new greeting message. The effect of resetting the mailbox database on unified messaging users is described in Microsoft TechNet's section, "Understanding Setup /M:RecoverServer."

The mailbox metadata are only temporarily lost and a subsequent section explains how to restore this information. Therefore, you should advise your users not to re-create this information on their own.

Recovery Storage Group Creation

Your next step is to create an RSG on your recovery server. The RSG is used to restore your last backup of the *MB4-SG1-PRIV1* database to recover your historical data.

The Database Recovery Management tool in ExTRA provides a GUI to simplify the steps and guide you in the recovery procedure. After you specify the Exchange server that you want to work with and the domain controller, ExTRA should connect to the menu that allows you to create an RSG (Figure 9-33).

ExTRA by default creates a subdirectory beneath the database and log file directory of your production storage group to host the RSG database and log files (Figure 9-34).

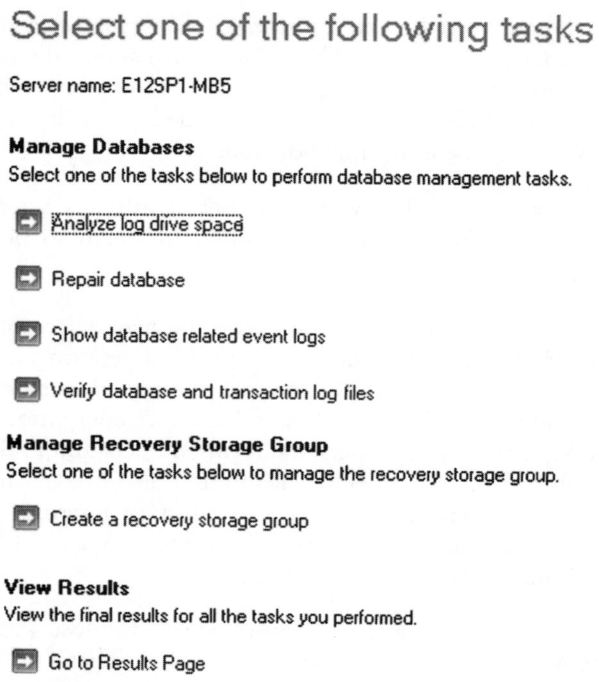

Figure 9-33
Creating an RSG

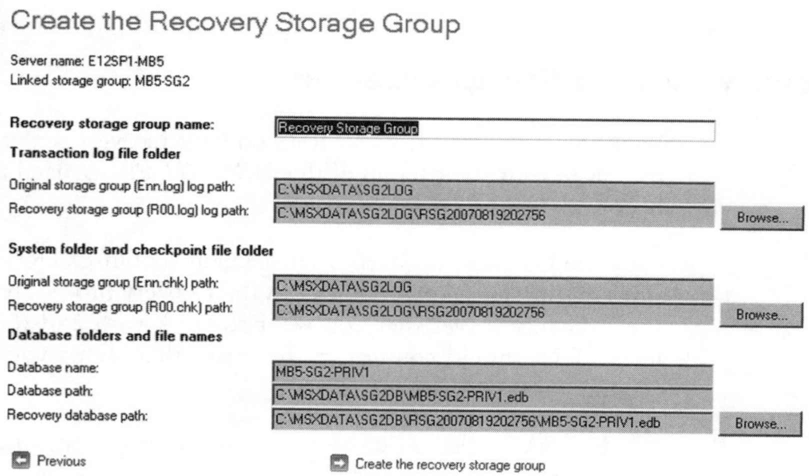

Select one of the following tasks

Server name: E12SP1-MB5

Manage Databases

Select one of the tasks below to perform database management tasks.

➡ Analyze log drive space

➡ Repair database

➡ Show database related event logs

➡ Verify database and transaction log files

Manage Recovery Storage Group

Select one of the tasks below to manage the recovery storage group.

➡ Create a recovery storage group

View Results

View the final results for all the tasks you performed.

➡ Go to Results Page

Figure 9-34
RSG directories

Create the Recovery Storage Group

Server name: E12SP1-MB5
Linked storage group: MB5-SG2

Recovery storage group name:	Recovery Storage Group
Transaction log file folder	
Original storage group (Enn.log) log path:	C:\MSXDATA\SG2LOG
Recovery storage group (R00.log) log path:	C:\MSXDATA\SG2LOG\RSG20070819202756 Browse...
System folder and checkpoint file folder	
Original storage group (Enn.chk) path:	C:\MSXDATA\SG2LOG
Recovery storage group (R00.chk) path:	C:\MSXDATA\SG2LOG\RSG20070819202756 Browse...
Database folders and file names	
Database name:	MB5-SG2-PRIV1
Database path:	C:\MSXDATA\SG2DB\MB5-SG2-PRIV1.edb
Recovery database path:	C:\MSXDATA\SG2DB\RSG20070819202756\MB5-SG2-PRIV1.edb Browse...

⬅ Previous   ➖ Create the recovery storage group

Restore

The next step is to restore a previous backup to recover historical data. You can use the Data Protection Manager (DPM) for the backup and recovery of Exchange. One benefit of the VSS-based recovery is that you do not have to adhere to streaming backup restrictions related to identical

Figure 9-35
*DPM Recovery
Wizard*

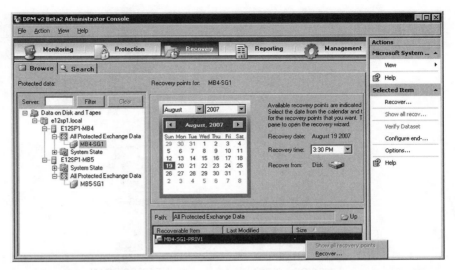

Figure 9-36
*Recovery Wizard
summary*

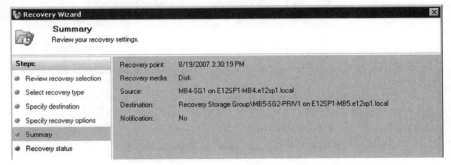

names for the storage group and database directory name. The previous section titled, "Database Portability," provided additional details about the restrictions.

Figures 9-35 and 9-36 show two steps of the Recovery Wizard in the DPM. Reading the event viewer entries that the VSS restore created is highly recommended. The descriptions of the events provide interesting insights to the VSS recovery process. This is a good opportunity to increase your knowledge about VSS.

Database Swap

Now you swap the databases in the RSG and your temporary dial tone database. The swap restores the historical data and metadata of the mailboxes. The metadata contain, for example, the delegate access permissions to inbox folders and your Outlook rules. It is *not* possible to recover the metadata by merging the mailboxes in the RSG and the production storage group.

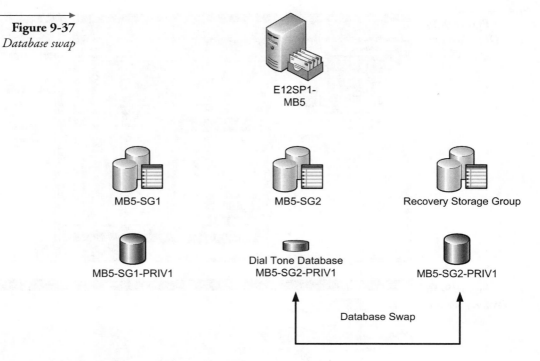

Figure 9-37
Database swap

Figure 9-38
Database swap in
ExTRA

Select Database Swap Option

Server name: E12SP1-MB5

Recovery storage group name: Recovery Storage Group
Selected database in the recovery storage group: MB5-SG2-PRIV1
Recovery storage group database path: C:\MSXDATA\SG2DB\RSG20070819202756\MB5-SG2-PRIV1.edb
Total recovery storage group database item count: 419
Total recovery storage group database item size (Bytes): 431044

Linked storage group name: MB5-SG2
Linked original database name: MB5-SG2-PRIV1
Linked original database path: C:\MSXDATA\SG2DB\MB5-SG2-PRIV1.edb
Total original database item count: 406
Total original database item size (Bytes): 378678

NOTE: If you select the 'Perform swap action' link below, both the original and the recovery databases will be dismounted, their database
file paths will be swapped and then both databases will be mounted. This will briefly interrupt mail service to users whose mailboxes are
located in the original database.

⬅ Previous   ➡ Perform swap action

➡ Go back to task center

Another benefit of swapping the database is that it is less time consuming to
copy emails from the small temporary dial tone database to the production
storage group, than copying several gigabytes of your restored backup from
the RSG to the production storage group (Figure 9-37).

Figure 9-38 shows a screenshot of ExTRA before you perform the database swap. In a production environment, the size of the database in the RSG would be much bigger compared to the size of the dial tone database. Note that ExTRA does not copy the database files but only modifies the attributes of the databases in the AD.

Performing the database swap manually instead of using ExTRA is possible. The manual procedure allows you to perform additional checks on the restored database or create a copy of the dial tone database as a safeguard.

Recovered Historical email and Metadata

Figure 9-39 shows that Robin Hood's historical emails are recovered after the database swap. Although his folder permissions and email rules are restored, these original metadata are present as hidden data in his Exchange mailbox.

Figure 9-39
Restored historical data

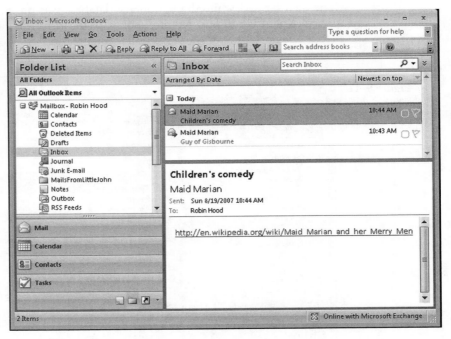

However, all emails sent and received while the dial tone database was active are missing. Therefore, you should expect the next flood of help desk calls after the database swap!

Merging the Databases

Now you have to use ExTRA to merge the contents of the database in the RSG with the restored historical data in the production database (Figure 9-40). This will restore the missing emails from the dial tone database back to the mailboxes.

Figure 9-40
Mailbox merge

Select Mailboxes to Copy or Merge

Server name: E12SP1-MB5
Recovery storage group name: Recovery Storage Group
Linked storage group name: MB5-SG2
Selected database name: MB5-SG2-PRIV1
Linked database name: MB5-SG2-PRIV1

Matched mailboxes

Display Name	Mailbox GUID	Exchange Legacy Distinguished Name
☑ Little John	6047a4af-99b8-45c2-8123-a28b36f41487	/O=MAIL/OU=EXCHANGE ADMINISTRATIVE GROUP (FYDIBOHF23...
☑ Robin Hood	870a3079-be7d-4303-82a3-56a70047a792	/O=MAIL/OU=EXCHANGE ADMINISTRATIVE GROUP (FYDIBOHF23...
☑ Maid Marian	d16a734b-59c3-49c7-8c32-f4d67dca7266	/O=MAIL/OU=EXCHANGE ADMINISTRATIVE GROUP (FYDIBOHF23...

The data created while the temporary database was online reappears in the inbox. Robin Hood now has an inbox with his historical data and the emails received during the recovery procedure (Figure 9-41).

Figure 9-41
Inbox after mailbox merge

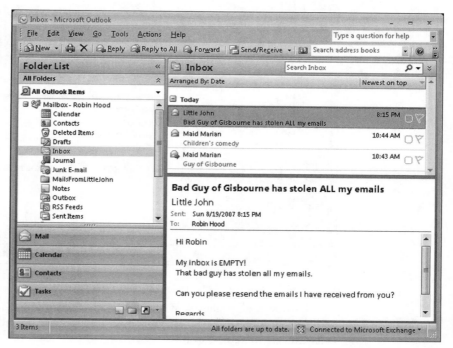

Cleanup

Your tasks are almost complete. You still have to remove the database in the RSG and delete the RSG, and it is likely that you will want to move the production database file to an appropriate file system location. The database file is currently located in the directory initially created by ExTRA for the RSG (Figure 9-42).

Figure 9-42
Database in RSG folder

Now you should run a series of Client Access tests to verify that users can access their mailbox using different clients and protocols. You also should verify mail flow to the moved mailboxes. Running a system state and storage group backup as the last step of your recovery procedure is recommended.

Short Recap of the Issues

Exchange Server 2007 introduced support for database portability. You can combine the dial tone recovery strategy of Exchange Server 2003 with database portability. This creates a new recovery option called dial tone portability. The dial tone recovery strategy and the use of the RSG are comparable with the process in Exchange Server 2003. The main difference is that you can perform the recovery on a different server, and the ExTRA of Exchange Server 2007 simplifies the steps.

Initially this looks great, but you should not forget the effect of the metadata temporarily lost when you create a new mailbox database file. You should carefully consider whether your end users will understand the Outlook dialog messages and can assess and understand the impact of the options they choose. We recommend inviting a few users to participate in a dial tone recovery test in your lab before you decide if this strategy is suitable.

The recovery procedure is complex and you have to regularly perform fire drills; otherwise, it is likely that you will make mistakes and the recovery procedure will take longer compared than a traditional database restore.

All these drawbacks are reasons to consider whether it is a good idea to create a database that is so large your users will not want to wait until the last backup has been restored. You can invest in LCR, CCR, Standby Continuous Replication (SCR), or storage array–based data replication to reduce the likelihood that you have to restore your last backup. However, nobody can guarantee that you never have to restore a mailbox database from backup. Therefore, you should think twice before you create a huge database. It might be more appropriate to create a database that you can restore in 30 minutes from tape media and only bother your users with the strange effects of the dial tone recovery strategy if a disaster occurs that destroys all the Exchange servers in a data center.

Server Recovery

Let's assume that one of your Exchange servers failed and you have to recover the server. Recovering a single server is relatively simple; the focus is therefore on recovering an Exchange Server 2007 Clustered Mailbox Server (CMS).

System State Restore Versus Reinstallation

One recovery strategy is to restore the last system-state backup to a rein-stalled server with the base operating system. Experience in previous projects is the reason for our recommendation to restore the system state only to an identical hardware configuration. It is likely that you will run into issues if the same PCI card is plugged in a different PCI slot. If the recovery server has a newer generation of the hardware than the failed server, it is also very likely that the server is using different chipsets on the motherboard or on expansion cards. It would be a surprise if restoring the system state works error-free with a different hardware configuration.

This is usually the case, although Windows provides Plug-and-Play, or should we call it Plug-and-Pray? Plug-and-Play is a hardware detection and installation technology. Data in the system state information is the end-state configuration for detected and installed hardware. Plug-and-Play is flexible, but the system state is fixed information. A system state restore is useful for completely restoring state to the exact same hardware, with the same compo-nents and configuration. Restoring the system state to a different hardware configuration is not recommended.

The preferred solution is therefore to reinstall the operating system from scratch. This allows you to recover an Exchange server to a different hardware. Creating an automated installation procedure for the base operating system is recommended. This is faster than a manual installation, and the likelihood of identical configuration settings is higher. How many times have you had to troubleshoot a strange error, and finally learned that somebody forgot to adjust the binding order of the public and private network card?

An automated installation is a must for an agile infrastructure. PowerShell lets you script the setup and configuration of Exchange Server 2007. You have to verify whether the installation and configuration of your add-on tools (backup software, virus scanner, monitoring software, etc.) can be automated as well.

Role of Active Directory

Exchange Stores a significant portion of its system configuration in the AD configuration container. Figure 9-43 shows the administrative group hierarchy in the configuration container with the Exchange server objects. If this information is still available, you can rerun the Exchange setup as

Figure 9-43
Server configuration in AD

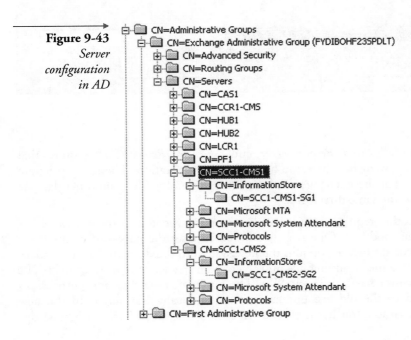

SETUP /Mode:RecoverServer for a single server, or *SETUP /RecoverCMS* for a CMS. The setup program uses the information in AD to re-create the configuration.

Information Stored in the AD includes, for example, the file system directory hosting the transaction log files (Figure 9-44) and the name of the database (Figure 9-45).

Figure 9-44
Log file path

Figure 9-45
Database file name

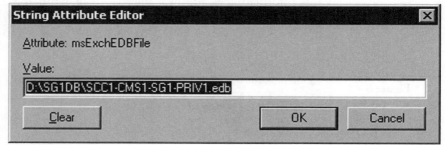

SETUP /Mode:RecoverServer and *SETUP /RecoverCMS* require that the new system has the same file system configuration. The setup program assumes that the Exchange databases, transaction log files, and other data are stored in the same directories.

Another requirement is that the computer account of the old server has not been modified. One is only allowed to reset the password of the computer account before you join the new system to the domain. If you accidentally delete the computer account, recreating the account will not help. The new account has a different SID. The group membership and permissions assigned to the old account are not automatically transferred to the new account although it has the same symbolic name. See Microsoft Knowledge

Base Article 840001 for additional information about restoring deleted accounts and their group membership in AD.

It is not a requirement that the IP address of the server is identical. If the IP address is different, you have to wait until the cached DNS information expires or force a flush of the DNS cache on the clients. The time-to-live (TTL) parameter of the DNS record determines when the cached information expires.

SETUP /Mode:RecoverServer

Figure 9-46 shows an example of recovering a single server. The article, "How to Recover a Lost Exchange Server," on Microsoft TechNet provides a list of items that you have to recover after the setup command finished. These items are not stored in AD.

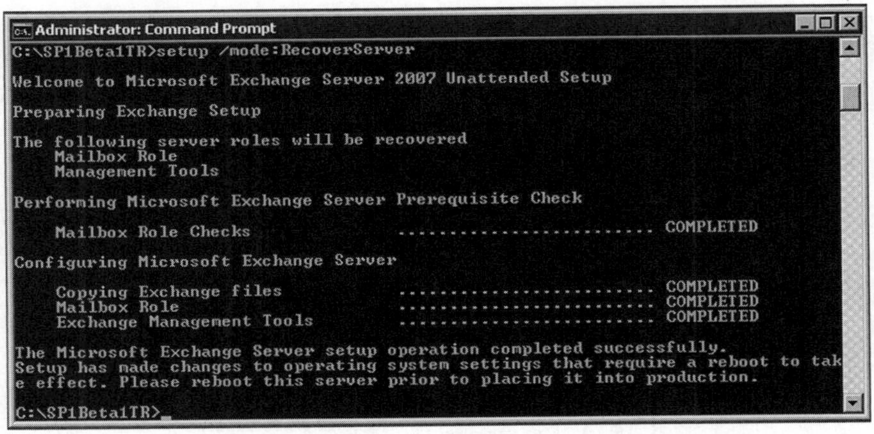

Figure 9-46
Setup /Mode:
RecoverServer

```
Administrator: Command Prompt                                            _ □ ×
C:\SP1Beta1TR>setup /mode:RecoverServer

Welcome to Microsoft Exchange Server 2007 Unattended Setup

Preparing Exchange Setup

The following server roles will be recovered
        Mailbox Role
        Management Tools

Performing Microsoft Exchange Server Prerequisite Check

    Mailbox Role Checks              ..................... COMPLETED

Configuring Microsoft Exchange Server

    Copying Exchange files           ..................... COMPLETED
    Mailbox Role                     ..................... COMPLETED
    Exchange Management Tools        ..................... COMPLETED

The Microsoft Exchange Server setup operation completed successfully.
Setup has made changes to operating system settings that require a reboot to tak
e effect. Please reboot this server prior to placing it into production.

C:\SP1Beta1TR>
```

Note that the Edge role does not store its configuration in AD. The Edge role uses AD Application Mode (ADAM). Therefore, you cannot use *SETUP /Mode:RecoverServer* to recover an Edge Server. You have to clone the configuration of the Edge Server to be able to recover it. The directory *C:\Program Files\Microsoft\Exchange Server\Scripts* contains the script *ExportEdgeConfig.ps1* to export the configuration to an XML file. The script *ImportEdgeConfig.ps1* is used to import the exported data to a new installed Edge Server with the same computer name. The abovementioned Microsoft TechNet article provides a detailed description of the steps.

If you recover a server with the Hub Transport (HT) role, you can add the switch */DoNotStartTransport* to *SETUP /mode:RecoverServer*. This allows you to restore a backed-up transport queue database before the transport service starts. On the other hand, backing up the transport queue database is not a common practice because it contains only messages in transit to a mailbox server.

You have to restore custom OWA files and virtual directories configured in the Internet Information Server (IIS) for the Client Access Server (CAS) role after running *SETUP /Mode:RecoverServer*. The above Microsoft TechNet article provides a description how to back up and recover the configuration data that the CAS role stores in the IIS metabase.

For a mailbox server, you have to restore the last Exchange database backup set. You can use the same procedure to move an Exchange server to a new hardware. This procedure is not limited to disaster recovery, but you cannot use it to upgrade Exchange Server 2003 to Exchange Server 2007. The only supported migration strategy is moving mailboxes from a server running Exchange Server 2003 to a server running Exchange Server 2007.

SETUP /RecoverCMS

The following section describes the recovery of a CMS hosted on a three-node single copy cluster (SCC). Figure 9-47 shows the configuration of the original server.

Figure 9-47
Original configuration

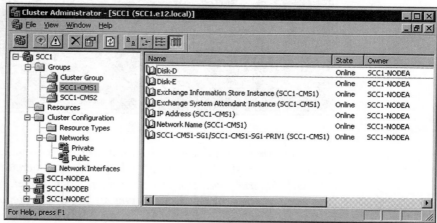

Let's assume that the nodes of your cluster failed because of a disaster. You have to recover the CMS to a new cluster. The remaining sections explain how you can recover the first CMS SCC1-CMS1. Recovering the CMS SCC1-CMS2 of your SCC can be performed using the same procedure.

It is important to note that splitting one cluster hosting more than one CMS into multiple clusters using SETUP /RecoverCMS is not supported by Microsoft. The reason for this restriction is likely an issue with the Message Transfer Agent (MTA). See Microsoft Knowledge Base Article 928811, and the Microsoft TechNet section, "How to Determine the First Clustered Mailbox Server Installed in a Single Copy Cluster" on.

It is required that the old cluster nodes are shutdown before you run SETUP /RecoverCMS. If you test the recovery procedure in a lab while the old cluster nodes are still running, the recovery will fail. *SETUP /RecoverCMS* will start the CMS on the old cluster instead of starting it on the new cluster.

The first step is setting up a new Windows cluster. It is important that you create a disk drive configuration that is identical to the one that was used by SCC1-CMS1. You need the disk volumes *D:* and *E:* in this example. It is not a requirement that these are the same disks. The disk volumes can have different disk signatures and have a larger capacity. It is only important that the volumes provide enough space to restore the last database backup, and the database and transaction log files can be hosted in the same file system directories. The file system paths on the new cluster have to be identical.

You should create a temporary cluster group for these two physical disk resources. Figure 9-48 shows the configuration of the new Windows cluster.

Figure 9-48
New Windows cluster

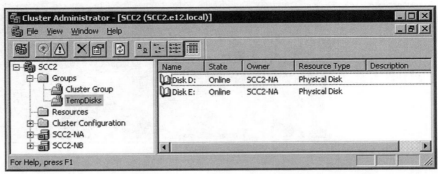

The next step is to create the same file system directories that the original CMS used and install the Exchange binaries for the mailbox role (Figure 9-49).

You should install the Exchange binaries on only one node of the cluster. This prevents the possibility of the cluster group failing over to the other node if it encounters any issue during the re-creation of the CMS in the following step.

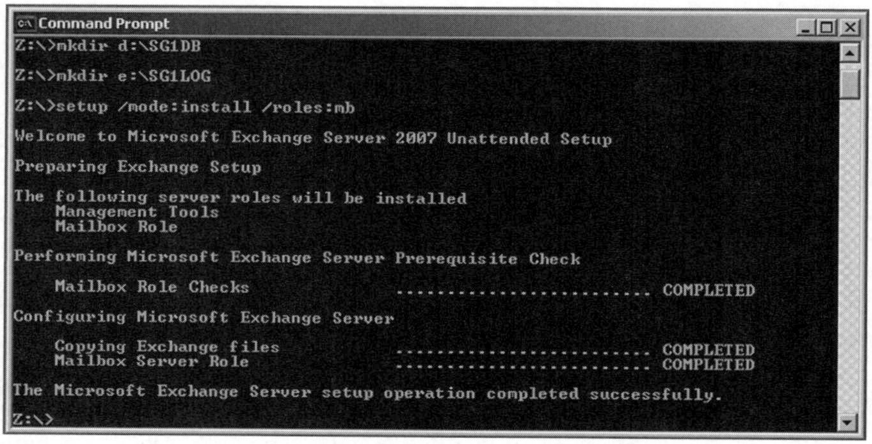

Figure 9-49
Install mailbox role

Figure 9-50 shows the command line to re-create the CMS. If you test the procedure in a virtualized environment, it is likely that this step initially fails. The start of the System Attendant resource does not finish in the default timeout Figure 9-51.

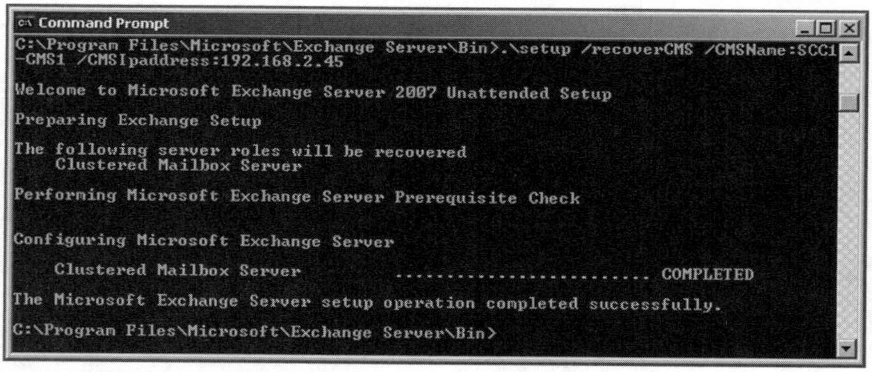

Figure 9-50
Setup
/RecoverCMS

You have to increase the timeout configuration of the System Attendant in the cluster administrator and run the same *SETUP /RecoverCMS* command again.

Following this step, the previously existing cluster resources on the original server have been re-created on the new cluster and all resources are online beside the System Attendant and the database resource. Figure 9-52 shows the corresponding screenshot.

It is important to realize that the dependency of the database cluster resource on the physical disks hosting the database file and the log files of

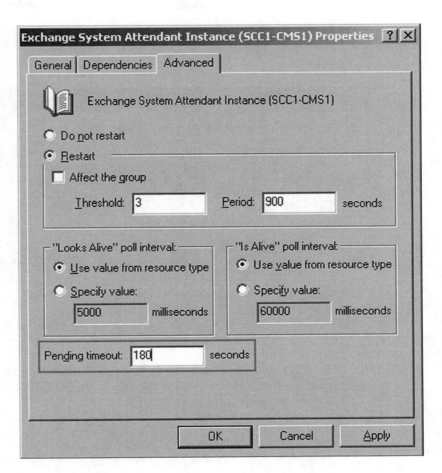

Figure 9-51
System attendant pending timeout

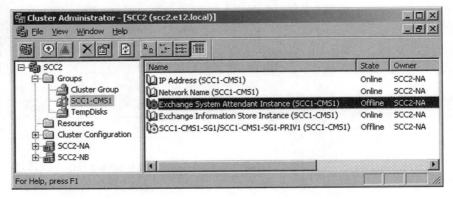

Figure 9-52
Cluster group after Setup /RecoverCMS

the storage group have not been re-created (Figure 9-53). This is one example of a configuration setting that is not stored in the AD.

Figure 9-53
*Missing data-
base resource
dependencies*

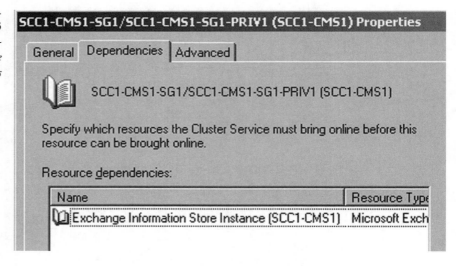

You have to move the physical disk resources from the *TempDisks* cluster
group shown in Figure 9-48 to the cluster group SCC1-CMS1, and add the
disks to the dependency list (Figure 9-54).

Figure 9-54
*Update resource
dependency list*

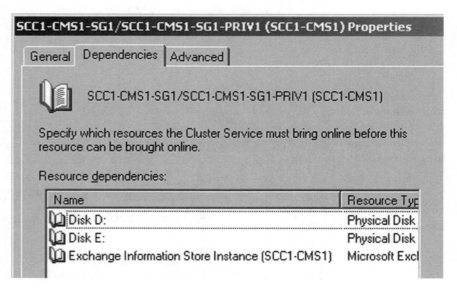

Manually start the System Attendant using the cluster administrator and set the *AllowFileRestore* parameter of the mailbox database using *Set-MailboxDatabase SCC1-CMS1-SG1-PRIV1 -AllowFileRestore:$true*. You can restore your last backup to the CMS, or move an offline copy of the database file to the correct location and mount the mailbox database.

Afterward, via the EMC, you should verify that the CMS was successfully recovered and the database mounted (Figure 9-55).

Figure 9-55
*Recovered CMS
and mounted
database*

It is possible that the user interface of the cluster administrator still shows that the database resource is offline, although the database is already mounted. You can resolve this issue by stopping and starting the CMS using *Stop-ClusteredMailboxServer* and *Start-ClusteredMailboxServer*.

Now that the CMS is up and running, it is time to configure your passive cluster node. Figure 9-56 shows that currently only one cluster node is able to own the CMS.

Figure 9-56
*Only one possible
owner*

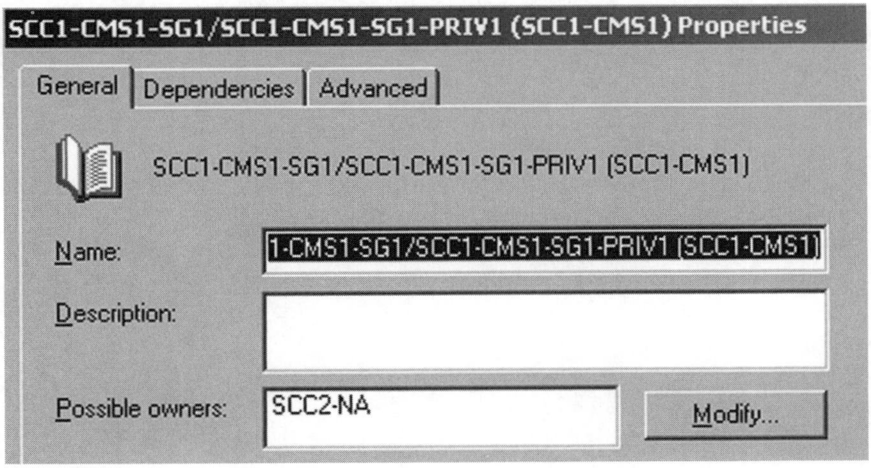

The other cluster node is automatically added to the list of possible owners of the Exchange cluster group and its resources after you run *SETUP /mode:install /roles:mb* on the passive node. Figure 9-57 shows a screenshot with the updated list of possible owners.

Figure 9-57
*Two possible
owners*

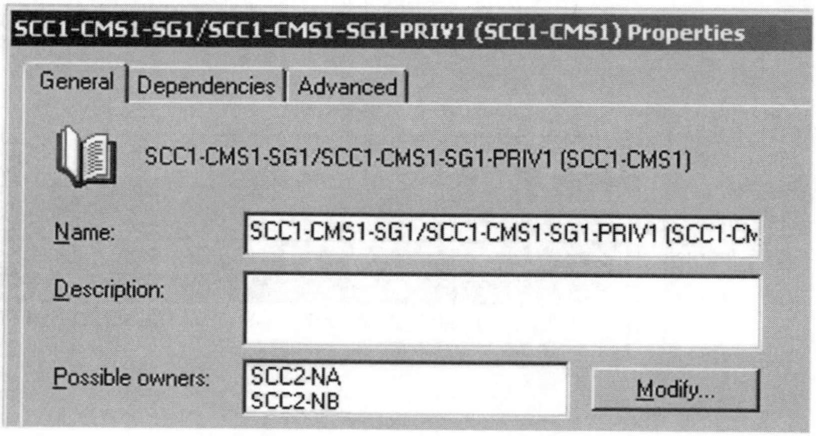

If the recovered CMS is a cluster continuous replication instead of SCC, you have to reseed the databases to the passive node and resume continuous replication. Backing up the recovered CMS as the last step of your recovery procedure is a best practice.

10

Storage Design Validation

You should include a proof-of-concept phase in your project schedule. This testing phase allows you to verify whether the theoretical assumptions were valid and the proposed solution architecture will meet your own or your customer's requirements. It is very important to take this phase seriously and not skip it because of time restrictions. Making architectural changes after the Exchange environment is already in production is more time consuming and expensive, and often requires a disruption of the messaging service. It is better to find your mistakes and know the performance of your environment before users complain about your inability to design an environment that fulfills their needs.

Several tools are available to test the configuration, starting from low-level disk exercisers like IOmeter, to an Exchange Store process simulator, and at the upper end a tool that simulates the actions users perform when they read and send emails or meeting requests.

Design validation is one use case of the tools described in this chapter. There are additional possibilities:

- Capacity planning—How many users can my infrastructure host?

- Impact of features—What are the impacts of enabling archiving, or adding an additional virus scanner engine?

- Identifying bottlenecks—What component in my infrastructure limits my backup and restore throughput? Is the CPU or the memory the bottleneck for the poor performance?

Starting from the basement is recommended. Don't try to build a high-rise building before you verified that your basement is rock solid. Start with testing the storage environment before you run a test that simulates users accessing the Exchange environment using Outlook Anywhere via ISA arrays and hardware load balancers. You really have to start from the bottom, and check to see whether the firmware and device drivers of the components used by your Exchange servers are reliably working together. For example, we had to run failover tests on a geographically dispersed Single Copy Cluster using HP StorageWorks Cluster Extension EVA. Initially, the cluster was not working reliably; as soon as there was load on the system the cluster service initiated an automatic failover to the passive node. The event viewer contained messages about lost network connectivity. It turned out that somebody had updated the firmware of the server but did not install the corresponding device driver update.

The following sections are mainly based on information shared by our colleagues in the the HP Customer Focused Testing (CFT) and Solution Alliance Engineering (SAE) teams. You can find whitepapers and tools created by these groups on the websites www.hp.com/go/hpcft and http://www.hp.com/solutions/activeanswers/exchange. They use the tools described in this chapter on a daily basis, and we are happy that they shared their experience with us. We received excellent support from the Microsoft team that develops the testing tools described in this chapter. This especially helped us to learn LoadGen.

The Risk of Running Tests in a Production Environment

We highly recommend running tests in a test environment and not in a production environment. Separating the test environment from the production environment removes the risks that your tests impact production systems. We often had to discuss the need of a dedicated test environment with colleagues who are responsible for project financials. The following list provides arguments for this discussion:

- If you share the storage subsystem with the production environment, the I/O load generated by your test cases impacts the response time that your production Exchange servers will provide to users.

- If you connect the test servers to the same network infrastructure, the network traffic generated by your tests will reduce the available bandwidth for the production servers.

- If you run a test that sends and receives emails on a mailbox server that is a member of the production Exchange organization, this will stress the production server holding the Hub Transport (HT) role. This will slow down email delivery for production users. If the test load is so high that the server with the HT role cannot handle it, you risk not meeting the Service Level Agreement (SLA) related to mail delivery.

- If you run a test tool in the production Exchange organization, you run the risk that because of a configuration mistake the test tool sends emails to a distribution list with customers or board directors as members. They will be more than unhappy with hundreds of test emails in their inbox.

- If you initialize mailboxes using real messages to improve the accuracy of your simulation, and your test system has connectivity to the Internet via production, the test tool might reply to those real messages. Your business partners or other external individuals might not appreciate receiving test mail in response to mail they had sent to your company.

- Additionally, you run the risk that these test emails received by production users will inflate the production databases and use all free space of the disk volume hosting transaction logs. Exchange will automatically dismount the databases of this storage group, and your production users will complain because they cannot access their mailboxes.

There may be cases where it is not feasible to totally separate the test environment from production. One example is testing a deployment in a geographically dispersed configuration. It is very likely that the link used to connect the data centers is the same for the test environment and the production servers. This is especially likely if you use storage array–based data replication solutions. Most of the time there is only one Dark Fibre connection available between the data centers. You must be aware that generating a high test load affects the latency of the write I/O from production servers. You may argue that you have the possibility of simulating the stretched deployment using a network delay simulator, such as a Hurricane II WAN Emulator from PacketStorm Communications. However, it is unlikely that you have access to such a device if you do not work for an engineering group.

Disk Exercisers

Why do we recommend that you familiarize yourself with low-level tools such as disk exercisers? The answer is that they do not require a lot of prerequisites. Full installation of the Exchange environment is not necessary; it is sufficient that the storage subsystem is connected to a Windows host. Therefore, you can easily use them and you have results in a short timeframe. Another reason for learning them is that you should understand the tools your storage administrators will use.

However, you have to be aware of limitations. They are not a perfect simulation of the I/O bursts that the Exchange Store process generates if the server is under a high user load.

IOmeter

The IOmeter tool measures performance of network I/O and I/O to a disk subsystem. Intel developed the tool in 1998, and in 2001 discontinued further development, but made the source code available as an open source project. You can download the current version from Sourceforge.net. As of this writing, there have been no new updates since fall 2006.

We encourage you to learn IOmeter because it is a tool that is well respected by your colleagues working in the storage department. Your colleagues might prefer to use IOmeter over any Exchange-specific tool, and if they are UNIX freaks, they might be even more skeptical of a tool provided by Microsoft. I (Juergen) must admit that I started as a UNIX system engineer but in the meantime I like both worlds, so please don't take this comment too seriously.

This section provides you with a fast start to IOmeter and will enable you to begin experimenting with it. You must consult the IOmeter user guide if you want to become an IOmeter expert. The aim of the section is to provide an IOmeter beginners guide that will help you to understand what your colleagues in the storage department are doing with IOmeter. Speaking the same language is always good. This is the first obstacle that you have to overcome if you want to have a productive relationship with the storage administrators. Collaboration between the Exchange team and the storage team is necessary for a successful Exchange deployment. This is still true, although Exchange Server 2007 is not as I/O bound as Exchange Server 2003, and the number of deployments using direct-attached storage has increased.

IOmeter can easily be configured to simulate the I/O characteristics of an application. You just have to determine the I/O pattern of the application, which is the more complicated part of the task.

The tool allows you to characterize disk subsystem performance without the need to set up the complete infrastructure that the application requires. Regarding an Exchange mailbox server, you need the server and the storage array, but you do not need the Active Directory (AD) and the other Exchange server roles to verify disk array performance. You only have to know the read/write ratio, the I/O size, and whether the I/O is a random or sequential access.

IOmeter is a client server application. *IOMETER.EXE* is the GUI that you use to configure the workload, and the GUI displays the measured performance. *IOMETER.EXE* runs only on Microsoft Windows operating systems. *DYNAMO.EXE* is the program that generates load by executing the configured workload. Dynamo, which has no GUI, is available for Microsoft Windows and a few other operating system versions such as several Linux distributions and Novell Netware.

Multiple Dynamo processes can run in parallel. IOmeter automatically starts one Dynamo process on the local system. This Dynamo process runs in a command window that immediately minimizes to the taskbar when you start IOmeter. If you open this window, you can see status information what Dynamo is doing, which can be helpful for troubleshooting purposes. Each Dynamo instance is called an "I/O Manager." In Figure 10-1 you can see the I/O Manager that was created for the Dynamo process running on the local machine—PC2.

Figure 10-1
IOmeter main window

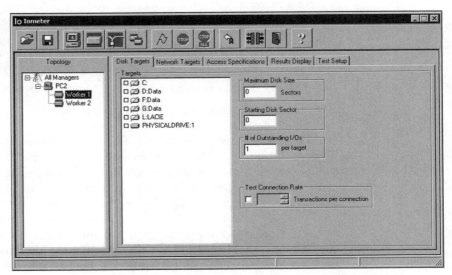

Dynamo is a multithreaded process. In Dynamo there are "worker" threads executing the configured workload. The I/O Manager controls the worker threads. The icon that represents a worker identifies it as a disk worker (■) or a network worker (▦). By default, Dynamo creates one disk worker thread per processor core available on the local system. You can create additional disk workers or network workers by pressing the corresponding icon in the menu bar.

You have to assign an I/O target to each worker. You can assign multiple targets to a single worker, and you can assign the same target to multiple workers, but the simplest configuration is to use a one-to-one mapping. If your server has more CPUs than disk targets that you want to test, do not assign a disk target to the remaining workers. Workers without a disk target assigned will be idle during the test run. For example, assume that your server has eight CPUs but you only have four disks attached to the server. In this case, you will assign one CPU to each of the four disks and four CPUs will have no disk target assigned—they will be idle.

A target can be a local disk or a network interface. You have to execute *DYNAMO.EXE /i IometerComputerName /m ManagerComputerName* on a remote server if you want to characterize network I/O. *IometerComputerName* is the computer name or IP address of the computer running IOmeter, and *ManagerComputerName* is the computer name or IP address of the system where you start Dynamo. The *ManagerComputerName* is afterward displayed in the IOmeter GUI as an additional I/O Manager. This happens only if no firewall between the computer running IOmeter and the computer running Dynamo blocks the communication between the server and the client process.

The following sections focus on validating disk subsystems. Therefore, topics specific to network I/O are not described. There are three kinds of disk targets:

- A yellow disk with a crossover red bar identifies an unprepared disk.
- A yellow disk without a crossover red bar identifies a prepared disk.
- A blue disk identifies a raw physical disk.

Preparing a disk consists of creating a container file, called *iobw.tst*. IOmeter creates this file in the root directory of the file system, and by default the file is as large as free space in the file system. Windows will complain when there are only a few megabytes of free space left on the disk. Creating an *iobw.tst* file that fills up the file system is not necessary. You should create a container file that is similar in size to the data that you are going to store on this volume. If this is the volume hosting an Exchange database, you should create a file that is as large as the production database that you plan to store on this volume. The file has to be larger than the storage controller cache size; otherwise, the test results are meaningless because the controller would be able to perform all I/O requests from cache.

IOmeter is not data destructive; it will create a container file but it will not delete existing files. This is a significant difference compared to a lot of other disk exerciser tools.

A disk gets prepared the first time you execute a test with a worker assigned to this disk target. If there is no container file on the file system, Dynamo creates the *iobw.tst* file. The following steps are used to prepare a disk:

1. Determine the size of the *iobw.tst* file that you want to use for the test.

2. Divide this size in bytes by 512, which is the sector size, and specify this figure in the Maximum Disk Size entry field shown in Figure 10-1.

3. Execute a workload assigned to the disk by pressing the green flag in the menu bar.

You will see that the icon for this disk has changed from the one used for an unprepared disk to the one identifying a prepared disk. It might be necessary to close and restart IOmeter if the icon showing the status of the disk does not change.

If you want to eliminate the influence of the NTFS file system, you have to use raw physical disks. One point where the NTFS file system can influence the test result is the level of fragmentation of the *iobw.tst* file. If you prepare a fresh formatted disk volume, you eliminate this issue. You can use the standard disk defragmenter tool to verify the fragmentation of the file.

The most interesting part of IOmeter is defining the workload. You define the workload in the Access Specifications tab. Figure 10-2 shows IOmeter providing preexisting workloads; they are shown in the Global Access Specifications window. If these preexisting workloads do not meet your requirement, you can create your own workload or edit an existing workload (Figure 10-3).

Figure 10-2
Access specifications

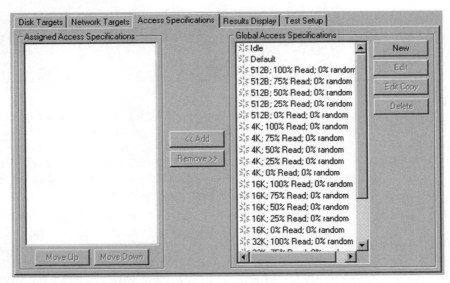

A workload is assigned to a worker, and all disk targets of this worker are under the same workload. If you have multiple workers, you can assign the same workload to the worker threads or you can assign different workloads to the workers.

You might wonder by which black magic art you can obtain the necessary figures to define the workload for a specific application. How can I simulate the Exchange Information Store process writing to the database volume or a backup application writing the backup file during a disk to disk backup? The best tip that we can provide you is to use *PERFMON.MSC* to capture the I/O pattern of the application in production and analyze the physical disk counters. Another option is to ask your colleagues from the

Figure 10-3
Edit access specification

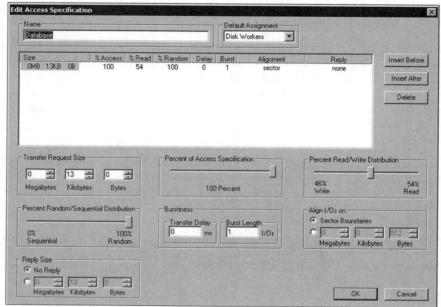

storage department for help. Often they have tools that can capture the I/O seen by the controller of the storage array. But be aware that the I/O seen on the controller might be different from what you measure with *PERFMON. MSC* on the Windows host. Not all storage arrays will expose performance counters that directly correspond to the physical disk performance counters seen by the Windows operating system.

Figure 10.3 and Table 10.1 provide a greatly simplified example for Exchange Server 2007. Exchange uses in reality several I/O sizes and not one fixed I/O size. Exchange I/O sometimes occurs in bursts and not as a continuous data stream. You have to create an IOmeter access specification with multiple I/O sizes and experiment with the delay and burst figure to simulate this behavior. However, creating an identical IOmeter access pattern is very time consuming. Additionally new releases of Exchange Server and even service packs can have a significant impact on the I/O profile. If you want to have a very close mirror of the I/O pattern then you should use Jetstress instead of IOmeter.

Table 10.1   *Exchange Server 2007 Log File Volume Workload*

Size	% Access	% Read	% Random	Delay	Burst
12 KB	100	0	0	0	1

The final step before running a test is defining the test setup. The fields in Figure 10-4 that you should pay attention to follow:

Run Time—Usually, after a few minutes, you can already tell how well your disk targets are performing. However, it is interesting to verify whether performance is changing over time. For certain workloads, such as backup and restore, it is appropriate to let the test run for the same amount of time that you expect it will last in production.

Figure 10-4
Test setup

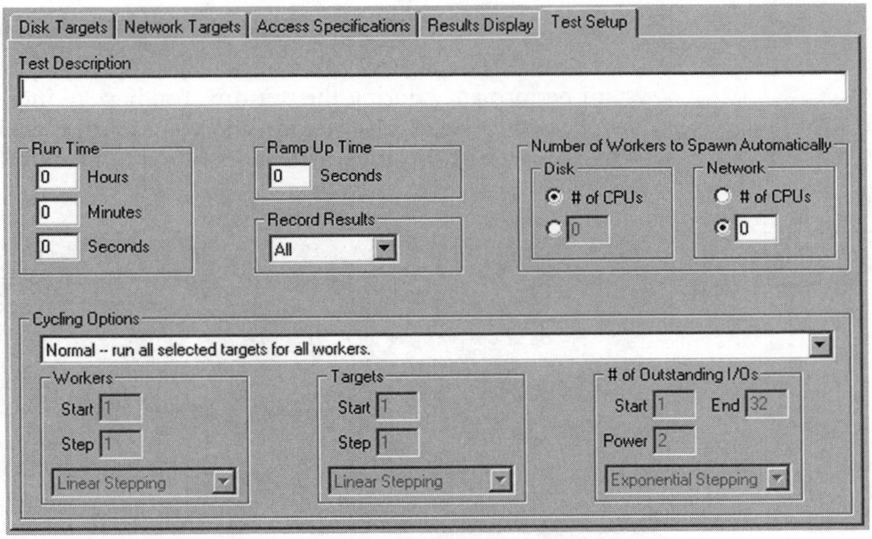

Ramp up Time—This specifies the ramp-up time during which the workers will be started. The default value of 0 seconds is usually okay.

Number of Workers to Spawn Automatically—This lets you define the number of disk workers and network workers. You can keep the default number of workers, or manually add additional disk or network workers by pressing the corresponding icon on the menu bar. If you think that you have CPU utilization issues with the default configuration, you can specify a fixed number of disk workers that is less than the number of CPUs in your server.

Cycling Options—This is the most interesting setting. The default option is "Normal—run all selected targets for all workers." Beyond running the actual test, it is sometimes appropriate to understand the behavior of the disk targets as the workload intensifies. By default, IOmeter will not generate more than one I/O at a time per disk target. This is typically the way that applications behave in sequential access mode, but it is not the case for random accesses, which tend to occur in either a sustained or burst mode to the disk target. We recommend that you use the default settings. Once you are certain of your workload, you should gradually augment the number of outstanding I/O; this will indicate the target queue depth of the IOmeter, and simulate multiple random I/O requests happening at the same time (similar to a production workload on database read and writes).

Saving the test configuration before you start a test is recommended. This allows you to repeat the test with the same workload specification and test setup parameters without manually redefining everything from scratch.

Figure 10-5 is a screenshot of the Results Display tab. This tab shows system performance during the test run. You have to increase the update frequency to see current performance, and you can drag workers or I/O managers to a progress bar to see performance of a specific object.

Figure 10-5
Results display

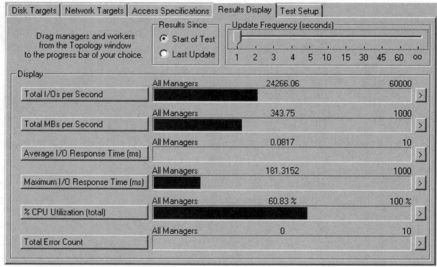

IOmeter also creates a CSV file with information about the workload and measured performance.

Microsoft Exchange Server JetStress

JetStress simulates disk I/O that the Exchange Store process performs. With JetStress you can check whether the system configuration will likely be able to handle the transactional workload generated by user activity with acceptable latency figures. JetStress is also able to simulate backup and recovery work-loads. JetStress is used in the Microsoft Exchange Solution Reviewed Program (ESRP) to verify the configuration of storage subsystems. The aim of ESRP is to facilitate third-party storage testing and publishing of storage configurations that are suitable for Exchange deployments.

One major advantage of JetStress is that it does not require a full Exchange and AD environment to run the tests. Installing the tool on a sin-gle server and copying the Extensible Storage Engine DLLs from a produc-tion Exchange server to the test system are sufficient. You need the following files from a production Exchange server:

- Ese.dll
- Eseperf.dll
- Eseperf.hxx
- Eseperf.ini

Copying the files from the Exchange Server 2007 installation media is not recommended because you should use the identical version that you use in production. The production version very likely includes updates made via service packs and hot fixes that are not included on the installation media. It is better to copy the files from an Exchange server with the corresponding service packs and hot fixes installed. You have to verify whether your JetStress version is compatible with these ESE files. There have been cases in which a JetStress build was not working reliably with the latest ESE files.

If you compare JetStress with IOmeter, then the main difference is that IOmeter allows you to define various workloads and thereby simulate dif-ferent applications. The workload generated by JetStress is Exchange spe-cific. You cannot use JetStress to simulate different applications. However, JetStress removes the burden of defining a workload that mirrors Exchange behavior. This is a significant advantage because you do not have to spend hours to verify whether the latest service pack modifies the I/O pattern of the Exchange Store process and you have to create a new IOmeter workload definition. You have to copy only the latest ESE files to the JetStress program directory and you are all set.

The JetStress installation package contains command-line and GUI ver-sions of the tool. The command-line version has the benefit that you can schedule the execution of a test run. Typically, you will use the GUI version.

The first time you start *JETSTRESSWIN.EXE*, it will check if the required database engine DLLs are available. Figure 10-6 shows that JetStress enables the advanced database performance counters. This pro-cess requires a few restarts of the application until the changes take effect. Microsoft Knowledge Base Article 556030 describes the registry change that

JetStress performs. You can see the famous Squeaky Lobster registry key in Figure 10-7. The key that actually enables the extended counters set is Show Advanced Counters above the Squeaky Lobster. The Squeaky Lobster registry key is added only for backward compatibility reasons.

Figure 10-6
Checking test system

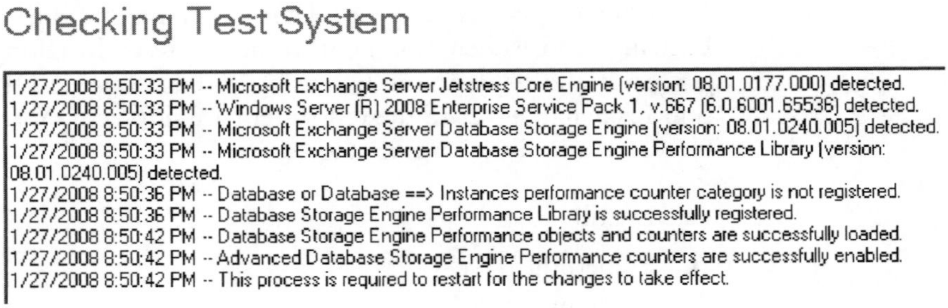

Checking Test System

1/27/2008 8:50:33 PM -- Microsoft Exchange Server Jetstress Core Engine (version: 08.01.0177.000) detected.
1/27/2008 8:50:33 PM -- Windows Server (R) 2008 Enterprise Service Pack 1, v.667 (6.0.6001.65536) detected.
1/27/2008 8:50:33 PM -- Microsoft Exchange Server Database Storage Engine (version: 08.01.0240.005) detected.
1/27/2008 8:50:33 PM -- Microsoft Exchange Server Database Storage Engine Performance Library (version: 08.01.0240.005) detected.
1/27/2008 8:50:36 PM -- Database or Database ==> Instances performance counter category is not registered.
1/27/2008 8:50:36 PM -- Database Storage Engine Performance Library is successfully registered.
1/27/2008 8:50:42 PM -- Database Storage Engine Performance objects and counters are successfully loaded.
1/27/2008 8:50:42 PM -- Advanced Database Storage Engine Performance counters are successfully enabled.
1/27/2008 8:50:42 PM -- This process is required to restart for the changes to take effect.

Figure 10-7
Squeaky Lobster

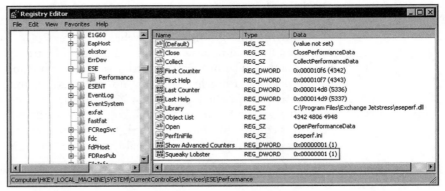

If multiple Exchange servers are connected to a single storage subsystem, you should run JetStress on all servers in parallel. Running JetStress on only one server while the other systems are idle will not produce a representative test result. This is a topic that you have to keep in mind in a shared storage environment. Whether using a shared storage infrastructure for Exchange is an acceptable design is a very interesting topic. However, this parallel execution of JetStress should not be your first test. First, you have to verify whether each server is working as expected individually. One thing is certain: Predicting the achievable performance of the transactional workload is more difficult in a shared environment. If the storage environment is used by additional applications such as file servers or Oracle databases, you have to collaborate with your colleagues and make sure that they simulate their workload at the same time.

JetStress does not include a function to simulate Exchange Server 2007 continuous replication; it does not perform the tasks that the Exchange

Replication service performs to ship closed transaction log files. If your production deployment includes Local Continuous Replication (LCR) or Cluster Continuous Replication (CCR), you have to add a storage group to your workload. To simulate LCR, you add a storage group to your single server, and to simulate CCR you run JetStress on the passive cluster node with the same workload configured on the active cluster node. With the Exchange Server 2007 Release to Manufacture (RTM) version, you had to increase the mailbox profile on the passive cluster node to account for the higher I/O load because of the inefficient batch processing of shipped log files. Starting with Service Pack 1, you can use the same mailbox profile on the active and passive cluster node because this issue has been fixed.

If you use a storage-based data replication solution, you should run a test with data replication disabled, followed by a test with replication enabled. This allows you to identify the impact of the replication on the storage performance.

You can use JetStress to verify the storage subsystem throughput or to simulate a mailbox profile. The "Subsystem throughput" test verifies the maximum performance that you can achieve with the storage subsystem. The aim of the mailbox profile is to verify whether the system can handle the predicted user load.

The following sections assume that you already have read the JetStress online manual. One note at the beginning: Setting your regional and language option to English US is recommended, as the tool was developed in the United States. You should not assume that performance test tools available free of charge have to pass the same quality assurance tests using all possible locales as it is the case for the Exchange Server product. We have seen tests failing because the tool did not "understand" the number format used in Germany. In Germany, the comma character and not the dot character is used as the decimal separator. JetStress works very reliably aside from this issue. You will have far less trouble with JetStress compared to the fun you will have with LoadGen.

Subsystem Throughput Test

If this is the first time you have used this kind of storage subsystem, we recommend starting with a subsystem throughput test. This test will provide you with a rough estimate of the achievable throughput. Afterward you can run a mailbox profile test to verify whether your specific mailbox profile can be handled by the subsystem with acceptable latency figures.

Letting JetStress automatically tune the number of threads is recommended for the first test run. For subsequent tests, you should disable automatic tuning and manually specify the thread count in Figure 10-8. This allows you to have comparable test conditions. Manually specifying the thread count is especially important if you run JetStress in parallel on multiple servers.

If you use automatic tuning, one system can still be in the tuning phase while other systems already execute the test. This would lead to inconsistent loads on the subsystem and the test results would be different for each test run.

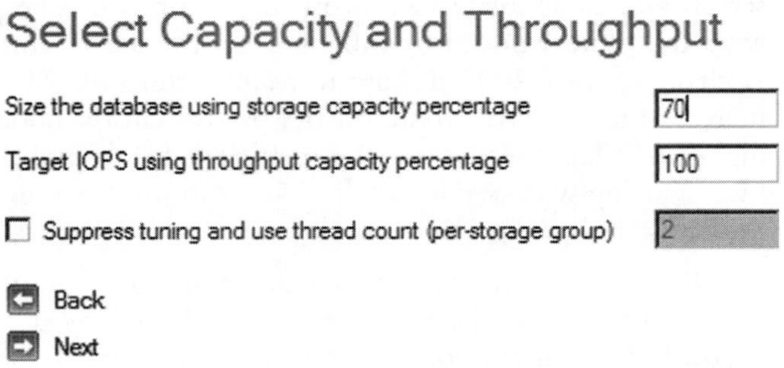

Figure 10-8
*Suppress tuning
and use thread
count*

Select Capacity and Throughput

Size the database using storage capacity percentage   [70]

Target IOPS using throughput capacity percentage   [100]

☐ Suppress tuning and use thread count (per-storage group)   [2]

⬅ Back

➡ Next

The section titled "Using Thread Count" in the online documentation provides a table that recommends thread numbers based on the expected log disk write I/O and disk transfer rate on the database volume. Note that when you increase the thread count, this increases the thread count per storage group. The change to the total workload for the server is significant different between a server with one storage group and a server with 20 storage groups.

The FAQ section of the online documentation notes that automatic tuning might fail if a single disk volume is used by multiple storage groups, or if you use a very high number of storage groups. In this case, you have to suppress tuning and specify a fixed thread count. Start with a low number and analyze the test results. If you are confident that the storage subsystem still has headroom, you can slowly increase the thread count. You can fine-tune the amount of I/O generated by JetStress with the parameter SluggishSessions in the XML configuration file. The default value for Exchange Server 2007 is 2. The value 0 would increase the load and generate an I/O pattern similar to the one used by JetStress 2004 with an Exchange Server 2003 *ESE.DLL*. The maximum value is 9; this would decrease the load (Figure 10-9).

The performance test simulates the transactions of the Exchange Store process during user load. Streaming backup simulates the workload that is generated by a backup application when it runs a streaming backup. There is no simulation available for a Volume Shadow Copy Services (VSS)–based backup. The Soft Recovery option measures the log replay rate that would occur after a database restore.

The Multihost test checkbox instructs JetStress to pause the test run after a performance or streaming backup test before it starts the process that validates the checksum of the databases. A popup window allows you to coordinate the parallel JetStress runs on multiple servers. This enables you to let a performance test run finish on Computer A before Computer B starts

Figure 10-9
Select test type

Select Test Type

⦿ Performance

○ Streaming backup

○ Soft recovery

☐ Multi-host test

◀ Back

▶ Next

its database checksum verification. The database checksum verification is very resource intensive and would affect the performance test result.

Figure 10-10 shows the step in the GUI where you define the number of storage groups hosted on the mailbox server, the number of databases per storage group, and the location of the database file and the directory used for transaction log files. JetStress determines how much RAM is installed in your server and only lets you create the number of storage groups that are supported with this memory configuration. The Microsoft TechNet section, "Planning Memory Configurations," provides a table that specifies the

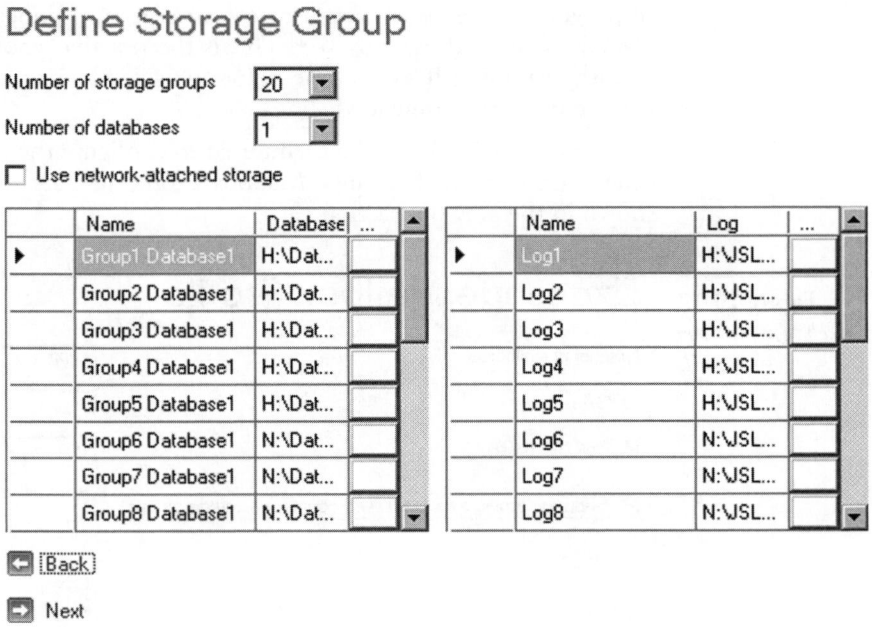

Figure 10-10
Define storage group

Define Storage Group

Number of storage groups   20 ▾

Number of databases   1 ▾

☐ Use network-attached storage

	Name	Database	...				Name	Log	...	
▶	Group1 Database1	H:\Dat...				▶	Log1	H:\JSL...		
	Group2 Database1	H:\Dat...					Log2	H:\JSL...		
	Group3 Database1	H:\Dat...					Log3	H:\JSL...		
	Group4 Database1	H:\Dat...					Log4	H:\JSL...		
	Group5 Database1	H:\Dat...					Log5	H:\JSL...		
	Group6 Database1	N:\Dat...					Log6	N:\JSL...		
	Group7 Database1	N:\Dat...					Log7	N:\JSL...		
	Group8 Database1	N:\Dat...					Log8	N:\JSL...		

◀ Back

▶ Next

minimum memory required based on the number of storage groups. You have to meet this requirement to get support from Microsoft.

For the first test run, JetStress has to create and initialize a new database. You should take advantage of the possibility to create a backup of the new database before it is used for the first test run. This allows you to restore the database later and skip the initialization phase, which saves you significant time (Figure 10-11).

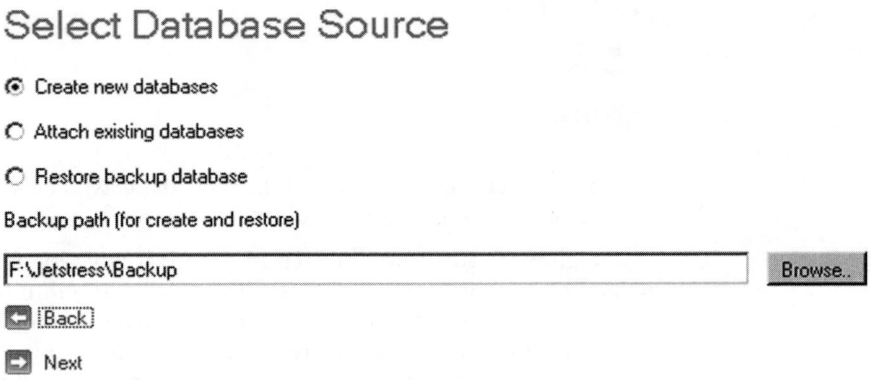

Figure 10-11
Select database source

Select Database Source

⦿ Create new databases

○ Attach existing databases

○ Restore backup database

Backup path (for create and restore)

| F:\Jetstress\Backup | Browse.. |

⬅ Back

➡ Next

Mailbox Profile Test

You can verify with the mailbox profile test if the subsystem is likely able to provide the necessary performance for a given number of users, assumed *IOPS/mailbox* and mailbox size. This is the test that you will run most frequently. Running it every time before you add a new mailbox server into production is recommended.

Figure 10-12 shows the menu used to configure the mailbox profile; the other menus of an Exchange Mailbox Profile test are identical to the one shown in the previous section.

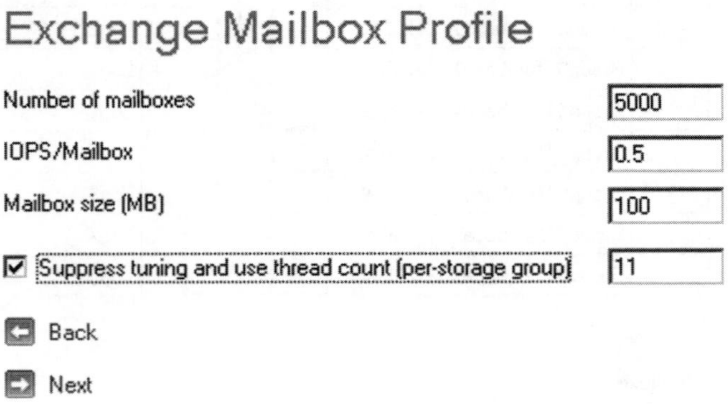

Figure 10-12
Exchange mailbox profile

Exchange Mailbox Profile

Number of mailboxes	5000
IOPS/Mailbox	0.5
Mailbox size (MB)	100
☑ Suppress tuning and use thread count (per-storage group)	11

⬅ Back

➡ Next

Test Result

During the test run, performance counters are collected in a *BLG* file. This file is analyzed at the end of the test and the result is presented as an *HTML/XML* file. Use the metrics described in Chapter 11 to interpret the summary report and judge if the measured performance fulfills your requirements.

Figure 10-13 shows the summary section of a test report from a mailbox profile test. The overall test result is pass or fail. You are encouraged to read the remaining sections of the report because they provide very helpful information.

Figure 10-13
Performance test result report—summary

Microsoft Exchange Server Jetstress

Performance Test Result Report

Test Summary

Overall Test Result	Pass
Machine Name	G1W1506C
Test Description	
Test Start Time	8/26/2007 6:21:08 PM
Test End Time	8/26/2007 9:27:13 PM
Jetstress Version	08.01.0177.000
Ese Version	08.00.0685.024
Operating System	Microsoft Windows Server 2003 Service Pack 1 (5.2.3790.65536)
Performance Log	F:\Jetstress\Results\Performance_2007_8_26_19_22_45.blg
	F:\Jetstress\Results\DBChecksum_2007_8_26_21_27_13.blg

Figure 10-14 shows the achieved I/O per second result and the target I/O per second figure. In this test, the achieved value was far above the required performance. The reason for this uncommon result was that we had to verify performance of a CCR system connected to a HP StorageWorks XP array. In the production deployment, the Exchange server would use a shared storage infrastructure, and during this first run in the test environment, the Exchange server was the only system connected to the storage array. Of course, this was not the most useful test to estimate performance in a production environment.

Figure 10-14
Database sizing and throughput

Database Sizing and Throughput

Achieved I/O per Second	10151.62
Target I/O per Second	2500
Initial database size	524335513600
Final database size	619579768832
Database files (count)	20

Figure 10-15 shows the system parameters used during the test. The JetStress command line tool would allow you to adjust the operations mix, such as increasing the proportion of read operations. Typically, we use the default values. The thread count is interesting if you want to compare results of two tests.

Figure 10-15
System parameters

┌─ Jetstress System Parameters ──────────────────────┐
Thread count	11 (per-storage group)
Log buffers	9000
Minimum database cache	640.0 MB
Maximum database cache	5120.0 MB
Insert operations	25%
Delete operations	10%
Replace operations	50%
Read operations	15%
Lazy commits	80%

Figure 10-16 is the most interesting part of the report; it shows the read-and-write latency during the test. This is the information you need to evaluate for deciding whether the storage subsystem can handle the transactional workload in an acceptable way. The subsystem should be able to achieve log writes at less than 10 milliseconds of latency and database read and writes at less than 20 milliseconds. Unfortunately, Microsoft has not yet published a performance troubleshooting whitepaper for Exchange Server 2007 similar to that for Exchange Server 2003. The above figures are provided in the Storage Validation section on Microsoft TechNet. In addition, see the blog article, "JetStress: Disk Sub-system Thresholds," published by the Microsoft Exchange Pre-Development Testing team.

Figure 10-16
Disk subsystem performance

Disk Subsystem Performance

LogicalDisk	Avg. Disk sec/Read	Avg. Disk sec/Write	Disk Reads/sec	Disk Writes/sec	Avg. Disk Bytes/Write
Database (H:\Data)	0.012	0.019	1304.542	1233.521	(n/a)
Database (N:\Data)	0.010	0.011	1302.863	1236.135	(n/a)
Database (O:\Data)	0.009	0.010	1300.220	1235.413	(n/a)
Database (R:\Data)	0.010	0.010	1303.312	1235.614	(n/a)
Log (H:)	0.000	0.001	0.000	725.310	12121.242
Log (N:)	0.000	0.001	0.000	734.579	11939.787
Log (O:)	0.000	0.001	0.000	733.369	11925.400
Log (R:)	0.000	0.001	0.000	737.037	11898.836

Figure 10-17 shows additional performance counters measured during the test run. The section titled, "Reading the Test Reports," in the JetStress online manual provides thresholds for these counters. Most of the thresholds provided in the online manual are only applicable for Exchange Server 2003 running on 32-bit Windows Server 2003; they cannot be used for Exchange Server 2007 on 64-bit Windows.

Figure 10-17

Host system performance

Host System Performance			
Counter	Average	Minimum	Maximum
% Processor Time	22.196	18.243	25.142
Available MBytes	8876.812	8866.000	9319.000
Free System Page Table Entries	16751789.376	16751755.000	16751790.000
Transition Pages RePurposed/sec	0.000	0.000	0.000
Pool Nonpaged Bytes	145758109.662	145588224.000	145997824.000
Pool Paged Bytes	195689444.209	195125248.000	196796416.000
Database Page Fault Stalls/sec	0.177	0.000	41.716

Figure 10-18 shows the report of a streaming backup test. This test verifies how fast Exchange databases can be read by a backup program using the streaming API. This allows you to estimate how long your backup will run. In Exchange Server 2003 deployments, you often had four storage groups, and backing up two storage groups in parallel was a common practice. The test in Figure 10-18 simulated this for an Exchange Server 2007 deployment. The total throughput was about 208 Mbytes/second. Let's assume that you have a mailbox server with 50 storage groups. How is the total throughput increasing if you run more than two backup jobs in parallel? What is the optimal number of backup jobs that you should run in parallel?

Figure 10-18

Streaming backup test result report

Streaming backup Test Result Report

Streaming Backup Statistics – All			
Database Instance	Database Size (MBytes)	Elapsed Backup Time	MBytes Transferred/sec
Instance4272.1	15630.27	00:02:29	104.71
Instance4272.2	15630.27	00:02:30	104.02

Figure 10-19 shows the test result with eight parallel backup streams. You can see that the total throughput is about 460 Mbytes/second. This test used four times the number of backup streams but the total throughput was not four times as high. This small example explains how you can use JetStress to assess the achievable backup throughput of your storage array, and how you can determine the optimal number of parallel backup jobs.

Figure 10-19

Eight parallel backup streams

Streaming backup Test Result Report

Streaming Backup Statistics – All			
Database Instance	Database Size (MBytes)	Elapsed Backup Time	MBytes Transferred/sec
Instance5252.1	16436.27	00:05:29	49.84
Instance5252.2	16020.27	00:04:45	56.21
Instance5252.3	15630.27	00:04:31	57.62
Instance5252.4	15630.27	00:04:30	57.89
Instance5252.5	15630.27	00:04:22	59.60
Instance5252.6	15630.27	00:04:22	59.48
Instance5252.7	15630.27	00:04:34	57.04
Instance5252.8	15630.27	00:04:21	59.71

However, please do not forget to assess the complete chain of devices that are involved in a backup. Do not forget the transfer speed from the Exchange server to the backup device and the speed of this target device.

Figure 10-20 is a soft recovery report from a test lab. The soft recovery test allows you to estimate the required time to replay transaction log files during a recovery. You can see that the replay performance of Exchange Server 2007 is far better than the performance of previous Exchange versions. The result in Figure 10-20 is 59.75/501 = 0.12 seconds per (1 MB) log file. Note that the log file replay speed it not directly linear, and that this figure is specific to this test environment. If you do not have a large storage array assigned to a single Exchange server, performance will be different.

Figure 10-20
Soft recovery test
result report

SoftRecovery Test Result Report

┌─Soft-Recovery Statistics – All─────────────────────┐

Database Instance	Log files replayed	Elapsed seconds
Instance3840.1	501	59.7507648

In an early Exchange Server 2003 project, we measured a replay time of about 7 seconds per (5 MB) log file. For the Recovery Time Objective (RTO), knowing how long log file replay will take is important. In this project, we were able to restore the database file from tape to disk in 30 minutes, but log file replay took far too long to be able to meet the 2-hour RTO requested by the customer.

Miscellaneous

By default, JetStress generates the same workload on all storage groups. The FAQ section in the JetStress online manual describes how you can configure various I/O characteristics for individual storage groups.

If you already had Exchange Server 2007 installed on the system before you installed JetStress, uninstalling JetStress may break the Exchange Server 2007 database performance counters. In this case, you have to unload the database performance counter and load them again. The related commands are *UNLODCTR.EXE ESE* and *LODCTR ESEPERF.INI*. Additional information about this issue is available in the troubleshooting section of the JetStress manual.

Microsoft Exchange Load Generator

With the release of Exchange Server 2007, Microsoft Load Simulator (LoadSim) was replaced by Microsoft Exchange Load Generator (LoadGen).

LoadSim was used to perform benchmark tests. LoadSim was the main tool that hardware vendors used to demonstrate the scalability of their servers. The goal was to simulate the largest number of users per server. Microsoft published the scores achieved by vendors on its Exchange Server 2003 benchmark performance website. This allowed customers to compare performance of the hardware offered by various vendors.

The benchmark tests were based on the MAPI Messaging Benchmark 3 (MMB3) standard. MMB3 describes the content of the inbox of the simulated users and the actions that the users perform during the test. For example, the actions include opening received emails or sending new emails using Microsoft Office Outlook 2003. LoadSim measured the latency of the Exchange Server responses to the client actions and calculated a score based on this information.

In November 2007, Microsoft announced that the MAPI messaging benchmark was being retired. The reason for this decision was that Exchange customers are more interested in comparing the complete messaging and collaboration solution of vendors than comparing performance scores for a single server. There is already a program available that is more focused on describing a solution than providing benchmark scores—the ESRP. As mentioned in the previous section, ESRP uses JetStress to test the storage subsystem. Although MAPI messaging benchmarks are being retired, Microsoft will continue to provide testing tools like JetStress and LoadGen to allow partners and customers to perform benchmark and scalability analyses.

During benchmark tests, only regular activities are simulated. You can combine these regular activities with real-world situations. Instead of testing only whether the environment can sustain the load of 5000 users sending and receiving emails, you can run in parallel a restore of a storage group and check whether performance is still acceptable, or you can use LoadGen to send emails containing the EICAR test virus pattern and verify how your environment reacts on this simulated virus outbreak.

LoadGen was redeveloped from scratch to address certain deficiencies of LoadSim. The initial version of LoadGen provided the same features that LoadSim had, and added several new features. For example, the new features are support for Microsoft Office 2007, cached Exchange mode profiles, or the possibility of installing the tool on the 64-bit version of Windows Server 2003.

The first release of LoadGen was limited to simulating users that use the MAPI protocol and RPC over HTTP to access their mailbox. The second release merged functionality of the Exchange Server Stress and Performance Tool (ESP) into LoadGen. Now you can use LoadGen to simulate Outlook Web Access (OWA), Post Office Protocol 3 (POP3), and Internet Message Access Protocol (IMAP), in addition to MAPI. Previously you had to use ESP to simulate clients using Internet protocols and LoadGen to simulate

MAPI clients. The possibility of using a single tool reduces your total effort dedicated to running load tests. You only have to learn a single tool.

The following sections assume that you already have read the LoadGen online documentation. Our objective is to provide a fast start in using LoadGen. We provide information that was difficult to locate and summarize our experience with the tool.

Important Note

The online documentation contains the following warning message:

Exchange Load Generator should be used only in test environments that have no connection to the production environment. This tool should not be used in a production environment, an environment that is mission critical, or one that contains important information of any kind anywhere in the network.

Exchange Load Generator uses many simulated user mailboxes to create the server workload. Because mailboxes must be part of a domain user's account, the Exchange Load Generator tool therefore creates many domain user accounts to support these user mailboxes. By design, Exchange Load Generator requires that the password associated with these domain accounts be the same. Because this most likely does not comply with your organization's security requirements, to lessen any risk this could present, we recommend that this tool be used only on isolated test networks that do not have connectivity to your production network.

Because load simulation works by using system resources, Exchange Load Generator is unsuitable for use on production networks because it could interfere with production operations by competing for those resources.

The End User License Agreement (EULA) contains this statement:

You may not test the software in a live operating environment unless Microsoft permits you to do so under another agreement.

This clause in the EULA forbids the usage of LoadGen in a production environment.

The Big Picture

Figure 10-21 shows the architecture of a LoadGen test environment. As seen here, you need a complete Exchange environment with all Exchange server roles, addition to the Unified Messaging (UM) role and the Edge role. Additionally, you need servers that provide all infrastructure services that Exchange depends on such as an AD domain controller. The test environment

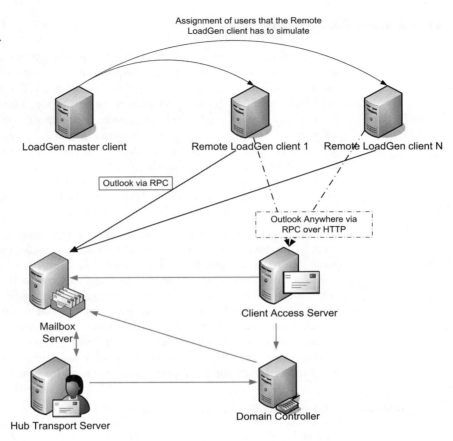

Figure 10-21
Big picture of a LoadGen *environment*

has no connection to the Internet because you do not want to send test messages to external recipients.

You do not need a full replica of your production environment to validate your Exchange design. If you designed a large-scale environment for 100,000 mailboxes, you do not need a test environment with the same number of mailbox servers. It is sufficient to have a representative test unit—for example, one mailbox cluster, two HT servers, and two servers with the Client Access Server (CAS) role. You should have some type of building block architecture under which you would add a block to your environment if you have to scale the environment. You only need the components of one building block to validate the design. The feasibility of this building block approach also depends on the kind of storage array you use at the back-end. For example, if you host Exchange data on one large storage array, it is more difficult to test a single brick of your solution.

Hardware Requirements

The minimum and recommended hardware configurations for a LoadGen client are available in the "System Requirements" section of the online documentation. Microsoft estimates that a client with 2 GB RAM and a current CPU can simulate up to 2000 users in online mode. The actual number of users that a single LoadGen client can simulate depends on the action profile of your test. If you simulate a heavy user profile, the number of users per client is reduced. Simulating an Outlook cache mode profile places higher demands on the amount of RAM installed in the LoadGen client compared with an online mode profile. Microsoft estimates in the online documentation that a single processor client with only 1 GB RAM can simulate approximately 1200 to 1500 Outlook Anywhere users.

If you want to simulate more users than a single client can handle, you need multiple remote load clients and an additional master client that distributes the workload to the remote client. The remote LoadGen clients are the clients that simulate user activity and thereby generate load toward the Exchange server. The master client should not simulate any user. The LoadGen master client is not used to verify whether the LoadGen clients are able to simulate the required number of users. You have to collect performance counters and manually verify whether the clients were overloaded. The following section explains how you can perform this verification. Table 10-2 provides example configurations that you can use to estimate the number of clients you need for your specific workload.

Table 10-2   *Example LoadGen hardware configurations*

Number of simulated users and user profiles	CPU	RAM
1500 users, various profiles including the heavy user profile	2 × 32-bit	2 GB and 4 GB RAM
5000 users, heavy user profile in online and cached mode	Four-way, 64-bit AMD and Intel	8 GB RAM

Network Requirements

The LoadGen client and the Exchange servers must be members of the same AD domain. Don't install the software on a standalone system that is part of a workgroup or is a member of a different AD forest.

LoadGen needs access to the Information Stored in AD. Therefore, it needs a network connection to an AD domain controller. It has to be a Global Catalog server. If you want to use LoadGen to create the user accounts and mailboxes for the test run, LoadGen must have a direct connection to the Exchange server.

You can configure LoadGen to connect to a network load balancer or a firewall such as an Internet Security and Acceleration (ISA) Server 2006 and not directly to the Exchange servers. This allows you to simulate users accessing an Exchange environment from the Internet without direct access to the back-end infrastructure. In this case, LoadGen does not require a direct connection to the servers with the Exchange server roles installed, but it still requires a direct connection to the AD. In this setup, you instruct LoadGen to use preexisting user accounts. These accounts can be created by a custom script. Another approach is to use one LoadGen client installed on the Exchange back-end network segment to create the mailboxes.

Software Requirements

You can install LoadGen on Windows XP, Windows Vista, Windows Server 2003, and Windows Server 2008. It is preferable to use a server operating system because of the support for multiple remote logins. You can use the x86 or x64 version of the operating system. A LoadGen client running the x64 operating system version is able to simulate more users because of the larger memory address space. On LoadGen clients running the x86 operating system version, you should use the */3 GB* switch to increase the user address space.

Disabling the firewall on the LoadGen clients helps to prevent issues with blocked ports that are used by the LoadGen master and the remote LoadGen client to communicate with each other.

You have to install the Exchange Server 2007 management tools and all its prerequisites before you install LoadGen. If you use the x86 version of the operating system, you have to install the 32-bit version of the Exchange management tools.

Environment Preparation

The Exchange environment must be installed and configured before you start using LoadGen. The mailbox databases that host the simulated mailboxes must exist before you start. Running the Exchange Best Practice Analyzer (ExBPA) before you start testing with LoadGen is highly recommended. Otherwise, you will waste hours in troubleshooting MAPI exceptions generated by the LoadGen clients, and in the end discover that a configuration error on an Exchange server was the root cause.

You should explicitly verify that all your servers have disabled the Windows Server 2003 Scalable Network pack. We recently wasted several days troubleshooting strange effects and it turned out that one server with the CAS role was not installed with our unattended installation script that disables this well-known troublemaker. The test environment had nearly 30 servers and a single server without the Scalable Network pack disabled was the root cause of our problems.

Installation

The installation of LoadGen is not difficult; it uses the standard Microsoft Windows installation wizard.

If you use a beta build of LoadGen received from the Microsoft LoadGen developers, it is likely that the Microsoft Installer Package (MSI) is not digitally signed and the installation will fail. You have to configure the *.NET* framework to skip strong name signature verification before you install the LoadGen MSI package. This can be achieved with the command *SN.EXE -Vr **. For information on the strong name tool (SN), see the Microsoft Developer Network article, "CLR Inside Out: Using Strong Name Signatures." *SN. EXE* is contained in the *.NET* framework Software Development Kit (SDK). Installing the SDK on every LoadGen client is not necessary; copying SN.EXE to each client is sufficient. However, you will only need this procedure if you work for a Microsoft partner company. The official LoadGen builds have a digital signature, and beta builds are not externally available.

You can use the defaults provided by the LoadGen installation wizard. Afterward you have a program with a GUI called *LOADGENWIN.EXE* and a command line tool *LOADGENCMD.EXE* in the directory *C:\Program Files\Exchange Load Generator*. This directory also contains several dynamic link libraries (DLLs), and it is the default directory for the LoadGen configuration file and any generated log files. Under this directory is the *Messages* directory, which contains the sample messages used by the tests with a MAPI profile, and the *Scripts* directory, which contains files used by tests with an Internet protocol, such as OWA or SMTP.

The installation adds the following performance counter objects to the system:

- Exchange Load Generator Engine
- Exchange Load Generator User
- Exchange Load Generator IMAP4
- Exchange Load Generator POP3
- Exchange Load Generator OWA
- Exchange Load Generator SMTP

These objects are used to monitor the LoadGen clients.

A LoadGen client has a different networking behavior compared to a standard client in that it will rapidly open and close new socket connections to the Exchange servers. The LoadGen installation program makes registry changes to adjust the TCP stack to enable this behavior. Therefore, you have to reboot the client after the installation. Note that uninstalling LoadGen does not revert these registry changes to the values before the installation.

You have to manually enable the extended ESE Performance Counters on the mailbox server. The required registry change is described in Microsoft Knowledge Base Article 556030:

```
HKLM\SYSTEM\CurrentControlSet\Services\ESE\Performance

DWORD Show Advanced Counters = 1
```

Configuration

LoadGen uses an XML file to store its configuration settings. The configuration file specifies every aspect of a test with the Outlook task module, such as the following:

- AD Organizational Unit (OU) with the test user accounts/test mailboxes
- How long the test will run, or to use LoadGen terminology, the length of the simulation day and duration of the simulation
- Which tasks are executed during the test, such as reading emails, browsing the calendar, or downloading the offline address book (OAB)
- The *MailboxStoreProfile* and the *PublicStoreProfile* defines how the inbox of the test users and the public folder will be initialized before the actual test run starts.

By default, the file is called *<LoadGenInstallationFolder>\LoadGenConFig. xml*. You can create this file using the command *LOADGENCMD.EXE /G* or *LOADGENWIN.EXE*. Creating the file with the GUI has the advantage that the menus allow you to specify the configuration settings without the need to understand all the parameters in the XML file. However, certain settings can only be made by using an editor to change the corresponding parameter, as not all parameters are exposed in the GUI. Using an editor that understands XML simplifies editing the LoadGen configuration file. For example, you can use Microsoft XML Notepad 2007.

The following sections describe how to create a LoadGen configuration file using *LOADGENWIN.EXE*.

Test Topology in Active Directory

LoadGen needs user accounts in AD for the mailboxes that it uses during the test. *LOADGENWIN.EXE* can be used to create these objects in AD or you can point it to an OU with existing test users. *LOADGENCMD.EXE* cannot create objects in AD; you have to point it to existing objects. If you use LoadGen to create these objects in AD, LoadGen will create the top-level container *OU=LoadGen Objects, DC=<domain>*. All LoadGen-created objects are located under this OU. The LoadGen configuration file contains two parameters to restrict users selected for the test: *LdapSearchFilter* and *LdapBaseDn*. By default, *LdapSearchFilter* will pick all user objects beneath *LdapBaseDN*, and *LdapBaseDn* points to *OU=LoadGen Objects, DC=<domain>*.

You can overwrite these parameters and specify a custom AD container. This is very handy if you have to run the test in an environment where you are not allowed to create additional top-level OUs and you have to create your test AD objects in a different AD container. In this case, you can use a custom script to create the user accounts and mailboxes, and direct LoadGen to this AD container when it searches for test user accounts.

If you use LoadGen in a root/child environment and want to create the LoadGen AD objects in the child, you have to run LoadGen with a user of the child AD domain.

In Figure 10-22, you define the length of the simulation day. LoadGen will divide this value by the number of tasks that a user performs per day. This determines the rate at which LoadGen dispatches a new task for the user. By default this is 8 hours. If you reduce this value, you increase the load on the Exchange server. The length of the simulation specifies how long a test will run. If you select stress mode, LoadGen will try to execute the tasks as fast as it can and ignores the deterministic distribution of the tasks over the simulated workday. You use stress mode only when you want to put the Exchange server under high load and do not want to simulate a specific user behavior.

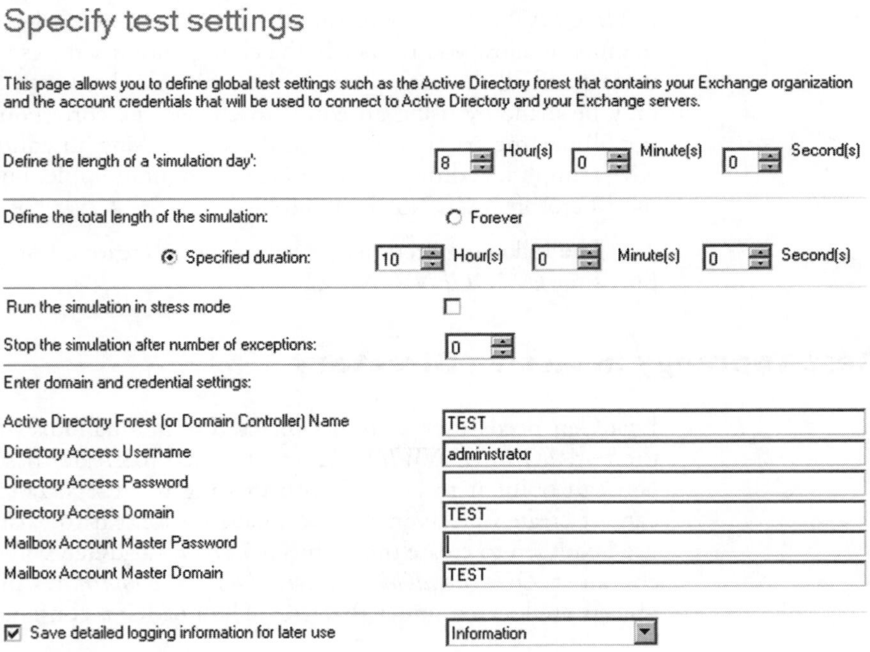

Figure 10-22
Specify test settings

Specify test settings

This page allows you to define global test settings such as the Active Directory forest that contains your Exchange organization and the account credentials that will be used to connect to Active Directory and your Exchange servers.

Define the length of a 'simulation day':   [8]   Hour(s) [0]   Minute(s) [0]   Second(s)

Define the total length of the simulation: ○ Forever

                                    ⦿ Specified duration: [10]   Hour(s) [0]   Minute(s) [0]   Second(s)

Run the simulation in stress mode   □

Stop the simulation after number of exceptions: [0]

Enter domain and credential settings:

Active Directory Forest (or Domain Controller) Name | TEST |
Directory Access Username | administrator |
Directory Access Password | |
Directory Access Domain | TEST |
Mailbox Account Master Password | |
Mailbox Account Master Domain | TEST |

☑ Save detailed logging information for later use | Information ▼ |

By default, LoadGen will continue even if an exception has been raised—for example, because the LoadGen client cannot connect to the Exchange server and a MAPI protocol error occurs. For official performance tests it is not acceptable that exceptions have occurred during the test. This is the reason why you should set this variable to 1, and instruct LoadGen thereby to stop the test after the first exception.

If you use LoadGen to create the test user accounts, you must have the required permission to create objects in AD and create new mailboxes. Note that all test users will have the same password. The password must meet the complexity requirements of the security policy defined in the AD domain Group Policy Object.

Figure 10-23 shows that LoadGen stores the password of the test users in clear text format in the LoadGen configuration file. In addition, it writes the username and password of the user account that you specify as a directory access account in clear text format to this file. (It would be nice if Microsoft would store the password in encrypted format and not in clear text.)

Figure 10-23
Clear text password

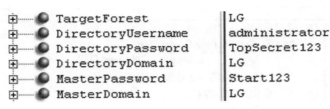

TargetForest	LG	
DirectoryUsername	administrator	
DirectoryPassword	TopSecret123	
DirectoryDomain	LG	
MasterPassword	Start123	
MasterDomain	LG	

Microsoft recommends using the enterprise administrator account to run LoadGen. You can try the following procedure to use an account with fewer privileges to run LoadGen.

- A full administrator creates the LoadGen topology and saves the LoadGen configuration XML file.

- The full administrator changes the directory access user account name and password, which is visible in clear text in the XML file, to random strings.

- The full administrator uses the AD Users and Computers MMC and selects the security tab on the LoadGen Objects OU; select Advanced view; add the regular user account; select Full Control; and Apply to "This object and all child objects."

- The regular user uses LoadGen to open the configuration XML file and specifies his user name and password as directory access credentials. Now it should be possible for the regular user to use the pre-populated topology to run LoadGen tests.

- If the topology in AD has to be modified, repeating the above steps is required. The regular user should still be a local administrator on the LoadGen clients and an Exchange administrator.

In the recipient management step, Figure 10-24, you can enter the number of test mailboxes this database should have. If mailboxes already exist in a database, LoadGen shows the corresponding number; if there are no mailboxes in the database, LoadGen displays 0. If you add mailboxes to a database, *LOADGENWIN.EXE* will create the corresponding AD user account and mailbox. LoadGen uses PowerShell for this process.

Figure 10-24
User settings

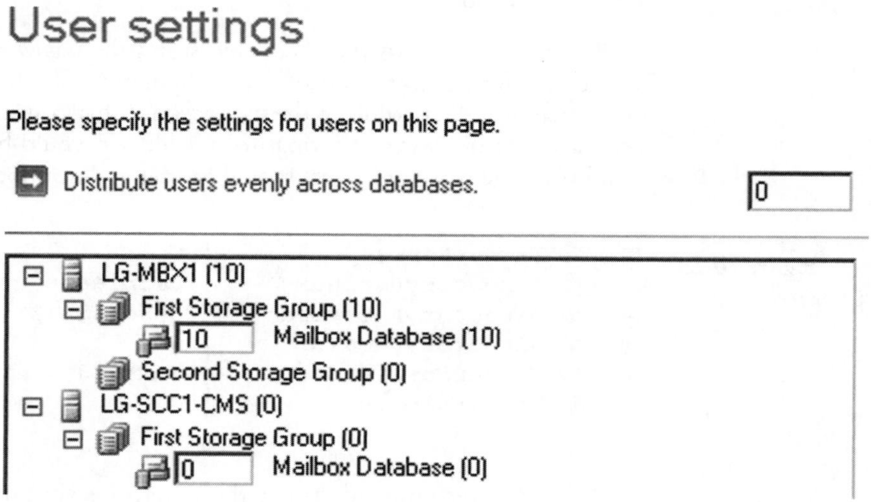

User settings

Please specify the settings for users on this page.

➡️ Distribute users evenly across databases.   [0]

```
⊟ 📋 LG-MBX1 (10)
    ⊟ 📁 First Storage Group (10)
        📑[10]      Mailbox Database (10)
      📁 Second Storage Group (0)
⊟ 📋 LG-SCC1-CMS (0)
    ⊟ 📁 First Storage Group (0)
        📑[0]       Mailbox Database (0)
```

In the following step found in the wizard, called Advanced Recipient Settings, you can specify whether the test will send emails to distribution lists, contacts, and external SMTP recipient domains. If you skip this step and do not include Distribution Lists (DLs) and external recipients, then the configuration is easier. However, you can give it a try and perform two runs, including one without DLs and the next with DLs. Then you can compare the test results and analyze the differences.

User Groups

The users that you are going to simulate have to be organized in user groups. All users in one group use the same client type and the same action profile. You can create multiple groups in one LoadGen configuration file. However, you usually have only one user group.

The meaning of the client type in Figure 10-25 is easy to understand. The action profile pull-down menu determines the *ActionProfile* and the

MailboxStoreProfile section in the XML configuration file. The *ActionProfile* defines how many times certain tasks are executed per user during the simulated workday, such as sending new emails or processing emails in the inbox of the user. The *MailboxStoreProfile* specifies the content of the user's inbox after the database initialization phase. With the Edit button, you can instruct LoadGen to search for test users under a custom AD container instead of the default LoadGen objects top-level container.

Figure 10-25
Specify test user group

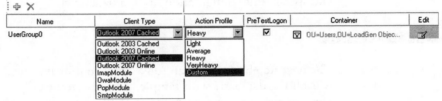

Specify test user groups

Configure one or more groups of users who will be simulated in this test.

Name	Client Type	Action Profile	PreTestLogon	Container	Edit
UserGroup0	Outlook 2007 Cached	Heavy	☑	OU=Users,OU=LoadGen Objec...	

Outlook 2003 Cached
Outlook 2003 Online
Outlook 2007 Cached
Outlook 2007 Online
ImapModule
OwaModule
PopModule
SmtpModule

Light
Average
Heavy
VeryHeavy
Custom

Remote Load Generators

In this step, you define whether the load will be generated by a single client or multiple clients. Figure 10-26 shows a configuration where the LoadGen master client uses the clients *LoadGen2* and *LoadGen3* to generate the load. The master client *LoadGen1* does not simulate any users; it only controls the other clients.

Figure 10-26
Remote load generators

Remote configurations

Configure one or more remote load generators if you want to enable the task engine to distribute the load to remote load generators.

☑ Enable the task engine to distribute the load to remote load generators

☐ Enable load balancing on remote load generators

Remote logging level   Warning

Remote Load Generators

LoadGen2
LoadGen3

If you do not enable load balancing, LoadGen will evenly distribute the number of users to the clients, and it will not adjust the number of simulated users per client during the test. If you enable load balancing, the master client will monitor the load clients and adjust the number of simulated users per clients. There is no guarantee that load balancing is working reliably. A fixed number of users per client is a less complex configuration, and therefore is the recommended setup. If you use load balancing, troubleshooting is significantly more difficult. Do not enable load balancing if you use a client type with a scripted module.

Configuration Summary

The last step of the test preparation shows the summary of the configuration settings. Now you should save the configuration as an XML file. You can either run a test with *LOADGENWIN.EXE* using this configuration file, or you can use the command-line tool *LOADGENCMD.EXE* to run the test and specify this configuration file as a parameter.

Database Init

The next step before you can run a test is to initialize the databases. LoadGen will fill the databases with sample messages. You can find these sample messages in the subdirectory *Messages* of the LoadGen program directory. You always have to initialize the databases independently of simulating a MAPI client or a client with an Internet protocol such as IMAP4.

The initialization can be done with *LOADGENWIN.EXE* or *LOADGENCMD.EXE*. The LoadGen GUI initializes the mailbox databases and the public folder databases. This comprises a single step in the GUI. The command line version allows you to initialize the private and the public Information Store separately. *LOADGENCMD.EXE /i* initializes the private store and *LOADGENCMD.EXE /p* initializes the public folder store.

Depending on the number of mailboxes and the size of the mailboxes, database initialization can take many hours. Initialization may run 24 to 48 hours if you host several thousand gigabyte mailboxes on a mailbox server. You can reduce the necessary time for a database initialization by running the database initialization directly on the mailbox server. For this approach, you have to install LoadGen on the Exchange mailbox server. This eliminates a possible network bottleneck between the LoadGen client and the Exchange mailbox server.

You can monitor the progress of the database initialization using the following performance counters:

- Exchange Load Generator Engine (_Total)\Task Queue Length
- Exchange Load Generator Engine (_Total)\Tasks Completed
- Exchange Load Generator Engine (_Total)\Tasks Dispatched

Tasks Dispatched is equal to the number of users that you are going to simulate. Tasks Completed is the number of mailboxes that have been initialized.

This counter is initially 0 and increases to the value of Tasks Dispatched. Task Queue Length specifies the tasks that have to be completed. If the initialization phase is finished, the value is 0.

Note that during database initialization, there is only a single task dispatched per user. During a LoadGen test run, the number of dispatched tasks per user is determined by the action profile assigned to the user.

By default, the database files and the corresponding transaction log files will consume the same disk capacity. Usually this is a problem because creating a log file volume with the same capacity that you reserve for the database volume is not a common configuration. You can solve this issue by enabling circular logging during the database initialization phase and disabling circular logging before you start the test run.

Deleting the database after each test run and re-creating a fresh database for the next test are common practices. Your first option to reduce the necessary time is to create a backup of the database after the initialization and restore this backup after each test. Another possibility is to run a database initialization on top of the used database. This reinitialization is very fast compared to creating a new database from scratch. LoadGen will reinitialization the mail environment to a prerun state by deleting additional items in the inbox and calendar. There has been concern that this database would be very fragmented, but such database is a better representative of a real-world database compared to a pristine database created by the first LoadGen database initialization.

Public folders

LoadGen creates two top-level public folders during the database initialization phase:

Folder <LongArbitraryHexadecimalNumber>

Swordfish PublicFolder

During the test run, LoadGen posts messages to these folders. The user who runs LoadGen must have the required permission to create top-level public folders.

The usage of public folders can be an issue if you run LoadGen in an existing environment. Usually there is only a well-defined set of top-level public folders, and the creation of top-level folders is restricted to a small group of administrators. If the user that runs LoadGen does not have the permission to create top-level public folders, the public folder initialization will fail. We also encountered the following issue: LoadGen tried to post messages in public folders that LoadGen did not create. These were preexisting top-level public folders. The user account that executed LoadGen did not have the necessary permission and the task failed. LoadGen posting messages only to folders that LoadGen created would be preferable.

If you do not want to populate the public folder store with messages, you have to modify the *<PublicStoreProfile>* section in the LoadGen configuration file. You cannot delete all message files in this section because LoadGen will complain. You have to set the **count* and **depth* parameters to 0.

Full Text Indexing

Exchange Server 2007, by default, creates a full text index of the databases. This process has a high CPU demand and is also very time consuming. The indexing service is the *MSFTEFD* process. You can verify whether the index creation is finished by monitoring performance counter, "MSExchange Search Indices/Document Indexing Rate."

The time to create the full text index has to be considered in the test schedule. The following figures are from previous tests. The LoadGen database was initialized with indexing off—indexing was started afterward.

5000 × 1 GB: 2.5 days + 7 days indexing

20 000 × 0.9 GB (on four servers): 4 days + 10 days indexing

One option to reduce the necessary time for index creation is to disable the search service and delete existing search catalog files before you begin the database initialization. After the database initialization, you have to start the PowerShell command *ResetSearchIndex -All -Force*. This crawl mode is faster than the regular indexing mode.

Note that in a test with an online profile, searches take place on the Exchange server, and in a cached Exchange mode profile, the client tries to search in its locally stored Offline Store (OST) file. In cached Exchange mode profiles, the client does not take advantage of the index created on the Exchange mailbox server.

LoadGen does not create OST files for the simulated users. It is not feasible to create OST files on the LoadGen client for the thousands of users this client is simulating. LoadGen simulates the OST files in memory; however, it does not cache the complete OST file for all simulated users in memory. This is not feasible. LoadGen skips the actual search in the OST.

Currently, the majority of the clients will use Outlook running in cached Exchange mode. Therefore, you can consider saving time by disabling the search indexer on the Exchange mailbox server. If you decide not to create a full text index, you should verify whether the Smart Folder and Rules activity in the LoadGen action profile for simulations of Outlook online mode are disabled. Otherwise, you will have significantly higher CPU load on the Exchange server. One of our customers tested approximately 10,000 mailboxes with nearly 1 GB mailbox size on one mailbox server with CCR. We had to disable content indexing because of time constraints. At the time we ran the test with the Outlook online mode, we were not aware of the tip to disable the Smart Folders and Rules activity. The CPU load was by far too high.

In a production environment, index files with a size of about 5 to 10% of the database size are common. The index that is created for the LoadGen initialized databases can be about 20 to 30% of the database size. This must be considered when you plan the disk volume size that your mailbox server needs for the test.

Test Run

We highly recommend verifying whether the Exchange environment is working before you start your first test.

You should use a regular client and verify whether you can use Outlook and OWA to manually send and receive emails. If you intend to run POP3 or IMAP4, set up a corresponding profile and verify that everything is working as expected. If you get errors with this manual test, LoadGen will fail as well. For example, if your IMAP4 client complains about certificates, LoadGen will have the same problems. You have to import the certificate of the CAS into the certificate store of the computer account on all LoadGen clients if you use Internet protocols. Importing the certificate into the store of the computer account is required because the LoadGen service on the remote client runs in the context of the Local System account and not in the context of your user account.

Additionally, you should use the ExBPA to check your setup and use the available PowerShell commands such as *Test-OutlookWebServices* or *Test-MapiConnectivity* to verify the configuration.

A recommended approach is to first initialize the databases with only a few users and run a test with them before you run your real test with thousands of users. This allows you to quickly assess whether you still have configuration issues. It is better to identify this in an hour instead of first waiting a day until your large database has been initialized.

For a performance test it is required to first initialize the Exchange databases. If you start a test run without an initialized database, the user inboxes are empty and some tasks of the action profile would not work as intended, such as reading new emails and replying to received messages. If you did not disable the search indexer on the mailbox server and start a test immediately after the database initialization is finished, performance results are not representative. There would be high CPU load caused by content indexing in addition to the load created by LoadGen.

You should restart the remote LoadGen client service before you run a new test. It saves you a lot of time if you create scripts for this purpose. We even prefer rebooting the complete test environment before we start a real test. In this way, all performance counters are reset, which makes the assessment easier.

If you are not using LoadGen for a performance assessment but rather to populate databases that you need for a backup and recovery test, for example, you do not have to bother with all these precautions.

The advantage of using *LOADGENWIN.EXE* for running a test is the status information that it provides. As seen in Figure 10-27, this test will soon fail because of the exceptions generated on a remote client. You can also start a test from the command line. The command line is handy if you have to troubleshoot a test. Instead of manually reopening the log file that LoadGen creates in an editor, you can instruct LoadGen to write traces to the console window. This is very helpful, as long as Windows does not provide one of our favorite UNIX commands, *tail -f.*

Figure 10-27
Simulation in progress

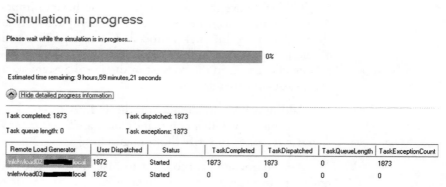

Figure 10-28 shows the corresponding command. You should use *PERFMON.MSC* to collect performance counters that LoadGen provides to check whether the test runs smoothly or whether the Exchange Load Generator Engine\Task Queue Length is constantly increasing.

Test results

At the end of the test run, a report is generated that provides information about the test setup and statistical data about the test results. Figure 10-29 provides an example of the generated HTML file.

The second part of the report, shown in Figure 10-30, provides detailed statistics about the individual tasks executed.

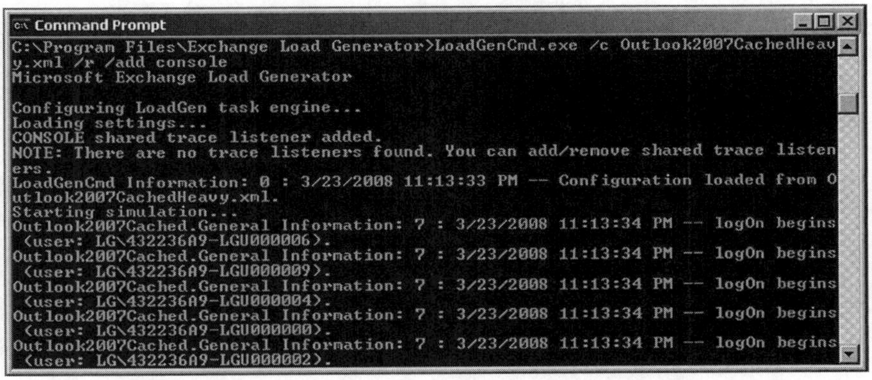

Figure 10-28
LoadGenCMD /
Add Console

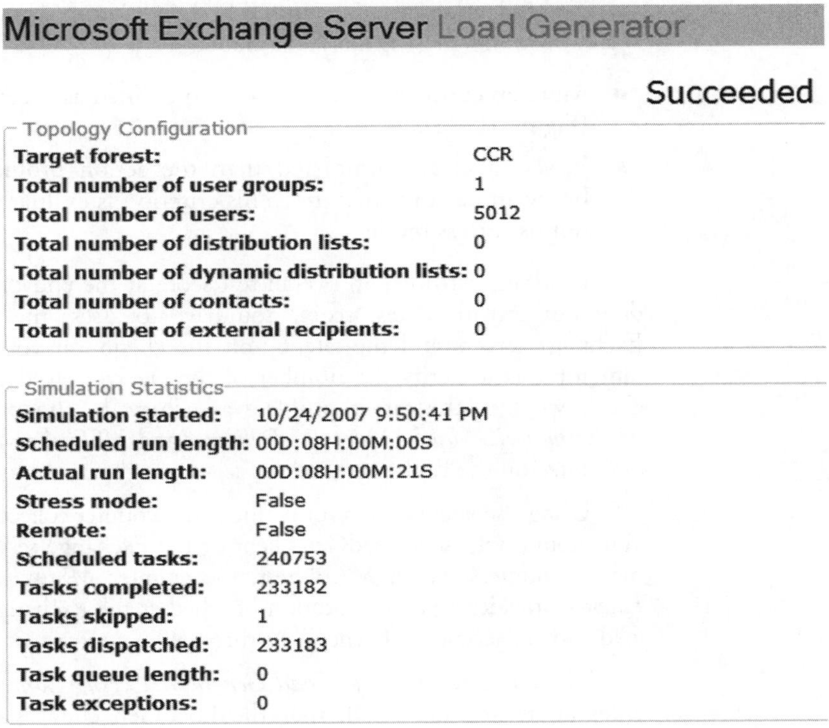

Figure 10-29
LoadGen Report—
topology and simu-
lation statistics

Microsoft Exchange Server Load Generator

Succeeded

Topology Configuration

Target forest:	CCR
Total number of user groups:	1
Total number of users:	5012
Total number of distribution lists:	0
Total number of dynamic distribution lists:	0
Total number of contacts:	0
Total number of external recipients:	0

Simulation Statistics

Simulation started:	10/24/2007 9:50:41 PM
Scheduled run length:	00D:08H:00M:00S
Actual run length:	00D:08H:00M:21S
Stress mode:	False
Remote:	False
Scheduled tasks:	240753
Tasks completed:	233182
Tasks skipped:	1
Tasks dispatched:	233183
Task queue length:	0
Task exceptions:	0

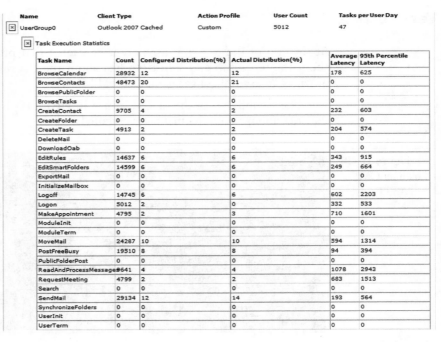

Figure 10-30
LoadGen Report—
user group task
statistics

Name	Client Type		Action Profile	User Count	Tasks per User Day
☒ UserGroup0	Outlook 2007 Cached		Custom	5012	47

☒ Task Execution Statistics

Task Name	Count	Configured Distribution(%)	Actual Distribution(%)	Average Latency	95th Percentile Latency
BrowseCalendar	28932	12	12	178	625
BrowseContacts	48473	20	21	0	0
BrowsePublicFolder	0	0	0	0	0
BrowseTasks	0	0	0	0	0
CreateContact	9705	4	2	232	603
CreateFolder	0	0	0	0	0
CreateTask	4913	2	2	204	574
DeleteMail	0	0	0	0	0
DownloadOab	0	0	0	0	0
EditRules	14637	6	6	343	915
EditSmartFolders	14599	6	6	249	664
ExportMail	0	0	0	0	0
InitializeMailbox	0	0	0	0	0
Logoff	14745	6	6	602	2203
Logon	5012	2	0	332	533
MakeAppointment	4795	2	3	710	1601
ModuleInit	0	0	0	0	0
ModuleTerm	0	0	0	0	0
MoveMail	24287	10	10	594	1314
PostFreeBusy	19510	8	8	94	394
PublicFolderPost	0	0	0	0	0
ReadAndProcessMessage	9641	4	4	1078	2943
RequestMeeting	4799	2	2	683	1513
Search	0	0	0	0	0
SendMail	29134	12	14	193	564
SynchronizeFolders	0	0	0	0	0
UserInit	0	0	0	0	0
UserTerm	0	0	0	0	0

The following criteria are used by LoadGen to determine whether a test was successful. A test is marked as failed if:

- More exceptions occurred than you defined as acceptable for the test (Figure 10-22).

- Fewer tasks are completed than the action profile (light, average, heavy, or custom) requires. This criterion is evaluated only if you did not use Stress mode.

LoadSim provided an overall test score at the end of each test. LoadGen does not provide a test score. You have to assess the performance of the Exchange servers and the latency on the clients on your own. One important topic is to verify the number of messages received and sent per user to check whether the target profile was achieved. The performance counters *MSExchangeIS Mailbox\Messages Delivered* and *MSExchangeIS Mailbox\Messages Submitted* on the Exchange mailbox server are the corresponding counters.

Using a separate system for performance counter collection is recommended. You should not use a LoadGen client or the Exchange servers to collect performance counters. For a MAPI test, the counter *MSExchangeIS\RPC Averaged Latency* provides a good indication of whether the Exchange server handled the load with an acceptable latency. The threshold is approximately 50 milliseconds.

The counter *Exchange Load Generator Engine\Content Cache Trims* provides an indication of whether the LoadGen client has enough memory.

This is especially interesting if you simulate a cached Exchange mode profile. Cache mode can reduce the number of users that can be simulated with a certain hardware configuration.

The counter *Exchange Load Generator Engine\Tasks completed* and *Exchange Load Generator Engine\Task Dispatched* should have a similar value. If this is not the case, then the client cannot handle the load. LoadGen automatically stops a test if it recognizes that the task queue is larger than one-half the numbers of simulated users.

The LoadGen clients write a log file, and you can define the logging level in the LoadGen configuration file. The log file is helpful if you have to troubleshoot LoadGen behavior, such as if a client generates a lot of exceptions and the test therefore fails.

Customizing LoadGen

LoadGen uses modules to implement various Client Access protocols. There are two types of modules available. Task-based modules have been available since the first version of LoadGen. The most commonly used task-based module is the Outlook module. The second type of module is script based. Script-based modules have been moved from ESP to LoadGen, such as IMAP4 or OWA. A significant difference between the module types is that a task-based module defines the user profile in the LoadGen configuration file. Script-based modules use a separate text file to define the user profile. The script file contains module-specific commands that are executed to simulate the user behavior. Examples of such commands are *CONNECT*, *STARTTLS*, and *SendMail*.

The *ActionProfile* of a task-based module specifies the tasks to be executed, and how many times a task has to be executed during the simulation day. Previous LoadGen versions used profiles defined by the MAPI Messaging Benchmark, such as MMB2 or MMB3. Additionally, medium and heavy user profiles were available. Microsoft stopped the benchmarking program, and in the new LoadGen version, the MMB2 and MMB3 profile has been removed. You now can select Light, Average, Heavy, Very Heavy, and Custom. Note that the I/O generated by these action profiles do not directly correspond to the IOPS figures used in the Exchange 2007 Mailbox Server Role Storage Requirements Calculator.

Another important topic is that LoadGen always generates a constant workload. It evenly distributes the tasks over the length of the test run. Real users do not have this constant behavior. There are peak usage times—often between 9:00 and 11:00 in the morning. If you want to be on the safe side, you can use an action profile that corresponds to the task rate during this peak time. In brief, put the environment for the complete duration of the test under the load that in reality only occurs between 9:00 and 11:00.

You can analyze the profile of your existing Exchange Server deployment with the Exchange Server Profile Analyzer (EPA) tool and compare the behavior of your users with the existing LoadGen profiles. If they do not match, you can create a customized LoadGen profile by editing the related sections in the configuration file.

Figure 10-31 shows the section in the XML file where you can modify the tasks executed during a test.

Figure 10-31
ActionProfile

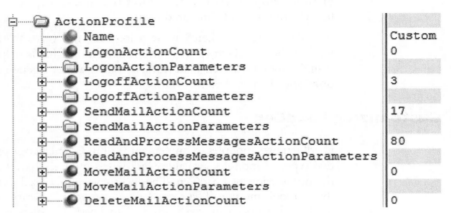

Another section that is frequently customized is the *MailboxStoreProfile* section. This section determines the structure and contents of your test users' inboxes. The action profile you selected in Figure 10-25 determines the number of items in the inbox of the test users and thereby the size of the mailbox database. Note that Microsoft sometimes changes the *MailboxStoreProfile* if a new LoadGen version is released. Therefore, we recommend creating a configuration file with a single user, initializing the Exchange database, and then checking the inbox size of the test user. LoadGen version 08.02.0032 created mailboxes with the following sizes: light ~50 MB, average ~100 MB, heavy ~185 MB, and very heavy ~272 MB.

If you want to run a test with a different mailbox size, you can customize the *MailboxStoreProfile* section shown in Figure 10-32. You can customize the mailbox size by modifying the *NewFolderCount* and *NewFolderMessageCount* variables. Note that too many items per folder have a negative impact on performance. Microsoft Knowledge Base Article 905803 recommends a maximum of 3500 to 5000 items per folder.

Outlook Anywhere is currently very popular, and you can enable the usage of RPC over HTTP in the configuration file. You have to add the section shown in Figure 10-33 and replace the string *yoursampleserver* with the name of the CAS or with the Fully Qualified Domain Name (FQDN) configured as the entry point in your ISA server.

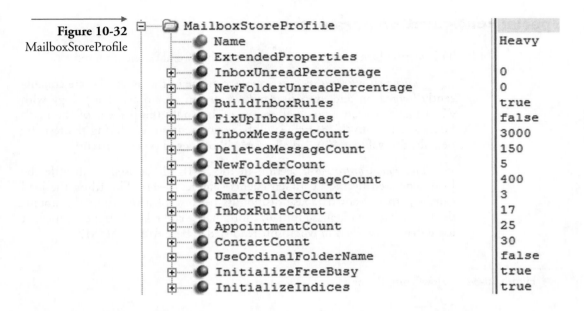

Figure 10-32
MailboxStoreProfile

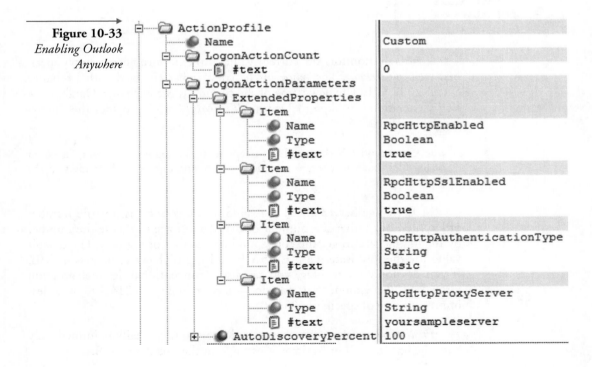

Figure 10-33
*Enabling Outlook
Anywhere*

Special configuration parameters

This section lists a few special parameters that we have encountered.

ConcurrencyPercent specifies the percentage of the users who are concurrently logged on and executing tasks. You can set up a test topology with 7500 mailboxes on your mailbox server, but only the percent of the mailboxes specified in this variable will be concurrently used during the test. By default, this value is 100 and all users will be logged on concurrently.

The *FlowControlPoint* section in the XML file is used to throttle the load generated by the LoadGen clients (Figure 10-34). Throttling the load can help to prevent database dismounts because of a too deep checkpoint depth during the database initialization phase. The related application event log entry is described in Microsoft Knowledge Base Article 925817.

Figure 10-34   FlowControlPoint

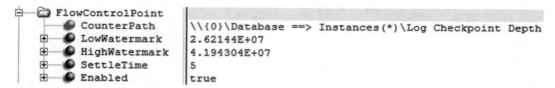

LoadGen monitors the current value of the performance counter specified by *CounterPath*. The name of the counter has changed with Exchange Server 2007 SP1. The new name of the counter is MSExchange Database → Log Generation Checkpoint Depth. *PERFMON.MSC* provides the following explanation:

Log Generation Checkpoint Depth represents the amount of work, in count of log files that will need to be redone or undone to the database file(s) if the process crashes.

In Exchange Server 2007, the value of the counter is not the number of log files, but rather the number of bytes. You have to divide the number by the log file size to get the corresponding number of log files. The default value for the low watermark is 25 MB and the high watermark is 40 MB. If you do not want to brag, you can use a conventional decimal notation instead of the exponential notation—for example, 26,214,400 is a less impressive way of specifying 25 MB.

PreTestLogon defines whether users log on to their mailbox immediately after the test starts. This variable is exposed in the LoadGen GUI.

InterLogOnControlInMsecs can be used to control the log-on behavior of simulated users. This value specifies the time that LoadGen waits between concurrent log-on actions, which can be used to stagger the log-on process. If you have large task queues, reducing the time that LoadGen sleeps between log-on requests can be helpful.

Simulating Internet Protocols with LoadGen

The following section provides an introduction to the new Internet protocol modules in LoadGen. They have been moved from ESP to LoadGen.

If we look back on my self-study of the scripted modules then the most difficult part was recognizing that we need a Certificate Authority (CA) structure. Exchange Server 2007 uses the secure variants of communication protocols. For example, if you want to test IMAP4, Exchange will communicate on port 993 (IMAP4/SSL) and not on port 143. This requires that you have the necessary certificates in place on your client and on the server with the CAS role. See the Microsoft TechNet article, "Certificate Use in Exchange 2007 Server," for details.

You will easily recognize this problem if you set up an IMAP4 profile in your email client. If you do not trust the certificate of the CAS, there will be many warnings and error messages at the time you try to connect to your mailbox using the IMAP4 protocol. The same is true if you want to use the SMTP protocol. The LoadGen clients have to trust the certificate of the server with HT role.

So why did I (Juergen) spend so many hours until I got it working? I must admit that I did not follow the best practices described in this chapter! I started with LoadGen from the beginning and did not run a simple test with a regular email client, nor did I run the PowerShell command to test connectivity. Okay, I paid the price and learned it the hard way. You should not make the same mistake, so manually test the setup with an email client and use the corresponding PowerShell test commands. We are sure you know "Get-Excommand test*".

Describing how to set up a CA is beyond the scope of this book. See the related documentation on Microsoft TechNet. Managing POP3 and IMAP4 is also explained on Microsoft TechNet. You have to enable the corresponding service on the CAS and enable your test users for the IMAP4 or POP3 protocol. The book *Windows PowerShell for Exchange Server 2007 SP1* is very helpful for learning the commands to set up the IMAP4 configuration and to verify the connectivity of all available client protocols.

One difference to the Internet protocol modules in ESP is that you do not have to define the users that are used by the test in a text file. LoadGen gets the users from the AD. You can use the same procedure to set up the test topology and the user objects that you already know from the Outlook module.

The scripted modules do not initialize the Exchange database, but they require that the mailboxes of the test users have already been initialized. A LoadGen configuration for an Outlook profile is used to create the topology in AD and initialize the Exchange databases.

After this has been completed, you create the LoadGen configuration XML file for the scripted module. You can do this with *LOADGENWIN.EXE* by selecting the corresponding user profile shown in Figure 10-25, or you can create the XML file with *LOADGENCMD.EXE*.

You have to replace the server name *sampleserver* with the name of your CAS server in the *ScriptProfile* section shown in Figure 10-35. There are several options how you can configure whether the communication occurs encrypted or unencrypted. The Port variable specifies the port that is being used initially, and this variable works together with the variable *EncryptedPort*. If you specify *Port=143* and set *EncyptedPort=false*, you have to use *STARTTLS* in the script file if you want encryption. If you specify *Port=993* and *EncryptedPort=true*, the communication starts encrypted and you do not need the *STARTTLS* command in the script file.

Figure 10-35
ScriptProfile
Section

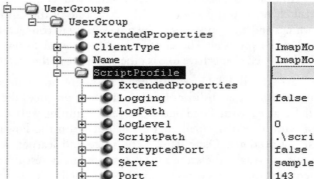

ScriptPath specifies the text file with the commands that the script module will execute during the test.

Figure 10-36 shows the beginning of the IMAP sample script included in the LoadGen scripts directory. See the LoadGen online documentation for a description of the commands that the Internet modules support. You should verify whether the sample script of your Internet module references other files such as sample emails. If this is the case, you have to ensure that your LoadGen installation uses the same drive and directory path. For example, the script that the OWA module uses assumes that LoadGen is installed on drive *D:* and not on drive *C:*.

Figure 10-36
IMAP Script

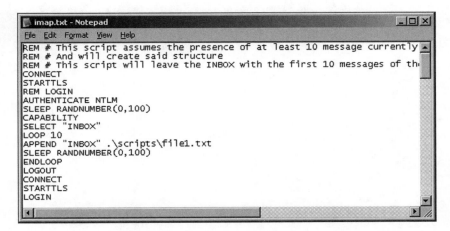

```
imap.txt - Notepad
File  Edit  Format  View  Help
REM # This script assumes the presence of at least 10 message currently
REM # And will create said structure
REM # This script will leave the INBOX with the first 10 messages of th
CONNECT
STARTTLS
REM LOGIN
AUTHENTICATE NTLM
SLEEP RANDNUMBER(0,100)
CAPABILITY
SELECT "INBOX"
LOOP 10
APPEND "INBOX" .\scripts\file1.txt
SLEEP RANDNUMBER(0,100)
ENDLOOP
LOGOUT
CONNECT
STARTTLS
LOGIN
```

You should execute script-based tests using *LOADGENCMD.EXE* and not with *LOADGENWIN.EXE*. The script-based modules do not have tasks or task queues. Therefore, the task-related status variables in the GUI stay at 0 during the test.

We recommend that you enable logging in the *ScriptProfile* section shown in Figure 10-35. You have to set *Logging=true*, specify a file name in the *LogPath* variable, and increase the *LogLevel*. Using a sniffer such as Wireshark is helpful for troubleshooting purposes as well.

Missing Pieces

Note that LoadGen will not provide a 100% simulation of Outlook. There are things that LoadGen cannot simulate, such as if your users have Outlook plug-ins installed. Thus, the effect of the plug-ins is not considered by a LoadGen test. Another topic is that LoadGen does not create the same number of TCP connections that an Outlook client will create. LoadGen directly connects to AD and does not use the Named Service Provider Interface (NSPI) like an Outlook client does to get directory information. This is something that you have to consider when you try to determine the scalability limits of your deployment. Luckily, Windows Server 2008 removes the 65,535 connection limit that exists in Windows Server 2003. With Windows Server 2008, you can have up to 65,535 TCP connections per IP address and not 65,535 TCP connections per server. Additional information about this topic is available in the TechNet article "Outlook Anywhere Scalability with Outlook 2007, Outlook 2003, and Exchange 2007". This is a very helpful document that was released after we provided the manuscript.

Performance Monitoring and Analysis

Description

Performance monitoring in Windows Server has evolved from the performance monitor as we knew it with Windows NT 4 (and still available from the Windows 2000 resource kit) into the following new tools:

- A system monitor, which displays current or saved performance counters information
- Performance logs and alerts, which capture counter values and manage log files and alerts
- Reliability and performance monitor in Vista and Windows Server 2008

The System Monitor GUI provides useful information, but to implement a proper performance analysis and assessment of a running Exchange server, you will require postprocessing tools to absorb the thousands of performance indicators on a Windows server running Exchange 2007 (Figure 11-1). Microsoft Excel can be quite handy for implementing basic statistical and mathematical functions (such as the use of the pivot table for screening HTTP errors on CAS server log files), and you may find some postprocessing tools from specific vendors.

In this chapter, we present a methodology to process and turn out something meaningful from several hundred megabytes of information captured during performance analysis.

The performance monitor in Windows comes with three basic features:

- The capture of performance counters capture into log files
- Trace information gathering (What do you do with this trace information?)
- Alert generation based on counter threshold, which can be utilized for triggering additional (perhaps more detailed) performance information

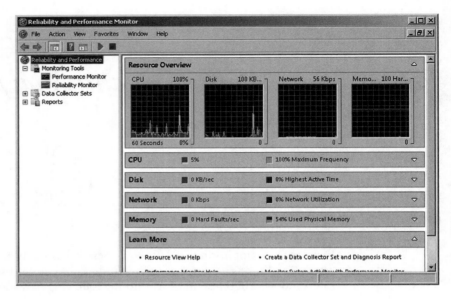

Figure 11-1
*Windows Server
2008 Reliability
and Performance
Monitor*

The Windows performance monitor is great because it lets you concentrate on the data acquisition task and does that well, by providing data in multiple formats, and by letting you schedule data acquisition (e.g., if you wanted to understand the stress put on your server during an online database defragmentation during off-peak hours). Granted, the performance counter selection dialog box hasn't changed much, and the acquisition time interval is limited to 1 second (just long enough). However, the monitor comes with interesting log file management features, such as the ability to stop acquisition after a given amount of time or at a precise date/time. Sequence numbering of log file names is also handy for trend analysis.

In addition to *Perfmon*, some tools that were in previous versions of the Windows Server resource kit are now included in the base operating system (Windows XP or Windows Server 2003), which allow rapid capture of performance data as well as refinement of performance data (*TYPEPERF* and *RELOG*, which we discuss later in this section).

Monitoring Exchange 2007 can be both an easy and rather complex task. It is easy because Microsoft, in both its operating systems and applications, has always provided detailed information about the behavior of running applications. With Exchange 2007, the presence of PowerShell commands (e.g., to test the operational status of some services) has greatly helped the Microsoft Exchange administrator.

On the other hand, monitoring can be complex; in the process of searching for performance bottlenecks for storage, you may be tempted to gather many performance counters, and having too much data to process can result in burying somewhat important information under irrelevant data. Too much data kills the data.

Therefore, you need to find a compromise that allows you to get essential data at a reasonable sampling interval. This way, you can easily report and make decisions while not overlooking essential elements, and you can have a sampling interval that does not mask peak loads, which often cause excessive queuing and bad response time. Simply put, you may design and monitor a server hosting 2500 users, but if the CIO or one of your IT directors happens to read a message (that translates into a set of client/server protocol commands, which themselves can be expressed as a set of transactions to the messaging service) at the wrong time, the response time may be mediocre and generate a complaint that the system is slow, even though it performs adequately on an average basis.

This section provides you with both key information to collect and a methodology for interpreting information, whether it is based on 10 samples or 100,000 samples. This methodology does not mask the peak loads but puts them into perspective.

Depending on your environment, you will need to choose a representative time period for the workload, or a time period during which you wish to satisfy a certain workload. For example, on several occasions, we worked for companies whose peak time (highest number of transactions) was between 8:30 and 10:00 on weekday mornings, and where the largest number of messages was transmitted between 15:00 and 16:30 on Friday afternoon. This provides an interesting perspective on what to monitor and when, and how to later decide whether your system architecture addresses the workload. If your system does not cope with this workload, you have at least the opportunity to tune the most appropriate components to achieve both the workload throughput and a satisfactory transaction response time (referred to as I/O latency in this chapter).

There are many tools and products on the market that address Exchange infrastructure monitoring. We usually classify them based on the number of applications and systems to monitor, the heterogeneous nature of the systems, and the level of detail requested. However, we do not believe that there is a single product that can address all problems. It is also important to consider the existing environment and the fact that operational staff may be used to a particular product and its interfaces and event monitoring and reporting system.

Things that you should value when selecting a proper monitoring and reporting tool for Exchange 2007 largely depend on answers to the following questions:

■ Can the tool interface with other operating systems (e.g., UNIX, among others)?

■ Can the tool monitor infrastructure components such as network switches, storage network switches, and controllers?

- Can the tool provide reporting functions that enable you to decide whether you have met the expected and/or committed service levels (e.g., time to deliver a message and response time to basic client operations such as reading a message)?

- Can the tool deal with a large number of objects (more than 100) scattered across a wide area network?

- Can the tool consolidate events and generate alarms that can be handled by the operational staff?

- Can the tool accurately provide both hot information (e.g., system activity during a 1-hour period) and more general information (system uptime over a 6-month period)?

- Can the tool interface with homegrown tools (e.g., integration of application-specific monitoring tools into enterprise management tools, or integration of hardware monitoring tools into enterprise or application or operating system–specific tools)?

Many products are available on the market and have evolved over time. Microsoft provides Microsoft Operations Management (MOM), now called Microsoft System Center Operations Manager. This product grew from NetIQ's technology and aims at monitoring a large number of systems (1000 or more). MOM is great because at Microsoft, the product groups are responsible for developing the Management Packs for MOM. The Management Pack is an application-focused component that can be used to collate reports and exploit performance and event information in the context of the application. Exchange has a pretty comprehensive Management Pack for MOM that can be used for real-time monitoring or more general operational monitoring and trending.

HP has a major operational monitoring tool from the OpenView family of products, OVO (OpenView for Operations), accompanied by application-specific plug-ins (called SPIs, smart plug-ins) that allow monitoring of application-specific components and performance aspects. Table 11-1 shows a succinct comparison of the two operation management products, HP OpenView Operations for Windows and Microsoft Operations Manager.

In this chapter, we will cover out-of-the-box performance monitoring tools—specifically, Perfmon, from Windows. Perfmon was introduced with the very first release of Windows NT; it is worthwhile, depending on how applications report their information and the relevance of performance counters. It is not the only solution for performance monitoring, but we found no limitations in using it to diagnose and monitor servers—other than the sheer quantity of counters available, which can sometimes make it hard to diagnose performance and service-level problems.

Table 11-1   *Summary comparison of HP OpenView and MOM*

Feature	HP OpenView	MOM
Manager–agent architecture	Yes	Yes
Built-in rules, policies, and filters	Yes	Yes
Built-in reporting	Yes	Yes
Add-on per application (Exchange and Active Directory)	Yes	Yes
Multiplatform support	Yes	Limited
Written by application-specific engineers	No	Yes
End-to-end management (hardware, server, network, storage, services)	Yes	Yes, with hardware monitoring add-ons (e.g., HP Insight Manager from HP)
Embedded knowledge base	Yes	Yes

Performance Monitor in Windows Server

The GUI for viewing performance counters is now provided as part of the System Monitor, another MMC snap-in, that can display either current system information or information captured by means of the performance log files. System Monitor has greatly improved the display of information, notably for multihour log file display. Figure 11-2 displays a snapshot of System Monitor, which you will find as Performance under the Administration Tools pull-down menu.

You can invoke the System Monitor by issuing the DOS command *PERFMON*. You may also use the NT4 Performance Monitor, which doesn't help very much in reviewing report data collected over a long period of time, but allows trimming the sampling interval to less than 1 second. This last point is very important. There is always an impact when monitoring a system or an application or one of its components. For example, Microsoft used to document that enabling performance counters for physical and logical disks was associated with a 10% performance impact. This impact can be on the response time, on the overall throughput of transactions to the volume or disk, and possibly on the quantity of data transmitted back and forth between the volumes and disks to the NT I/O subsystem. Should this be really an issue? We do not believe so. If you tune your environment such that you take into consideration the impact of performance monitoring, you place yourself in a worst-case scenario that: you add margin of operation (present when performance monitoring does not run) that is beneficial for

Figure 11-2
System Monitor
with Windows
Server 2003

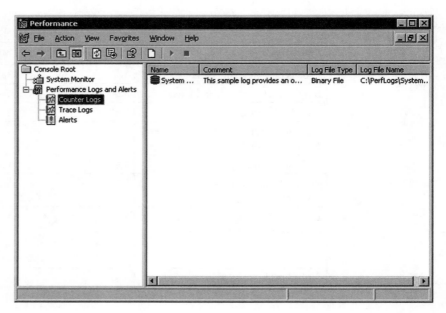

production use. If you consider that your systems should not have disk counters permanently enabled for performance reasons, ask yourself, "Is it wise to run a system with so little headroom in a performance capacity?" With Windows Server 2003, the physical disk performance counters are enabled by default, and if you use partitions on your disks, or if you use some form of host-based volume management (e.g., by using dynamic disks), you will have to enable logical disk counters as well.

Another question is whether you should monitor a particular counter using a 1-second sampling interval, a 15-second sampling interval, or a 15-minute sampling interval. The answer depends very much on the counter and what you wish to get out of it.

For disk counters, a sampling interval of 5-second is definitely appropriate. For determining the overall number of messages sent by an Exchange server or the number of active users (in the Exchange terminology), a 15-minute sampling interval is more than sufficient. You may have an appropriate sampling interval, decide on which counters to monitor, and end up with a bunch of numbers. Are they good or are they bad? The result of the sampling and reporting will not answer that question unless you have a baseline to work with.

As described in the previous section, this baseline can be established by implementing a load simulation test that provides a ballpark figure. The baseline can also be determined by your knowledge of the system's components.

For instance, we know that 5 milliseconds for a sequential noncached write operation is "decent" for a disk drive. It may not be optimal, but it is decent. So, you may decide to enable write caching on your disk controller and go below 1 millisecond for similar operations, and you will know that you have realized a certain gain, one that should translate into better performance for the overall system.

The goal of this chapter and this book is to provide you with information and experience that we have collected from many customers and real-world scenarios, along with baseline figures. It is not an end in itself, since you will also need to put these data into the perspective of your own environment (which includes hardware components, software operating systems and applications, and overall logical topology), and decide whether the information gathered brings value and whether it requires attention.

Toolbox

The performance analysis engineer typically has a toolbox that contains a series of tools and scripts, Excel sheets, and homegrown processes that facilitate making rapid performance analyses. In the last 10 years, we have been working on performance analysis in general, and for Windows and Exchange in particular, we have developed our own methods. We have also had the opportunity to meet, interact, and exchange ideas with talented engineers inside and outside of HP.

To be efficient in finding needles in haystacks, or pinpointing a painful area in hours instead of weeks, the performance engineer for Exchange should be proficient in the following tools:

Perfmon: For both interactive and batch capture of performance data.

Relog: For extracting subsets of performance captures and transforming data into a manageable set (Figure 11-3).

Figure 11-3
Using relog *to convert a binary performance data file into a CSV file*

```
C:\Documents and Settings\bijaoui\Desktop>relog 092905-counters_000009.blg -f cs
v -o 092905.csv

Input
----------------
File(s):
    092905-counters_000009.blg (Windows 2000)

Begin:     10/10/2005 8:00:00
End:       10/10/2005 16:59:57
Samples:   6480

7.41%
```

Typeperf: To quickly enable performance counter capture, such as in the midst of an event.

Microsoft Excel: To use mathematical functions that go above and beyond the minimum, average, and maximum calculations, such as using percentiles.

Charting and analysis tool: You might find using a specialized charting and analysis tool that helps you run through correlation and charting of information to be advantageous. HP has one, called TLVIZ, that you can obtain from searching www.hp.com. The most recent link to this tool is http://h71000.www7.hp.com/openvms/products/t4/index.html?jumpid=reg_R1002_USEN. (Note that the link may have changed by the time you read this.) TLVIZ was developed for analysis of comma-separated value files from OpenVMS. The translation of Windows Perfmon CSV files into TLVIZ files is quite trivial.

Sysinternals Process Monitor: You can download Process Monitor from http://www.sysinternals.com. This is a great tool to determine what is happening on a server. If you are unsure of the activity on a particular disk unit, Process Monitor will let you trace all I/Os made to the server's file systems.

IOmeter: Intel's donation to the open source community. It is an I/O exerciser that is quite popular among storage specialists, and it can be used to assess performance of storage units, using varying workloads (sequential or random, large or small I/O size).

Microsoft Exchange Performance Troubleshooting Analyzer: This tool is integrated with the Exchange 2007 Management Console (Figure 11-4).

Figure 11-4
Microsoft Exchange Performance Troubleshooting Analyzer

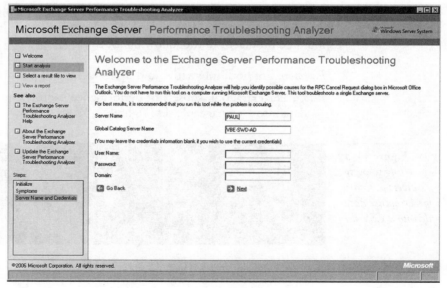

Prepare to allocate enough storage for your analysis; it is not uncommon to collect over 1 GB of performance data in a single working day. There are many ways of collecting performance data; the best results are obtained if you use the same machine to collect performance data across the environment. That way, information from multiple servers, such as mailbox or Hub Transport Servers, is collected in the same file and correlation can be established more easily.

Sometimes, the analysis of this information will outperform common laptop environments. We found that an old server with 2 GB or more of RAM was adequate.

In subsequent sections, we will use outputs from "the Monkey," an underground (private use only) performance analysis tool that we could summarize as being "what Microsoft would have always wanted to turn Perfmon into." The author will recognize himself in this paragraph, and we still have a hard time finding the right words for thanking him for the work he did.

What Should you Monitor in Your Microsoft Exchange Storage?

This section describes the basic performance counters that can be obtained using PERFMON in Windows 2003. Sometimes you will find that you can use these counters directly with PERFMON and gather information in data files that can be later exploited. At other times, you can use this information as input to integrated monitoring products in order to define threshold values that can trigger alarms or to establish trends that can be used in capacity planning and overall system monitoring.

The next section provides a method for analyzing performance data based on the use of percentiles, which is a common practice in the transactional world, of which Exchange 2007 is definitely part.

Workload monitoring

Workload monitoring with Exchange 2007 is a challenging task. There is an unmatched number of elements that relate to Exchange 2007 server activity that can provide information. The set of counters to monitor in Exchange 2007 depends on the role of the server. When dealing with storage of Microsoft Exchange, you might wonder why you should care about this. The reason is simple: If you find your storage subsystem under pressure (large number of I/Os per second, high data rate [MB/second], or high latency), you will need to relate this to application activity. Storage performance directly depends on application demand. Understanding the reasons why you have an application demand will help you determine if you need to throw more storage in your environment, fine-tune a RAID level, or perhaps change some configuration rules.

Monitoring Exchange 2007 performance can be done from two key sources:

- Performance objects
- IIS Log files

Performance objects are numerous, and trying to get them will provide a large quantity of information to process. Subsequently, we describe methods and tools for managing this information. IIS log files are optional as is tracking message traffic information. They can be useful to determine message-oriented workload, or client protocol utilization (MAPI, IMAP, POP, HTTP-DAV, or any other). Do not neglect the value of IIS log files: They contain valuable information regarding the activity of your systems and the ability of intermediate servers, such as the Client Access Server, to deal with client requests.

Keeping a scorecard of Exchange activities

For proper workload monitoring, you should attempt to define and maintain a scorecard for Exchange activities that you can plot and visualize across a given time period. You can compare this scorecard with your baseline (established, for example, and, if appropriate, from a legacy Exchange activity) and determine workload evolution.

For example, in Figure 11-5, we can see the ramp-up of connections in the environment (from several CAS servers), and from there, deduce "peak" client activity to your server environment.

The scorecard can vary depending on your client profile. If you have only MAPI clients, you should concentrate on capturing information about those clients. However, if you have a mixture of MAPI, RPC/HTTP (Outlook Anywhere), OWA (HTTP), IMAP, POP, or even NNTP clients, remember to create the workload scorecard for each of these protocols. Fortunately, there are performance counters in Exchange 2007 to allow capture utilization (in terms of transaction issues) for each of the different access types (Figure 11-6).

For a good example of storage resource utilization, consider the Microsoft Exchange Profile Analyzer tool (see a sample report in Figure 11-7), which allows scrubbing a database and enumerating the mailboxes and their contents (in terms of item and folder count and size, not actual text content).

Beyond the actual utilization of the storage and the database contents, throughput (requests that can be handled per second) and latency (response time for a given transaction) are equally critical, as your environment grows.

Figure 11-5
Connection ramp-up during weekday morning

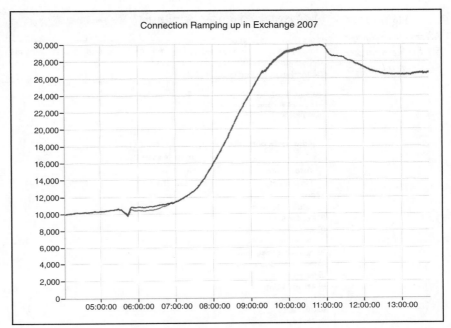

Figure 11-6
Monitoring the user count on a mailbox server

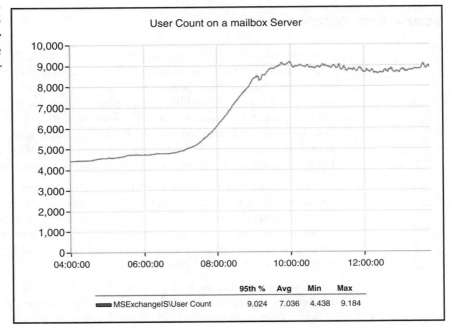

Figure 11-7
Microsoft Exchange
Profile Analyzer
sample report

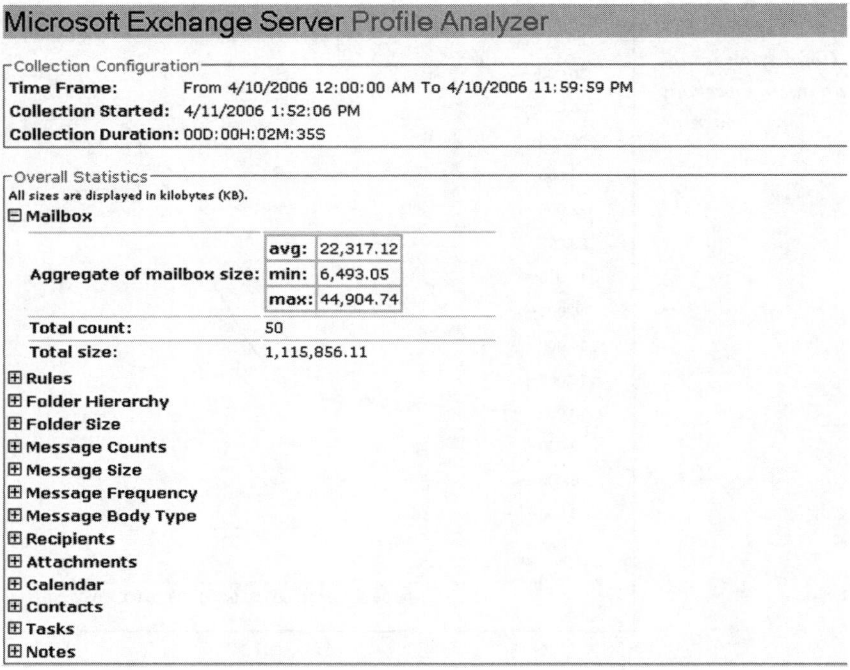

Microsoft Exchange Server Profile Analyzer

Collection Configuration
Time Frame: From 4/10/2006 12:00:00 AM To 4/10/2006 11:59:59 PM
Collection Started: 4/11/2006 1:52:06 PM
Collection Duration: 00D:00H:02M:35S

Overall Statistics
All sizes are displayed in kilobytes (KB).
⊟ **Mailbox**

		avg:	22,317.12
Aggregate of mailbox size:		min:	6,493.05
		max:	44,904.74

Total count:	50
Total size:	1,115,856.11

⊞ **Rules**
⊞ **Folder Hierarchy**
⊞ **Folder Size**
⊞ **Message Counts**
⊞ **Message Size**
⊞ **Message Frequency**
⊞ **Message Body Type**
⊞ **Recipients**
⊞ **Attachments**
⊞ **Calendar**
⊞ **Contacts**
⊞ **Tasks**
⊞ **Notes**

Scorecard design

A scorecard for application activity—in our case, Microsoft Exchange 2007—should report on meaningful transactions, and, if at all possible, throughput information (transactions per second) and latency (transaction completion time). By linking (correlating) the scorecard information with the computing resource utilization (network, CPU, memory, storage), you can determine whether Microsoft Exchange 2007 makes efficient use of these resources, especially with the support of 64-bit Windows, and whether any of these resources is not meeting a satisfactory service level.

For example, if you have 1000 transactions per second (RPC operations per second) and high (above 80%) CPU utilization, you have a good indication that with this particular workload, your CPU processing capability is maxed out, so you should plan for a hardware upgrade that benefits the processing capacity of your server. For example, you can add more processors or more cores, or change the processors' clock rate.

A day in the life of an Exchange 2007 server usually starts with morning log-ons, users starting up the Outlook client, requesting Inbox contents, or synchronizing the mailbox if Outlook operates in cache mode (regardless of the MAPI or RPC/HTTP access mode), processing mail rules that move messages around or delete them. All of these operations occur during a short time period, say between 8:00 AM and 9:00 AM, depending on the opening hours of the user environment. Then you have the day's activity; activity is likely to decrease during lunch breaks, and finally resume toward the end of the day when users complete their work.

Background work happens later, that is, the work that is not transactional per se but which can put a severe resource demand on the Exchange 2007 server and the components it depends on, especially the back-end storage infrastructure. These include backup jobs and system attendant maintenance tasks (online defragmentation being the main one, and records management, or archiving add-on software solutions). During the day non–user-related transactions also occur, such as virus checking, mobile user connectivity links, content indexing (this is not negligible), desktop search engines, and exceptional operations such as database restore operations. Note that they may or may not directly reflect on the back-end server performance, depending on whether the Outlook client is running in cache mode or in online mode (option configurable from Outlook 2003 onward).

MSExchange Database performance object

The MSExchange Database performance object has generally one instance on an Exchange 2007 SP1 server, which is the Information Store instance. For this particular instance, there is a further breakdown per storage group. This performance object is named "Database" for pre-SP1 versions of Exchange 2007.

The MSExchange Database performance object focuses on the _Total instance of each MSExchange Database ==> Instance object (Figure 11-8).

This section focuses on the MSExchange Database (Information Store) performance object's instance, since it the most revealing and critical for the Exchange 2007 mailbox server role. Database counters are useful for determining the stress applied on the Exchange 2007 database engine. As mentioned previously, the database cache size indicates how much system memory can be used for database operations.

It is normal for an Exchange 2007 server to have a reduced amount of physical memory available, because the ESE database engine cache is precisely designed to use as much RAM as possible. With 64-bit Windows and a large memory model, you will not necessarily use all of your RAM, but the store will attempt to allocate as much RAM as needed for the database cache (Figure 11-9).

Figure 11-8
*Database and
database instances
performance objects*

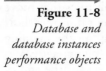

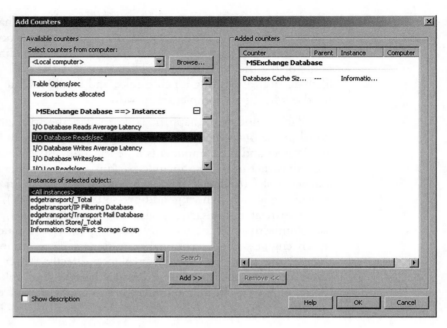

Figure 11-8
*Database and
database instances
performance objects*

Figure 11-9
*Memory usage on
an Exchange 2007
server*

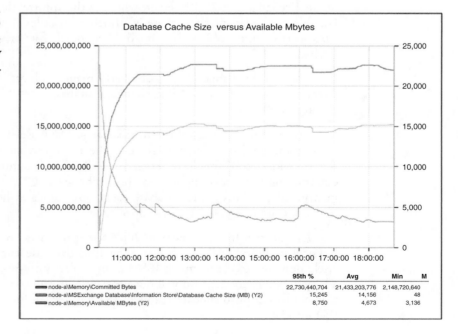

The size of the database cache and log buffers will affect the following two operations:

Frequency of disk access for log writes. This can be critical if you have many transactions to log (i.e., a high rate of information to be stored in the Exchange databases or a high rate of user activity), but is not necessarily critical if the underlying disk subsystem can process log writes fast enough. Nevertheless, the less you go to the "slow" storage systems, the better your system overall performance is because of latency incurred less often, and because of fewer CPU cycles are spent in processing the I/Os in the NT I/O subsystem.

Frequency of disk access for database reads. A database cache that is too small (trimmed automatically by the database engine because of a shortage of RAM) can cause longer response time to user transactions that require database read operations. You can therefore determine and demonstrate whether adding more RAM or changing the cache size has a positive effect on the system's performance if the result is *decreased* I/O reads to the database volumes. Less read I/O means better caching, which means that the device has more capacity to handle extra load and transactions, something very desirable in a high-growth, high–throughput and transaction rate environment. Tracking this rate can be complex in a multivolume and multidatabase environment, and requires dedicated attention for accurate reporting.

Frequency of disk access for database writes. The Microsoft Exchange Information Store can use many database engines (storage groups, up to 50). For each storage group, a "checkpoint" depth indicates the number of dirty pages in the cache. Set to 20 MB by default, this depth is per storage group. The more storage groups, the greater the quantity of dirty pages; if you can host many more pages in the cache, you increase the chance of I/O coalescence, thereby reducing the I/O number by accessing contiguous pages as one block instead of several.

The actual response time of the database write operations does not impact the user's response time, nor the message transfer, since this operation occurs in the background. However, because the database volume is receiving both reads and writes, quite understandably, fewer writes to perform means a higher transaction rate (I/O per second) available to read operations. So, while the write response time is not a valid indication of good performance, the actual number of write operations, combined with the volume capabilities—depending mainly on the controller model, the storage network, the controller cache size and fetch method, the number of disks, and the data protection level (i.e., the RAID level)—do impact on the overall volume transaction rate and data rates, which include the read transactions, critical for user response time and system throughput.

The MSExchange Database (Information Store)\Log Writes/sec performance counter provides the rate at which the database is writing to the log device. You will need to ensure proper write throughput if you do not wish to turn your log drive into a performance bottleneck. You should attempt to qualify your log volume(s) first.

Use tools such as IOmeter or JetStress to determine the data rate and the request rate of the volume. Once determined, you will know how much headroom you dispose of by checking the Log Writes/second counter. Another related counter is MSExchange Database(Information Store)/Log Threads Waiting. On a single Storage Group server, this parameter will range between 0 (what you should aim for) and the number of active threads. How often it is not zero will in fact indicate a log write performance problem—the transaction log device has trouble keeping up with the log request rate. Either the system is too loaded or the log device is too slow. In either situation, improving the write request rate of the transaction log drive will improve not just the counter situation but also overall system performance.

Note that you should expect an initial lower performance if your database has been upgraded from a previous version of Exchange (going from Exchange 2007 to Exchange 2007 SP1 with an in place database upgrade).

Finally, since Exchange 2003 SP1, Microsoft has added a number of advanced performance counters that can be helpful for sizing purposes. You can now measure right off the database engine the I/O request rate (reads per second, writes per second), without necessarily having to monitoring and analyze the physical disk. This is particularly useful if you wish to:

- Compare storage groups pressure on the I/O subsystem
- Calculate IOPS per user (see later in this section)
- Measure the I/O workload generated by the database engine.

You will benefit from using the database engine to report its own view of the I/O subsystem. Figure 11-10 illustrates the actual reduction of I/O during a load simulation as the cache warms up.

Remember that regardless of the performance reported by back-end storage subsystems, the important performance data are the one perceived by the application. From there, you can quickly determine if the databases are demanding too much from the storage subsystem (and therefore, you can see the real need for characterizing or baselining your storage subsystem).

We cover the exact counters to follow later on in a summary table, but they are found prefixed by "I/O Database" for the database I/O traffic and "I/O Log" for the transaction log files prefix (Figure 11-11).

Figure 11-10
Cache warming during a load simulation

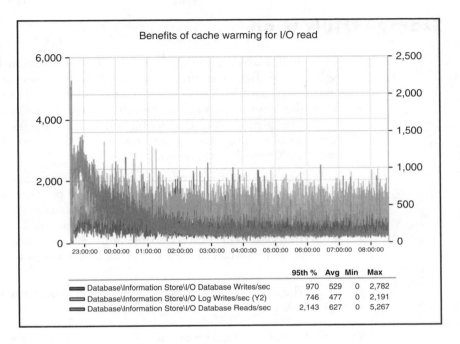

Figure 11-11
I/O counters from the database performance object

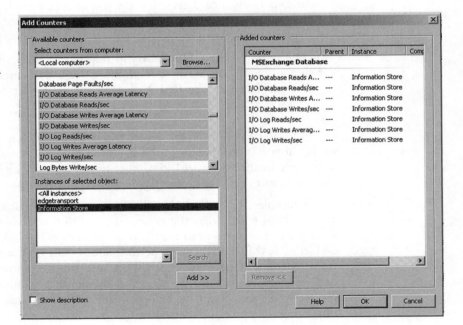

Storage Utilization

How well Exchange can get access to the information from the storage subsystems often determines the overall performance of the application. Fortunately, in Windows, there is a lot of information that can be gathered from the I/O subsystems. The benefits brought by Exchange 2007 and the very large memory (VLM) of 64-bit Windows have significantly diminished the impact of lousy storage performance to the end user (especially if the user runs Outlook in cache mode).

Regardless of the mode of connectivity for your storage (DAS or SAN), you will have to ensure that the storage performance is adequate for your Exchange 2007 deployment, and for all server roles. The main candidates for storage performance analysis are the mailbox servers; however, Hub Transport (HT) servers do require some caretaking for ensuring that the storage performance does not come at the detriment of rapid message delivery.

When you monitor storage performance, you need to watch for two characteristics:

- The rate of requests or data. We saw earlier that the data rate, outside of backup operations, is of little importance, given the I/O size. Nonetheless, for any disk or storage unit that hosts databases and transaction log files, you need to understand the IOPS (I/O per second) performance. This will allow you to determine how fast you can run your backup, how you can recover data, or seed databases in a replication scenario.

- The response time. How fast you respond to I/O can have more or less influence on server operations. It can also determine whether the LUN layout, the RAID level, or the controller configuration is correct.

Additional performance monitoring counters, such as queue length, are of less importance, because of the ability of modern storage systems to deal with large quantities of I/O in a short time period. A high queue length is less important than how long this queue was.

The objective of Exchange 2007 storage performance monitoring and analysis is to ensure that the system deals with a responsive (good quality) storage subsystem. You can configure an Exchange 2007 mailbox server with 64 GB of RAM, but if storage performance is not on par with the demand from Microsoft Exchange, you will get into trouble, either directly because of bad user performance or failure to maintain continuous replication, or indirectly because you have trouble running backup and recovery without impacting the production workload.

Response time

For disk utilization, response time is the most important counter. Queue length may indicate some level of latency and busyness of operations, but response times will indicate whether the disk subsystem is responding satisfactorily. Beyond the actual values, you will need to understand the actual repartition of the response times reported. It is acceptable that 5% of the response times are above 50 milliseconds. It is not acceptable than 15% or more are above 50 milliseconds. In that case, you may hit the storage subsystem too hard and turn it into a performance bottleneck. At this point, you will need to look into other performance counters such as the disk queue length. The response time counters are as follows:

- Physical disk(<instance>)\Avg. disk sec/Read
- Physical disk(<instance>)\Avg. disk sec/Write
- Physical disk(<instance>)\Avg. disk sec/Transfer

The Avg. disk sec/Transfer counter is effective for quickly getting a feel for the volume performance—a value consistently above 30 (milliseconds) calls for improvement. In Figure 11-12, the latency is fine most of the time, with a 95th percentile that is around 13 milliseconds, even though the 99th percentile is higher (31 milliseconds), and the absolute peak is slightly above 600 milliseconds.

Figure 11-12
Avg. disk sec/Write on database disk unit

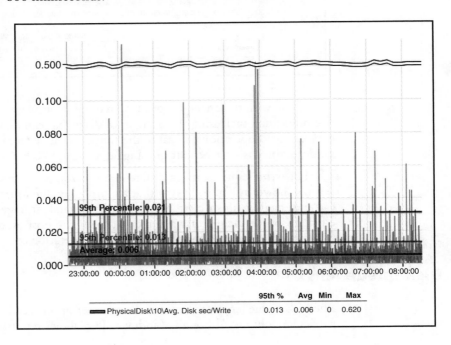

Further analysis, such as determining the efficiency of a read or write controller cache may require you to drill down at the "Avg. disk sec/Read" and "Avg. disk sec/Write" counters. Typically, read operations should be in 15 to 20 milliseconds and write operations should be less than 5 milliseconds (if you have enabled the write-back cache on your RAID controller). Figure 11-13 shows a good example of a disk controller that does an effective job at caching write requests (consistently under 5 milliseconds), but has trouble dealing with read requests.

Figure 11-13
Splitting response time between reads and writes

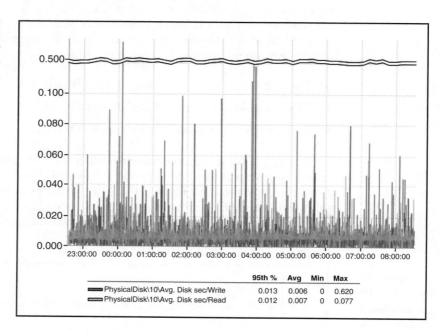

If you wish to accelerate your read request latency, you have little alternative other than increasing the number of disks that can be used for Exchange database read operations. Because the traffic to the database volumes is quite random, there is little benefit in using large cache (4 GB and above) arrays.

For write requests, it is a different story: You may have some high latencies (as shown in Figure 11-13) that are probably due to transient latency for cache destaging (flush of transactions). In general, storage arrays can do an efficient job of caching a write request from the host, and then proceed to free the cache memory for subsequent write operations.

Disk queue length

The disk queue length reports on the number of outstanding operations to a particular volume. Although Windows 2003 allows reporting separate queue length for read and write operations, the current aggregate value is really the one that matters. A good rule of thumb is that there should never be more than half the number of spindles in the queue length. If you have a 10-disk RAID volume, the queue length should be less than 5. Such a recommendation calls for capacity headroom to enable peak handlings.

You should be careful about monitoring queues on storage devices: Although queues greater than the number of disk drives supporting the logical unit was considered barely acceptable, with the implementation and adoption of Storage Area Networks (SANs), a large disk queue length (e.g., 200) should not be of major concern because of the SAN array's ability to absorb these I/O at a higher rate than direct-attached RAID controllers. Figure 11-14 shows a disk queue length that peaks well above 20.

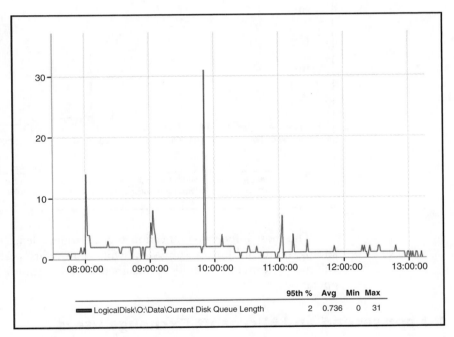

Figure 11-14
Disk queue length for a database disk

	95th %	Avg	Min	Max
▬▬▬ LogicalDisk\O:\Data\Current Disk Queue Length	2	0.736	0	31

In this particular case, the queue peak is just an indicator of a contention that does not repeat during the day and can be safely ignored. However, consistently high values indicate that the volume cannot keep up with the request rate from the application, which, in turn, will generate long response times (and therefore long application response times).

In the case of Exchange database transaction log volumes, the queue length is never greater than 1, unless you combine multiple transaction log sets on the same device. This is because transaction logging is a synchronous process, which triggers a new write only after the current write has been completed. In this case, only the response time actually matters; it indicates whether performance of the overall application is suffering from these response times. In Figure 11-15, we can see that the transaction log disk for the corresponding database disk shown in Figure 11-14 does not exhibit the same queue pattern.

Figure 11-15
Comparing disk queues between transaction log and database disks

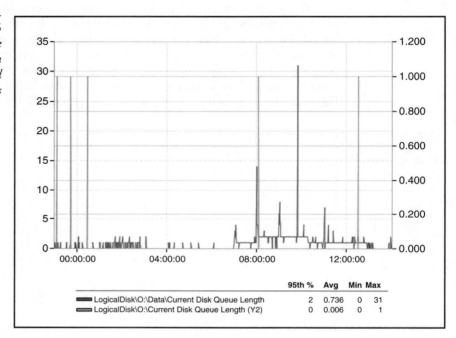

	95th %	Avg	Min	Max
LogicalDisk\O:\Data\Current Disk Queue Length	2	0.736	0	31
LogicalDisk\O:\Current Disk Queue Length (Y2)	0	0.006	0	1

The most important indication the disk queue length gives is whether adding more disks to a subsystem will improve its performance. Actual volume performance should be qualified by the response time of the I/O operations.

I/O per second and Microsoft Exchange users

Storage being quite critical for Microsoft Exchange performance, there have been many attempts during sizing exercises to not only sizing storage per capacity (GB), but also per transaction throughput (IOPS).

The idea during the storage sizing exercise is to make sure that the volumes hosting data (databases, transaction log file and other transient data areas) for the Microsoft Exchange application do fulfill on the throughput (IOPS) and response time (seconds per I/O), and possibly, depending on the storage infrastructure, the data rate (megabytes per second, sometimes expressed in gigabytes per minute or per hour).

For this sizing, we can start from known and well-defined profiles, or even better, calculate the user transaction rate (I/O per second per user/mailbox) based on the existing production environment. Microsoft provides load simulation tools, such as LoadGen; however, simulated users are just that—simulated.

In a day in the life of a Microsoft Exchange server, there are weekends, morning peaks, week peaks (on the Monday if you happen to be in a country where the work week starts on a Monday), and monthly and even quarterly peaks.

For determining the existing transaction workload based on your production system, you must work with Perfmon objects, where the basic rule is to bring together physical disk utilization and application-level workload.

The physical disk utilization is measured using counters presented later in this chapter. The goal is to first determine the response time and transaction throughput together.

The application workload is measured using various counters, depending on how you wish to reuse this information. For example, you may decide to measure the number of mailboxes defined on the server. However, this measurement does not take into account the fact that mailboxes may or may not be logged in—this fact depends upon your user profile and the time of day, day of the week, week of the month (and so on).

You may then decide to measure the number of users "connected" to the server. This is getting closer to the actual ratio between server activity and disk activity; however, it does not account for two key aspects:

- Users might be connected but not active
- A connected user might be using more than one mailbox (common in delegated environments, where assistants will access their mailboxes as well as their boss's mailbox)

Outlook 2003/2007 in cache mode may use more than one connection to the server during its background synchronization process.

To further make the distinction, you can then decide to measure the "connections" to the server. In that case, you take into account the facts that users are logged in and that a single user might have more than one connection, but you still miss the "activity" factor. Depending on the industry you're in, the user profile and population, and the type of client, the actual number of active users (users doing "something") might be significantly different from the number of connected users, which in turn is different from the number of mailboxes defined on the server. Note that this activity factor largely depends on the client protocol. With POP and IMAP users, you do not have the concept of being connected yet idle: You establish connection to the server, you synchronize your email and that's it. The activity factor is primarily used in MAPI clients (e.g., Outlook) environments, where opening the client in the morning and closing it at the end of the workday is common, maintaining a connection between the client and the server, but not necessarily using it.

For taking into account the "activity" factor from MAPI clients, the "MSExchangeIS\Active User" performance counter can be utilized: It describes the number of users who have performed a MAPI operation in the last 10 minutes.

Similarly, and probably more applicable to Outlook 2003/2007 cache-mode environments, the "MSExchangeIS\Active Connection" counters account for the users themselves as well as additional connections to the servers, either due to user connections or other peer server/component connections (e.g., connections to delegates and shared calendars).

What is a percentile?

A percentile is a mathematical function that analyzes a set of samples (they can be marks from student exams or performance data points), and returns the highest value of a given percentage of the samples. Percentiles are used in statistical analysis, and interestingly enough, in education, as a way to rank students. In fact, in certain universities or colleges where a fixed number of seats are available to candidates (e.g., 80 seats for 2000 contenders), this method is used rather than defining a passing "mark." No matter how good or bad the results of the exam are, only 80 of the 2000 students (4%) will pass the test.

In storage performance measurement, percentiles permit determining the score for a percentage of the measurement. In other words, if 95% of your I/O are at 20 milliseconds or less, we consider that the 95th percentile is 20 milliseconds or less. Because averages tend to erode the differences between values, by using percentiles you can quickly determine if high latency (for when you measure I/O response time) is meaningful or not.

You can use the percentile function in Microsoft Excel in order to rapidly calculate a percentile value out of a data set, as shown in Figure 11-16.

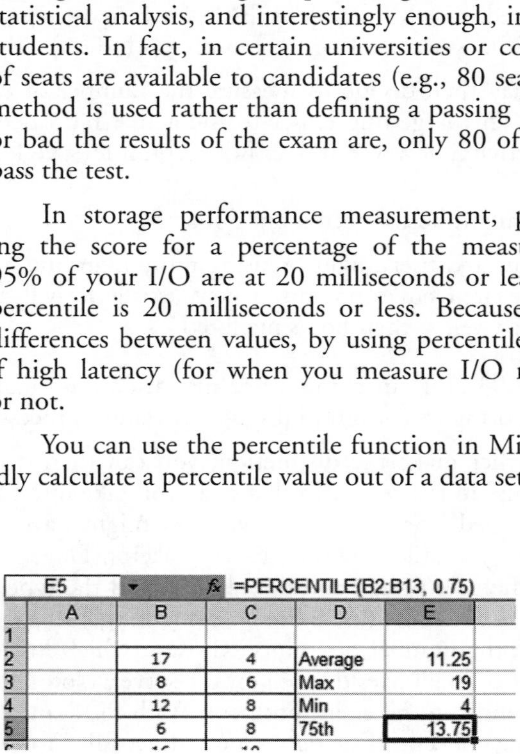

Figure 11-16

Using the percentile function with Microsoft Excel

E5	▼	*fx*	=PERCENTILE(B2:B13, 0.75)	
	A	B	C	D	E
1					
2		17	4	Average	11.25
3		8	6	Max	19
4		12	8	Min	4
5		6	8	75th	13.75
		16	10		

Putting it all together

There are shortcuts that you may take in the procedure described below, but this varies, depending on your data set and user behavior. The basic steps for getting your I/O per second per user/mailbox follow:

- Monitor the user activity (10-minute interval)
- Pick a representative time slot of 2 hours (or more): reference time
- Monitor the disk activity (1-second interval) during the reference time
- Merge data together and for *each* sample, calculate the following ratios:

Write/second ÷ user

Read/second ÷ user

Write/second ÷ active user

Read/second ÷ ctive user

Active user ÷ user

Next, obtain a set of rows of calculation that include both raw numbers and ratios. The result is that you may view the instantaneous write-and-read transactions per user and active user. In fact, based on your reference time and user profile, the user versus active user ratio might be predictable enough so that you only need to care about the user ratio and dismiss the active user ratio.

From these rows, calculate the following values:

- Minimum
- Maximum
- Average
- 95th percentile
- 99th percentile

These values will bring a sense of statistics to your data set: Because addressing 100% of the workload (i.e., the maximum throughput ever seen during sampling) might require too many resources, you may have the up-front and conscious decision that part of it (1%, 5%, or other) will exceed your environment, and you are happy with this. One percent of 2 hours is slightly more than 1 minute—maybe your users would be happy if the system was performing excellently for all of 2 hours except for 1 minute. Maybe they just would not notice.

For a production machine data set, let's have a look at the ratios and the statistical values to further illustrate the relevance for such analysis.

	User count	Active user count	Active user ratio	Log I/O rate	Database I/O rate	Log ratio	I/O rate per user	I/O rate per active user	Database I/O rate per active user
Average	1007	958	95%	23	159	19%	0.182	0.191	0.167
Minimum	859	834	89%	0	0	0%	0.000	0.000	0.000
Maximum	1078	1055	105%	229	1818	100%	1.721	1.723	1.723
95th percentile	1073	1055	104%	61	508	55%	0.550	0.578	0.535
99th percentile	1077	1055	105%	94	699	78%	0.779	0.812	0.752

The absolute values are of little importance in the context of this analysis (don't get upset about the active user count ratio being above 100%). What is more important is the difference among the average, minimum, maximum, and 95th and 99th percentile values.

First, the user count indicates to us that the reference period includes a fair number of connected users that we will need to put in perspective with the actual number of mailboxes. Usually, 80% of the registered mailboxes have connected users in a normal work day in a corporate environment. In service provider environments, this can be as low at 10%. Note that the active user count is quite close to the user count in a consistent manner: The minimum is 89%, the maximum is 105% and the average is 95%. This is normal—the variation between the two counters is quite small for our sampling time (peak 2 hours of the first working day of the week).

Next, we look at the log I/O rate: This is simply the number of writes per second issued to the transaction log files area summarized for all storage groups defined on the server. The maximum value is *twice* the 99th percentile. This means that 1% of the time, the I/O rate to the log area was comprised between 94 and 229. If you were to pick the maximum value for further sizing consideration, you realize that you could significantly oversize your configuration 99% of the time. For the database I/O rate, the difference between 99th percentile and maximum is three times as much!

This back-of-the-napkin analysis so far (which took only a few minutes to make after displaying the data set) shows that maximum values are much larger than percentile values—it is indeed worthwhile to dismiss 1% of the workload for future sizing exercises.

Finally, we look at the actual ratios, and given that the user variation is not that important in the data set, the ratio would basically follow the same trend as the data rates. This time, we look at the difference between the average value and the percentile and maximum values: The overall I/O rate per user differs by almost a factor of *ten* from the maximum value. This maximum is three times more than the 99th percentile, and twice the 95th percentile, and almost *ten* times the average.

Which to trust? It depends from your environment, from your workload and users and from the sampling time. We have found, in production environments and during design efforts, that using the 95th percentile gives a good "minored" peak value—which does not take into account the sudden and seldom burst of transactions to the volumes or the frequent moments where no disk activity is present, most likely due to effective in-memory database buffering and caching.

In the above example, our I/O per second per user is 0.550, and 0.578 per active user, for the 95th percentile. Our target tuning and capacity planning will use 0.6 I/O per second per user, well away from the 1.720 maximum and 0.182 average rates.

Logs versus databases

From the previous example, we did not discuss the log to database I/O ratio: This factor is interesting because in storage design, reads and writes do not necessarily have the same path. For instance, a read operation is typically not cached (because it is highly random), while a write operations is almost 100% cached (or should be). Also, the write performance to the transaction log areas are synchronous, single threaded, and in the foreground to a transaction, while the writes to the database are performed in the background, independently (almost) of the user activity. One hundred milliseconds for write latency to the database drives is far better than 5 milliseconds of write latency to the transaction log areas. Furthermore, the write throughput to the logs, because sequential and synchronous, directly depends on latency: The higher the latency, the lower the writes per second to the logs, and therefore, if you focus your attention only on the writes per second, you might think "my log traffic is not very high" and not be focused on what you should be, to fix a potential problem.

Other approaches

Based on technical publications and communications, Microsoft Exchange has a similar way of computing I/O rates per user (IOPS in Microsoft literature). The simple formula can be expressed as:

```
IOPS/mailbox = (average disk transfer/second) ÷ (number
of mailboxes)
```

In most environments (remember, 90% of Microsoft Exchange deployments are in the SMB space, with less than 1000 users per server), this formula will work well. However, in atypical environments, such as 5,000-user servers or service providers, you will want to get closer to the numbers and figure out how you may "oversubscribe" your environment while preserving a good service for "most" of the time ("most" = percentage of time/operations that will be satisfactorily serviced by the storage subsystem).

In summary

With the above method, we have reviewed how to sample counter information, quickly identify a reference time period using timeline analysis, and use mathematical formulas (use Microsoft Excel) for simple (yet not simplistic) statistical analysis.

You might want to automate this information reporting if you wish to perform baseline analysis, and possibly report on excessive server utilization—as a matter of fact, the data presented here was taken from a customer case where eventually a faulty add-on to the Outlook client was identified as the root cause of the excessive storage request rate. We identified the norm (baseline) for the request rate and further sampled several servers and brought the data together.

At the same time, you will want to be somewhat careful about these calculations. The request rate per user depends on many factors: the type of the client, and eventually, the version of Microsoft Exchange. In Exchange 2003 SP1 and further, efforts were made to "flatten" the request rate for the database volumes, resulting in less spiky workload, less inactivity, and less rush. The result is that peak-based analysis can be affected and yields smaller "peak" I/O ratios.

The consequences can be quite significant if you intend to use the I/O ratios for storage sizing exercises—a 20 or 50% difference is directly (linear) impacting the cost of acquisition for such storage infrastructures!

Reporting Performance Results

This section focuses on how to best interpret and report performance information. There will be times when a time-based graphic is of value. The sampling interval to use depends largely on the type of counter. For example, if you monitor the Send Queue Size for the MSExchange\IS Mailbox, a sampling of 1 minute is enough, because that value does not change very often. On the other hand, if you focus your attention on the disk counters, an interval of 5 seconds is necessary. Using more would cause some extra averaging between two samples that would erode the peak values.

On the use of percentiles and moving averages

Percentiles provide a much better view of the repartition of the various values in a series, as opposed to peaks and averages. They allow understanding the proportion or determining the importance of peak values versus minimum common values. I have found that customers preferred assertions like "CPU utilization was below 60% for 80% of the time" rather than "CPU average utilization is 33%."

Furthermore, you will find it quite expensive to build a system that handles 100% of the load. Generally, 5% is considered acceptable for decreased or nonoptimal performance. For example, Microsoft uses the 95th percentile of all the transaction performance readings during a load simulation as an indicator of good system performance.

Figure 11-17 is an example of sampled response time for a database volume taken during production hours of a *very* busy server. As seen in the figure, a fair proportion of operations are above 20 milliseconds. In fact, the server is not producing great response times, and the users of that machine complain about performance. Still, it is hard to really quantify and determine relative values.

If, instead of bluntly reporting on the actual values, you proceed to sort them by arranging them by order of percentile (5th percentile, 10th percentile, etc.), you can get a much clearer view of the proportional information

Figure 11-17
Sampled response time for a database volume

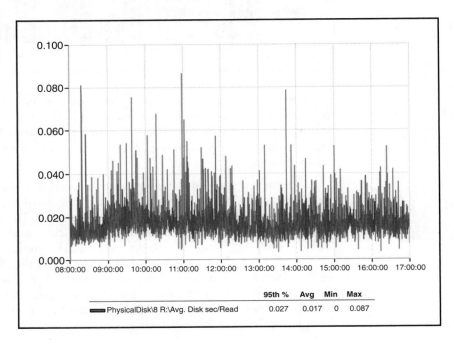

	95th %	Avg	Min	Max
PhysicalDisk\8 R:\Avg. Disk sec/Read	0.027	0.017	0	0.087

(Figure 11-18). At this point, peak values still appear, but they are of lesser importance. What is really important is to determine the acceptable response time (20 milliseconds, for instance) and determine that 80% of the operations "only" are satisfying this performance criteria. In fact, 20% of the time, the disk is not producing a good response time, and in a day, 20% of the time is a *lot*.

Figure 11-18
Response time distribution

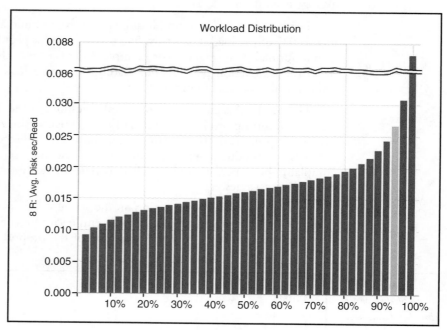

There are many ways to plot diagrams and percentile information, and there are no superlative tools freely available on the market. You may develop a simple Excel spreadsheet that gathers percentile figures and allows you to make quick decisions regarding your server performance analysis and troubleshooting.

Moving averages, on the other hand, are useful if you wish to measure the duration of a peak. A moving average is calculated over a defined number of samples. If your moving average is more than 10 (for example), you have certain evidence of the duration of a particular peak of throughput or response time. In Figure 11-19, we have added a moving average. It does not really express the same information as the percentile. When the percentile data indicated that 20% of the samples showed poor response time (i.e., above 20 milliseconds), the moving average navigates between 20 milliseconds, but erases (way too much in our opinion) the peak values, which can deter performance problem detection.

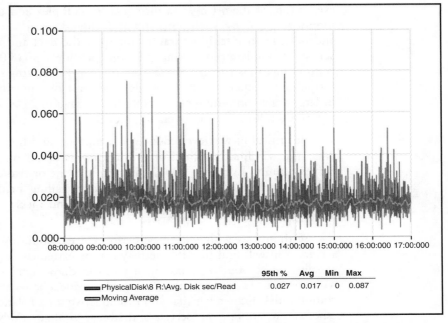

Figure 11-19
Using a moving average

You will find that moving averages are useful for detecting spikes over a short period of time, but fall short of global performance analysis across a workday. They are appropriate for threshold and event alarming, while percentiles are more appropriate for dealing with the overall timeline of a performance capture/analysis.

In Summary

Performance monitoring and system tuning are not far from being an art form, and it would be very presumptuous of us to say that we are masters of this particular art. Great artistic work, in our opinion, is typically a combination of talent (often a gift) and know-how. We hope that with the information provided here, you have enough know-how to check and monitor your Exchange storage performance, and we trust that you will have the talent to interpret and fine-tune the data. We cannot transmit any kind of talent, but we hope to provide you with best practices that can be helpful in your daily work.

Among the key things to remember, we would like to mention the following: do not hesitate to equip your messaging infrastructure with vertical and complete monitoring solutions. They will let you sleep peacefully and take care of properly interfacing a complex messaging environment with operational support staff, by providing events and associated actions that can help the system run smoothly, and address problems before the users are even aware of them (this is a nice goal for complex and distributed system monitoring). Vertical solutions aim at drilling down a particular application and provide an intelligent way to interpret the data and report events and activity. Complete monitoring solutions provide a 30,000-foot view of the computing infrastructure and *federate* the many operating systems and application environments under a single viewpoint of reporting, often required in large-scale computing environments that require 24×7 monitoring and typically a follow-the-sun operating model.

Be critical of whatever counter you monitor and how you interpret the data. You will find hundreds of performance counters on a Windows 2003 Server running Exchange 2007, but with just one or two counters, you can quickly determine whether your machine is falling behind or providing a good service level, from user response time and message throughput and background activities perspectives.

With this, we wish you a great performance monitoring of your Exchange servers. You will find that this activity can be extremely rewarding both personally and to your organization if you can draw conclusions that help in reducing your IT infrastructure costs and provide a better service to your user communities. Remember that you should strive for a balanced infrastructure, especially regarding your servers and storage configurations, where you can, using acceptable budgets, meet a certain service level. Throwing CPU and RAM into a box do not help if your storage component is falling behind.

Knowing that a server is not performing adequately is useful information, and it is very important to address before your users complain. Knowing *why* the server is not performing up to your standards is better. Knowing how to improve your server performance is the best approach.

Without a sound analysis and comprehension of Microsoft Exchange 2007 performance and monitoring, you don't stand a chance of achieving the three abovementioned points.

12

Best Practices and Sample Configurations

There are many ways to achieve a given result (service level) with Exchange 2007. That is probably the most challenging aspect of Microsoft Exchange. Because the technology gives us more choices every day, we have to make more choices, or at least we have more decision points. Thus far, we have presented to aspects of storage and Microsoft Exchange technologies. In this last chapter, we would like to present several design types that support various users. From the consolidated data centers, as found inside Microsoft or HP, to the distributed offices of a pharmaceutical company, there is a range of solutions that you should consider.

Key Attributes

In the solutions we present, there are a number of key attributes that characterize the solution. For example, deployments that leverage on SAN infrastructures are quite common, while other deployments focus solely on direct-attached storage.

- Centralized versus Distributed: We often study designs that consolidate all mailboxes in a discrete number of data centers (regional, continental, or worldwide). In the most extreme consolidation—one logical data center—you will still need to consider the time zone of the users, and ensure some off-peak hours for your Exchange server to perform maintenance activities, such as database maintenance or backup and recovery.

- Building Block: The first thing you need to identify in a design is the building block unit that can be replicated in order to create scalability (i.e., adding more users). Building blocks can consist of one or two servers, and support from 2500 and to 5000 users.

- Backup and Recovery Strategy: The next step is to define your backup and recovery strategy and decide if you wish to adopt the built-in continuous replication mechanism of Exchange 2007. If you go with continuous replication, you have more flexibility in the frequency and use of backup media.

■ SAN versus DAS: This is likely to be the major debate for your Exchange 2007 deployment and more so with future versions of Exchange that will enhance the application-based storage management functions. Keep in mind that continuous replication is not mutually exclusive from SAN.

The above attributes can be somewhat interlinked. For example, a SAN-based design allows SAN-based backups, whereas a DAS-based design with CCR clusters will be more appropriate for near-continuous data protection, using solutions such as Microsoft Data Protection Manager.

While we focus a lot on the mailbox server role for the storage configuration, do not forget that the Hub Transport (HT) server role requires attention if you wish to send or receive a high rate of messages from a single server (e.g., 50 messages per second and above, or approximately 1.5 million messages per working day).

Tools

In this chapter, we discuss a number of Microsoft tools that help with the management of the storage resources and performance and reliability of the messaging service. ExBPA, for example, is a key tool for regularly auditing your Exchange 2007 environment and spotting potential storage-related configuration issues, such as device driver mismatch or incorrect tuning parameters. JetStress is key for storage validation, and we found benefits in using JetStress as part of the release to production process, during which you will "burn in" the storage solution. In fact, in one of our customer projects, we spotted a couple of instances where the storage was not correctly configured (although it appeared to be correct) and we corrected a problem before users were affected.

In your infrastructure, and as part of the "standardized" build of Microsoft Exchange servers, you should include a network share with tool repository, or include them in the installation (e.g., in case the servers are in a perimeter network). This will save you valuable time.

DAS Design: The Microsoft IT Case

Microsoft has been a long-time user of SAN solutions for internal deployment of Microsoft Exchange. However, as explained in the excellent article titled, "Storage Design for Exchange Server 2007" (http://technet.microsoft.

com/en-us/library/cc500980.aspx), Microsoft made a move to CCR technology and direct-attached storage for the company's consolidated deployment. Microsoft uses a 4000-user, 2 GB-mailbox server design, as shown in Figure 12-1.

Figure 12-1
*Microsoft IT
Server Design
(Source: Microsoft
TechNet)*

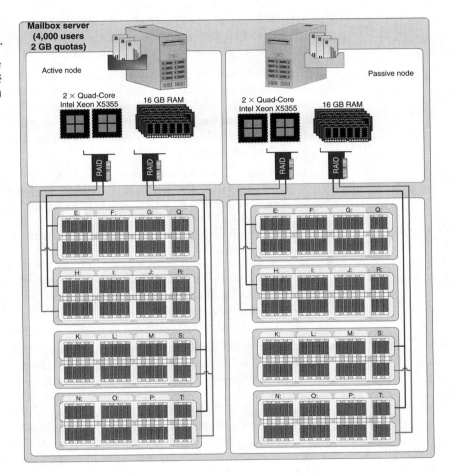

The first thing that strikes the reader is the server count: All servers for mailboxes operate in CCR active/passive mode. This means that such a design will double the server compared to a conventional server design that does not use active/passive clustering. The second observation we can make is the utilization of many disks for the DAS configuration, based on two RAID controllers per server, to which four disk shelves attached in a daisy chain mode (two per SAS bus). Each shelf contains 25 disks.

As seen in Figure 12-1, each controller can address four shelves, and spreads volumes across two shelves, such that the controller can sustain, in theory, the loss of an entire shelf. If however, the RAID controller fails, the access to those four shelves is lost. Is this a problem? Not so much, because of the CCR asynchronous replication and the ability to resume service from the passive node, on the condition that all databases have properly been replicated and available to be mounted (controlled by the LLR settings described in Chapter 7). The quality of the data after a failover will also depend on the HT dumpster size, and therefore the ability from the HT server to redeliver messages previously transmitted to the mailbox server.

The other benefit of the CCR replication is that you have a spare copy of the database for backup! This results in a significant benefit: The application server is left untouched during backups, meaning that you can run backups during peak work hours with no impact on production. On the flip side of this, you should be careful to allow enough headroom to permit continuous replication to operate satisfactorily.

Attempting to match your design with Microsoft's would be a somewhat extreme approach. For example, you may not have the same storage scale for your users simply because you will not enable a large mailbox quota (i.e., 2 GB or more). On the other hand, based on the storage design at Microsoft IT, emphasizing some key principles is worthwhile:

- Attempt to eliminate as many single points of failure as possible. This seems fairly straightforward, but is not so easy when dealing with DAS. The tactic to employ is to enable as much resilience as is available from the DAS controller, such as using RAID1 or RAID5 for the disk volumes and spread mirrors across separate buses and shelves.

- Use basic disks and refrain from host-based disk management. The use of third-party solutions, such as Symantec's VVM (Veritas Volume Manager) can deliver significant advantages in a DAS environment, such as the ability to combine several volumes across multiple controllers. This further extends the first principle by being able to withstand a single disk controller failure. However, if you have little or no experience with a volume manager, you will find it harder to manage your storage because in addition of your regular RAID manager, for you now have an additional storage management tool to manage and support.

- Do not create RAID5 volumes with a large number of disks (>20). Because the rebuild of a RAID5 volume implies accessing all blocks of all remaining disks in the RAID set, a considerable amount of time can be spent during a volume rebuild. Figure 12-2 shows the difference between the rebuild time of a RAID0+1 (striped mirror) and a RAID5 volume build.

- During rebuild time, the RAID5 volume has no protection. A second disk loss means that you lose the entire volume. To work around

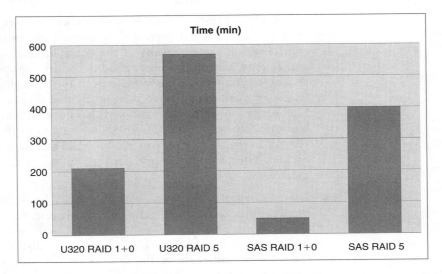

Figure 12-2
*Comparing array
rebuild times
(Source: HP)*

this, vendors have implemented techniques such as RAID6 (known as "advanced data guarding" at HP) with a double parity scheme and twice the impact of write operations for parity block update. Instead, you should either use RAID0+1 or RAID5 volumes that can rebuild in a relatively short period of time (less than 3 hours is acceptable). Consult your vendor and make tests (e.g., JetStress during a volume rebuild) before finalizing your configuration.

■ Refrain from deploying DAS without CCR. While the use of DAS for Exchange 2007 is appealing for its significant acquisition cost savings (compared to full-blown SAN solutions), it has drawbacks that can only be addressed with the continuous replication mode of Exchange 2007. SCR (standby continuous replication) does not provide the same level of functionality and recoverability as CCR. It is more time consuming to activate a SCR target compared to a CCR failover. We recommend SCR if you lose the complete data center, but it is not a solution for maintenance work or if you lose a single server in the data center. For medium and large servers (500 users and above), DAS makes sense with the additional data duplication from Exchange. Otherwise, you may have a tough time explaining repeated downtime due to hardware failures or maintenance.

■ Use controllers that have a removable battery–backed-up cache. In the unlikely (yet possible) event of a controller failure, you will want to replace this controller. A battery-protected write cache is a memory module with a battery attached to it. When you replace the failed controller, you can insert the memory module into the new controller, connect the disks of the failed controller, and the new controller will resume operations and flush the cache contents to disk. If the controller cache is not protected by battery, the replacement of the controller will cause the loss of the controller cache. (You may be able to reuse the same memory module, but the contents will be lost as soon as you unplug the module from the controller board.) After failure of a controller, there is no guarantee that all data from the local cache (onboard memory board) has been flushed to disk. In the best case, you will have a CHKDSK running to verify the NTFS file system. In the worst case, you will lose data and have to revert to the backup. This last point is mitigated by the use of CCR or LCR, for example.

■ Do not (repeat: *do not*) enable disk cache. SAN disks come with the local disk cache disabled by default, because that level of performance is not required due to the accrued performance available in SAN controllers. However, DAS disks (especially SATA disks) have the possibility of enabling the disk cache. The disk cache is *unprotected* and *local*, which can be enabled (disabled by default) for better performance. Power loss means cache loss, which in turn means possible drive corruption. Do not attempt to enable this cache. If you need improved performance, get a better DAS controller or move to SAN, but stay away from local disk cache. (Please.)

■ Use monitoring systems to report on disk failures. Because the purpose of RAID is to protect you from disk failures, a single disk failure in a RAID volume will not cause downtime. How do you know if a disk failure actually happened? The days where you could walk into computer rooms and change disks with a red fault LED are over. Servers tend to be operated remotely, and do not have local consoles. It is therefore essential to use a server management and monitoring environment (e.g., HP Insight Manager in Figure 12-3) that can report the *physical* status of a server farm. Some of these tools actually integrate into high-level management tools. It's important, however, that you consult your server vendor for proper implementation.

In summary

The deployment of DAS solutions for Exchange 2007 should be linked to implementation of continuous replication features of Exchange 2007. As discussed previously, DAS has benefits such as simplicity and low acquisition costs. Simplicity means that you need to make an extra effort in storage management, and implement the built-in replication features of Exchange 2007. It also means that you need to spend more time in managing the Exchange 2007 – specific storage functions, such as ensuring the health of replication.

Figure 12-3
*HP System Insight
Manager*

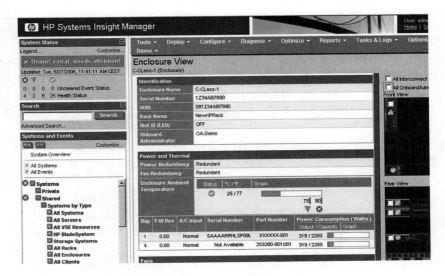

SAN: Large Enterprise with Consolidated Deployment (>50,000 Mailboxes)

Storage Area Networks deliver the most benefit in consolidated deployments, where you can provision storage to many servers (with different operating systems, different applications) from a single place, using the same processes. SAN designs for Exchange 2007 are not incompatible with continuous replication. In fact, one of the first designs for Exchange 2007 on which we worked used SAN *and* CCR for creating a stretched cluster across two data centers with a high-speed intersite link.

Figure 12-4 shows a sample SAN-based design with single copy clusters (SCCs), in either 6+1 or 7+1 mode (i.e., 6 active nodes, 1 passive, or 7 active nodes, 1 passive). In such as design you can see that the actual disk configuration is totally abstracted by the presence of the SAN controller. Each server has a dual attachment to the Fibre Channel SAN infrastructure, and this is the only piece of storage configuration that is local to the server. This attachment is done such that if a connection fails, the SAN multipath I/O will ensure that access to the disks on the storage network is preserved.

The notable difference is the presence of a tape library connecting directly to the SAN. In this example, SCC is utilized, which means that CCR is not used, and therefore we cannot take advantage of the passive node replica for running backups. However, the tape being attached to the SAN means that the data traffic, although processed by the servers, will not go over the data network (e.g., otherwise used for the client/server traffic and messages transfer) and instead will stay local in the high-speed storage network infrastructure.

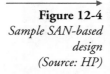

Figure 12-4
Sample SAN-based design (Source: HP)

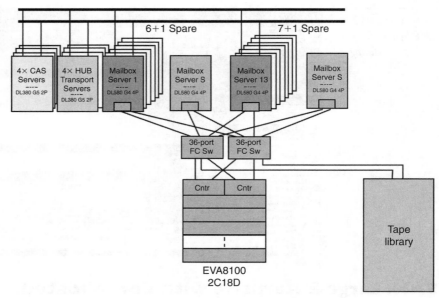

This particular topology aims at favoring the service availability by providing a 6+1 or 7+1 clustering model. What does this mean? It means that on a 7-node cluster, 6 nodes run Exchange and a 7th one is in passive mode. It means that you may only withstand the loss of one single node. Losing 2 nodes would result in service outage, because you only have one spare machine.

The second observation is the utilization of a single HP EVA storage array. This means that here we do not use the data replication feature of Exchange 2007 nor of the EVA. If, for some reason, the EVA becomes unavailable, you will get an outage, because the array is not replicated, either by Exchange or through its own replication mean.

This type of approach is interesting for dealing gracefully with application and operating system updates. In the case of a major outage (e.g., site failure), this setup does not allow graceful recovery. If you want a fully redundant setup, you would start by having as many passive nodes as there are active nodes in the cluster. Then, you would *duplicate* the live data available. This duplication is typically done by array or Exchange replication. Finally, spreading the configuration across two sites will finalize the setup.

Finally, note the benefit of using a SAN, expressed by the direct connectivity of the tape library to the storage network: it means that the backup traffic, although originating from the mail servers, will not go over the data network, and instead will be occurring on the dedicated, high-speed, storage network. In a DAS deployment, all your backups will have to go over a TCP/IP network. This can be an issue for the initial creation of the backup set, and subsequently you may want to use a dedicated data network for the backup traffic. If you do so, you might even ask yourself the question again: How about using a specially dedicated network for storage, designed for this kind of data flow?

SAN: Mission-Critical Email

Mission critical email usually means that you have little time for downtime (including unplanned) and zero time for data loss. This kind of setup is often observed in companies that use email for their business, and which are liable for the email usage. From a storage configuration viewpoint, the resolution is actually quite simple. You must duplicate any data that you have on disk. The extent of duplication will then depend on your budget and the likelihood of data loss. For example, individual disk failures are common, so RAID is commonly used for dealing with individual disk failures. On the other hand, a complete data center outage is quite rare; therefore, fewer companies will actually implement replicated storage across physical sites. In the case of those for whom data loss jeopardizes their business, however, physical storage replication across one or more sites is mandatory, and the use of Exchange 2007 continuous replication must be carefully considered and compared with array-based replication.

Let's examine the topology shown in Figure 12-5. This solution focuses on the "no-data loss" paradigm, and utilizes for the environment a local cold standby server and a remote cold-standby server. You may be surprised by the use of cold standby servers instead of clusters. The reason is that you create in such an environment, fairly simple and independent components: The servers are standalone, and therefore they do not require the added management complexity of clustering. Of course, this complexity can be a nonissue if your IT operations staff is well versed in Microsoft clustering. Most importantly, the servers can be located in various subnets and still run Windows Server 2003. Indeed, you may remember that pre-Windows 2008 clusters need to operate in the same subnet, and extending a subnet between two locations can be an issue for your network administrators. In the scenario illustrated in Figure 12-5, the two sites are more independent from a networking standpoint. This confirms disaster-tolerance and recovery-networking designs, and prevents situations where mailbox servers in one site would access HT servers in the other site (for recovering items during a lossy failover, for instance).

To further simplify individual components, a replication link is created between the SAN on the two data centers: This replication happens "both" ways, such that both data centers can be active at the same time. The value of doing so is that you can *spread* the workload across two data centers, and therefore realize better utilization of your assets overall, instead of having one local site hammered by transaction processing and another handling differential changes resulting from SAN replication.

Figure 12-5 *Taking advantage of SAN-based replication*

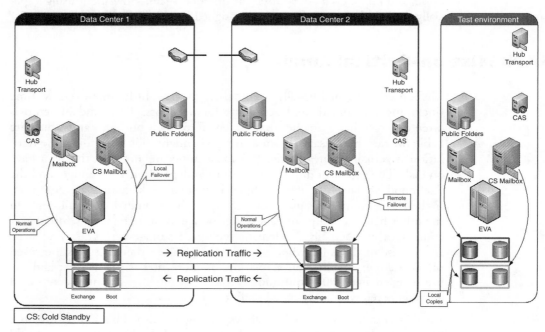

Finally, Figure 12-5 shows a dedicated test environment that represents production, which is required to validate your processes, tools, and technologies.

All of this seems positive, but what type of drawback does this environment have? Well, first of all, it does not use clustering: This means that the decision to use one server or another in a cold standby scenario has to be made by something other than the Microsoft Cluster Resource Manager. In the same vein, the decision to use one site or another from a storage perspective has to be made in concert with the whole site failover. Considering that you may not have to perform this operation routinely, this setup is in fact quite efficient. The primary constraint is, in fact, the replication path between the two data centers, because you must ensure that data are replicated safely and quickly (especially for the transaction log files). This means that link latency should probably not exceed more than 3 or 4 milliseconds, which probably requires some type of Dark Fibre implementation. While this may appear quite expensive, keep in mind that such a setup (SAN-based replication) is independent of servers, and can probably fulfill the needs of *other* mission-critical applications for your enterprise. The result is that you can build a common infrastructure that benefits many applications, including Microsoft Exchange and SAP/R3.

Storage replication and cluster integration

When you implement storage replication with Exchange 2007, you basically depart from the application-specific replication to use a general-purpose storage replication. From an operation viewpoint, you will encounter a challenge when performing failover of servers and/or storage: How to ensure that the overall state of the environment is consistent? To achieve this consistency, you must consider tight integration between the server and application operations management and storage management.

We found that the best way to deal with failover between nodes is still Microsoft clustering. Thus, if your design and operations teams are familiar with clustering, you should employ this technique. If they are not, you should ensure that they become familiar with clustering. The main benefit of clustering will be the automatic monitoring of resources, such as disks and services, that contribute to automating the implementation. Understand that if you do not use clustering, you will have to implement this watchdog and decision-making process that consists of verifying that the local services are up and running, and if they are not, they are doing a failover in a concerted way with all resources.

If you implement clustering, in conjunction with storage replication, you should ensure that both the node-level failover and the storage failover happen in a graceful way. Technologies are available that enable instrumentation of the storage failover directly from within cluster resource management. One of them is HP's Cluster Extensions for the EVA (short name is CLX), shown in Figure 12-6. A purpose of CLX is to interface with the cluster resource manager and ensure that when you fail over from one site to another, you also make a proper failover of the storage components and ensure that the passive node of the cluster has access to a consistent set of data from a storage

Figure 12-6
Using HP StorageWorks EVA or XP technology in clusters with CLX

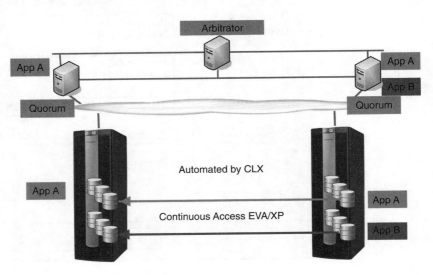

replication viewpoint. In the clustering dependency tree, CLX will intervene as a dependency for a physical disk, as shown in Figure 12-7.

CLX appears as a resource in the Microsoft cluster resource management and can be configured for failover policies (Figure 12-8).

Figure 12-7
Physical disks depend on CLX

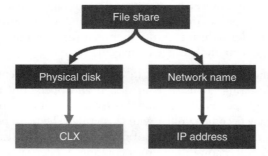

Figure 12-8
Configuring CLX (Source: HP)

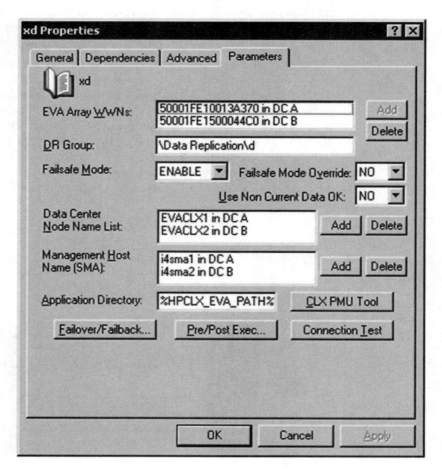

In the end, you will have created a stretched cluster (which can be implemented without SAN and replication using DAS and CCR), based on infrastructure components. This means that the same topology and hardware can be utilized for other applications. Obviously, the more applications that use your infrastructure, the better your return on investment. In Figure 12-9, we have a real-life topology in which two production sites are used in Locations A and B, and a third location is used for vaulting tape media.

Figure 12-9
Multisite stretched
cluster
(Source: HP)

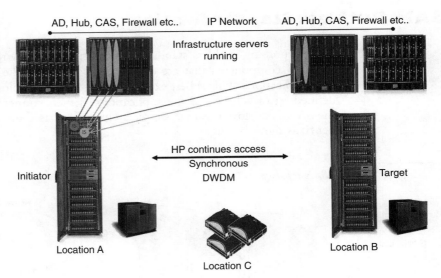

Such a design requires the intersite link to be fit for single subnet deployment (pre-Windows Server 2008) and for synchronous storage replication (low latency). You will find that this is one of the most challenging and show-stopper implementation items for such a solution. Because many customers do not have the necessary infrastructure for synchronous replication, the CCR functions of Exchange 2007 typically will be used instead at lower cost and simpler storage topology. Again, the downside is the application-specific nature of data replication and recovery.

In summary

The use of SAN for mission-critical deployment prevents all types of information loss. To achieve this, you need to implement two things:

■ Storage replication for duplicating data written to disk in separate environments (arrays, sites, or data centers)

■ Operational processes to manage replication and integration in a clustered environment (preferably)

Do not risk your organization in a replicated storage environment that is not closely linked, whether by technology or processes (or both!), to the Microsoft Exchange environment. If you do so, failure is almost guaranteed in performing failovers and reuse of duplicated data. If you cannot use these duplicated data, you will be questioned about why they were created in the first place.

SAN: Ruthless Standardization

The purpose of "ruthless standardization" in a SAN environment is to create SAN components that are the same, regardless of the operating system and applications. This is best expressed with a SAN topology that provides a defined set of volumes to the applications. Servers connect into a SAN and the SAN is deployed using a simple architecture based on core-edge components, as shown in Figure 12-10.

Figure 12-10   *SAN topology*

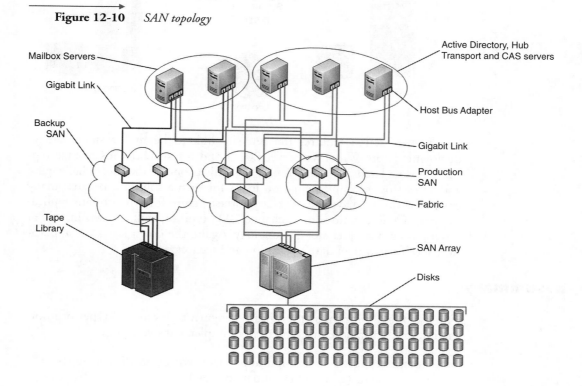

From a networking and infrastructure standpoint, the standard implies that all servers boot on the SAN, they have only local disks for paging purposes, and servers that must be backed up (e.g., mailbox servers) have a third attachment to a dedicated backup SAN.

What benefits derive from such an environment? First, all servers are replaceable, and do not have local data. This means that backup and recovery only need to focus on SAN components, and that the provisioning of significant storage is done exclusively from the SAN. Next, a dedicated backup fabric is used for backups. This has the benefit of preventing *any* mutual disruption from backup or production SAN topology changes, which is a moot point with Windows Server 2003 and the generalization of the Storport for Windows servers. The server connection becomes slightly more complex because you get a third option instead of a dual attachment. Figure 12-11 shows the topology visible in a closer view of the server connectivity.

Figure 12-11
SAN attachment details

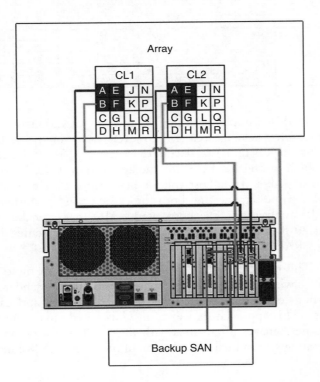

Each connection is doubled and the architecture of the back-end array is such that it can withstand the failure of several processing units. Yes, using a SAN means putting all your eggs in the same basket, and this requires that you watch it carefully.

To the SAN administrator, Microsoft Exchange is just another application. SAN management focuses on excellence of administration, monitoring, and provisioning. It also implements automation to allow for rapid provisioning of storage to any kind of server model. This latter point is achieved with the utilization of fixed-size SAN logical volumes, arranged locally at the server for matching the Microsoft Exchange requirements (Figure 12-12).

Figure 12-12
Providing storage to Microsoft Exchange servers

		Exchange Requirements			Storage Config		
	Volume	Description	Vol size	IOPS	Lun size	Lun qty	Lun to Volume tool
Database config	H:\mnt	Database	384	1600	64	6	Dyn-Disks
	H:\	Transaction Log	64	160	64	1	Lun
	N:\mnt	Database	384	1600	64	6	Dyn-Disks
	N:\	Transaction Log	64	160	64	1	Lun
	O:\mnt	Database	384	1600	64	6	Dyn-Disks
	O:\	Transaction Log	64	160	64	1	Lun
	R:\mnt	Database	384	1600	64	6	Dyn-Disks
	R:\	Transaction Log	64	160	64	1	Lun
Other	E:\	Exchange Binaries	64		64	1	Lun
	F:\	Utility	256		64	4	Dyn-Disks or LUSE
	P:\	SMTP	64		64	1	Lun
	V:\	Bkp and Recovery	896		128	7	Dyn-Disks or LUSE
	W:\	Bkp and Recovery	896		·128	7	Dyn-Disks or LUSE

In this example, note that volumes are of various sizes at the host level (Microsoft Exchange server); however, each volume is provisioned using LUNs (logical units) of fixed size (8, 15, 32, 64, and 128 GB). Therefore, to obtain a 384 GB LUN for the application, 6 LUNs of 64 GB each are provisioned, and the host volume management arranges these volumes in a RAID stripe set, meeting both the capacity and performance requirements of the application. The host-based RAID may even be implemented as a RAID0 if disk-level redundancy is already implemented in the SAN (e.g., using RAID1 or RAID5).

This particular mode of operation is suitable for multivendor, multi-OS SAN environments, enabling the provisioning of standardized LUNs, and shifting to the application server the definition of application-specific volumes. This approach derives from Unix-based environments where a local volume manager often ships with the product (for example, HP's HP-UX operating system includes a version of the VERITAS Volume Manager).

In summary

The use of a fully standardized SAN is recommended in high-end environments where a large number of hosts are provisioned. If you have Microsoft Exchange as the only consumer application on your SAN, you should not attempt a too-complicated setup, and focus instead on responding to the application requirements. We have determined that the simpler the setup, the easier the troubleshooting. In a SAN with previous versions of Microsoft

Exchange, the storage demand from Exchange and the storage design could be largely incompatible. With the vast improvement of the I/O request rate requirements found with Exchange 2007 and the 64-bit computing mode, Microsoft Exchange has never been more appropriate for SAN, and the chances of performance bottleneck inside the storage network are quite diminished. SAN does not prevent you from qualifying the storage using JetStress, but it does make things easier to match both capacity and performance requirements.

IP SAN: Using iSCSI for Midrange Servers

With the standardization of IP-based block-mode storage, namely iSCSI, it is now possible to provision storage LUNs over IP networks. The benefits are easy to understand: Instead of creating a specific infrastructure for storage networking, you can capitalize on IP-based data networks, which are ubiquitous in modern data centers.

Using iSCSI significantly simplifies the hardware configuration of your server. You can use the Ethernet NIC interfaces on your server to connect to the storage network. If you wish to boot from an iSCSI LUN, however, you may have to use a specific HBA/interface (e.g., Qlogic has an iSCSI HBA that allows booting a server from a networked-storage LUN).

Figure 12-13 shows a simple configuration using iSCSI. Two iSCSI modules (here, HP's mpx100) are used to bridge the data network to the back-end of a SAN array (EVA 8000). The mpx100 modules are connected to a private iSCSI gigabit Ethernet network. However, they could be connected to the same data network as the clients; performance, reliability, and security are major requirements for using a dedicated gigabit Ethernet infrastructure. (We will return to discussion of the appropriateness of such a setup.)

From a pure I/O standpoint, there is little difference between each storage solutions. The configuration in Figure 12-13 generated a reasonable number of I/O per second per user, regardless of the number of storage groups and databases. This is better viewed in Figure 12-14.

You may wonder what is so special about an iSCSI configuration. At this point, it's important for to recall the origins of TCP/IP: 1970s, unreliable networks, and so on—all were conditions for creating a protocol that could deal with a high rate of errors during transmission, disordered packets, and error checking required at each level of the frame. To return to our example in Figure 12-13, it means that the *overhead* of processing TCP/IP frames for the SCSI protocol encapsulation, instead of using a powerful Fibre Channel host-bus adapter, is shifted to the CPU of the Microsoft Exchange server. To mitigate this additional workload, you should use

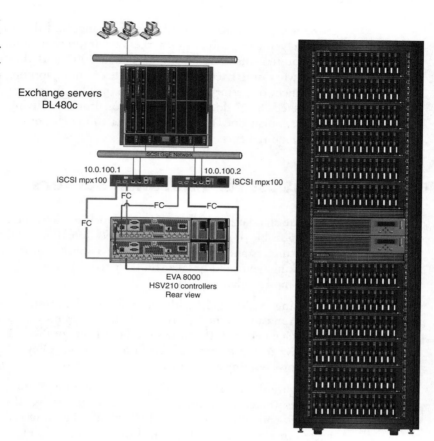

Figure 12-13
*iSCSI setup for
a single mailbox
server (Source: HP)*

multifunction network interface cards (NICs). NICs have built-in intelligence for assembling and disassembling TCP and IP frames and offload the CPU from the overhead of the TCP/IP protocol. This feature is commonly referred as a TOE (TCP offload engine). Figure 12-15 shows how latency is affected by the use of iSCSI, compared to Fibre Channel.

In the environment presented here, we observed that the overhead of using non–TOE-capable NICs was estimated at 5 to 10%. In other words, we could observe an increase of 10% (maximum) of CPU consumption when using non-TOE-capable NICs. In modern computing, you should not see this difference as a major gating factor for the adoption of iSCSI.

For such an environment, you should ensure that you remove any single point of failure by using several NIC and several iSCSI routers (mpx100). This will ensure that each LUN is presented several times to the server and that Ethernet jumbo frames are enabled on your server: This allows transmission of large data packets in a single Ethernet frame.

Figure 12-14

I/O per second per use for 5000-1 GB mailbox workload

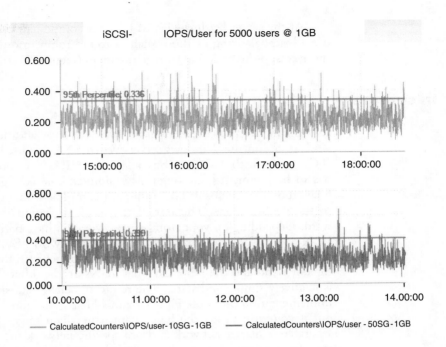

Figure 12-15

Comparing latency between Fibre Channel and iSCSI (similar workload)

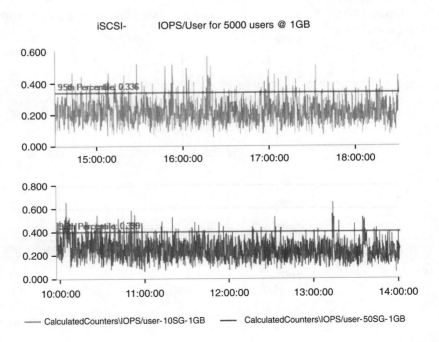

At the server level, the iSCSI initiator component can be configured to use a load-balancing method, such as round robin in order to load balance the access to the back-end storage resources (Figure 12-16).

In summary

As seen in the presented environment, you have additional configuration work to do on the Windows server. When a SAN is used in Fibre Channel (FC) mode with FC host bus adapters (HBAs), a similar configuration has to be performed, although a bit simpler. The configuration should be focused on the Microsoft iSCSI initiator component that connects the server to the iSCSI targets. The rest of the implementation is fairly straightforward: Depending on your storage array, you will have native exposure of the LUN over iSCSI. In the case of the HP StorageWorks EVA and the mpx100 iSCSI router, you must configure the mapping between the iSCSI targets on the one hand and the Fibre Channel LUNs on the other. This configuration is relatively simple and static. The resulting benefit is a simplified hardware implementation (no more Fibre Channel HBAs, no Fibre Channel network), but if you wish to get the best performance, you might end up creating a separated Ethernet network and use specific network interfaces, and in the end, have an environment more complex than with Fibre Channel storage

Figure 12-16
*Using round robin
for iSCSI targets*

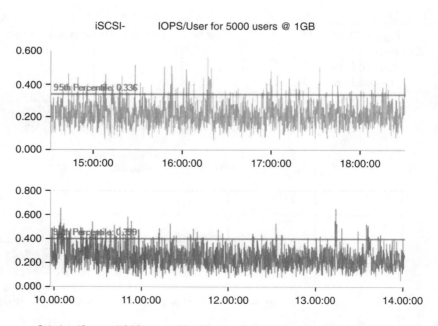

networks. Therefore, you must weigh your requirements correctly and make sure that you do not create extra complications.

ESRP: Microsoft's Exchange Storage Reviewed Program

Microsoft has established the Exchange Storage Reviewed Program (http://technet.microsoft.com/en-us/exchange/bb412164.aspx). Version v1.2 focused on Exchange 2003, while v2.0 focuses on Exchange 2007. See http://www.microsoft.com/technet/prodtechnol/exchange/2007/esrp.mspx for more information about the program. Whether you are a vendor, a partner or a customer, you should consult this program for several reasons:

- It provides noncompetitive storage configurations that are suitable for Exchange 2007.

- The configurations are suitable for production use: RAID0 or low-resilience solutions are no longer found, as in the early days of the MMB program (but these had another objective).

- The ESRP solution documentation contains characterization data. This characterization will basically provide you with the capabilities of performance of a particular storage configuration.

- For each configuration, you will find vendor-specific information regarding fine-tuning, such as the partition alignment parameters, when relevant.

The ESRP tests are based on JetStress tests, using varying configurations for transactional workload and backup and recovery workload (streaming in and out of storage components). The information provided in the reports will not allow you to build your production solution out of the box. Some level of solution engineering will still need to take place to encompass more requirements that are specific to the deployment scenario that you envisage. However, it will provide you with fully characterized reference configurations that can be used as a starting point for your deployment.

Figure 12-17 shows an example from the Sun report on a 20,000-mailbox Fibre Channel-based configuration (http://www.sun.com/storagetek/exchange/ESRP_20000_User_Configuration_6540.pdf). The table contains the results of the JetStress runs. Focus on the disk latencies and throughput. In this example, the volume is able to perform 1773 reads per second with a 12-millisecond response time. Twelve milliseconds is the access time you would expect from a moderately loaded high-performance disk drive. The write latency is lower (better) at 7 milliseconds, with a write request rate of

Figure 12-17

Example of ESRP report (Source: Sun Microsystems)

Primary Storage Performance Results

The Primary Storage performance testing is designed to exercise the storage with maximum sustainable Exchange type of IO for 2 hours. The test is to show how long it takes for the storage to respond to an IO under load. The data below is the sum of all of the logical disk I/O's and average of all the logical disks I/O latency in the 2 hours test duration. Each server is listed separately and the aggregate numbers across all servers is listed as well.

Individual Server Metrics:

The sum of I/O's across Storage Groups and the average latency across all storage Groups on a per server basis.

Database I/O	
Average Database Disk Transfers/sec	3202.92
Average Database Disk Reads/sec	1773.321
Average Database Disk Writes/sec	1429.599
Average Database Disk Read Latency (ms)	12
Average Database Disk Write Latency (ms)	7
Transaction Log I/O	
Average Log Disk Writes/sec	830.962
Average Log Disk Write Latency (ms)	1

Database I/O	
Average Database Disk Transfers/sec	3429.772
Average Database Disk Reads/sec	1892.125
Average Database Disk Writes/sec	1537.647
Average Database Disk Read Latency (ms)	11
Average Database Disk Write Latency (ms)	8
Transaction Log I/O	
Average Log Disk Writes/sec	882.556
Average Log Disk Write Latency (ms)	1

1429 writes per second. You may wonder why writes are better, as normally they should be slower due to the redundancy implied by RAID logic (mirrors or parity stripes). This is due to the ability of the disk controller to *cache* the write operations. For transaction logging, the latency is even smaller (1 millisecond), which indicates a cache hit (i.e., the I/O always returns as soon as the data are in cache): This is due to the sequential nature of the write operations, found with the transaction logging of the ESE database engine.

Figure 12-18 shows the backup/recovery performance data from the same report.

From this table, you can determine the raw speed (data rate) for the volumes. This speed may improve if you decide to make certain changes in the environment (fabric, controller, cache, or disks are components that can influence the data rate of a disk volume). However, assume that you know for sure that with the configuration documented in this report, you will have

Figure 12-18
ESRP streaming
backup
information

Microsoft Exchange Server Jetstress

Streaming backup Test Result Report

Streaming Backup Statistics - All

Database Instance	Database Size (MBytes)	Elapsed Backup Time	MBytes Transferred/sec
Instance996.1	236687.65	01:26:22	45.67
Instance996.2	236359.65	01:26:22	45.61
Instance996.3	236247.65	01:26:22	45.59
Instance996.4	236455.65	01:26:22	45.63
Instance996.5	236333.65	01:26:22	45.61
Instance996.6	236611.65	01:26:22	45.66
Instance996.7	236421.65	01:18:55	49.92

this speed. If you cannot reproduce it in your environment, you know that you can search for potential problems (e.g., incompatible firmware/driver combination).

Of course, you can (should?) consult other vendors. Note that the information in the ESRP reports does not contain any competitive information or pricing information. This is why we like these reports: They are free from commercial positioning and focus on the facts, and just the facts! On the other hand, the ESRP reports do not go beyond storage characterization, nor do they test special scenarios. For example, a restore speed of 45 MB/second on a disk volume is good information, but this assumes that there is no other activity on the server: in reality, if you restore a database, are you really sure you can decide when to make this restore? Typically, you have no choice, and must restore (or seed) the database ASAP, while there is production workload that may impact your figures.

HP: Storage Solutions and Active Answers

HP takes the problem where the Microsoft ESRP left it: After running JetStress on a production-level configuration, you will want to exercise the solution in a "more realistic" manner, by combining additional parameters such as networking latency (for CCR), and possibly LoadGen load testing that simulates Outlook connections (JetStress only tests the I/O request and data rate capabilities of a given storage solution).

For more information on the HP reports, see http://h18006.www1.hp.com/storage/solutions/storagesolutions.html, and Active Answers, at http://www.hp.com/solutions/activeanswers.

The HP publications are often driven by actual customer requirements. As a consequence, the configurations tested are typically more complex than the ESRP tests, and they address complex enterprise-level deployment scenarios. They are also more restrictive, given that they are made of HP hardware only and seldom include third-party software solutions (except when covering Oracle 10 g, for example). One of the configurations described in this chapter originates from the HP Storage Solutions web portal. A great example is the paper that describes backup and recovery for Exchange 2007. The table of content is reproduced in Figure 12-19.

The significant value that you will find above that of the ESRP is that the tests were carried out with different configurations and beyond the raw speed of the storage. For example, tests have been done with NTBackup (guaranteed to be found on the server), but also in other modes such as VSS, using a varying number of tape devices, and so on. Finally, the paper finished with a set of best practices (common in HP's publications) that summarized key learning points in the document.

Figure 12-19
Example table of
contents for HP's
whitepapers on
storage

Backup and recovery best practices for Microsoft Exchange Server 2007 with HP servers and HP StorageWorks array and tape products

Active Answers will provide you with solution sizing tools (previously referenced in this book) and articles focusing on reference implementations that cover both server and storage sizing and design (Figure 12-20).

You will also find the Performance Briefs series, which advantageously replaces the Microsoft MMB program, now discontinued by Microsoft (Figure 12-21).

In Summary

In addition to the best practices described in this chapter, we would like to share some more general best practices typically found in successful environments (and not just HP's IT environment, for example).

First, standardize. You will find endless benefits in having a standard server build and layout across your infrastructure. We found that server models (building blocks), such as small, medium, large and huge, are excellent for deployment and maintenance. In the long term, if you consolidate to a reduced number of data centers, you may even consider reducing the number of server models.

Figure 12-20
Active Answers Web portal for Microsoft Exchange Server

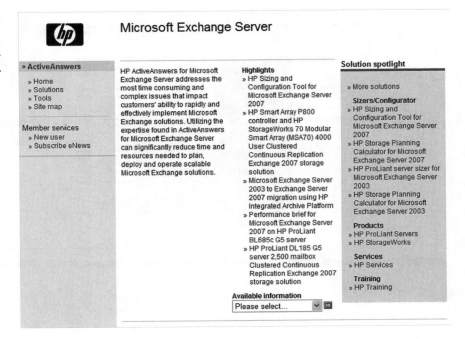

Figure 12-21   *Sample extract from an HP Performance Brief*

Mailbox simulation using LoadGen

Testing was performed with Microsoft's Exchange load generation tool, LoadGen. LoadGen requires the complete Exchange topology, including the Active Directory domain, Client Access Server (CAS), the Hub Transport Server (HUB) and mailbox server roles to be installed. LoadGen is used to simulate some of the key functions of the Microsoft Office Outlook 2007 client, to exercise the mailbox server. For more information on LoadGen, go to
http://www.microsoft.com/downloads/details.aspx?FamilyId=0FDB6F14-1E42-4165-BB17-96C83916C3EC&displaylang=en

LoadGen setup

• 8000 mailboxes - 1000 per database

• Office Outlook 2007 cached mode with very heavy action profile

• Pre-logon enabled

• 8 hour simulation day

• 12 hour test duration (4 hour cache warming + 8 hour steady state)

Two comparison tests were performed to simulate 8000 very heavy mailbox users. The first test of 8000 users was configured with eight processor cores which resulted in an average CPU utilization of 49%. The second test with 8000 users and 16 cores resulted in an average CPU utilization of 30%. Results indicate a 38% reduction in CPU utilization moving to 16 cores, as seen in figure 2 below.

Figure 1. Average CPU utilization

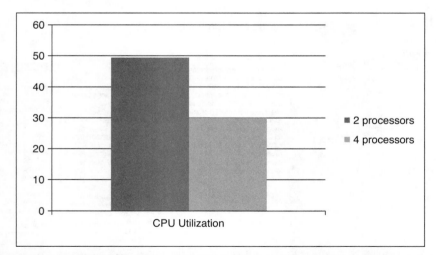

Second, automate. There is nothing worse in the life cycle of an infrastructure than the disparate deployment of servers that are similar in function. You do not want to have two mailbox servers in the same data center to be configured differently. There are several ways to achieve this, and the most effective one is to automate the setup and configuration of your servers. If you can link with the provisioning of the storage, you have done a superb job; not only you can save on the time to deploy a server, but most importantly, you can reproduce known-to-be-working configuration with no risk of manual intervention and mistake.

Third, monitor. Storage is not always easy to monitor. If you have direct-attached storage, the use of local performance monitor counters, as described in Chapter 11, will suffice. If you have networked storage (Fibre Channel or IP SAN), you will need to correlate that local Windows monitoring with the monitoring of the SAN. It is not always easy to perform; however, it is feasible, depending on the storage vendor you use. Remember always that the performance information that counts is seen by the Windows server and eventually, the end user!

Index